The Popes
Histories and Secrets

by Claudio Rendina

The background and mysteries of the Holy See,
together with Antipopes, Jubilees, Conclaves and
Ecumenical Councils revealed through
the biographies of the 2 6 4 Roman Pontiffs

Translated from the original
by Prof. Paul D. McCusker, J.D., Cornell Law School
and J.D., University of Rome, Italy

SₗP

SEVEN LOC

Santa Ana, (
Minneapolis,
Washington, D.C.
Helena, Montana

Pharos Publications Ltd.,
2nd Floor, Atlantic House, Circular Road,
Douglas, Isle of Man
e-mail: pharospublications@mail.com

Seven Locks Press
P.O. Box 25689
Santa Ana, CA 92799
(800) 354-5348

Printed in the United States of America

Library of Congress Cataloging-in-Publication Data
is available from the publisher
ISBN 1-931643-13-X

Cover and Interior Design by Sparrow Advertising & Design

CONTENTS

Foreword

The biographies of the 264 Roman pontiffs, presented chronologically from St. Peter to John Paul II, have been written bearing in mind the human aspect of the vicar of Christ, eschewing *ex cathedra* pronouncements while reassessing the myth of the personage, yet avoiding undue theological evaluations.

The references to historico-political events appear on certain occasions in the foreground and at others in the background, while at times the biography of a pope is interlaced with those of one or more antipopes, or of that of an emperor. And again, a council or a conclave can have best reflected the real face of a pope. Attention has also been given to legends and anecdotes, chronicles and poems, from Dante to those in dialect of the Roman Belli, as well as to the popular sayings of the *"Pasquinades."*

Regarding the chronology of the popes, I have respected the dates given in the Vatican's *Annuario pontificio*, hazarding only the beginning of the papacy at the year 30 A.D., and this on the basis of the latest studies on the life of Jesus Christ. I have also respected the tradition which considers the first 54 popes as saints, despite the fact that the Church's new *Universal Calendar* has struck certain of them off the list because their cult had no foundation, and this has been noted in their respective biographies.

Another problem was that of the term "pope," feasible only as from a specific moment in history and related to the recognition of the primacy of the Roman Church over the others. Until then I should have used that of "bishop of Rome," but I reckoned it was opportune to follow the decision of Gregory VII who assigned the title of pope to all his predecessors back to St. Peter.

Finally, I decided on an appendix which, apart from presenting in a rational, synoptical manner the chronological lists of popes and antipopes, jubilees and ecumenical councils, could satisfy the reader's curiosity regarding the world of the papacy.

INTRODUCTION

For over two thousand years, from Peter of Galilee to Karol Wojtyla, the "rock" has not given way and the forces of hell have not prevailed. Of course, ill winds have not been absent; many have been the metamorphoses of an institution which was attacked from outside, assailed from within, engulfed by the storms to the point of scandal, but which survived principally because of the faith of believers convinced of the eternity of Christ's promises to Peter. Indeed, the institution of the papacy has endured precisely because this base of the faithful has stood firm continuing, despite everything, to see in the pope the Church itself. *Ubi Petrus, ibi Ecclesia.*

The "rock" in its origin is the "cornerstone" in the catacombs; excluded by the pagan temple and by the divine Augustus, it succumbs to the power of the State. Many popes of this era are martyred. They do not deny their faith and the "rock" is soaked with their blood, while for other popes there is exile and imprisonment. And yet the bishop of Rome manages to guide his community, maintains contact with those far away, and asserts himself as the custodian of unity in Christ. Some are lost on the way, or abjure the faith and terror produces saints or apostates. The young Church, sprung from the ancient olive tree of Galilee, somehow roots itself in the heart of the empire, transplanted from Jerusalem to Rome. *Stat crux, dum volvitur orbis.*

As a result of the Edict of Milan, the Church of Rome comes out of the catacombs and acquires the rights of citizenship, and after three centuries of persecution, practices its own religion publicly. The State slowly becomes Christian, and the emperor would like to manipulate that "rock" in the most appropriate corners of his palace. The crisis of the empire accompanies the spread of heresies while military strength is lost gradually. But the bishop of Rome stands firm and without seeking it, discovers his civil role. When the barbarians arrive, his authority replaces that of the emperor and the pope becomes the *defensor Urbis.* By this route the Church acquires a universal dimension. The "rock" has raised a structure in which spiritual power is asserted in all its dignity, which is the *civitas Dei*; built in the heart of the city of men it leads to the Kingdom of God. The authority of the pope in controversies about dogma is recognized from the time of Leo the Great; it is the primacy of the apostolic see.

But the "rock" of this holy structure, viewed as a community of the faithful of an exclusively spiritual nature, inserted as it is within the State, inevitably leads to compromise. Even if initially only on religious matters, the pope now enjoys an authority equal to that of a "Caesar," and politics and imperialism

slowly grow together in the upper levels of the structure. With the collapse of
the Western empire, Rome finds in the pope the bastion of civilization as
Byzantium is far away and weak, apart for the Justinian ray of light. But
Gregory the Great is unique in his integrity as *Consul Dei.*

Italy breaks apart, and the pontifical supremacy becomes its safeguard,
although its ecclesiastical imprint is altered. The compromise is the false
Constitutum Constantini and the arrival of the Franks with the grants of Pepin.
The Church becomes a political organism, discovers temporal power, and cre-
ates the future ecclesiastical State.

"However, with the foundation of this State," Gregorovius observed bitterly,
"came to an end the most glorious period of the Roman Church, whose character until then had been purely episcopal and priestly. The Church became
territory. The popes who, contrary to the teaching of the Gospel and the doctrine of Christ, united the priesthood to the secular state, could no longer protect
the purity of their apostolic office, and the dual and contradictory nature of their
position drew them increasingly towards a policy of ambition. They were constrained by the necessity of things to undertake debasing struggles to preserve
their temporal entitlements; they faced up to civil wars against the city of Rome
and sustained fierce battles against the political powers."

These are the extreme words of a condemnation that others might prefer to
mitigate by giving more credit to that phrase "the necessity of things" which
were historically irreversible. The pope was probably forced by circumstances to
set up his own temporal authority because only political independence could
have protected his freedom of political action. This is debatable, but it is substantially correct to consider this doubling of power to be the birth of a symbolic
aspect of the figure of the pope. The recourse to false papal decrees, such as
those of the *Pseudo Isidore* is perhaps the most striking show of this desire for
power, which one tries to legitimize on a juridical level. And this is shameful.

The only redemption is universal sovereignty in the wake of Nicholas the
Great; it is, despite everything, the *Dictatus papae* of Gregory VII, the attempt
at a theocratic State with Innocent III, in the absolute right acknowledged in the
pope to command spirit and matter, both the ecclesiastical world and the secular world. This utopia will last for more than two centuries, a utopia in
which is carried out exacerbated reach for power, while the pope often loses
the stimuli of Christian edification and encourages the germination of dis-
cords which demand, unheard, a return to the evangelical spirit. Every
renunciation of temporal power is suffocated by the "grand refusal," from
which derive the slavery of Avignon, the schism of the West and the definite
rupture of the religious unity of Europe.

The pope loses credibility. In the widespread conviction of a reform, which
will not be carried out, the authority of the Council is asserted at Pisa, at

Constance, at Basel. Pope and antipope at the same time, the "vicar of Christ" has his revenge on the national States, with his role of the "sovereign" pontiff, the pope-king. And this is "not a legal abstraction but rather a daily reality," according to Paolo Prodi, "in which it is left, in the first place, to the subjects-believers to pay the price of the development of the monarch's absolute power."

The result is the carnival of eroticism and simony, of crime and nepotism of the popes of the Renaissance; it is Luther, and it is the split in the Christian world. The Chair of Peter is saved by the terror of the Inquisition, finds again its primacy in the Counter Reformation, but closes itself in its State and makes compromises with the Spanish, the French, and the Austrians. Thus the judgment of Machiavelli, who identified in the temporal power of the papacy the cause of the failed unification of Italy and of the many foreign invasions, appears in great part true. And, similarly, the attachment of the Church to the pontifical State caused, as a reaction, the birth of a laic awareness in the Italian faithful. From then until now, that awareness has experienced a dissension between civic duty and religious obligation, and a kind of inevitable nihilism (anarchy) has crept into its soul.

This accompanied the final metamorphoses of the temporal power of the popes right up to its territorial realignment within the Vatican City, although the financial interests which the Holy See has conserved remain vast. From the concept of the "free Church in a free State" in the Concordat of 1929, the material power of the papacy remains intact; masked and transmuted into other forms, it invests its capital.

On the other hand, liberalism and nationalism, socialism and communism have helped to augment in the believer of today, both in Italy and the world over, an increasingly secular conscience which has, however, often seen personal and civic values collapse after loss of faith. In this regard, the observation of the writer Dino Buzzati in an interview released shortly before he died is significant: "If religious feeling has fallen away in Italy, it is due to the temporalism of the Church and to the related errors which follow therefrom." Recalling Pius XII and the events of the Second World War, he reproached him, saying that, "if the pope knew what was happening at Auschwitz and Buchenwald, he should have raised his voice in a definitive condemnation, risking everything, even if he might have been shot and all the cardinals with him, and the Vatican were to have been burnt to the ground. He would have saved the Church and we would all have believed in him. If it did not happen, it means that opportunism intervened, the pre-eminent problem of "surviving." And certain failures of the spirit have to be paid for."

The thesis of *The Vicar* by Hochhuth, however arguable it may be, weighs on a certain aspect of the papacy, and it needed John XXIII and the Second Vatican Council to shake the power of the Church of Rome to its foundations.

Since then the "Vicar of Christ" has been seeking an authentically spiritual and evangelical dimension, which it is trying to prove to the world through a recovered credibility. With the statement of John that "the Church belongs to everyone, but especially the poor," as Giancarlo Zizola has noted, "the impetus is towards a Christian community which has at its center those who are oppressed, excluded and are powerless." Utopia?

The most recent developments of the I.O.R. would appear not to demonstrate an impartial attitude. The Vatican always appears to be "a State with its own Minister of Finance who invests and increases the reserves rather than living in the evangelical present," Zizola emphasizes again, clarifying that, in the final analysis, "one is not asking for the end of the papacy, just the end of its temporal power. Not the end of an authority, but the end of the worldly means to which this authority has recourse."

One can only await a concrete program in answer to the cry launched by John Paul II: "We live only on offerings!" And perhaps for once it is not simply a matter of words. Karol Wojtyla, "a pope come from afar," so similar in name and origin to the character of Kiril Lakota, "a pope come from the steppes" in the novel by Morris West, *In the Shoes of Peter*, really could, as that imaginary pontiff had planned, "change the course of history by establishing the Kingdom of Christ in the hearts of men so they can establish for themselves a temporal system solidly based on truth, justice, charity and moral law."

THE POPES

1. ST. PETER (30—67)

He was called Simon and he was a fisherman from Bethsaida on the eastern shore of the Lake of Tiberias in Galilee. He was married and he had moved with his wife, his father, his mother-in-law and his brother Andrew to Capharnaum, where the fish business offered good prospects. At Bethany, he and Andrew had joined the disciples of John the Baptist who was preparing people for the coming of the Messiah. This was, in fact, a period when the Galileans were very receptive to the Messianic concept and ready to shake off their miserable existence in bondage to Rome, had they found a leader. Then, all of a sudden, one day there was the meeting with Jesus of Nazareth between February and March of the year 28. Jesus gazed at Peter intently and, as St. John recounts it (I, 42), said to him: "Thou art Simon, the son of John; thou shalt be called Cephas;" that is "Rock," and so his name was changed to Peter. No doubt the fisherman in question did not understand, right then, the significance and scope of this declaration, but there was something mysterious and disturbing about the young Nazarene.

And more or less from that day began the experience of Simon whose faith in Jesus-Messiah slowly grew as he witnessed the manifestation of His extraordinary miraculous powers, observed the young Rabbi's new attitude and disregard for social and religious taboos and trustfully heard the promise of a kingdom. He became fully convinced that he was following a political Messiah.

Once the center of His preaching was fixed at Capharnaum, Jesus developed a preferential relationship with Simon, and performed for him the miracle of the fish as told by Luke (V, 8), an event which aroused Simon's fear in the face of the Divine, since he says: "Depart from me, for I am a sinful man, O Lord!" revealing thereby that he was beginning to understand the completely religious nature of the Messiah whom he has been following. And Jesus reassured him, indeed, invited him to take on a task of which the fishing catch was merely a symbol: "Do not be afraid; henceforth thou shalt catch men."

Then, one day in July of the year 29, came the promise of the primacy. Travelling up the valley of the Jordan towards Caesarea Philippi followed by the twelve apostles, Jesus asked from them a profession of faith: "Who do you say that I am?" Answering for them all was Simon: "Thou art the Christ, the Son of the living God." It was not yet that faith which will live in him after the Resurrection and Pentecost, but it was such that Jesus considered it to be a revelation from God: "Blessed art thou, Simon Bar-Jona, for flesh and blood have not revealed this to thee, but my Father in heaven." Then, referring to what he had said during their first meeting, He called him "Peter," adding an explanation of the change of name by stating that "upon this rock I will build my Church, and the gates of hell shall not prevail against it. And I will give thee the keys of the Kingdom of Heaven; and whatever thou shalt. . . loose on earth shall be loosed also in heaven" (Matthew, XVI, 13–19).

In these words, the Catholic Church recognizes the creation of the Papacy, prescribing a function to be carried out throughout the centuries in a community of living "rocks," among which Peter appeared as the one which assured the stability of the building. He also took on the power to make decisions on doctrinal issues among men to whom the will of God is extended. In this sense, the function of the primacy could not end with Peter, and hence the succession of Roman pontiffs.

The promise of the primacy was in any case confirmed after the Resurrection. Following the threefold declaration of love by Peter, Jesus conferred on him the primacy over the entire Church ("Feed my lambs") naming him the first Pope. This was in April of the year 30.

Peter carried out his function as head of the Church in various places. To begin with in Jerusalem, where the first Council of the Church took place in 48–49, then at Antioch where a tradition of the second century has it that he governed the episcopal see for seven years, and perhaps at Corinth, where the Church was considered to have been "founded by Peter and Paul," according to a letter of the bishop Dionysius in the second half of the second century. And finally in Rome where, by tradition, Peter guided Christianity for 25 years, from 42 to 67, not without interruption, as his presence in Jerusalem for the Council in 48–49 shows. Also St. Paul, in his *Letter to the Romans* in the year 58, does not list him among the Christians whom he greets, and the *Acts of the Apostles* make no mention of Peter when they describe the arrival of Paul in Rome in 61.

With regard to the presence of Peter in Rome, the literary testimony is generic (Clement of Rome, St. Ignatius of Antioch, Clement of Alexandria, Eusebius of Caesarea), apart from that of the Apostle himself who, in his *First Letter*, alludes to the city from which he is writing as Babylon, a symbolic name which refers to Rome, like John in the *Apocalypse*. He is supposed to have come with his wife who, according to Clement of Alexandria died a martyr, and with his daughter whose name is known as Petronilla, though this could well have been the name of a disciple of his, converted and baptised by him.

Numerous, however, are the legends related to places and monuments in the city which recall the presence of Peter. First of all, there is the Mamertine prison where, at the top of the staircase leading to the lower cell of the prison, the Tullianum, an inscription on the marble records that "on this stone Peter laid his head, forced down by the police, and the miracle remains." And indeed, the stone below it appears hollowed with the imprint of a head. There is another inscription in the Tullianum behind the remains of a marble column: "This is the column where the Apostles Sts. Peter and Paul, being bound, converted their jailers Processus and Martinianus, who were martyred, and baptised XLVII others in the faith of Christ with the water from this fountain which miraculously sprang forth."

Belli recalled the incident in his sonnet, *St.Peter in Jail*:

The best thing they did at the "cow pasture"
(the Forum]
in the time of Nero was to put
a prison at the foot of the Capitol
where everybody spoke Latin.

That place was called the Mamertine;
and don't believe me, a nut,
but let a certain little lawyer
give the explanation.

It is that very prison where
they put Saint Peter
before he went to the new prison.

And he made that new well so full
that for so many years, in rain
or shine, is always full and never
has run dry.

The Church of Sts. Nereus and Achilleus, which already in the fifth century was called *in fasciola*, is supposed to recall the *fasciola*, the bandage that covered the wound on St. Peter's foot, which he got while he was leaving Rome after he had escaped from the Mamertine jail. Also famous is the tiny church of *Domine, quo vadis?* on the Appian Way, built where Christ is said to have appeared to Peter fleeing from Rome, and to the Apostle's question: "Lord, where are you going?" replied "to Rome, to be crucified again," causing Peter to turn back and accept his martyrdom.

In addition, the Chapel of the Separation on the Via Ostia was where Peter and Paul arrived from the jail, then to part towards their different places of death. Later dedicated to the Most Holy Cross, it was located on the left side of the Basilica of St. Paul until 1568 when it was knocked down and reconstructed on the opposite side where it remained until 1910, when it was finally demolished. A bas-relief showed the scene of the separation on a stone frieze now in the Church of the Most Holy Trinity of the Pilgrims.

IN THIS PLACE ST. PETER AND ST. PAUL SEPARATED
ON THEIR WAY TO MARTYRDOM AND PAUL SAID TO PETER
MAY THE LIGHT BE WITH YOU FOUNDATION OF THE CHURCH
AND PASTOR OF ALL THE LAMBS OF CHRIST
AND PETER TO PAUL GO IN PEACE PREACHER
TO THE GOOD AND GUIDE OF THE HEALTH OF THE JUST.

And finally, the chains that bound him are reputed to be those kept at St. Peter in Chains in an urn of gilded bronze. It is said that there were two different ones that had enchained the Apostle, one in Palestine and the other in Rome itself. St. Leo the Great placed them in the urn and, when they came into contact, they miraculously fused, forming a single chain of 38 links.

Peter is thought to have lived on the Esquiline, in the palace of Senator Pudente, located on *vicus Patricius*, where he set up an oratory in which he baptised the virgins, Pudentiana and Prassede Tradition has it that Rome's oldest church, that of Saint Prudentia, was built on the site. However, according to another tradition, Peter is said to have also been a guest on the Aventine of a couple, Aquila and Prisca, on the remains of whose house the Church of St. Prisca was built in the fourth century.

The most colorful legend is certainly the one about the stone, kept in the Church of St. Francesca Romana in the Forum, which bears the impression of the knees of St. Peter as he prayed to God to punish Simon Magus (the Magician) for his pride in elevating himself into the air. The Apostle recounts this flight in the Apostolic Constitutions (end of the fourth century). "I had met Simon in Caesarea," recalls St. Peter, "and I had forced him to admit his defeat in a public confession. He then came to Italy from the Orient and arrived in Rome, where he began his war against the Church, causing many brothers to lose their faith through the seductions of his magic arts. One day he invited people to come to the amphitheater at noontime, and summoned me as well, promising he would fly. Everyone was watching him. In the meantime, I was silently praying. And then he raised himself heavenwards, supported by demons, and said: 'I lift myself towards heaven and I shall rain blessings upon you.' The people applauded and hailed him as a god. With my heart and my hands raised to heaven, I prayed to God, through our Lord Jesus, to strike at the pride of this impostor, to humble the power of the demons who seduce men, dragging them to their death, to cause that infamous being to fall ignominiously and to break his neck, yet to keep him alive. Then, looking at Simon, I shouted: 'If I am truly the man of God, the true Apostle of Jesus, doctor of honest devotion and not an impostor such as you, wretched Simon, I command the powers of evil who are accomplices in your perverseness and are holding you up in this flight, to abandon you immediately. Fall from your heights and come and hear the jeers of the crowd seduced by your magic tricks.' As I ended these words, Simon, abandoned by the demons, suddenly fell into the amphitheater. He broke a leg and disjointed his toes. The crowd thereupon cried out: 'The only true God is the One declared by Peter!' And a great number of people renounced the teachings of Simon."

Peter died in Rome sometime between the fire of 64 and the death of Nero in 68, and tradition fixed the date as 29 June of the year 67. He was one of the victims of the emperor's persecution following the burning of the city, for which Nero blamed the Christians.

No document exists which shows the exact date but, from a series of plausible inferences, Margherita Guarducci reached the conclusion that his death occurred on exactly 13 October 64 A.D. The uncertainty about the two dates continues even in the most recent *Annuari pontifici*.

Apocryphal writings give the place of his crucifixion (head downwards, as he himself requested, deeming himself unworthy to die like Christ) as "on the site called *naumachia* close to the obelisk of Nero towards the *monte*," that is, in the Circus of Nero near the Vatican Hill. He was buried there, as the Roman presbyter Caius wrote at the beginning of the third century to the Montanist Proclo: "Go to the Vatican Hill and along the Ostian Way, and you will find the *tropei* of those who founded this community," in other words the tombs of the two apostles, Peter and Paul.

According to one tradition, during the persecution of 258 under Emperor Valerian, the remains of Peter and Paul were removed from the original tombs and carried *ad Catacumbas*, (or to the cemetery of St. Sebastian), to be protected against possible desecration. A century later, Sylvester I had them returned to the original burial place, and so the remains of Peter returned to Vatican Hill where they were placed in a sarcophagus of Cypriot bronze, fixed to the ground, on top of which, it seems, Constantine had built the oldest basilica of St. Peter. The legend goes that the emperor himself dug up the first spadeful of soil for its foundation, and carried twelve baskets of earth in honor of the Prince of the Apostles.

Attempts were made at various times to discover the sepulcher of the first pope, which had been placed amongst other tombs of the second and third centuries in various strata of a necropolis, so the task proved a difficult one.

Only in 1939, under the patronage of Pius XII, were systematic excavations carried out in a series of efforts which led to concrete results, in the 1950s, when a small shrine attached to a wall of red plaster was discovered and identified by archaeologists as the *tropeo* cited by Caius, and on which was inscribed the word *Petr(os)eni*, that is, "Peter is (buried here) inside." The tomb, however, turned out to be empty.

In 1965 the archaeologist Margherita Guarducci managed to find the remains of the Apostle, not in a sarcophagus of Cypriot bronze but in a "shoebox," an incident which took on an air of mystery and has become part of the city's archaeological history. Luciano Zeppegno recalls it with lively irony. "A denizen of St. Peter's reminded Margherita Guarducci that at the time of the discovery she had received from the steward of the Workshop at St. Peter's some material which had been found in the mysterious storage place. The material had been put into a shoebox and put aside somewhere.

"Margherita Guarducci's investigative nature was rewarded when the box was found in a storeroom of the Vatican Grottoes. Inside were human bones, those of animals, cloth fragments, little pieces of red plaster, little scraps of silver and medieval coins. The investigation carried out by experts established that the human bones were those of a man, fairly tall and sturdy, between sixty and seventy years old, the fragments of textile came from a purple cloth with gold threads, the plaster from the Red Wall, while the dirt inside was identical with that in the shrine. Guarducci came to the conclusion that the bones were the remains of the Apostle, removed from the shrine and put in the storeroom to protect them from water infiltrations. And the medieval coins? They probably fell through cracks in the wall into the storeroom, the same way the rats, whose remains were still there, had come."

Mystery apart, the laboratory test results linked to a series of circumstantial evidence, if not of proofs, have served to confirm the tradition, never contradicted in nineteen centuries, that, in fact, "Peter is (buried here) inside," that is, in the basements of the actual basilica.

These are the most recent of Peter's mishaps in what has become, in the course of centuries, his city—by popular decree. The first pope, yes, if we want to use this term as from him, but basically the first bishop of Rome and its patron, ready from the top of the Muro Torto to blind the enemy who would dare profane the center of Christianity, as Procopius has passed onto us with one more legend concerning the siege of the Goths in 537. And Saint Peter has always been an object of veneration by the people, almost as a sign of gratitude for his protection.

Even today this devotion is evident by the bronze statue which dominates in its severe and sullen majesty the central nave of the Vatican Basilica. According to one tradition, the statue is supposed to have been cast from the remains of a statue of Jupiter by order of Pope Leo the Great in the fifth century, but a more generally accepted version is that it may be the work of Arnolfo di Cambio. It is, nonetheless, a fact that the devotion of the Romans has always been great for this statue of Saint Peter, depicted in the classic gesture of the vicar of Christ imparting the solemn blessing, with his right foot worn by having been rubbed for so many centuries by the hands and lips of the faithful.

2. SAINT LINUS (67–76)

Linus, son of Ercolano of the Moors (Mauritanians), is said to have been born at Volterra, and tradition has it the Tuscan city built a church in 1480 to him on the emplacement of his father's house.

A disciple of Peter, he probably preached in France while he was bishop of Besançon, and stood in for the Apostle, heading the Roman community during the latter's absences from the city. He was the pontiff as from the year 67, through the reigns of five different Roman emperors: Nero, Galba, Otto, Vitellius, and Vespasian.

We learn from the *Liber pontificalis* that it was Linus who ordered women to cover their heads in church, a rule that prevailed for a long time, considering that it was only in the past twenty years of the twentieth century that it disappeared.

He is said to have added to the canon of the Mass the part which, up until the new liturgy adopted with the Second Vatican Council, was called *Communicantes*, and also introduced the pallium as an ornament and symbol of papal authority. This was a simple strip of white wool bearing the imprint of black crosses and worn as a stole over the vestments. Books attributed to him on the passion of St. Peter and Peter's dispute with Simon Magus are, however, to be considered apocryphal.

For the spread and the application of the Gospel, the Christian community of Rome in the days of Linus could count. on "presbyters" and "bishops," two terms which seemed originally to be synonymous but quickly acquired the meaning they have today. The bishops were the true heads of the community, who celebrated Mass and administered the sacraments, while the presbyters, or the priests, exercised such functions only with the approval of the bishops. Other persons worked too within the Church to take care of the apostolate, like the "deacons" who were charged with administering the ecclesiastical property and assisting bishops and priests. Then there were the "prophets" who were the same as those later called catechists or instructors, assisted by a group of younger persons called "didacticians," and finally the "paracletes" who were concerned with the aid to the sick and the poor. The other two large Churches at Corinth and Ephesus were structured more or less in the same way.

So the Roman community, established only a few years earlier, was already organized, but it had to protect itself from certain restless souls who insinuated themselves among the initiated and, not content with the Christian revelation, stained its purity by attempting to reconcile different, and even contradictory, tendencies.

Linus, in fact, had problems with the heresies that were circulating. Apart from that of Simon Magus, with whom St. Peter had been in direct conflict, and carried on by the disciple Menandrus, the thorniest heresy was that of the Hebionites, Jewish-Christians who were defending Mosaic law while recognizing Jesus as the Messiah. The marginalized status of these became clear with the destruction of the city of Jerusalem in the year 70 by Titus, son of the Emperor Vespasian, the most important event during the pontificate of Linus.

For Christians, that event could have meant the fulfilment of Jesus's prophecy when He predicted that not a stone would remain of the Temple, a sure sign of the imminent end of the world, and at the same time of the advent of the Kingdom of God! Or the destruction of Jerusalem could have been interpreted as a revenge, "the revenge of the ancient sin," to quote a verse of Dante, spokesman of a Christian way of thinking up to the Second Vatican Council. The Jews were viewed as directly guilty of the death of Christ, even though the death was necessary to achieve redemption (the "revenge") from original sin, so God used the Romans to punish them.

Moreover, the destruction of Jerusalem was the result of an uprising in Judea beginning in the year 66, a revolt which clearly could not have succeeded against the empire, and sooner or later had to be paid for. Josephus Flavius tells of the siege of the city with a realism which remained linked to famous episodes such as that of a woman named Mary who, starving, killed and ate her own son.

It is a fact that the Christians, as soon as they heard that the Jews, because of their rebellion, had fallen foul of Roman authority, lost no opportunity to convince the Romans that they themselves were not contaminated by Judaism. Starting with the heresies that had developed among the Jewish Christians, they distanced from these, openly condemning them. The Hebionites thus wound up discredited in the eyes of the Romans. Grant notes, "just like the Jews, and as a result gradually disappeared into the number of meaningless sects which failed to survive in the modern world. Instead, the Gentile Christians escaped this branding by Rome and became the strength and the dominant theme of Christianity to come." It was, if one wants, a purely tactical move of a "political" nature, the first of many such moves by the Christians during their long history.

These were certainly difficult times for a clear propagation of the words of Christ, and some shrewd tricks were used not much in keeping with the Christian ethos as preached by St. Paul. Obviously another obstacle was imperial persecution against which the clerical "policy" could not do much. But, for a while, following the terror of the times of Nero, it seems that Vespasian had vented his wrath by destroying Jerusalem, exterminating the Jews and putting an end to the national existence of Israel.

Nevertheless, the *Liber pontificalis* has Linus dying martyred, beheaded by the Consul Saturnine on 23 September 76, and it notes that he was buried the following day next to St. Peter. In fact, there is reason to believe that he was not martyred, and the commemoration of St. Linus is no longer to be found in the *Universal Calendar of the Church*.

3. ST. ANACLETUS (76 – 88)

Up until 1946 an Athenian Anacletus was considered the fifth pope, following on Saint Clement, and a Roman, Cletus, a disciple of Saint Peter, was classified as the third. Since the *Annuario pontificio* of 1947, however, the idea has been finally accepted that the Anacletus mentioned in the *Catalogo liberiano* is the same person as the Cletus described in the *Liber pontificalis*, said to have succeeded St. Linus in 76.

He lived under the Emperors Vespasian, Titus, and Domitian and probably followed the direction given to the Christian community of Rome by his predecessors, including the naming of bishops and priests. He is thought to have ordered the ecclesiastics to wear their hair short and to have begun the building of a Workshop of St. Peter above the tomb of the first pope.

The eruption of Vesuvius, on 24 August of the year 79, took place during his pontificate and the phases of that tragic event have been described for us by Pliny the Younger in two letters written to Tacitus, who had asked him for information on the circumstances of the death of his uncle, Pliny the Elder, who had gone too close to the area where the lava had fallen. It is terrifying to read about the torments suffered by the peoples of those buried cities: "I listened to the groans of the women, the cries of the children, the shouts of the men, some cried out loudly seeking their parents, or their children, or their spouses, recognizing them by their voices. There were those who pitied themselves, who worried about their own dear ones and some who prayed for death, out of fear of death. Many raised their arms to the gods, even more declared there were no more gods and that it was the last night of the world."

For Christians, the volcano's eruption coming after the destruction of Jerusalem could only be taken as a final warning to expect, terrorized, the advent of the Kingdom of Christ, and that Rome would disappear along with its idols.

But a year later came the confutation of these beliefs, with the superb inauguration of the Flavian Amphitheater by Emperor Titus, and impressive ceremonies and games lasting a hundred days and costing the lives of thousands of gladiators. Later came Domitian's planning of a stadium for athletic and gymnastic competitions at the Campus Martius, between the Baths of Nero and the so-called pool of Agrippa. Its inauguration must have been around the year 85, if it is true that a year later the *Certamen capitolinum* took place, for which athletic, equestrian and musical competitions were to be held, and hence the stadium must have been usable by then.

In the Middle Ages the stadium was to become the *Campus agonis* and, later, *Circus agonalis*, even if a stadium is certainly something other than a circus. In any case, from *agone* (athletic combat) it became in *agone* and *inagone*, then "Navona," the name which was applied in modern times to the square, with its intense and individual life, linked to popes such as Innocent X and Clement XI.

So pagan Rome erupted triumphantly, assisting at gladiatorial games in the Flavian Amphitheater and at athletic competitions in the Stadium of Domitian. The people demanded nothing more than *panem et circenses* (bread and circuses) and the Christians were forgotten. Basically, Titus was tolerant toward them, and Domitian himself seemed to stick to that attitude at the beginning of his reign.

It is very probable that Pope Anacletus, who died in the year 88, in fact was not martyred and, as a result, whether his name was Cletus or Anacletus, he wound up being removed from the *Universal Calendar of the Church*.

4. ST. CLEMENT I (88−97)

Clement was a Roman, but of Jewish origin. A disciple of St. Paul and his collaborator at Philippi, he had been nominated bishop by St. Peter and became pope in 88. Tradition has him as a son of Senator Faustinus of the Flavian family, and hence related to Emperor Domitian, so perhaps it was his origins that saved him from the very brief but intense persecution unleashed by the emperor in 95.

There were many famous victims of that "reign of terror," including the Consul Flavius Clement, husband of Domitilla, niece of Domitian. According to Cassius Dion, the reasons why these people fell from grace were "atheism and Jewish practices," a term which could mean that they were Christians. Flavius was executed and Domitilla was exiled, while her name was given to the catacomb on the Via Ardeatina in Rome, a part of which moreover is called the Crypt of the Flavians.

Another victim of note was St. John the Evangelist, who escaped unharmed martyrdom in boiling oil, which he suffered near Porta Latina, but was exiled to the island of Patmos where he wrote his *Apocalypse*, providing even greater credence to the hopes of an imminent coming of the Kingdom of Christ.

A year later in 96, a conflict broke out within the Church at Corinth when a group of young ecclesiastics contested the policy of certain presbyters regarding the Christian community in that city. Clement responded firmly by letter, reminding them of the necessity to obey the traditional authorities of the Church, and exhorting them to flee from the false doctors. The letter was received with great respect and became a subject for meditation during the Mass on Sunday. It is the first text, which affirms, in practice, the superiority of the bishop of Rome over all the Churches scattered around the world.

So Christianity, under the pontificate of Clement I, gained new proselytes and developed considerably in the East. At Rome, Clement himself carried on his apostolate with diligence and was destined to leave a popular mark which gave rise to various legends, such as that of Sisinnius, connected to a miracle conserved in a fresco on a wall of the Church of St. Clement. This was founded in Rome three centuries after the pope's death, and, according to tradition, right on the site of his paternal home.

What purportedly happened was that the Saint, while converting a certain Theodora, wife of the prefect Sisinnius, had convinced her also to make a vow of chastity, obviously arousing the ire of the husband. The latter, together with his soldiers, followed her one day and surprised her inside a catacomb in a room where St. Clement was celebrating Mass. Furious, Sissinius ordered his soldiers to arrest the pope, but it seems God did not permit this to happen, and blinded Sisinnius and his thugs. Theodora took her husband home where he then recovered his sight.

But, under the part about the miracle, the fresco depicts the rest of the legend with the comic side of the soldiers who, blinded, drag along a column instead of the pope.

After St. Peter, St. Clement seems to have had the strongest personality among the first popes of the Christian community in Rome, and provoked considerable distrust of the Christians at the top ranks of imperial power. As a result, in 97 the new Emperor Nerva exiled the bishop of Rome to Crimea. There at the Black Sea, Clement carried on the apostolate with two thousand Christians condemned to forced labor in the marble quarries, while Evaristus filled in for him at Rome during a period of what, in fact, was a forced abdication from the See of Peter. Urging them to have faith, he achieved new conversions, and this angered the new emperor, Trajan, who looked upon Christianity as a plague for the human race. Clement then was ordered to offer sacrifice to the gods, which he obviously refused to do. With the result that the sentence against him to be thrown into the Black Sea with an anchor around his neck was carried out. And behold, another miracle, also immortalized in a fresco in his church in Rome, which narrates the legend by which the waters of the Sea opened up once a year, permitting the faithful to build a chapel around his relics, and later to walk down to it in a procession, always making sure though to leave before the waters closed in on top of them. And one year, a widow lost her only child there but the next, coming back in the procession, found her little boy safe and sound as though nothing had occurred.

However, in the year 869, the body of St. Clement was brought to Rome by St. Cyril and St. Methodius, through the intervention of Pope Nicholas I, and finally buried in his basilica.

5. ST. EVARISTUS (97—105)

Evaristus was born in Bethlehem of Jewish parents, who had him educated in Greece, and he became a Christian while with Clement at Rome. According to tradition, he took the place of his teacher at the time of the latter's arrest and extradition to the Chersonesus, becoming head of the Church of Rome in the year 97. Very little is known about him from the usual sources, particularly unreliable and fragmentary, but what is curious is that Clement was not considered still in command even though in exile. Perhaps he should be considered the first pope to have abdicated, even if forced to by being sent into exile. The *Pontifical Annual* is of that opinion.

Evaristus divided the city into parishes or *tituli*, a term indicating places sanctified by the martyrdom of a Christian which, marked with a memorial cross, were to become places on which churches were to be built. Every "title" was assigned to a priest and the church thus became the personal "see" of the titleholder.

These were more like embryonic churches that would be developed in the course of time, and to begin with were simply meeting places, but entrusted to assistants of the bishop as co-responsible for the Church of Rome.

Evaristus also ordered that seven deacons were to assist the bishop while he preached, in order to offer guarantees of his orthodoxy against the false claims of heretics. It is also said that he was the one to prescribe that marriages were to be celebrated in public and with the benediction of a priest.

He died in the year 105 but it is not certain that he should be considered a martyr, or that he was interred near the tomb of St. Peter, as tradition would have it.

6. ST. ALEXANDER I (105—115)

Alexander was born to a noble family at Rome, in the region of the *Caput Tauri* (Head of the Bull) and his father's name was also Alexander. He was elected pope in 105, a few days after the death of Evaristus, and while still very young, between twenty and thirty years old. His was probably the first election which did not take place by testamentary designation from teacher to disciple, still in practice, but was based on a choice of the bishops present in Rome, with the testimony of priests and deacons and the vote of the faithful.

He is supposed to have had numerous adherents in the imperial court, persons such as the prefect Ermetes and the tribune Quirinus, but this did not help him avoid martyrdom in 115 and he was beheaded together with Ermetes and two priests, Evenzius and Teodulus. However, according to a different version, the Alexander in question, buried at the seventh mile on the Via Nomentana, was not the pontiff but another Alexander.

What is certain, though, is the notice of a decree of his approving the addition of water to the wine in the sacrifice of the Mass, as well as the introduction of holy water.

A manuscript uncovered in the seventeenth century, considered apocryphal, contained a fragment from the time of Alexander I which told of legendary battles between this pope with the Gnostic heretics.

However, it was a golden era for the Roman empire and the prophecy of the coming of the Kingdom of Jesus seemed a thing of the past. And Trajan, after his victories over the Dacians, built his own Forum with, at its center, the famous Column, at the top of which stood the statue of the emperor, replaced in 1587 by a statue of St. Peter.

On the subject of arrests of Christians and their convictions carried under Trajan, Eusebius of Caesarea, citing some testimonies on the situation in the East in the *Storia ecclesiastica*, notes that, at a certain point, the persecution "increased so much that Pliny the Younger, greatly esteemed among the governors, wrote to the emperor about the multitude of those who had been put to death for their faith. At the same time he informed him that he had not found that these people had committed any impieties or illegalities. They merely rose at dawn to sing hymns to Christ, as to a God; they rejected adultery, felonies and similar crimes and did everything in accordance with the laws.

"Then Trajan issued a decree not to seek out specifically the Christian 'tribe' but to punish it only when found, thus eliminating the threat of persecutions which had become terrible. But there was no lack of pretexts available to those who wanted to do harm. At times it was groups of people, at others the local authorities themselves who prepared pitfalls." And these underhand maneuvers to get round the basic problem and hit at the Christians, in any case, spread throughout the empire. Probably Alexander I himself was a victim of it since he openly preached the Gospel and died, if not with those companions in martyrdom mentioned above, still a martyr, interred beside St. Peter.

A famous victim was the bishop of Antioch, St. Ignatius, who was arrested with two companions, Zosimus and Rufus, and was brought to Rome to be thrown to the beasts. Detained for some time during the trip to Smyrna, he learned that the Christians of Rome were trying every possible way to free him. But Ignatius did not give a second thought about recommending that no finger be lifted to help him, addressing a letter to them which is considered the spiritual testament of these first martyrs, and the symbol of the redemption to which all faithful Christians should fearlessly aim. "Let me be immolated. . . let me become the prey of wild beasts; by way of them I shall arrive at God: I am the wheat of God; may I be chewed up by the teeth of the wild animals in order to become the white bread of Christ." He died in 107 or 108.

In fact, during the times of Trajan, there was a strange situation in respect to the persecutions and one which would characterize, for a century and a half, the relationship between the Imperial authorities and the Christians. As a result the latter could openly carry on the work of the apostolate, celebrate the rites and meet together, without causing reaction on the part of the authorities. But hanging over them would be the sword of Damocles of antipathy and hostility, which could lead to an accusation and thence to a death sentence.

7. St. Sixtus I (1 1 5 — 1 2 5)

A Roman from the Region of Via Lata and the son of a certain Pastor, Sixtus I was elected pope in 115 while Hadrian was emperor.

Hadrian turned out to be well disposed towards the Christians and, although he maintained in substance the methods used by Trajan, he warned about false accusations and wrote to this effect to the Proconsul of Asia: "If someone makes accusations and proves that the Christians are violating the laws, then you will punish according to the gravity of their responsibility; but, by Hercules, if someone uses it as a pretext to slander another, you decide according to the seriousness and have that person punished."

Sixtus I is said to have introduced numerous rules in religious practice. He prohibited lay persons from touching the chalice and the paten, reserving that privilege to the priests, and ordered that bishops sent to the apostolic see present a letter of salutation to the faithful on their return, in order to keep all the Churches in direct communication with Rome. Attributed also to him was the introduction of the triple *Sanctus* during Mass but in fact that must have occurred at an earlier date.

In any event, the first concrete differences between the Church of Rome and that of Asia may be due to Sixtus I, if it is true that Easter was already celebrated in the Orient whereas it was not yet declared obligatory in the West. However, that he sent Bishop Pellegrinus to evangelize Gaul was pure legend.

To Sixtus I are attributed two apocryphal letters which concern the doctrine of the Trinity and insistence upon the primacy of Rome.

He was probably not martyred and, as a result, has been removed from the *Universal Calendar of the Church*. It is thought that his sepulcher is in the cathedral of Alatri and not beside St. Peter, as according to an ancient tradition. In any case, Alatri celebrates him as its patron saint.

8. St. Telesphorus (1 2 5 — 1 3 6)

Of Greek origin, Telesphorus is thought to have been born at Terranuova in Calabria, where he lived for a long time as a hermit. Once in Rome, he was elected pope in 125 at a time when a large number of heresies were increasingly threatening the Christian faith. And it was in Rome, especially, that numerous heretics had gathered in those years, aware that the importance of the city would give them greater credit for possible converts.

The heresy gaining most ground was that of the Gnostics. This was based on the concept that, in order to purify and enlarge the idea of the Divine, God must be viewed as something completely separate from man and the earth, like a god of the Abyss and all mixed with acts of magic, along the lines of Simon Magus's teachings. The propagator of these ideas in Rome was a man named Valentinus, a native of Egypt, who, remaining in the City for about twenty years, succeeded in gaining a number of followers. He wrote works inspired by profound mystical impressions, chiefly psalms and homilies.

Telesphorus brought all his strength to bear against this heresy, and the austerity of his life as a hermit no doubt accounted for the intransigence with which he condemned it.

According to the *Liber pontificalis*, he is believed to have instituted the Lenten fast, extending it for the clergy to seven weeks, and the celebration of midnight Mass at Christmas. Perhaps he himself composed the *Gloria in excelsis Deo*.

However, two different persons may be mixed up in this name of Telesphorus; the pope mentioned above who is said to have died in 136 and who, as a saint, has nevertheless been cancelled from the *Universal Calendar of the Church*, and another Telesphorus, martyred under Hadrian and recorded as such in the *Roman Martyrology*.

9. St. Hyginus (1 3 6 — 1 4 0)

Reknown for his virtues, the Athenian Hyginus, whom tradition credits with being a philosopher, entered the clergy of the Roman community and was elected pope in 136. He carried on the organization of the Church of Rome, dividing the ecclesiastical hierarchy into various groups, which probably led to a clearer distinction of functions between presbyters and deacons, and to the institution of the subdeaconate. It seems to have been he who required a godfather and a godmother for baptism and prescribed the method by which the Holy Chrism was to be preserved.

From those years dates another grandiose Roman monument—the mausoleum of Hadrian. Begun by that emperor in 135 in the area of the Domitian Gardens to serve as the tomb for himself and his successors, it was completed in 139 by Antoninus Pius. Transformed into a castle during the tenth century, it is considered an important "personage" in city's history. Bastion of defense, fortress, prison, setting for theatrical performances and for celebrations, it comes up often in the biographies of the Roman pontiffs as a witness of events, both sad and happy.

But at the time, the mausoleum served only to attest to the glory of the emperors. The angel of bronze had not yet arrived on its summit and in its place was a four-horse chariot with the statue of Hadrian. In the meantime, the bishops of Rome had problems of survival on the one hand and an ocean of internal polemics on the other, due to the emerging heresies. At Rome, Gnosticism was still spreading with the arrival of Cerdon from Syria, who obviously found grist for his mill in Hyginus's philosophical disposition.

Nothing further is known about this bishop who died in 140 but not martyred, and he does not even appear as a saint in the *Universal Calendar of the Church*. St Hyginus was buried next to St. Peter.

10. St. Pius I (140–155)

The first Pius of the twelve pontiffs to have this name was born at Aquileia in Friuli, the son of Ruffinus of the Aurelian family. His brother was called Erma and they probably came together to Rome. Pius, ordained as a priest, obtained a title which tradition identifies with what is supposed to be the oldest church in Rome, Saint Pudentiana, mentioned in the biography of St. Peter. More probably, however, the church dates from the fourth century. Pius was elected pope in 140.

His brother Erma wrote *The Pastor*, a peculiar work that was widely circulated among the Christians. In it the author calls his brothers in faith to a more attentive moral engagement to put a stop to the relaxation of customs. The principal means which could bring about a moral reform was, according to Erma, the remission of sins following sincere repentance. To understand the significance of this work one must recall that, at the time it was written, the Church did not yet have precise ideas what position to take with regard to those Christians who, once having obtained pardon of their sins through baptism, fell back into sin. The concept of a repetition of the remission of sins committed later, through what was called "confession" or "reconciliation," was not yet clear and we can understand the traumatism which the consciences of a good many Christians were experiencing.

It was precisely due to these psychological situations that the heresies continued to circulate and gain credence in Rome, where Cerdon was still proselytising, joined by Marcellina who appeared as the spokeswoman for Carpocrates of Alexandria. Against them, once elected pope, Pius continued to struggle diligently, helped by St. Justinus, author of *Dialogue with Trifone*, an ongoing controversy with the Jews.

Indeed, as a result of Justinus's interest in the relations with the Jews, Pius I ordered that the heretics of the seven Jewish sects which had been converted should be accepted by the community and be baptised, which was putting into practice the most open evangelical spirit.

He also prescribed that the Christian Easter should be celebrated on the Sunday following the full moon in March, in order to distinguish it from the Jewish Easter which was celebrated on the day of the full moon, an issue which would bring disputes in later years with the Church of Asia which followed the Jewish tradition.

According to Petrai, Pius was a good man who "lived on bread, water and fruit, who banned the use of possessions donated for divine worship for any other purpose, who threatened with very serious punishments priests who lived in concubinage, and who was so scrupulous in his ministry as to adopt similar punishments for those priests who, during the Mass, had negligently spilled a drop of wine from the chalice." These were sayings probably based on rumors transmitted from generation to generation over a span of eighteen centuries, since Petrai was writing in 1903, and gives the impression that they were colored by a substantial dose of imagination.

Pius I was the pontiff under Antoninus Pius, the emperor who kept on reasonably tolerant laws towards the Christians, and no document speaks to us of a martyrdom of this pope. Instead, even for his death in 155, Petrai leaves us some original, if not fantastic, ideas: "He was probably assassinated by someone, or on the orders of someone to whom his excessive severity was displeasing . . . He was an inconvenient pope and they got rid of him." So we discover that Pius I was the first pope "assassinated" by history, but the story seems more fantasy than fact.

1 1. St. Anicetus (1 5 5 – 1 6 6)

Anicetus came to Rome from Syria, where he was born, and joined with the Christian community of Justinus in the battle against the heretics. Indeed, the new propagators of heresies in Rome in those years were numerous, amongst whom was a certain Marcion, son of a bishop of Sinope and author of a doctrine which coincided in part with that of Cerdon. Rejected by the Eastern community, and called by the bishop of the Church at Smyrna "the first child of Satan," he had founded a personal center of worship, strongly attacked by the Church of Rome.

Elected pope in 155, Anicetus concentrated his efforts against the mob of heretics circulating in the city, and he found, like Pius I, strong support in the school which Justinus had established, and which defended the faith in the apostolic tradition.

He increased the number of participants in the community with new nominations of deacons and priests, insisting on a rather rigid standard of conduct that included the instructions recommended by St. Anacletus regarding short haircuts.

With respect to liturgy, he confirmed what Pius I had decreed as to the day for the celebration of Easter, and this led to controversy with the Greek Church, whose bishops, though tenacious in their tradition, nevertheless decided to discuss the matter with the bishop of Rome before coming to a rupture.

So in 160 St. Polycarp, aged eighty, and last survivor of the disciples of the apostles made the journey to Rome. St. Irenaeus relates the encounter in diplomatic terms: "Anicetus was just as unable to convince Polycarp to give up the custom which he had always observed with John, disciple of Our Lord, and with the other apostles with whom he had been in contact, as Polycarp was to move Anicetus to adopt the custom, since Anicetus declared his obligation to maintain the usage of his predecessors. However, they did not break relations and Anicetus, to honor Polycarp, had him celebrate the Eucharist in his own church and they then separated in peace." As much as to say that each stuck to his positions, but—and this is important—they did not arrive at a schism.

In 161 Marcus Aurelius became emperor and, under him, the controversy about the Christians grew more bitter on account of the spread of Montanist ideas which disputed the claim of the hierarchic Church to be the depository of a more direct inspiration from the Divine Spirit and resulted in a form of exaltation with manifestations of hysteria. This cast Christians in general in a bad light with the emperor making them appear anti-social and against the State.

There were arrests and prosecutions and in the East even the aged Polycarp was martyred. Anicetus would certainly have heard the news with a broken heart, remembering the man he had welcomed in his church, so good and full of understanding, and with whom he had agreed to maintain the unity of the Christians despite differences of cult.

Anicetus died in 166. It appears that he was not martyred and was "cancelled" as a saint from the recent *Universal Calendar of the Church*. He was probably the first bishop of Rome to be buried in the Catacombs of St. Calixtus.

12. ST. SOTER (166—175)

Though born at Fondi in Campania, his father came from Greece which, as soon as he was elected pope in 166, seems to have made Soter particularly interested in the problems of relations with the Greek Church. In fact, he sent to the Church of Corinth a collection of funds to be distributed to the poor, and the letter of gratitude from Dionysus, bishop of Corinth, underlines Soter's charitable spirit.

"Right from the beginning, you introduced the custom of distributing to your brothers various benefits, and of sending to many churches scattered in individual cities the needed support. You thereby respond to the poverty of the wretched and you offer what the brothers who work in the mines really need"— a reference to the quarries of the Chersonesus where St. Clement had already done his own good works— keeping alive," Dionysus pointed out, "the traditionally generous spirit of your forefathers. Bishop Soter has not only maintained that practice, but he has increased it by sending ample alms, consoling his afflicted brothers by his word and treating them like a father."

The Church of Rome, in the person of Soter, really manifested a universal, charitable disposition never seen before, and appeared really able to embrace within itself all the other Churches, ready to help them in their need, but also, evidently, ready to guide them along the way as shown in the evangelical message.

Under his pontificate, the Montanist heresy spread together with its anti-state attitudes and Emperor Marcus Aurelius continued with his policy of repression with trials and convictions throughout the empire. Faithful to the State, he was not moved by the serenity with which the Christians faced martyrdom. The report by Tertullian that the emperor, at a certain point, issued an edict of tolerance towards the Christians following what had happened to a Roman legion in 174 in Germany, an event handed down to us as the *Miracle of the Lightning Legion,* is not at all convincing. The tale is that, during the campaign against the Quadi, a Roman legion was threatened by a terrible drought which would have caused all the soldiers to die of thirst at a critical moment of the enemy's assault. It seems that a group of Christian soldiers began to pray for rain and, sure enough, the rain came accompanied by lightning flashes that routed the barbarians and saved the entire legion.

This event, immortalized in the bas-relief on the column of Antoninus Pius showing the soldiers collecting the pouring rain in their helmets, no doubt did take place, but it would certainly have been interpreted by the imperial powers as a favor granted by Jove, the god of rain, that is, by pagan gods. So nothing leads us to think that the emperor performed an act of mercy; indeed, thereafter he increased his persecution.

Soter reacted to this severity by exercising considerable authority in the development of his functions as bishop of Rome. A decree, which enables us to understand this, is the one that prohibited women from touching the paten and chalice and from burning incense during ceremonies. The deaconesses constituted an important group during the first years of the Church. Giovini Bianchi reminds us, in that rather old-fashioned yet meaningful style of his, that "the institution of the deaconesses goes back to the cradle of Christianity and was contemporary with or even prior to the institution of the deacons. Phoebe, sent by St. Paul to carry his epistle to the Romans, was a deaconess of the Church of Cencrea; and we see that, already even then all the churches in Greece had deaconesses. For this office, widows over sixty, and later over forty, were selected and stood at the door of the church in charge of the entrance. They instructed the young catechumens, while for baptism, which meant immersing the entire body in a bathtub, they helped the women to undress and then put the white gown on them. They also assisted the bishop when he anointed them and administered holy oil to sick women and washed the bodies of deceased women and placed them in the coffins. In times of danger they were the bishop's messengers, carrying his orders, doing his errands and replacing deacons in giving out alms. And it is probable that their diligence was outstanding, because the local people spoke quite a lot about these women whom they called 'fanatical little women' and gave Christianity a reputation of old women's superstitions. The deaconesses were part of the ecclesiastic body and shared in the income but, as the discipline regarding age was relaxed and young women, even spinsters, were admitted under the pretext that they dedicated themselves to chastity, scandals arose, and the bishops stopped ordaining deaconesses in order to avoid them."

In any case, with reference to Soter's decision, A. Saba emphasizes that "the decree regarding women. . . leads us to depict circumstances in which the influence of the heretics brought the feminine element in ecclesiastical discipline a little too high when prudently it would have been better to keep it in due submission!" Aside from the *machismo* tainting that judgment, the reference to heretical motivations is interesting, and it is important to recall the institution of the *sinisacte*, as told by Giovini Bianchi.

"The Greeks called *Sinisacte* those women who embraced the costume and the customs of the philosophers and who attended the academic lectures of esteemed teachers in the company of men. Then, in the first centuries of Christianity, with the ideas of an exalted platonic love, exempt from the concupiscence of the flesh, the term *Sinisacti* and *Sinisacte* was applied to those men and women who lived together under the severe discipline of platonic or pythagoric mysticism, and who claimed to love each other with a love completely contemplative and free from the demands of nature and of sex. Indeed, this obstinate disdain for the physical love was judged by them to be an exercise in virtue and a refinement in the overcoming material appetites. Christians who adopted those mystical prejudices adopted also the custom of the *Sinisacte*, otherwise known as *Agapete* or charitable women and by Latin-speakers as *Subintroductae* (under-introduced). And these were for the most part young women who dedicated themselves without pay to the service of religious persons. They lived with the priests and sometimes slept in the same bed, in order, they said, to put concupiscence to harder test and to have the glory of defeating it. But one may well believe that failures were more frequent than successes."

Giovini Bianchi records further in a footnote that "the name of *agapete* or *sinisacte* was also used by a sect of heretics called the first Origenists whose loose customs were described by St. Epiphanius in his *Heresy*," where, regarding the Adamites, he stated "that some of them, vaunting their self-restraint, had several virgins with them, which resulted with all being fooled."

If the Origenists were heretics in the fourth century, the Adamites were already around in the days of Soter, so his attitude towards the deaconesses appears to be in good measure justified, as protection against the lack of discipline among the heresies in vogue, that of the Adamites, of the Nicolaitans, and of the Gnostic. Thus a certain severity can be understood with regard to women who, in fact, were excluded from the ecclesiastical hierarchy.

Soter died in 175. He was cancelled from the list of the saints in the *Universal Calendar of the Church*, together with Caius, because both of them "under no title are to be listed in the number of martyrs." Wrapped in mystery is the original place of his burial. To begin with he was buried either next to St. Peter or in the Catacombs of St. Calixtus and later his body was moved, under Pope Sergius II, to the Church of St. Sylvester, then to the Church of St. Sixtus. But some of his remains are thought to have actually wound up in Toledo, Spain.

13. ST. ELEUTHERUS (175—189)

A native of Nicopolis, a city in present-day Bulgaria, he was a disciple of Anicetus whom he had followed to Rome when he was elected pope. He was his personal deacon and acted as his secretary during the meeting he had with Polycarp regarding the controversy over Easter.

Elected pope on the death of Soter in 175, he is said to have sent the priests Fugazius and Damian to preach the Gospel in Britain at the request of King Lucius, but the story is doubtful. More realistic are the relations that he had with the new-born Churches in Vienna, and at Lyon in Gaul where the persecution of Marcus Aurelius erupted in 177. The story of the martyrs of Lyon, amongst whom were the bishop St. Fotinus and the famous St. Blandina, is related in a document which dwells on the cruelty and sufferings endured by the martyrs, including decapitations and being fed to beasts in the amphitheater of the city.

The year 177 was a terrible one for the Christians due basically to the increase of Montanism and its radical diffusion not only in Rome, but also in all the provinces of the empire. The Christians reacted by addressing four separate explanations to Marcus Aurelius to emphasize the clear distinction between themselves and the Montanists, and to reaffirm their loyalty to the empire.

However, there was a famous victim in Rome also between 177 and 178— the young Cecilia. According to the legend, the Roman girl had agreed to marry the pagan Valerian, but wanted to remain a virgin. She had succeeded in convincing the groom of this, so much so that he himself was converted, as was his brother, Tiburtius. Discovered by the prefect Almachius, they were condemned to death. Cecilia should have died by suffocation from the steam rising from boiling water in a *calidarium*, still preserved in the chapel named the Calidarium in the basilica of St. Cecilia in Trastevere. But after three days of martyrdom she emerged unharmed, so she was beheaded.

Pope St. Paschal I built the basilica on the spot where the martyr's home had stood, the ruins of which are visible under the crypt called "Crypt of the remains." Cecilia was buried in the Catacombs of St. Callixtus and in 1599, Cardinal Sfondrati, having ordered excavations in those catacombs, found the body of the saint miraculously intact. She seemed to have been laid to rest in such a way as to conceal her face, with her hands placed to show one hand with three fingers and the other with a single finger, a way of demonstrating to the very last the sign of her faith, recalling with this gesture the mystery of the Most Holy Trinity. Stefano Maderno immortalized her thus in the prostrate statue to be found under the altar where her sepulcher is located.

As is well known, Cecilia is also considered the patron of music, but this was as a result of the misinterpretation that she "was singing in her heart" on her wedding day, and the Academy of Music at Rome was given her name.

On the death of Marcus Aurelius, his son Commodus became the emperor and there followed a period of peace for the Church, during which Eleutherus was able to devote his attention to problems of internal organization more calmly.

In fact, Eusebius of Caesarea declared that under Commodus "the Church enjoyed peace everywhere and the word of God could be spread." Nevertheless, trials involving Christians continued, the most important of which concerned the future Pope Calixtus, freedman in the service of the banker Carpoforus. When he appeared in the synagogue to request the payment of certain debts, he was accused by the Jews of disturbing their services. There was a trial and the prefect Fuscianus had Calixtus flogged and condemned him to forced labor in the mines of Sardinia for having disturbed public order. That was in 186.

As to Eleutherus's attitude towards the Montanists, it appears that his delay in condemning them was due to the fact that he agreed to a specific request for such a delay from the Christians jailed in Lyon which was brought to him in Rome by St. Irenaeus, bishop of Lyon after Potinus. But it seems that nothing came of it, so it should certainly not be viewed as a consent to the heresy but as a diplomatic tactic, perhaps political, which preceded the energetic action which was to take place shortly afterwards. Eleutherus died in 189 and was buried in the Vatican.

14. St. Victor I (189–199)

In 189 Victor I, an African, was elected pope. It was a period of tranquillity for Christians during the last years of the reign of Commodus and the first of Septimius Severus, all thanks to a lady, a certain Marcia. One of the favorite mistresses of Commodus, it seems she was ready to sacrifice her virtue for the cause though a Christian, with a spirit of emancipation astonishing for those times. It is true, however, that once she became Commodus's wife, Marcia succeeded in obtaining the freedom of all the members of the community who had been jailed or condemned to work in the Sardinian mines.

Entrusted with this task was a presbyter of the Church, the eunuch Hyacinthus who, upon his arrival in Sardinia, appeared before the Procurator with the list of Christians who had been pardoned. But freedom came also for those not on the list, such as Calixtus, which shows the extent of Marcia's prestige. And the pope, opposed to the nomination of subdeaconesses and ready to excommunicate the *agapète* as heretics, wound up making use of a woman who called herself a Christian but was ready evidently to use any means to liberate her brothers. Nevertheless this was politics, dirty politics, and religion was another matter even if the two were intermixed in this instance.

And again it was a woman who succeeded in bringing tranquillity to the bishopric of Victor when Septimius Severus became emperor— the emperor's wife Julia Domna. Coming from an ancient priestly family in Syria attached to service of the temple at Emesa and daughter of the great priest Bassianus, she was a woman exceptional for her culture and political astuteness. Interested in all eastern religions, she did not openly defend the Christians but made their existence bearable, amongst the other religions that were flooding Rome. But if Julia Domna was somehow able to make her husband listen to her to begin with, it is certain that, from 197 onwards, Septimius Severus found in Gaius Fulvius Plauzianus, the prefect of the Pretorian Guard, the person capable of fully carrying out his political aims. This man was the future father-in-law of Caracalla, and he did not nourish any particular sympathy for the Christians, which became clear a few years after Victor's death.

So this pope, safe from pitfalls and persecutions, and able to give himself completely to the problems of the Church in matters of liturgy and theology, was determined to settle the problem of the Easter celebration, and to reject all heresies. He wrote to the various Churches urging them to discuss the issue of the Paschal rite, and, as a result, numerous bishops agreed to celebrate the feast day on Sunday, according to the Roman custom. Only the province of Asia was against it, and Policrates of Ephesus replied to Victor that the Christians of that Church intended to maintain the custom of celebrating Easter on 14 Nisan, according to the so-called fourteenth practice.

Victor was decisive and immovable. He declared all adherents to this practice outside not only the Church of Rome but all the others as well. Some people
criticized his unbending attitude, including Irenaeus who, as he had demonstrated at the time of the persecutions in Lyon, was by nature docile, tending
never to condemn anyone openly. But Irenaeus's intervention had no effect and,
albeit slowly, even the Churches in Asia adapted to the Roman custom.

What becomes evident from this whole question is Victor's forceful and confident character, and hence the prestigious personality which, through him, the
bishop of Rome came to assume. He issued instructions after a close examination of a problem, which he invited the bishops of all the Churches to do and,
once taken, his decisions were unchangeable. It is quite true, as Renan has
observed that with Victor I, "the papacy is now born, and born as it should be!"

Regarding heresies and questions of dogma, Victor was equally firm. Around
190 Theodotus, arriving in Rome from Byzantium, maintained that Christ was
a mere man. Victor expelled him from the community. However, Theodotus
made converts, among whom were Asclepiodotus and a namesake, Theodotus,
and succeeded in setting up a small community to elect as its chief the confessor,
Natale, who became a sort of "antibishop.' So maybe he can be considered the
first antipope, although a few years later he repented and, pardoned by Victor,
returned to the Church.

In those same years another heresy arose, that of Noetus at Smyrna who considered Christ only an apparent form, a *modus* of the Father. But this heresy did
not go far, and, condemned by the very Church at Smyrna, Noetus was excommunicated.

Clearly the problem of heresies was not resolved by Victor as they were to
erupt by the thousands in the various ecclesiastical sees during the initial period
of Christianity. But Victor showed the right way to combat them, and his successors were to follow in his footsteps.

Victor died in 199. He was not martyred and was buried near the sepulcher
of St. Peter.

15. St. Zephyrinus (199—217)

He is sometimes referred to as Gepherinus or Severinus, but the more exact
spelling is Zephyrinus. A Roman, son of a certain Abondio, he was pope from
199, during the last period of the reign of Septimius Severus and then under
Caracalla. But with the former there were suddenly hard times for the
Christians, following the peaceful years of the "protectorate" of the emperor's
wife, Julia Domna. In 202, on the tenth anniversary of his reign, *pro salute
imperatorum* celebrations were announced which, in many provinces, the
Christians did not attend since they were pagan.

Irritated by their behavior, which he judged offensive, the emperor issued special decrees against the recalcitrant Christians. These resulted in a series of persecutions which, however, died down a year later when the Christians adopted a milder attitude and participated in those celebrations which did not violate their principles.

Zephyrinus, once elected, named Calixtus as his secretary and entrusted to him the administration of the places of worship made available by wealthy individuals and protected the rights that guaranteed private ownership of property. These were the first assets of a Church emerging from clandestinity, and which took advantage of the imperial tolerance, but risked, by coming out into the open, unexpected changes of humor on the part of the government and society itself.

Calixtus was charged in particular with reorganizing the cemetery, which at that time was on the Via Salaria, moving it to the Via Appia near the existing one of Pretestatus and Domitilla. He arranged it in such a way that numerous bishops of Rome were buried there in what came to be called the "Crypt of the Popes," between 235 and 314.

Under Zephyrinus the heresy of Patripassion Monarchianism flourished. Originated by Marcion and Noetus, it held that Father and Son were one Person and that the Father was incarnated and had been crucified. A tenacious enemy of this heresy was Hippolytus, a disciple of St. Lawrence, who did not consider Zephyrinus forceful enough in his stand against it. He accused the pope of being influenced by Calixtus for any and all decisions, of being an ignoramus and, in effect, of favoring the Monarchians.

According to Hippolytus's own report, Zephyrinus was supposed to have declared that he acknowledged "only one God, Jesus Christ, and apart from Him none other was born or suffered," a formulation which was linked, for the sake of clarity, with Calixtus's dogmatic statement: "It was the Son and not the Father who died." Zephyrinus showed himself in this entire issue to be a man more endowed with great virtue than with great theological culture, and Hippolytus was probably right to call him an ignoramus.

As Seppelt observes: "In the interpretation of the formula used by Zephyrinus for the divinity of Christ and the unity of nature in God, one senses the advice and the influence of Calixtus, and this appears to support Hippolytus in that it is expressed in such a way as to avoid increasing the danger of a schism within the community of the faithful at Rome which unfortunately persisted." It was a very diplomatic and rewarding tactic; in fact, "by acting in this manner, he had on his side, as his very own opponents admitted, the majority of the faithful in the Church of Rome who, perturbed by the subtle doctrinal speculations, wanted only to remain firm in the faith they had inherited by tradition."

The basic suspicion is that Hippolytus was motivated in this dispute by a personal resentment towards Zephyrinus on account of the nomination of Calixtus to a prestigious post to which he himself aspired. His spite and rancour grew and, upon the death of Zephyrinus, this produced the first schism in the Church of Rome. Zephyrinus died in 217 and was buried in a modest mausoleum above the cemetery of Calixtus.

16. St. Calixtus I (217–222)

Calixtus, a Roman, came from the region of the city called Ravennatius, or Trastevere. The slave of Aurelius Carpoforus, a relative of Emperor Commodus who reigned from 180 to 192, he had the good fortune to have a Christian master who, in the name of the Gospel, liberated him and educated him in his own religion.

Carpoforus took to heart Calixtus's future and gave him the funds to open a money-changing shop near the "public swimming pool," that is, where Caracalla later built the baths.

But apparently Calixtus strayed from the straight and narrow path and wasted the money and probably even stole some from his former master since, one day, he fled to the port to escape aboard the first ship he could find. Carpoforus caught up with him, and Calixtus, who had tried to escape (or to die?) by jumping into the water, was caught by the hair by two boatmen. Carpoforus took him back to Rome, made him a slave again and forced him to work in his gristmill, determined to keep him there until the stolen money had been repaid.

Yet Carpoforus must indeed have been a saintly man, and Calixtus a very lucky and charming one, as so many crooks are, because Carpoforus finally gave way to the pleads of many in the community and not only freed Calixtus again, but waived any financial claim against him. So Calixtus was able to go back to the business for which he had a definite flair. But this "banking" activity involved him in usurious loans with Jews, and regrettably one day, searching for a debtor, he found him intent on the rites in the Synagogue on the Sabbath. As a result he had to say goodbye to the money he was trying to recover and wound up in jail. In fact, the Jews presented an accusation to the prefect Fuscianus that he had disturbed a religious ceremony, so he was whipped and sentenced to forced labor in the mines of Sardinia. This all happened during the pontificate of Eleutherus.

Then came Pope Victor I and Marcia, the mistress and later the wife of Commodus, responsible indirectly for the salvation of Calixtus. It seems though that Victor I was against his release, and when he saw him back in Rome, he sent him to Anzio on an errand of little importance just to get rid of him.

Pope Zephyrinus, who trusted him completely, recalled him from Anzio in 199 as Calixtus appeared finally to have got his act together and he distinguished himself in administrative activities. Then, as the secretary of the pontiff, he was able to get away from these and become the papal advisor on delicate questions such as those relating to the heresies, even challenging Hippolytus, the great priest and author and defender of dogmatic strictness, who also aspired to a position of prestige in the Church of Rome. Naturally, the two hated each other.

When Calixtus was elected pope in 217, Hippolytus did not accept this thwarting of his ambitions. He created a separate community with his followers and certain bishops with sees near Rome, and declared himself "successor of the apostles and participant in the same grace of the supreme priesthood and magistracy." This was the first schism in the history of the Church of Rome, with Hippolytus becoming an antipope, the first to be recognized in the *Annuario pontificio*. He held this "position" through the pontificates of Calixtus, Urban, and Pontianus until his death in 235.

With Calixtus it was open warfare on the level of ecclesiastical discipline. Hippolytus accused his adversary of having consecrated as bishops deacons or priests who had already been married two or three times, of having allowed certain bishops to marry and, in general, of being too lenient with adulterers and prostitutes even if they had done public penance. Hippolytus found an ally in the person of Tertullian, once a great apologist, who became a Montanistic heretic and attacked Calixtus in his *De pudicitia*: "The supreme pontiff, bishop of the bishops, forgives adulterers and fornicators. And where will this generous edict be posted? On the door where the prostitutes live? Oh, no! It is to be placed in the Church, the virgin spouse of Christ!"

In reality, Calixtus was moving away from an exaggeratedly rigorous attitude and now interpreting the purest spirit of Christianity by social progress. One must note this in his favor and recognize that Hippolytus instead, through personal hatred, came to betray a certain spiritual avant-gardism which originally had seemed more in keeping with his defiance of authority.

Destiny had martyrdom in store for both of them. Calixtus was the victim of an uprising of the population in reaction to the attitude of goodwill shown by Heliogabalus to the Christians throughout the empire (217–222). This emperor had gone as far as to express his wish to establish in the Temple of the Sun, which he had erected on the Palatine, even the cult of Christ.

However, he ended up being hated and was killed, together with his mother Julia Soemia in 222, and their bodies were thrown into the Tiber. The new emperor, Alexander Severus, was not able to control or, perhaps, did not want to restrain the anger of the populace that then turned against Christians. Calixtus was seized, together with two priests, Calepodius and

Asclepiades, who were promptly executed and their bodies were dragged through the streets of Rome.

Calixtus was thrown from a window of his house into a well and then stoned to death. The well is still in the garden of the former monastery of St. Calixtus annexed to the church of the same name, alongside the basilica of S. Maria in Trastevere, which tradition has it, was built by Calixtus himself. He was not buried in the "Crypt of the Popes" which he had prepared in the cemetery named after him, but in the cemetery of Calepodius on the Via Aurelia.

The death of Hippolytus instead is traditionally linked to that of Pope Pontianus, who was exiled with him to Sardinia and was the victim of the unhealthy air and many privations. But they were united and reconciled in martyrdom, after which their remains were transported to Rome and buried with the same honors.

Hippolytus was interred in the cemetery near Via Tiburtina named after him. In 1551 a headless statue without hands was discovered there which could well represent him since a list of works attributed to him is carved on one side of it.

17. St. Urban I (222–230)

Information about this pope is scarce and in some texts he is even confused with another unidentified bishop. According to the *Liber pontificalis* however, he lived at the time of the Emperor Diocletian.

It seems that he was by birth a Roman, and pope at the time of Emperor Alexander Severus. Once the initial period of anti-Christian riots, of which Calixtus I had been a victim had passed, Christianity enjoyed a period of true tranquillity under Urban. The emperor was even supposed to have accepted in his residence images of Abraham and Christ, along with those of pagan divinities, perhaps to please his mother, Julia Mamea who, according to Orosio, was a Christian.

Alexander Severus granted the Church a *locus publicus* situated in the area where Calixtus I had died, and where later arose Santa Maria in Trastevere, perhaps as a kind of compensation for his assassination. And Urban I increased the temporal possessions of the Church, as is evident from a lawsuit which, during his pontificate, was debated between an association of Roman innkeepers and the Christian community over the ownership of a building.

Urban I is thought to have been killed through the treachery of the prefect Almenius on 19 March of the year 230, and his body to have been tenderly recovered by the emperor's mother and buried in the cemetery of St. Calixtus.

18. St. Pontianus (230–235)

There is little information about this pope, probably Roman by birth. He is, however, the first about whom the *Annuario pontificio* gives the date of consecration as pope, which was on 21 July 230, as well as that of his forcible removal on 28 September 235, the result of a sentence by Emperor Maximinus Thrax.

This emperor, in reaction to the conciliatory policy of his predecessor, Alexander Severus, ordered a violent purge of magistrates faithful to the latter, and many Christians in the imperial court were executed.

Apparently Pontianus can be considered the second pope, after Clement I, to have made "the great refusal," though not through cowardice since before leaving for his involuntary exile he abdicated, so that the Church of Rome could elect a bishop who was a member of the community.

He died in 237 in Sardinia a martyr, either from the suffering which he endured or because of a special punishment inflicted on him. His corpse was brought back to Rome by Pope Fabian, who had him buried in the papal crypt in the cemetery of St. Calixtus.

19. St. Anteros (235–236)

Again what little information there is about Anteros is vague. Greek by birth, he was pope for only a few months, while Pope Pontianus was still alive in his forced exile in Sardinia. Anteros was consecrated on 21 November 235 and died on 3 January 236.

He should be considered a martyr, since he was condemned to death for having put together a collection of documents about the acts of martyrs. He was buried in the papal crypt in the cemetery of St. Calixtus.

20. St. Fabian (236–250)

Fabian was an ordinary man who, one day in January of 236, was returning to Rome from the country just as the Christian community had got together to elect, amidst considerable uncertainty, a new pope. But, lo and behold, as Eusebius recounts it, a dove suddenly landed on Fabian's head, as if it were the Holy Spirit. So, no further discussion was needed since he had obviously been chosen by God Himself, and was promptly elected pope. According to the *Annuario pontificio*, his consecration took place on 10 January 236.

However, once ascended to the seat of Peter, Fabian proved to be a good administrator and established, in particular, the framework of Christian Rome, dividing the city into seven deaconates or regions and naming for each of these a deacon with the function of supervising and running the hospitals, shelters and chapels either already built or to be so, and with each in touch with the priests who held a *titulus*. In effect, he consolidated what Pope Evarestus had already decreed during his pontificate. From then on there began to be a difference between those who had a fixed *titulus* and those who had merely temporary functions: the former were called "cardinal points," later "cardinals" and constituted the first pontifical council, a Sacred College in embryo.

Part of Fabian's pontificate took place under Emperor Philip the Arab (244–249), considered by St. Girolamus to have been the first Christian emperor and on whom Babel, the bishop of Antioch, is supposed to have imposed a public penance before admitting him into the church. It was a moment of tranquillity, though, according to St. Cyprian, this had a negative influence as it brought about a certain relaxation of customs.

"Everybody was intent upon accumulating wealth, forgetting what Christians had done at the time of the Apostles and of what they themselves should be doing. They developed an insatiable desire for riches and could think of nothing else. Religious feeling among the priests and faithfulness and integrity among the ministers were dead. Charity was no longer part of the life of the Christians, and there was no more discipline in the customs. Men combed their beards while the women put make-up on their faces and even around their eyes, and had their hands manicured and their hair dyed. They used ruses and tricks to fool the simple people, and took advantage of their brothers by infidelities and sharp practices. They married pagans, prostituting their Christian bodies. They swore oaths without good reason and also perjured themselves. They arrogantly disdained their prelates, insulted each other and hated each other unto death. They disdained the simplicity recommended by the faith and were attracted by all that is vanity. They renounced the world in words but not in deeds, and each loved himself so much that he could not be loved by anyone else." And so almost as a divine punishment, as the pure in heart of that time (including St. Cyprian) would have thought, came another terrible persecution for which the new emperor, Decius (249–251), was responsible. He was convinced that the Christians were politically dangerous as they had succeeded in infiltrating the highest levels of power, so he issued an edict which obliged every subject to appear before a committee of five members and offer a sacrifice to the gods to prove his devotion to the State religion. Each was to receive a certificate called a libellus.

Refusal to obey the edict involved torture, property confiscation, prison and, in certain cases, death. The reaction of the Christians was to some extent a logical consequence of the type of life in which they indulged as described by Cyprian.

Defections were numerous, with real cases of apostasy. To avoid the penalties, some committed sacrilege; these were the so-called *lapsi*, the "fallen" into idolatry. Others, the rich especially, took a cowardly way out and bought *libelli* from the authorities. In this way they put themselves right with the law but probably not with their conscience. They were called "libellatics."

There were also many martyrs, amongst whom the bishops of Jerusalem and of Antioch, Alexander and Babel, were killed, though Cyprian managed to save himself by hiding near Carthage all the while remaining in touch with his community. Pope Fabian was condemned to death at Rome on 20 January of the year 250 and was buried in the papal crypt at the cemetery of St. Calixtus.

21. ST. CORNELIUS (251—253)

The Decian persecution made it impossible to elect a successor on the death of Fabian. As Cyprian wrote, "the tyrant declared that he would rather have welcomed the news that a rival had appeared on the scene to claim the empire than that of the election of a new bishop of Rome."

The "vacant see" lasted for more than a year, during which presbyters and deacons led the Church. There were many disputes, especially regarding Cyprian, bishop of Carthage, who had gone into hiding to avoid Decius's persecution. Particularly opposed to him was Novatus, who arrived in Rome in order to put pressure on the Roman Church to consider Cyprian a traitor. Lacking a leader, the Roman community was unsettled, and Novatus found an ally in Novatianus, a Gentile converted to Christianity who had become a priest even though professing the Stoic philosophy. Together they tried to gain to their cause the most destitute Romans, but Novatianus had a bad reputation. During the Decian persecution, he had even denied being a priest, and it was rumored that he had caused his wife to abort by a kick in the stomach.

Then, unexpectedly, Decius died in March of 251. Novatianus boldly put forth his candidature for the see of the bishop of Rome, but without success, and a high member of the Roman aristocracy, Cornelius, was elected. A moderate, he was clearly opposed to the apparent severity of Novatianus and Novatus.

Yet Novatianus did not give up. According to Eusebius, he picked out two of his group "who were lost souls and sent them off to a small, unknown Italian town to bring back to Rome three simple, uneducated bishops, urging them to return to Rome as quickly as possible so that, through their mediation and that of other bishops, the problems could be rapidly resolved.

"These simpletons, once in Rome and unaware of the wiles of this miscreant, were put under lock and key with ready to do his bidding. Then at ten o'clock in the evening, inebriated and incapable of thinking straight, they were forced to give him a fraudulent laying on of hands."

In other words, by these gangster-like methods, Novatianus got himself named pope, though in fact he was an antipope. And once he had this nomination, he manoeuvred to get the support of the important bishops, since it was not enough just to have the signature of three drunkards. He managed this on the grounds of a certain "doctrinal" position and through accusations that Pope Cornelius had been an apostate during the Decian persecution.

He sent letters in this sense to the Churches of the East, but only Fabian of Antioch paid any heed to his calumnies. Dionisius, bishop of Alexandria, enjoined him to give up the position for the good of the Church, and Cyprian even refused to receive his envoys.

Nonetheless, Novatianus had followers in Italy, Africa, Asia and Gaul. Following his suggestions, they opposed the readmission to the Church of the *lapsi*, even after a public declaration of repentance, as Cyprian had decided to do for the Church in Carthage. They became advocates of a Puritanism *ante litteram*, which turned into an excuse to promote a cause that was probably lost before it had even begun. By claiming to be the sole pure interpreters of the Evangelical message, the Novationists appeared to be maintaining an attitude which did not hold water, and yet there was here the elements of a schism. So Cornelius convoked a council at Rome attended by sixty bishops who condemned Novatianus and his teachings, and approved Cyprian's attitude at Carthage regarding the *lapsi*. The Church of Rome acted in the same manner. The condemnation was transmitted to all the Churches, but the Puritanism of Novatianus left its imprint, especially in Africa, where the antipope died, perhaps a victim of the persecutions.

In 252 Cornelius was exiled to Civitavecchia by order of the new emperor, Trebonianus Gallus, where he died in June of the following year, probably without having suffered martyrdom, otherwise, what Cyprian said about him in a sort of epitaph would make no sense. "Isn't he who was for so long exposed to the furor of the aides of a barbarous tyrant to be numbered among the confessors and martyrs? One who was continually in danger of being beheaded, burned, crucified, torn apart by cruel and unusual tortures, who opposed terrible laws and who, by the strength of his faith, scorned the atrocious suffering with which he was threatened? Even though God saved him, he gave ample proof of his love and fidelity, ready to suffer any torment and to triumph over his tyrant in the name of the faith."

His remains were brought to Rome in 283, only thirty years after his death, and buried by the matron Lucina in a crypt belonging to her near the cemetery of St. Calixtus.

22. St. Lucius I (253–254)

Little is known about Lucius. Elected pope on 25 June 253 as soon as the news of Cornelius's when death had reached Rome, he probably hardly had time to sit upon the throne, he was sent into exile, destination unknown, on 6 March of the following year. According to the *Liber pontificalis*, however, he did issue a decree that required every bishop to be accompanied by two priests and three deacons who would report on his behavior.

Emperor Valerian, fairly benevolent toward Christians at the beginning of his reign, let him return to Rome, where he died shortly afterwards on 5 March 254, of natural causes. He was buried in the papal crypt in the cemetery of St. Calixtus. Because he was not martyred, his name was "erased" as a saint from the *Universal Calendar of the Church.*

23. ST. STEPHEN I (254—257)

Stephen was a Roman patrician named to one of the seven deaconates established by Pope Fabian. He was elected pope at the cemetery of St. Calixtus on 12 May 254, by the priests who held a title and the deacons who had a function in the community of the faithful.

Stephen was bishop of Rome in the "tranquil" period of the empire under Valerian, and had time to devote himself to the internal problems of the Church. He wanted to affirm the supremacy of the see of Rome over others, but started off on the wrong foot and really did not cut much of a figure to begin with.

Two Spanish bishops, Basilidis and Martial, had been deposed from their sees because they had been identified by the Church of Spain as "libellatics," that is, of having purchased the *libellus* which served as a warranty during the Decian persecution. They appealed to Rome and Stephen, considering the accusations groundless, overruled the condemnation reckoning them to be honorable persons.

The Church of Spain did not accept this and presented an appeal to the Church of Carthage, whose bishop was Cyprian. He called a council, evaluated the evidence carefully, and declared Basilidis and Martial unworthy to be bishops. But he was very correct with Rome and personally explained his decision to Stephen saying that presumably his "colleague" had been duped, being so far away from the bishops' sees and not fully informed of the true state of affairs.

After which, for a certain period, Rome and Carthage did not speak the same Evangelical language, since obviously a question of supremacy was involved. This became clear with the problem that arose over baptism administered by heretics.

Cyprian considered it null and void, and that whoever had abandoned a sect and wanted to come back into the Church had to be re-baptised. In 255 another council met in Carthage and approved Cyprian's doctrine which Stephen immediately disputed, countering that it was right to follow tradition and accept the heretics already baptised, imposing a penance on them but not requiring a new baptism.

At this point, Cyprian did not want to disagree openly with the decision of the bishop of Rome, regarding it as little more than an opinion. "Each one of the heads of the Church," he observed, "is free to act as he wishes and must account of it only to God." Still another council in 256 confirmed the position of the Church of Carthage, and though the authority of the bishop of Rome was not put in question on this occasion, it was not mentioned either.

Stephen saw that the prestige of his see was at stake and asked all the Churches to follow Rome's attitude. The dispute intensified. Firmilianus of Cesarea allied himself with Cyprian and accused Stephen of spreading heresy. Dionisius of Alexandria tried to calm the waters but was unsuccessful. The issue would only be settled by the successors of Stephen, by which time Cyprian had died and Rome's opinion triumphed.

But there were difficult times again for the Church, and little opportunity to delve deeply into the dispute. In August 257, Valerian was convinced by Macrianus, a member of his household, that the Church was obtaining State property, so he issued a first edict of persecution against bishops, priests and deacons, ordering them to recognize the pagan deities while permitting them to practice privately their Christian faith.

It is hardly likely that Stephen escaped martyrdom or at least exile, but nothing is known for certain about his death which occurred on 2 August 257, just as the new persecution was beginning. He was buried in the papal crypt in the cemetery of St. Calixtus.

24. St. Sixtus II (257–258)

A native of Greece, this "good, peace-loving priest," as Cyprian's biography describes him, became pope on 30 August 257 at the height of the Valerian persecution.

He immediately set about calming relations between Rome and Carthage, strained by the question of baptism administered by heretics, but the rigid attitude of the State towards the Church hindered getting to the roots of the disagreement.

In 258, a new Imperial edict ordered bishops, priests, deacons and normal lay followers of Christianity to abjure their faith under pain of confiscation of their property as well as decapitation. On 6 August, Sixtus was surprised while celebrating the Eucharist in the catacombs of Pretextatus. He was arrested, pulled into court, convicted and immediately brought to the cemetery to be beheaded.

According to the poet Prudentius, on his way there he met the deacon Lawrence who, seeing his bishop being taken to martyrdom, cried: "Where are you going, Father, without your son? You who have never offered a sacrifice without your deacon, you now intend to die alone?" Sixtus comforted him, prophesying for him a "more beautiful crown." The crown was the special martyrdom which, four days later, on 10 August, Lawrence suffered by being burned alive on the grate as so many paintings have since depicted.

Sixtus was himself brought back to the cemetery of Pretextatus where he was killed on his own episcopal throne, which was then put near the place of his burial in the papal crypt of the cemetery of St. Calixtus.

25. ST. DIONISIUS (259—268)

A simple priest of unknown origin, he became pope only when Emperor Valerian, concerned by urgent military problems on his eastern borders, eased up his persecution. As a result, between the death of Sixtus II and Dionisius, there was almost one year of "vacant see" and the new bishop of Rome was only elected on 22 July 259. But Valerian died in 260 in the war against the Persian king Sapor, and his son Gallienus, the new emperor, had very different feelings toward the Christians. He revoked the edicts, returned confiscated properties, and the pope was able to devote himself completely to internal problems of the Church.

In the meantime, Cyprian, bishop of Carthage, had been martyred on 14 September 258, so Rome's position on the question of baptism of heretics triumphed. Of great help in winning this temporary halo of supremacy was the charitable attitude of Dionisius, who was able to put the see of Rome into a good light by sending gifts of money to the eastern Churches afflicted by invasions of barbarians. He was also involved in the ransom of many imprisoned Christians, and with the reconstruction of numerous churches which had been destroyed.

But other theological controversies arose in those years, particularly in regard to the Trinity of God. Sabellius, a writer from Ptolemais, saw the Trinity as a semantic question and re-elaborated the Monarchian theory previously contested by St. Hippolytus. In a council at Rome in 262, Dionisius set forth in clear terms the doctrine of the Trinity and condemned the ideas of Sabellius as heretical.

More "worldly" was the character of another theoretician on the Trinity, the bishop of Antioch, Paul of Samosata, an intriguer connected with Zenobia, the queen of Palmyra, who had entrusted to him the administration of affairs of State as governor of the city. It appears that, as a quid pro quo, in order to satisfy the "theological" caprices of the queen, he promulgated the idea of Christ who became God progressively by adoption. Between 264 and 268 three councils at Antioch were in favor of declaring Paul a heretic, but he cleverly managed to justify himself until the learned priest Malchion, professor of rhetoric, unmasked his attitude as not exactly episcopal.

Paul was excommunicated, deposed and replaced by Domnus, a son of bishop Demetrian, the predecessor of Paul. The verdict was sent to Rome when Dionisius was already dead but was received and approved by his successor,

Felix I. Yet Paul did not in fact leave his episcopal palace, well defended by Queen Zenobia until Emperor Aurelian, the first Head of the Roman State to concern himself with administrative questions regarding the Church, looked into the matter two years later. At war with Zenobia for the recapture of the kingdom lost by Valerian, Aurelian seized Antioch and took over the bishop's residence, leaving it for whomever "the bishops of Italy and of Rome were in relation with."

Dionisius died on 26 December 268, and was buried in the papal crypt of the cemetery of St. Calixtus.

26. ST. FELIX I (269–274)

Probably a Roman by birth, Felix was bishop of Rome more or less while Aurelian was emperor and he was consecrated on 5 January 269.

The period of peace for the Church continued as the emperor was taken up with other problems. The barbarians were threatening the borders, and he had decided to protect the city with that defensive circle that consisted of the Aurelian Walls, a grandiose structure of which numerous sections still exist, and a testimony to the military crisis permeating the empire and making Rome the "last beachhead" of a vast but now decadent power.

The pontificate of Felix is shrouded in darkness. A letter is attributed to him on the question of the Trinity that he is thought to have sent to the bishop of Alexandria, Maximus and considered by the council of Ephesus in 431 as an interesting document defining the dogma. This is the text: "Our faith in the Incarnation is that handed down by the Apostles. We believe that our Lord Jesus Christ, born of the Virgin Mary, is the Word, the eternal Son of God, and not a man diverse from God, raised by God Himself to this honor. The Son of God did not choose a man to associate Himself with; there are not two persons in Christ. The Word, perfect God, was incarnated in the womb of the Virgin and became perfect Man."

Felix died on 30 December 274, and was buried in the papal crypt of the cemetery of St. Calixtus. His name no longer appears in the *Universal Calendar of the Church*.

27. ST. EUTYCHIANUS (275–283)

According to the *Liber pontificalis*, Eutychianus was born at Luni in Etruria and was consecrated on 4 January 275. However, information about his pontificate, which took place mostly while when Probus was emperor (276–282), is virtually non-existent. He is thought to have instituted the Offertory of the Mass. The tradition that Eutychianus was a martyr is also erroneous.

He died on 7 December 283, and was buried in the papal crypt in the cemetery of St. Calixtus, but in 1659 his remains were taken to the Gothic cathedral
at Sarzana where an imposing marble statue of him was erected.

28. ST. CAIUS (283—296)

According to a legend, this Caius was related to the Emperor Diocletian, a
Dalmatian like him, which could explain the fact that, as long as he was the
bishop of Rome, Diocletian did not lift a finger against the Church. Caius was
consecrated on 17 December 283.

It is true that the emperor had several Christians among his collaborators,
and Eusebius reports that the bishops easily obtained from the magistrature permits for the construction of churches and the enlargement of buildings in the
cemeteries.

But heresies multiplied, and the Manichaean one gained ground while the
cult of Mithra arrived in Rome from the East and, for a while competed with
Christianity. Yet, according to Duchesne, though the Church of Rome grew in
prestige more than the others, in those days its authority was "more felt than
definite."

The *Liber pontificalis*, based on the anonymous *Passion of Santa Susanna*,
states that Caius is thought to have been beheaded for having suggested to his
cousin Susanna to take a vow of chastity. However, the *Universal Calendar of
the Church* now states that "by no means are St. Soter and St. Caius to be listed
among the martyrs."

He died on 22 April 296, and was buried in the cemetery of St. Calixtus but
not in the "Crypt of the Popes." The house in which he lived was consecrated
as a church where, in 1631, his remains were placed under the main altar. When
in 1880 the church was demolished to make way for the construction of the
Ministry of War in Via XX Settembre, these were transferred to a private chapel
belonging to the Barberini.

29. ST. MARCELLINUS (296—304)

A Roman by birth and son of a certain Proietto, he was a very pious priest
praised by St. Augustus for his *fama et pietate notissimus*, and he worked his
way up the Church hierarchy until he was consecrated bishop of Rome on 30
June 296.

All information about the pontificate of Marcellinus relates to the final two
years, when Diocletian's terrible persecution took place. This emperor had
already established the tetrarchy, by which he governed the East with Galerius
as the Caesar, while the West was entrusted to Maximianus, whose Caesar was
Costantius Chlorus.

The one really responsible for the persecution was Galerius who, during the winter of 303, after lengthy discussions at Nicomedia with his Augustus, managed to convince him of the need to fight the Christians. In effect, Galerius was motivated only by blind pagan fanaticism, and it was in the name of an ardent traditionalism that he succeeded in convincing Diocletian to take the decision, by provoking fires, like Nero.

To begin with on 23 February of 303 the church of Nicomedia was set on fire but when, a few days later, another one destroyed the imperial palace, Galerius accused the Christians. Diocletian vented his anger on the palace staff and had them tortured, then, when a second fire broke out, the emperor decided that an iron hand was needed.

He issued an edict which ordered the destruction of the churches and sacred books, prohibited religious ceremonies and commanded Christians to abjure their faith. Diocletian forced his wife Prisca and his daughter Valeria, who were favorable to the Christians, to make sacrifices to pagan gods. The edict did not include death sentences but, by the use of false evidence, many Christians were classified as "arsonists" or else were accused of resisting the "forces of the State" by failing to turn over the sacred books, for which they paid with their lives. Once again the hounding of Christians began, spreading from the East to the West.

In Rome sacred texts were seized, the bishopric's files turned upside down, and property of the Church confiscated. It is not clear how Marcellinus reacted to these blows, though, according to the followers of the heretic Donatus, he is said to have given in to the authorities, surrendering the sacred books and even burning incense before the pagan gods.

St. Augustine called this information calumnious, but it is a fact that the *Liber pontificalis* itself reports that Marcellinus did make sacrifice to the pagan gods, even though he repented a few days later and was beheaded by Diocletian's order on 25 October 304. Moreover, his name is missing from many lists of pontiffs in antiquity, and this leads one to think that his image was somewhat tainted. Yet his sepulcher in the cemetery of Priscilla, considerably more modest that those of the papal crypt in the catacombs of St. Calixtus, was much venerated for many centuries. The story of this pope smacks of betrayal, even if followed by repentance, though it is humanly understandable that his faith in certain tragic situations could have given way, or at least have been bent. Diocletian issued three other decrees against the Christians, and with the fourth began mass executions. According to legend, the twelve-year-old Agnes was martyred in the brothel in the vaults of Domitian's Stadium in which she had been sentenced to live, by order of the prefect of Rome.

30. St. Marcellus I (308–309)

For about four years Rome was again a *sede vacante* (vacant see), and only at the beginning of the reign of Maxentius, when calm had returned, was it possible to reelect a bishop in the person of Marcellus, a Roman, on 27 May 308. To him fell the arduous task of starting the reorganization of the Church of Rome, so devastated by the persecutions, and of rebuilding the places of worship. It appears that he set up twenty-five "titular" churches with precise limits of jurisdiction.

Then there was the problem of the apostates who wanted to rejoin the community, and riots broke out because Marcellus was against this, at least not without the imposition of severe penalties for readmission.

The dispute reached a point where the intervention of the lay authorities was required, and Maxentius decided to restore order by sending Marcellus into exile where he died on 16 January 309. His remains were brought back to Rome and he was buried in the cemetery of Priscilla.

According to one legend, Maxentius forced Marcellus to perform the humblest of labors in the rooms of the imperial servants until he died of exhaustion. It is said that the oldest church of St. Marcellus was built on the ruins of the *catabulum* between the fourth and fifth centuries, but nothing of it remains. The church now in the Via del Corso at Rome dates back to the beginning of the sixth century and was probably rebuilt on the original one.

31. St. Eusebius (309)

The successor of Marcellus, Eusebius, was probably Greek. His pontificate was very brief, only four months, from 18 April to 17 August 309.

He too wound up in exile because of the continued rioting carried on by the apostates who wanted to come back into the Christian community. These found a supporter in a certain Heraclius, obviously the proponent of less rigid principles in their regard. But the situation continued to be chaotic, as Maxentius put a stop to the riots by bloodshed, not through any sectarian, bias since the matter did not concern him from a religious point of view, but to maintain public order.

For this reason he sent into exile both Heraclius and Eusebius, the latter to Sicily where he died. His remains were brought back to Rome and buried in the cemetery of St. Calixtus, but not in the papal crypt. Meanwhile Maxentius confiscated part of the Church's property and refused to permit the election of a successor, so Rome was again a vacant see.

32. St. Miltiades (311–314)

Miltiades, or Melchiades, an African priest, was able to be elected bishop of Rome about two years after the death of Eusebius, on 2 July 311. That year, in fact, there was a change of attitude towards Christianity by the rulers of the empire which, at the time, was split into two parts: the Eastern with Galerius and Maximinus Daia, and the Western with Constantine and Maxentius. Yet the momentum came from the East where Galerius, the perpetrator of the last great persecution, confronted by the moral resistance of the Christians, gradually realized that their persecution was politically unpopular. Moreover, in 310 Galerius was struck by a terrible illness which was slowly killing him and, feeling his end near, issued an edict on 30 April 311 which permitted Christians to profess their faith and allowed them to hold meetings for services of cult. One edict seems dictated by his fear of impending death, since he ended it by saying: "In recognition of our magnanimity, they must pray to their God for our good health." He died six days later.

Maxentius, in Rome, upheld the edict, restored confiscated buildings and real estate to the Church, and permitted the election of the bishop of the city, which took place on 2 July. Then, on 28 October 312 came the Battle of the Milvian Bridge. The cross that appeared in the sky with the inscription *In hoc signo vinces* and the banner in the form of a cross which mysterious messengers are supposed to have delivered to Constantine, were evidently a product of the public's imagination. The reality was the victory of Constantine and the issuance of the Edict of Milan between February and June of 313, which declared the freedom of all and any religious cult.

As a result, the person of the emperor became popular with the Christians, appearing as a protector of their religion, and Constantine found himself caught in a situation from which he neither could nor wanted to retreat.

A first occasion came from Carthage when Bishop Cecilianus was accused by the followers of Donatus of *Casae Nigrae*, the latest Puritan of the times, of having betrayed his faith during the most recent persecution, and as a result, was deposed.

Riots broke out between the opposing groups, and the Proconsul of Africa, Anulinus, asked Constantine to intervene, which he did, deciding to put the issue to the bishops of other churches, such as those of Autun, Cologne and Arles, under the chairmanship of Miltiades in Rome. Cecilianus and Donatus were ordered to appear, each accompanied by ten of their supporting bishops.

It was in effect the convocation of a Council, the first to be organized in full agreement with the civil authorities. It took place from 2nd to 4th of October 313 *in domo Faustae in Laterano*, that is to say, in the house of Empress Fausta, the second wife of Constantine. This was the Lateran Palace which was to become the residence of the bishop of Rome and one of the donations made by the Emperor to the Church.

The Council ended by condemning Donatus and absolving Cecilianus. Miltiades, the chairman, after proclaiming the judgment, gave Constantine notice of it. Clearly the followers of Donatus were unhappy with the verdict and, when they returned to Africa, resumed their conflict with Cecilianus by rioting. But Miltiades was unable to follow developments, dying on 11 January 314. He was the last bishop of Rome to be buried in the papal crypt of the cemetery of St. Calixtus. He certainly was not a martyr and therefore has been eliminated from the *Universal Calendar of the Church*.

3 3. St. Sylvester I (3 1 4 — 3 3 5)

On 31 January 314, a Roman named Sylvester was elected bishop of Rome. Destined to hold the position for more than two decades, his was a lengthy pontificate during which one might have expected to see important and well-documented events at what was a decisive historic moment for the future of the Church of Rome. Instead, as Caspar observed, this pontificate was "the emptiest of the century." in the sense that Sylvester, a colorless pope, did not have a personality such as to involve him in the grand events of the period. The Emperor Constantine, on the other hand, was full of vitality and determined to set the Church on its future course.

One could say that Sylvester was simply a figurehead for Constantine who, in fact, made full use of him. A clever statesman, the emperor realized the strength of Christianity as compared to the pagan cults, and decided to make it the state religion in lieu of other ones, and to give stability to the doctrines of the new religion. This led him in a certain manner to step into Sylvester's shoes to ensure respect for his decisions, not only as head of state, but also as virtual bishop of Rome, which he came to be considered in the East especially where he was called "Isapostle," the equal of the Apostles.

As Falconi recalls, "Constantine really thought he was above the Church," a "bishop of the bishops" (to use his own description), for "external affairs" which rapidly turned out to be for the "internal" ones also. But he did not understand the profound spiritual significance of Christianity. He imposed it for purely political motives that, for him, meant above all the security of the State. And for it he even resorted to assassination, liquidating his colleague of the East, Licinius, and condemning to death certain family members, like his second wife Fausta and his son Crispus.

What happened during Constantine's lifetime was sufficient to overshadow a personality like Sylvester's, but not in the centuries to come for the papacy. Sylvester, the first pope of the Church to be recognized by the State, had to be shown as equal, if not superior, to the emperor. So a legend began to circulate around the middle of the fifth century, thanks to which Sylvester could finally appear as a great pope.

According to this legend, Constantine had been a persecutor of Christianity, and as a result Sylvester had hidden himself away on Mount Soracte. The emperor, ill with leprosy, was counselled by pagan priests to bathe in the warm blood of slaughtered babies, but he was touched by the cries of the mothers and refused such a cruel cure. One night the Apostles Peter and Paul appeared to him in a dream and advised him to turn to Pope Sylvester. Summoned by three messengers the next morning, Sylvester came immediately and immersed Constantine three times in a pool, baptising him and curing him of his illness. Out of gratitude, the emperor granted the Christians freedom of religion and established many churches. Connected with this legend were numerous miracles by Sylvester who, among other things, was the winner in a religious dispute with twelve Jews, and had liberated Rome from a fearful dragon by shutting it in a cave, the iron gates of which would reopen only on universal Judgment Day.

These were myths which tended to belie the reality of a Constantine baptised of his own will at the moment of death by an Arian, and of a Sylvester who had carried little weight in the theological disputes of the age.

But the legend served not only to make the image of Sylvester "great," but it also became the origin of one of the best known medieval documents, the *Constitutum Constantini*. This forgery was published in Rome around 753, and it allowed the Church to claim that the basis of its own supreme power, civil as well as religious, went back to a law enacted by Constantine. It was for this reason that Pope Innocent IV in 1248 took pains to immortalize the legend on the walls of a chapel in the church of the Santi Quattro Coronati in Rome. These paintings were in effect a means of propaganda to demonstrate the superior power of the Church of Rome over that of the empire. The scenario on the walls of Santi Quattro ends with Constantine, on his knees, passing the imperial tiara to St. Sylvester as symbol of the concession to the pope of civil authority over Rome, and therefore over Italy and the West.

In a sonnet, Belli recalls St. Sylvester as he hastens to Rome from Sant'Oreste, a village on Mount Soracte, once the persecutions were over. All this haste (alas! on the back of a mule!) seems to have been inspired by the avid desire to possess supreme powers.

> Saint Sylvester, once certain troubles were quieted,
> eager to reach Rome for some fast deals,
> spoke to a cute little pack mule:
> "Gallop, by God, faster than the wind!"

The mule eyed the papal crest
and in no more than three jumps,
leaving its hoofprints on three stones,
flew to Rome from Sant'Oreste.

Good Christ! With neither spurs nor bridle,
just the whip of the Faith,
it did sixteen miles with every jump.

Well, the deed was done by the mule,
either the devil or his daughter,
who made the trip in three leaps
and had one hoof left over!

Such was the legend, and the *Constitutum Constantini* was a forgery, intentionally created in such a way as to influence throughout centuries so much of Rome's and of Italy's history. The biographies of Sylvester and Constantine, however, tell a very different story.

Sylvester was already the bishop of Rome when, on 1 August 314, Constantine, faced with the riots provoked by the Donatists in Africa, convoked on his own initiative a great Council in Gaul at Arles at which bishops of opposing camps took part, but not Sylvester. Beyond condemning Donatus, openly recognized as being outside of the Church, the council decided on certain points of ecclesiastical discipline, and the council fathers sent Sylvester a letter, no doubt inspired by Constantine given its tenor, which emphasized the authority of the bishop of Rome.

"Very dear Father, heaven should have seen to it that you were present for this grand spectacle! You would have helped to render more severe the judgment against certain criminals!

"Had you been with us, the joy of the entire assemblage would have been great. But, since you could not leave the city, the preferred seat of the Apostles, where their blood is witness to the glory of God, we report to you that we felt duty bound to examine matters other than those for which we had been convoked. Since we come from various provinces, we felt it was advisable to discuss various problems, with the assistance of the Holy Spirit and the angels. And we wish that you, whose authority is the most recognized, may be the one to convey our decisions to all of the Churches."

However, the schismatics went on disturbing the Church in Africa, so Constantine had their churches shut. But the Donatists did not give in. Faced with a violent repression, they proceeded to die as martyrs.

In any case, the emperor was the real protagonist of the era. We find him dedicated to christianizing the State through a series of decrees, amongst which was the one by which only the ecclesiastical tribunal had jurisdiction over religious questions, so that judgments rendered by the bishops were to be executed just like those of the civil courts. The Christian clergy was exempted from all civic duties and Sunday (so named, according to the *Liber pontificalis*, by Sylvester) was recognized as a non-working day by the State as from the year 321.

Donations in favor of the Christian cult were numerous. First of all, there was the Domus Faustae, the Lateran Palace, seat of the bishop of Rome from Sylvester I to Benedict XI and, next to it, the Lateran Basilica, erected by Constantine who is said to have donated so many gold statues, candelabras and vessels, that it was called the Golden Basilica or the *Constantiniana*.

Again according to the *Liber pontificalis*, Constantine is said to have also founded, at the request of Bishop Sylvester, the ancient church of St. Peter over an earlier temple of Apollo, burying the body of the Apostle in a sarcophagus of Cyprian bronze. And in response to the pleas of Sylvester, the emperor is thought to have built the Basilica of St. Paul, and for his mother, St. Helen, the Basilica of Santa Croce in Gerusalemme, in which she placed a piece of the true Cross of Christ, discovered by her during a voyage to the Holy Land.

On the subject of churches, the first structure of S. Martino ai Monti was carried out during that period and should be identified with the *Titulus Equitii*, from the name of a priest, a certain Equitius, who built it on orders from Sylvester.

When Constantine became sole emperor, he introduced Christianity into the East as well, though he found that area of the empire plagued by Arian turbulence.

Arius, a priest of the Church of Alexandria, had gone about preaching his own doctrine of the Trinity, which was that the second person was a common man "adopted by God as son in foreknowledge of his merits." Arius, who in effect denied the divinity of Jesus, immediately found a strong opponent in his bishop, Alexander, who had him excommunicated by a Council, without actually discrediting his doctrine. Among his defenders were the bishops of Nicomedia and Caesarea, both named Eusebius. As Alexander did not succeed in stopping the development of the movement, he wrote to Sylvester to keep him informed of it. But forestalling him, Constantine sent Arius and Alexander his own adviser, Osius, bishop of Cordoba, to assess the situation. The attempt at an agreement failed and the emperor, recognizing that a whole series of questions needed answers, convoked a Universal Council of the Church at Nicaea, in Bithynia, the first ecumenical council in history.

Eusebius commented that Constantine had committed himself to "convene all the bishops on earth to oppose the invincible enemy of the Church with the battalions of an enemy force;" another instance in which the personality of the emperor overshadowed that of Sylvester.

In May of 325 three hundred bishops gathered at Nicaea. For the opening of the assembly, which took place on 14 June, Constantine, as honorary president, was expected to be present even if the actual president was Bishop Osius, assisted by two priests, Vitus and Vincent, representing Sylvester, whose absence was justified because of his advanced age. In any case, the role of the bishop of Rome appeared very limited.

The Arians were condemned, and the famous Nicene phrase was introduced: "I believe in one God, the Father Almighty, the Creator of all things visible and invisible." But, for the East, it was not the end of the question. The decisions of the Council proved unable to overrule the Arians, and Constantine's obvious ignorance of theological issues was to have its consequences, sooner or later.

Eusebius of Caesarea, an Arian, took over the job of Osius as the emperor's favorite adviser on ecclesiastical problems, and once Constantine had founded Constantinople as the "New Rome" with a solemn ceremony on 11 May 330 at the ancient port of Byzantium, he gave up his interest in the other part of the empire thus, in a sense, confirming the medieval "myth" of his donation of the West to the bishop of Rome.

Constantine settled, in his own way, the religious problems in the East where Arius, through Eusebius, succeeded in convincing him again about his particular profession of faith, and the emperor, poorly advised, figured that his rehabilitation might help bring peace in the Eastern Church, without realizing the universal value of the Nicene Creed. So he asked Athanasius, the new bishop of Alexandria, to take Arius back into his Church.

When the bishop refused to do so, Constantine, without even informing Sylvester, convened a council at Tyre in 335 composed only of Arian bishops and Athanasius was dethroned. Sylvester was unable to intervene and died on 31 December of the same year. He was buried in the cemetery of Priscilla, in the church he had built in honor of the martyrs, Philip and Felix. Later Paul I arranged to have his remains laid in the church of S. Silvestro in Capite.

34. ST. MARK (336)

A Roman, like Sylvester, Mark was pope for a very brief period from 18 January to 7 October 336 and was even less esteemed by Constantine than his predecessor. Nonetheless he was already bishop of Rome when the new bishop of Alexandria protested against his own removal and went directly to Constantinople. Athanasius was exiled to Treviri by the emperor who, instead, granted Arius, freshly arrived at the imperial see, readmission to the clergy of Alexandria. On the following day, however, Arius died.

The *Liber pontificalis* attributes a longer pontificate to Mark as well as the issue of the decree by which the right to consecrate the bishop of Rome was given to the bishop of Ostia. In the name of Mark the Evangelist, he built the *Juxta Pallacinis* basilica, identified with the present Church of S. Marco. Subterranean remains of the earlier basilica have in fact been discovered, together with fragments of wall paintings and of a mosaic pavement, as well as the eleventh-century crypt which held the corpse of Pope St. Mark. Buried first in the cemetery of St. Balbina on the Ardeatine, his body was later moved there by Pope Gregory IV.

35. St. Julius I (337—352)

The Roman, Julius, consecrated pope on 6 February 337, was an energetic man, destined to play a central role in the defense of the orthodox faith, and in recouping the authority of his episcopal see. The death of Constantine on 22 May 337, a few days after having been baptised by an Arian, evidently helped Julius. Constantine's three sons divided up the empire, making the continuation of an ecclesiastico-political system difficult, and so gave the episcopal authorities more of a free hand in theological controversies.

Athanasius, bishop of Alexandria, who had been exiled by Constantine, was reintegrated in his post, as willed by the emperor on the point of death. Constantine II, who was at Treviri, communicated this to his brother Constantius in the East who acquiesced, despite his Arian sympathies. But the Arians did not give up and submitted the candidacy of Pisto directly to Julius, whilst Athanasius wrote a series of letters to the pope and the bishops of Egypt, proclaiming his own rights. In brief, the names had changed, but the situation remained uncertain and turbulent as ever.

A council favorable to Athanasius was set up in Alexandria, but Constantius cancelled its decisions. He sent Athanasius back into exile and raised Gregory of Cappadocia to the episcopal throne. Athanasius went to Rome and, at this point, Julius intervened.

In 340, the pope convened a council attended by fifty bishops and Athanasius was fully and definitively rehabilitated. A letter sent to the bishops of the East reflects a firm authoritarian position, and sets forth clearly the primacy of the Church of Rome: "Whenever accusations are made against the bishop of Alexandria and other bishops, it is necessary, in accordance with the custom, to write first of all to us in order to resolve the dispute with justice."

The decision of Rome, however, was only theoretical as in practice Athanasius still could not return to Alexandria. The Arian bishops organized their own council at Antioch in 341 in opposition to that of Rome, provoked incidents in Constantinople and tried to win Emperor Constans to their cause. In April 342, Constans met Athanasius who convinced him of the justice of his position. He became his protector and, in full agreement with Julius, convened a new council at Sardica, today's Sofia.

This next council was presided over by Osius, bishop of Cordova, and formerly the adviser to Constantine on religious affairs, who had been set aside but was once again in favor. Julius was not present this time to assure by his absence a calm judgment, and the Arians, realizing that they were in a minority left the assembly, with the result that Athanasius was fully reintegrated in his post.

The canonical rules developed by this council were of particular importance as they established the supreme jurisdiction of the Church of Rome, considered the only see which could decide on appeals against decisions taken by councils, and issue final judgments. However these rules were not applied immediately (although they were deemed obligatory like those earlier set forth at Nicaea) because the situation in the eastern part of the empire was still tense.

The Arians, in fact, succeeded in gaining Constantius to their side and a sort of politico-religious Reign of Terror took place in the East, which did not facilitate the decisions of councils. Athanasius had to wait for Gregory's death to return to Alexandria, and only in 346 reached his see in a climate of apparent serenity. The following year some of the Arian bishops, in a council at Milan, withdrew their accusations against him, and Julius had the satisfaction of gaining ground against the heresy which, all the same, continued to spread due to the political chaos of that period.

Indeed in 350, Constans was assassinated by Magnensius in a church where he had sought refuge, in open violation of the right of asylum. But if the usurper had no religious qualms, he certainly had to be on his guard against Constantius who succeeded in overcoming him in 353, thus becoming the absolute sovereign.

Julius died on 12 April 352 and was buried in the cemetery of Calepodius where he had built a church. Two other cemetery churches have been attributed to him, the one of St. Valentine on the Via Flaminia and that of St. Felix on the Via Portuense, in the catacomb Ad Insalsatos, a term the meaning of which is uncertain.

36. St. Liberius (352—366)

Liberius, again a Roman, succeeded Julius I on 17 April 352, and was promptly plunged into the religious battles of which Athanasius, bishop of Alexandria, was the main protagonist. The Arians wanted to get rid of him and sought to involve the West in his removal by sending new accusations to the newly elected Liberius. The immediate answer was a council at Rome at the end of 352 that deemed the accusations groundless. But the Arians, aiming to nail Athanasius, chose to attack the Nicaean Creed. So Liberius realized that all previous councils would have served no purpose if the whole matter were not

confirmed again with authority, since the decisions of the Great Council of
Chalcedon had never been put into effect, even if this new council had been,
under certain aspects, an ecumenical confirmation of the Nicaean Council.

In October 353, Liberius asked Constantius for authorization to hold a
council at Aquileia, but the emperor wanted it to be held at Arles in his presence. It took place speedily, and in practice the emperor made all the decisions.
Athanasius was condemned with the approval of all participants intimidated by
the pressures exerted by Constantius, and even the pope's emissaries were unable
to react. The only one to oppose Constantius was Paolino of Treviri, who was
exiled in Phrygia.

Liberius deplored the behavior of the bishops and wrote as much to Osius,
hinting at a kind of treason and stating that he personally could not approve
such decisions. He urged Constantius to convoke a new council, and this
took place at Milan in the spring of 355. The emperor proved more decisive
than ever and, with Athanasius condemned once again and the refusal of the
Nicene Creed, he decreed that whatever was decided was to be considered
law, and that any bishop who opposed it would be sent into exile. It looked
as if Arianism was to become the dogma of Christianity, but the support of
Rome was missing, and Constantius was aware that, if he really wanted to
win, its approval was necessary.

So he sent the eunuch Eusebius to Rome with orders to induce Liberius
through fair or foul means to approve the condemnation of Athanasius and to
recognize Arianism. The eunuch offered sumptuous gifts in St. Peter's which
were refused by an indignant Liberius. Every attempt having failed, Constantius
had him arrested and brought to his court in Milan. This was done at night
because Liberius was loved by the people, and a revolt by the Romans was to be
avoided at all costs.

A pathetic dialogue took place between Constantius and Liberius, in the
presence of the eunuch Eusebius and the Arian Bishop Epictetus, as narrated by
Theodoretus, bishop of Cirus, in his *Ecclesiastical History*.

"You must ban Athanasius from the Church," Constantius ordered him. "A
council has already excommunicated him."

Liberius replied: "To become executory, judgments must be just. Put
Athanasius before a tribunal which will adhere to ecclesiastical law."

"But he has already been convicted by the whole world!" the emperor
insisted.

Liberius retorted: "Those who signed his conviction ignore the facts. Some
have acted out of ambition, others out of fear."

"And who do you think you are," Constantius shouted at him, "that you
alone can defend a crook against the entire world?"

"Even if I am all alone, that does not diminish the high ideal that I am defending: the faith and unity of the Church. I demand that all the bishops sub-scribe to the Nicene Creed; let them be free to return to their sees and there render a free opinion about Athanasius."

The eunuch Eusebius reproved Liberius for treating Constantius like a Nabuchodonosor; Epictetus poked fun at him. The emperor cut this short: "Become an Arian and you will return to Rome." But Liberius's answer was one worthy of a great pope: "At Rome I have already taken leave from my brothers. For me the laws of the Church take precedence over all else. I shall never betray them in order to live in Rome."

Liberius was sent to Berea in Thrace under the surveillance of an Arian bishop, Demophilus. Constantius arranged for three Arian bishops to have a Roman archdeacon, Felix, replace him but forcing him, the clergy and the whole Roman population to swear under oath not to name a successor to the exiled Liberius. Felix was in fact an antipope, and the example of firmness set by Liberius made a profound impression on the people who continued to consider him their legitimate pontiff. This antipope, confused with one of the more pop-ular martyrs of Rome, was listed in the *Liber pontificalis* as a pope and represented in the mosaics at St. Paul's with the name Felix II. This was why in the list of the popes who had this name the symbol II no longer appears.

In the meantime, terror reigned throughout the empire and not even the Arian party appeared united. Athanasius was exiled and St. Hilary, bishop of Poitiers, suffered the same fate. Constantius finally became aware of the unpop-ularity of Felix when, in May of 357, while visiting Rome, he received numerous requests, especially from matrons of the city, to do something. So he decided to recall Liberius from exile during the summer of 358 for a council at Sirmio, where the pope signed a rather imprecise formula on the nature of the Word. It was one which in substance attenuated the Nicene Creed and was very close to the Arian thesis. According to Athanasius, who at this point had been aban-doned by all, Liberius "has become weak and has signed through the fear of death that threatened him." St. Hilary and St. Gerolamus confirmed this in their writings, and so one wonders whether his was the attitude of a renegade or of a weak man, though in either case his behavior was inexcusable. As Falconi has remarked, "if one reflects that Liberius, by so doing, definitely reneged both on himself and on his consistent and indomitable past, one must conclude with Duchesne that his was "a weakness," or better "a give-in."

Above all, the bishops of the council at Sirmio and the emperor forced a compromise on Liberius for his restoration as bishop of Rome, namely a joint administration with Felix. But here the Roman people intervened and, once Liberius had been triumphantly received, they threw the antipope out and denied him any possibility of returning to Rome. He was to die as an exile in Campania on 22 November 365, abandoned by all.

This episode is significant because, for the first time, the population takes part in the life of a pope. It is a "personage." destined to play a fundamental role on various occasions in the future that succeeds in imposing its will both to elect a pope and to throw one out. It will be a centuries-long love-hate relationship with its own bishop-king, which at times will reveal Christian and pious feelings, at others lay and anti-clerical ones. However, we cannot talk about "the population" in those years in the broad sense of the term. It is not yet that of the commune or of the curia that will make itself heard through the *Pasquinades* by more or less anonymous men of letters. Nor is it Belli's populace or today's citizens, who are mostly laicized and probably indifferent to the characteristics of "its" bishop and his "Romanness," because of the way the figure of the pope has been projected in a truly universal dimension that involves humanity everywhere and not just the population of Rome. At the time of Liberius, without forgetting that a part of it was still pagan, one can well speak of "community," a very large one and such as to influence a popular movement which, from then on, would become committed to an active participation in the episcopal events of the city. Factions, parties, clienteles would come into play, patricians would give way to plebeians, and the noble Roman families, very distinct from the "plebe," would appear on the scene.

So Liberius regained possession of the bishop's throne with full authority, even if in the shadow of an indelible disgrace, but of which the people seemed to take no heed or were unaware. And the theological disputes went on from one council to the next.

Two new councils convened by Constantius, one at Rimini for the West, the other at Seleucia for the East, failed to solve the Arian problem. So the emperor tried to resolve it all by an ambiguous term called "Nisenic," from the city of Nis in Thrace, which accepted a "similarity" of the Father with the Son. Notwithstanding appearances, this was the triumph of the Arian doctrine and St. Girolamus wrote, "the world, groaning, was amazed to find itself again Arian." But there was not the slightest reaction.

On 3 November 361, Constantius died. He was succeeded by Julian, son of a brother of Constantine who had replaced him, a year before, by military acclamation as the emperor of the West. He revoked the sentences of exile and all the orthodox bishops returned to their sees, including Athanasius who, during a council in 362, made a peace overture by declaring that he was in favor of accepting repentant heretics back into the community.

This measure was approved by Liberius who, in a letter to all the bishops in Italy, recommended that they act in the same manner, a diplomatic move to make peace again with a bishop who, formerly, had been abandoned by all.

Julian died in June 363 and his successors followed a rather ambiguous policy. Valentinian I was a sincere believer in the Nicene Creed. The Council of Lampsacus in 364 rejected the formulation of Constantius and condemned the most famous of the Arian bishops, while Valens, the brother of Valentinian I and joint emperor, defended them, so the situation remained in a flux.

In Rome a new political force, mentioned earlier while speaking of the people, began to take form, i.e., the patricians. During these first years the aristocracy proved to be a bulwark in defense of the pope. An indirect confirmation of that is the legend connected with the foundation in Rome of the basilica later called St. Mary Major, originally the Liberiana after Liberius who built it, as Gregorovius tells us, "on the Esquiline, next to Livia's butcher shop, in the market place, restored in the fourth century by Valentinian, Valens and Gratian for the inhabitants of the crowded quarter around it.

"According to the legend, the foundation of the church is related to a vision. A rich nobleman named John, during the night of 4 August, is supposed to have seen the Virgin Mary in a dream who told him to build a basilica at the place where, the next morning, he would find fresh snow. The wealthy patrician ran to Liberius and told him of his dream; Liberius admitted that he had had the same one. Since the prodigy in the meantime had taken place, Liberius had someone trace the plan of the basilica in the miraculous snow and the nobleman duly furnished the money for the construction."

However, Gregorovius also offered a plausible explanation of the legend. "The new basilica was in fact a monument to the Nicene symbolism and to the orthodox teaching of Athanasius, for whom Liberius himself had had to suffer two years of exile."

Liberius died on 24 September 366, and was buried in the cemetery of Priscilla.

37. ST. DAMASUS (366–384)

When Liberius died on 24 September 366, the election of a successor caused the formation of two factions within the clergy and the people of Rome, one in favor of, and the other against a conciliatory policy towards repentant heretics and the clergy formerly obedient to the antipope, Felix II.

The groups met separately. One made up of seven priests and three deacons with a small number of the faithful, all displeased by the leniency of the deceased pope, hastily elected a deacon, Ursinus, in the basilica of Santa Maria in Trastevere and, contrary to the canons, had him consecrated by a single bishop, Paul of Tivoli. Meanwhile, the majority of the clergy and the people gathered at San Lorenzo in Lucina and elected Damasus, a Spaniard of patrician lineage.

The supporters of Ursinus reproached Damasus for having sided with Felix II when Liberius was in exile and for being protected by Roman patricians, and

the two basilicas became the fortresses of the two factions. There were skirmishes for three days with dead and wounded but, nevertheless, Damasus
succeeded in having himself consecrated pope in the Lateran basilica in the presence of the bishop of Ostia on 1 October.

"The eagerness of Damasus and Ursinus to occupy the episcopal seat,"
narrates Ammiano Marcellino, "surpassed all possible human ambition.
They confronted each other like two political adversaries and even arrived at
armed conflicts with wounded and dead. The prefect, unable to impede or
suppress the riot, had to keep out of the battle. Damasus got the upper hand
and victory went to his party in the basilica of Sicinnius, where the Christians
had gathered. 137 were found dead, and much time passed before the people
calmed down. But it was not surprising, considering the splendor of Rome,
that such a desirable prize should ignite the desire in malicious men and give
rise to the most furious and dogged struggles. Once having reached the goal,
one could enjoy in peace a fortune assured by the donations of the matrons,
go about elegantly dressed in a coach-and-four, and attend banquets superior
even to those at the imperial table."

This ecclesiastical immortality, however, was not condemned only by a pagan
writer such as Ammiano Marcellino, who possibly exaggerated certain events.
Even St. Jerome, referring to Damasus to whom he was secretary, recalls that,
when a bishop, he had tried to convert Pretextatus, the Prefect of Rome, and had
received this response, which reflected an attitude that had obviously become
commonplace: "Certainly, but I want to be elected bishop of Rome!"

St. Jerome is the source of other information that shows the considerable
degeneration of ecclesiastical mores. "There are some who get ordained as deacons and priests simply to be able to visit women freely," he complains in one
letter. "They think only about dressing well and using perfume with a thousand
fragrances. Their boots must be perfect and they use curlers in their hair; their
fingers sparkle with rings; for fear of soiling their shoes with mud, they are seen
walking as if on their toes. To watch them going around in this manner, one
takes them more for gigolos than for acolytes. The work and knowledge of
many of them consists exclusively in knowing the names, the homes and the
standard of living of the matrons."

The prefect of Rome mentioned by Ammiano Marcellino was a certain
Vivenzius, and he was the Pilate of the situation. When he saw that things were
taking a bad turn, he thought only about saving his own skin, and left the city
for the countryside to wait for developments. Once the waters had calmed, he
returned to the city and saw that the situation was in favor of Damasus, i.e., of
the more numerous group. So he recognized Damasus and expelled Ursinus with
his deacons. However, the Ursinians did not give up and barricaded themselves
in the Liberian basilica. The supporters of Damasus attacked the basilica on 26

October and, as Ammiano Marcellino tells us, when the battle was over there were all those dead bodies.

A year later, Ursinus was allowed to return to Rome, but when troubles began again, Emperor Valentinianus I sent him into exile. Ursinus never gave up his claims. On the contrary, living at first in Gaul and then, by a concession from the emperor, in Milan, he continued to plot against Damasus. In 370 he managed to corrupt a Jew named Isaccus, a convert who later apostatised, and got him to accuse Damasus of serious crimes before the imperial court. Maximianus, the vicar of Rome, had to set up an investigation of Damasus, but left the verdict to the new emperor, Gratian. In 372, Damasus was acquitted and his accusers, Isaccus and Ursinus, ended again in exile, the former in Spain and the latter at Cologne.

Notwithstanding those accusations which, whether true or false, certainly damaged the dignity and the decorum of his episcopal authority, Damasus managed to impose the supremacy of his see through his strong personality. The councils of Rome in 369 and Antioch in 378 established the rule that a bishop would be considered legitimate only when recognized as such by the bishop of Rome. Using this right, Damasus deposed the Arian bishops, and St. Ambrose, bishop of Milan, set forth in a very clear formulation the essence of Christendom for the East and the West: "Where Peter is, there is the Church," this was simply a rephrasing of Jesus's: "Thou art Peter and upon this rock I shall build my Church." Damasus recalled this in the council at Rome in 382: "The Holy Church of Rome has precedence over all, not because of deliberation by one or another Council, but because the primacy was conferred by the declaration of Our Lord and Saviour as reported in the Gospel."

As a result of this recovered authority, and thanks to the support of a mover of masses such as St. Jerome, Arianism gradually lost ground. The two joint emperors, Gratian and Theodosius, had a policy which was decidedly orthodox in ecclesiastical terms, and heresy was no longer tolerated. They even went as far as death sentences, which was what happened at Saragossa in 380 with Priscillianus guilty of a rather personal interpretation of Holy Scripture.

Following on this imperial dogmatism, the Church tackled important problems of doctrine in a series of councils, such as the ecumenical one at Constantinople in 381, where the divinity of the Holy Spirit was affirmed.

Christianization was in full swing in Rome as well, where Damasus made full use of St. Jerome, and the lectures he gave to a group of Roman matrons, gathered together by the patrician Marcella in her home on the Aventine, became famous.

In brief, Damasus managed to energize the community in Rome, embodying it in an ecclesiastical structure which virtually had no precedent. He continued the building activity of his predecessors, as bear witness the churches of Saints

Nereus and Achilleus, as well as the *titulus* Damasi, San Lorenzo in Damaso, located near the Curia where Caesar was assassinated, though demolished and subsequently reconstructed in the fifteenth century. Moreover, he was devoted to the restoration of the catacombs, and was the "poet of martyrs." the author of metrical inscriptions which he arranged to have carved on sepulchers in various cemeteries by an expert calligrapher, Junius Dionigius Filocalus.

Damasus, an artist surrounded by artists, was a Maecenas-like pope, the first in history, and it was thanks to him that St. Jerome took on the task of revising the Latin text of the Gospels, a unique labor in the Christianization of East and West. It was perhaps the most enduring achievement of his pontificate, destined to remain for centuries the point of reference for peoples of diverse languages who were united by reading the word of Christ in Latin.

Damasus died on 11 December 384. He had composed an epitaph for himself in Latin which goes as follows in the vulgate:

> He who walked on salty water,
> who gave life to seeds dying in soil,
> who could dissolve lethal ties
> after the darkness of Death,
> who for Martha could revive her brother,
> three days after death, I believe
> will resurrect Damasus when he dies.

38. St. Siricius (384—399)

Siricius, the son of Tiburtius, a Roman, had been a deacon under Liberius and Damasus. He was elected pope on an uncertain date, either on 15, 22 or 29 December 384, but not without opposition from followers of Ursinus. We have evidence of this in a letter from Emperor Valentinianus II to his prefect, Pinianus: "Hello, my dear Pinianus! That the people in Rome are united and elect an excellent priest, we consider to be an event worthy of the Roman people and we are pleased that this has occurred in our time. Therefore, considering that Siricius, a most virtuous bishop, was chosen to preside over the priesthood when the dishonest Ursinus was being acclaimed, it is with our approval and our joy that we wish Siricius to hold his post as bishop. Dear, sweet Pinianus, it is certainly a great sign of innocence and wisdom that he has been elected by acclamation and that the others have been rejected." St. Jerome did not think highly of him, but one must take into account that he was openly critical of the Roman clergy in general, and it is therefore likely that his judgment was biased.

In principle, Siricius must have felt obliged to follow the line laid down by Damasus, because two months after his election, on 11 February 385, he wrote a letter to Bishop Imerius of Tarragona considered the first "decretal" of history, that is, the first letter written by a bishop of Rome which goes beyond the tone of simple admonition or a loving instruction, and assumes the semblance of a law. The style of this letter is that "of the absolute monarch who uses concise expressions of command or prohibition with a tone both moving and dramatic, without setting forth juridical reasons for orders from the authority whose will is law and needs no other justification," as Seppelt notes in reporting an opinion of Getzeny. This first "decretal" was in fact the reply to questions raised by Imerius with Damasus who had died before he could answer him. Seppelt goes on to observe that, "the answers by Siricius to the questions posed by Imerius are in the form of proper orders as in imperial letters; these not only set forth and instruct on the existing ecclesiastical law but dispose of doubtful cases and create new rules. Imerius's questions related in particular to various issues of ecclesiastical discipline which Siricius resolved authoritatively, pointing out that he was responsible for all the Churches and bore the burden of those which were oppressed, or rather that Peter the Apostle was still bearing it."

In 386 a council in Rome once again confirmed the primacy of the bishop of Rome over the others, and the year 386 is an important one in the history of Christianity because it saw the conversion of St. Augustine, baptised the following year by St. Ambrose. Augustine was bishop of Hippo from 397 on, and is one of the greatest Fathers of the Latin Church. At that time, Manichaeism had reached Rome from the East, in a form of exaggerated asceticism but , upon entering into the life of a great city such as Rome, the Manichaeans abandoned themselves to a disorderly existence without precise rules. A certain Jovinianus reached notoriety after having lived Manichaeism to the full, including fasting and mortification, then changed to a very personal doctrine marked by dissoluteness. For him there was no difference between chastity and lust, and the true Christian could never commit sin if he had assimilated profoundly the meaning of baptism. Hence, everything was permitted.

He was opposed by St. Ambrose and St. Jerome in writings which became famous in the Christian literature of those years. Condemned as a heretic by Siricius, he was expelled from the community together with his followers.

Siricius continued the policy of construction that had been promoted by Damasus. He furthered work on the churches of San Clemente and Santa Pudenziana, but, above all, he rebuilt the basilica of St. Paul on new foundations, as recorded on a column of cipolin marble preserved under the north portico: "*Siricius episcopus tota mente devotus.*"

He died on 26 November 399, and was probably buried in the cemetery of Priscilla until Paschal II had his remains transferred to S. Prassede.

39. St. Anastasius I (399—401)

Anastasius I was consecrated pope on 27 November 399, but proved to be an insignificant figure. The *Liber pontificalis* attributes to him the decree concerning the duty of priests to stand during the reading of the Gospel by the deacons, a measure probably due to the fact that the two ecclesiastical orders were not on good terms. He is said, moreover, to have erected a basilica named Crescenziana, not readily identifiable.

In letters sent to the bishops he speaks with authority about the controversies going on between the followers of Origen and of Donatus, and in the year 400 he condemned the writings of Origen and their translator, Rufinus, who was in disagreement with St. Jerome.

Another problem, however, was threatening the empire in its decadence, Rome and the Christian world generally at the dawn of the fifth century, namely, the Barbarians. In November 401, Alaric, king of the Goths, invaded the northern part of the peninsula as far as Piacenza and threatened Milan, where Honorius, the emperor of the West, resided.

Anastasius I died on 19 December 401 and was buried on the Via Portuense, above the catacombs of St. Pontianus.

40. St. Innocent I (401—417)

Innocent, a native of Albano and, according to St. Jerome, son of Pope Anastasius, was elected on 22 December 401.

With him, Rome's primacy over the entire Church increased notably. His "decretals" attest to this, and from them emerges the rather authoritarian personality of Innocent, deemed by many to be "the first pope." What Falconi says about this is essentially correct: "He was the first pope in an extremely embryonic manner and hence discernible with difficulty, whereas with Leo I the characteristics and the historical functions of the Roman pontiff appear at a stage of development which is unequivocal and clear."

As I have indicated in the introduction, I am using without distinction the terms "bishop of Rome" and "pope" from the time of St. Peter, and as a result the question of attribution of 'first pope' to Innocent I or to Leo I, I consider of marginal importance.

During the first phase of his pontificate, Innocent was occupied with the tragic misfortunes of St. John, called Chrysostom, or "Golden Mouth," obviously for his outstanding oratorical gifts which, however, caused him enemies in Constantinople where he was the bishop from the year 398. Eudoxia, wife of the East Roman emperor, was especially put out by the severe tone of his sermons, and she found support in Theophilus, the patriarch of Alexandria, who held a meeting of thirty-six bishops in the Villa of the Oak Tree near Chalcedon in Bithynia in 403, and succeeded in having Chrysostom deposed and exiled. Recalled because of the uproar among the population, he was exiled a second time to Armenia, guilty of having disapproved of a big party organized at the court in honor of Eudoxia, a criticism which she, of course, resented. Innocent came into the picture when he received letters from both Chrysostom and Theophilus, each making reciprocal accusations and defenses. The pope was convinced of the innocence of Chrysostom and tried to have Honorius convene a council, but the emperor already had problems with the Barbarians roving around Italy, so the council did not take place. Innocent had no choice but to send a delegation of bishops to Constantinople, but they were not even received and the situation did not change. St. John died in exile in 407. Thus, the letters from Innocent served only as moral comfort to Chrysostom, and it must be admitted that under certain aspects the bishop of Rome had suffered a defeat, even if he showed firmness in the whole matter.

Another important event during the pontificate of Innocent was the sack of Rome in 410, carried out by the Goths under Alaric. This was the logical result of a badly defended empire left to improvisations, perhaps courageous but inadequate, by generals such as Stilicho (fated to fall into disgrace and be condemned to death) and in the hands of incapable emperors like Honorius who showed only fear at the threats of the Goths. Hiding in Ravenna, he left responsibility for the defense of Rome to a Senate totally unprepared and unable to do anything but pay tribute, as actually happened in 408. But the ransom payments were too little to assuage the greed of Alaric who wanted land as well as gold, land such as Pannonia. The Senate gave in, even to the point of recognizing the prefect Attalus as pretender to the imperial crown, though he did not have the personality to supplant Honorius. Disappointed, Alaric got rid of him.

Then came the idea to send a delegation to Ravenna to convince Honorius to give in to the demands of the Goth. The delegation of Senators included Innocent. This was an important moment for the Church of Rome which, engaged in a civil matter, gave a new image to its bishop. But all was in vain; at the end of his patience with Honorius's delays, Alaric gave a free hand to his Goths who entered Rome on 24 August and pillaged it for three full days.

However, Alaric, an Arian yet nonetheless always a Christian, must have given Innocent some guarantees should things go badly. Certain events, recorded by Gregorovius and based on legends and tales of the period, would confirm this: "Alaric had given his warriors full permission to pillage but he ordered them not to kill any residents and to respect the churches, particularly the basilicas of the two Apostles in which the Romans were accustomed to seek refuge."

When the Goths burst into the house of Marcella on the Aventine, she, "the first Roman nun of noble birth was wearing her humble clothing of a penitent and, despite the ferocious blows of the assassins, begged them clutching their knees to spare the virtue of her adoptive daughter, Principia. The hearts of the Barbarians were touched and they themselves led these pious ladies to the asylum of St. Paul." And again, "one of the Goths, having entered a house, found there a young girl who, alone and undefended, was fearlessly guarding a collection of precious household goods, piled up all together. The Goth was about to seize the goods when the calm tone of the young woman scared him off. He could do what he wanted, she said, but these objects belonged to Peter the Apostle, who would surely know how to make him pay for his sacrilegious seizure. Hearing those words, the Barbarian would have rather thrust his hand into a fire and, having told Alaric what had happened, was ordered to escort the treasures of the Apostle and their custodian to the safety of St. Peter."

All this went to boost the image of an Innocent, forerunner of Leo the Great, as *defensor Urbis*, personally carrying out temporal responsibilities. "Innocent is believed to have forestalled, even if in a more modest way, the same gesture that a legendary figure of Leo the Great made when he went all the way to northern Italy to meet Attila," Falconi notes.

In Rome, once the Barbarian horde had left, Innocent flung himself into the battle against the heresy of the last Manichaeans, as well as against that of Pelagius, denounced by St. Jerome. At a council held at Carthage in 411 he excommunicated Celestius, a disciple of Pelagius. The Pelagian doctrine, which did not admit original sin and attributed to free will alone resolutive importance for salvation, had gained numerous followers in the East, especially in the Holy Land, where the bishop of Jerusalem, John, had shown himself favorable to it, despite official condemnations. A kind of fanaticism characterized the Pelagians, who perpetrated acts of vandalism against monasteries opposed to their ideas. Even St. Jerome himself was saved only with difficulty from a fire started by them.

Made aware of these events, Innocent convened a council at Rome in 417 that condemned Pelagianism.

Finally, the building activity of this pope must be noted. He built the basilica of Saints Gervasius and Protasius, erected out of legacies left by the matron Vestina, which was later dedicated to San Vitale, and also provided for improvements to the basilica of St. Agnes.

Innocent I died on 12 March 417, and was buried in the cemetery *ad Ursum pileatum*, together with his father Anastasius I, on the Via di Porto.

41. ST. ZOSIMUS (417—418)

A Greek priest, Zosimus succeeded Innocent I on 18 March 417, probably at the latter's suggestion on the recommendation of John Chrysostom. Also much in his favor was Patroclus, the bishop of Arles who, as soon as he was consecrated, Zosimus named vicar of all the Gauls.

His pontificate was brief and full of difficulties caused by Pelagianism which, notwithstanding severe condemnation by Innocent, had not ceased to gain ground. Indeed Celestius, the disciple of Pelagius, came to Rome to submit himself to the new pope's judgment and to clear himself of false accusations. But it was a trap that Zosimus fell into. After being interrogated by him at San Clemente, Celestius replied that he was prepared to repudiate all that the council of Innocent had condemned, with the result that Zosimus recognized him as being fully Orthodox.

Zosimus sent his decision to St. Augustine and the other bishops, reproving them for the haste of their decision, and called for the accusers of Celestius and Pelagius to appear in Rome. The African bishops begged Zosimus not to annul Innocent's decisions, explaining to him that he had been hoodwinked by Celestius. The pope did not want to admit that he had made a mistake and declared indignantly that what was decided by Rome should not even be discussed. But at the same time he did not dare go back on the decisions of his predecessor, wanting to maintain a kind of *status quo* while awaiting clarification of the issue.

This came from a council held in May 418, at Carthage which again condemned the Pelagian doctrine. At the same time, Honorius issued a decree deploring the spread of this doctrine which he saw as a disturbance to the public order. Celestius became alarmed and left Rome.

At this juncture, Zosimus could not but give a definitive judgment. He set it forth in a lengthy letter, the *Tractoria*, in which he specifically condemned Pelagianism, defined the dogma of original sin and emphasized the fundamental and unique importance of grace as the way to salvation.

Having corrected his somewhat imprudent behavior, Zosimus suddenly found himself involved in a new scandal and made another mistake. A priest called Apiarius, who was excommunicated by a bishop named Urban of Sicca, had sent an appeal to Rome, ignoring the African canon law that did not permit such appeals. Zosimus accepted it and, furthermore, sent Faustinus, bishop of Potenza, to Carthage with instructions that, among other things, deacons and priests excommunicated by African bishops were to be permitted to appeal to bishops of nearby Churches, and Bishop Urban was to be excommunicated if he failed to make good the wrongs done to Apiarius.

This was a grave diplomatic mistake, but fortunately the African Church was not rigid in its views, otherwise there would have been a schism. However, the issue did involve the immediate successors of Zosimus, Boniface I and Celestine I, and naturally resulted in a refusal of Rome's requests which, once Zosimus was dead, could in substance be shelved or even ignored.

Certainly Zosimus was disconcerting in his attitude, but what Seppelt has observed is true: "The obvious mistakes which occurred during the brief pontificate of Zosimus must certainly be blamed on his way of doing things and on his character, ready to take hurried and ill-considered decisions, but can also be explained by the fact that, being Greek, he did not easily assimilate the mentality of the westerners, so different from that of the easterners. Indeed, in Rome he was not at all popular, on the contrary, some of the Roman clergy were quite hostile towards him, and schemed to distance him from the imperial court at Ravenna. Zosimus himself complained about this in a letter written shortly before his death," which occurred on 26 December 418. He was buried in the basilica of San Lorenzo.

42. St. Boniface I (418—422)

The funeral of Zosimus was not yet over when a tumultuous crowd went to the Lateran basilica and elected as pope the archdeacon Eulalius. Shortly afterwards a majority of the clergy, supported by a good part of the people, gathered in a basilica, not clearly identified but said to be that of Theodore, and there elected an elderly Roman priest, Boniface. It was December 28th or 29th. As a result there were riots, since neither of the two factions was prepared to cede, and the pagan prefect, Aurelius Anicius Simmacus, who was on the side of his friend, Eulalius, sent a report to the Emperor Honorius which put Boniface in a bad light. Honorius naturally supported Eulalius.

But the populace would not give in, and it was the times of Damasus and Ursinus all over again. However, since Honorius's decree was in force, Boniface withdrew to the basilica of St. Paul where a tribune, ordered by the prefect to arrest him, was beaten up by the population. Simmacus thereupon closed the gates of the city to prevent him from reentering. But the supporters of Boniface sent a plea to the emperor, pointing out that their bishop had been elected by the necessary majority according to the rules, while canon law had been broken where Eulalius was concerned.

Honorius decided to solve the problem by a council and the two parties appeared first at Ravenna and then at Spoleto. But, pending a decision, both were banned from coming into Rome. Boniface obeyed, staying at the cemetery of Felicita on the Via Salaria while Eulalius went instead from Anzio to Rome on Easter Day to celebrate Mass in the Lateran, defying the imperial orders.

Honorius did not forgive him. He banned him from the city once and for all, detaining him in Campania, and recognized Pope Boniface who was consecrated on 10 April 419. Honorius issued a rescript to clarify that in the future, "in the event of an election in dispute between two contenders, only he who shall be designated by a new election on the basis of unanimous consent shall be bishop."

During his pontificate, Boniface was particularly busy with the Pelagian heresy: in effect, respecting the decisions of Innocent I and reaffirming them.

St. Augustine greatly admired him for this, so much so that he dedicated to him the four volumes of his work, *Against Two Letters from the Pelagians.*

But perhaps Boniface did not really merit this dedication, as he did not behave well with the bishop of Hippo, cutting more or less the same poor figure his predecessor had with the Church in Africa.

When a certain Antonio, named by St. Augustine as bishop of Fussala in the district of Hippo, was removed from his post because the author of the *Confessions* had had second thoughts about the choice, Antonio travelled to Rome to present an appeal to Boniface who granted it and restored him to his post.

Between appeals, letters and councils, the situation between Rome and the African Church remained unsettled. Apiarius versus Zosimus and Antonio versus Boniface had led to a certain tension. However, this did not provoke a schism probably more to the merit of the Church of Africa than to Rome, and the atmosphere was to become less tense with Celestine I.

Boniface died on 4 September 422.

43. St. Celestine I (422—432)

The election of Celestine, a deacon born in Campania, was peaceful and took place on 10 September 422. He was a friend of St. Augustine and this facilitated the settlement of disputes with the Church of Africa concerning Apiarius and Antonio, which had brought no honor to Rome since it had taken the defense of persons who did not deserve it. Celestine, in effect, reaffirmed the autonomy of the African Church in disciplinary matters, to which it was jealously attached, without damaging the primacy of Rome. On the other hand, as Seppelt notes, "the events which took place soon after in Africa turned out to be favorable to Rome, since they guaranteed the rights it claimed. In fact, the blossoming African Church was reduced to almost nothing a few years later by the terrible invasion of the Vandals, and it lost the exalted position it had earlier enjoyed in the Catholic Church."

But Celestine is remembered chiefly for the important role he played in the settlement of Christological controversies. In 428 Nestorius, the aged abbot of a monastery in Antioch and, at the time patriarch of Constantinople, opposed the title "Mother of God" for the Madonna, preferring for her that of "Mother of Christ." Cyril, patriarch of Alexandria, complained about this to Celestine who condemned Nestorius during a Roman council held in the month of August 430.

But Emperor Theodosius II, supported by John of Antioch, declared that he thought Nestorius was right. The result was an ecumenical council convened at Ephesus for 7 June 431. For various reasons, many Eastern and African bishops, as well as the representatives of Boniface, did not appear. So, as chairman, Cyril called the meeting for 22 June when 150 of them met and decided in great haste to condemn Nestorius and to proclaim the legitimacy of the term "Mary, Mother of God."

This smacked of fraud, and Nestorius, supported by John of Antioch, presented an appeal to the emperor to ask him to have the case examined again by a plenary assembly. The representatives of Boniface arrived in Ephesus during the first days of July when the eastern bishops also showed up. The case was reexamined and the judgment of the first session was confirmed. This time Theodosius II could do nothing other than approve the judgment, but he insisted that both Nestorius and Cyril be deposed. The latter succeeded in bribing the courtiers and was rehabilitated. Nestorius lost his case, withdrew to a monastery in Antioch and ended his days in Egypt where he passed away.

The priest Philip, head of the delegation from Rome, approved on his part the decisions of the Council and proclaimed in his allocution the primacy of the bishop of Rome in customary terms, not realizing that the East was slipping away from Rome's control. However, new Christians were being gained for the West with St. Patrick in Ireland and Palladius in Scotland and the work of evangelization proceeded.

Rome registered the construction of a new church. A certain Peter, a priest from Illyria, built the church of St. Sabina on an ancient *titulus Sabinae*, probably within the home of a matron named Sabina. Of the original wall decoration there still remains, above the main portal, a large mosaic strip bearing a metrical inscription, attributed to St. Paulinus of Nola, with the names of Peter of Illyria and Celestine I. But the latter could not have witnessed its completion, since he died before it was finished, on 27 July 432.

44. St. Sixtus III (432—440)

A Roman priest and, on the basis of a letter written to him by St. Augustine, a Pelagian in his youth, Sixtus was elected pope on 31 July 432, the third with that name.

During his pontificate the last disputes arising from the council of Ephesus were resolved. John of Antioch, defender of the stand taken by Nestorius, finally came to more moderate views and agreed with the affirmation of Ephesus. By acknowledging an equal identity in the various terms for God, Christ, Lord and Son and the union of the two natures in the person of the Word, the Virgin Mary was automatically recognized as the "Mother of God." In messages sent to Cyril and John, Sixtus III expressed his joy over the settlement of the dispute.

But Sixtus III is best remembered for having increased the number of churches in Rome. First, the construction of Santa Sabina was finished, then San Lorenzo in Lucina was built, so called because it was built next to the house of the matron, Lucina, even if it lost its original structure when it was rebuilt by Paschal II.

Sixtus III also reconstructed the baptistery of St. John which had been built by Constantine in a circular shape, giving to it the octagonal form that it still has. Significant is the inscription in distichs dictated by him for the architrave supported by eight columns of porphyry surrounding the baptismal basin, an inscription which praises baptism in anti-Pelagian tones. "Here takes place the birth of a holy lineage from a noble seed: the Spirit of God impregnates the waters and is the generator. Nothing separates the new-born from the new life; the same fountain, the same Spirit, the same faith makes them one whole person. Neither a paternal fault nor any fault of yours will weigh upon you. This is the fountain of life which washes away the sin of the whole world; it springs forth from the wound in the side of the dying Saviour."

But the grandest work was no doubt the restoration of the basilica of Liberius, damaged during the riots over the election of Damasus. Sixtus dedicated it to the Madonna in honor of the dogma decreed by the council of Ephesus, as the inscription states: "*Virgo Maria, tibi Xystus nova tecta dictavi*" ("Virgin Mary, for you Sixtus provided a new dwelling"), and ever since it has been called St. Mary Major.

He had it adorned with splendid mosaics depicting the story of Mary and of the infancy of Jesus, with numerous precious sacred objects, including a gold chalice weighing 50 pounds, an altar covered with silver weighing 300 pounds, a deer made of 30 pounds of silver from whose mouth water flowed into the baptismal font, as well as a tabernacle of silver weighing 511 pounds, a special gift of Valentinianus III.

Rome, in effect, was being rendered sumptuously beautiful. But was all that luxury a sign of a true Christian spirit? St. Jerome condemned it: "The true servants of Christ stay far away from luxury. Somebody will tell me that in Judea the Temple was richly decorated and the table, the candelabra, the thuribles, the cups, the chalices and all the other furnishings were made of gold. But, as the Lord made his Temple out of poverty, we must think about the Cross and consider wealth as nothing other than mud."

"But the vain clergy of Rome thought otherwise," observed Gregorovius, "so they tried to make every church a copy of the Temple of Solomon and to reproduce the sumptuous oriental pomp in the sacred vessels and priestly garments. Within the period of only forty years a new and rich booty was amassed in Rome for those barbarians whom audacity and luck were to bring back to the city."

Sixtus III did not live to see the barbarians again attacking the riches of Rome: he died on 19 August 440, and was buried at St. Lawrence outside the Walls. He no longer appears as a saint in the *Universal Calendar of the Church*.

4 5. St. Leo I, the Great (440–461)

Leo, a deacon and a native of Volterra in Tuscany, was unanimously elected pope by the clergy and the people on 29 September 440.

His reign left a mark in the history of the papacy and was a turning point, giving the episcopal see of Rome that characteristic stamp which confirmed its primacy. For this reason Leo is generally considered "the first pope." However, as Falconi notes in a rather polemical tone, the Church, "unable to call him the 'first pope' without a serious danger of proclaiming human an institution which it already claimed to be divine, named him instead 'great.'" And it is true, as the famous scholar points out, that "Leo was not only the 'first pope' because none of his predecessors equalled him in attributing explicitly to himself this role and in concretising the resulting functions, but also, and above all, because he constituted in an exemplary fashion the prototype of the ideal figure of a Roman pontiff for centuries to come."

Let us therefore indicate the essential events in the biography of this pope *ante litteram*, who faced the two fundamental threats to the Church of that period, heresy and the Barbarians, in a role both religious and temporal. And we will begin by noting that, even as a simple deacon, he had become known in this double role under both Celestine I and Sixtus III, by defending orthodoxy against the Pelagians and by bringing to a successful conclusion in 439 a mission entrusted to him by the Empress Placidia to mediate a dispute in Gaul between the generals Ezius and Albinus.

As soon as he was elected, he continued the fight against the heretics, first of all against the sect of the Manichaeans, by obtaining from the emperor, Valentinianus III, the promulgation of very stringent laws. Then he insisted that the Pelagians make a retraction in writing in order to be readmitted into the Church and also gave Turibius, bishop of Astorga, the task of condemning the adherents of Priscillianism in a council at Toledo, with instructions in a letter specially prepared by him.

But the heresy which gave him the biggest problem was the monophysitism of Eutiche, a monk and the head of a large monastery near Constantinople who, around 448, began preaching in the East a doctrine which emphasized the divine nature of Christ to such a point that it no longer recognized His human nature, a position in certain aspects opposite to that of Arius.

The patriarch of Constantinople, Flavian, summoned Eutiche to a council in which his ideas were judged indisputably heretical. Eutiche was expelled from the priesthood as well as from the post of archimandrite, and was excommunicated. The monk submitted an appeal to Leo who replied in a fatherly tone, stating that Rome would quickly clarify its point of view. However, as soon as he had received from Flavian a detailed report, the pope immediately declared the opinions of Eutiche erroneous and the position of the council correct.

But Theodosius II, emperor of the East, supported Eutiche and, wanting to reinstate him, summoned an ecumenical council at Ephesus which was held in 449. Following a century old tradition of the bishop of Rome, Leo did not himself go but sent three legates with letters to the emperor, to the assembly, to the monks in Constantinople and to Flavian, whose letter was the most important as it gave precise explanations of the dogma of the incarnation and about the dual nature of Christ.

However, the letter was not read to the council at the opening session on 8 August. The imperial court managed to put pressure on the majority of the bishops and to manipulate the phases of the meeting, while the papal legates were treated hostilely and were even threatened. There were scenes of violence, and the police had to intervene. Flavian protested and was manhandled and injured, but managed to hide somewhere with his followers and to send an appeal to Leo. Eutiche was acquitted and the bishops who remained in the assembly hall with the doors barred, willingly or unwillingly signed the documents of what the pope immediately defined as the "larceny of Ephesus."

Indeed, Leo refused to recognize the validity of any decision made by such an assembly, and he protested to Theodosius II, requesting the convocation of a new council. The only response from the emperor of the East was a law approving the decisions of the council. Flavian was forced to go into exile and he died a few days later.

In February 450, the emperor of the West, Valentinian III, with his wife, Eudocia, and his mother, Placidia, arrived in Rome from Ravenna for a pilgrimage to the tombs of Peter and Paul. The pope, after delivering a homily in their presence, begged the emperor to intervene with Theodosius II and have him arrange the convocation of an ecumenical council in Italy. From the East came only vague promises until Theodosius II died in July, when things changed. His sister Pulcheria, orthodox and faithful, put Senator Marcian on the throne with her, annulled the laws issued by her brother, sent Eutiche into exile, and agreed to a new council.

But at this point Italy did not seem to be a suitable place for an ecumenical assembly. Attila, with his Huns, was massing troops at the borders, and although Ezius had defeated him in Gaul, he was still an impending danger. So it was better to convene a council in the East which was set up at Chalcedon in October 451. More than 500 bishops took part in it and Leo was represented by three legates who were to manage the assembly proceedings.

At Chalcedon, two fundamental decisions were taken: a dogmatic decree on the Incarnation, linked to the Nicene Creed, and the acceptance of the letter from Leo to Flavian, which the pontifical legate had not been able to read at Ephesus. The comment by the assembly on this letter was: "Through the mouth of Leo, Peter has spoken!" It was the recognition of the primacy of Rome.

The council of Chalcedon also declared that it was in favor of considering the see of Constantinople superior to all the others in the East, but Leo categorically refused to recognize this. "By virtue of the authority of St. Peter the Apostle," he declared to be without validity any decision contrary to those of the Council of Nicaea that recognized the primacy of Alexandria and Antioch. Instead he considered it appropriate to establish at Constantinople a permanent delegation from the Roman see, which he entrusted to the bishop of Cos, Julian. This was, in a way, the first nunciature.

Meanwhile by 452, the Attila danger had become a reality for Italy with the Hun king already at Aquileia. Nothing seemed able now to halt his advance toward Rome, where Valentinianus III himself had taken refuge. Yet, "the scourge of God" hesitated. Perhaps the City still had a prestigious name, despite everything, or, as Gregorovius noted, "most probably this superstitious man had been shaken by the sudden death of Alaric right after his conquest of Rome, and apparently his friends tried to dissuade him from going ahead, reminding him the example of the great Goth *condottiere*."

While Attila was in this uncertain frame of mind, discussions of what to do went on in Rome. The most logical would have been to recall Ezius, but jealous of again giving glory to the general prompted Valentinianus III to oppose this. So they opted to send a delegation in which all the powers would be represented, and which Attila would receive near Peschiera on the Mincio. Taking part were the old consul, Avienus, the prefect Tricezius and Pope Leo I, the most important interlocutor. We have no idea what he said to Attila, but it is a fact that the Hun king withdrew.

It is probable that the pope resolved the issue by using the same method that Gregory the Great would later use with Agilulfo, that is paying a huge tribute of gold from the "coffers" of St. Peter, an action which would furnish an explanation of the legend that arose from the event, and enable whoever spread the story to put to advantage the Apostle's personality.

Indeed, the legend describes an Attila who, while Leo is speaking, sees next to him an old man wearing a priestly robe, brandishing a sword and who orders Attila to obey the exhortations of the holy bishop; a legend which takes on effects and artistry in the works of painters such as Raphael and Algardi, even if losing thereby its genuineness. In these works of art, the old man becomes two persons, those of both the Apostles Peter and Paul, brandishing unsheathed swords behind Leo who is moving towards the Hun king. Attila, terrified, retreats.

And again, a "historical" phrase is attributed to Attila who, thinking of Leo and of the bishop of Troy, Lupus, believed like the pope to have prevented the sacking of his city, is said to have stated: "I can conquer men, but a lion and a wolf have been able to conquer a conqueror."

That same period gave rise to another legend, a sort of consequence of the earlier one, the purpose of which was to exalt the figure of St. Peter, elected patron of the city. Leo, back from his mission to render thanks for the assistance provided to him by the Prince of the Apostles, is supposed to have melted down the statue of the Capitoline Jupiter and to have used the bronze from it for the statue of St. Peter, still to be found in the middle nave of the Vatican basilica.

It was also at that time that a church was erected in honor of the Apostle by Eudoxia II and called by her the basilica of Eudoxiana, later St. Peter in Chains. Eudoxia in fact did give this church the chains from St. Peter's prison in Jerusalem, a gift to her from her mother, Eudocia. However, the chains from the Mamertine prison were already preserved in Rome and when Pope Leo placed the two sets of chains next to each other they apparently fused forming a single chain with 38 links, as already noted previously in the biography of the first pontiff.

But, legends aside, it is a fact that the Romans, once the danger had passed, gradually stopped going to the numerous religious ceremonies established by Leo in honor of St. Peter to commemorate the saving of the city. They preferred watching the games at the circus to praying over the tomb of the Apostle, and of course, Leo reproached them this in one of his famous sermons.

"The religious feast, in honor of the day when we were first punished and then liberated, when all of the faithful would come together to give thanks to the Lord, has already been forgotten by everybody, as is clear from the few who are here, and this has both saddened and disturbed my heart. I am ashamed by what I am about to say, but I cannot be silent about it. The devil has more followers than the Apostle, and the shameful, profane shows attract the people more than do the tombs of the martyrs. Who, then, saved this city, who broke out of his chains, who removed the disaster from it? The games at the circus or the solicitude of the saints?"

We do not know whether the Romans returned to pray to their patron, but what is certain is that all Rome in those days was taken up with the games and with vice, and not ready to beat its breasts and do penance. The emperor himself, now established in Rome, was not a role model, and his luxurious living style brought about, if indirectly, the sack of the city by the Vandals.

In fact, he was assassinated by Senator Petronius Maximus for having insulted the latter's wife, Anicia, an act of revenge which enabled this senator to gain the imperial throne. And after Anicia had died, Maximus succeeded in marrying Eudoxia who was unaware that he was Valentinianus III's assassin. Once she learned about it though, the proud daughter of Theodosius took her revenge in the worst possible way, by secretly calling to Africa for the intervention of Gaiseric, king of the Vandals. So in May 455, he and his troops disembarked at the port of Rome.

The Vandals were famous for their cruelty. They had reduced Africa to a land ravaged by cut-throat gangs that destroyed churches and monasteries and killed and captured bishops. Terror ran rampant in Rome with the people victims of unrestrained disorders and Maximus unable even to plan the city's defense, capable only of dismissing the court and giving them all permission to flee wherever they could. The indignant population killed him and tore his corpse to pieces while Gaiseric advanced along the Via Portuense.

Once more, Leo tried to save the city, as he had done with Attila, but the "miracle" was not repeated, or Gaiseric was not content with a simple ransom, as the Hun king had been. The pope obtained only the promise that the three great basilicas, St. Peter, St. Paul and the Lateran, would not be touched. Beginning on 15 June of that year, there began fourteen days of plundering.

The pillaging was carried out systematically in all parts of the city and many treasures from existing ancient pagan temples and from the imperial palace were taken aboard the ships moored at the banks of the Tiber. These included statues and precious vessels from the Temple of Jupiter on the Palatine, and all the sacred ornaments from the Temple of Jerusalem brought to Rome by Titus to embellish his triumph. Gaiseric dragged off to Africa thousands of Romans as slaves of war, as well as Eudoxia who had caused all this ruin.

Once the Vandals had sailed away, there was another slow period of reconstruction under emperors of little initiative, though Leo was active as ever. As Platina wrote, "he survived a calamity painful beyond belief, and turned all his energy to the restoration of a desolate city and its burned-out churches."

Besides, he loved Rome because it was the city where Peter, according to him, "in the same flesh by which he was our supreme head, sleeps the blessed sleep of death; the city which, by virtue of the Princes of the Apostles, from teacher of errors became disciple of truth; the city which Peter made the Head of the world." His numerous letters and sermons are almost always centered on the figure of the Apostle, because "as is eternal verity that which Peter believed of Christ, so is also eternal that which Christ instituted in Peter." In effect, Leo understood the symbolic significance of the personality of the first pope, explaining it in his own words to the point of personifying him as his descendant, and appearing to the Romans of the time as the new Peter.

Notwithstanding "the ingenious poetical creation" of the legends and his attempts to attribute the saving of the city to the Apostles Peter and Paul, it was Leo who was recognized as *defensor Urbis*. The Romans, while he was alive, thought they could sleep peacefully without a lot of prayers of thanksgiving, once the danger from Attila was averted. Their behavior proved to be then what has always been, typical of the Romans right up to the present day. Leo was the first pope to verify it in person and, probably, to understand it as the genuine "Roman" that he was.

He died in November 461, probably on the 10th, and was buried in the old basilica of St. Peter and when the new one was built, his remains were relocated during the reign of Clement XI under the altar dedicated to him bearing the marble relief by Algardi.

46. St. Hilary (461 – 468)

The deacon, Hilary, a Sardinian, was elected the successor of Leo the Great on 19 November 461. He had already acquired a reputation as a papal legate at the council of Ephesus, from which, however, he had to escape, an unwilling hero of that "larceny."

He was certainly not of the same stature as his predecessor and was classified by some as a "modest counter-image" of Leo. The scarcity of documentation on him certainly contributes to a negative judgment about his "pastoral" work, but the little one knows about him is at least indicative of the "school" in which he was trained, that of Leo the Great.

One must not forget, therefore, his behavior towards the Emperor Anthemius, at whose court had been established a heretical community led by a certain Philoteus. When the new emperor went to call on Hilary in the basilica of St. Peter, the pope met him surrounded by the faithful and would not let him proceed until he had assurances that the heretical group would be suppressed.

Hilary also showed his strength of character in questions about certain violations of the canon rules that had taken place in the Church of Gaul. In 462 he issued a decree which fully maintained the prerogatives given the bishop of Arles over the other bishops of that Church, and stated that only the most difficult problems were to be submitted to Rome. Similarly, during a council held in Rome in 465, he confirmed Tarragona's priority to consecrate bishops in Spain.

The negative opinion expressed with regard to this pope is perhaps due to "the imprudent Maecenas-like passion frivolously displayed by Hilary for the decoration of the Christian temples in his city," as Falconi has described it. According to the *Liber pontificalis*, he erected monasteries in St. Lawrence ad Balneum, in the pretorium of St. Stephen, and in the area called ad Lunam, as well as two libraries in the neighborhood of the Lateran.

He showed special interest in the construction of two oratories annexed to the baptistery of St. John. One was dedicated to the Evangelist, considered by Hilary his protector from when, near Ephesus in those famous days of the "larceny," he had found shelter in a burial chapel consecrated to the apostle, as attested by the inscription still legible there: "*Liberatori suo, Iohanni Evangelistae, Hilarus episcopus famulus Christi.*" In the splendid mosaic vault preserved there, one sees in the center the Lamb among garlands of flowers, with decorations of platters of fruit among birds and vines bound together by sticks.

The other oratory, dedicated to John the Baptist, is characterized by the famous "singing doors" so called because the ancient bronze portals, rotating on their hinges, emitted a harmonious sound. Time obviously created this particular "sonority," which, nevertheless, was well suited to the ostentatious opulence that typified the decoration of certain religious buildings. It is thought that more than a hundred pounds of silver were used for the altars of the two oratories and the decoration of the doors and fixtures were also made of silver and gold.

A third oratory built by Hilary in the Lateran complex must have been in the same style; dedicated to the Cross, it was joined to the baptistery by means of a portico. There were still considerable traces of it at the beginning of the seventeenth century, and it seems that a golden lamb was kept under an arch which was itself made of gold and supported by onyx columns. However, the apotheosis of unrestrained opulence was reached in the decoration of the baptistery. On the edges of the font, according to the *Liber pontificalis*, were placed three sculptures of deer, each made from thirty pounds of silver, of which sprouted the water for those to be baptised. Sixty pounds of silver were apparently used for a tabernacle or "tower" bearing a frieze of dolphins in the center of the circle of water, while on top of it stood a stupendous lamp of gold with ten flames to illuminate the baptismal ceremony at the Easter vigil. Crowning all was a golden dove, symbol of the Holy Spirit, aloft over the "waters of regeneration."

But Hilary's mania for grandeur did not stop here. The *Liber pontificalis* contains a mindboggling list of sacred utensils of gold and silver which he provided to enrich the sacristies and treasure rooms of the basilicas of St. Peter, St. Paul and Saint Lawrence. All of this, as Grisar noted, "shows the inexhaustible source of wealth that at that time flowed to the Church of Rome from donations by well-known families of senators, and from the extraordinary generosity of the court."

Moreover, the Roman Church was able to rely upon a vast number of parcels of real estate "the size of which was such as to permit a constant source of rental income," as Gregorovius observes.

But wasn't it really a waste to use such limitless wealth for works which brought no advantage to the city in terms of its civil rebirth? "While Rome was falling into wretchedness and was dying," Gregorovius fulminated, "the churches were being covered with precious gems and the basilicas were bursting with fabulous treasures, before the eyes of a people that had bled itself dry in an effort to mobilise an army and a fleet against the Vandals."

It is through these excesses that the figure of Hilary clearly loses prestige, precisely because the "social" aspect which Leo the Great had adopted was missing. The use of so much wealth for an external aspect of religion in Rome became an indictment which the passage of time would not fail to launch against popes of Hilary's stamp. As a result, Falconi's similar negative judgment is correct: "If the generosity of the wealthy faithful allowed the Church to dispose of ever larger quantities of wealth in order to do what was necessary to improve the general situation of the people, then it would have been wiser to set aside that wealth to cope with more ominous situations which unfortunately, as anyone could see, were looming on the horizon."

Hilary died on 29 February 468 and was buried at San Lorenzo fuori le Mura.

4 7. ST. SIMPLICIUS (4 6 8 — 4 8 3)

A native of Tivoli, Simplicius was elected pope on 3 March 468. During his pontificate, which lasted fifteen years, three dramatic events in the history of Rome occurred: the third sacking and the plague, both in 472, and the end of the Western Roman empire in 476.

The sacking was made by Ricimerus, minister and son-in-law of the Emperor Anthemius, as a result of an agreement by the latter with Senator Anicius Olybrius who, having married in Constantinople Placidia, the daughter of the Empress Eudoxia, aspired to the throne of Rome. The city in which famine and pestilence were on the rampage was defended by Anthemius and by the Goth king Bilimerus, who had arrived with his troops from Gaul, but it collapsed on 11 July 472. Bilimerus and Anthemius were killed and the same year the plague did away with Ricimerus and the new Emperor Olybrius.

Chaos ensued with a succession of useless emperors up to the insignificant Romulus Augustulus who was deposed by Odoacer, a nomadic tribal chieftain with a mixed band of Rugii, Heruli, Sciri and Turcilingi followers who became the masters of the peninsula. On 23 August 476, Odoacer assumed the title of King of Italy, rapidly confirmed by the city's Senate. The Eastern emperor, Zeno, replied disdainfully to this approval by the Senate, guilty of having sanctioned the loss of a part of the ancient Roman empire, but in the end gave to Odoacer the title of *Patricius*. Italy was now in the hands of the Barbarians.

The papacy could do nothing but accept the situation, notwithstanding that Odoacer was an Arian. Yet one must note that the prospects for the Church of Rome had changed. As Gregorovius has noted, "freed of the emperor of the West, the papacy began its ascent and the Church of Rome grew powerful on the ruins of the empire. At its fall, the Church was already a solid and imposing organism which could not be touched by the tragic fate of the ancient world; on the contrary, filling immediately the gap created by the disappearance of the empire, the Church built the bridge which was to link antiquity with the new world. Recognizing the right of citizenship for those tenacious Germans who had destroyed the empire, the Roman Church acquired the vital elements which allowed it to raise itself to a dominant position until, through a long and memorable process, the Western empire was able to rise again as the Roman-German empire."

But the relationships with the East, or rather with the Oriental Church, went through critical times. The Monophysites had taken over the Patriarchate of Constantinople, and even the see of Antioch had fallen into heretical hands, thanks to the support from Basiliscus, usurper of the throne of Emperor Zeno. The situation became calmer when Basiliscus died and Zeno regained possession of the imperial throne by agreement with Acacius, who was reinstated as patriarch of Constantinople. He hastened to publish a decree on the union called *Henoticon*, addressed to the bishops, clergy, monks, and the faithful of the Eastern Churches, which proposed the Nicaean symbol as the Faith but was equivocal on other subjects. For example, while it condemned Eutiche, it made practically no reference to Chalcedon and the "tome" of Leo the Great.

The *Henoticon* decree arrived in the West after the death of Simplicius. Nonetheless, he had been in a position to ascertain that affairs were not going well for Rome when he received news of the replacement of the bishop of Alexandria, Talaia, accused of perjury by Peter Mongo, who had hastened to sign the *Henoticon*. Simplicius wrote twice to Acacius to get an explanation of the replacement, but the latter did not honor him with a reply. In effect, Rome was sidelined on these difficult matters, and Simplicius certainly failed to handle them with the authority that Leo the Great had tried so hard to impose. Rigid but just is Falconi's judgment in this regard: "If Hilary had little of the personality of Leo, one could say that he was, in a certain way, his rather pathetic imitation. Even a bold-faced, but cautious, intriguer like Acacius would surely have behaved differently towards him if he had shown a stronger character. Simplicius ignored the fact that Rome without an emperor had by now become, and was considered, a distant provincial city which had outlived its reputation."

Perhaps Simplicius can be redeemed, if he is viewed only as far as Italy and Rome are concerned and where he was engaged in the organization of the pontifical assets. He was above all an excellent administrator, even if the details of his management are not very clear from what has come down to us. It was probably a question of decentralizing power through assignment by rotation of the various functions which had become burdensome for the clergy with the increase in the number of churches.

Also, Simplicius did not want to fall short of his predecessor, and pursued the necessary construction work following the third sacking of the city, from which he probably succeeded in saving only the basilica of St. Peter and the area of the Vatican.

On the Celian Hill, a basilica was consecrated to the First Martyr, Stephen, called Santo Stefano Rotondo, said to be the first church recovered from an ancient temple dedicated to Faunus. Another one was in the vicinity of St. Lawrence outside the Walls together with one near Sant'Andrea on the Esquiline Hill which, in the ninth century, received the strange name of Cata Barbara Patricia. Built on a *fundus* left to the Church of Rome by the Goth general Valila, it was subsequently adapted as a place for religious functions but destroyed at the beginning of the seventeenth century. Lastly, the church of St. Bibiana was built near the gate of San Lorenzo, later redone by Bernini.

So the usual squandering of huge ecclesiastical incomes went on. The Church of Rome continued to use its substantial assets to build new churches and, as the number of churches rose, the population of Rome shrank, while the pontifical see itself seemed to be in crisis, its mystique shaken by the Eastern Church with which it was now close to a schism.

Simplicius did not live to see it. He died on 10 March 483.

48. St. Felix III (483—492)

For many years now the election of a pope had not given rise to disorders in Rome. This came about normally through a choice made by the people who formed the community of the Church of Rome, and ratified by an imperial official who verified the validity of the election itself. As there was no longer an emperor in the West, Odoacer exercised his right to the ratification as a patrician and king, by sending to Rome as his plenipotentiary the prefect Cecina Basilius, chief official of the kingdom, who summoned the laity and the clergy to the mausoleum of Honorius near the basilica of St. Peter.

He unrolled a decree said to have been signed by the deceased Simplicius according to which from then on the naming of the pope should take place in consultation with the royal representatives. The decree was accepted and from the consultations that followed, Felix III, a Roman of the noble Anician lineage was elected. The consecration took place on 13 March 483.

During the nine years of his pontificate, he was assisted by the archdeacon, Gelasius, his future successor, and gave back to the see of Rome some of that forceful prestige that had not been seen since the times of Leo the Great.

Felix III focussed on the question of the Eastern Church and sought to resolve whatever was behind the discord between the two Churches. In fact, Rome was still demanding explanations about the deposing of Talaia as bishop of Alexandria as well as clarifications about the Henoticon. For this reason, two bishops were sent to Constantinople as pontifical legates with letters for the Emperor Zeno and for the patriarch, Acacius, in which the restoration of Talaia to his see was requested and the doctrine of the council of Chalcedon was restated. The letter to Acacius contained reproaches and an invitation to come to Rome to justify his behavior.

Acacius did not comply and, by agreement with Zeno, frightened and corrupted the legates who refrained from any public condemnation of him,

participated in the ceremonies which he celebrated and made no objections to
the insertion of the name of Peter Mongo as successor of Talaia amongst the
Dittici, the official list of the bishops recognized as orthodox.

The Church of Rome was, in effect, ridiculed by the performance of its representatives and Felix, as soon as he learned about it through the faithful
Orthodox monks, decreed the excommunication and the removal of the legates
as well as of Acacius. This was communicated to Constantinople by a new representative. Acacius, sure of the support of Zeno, simply refused to recognize the
validity of the excommunication and succeeded in corrupting the new pontifical
legate. As a result there was an open break between Rome and the East, a real
schism between the two Churches, called the "Acacian" schism, which lasted
from 484 to 519.

The question of Zeno was settled separately. The pope did not want to
excommunicate him, even if he was the one directly responsible for the
Henoticon, since he had promulgated it. But he was, after all, the emperor, and
the medieval times when a pope would not think twice about deposing or
excommunicating an emperor, and not just for heresy, were still to come. Felix
went no further than a scolding, speaking to him as a father to his son. For the
salvation of his soul, he advised him to submit in matters relating to God to the
orders of the bishops of Christ: "You must desist from trying to dominate the
prescriptions of Him to whom, according to the divine will, your goodness must
be submissive with pious devotion, or otherwise you will be going beyond the
limits of the divine order and insulting the lawgiver Himself."

But Zeno put a deaf ear to them. Indeed, he urged Theodoric, king of the
Ostrogoths, to throw Odoacer out of Italy, as he was guilty of having influ-
enced the election of Felix III. The war between those two was a long one
and, following a battle favorable to Theodoric in 490, Odoacer retreated to
Ravenna, resisting the siege for three years. There he was killed and
Theodoric became king of Italy in 493, when Zeno was already dead and
Gelasius I had become pope.

Felix III died on 1 March 492, and was buried in the basilica of St. Paul, the
only pope in history to be buried there. He no longer appears in the *Universal
Calendar of the Church* as a saint.

49. St. Gelasius I (492–496)

The secretary of Felix III, the African archdeacon Gelasius, was elected pope
on 1 March 492. Possessing a strong character and conscious of the primary
authority of the see of Rome, he pursued the efforts made by his predecessor to
end the schism with the Eastern Church without surrendering the orthodoxy of
Christian doctrine.

He sought the support of Emperor Anastasius I by notifying him of his election, to which he did not receive even an acknowledgement. Yet, later when Theodoric sent ambassadors from Rome to Constantinople for questions of a political nature, as well as acting as spokesman for Gelasius with regard to condemnation of the ideas of Acacius, the deceased patriarch of Constantinople who had brought about the schism, Anastasius expressed astonishment that the pope did not send him a personal letter.

Then Gelasius did send him an epistle which, by its structure and tenor is considered a milestone concerning the interaction of the Church and of the State and the primacy of the spiritual power over the temporal. It is the basis of a doctrine which was to characterize the Middle Ages.

"August Emperor," wrote Gelasius, "the powers that chiefly govern this world are two: the sacred power of the bishops and the temporal power of the kings. Of these two powers, the ministry of the bishops has the greater weight, because they must account to the tribunal of God also for the kings of the mortals." He continued, "You are also aware that, to take part in the divine mysteries, you have to fulfil the precepts of religion, which are not given to you to determine, because in such matters you depend on the judgment of the ministers of the sanctuary whom you cannot bend to your own will." And at the same time he explained, "In temporal matters, on the other hand, concerning the State, those dedicated to the worship of God also obey your laws because they know that, by divine power, you were given imperial power so that with regard to temporal matters all resistance is to be excluded." And, finally, he could not fail to reconfirm the primacy of the see of Rome: "And if it is fitting that all of the faithful submit themselves to the bishops, who correctly administer sacred matters, how much more necessary it is to proceed with the head of that see which God has set above all the others and which has always been venerated with filial devotion by the Universal Church."

These words alone suffice to illuminate the image of Gelasius I, a pope profoundly convinced of the dignity of his office, and who set forth in clear terms such as no pope had expressed before him that the distinction between politics and religion was a clarification of the concept in the phrase of Christ: "Render unto Caesar the things that are Caesar's and unto God the things that are God's." The good Gelasius wanted to be the "vicar of Christ" and nothing more, but the future would belie those good intentions. The religious spirit of the pope was seen above all in his firm opposition to the *Henoticon* that had caused the schism, yet the schism remained.

During his brief pontificate, Gelasius I proved to be a towering defender of the Orthodox faith, determined to keep it free from any blemish of heresy and uncontaminated as well by pagan traditions which superstition could still have kept alive. An example of this was the feast of the Lupercalia between 15

February and 18th, culminating in the *Februatio*, that is, the purification of the city from the influence of the demons. The attachment of the Romans to this very ancient celebration was so strong that, even after their conversion to Christianity, they did not want to give it up. On the contrary, to the bishops who condemned the Lupercals these Christians replied that the plague and the famine in Rome, as well as the sackings by the barbarians and the fall of the empire, were caused by the abolition of the old sacrifices to the god, Februo.

Gelasius I was firm in getting rid of these superstitious celebrations, so unchristian and orgiastic, and he sent Andromachus, head of the Senate and supporter of the Lupercalia, a proper theological dissertation on the subject. He decreed that one could not "serve two masters," God and Mammon, nor approach the table of the Lord and that of Satan, and that the Lupercals had never been any good for Rome. Indeed, the fall of the city had to be blamed on the vices of the population, on pagan superstition and on the survival of sacrilegious practices. It seems that he succeeded in getting the Senate to abolish the Lupercalia, and he replaced the pagan ceremony of purification by the feast of the Purification of the Madonna, introducing the procession of the Blessing of the Candles on 2 February.

The *Liber pontificalis* reports that Gelasius I saved Rome from famine. History does not confirm this, but it is probable that the city had had problems of the sort and that the pope put his own wealth at the disposal of the populace. Thus, no more building of new churches with the waste of money in works of marble, silver and gold, but rather the use of the funds for the public good, for the poor people.

It is a fact that Gelasius himself liked to call the assets of his episcopal see the "property of the poor" and, also from this point of view, his papal persona appears really unusual because of the "Franciscan" spirit which characterized it. Dionisius il Piccolo remembers him in the foreword to the collection of his decretals as follows: "Having assumed the government of the Church by the Will of God and for the welfare of many, Gelasius seemed more of a servant than a sovereign. To the merit of chastity he added that of wisdom. He was devoted to prayer, to studies and, at times, to writing. . . Under the loving guidance of God, he spent the poor days of his earthly life patiently and constantly in the midst of many difficulties, preferring penance and fasting, conquering pride by humility, so full of charity and generosity toward the poor that he himself died poor." That happened on 21 November 496 and he was buried in St. Peter's.

50. St. Anastasius II (496–498)

Anastasius II, a Roman, was consecrated pope on 24 November 496.

Up to his time, all the bishops of Rome had taken a firm position against the Eastern Church because of its adherence to the Monophysite heresy of Eutiche, but Anastasius II, wanting to put an end to the schism, was prepared to make big concessions.

This benign way of giving made him extremly unpopular in Rome, creating a division within both the clergy and the entire community. Certain contrasts were also fanned by the faction which had resented Gelasius I for his condemnation of the Lupercalia and which hoped to gain ground again under a weaker pope. There was also the fact that the Consul Festus, sent by Theodoric to Constantinople to have himself recognized as king of Italy, promised the emperor that he would persuade the pope to sign the famous *Henoticon*, which had been rejected by his predecessors.

However, Anastasius II, even if he was unable to disavow Festus since he was already dead when the latter returned to Rome, had given rise to other suspect rumors by readmitting to the Church a certain Photinus, a deacon at Thessalonica, who had been excommunicated as a follower of the Monophysitic heresy.

The record of his disfavor was handed down through the centuries by the *Liber pontificalis*, according to which the pope was struck by the will of God (*nutu divinu percussus est*) precisely for having readmitted Photinus. The chroniclers of the 13th and 14th centuries said he died the same way as Arius, with his bowels scattered, and Platina himself reports how "as he made himself comfortable to unload his stomach, he sent his intestines down, and died."

Following this tradition, Dante put him in the *Inferno* (XI,6–9) among the heretics:

> We approached it under cover
> of a great tombstone, whereon I saw a writing
> that said: 'I hold Pope Anastasius
> whom Photinus drew from the straight path.

And there were those who, in an effort to redeem the figure of the pontiff, launched the idea that in the *Liber pontificalis* there had been confusion between Pope Anastasius II and Emperor Anastasius I, a follower of the Monophysitic heresy.

In any case, it is certain that Anastasius II was the opposite of Gelasius I, whether the information about his very conciliatory tone towards the Monophysites was true or not. Lacking the energy and basically incapable of maintaining the position of prestige which the see of Rome demanded, he was, because of his weakness, the decisive cause of the disorders which occurred in Rome at his death on 19 November 498. In certain calendars he appeared as a saint on 19 November, in others on 8 September, but he is not recognized in the *Universal Calendar*.

5 1. St. Symmachus (4 9 8 — 5 1 4)

When Anastasius II died, Rome found itself with two bishops who were both elected by the two factions in the city. The orthodox faction which had disapproved of the conciliatory behavior of Anastasius II with regard to the Eastern Church, headed by Senator Faustus, elected the Sardinian deacon, Symmachus. The other one, a minority that favored ending the schism, headed by the consul Festus who had just returned from his mission to Constantinople, chose the archpriest, Lawrence. They were consecrated on the same day, 22 November 498, Symmachus in the Lateran basilica, Lawrence at St. Mary Major.

The battles of the previous years returned in a climate of civil war with rioting and fighting in the churches and on the streets. Recourse was made to Theodoric at Ravenna who delivered the verdict that "he who is elected first or has obtained the greater number of votes is to be considered the pope." In these circumstances, the favorite was Symmachus, suspected however of having bribed people at the Ravenna court to influence Theodoric's decision. But apart from this, Symmachus was well thought of by the king, precisely because Byzantium did not hold him in esteem, and would, hopefully, become a tool in his hands to make the emperor understand that in Italy it was the king and not the emperor who counted.

Symmachus, having returned to Rome, convened a council on 1 March 499, at St. Peter's in which seventy-two Italian bishops took part. "I have summoned you," he said, "to seek a way to stop the intrigues of the bishops, the scandals, and riots among the people like those provoked during my election." For the first time it was established that electioneering for a future pope was forbidden while the predecessor was still alive and unaware of such discussions, and that the pontiff had the right himself to designate a successor. In the event of the unforeseen death of a pope who had not named a successor, "he shall be consecrated who shall have gained the votes of all the clergy or, at least, the greater number of votes." It seems that the laity was excluded and the idea of a "majority" vote, in contrast to the "unanimity" desired originally by Honorius gained ground. Lawrence himself, attending the council, subscribed to these decrees and, in effect gave in to Symmachus. As a token of reconciliation he was assigned to the diocese of Nocera in Campania.

These rules on the election of a pope lasted only and, briefly, for the moment, the laity continued to be a significant element. Moreover, the popes would never obtain the right to name a successor.

The council of 499 was particularly important for the history of Rome since, from the signatures of the bishops who subscribed to the decrees, one learns that the titles of the basilicas then existing in the city were twenty-eight. Distributed among the various "regions," they were originally placed under a single presbyter or pastor but were later entrusted to three or more priests, the most senior of which was an *"incardinatus,"* or a priest-cardinal. Distinct from these parishes were the five patriarchal basilicas of St. John Lateran, St. Peter, St. Paul, St. Lawrence outside the Walls, and St. Mary Major, which were directly assigned to the bishop of Rome, their congregation not being limited to a particular quarter of the city but consisting of all the faithful there. These privileges were granted also to the basilicas of St. Sebastian and Santa Croce in Gerusalemme which, together with the others, constituted the so-called "Seven Churches" of Rome that during the Middle Ages were goals of pilgrimages.

After this council, Rome seemed to experience a period of tranquillity, and the visit which Theodoric made to the city in 500 provided the official approval to this state of peace. "When he entered the city, the Romans gave him the honors of an emperor and greeted him with the flattering title of the 'new Trajan,'" as Gregorovius recalls it. "The Senate, the people and the clergy, with the pope at their head, went to meet him outside the city and welcomed him, it seems, at the bridge over the Aniene or perhaps at the foot of Monte Mario. In deference to prudence, the Arian king went immediately to the basilica of St. Peter where he prayed at the tomb of the Apostle 'with great devotion and like a true Catholic.' Finally, with triumphal pomp, he entered Rome across Hadrian's bridge."

The donations to the churches, the resumption of the Circus games and the orders given for the restoration of certain monuments were decisive in gaining the hearts of the Roman people, just as the speech which he gave in the Forum, however brief, aroused a general enthusiasm. For a while Rome had the illusion of being "great" again, and in peace. But peace was far from certain among the Roman faithful and, as soon as Theodoric returned to Ravenna, the Senate faction hostile to Symmachus reappeared and sent the king a circumstantial accusation against the pope, guilty of having celebrated Easter in 501 without respecting the computation of the date established by Alexandrian tradition. It was simply an excuse to bring him before the king at Rimini. And Symmachus did go, but when he realized that the accusations were basically quite different and concerned illicit relations with women and the wasting of the Church's assets, he hurriedly returned to Rome. But back there, feeling abandoned by his own faithful, he became frightened and sought refuge in Saint Peter's.

Theodoric was ill at ease since Symmachus's behavior appeared to be an acknowledgement of guilt, so he convened a council at Rome which judged him and, as if the see were now vacant, nominated the bishop of Venice, Peter of Altino, "visitor" or regent of the Church of Rome. This man immediately joined the faction opposed to Symmachus, summoned Lawrence from Nocera and approved the confiscation of the pontifical ecclesiastical property.

In effect, the council seemed conditioned by the attitude of Theodoric. Nevertheless, Symmachus appeared at the first session in May 501, and declared himself ready to be tried, on condition that Peter of Altino be sent away and the confiscated goods be returned to him. The request was submitted to Theodoric and rejected. Symmachus decided, notwithstanding, to appear also at the second session that began on 1 September. But while he was on his way from St. Peter's to the Sessorian basilica where the council was meeting, he was attacked by a group of armed men who killed two priests of his entourage and he himself barely escaped from being stoned. After which, he wanted nothing more to do with the council.

Then, following another period of rioting, the bishops found a way to meet again in a place called *Ad palmam*, probably in the vestibule of St. Peter's. This time they decreed that none of them had the authority to judge the bishop of Rome, as it was universally acknowledged that the accusations against Symmachus had to be left to the judgment of God, and that all the clergy, therefore, owed obedience to him.

It was obvious that such a verdict would be ignored. In practice the anti-Symmachus faction won the day and the city's titular churches passed into the control of Lawrence who, to prove the legitimacy of his own pontificate, had a bust of himself placed in the basilica of St. Paul, next to the mosaic portraits of the bishops of Rome. Symmachus barricaded himself in St. Peter's and for four years the city was the scene of violence and bloody battles.

Peace returned only in 505, when Theodoric finally listened to the continued protests of Dioscurus, deacon of Alexandria, sent to him by Symmachus. He ordered the supporters of Lawrence to return the churches to Symmachus and Lawrence, himself, to leave Rome. The latter obeyed and retired to a villa of his protector, Festus.

Thus ended the schism of the see of Rome, but the one with the Eastern Church continued. The Emperor Anastasius I was now completely on the side of the Monophysites. In an edict he treated Symmachus in an insulting way, accusing him of being a Manichaean and declaring that his consecration was illegitimate. The pope responded in equal tones, reviving for the occasion the authority of some of his predecessors: "Respect God in us and we shall respect God in you. If you do not respect God, how can you assume the prerogatives of Him whom you fail to honor? Remember, Emperor, the long line of those who, from the beginnings of Christianity, have persecuted the Faith: they fell, but the Church, the more it is persecuted, the more it shines forth in all its power."

Regardless of the disorders that troubled the first years of his pontificate, Symmachus managed to embellish Rome with new buildings. And perhaps, as Gregorovius ironically puts it, "the fact of having luckily escaped so many dangers increased the zeal of this priest with a somewhat soiled conscience who, out of gratitude to his protector saints, hastened to decorate their churches or to build new ones."

In fact, he built the churches of St. Pancrazio on the Janiculum and St. Martin ai Monti on the ancient *Titulus Equitii*, as well as an inn at Porto for pilgrims coming by the sea to Rome. He also restored St. Paul's, but it was chiefly in the basilica of St. Peter that he made the greatest improvements. He covered the pavement of the atrium with slabs of marble and built over the *cantharus* a small temple supported by columns of porphyry. A well was dug in the large square in front of the basilica, precursor of the Bernini fountains, while the staircases in the courtyard were widened and residential quarters were constructed, the first nucleus of the Vatican palazzi.

Symmachus died 19 July 514.

52. St. Hormisdas (514–523)

When, on the day after the death of Symmachus, 20 July 514, a deacon named Hormisdas, born in Frosinone, was consecrated pope, the situation in the Roman community was calm. Hormisdas had become a deacon after being married, and had a son Silverio who, in turn, would become pope, a unique case in the history of papacy. Hormisdas had been elected unanimously, even though his predecessor, Symmachus, had not designated him. So the partisan motivations which had divided the city up to then were for the moment stilled.

As for the Eastern Church, many bishops requested and were permitted to be readmitted into communion with Rome. In reality, the schism existed now only because the Emperor Anastasius I wanted it, and while he was alive, vain were the attempts by Hormisdas to eliminate once and for all the points of disagreement. Only with the new emperor, Justin, were there the determinant conditions ready for a reconciliation and a return to the orthodoxy of the council of Chalcedon.

Indeed, the emperor convened a council at Constantinople which condemned the doctrine of Eutiche in favor of a full adherence to the decrees of Rome, and of Leo the Great. Further, Justin wrote to the pope requesting him to send legates for the restoration of religious unity. The legates were solemnly received at Constantinople, and the patriarch subscribed to the so-called "formula of Hormisdas." "I consider the holy churches of God, that of old Rome and that of new Rome, as one and the same church, the See of Peter the Apostle and the episcopal see of Byzantium as one and the same see . . . I agree with the pope's profession of the doctrine and I censure all whom he censures."

It was 28 March 519. Rome had won and the schism was over. Two thousand five hundred Eastern bishops signed this statement of adherence to Rome which then remained the fundamental point of reference between the Church of the East and that of the West.

The significant effort which Hormisdas put into the settlement of the schism did not, however, lead him to forget the problems of Western

Christianity, especially in Rome, There a group of schismatic monks stubbornly insisted on presenting to him for approval a thesis based upon the affirmation that "One of the Trinity was crucified." This phrasing, in itself not heretical, appeared also in Constantinople where it enthused some hot heads and could have easily given rise to heretical interpretations. At first Hormisdas sought to throw water on the fire but, faced with the protests of the monks who wanted an official approbation of the formula, he opposed it openly with the following phrase: "One of the three divine persons suffered in the flesh."

According to the *Liber pontificalis*, Hormisdas had to deal with another group of Manichaeans in Rome, who were tried and condemned to exile and their books burnt in the square in front of the basilica of St. John Lateran.

Hormisdas died on 6 August 523, and was buried in the basilica of St. Peter.

53. ST. JOHN I (523—526)

An elderly native of Tuscia named John succeeded Hormisdas on 13 August 523. He had a brief pontificate, but one that was pretty stormy.

In 523, Emperor Justin issued an edict against the Arian heretics. Many of these abjured out of fear, others suffered martyrdom and several of their churches were taken over and given to the Catholics. When Theodoric learned what had happened to his brothers in faith, he felt directly threatened by this edict.

His irritation, increased by his awareness of having demonstrated complete tolerance toward the Catholic faith, led him to declare that the persecutions against the Arians of the East were to be avenged by the suppression of the Catholic faith in Italy. As an initial warning, he had the Oratory of St. Stephen in Verona demolished. But he did not stop there, for in his heart he suspected that Rome was trying to undermine him from afar, which was true partly of certain members of the Senate.

He, therefore, forbade Roman citizens to use weapons and began to distrust those in his entourage. The consul Albinus, who had exchanged correspondence with Justin, was accused of high treason and the same charge was made against Boethius who was only guilty, in fact, of having defended the Roman consul. The famous writer was tried and convicted and the head of the Senate, Symmachus, father-in-law of Boethius, suffered the same fate.

Their "accusing shades darkened the reputation of the noble Goth king," notes Gregorovius. "It is certainly possible, as some historians have done, to justify their execution by invoking the 'Reason of State,' but a man like Boethius, universally known as the author of *De consolatione philosophiae*, is too authoritative an accuser to allow his death to be deemed anything less than barbaric, even though it occurred in the darkest age of history."

In this state of violent anger which was overwhelming him, Theodoric summoned Pope John I to Ravenna in 525 and ordered him to go to Constantinople with a delegation consisting of a few bishops and four distinguished Senators. The mission entrusted to him was to induce Justin to withdraw the edict against the Arians, to return the churches to them and to allow those who had been constrained by fear to abjure, to return to the Arian religion. While John I firmly refused to present the third request, contrary to his conscience as a Christian, he departed.

Constantinople welcomed him enthusiastically, not as an ambassador from Theodoric but as the head of Christianity. He was, after all, the first pope to visit the capital of the Eastern Empire. He was carried in triumph into the church of Saint Sofia where he celebrated Easter that year. As to the outcome of his mission, he only partly managed to satisfy Theodoric, as he did not present the request for permission for the new converts from Arianism to return to the heresy, as he had promised to when he had left.

The consequences were to be foreseen, and the members of the delegation were sent to jail as soon as they returned to Ravenna. John I died in prison on 18 May 526 and his remains were later transferred to Rome where he was buried in the portico of St. Peter's basilica as set forth in a metrical inscription as "victima Christi."

54. St. Felix IV (526—530)

In the climate of terror in which the Church in Italy was living at the death of John I, there was no reaction at all to the imposition by Theodoric of his own candidate for the pontifical post, a Roman named Felix and a native of Sannius. The terrified community of Rome consecrated him as pope on 12 July 526, the fourth with this name.

A few weeks later, on 30 August, Theodoric died and a series of legends arose about his death. One had him dying a few moments before making operative a decree by which the Catholic churches would have passed to the Arians. Another, reported by Procopius, was that Theodoric fell victim to a sudden fever caused by his remorse for the death of Symmachus, whose head he thought he saw again in a huge fish served to him at a banquet. And, again, that his soul was carried away in the air by the angry spirits of Pope John and of Symmachus and was cast into the crater of the volcano on Lipari.

Felix IV did not make the Roman clergy regret that they had elected him. In fact, he had good enough relations with Amalasunta, regent of the child Goth King Athalaric, to obtain an edict which conferred on the bishop of Rome the right to judge disputes between lay and religious persons. On this basis, whoever might have a case against a representative of the clergy had to appeal to the pope, and only in the event that the latter had rejected the complaint could the lawsuit pass into the hands of a lay authority. As Gregorovius observes, "the beginning of this privilege can be viewed as the prerequisite for the exemption of the clergy from the secular courts and the basis of its future political strength."

Furthermore, Felix IV succeeded in manoeuvring between the two parties in the city, the one favorable to the Goths, the other to the emperor of Byzantium. And perhaps it was in deference to the Eastern Church that the pope built in Rome the basilica of Saints Cosmas and Damian, since these were the first saints of eastern origin to whom the city dedicated a church. "Perhaps it was a case of diplomatic courtesy toward the Orthodox emperor, with whom the Roman Church was maintaining friendly relations in those days." observes Gregorovius again, and "it is even possible that one wished to flatter the Greeks for fear of the Goths."

In any case, Felix IV, during the lengthy illness which brought on his demise, wanted to protect himself against possible disorders which might occur at his death. The idea of a new schism within the see of Rome worried him, and as a result he resolved to take advantage of what had been decided by Symmachus in the synod of 529, that is, the possibility for a pope to designate his own successor. So, in the presence of the clergy and the Senate, he consigned his own pallium to the archdeacon Boniface, thereby nominating him his successor. Moreover, he gave notice in writing of his personal choice, which was affixed in all the titular churches in Rome, threatening to excommunicate whomever might disturb the peace of the Church. For its part, the Senate threatened to confiscate the property and exile anyone who instigated disorders of a political nature while the pope was still alive.

A major event during these years was the spread in Italy of monasticism, thanks to St. Benedict from Norcia who founded the famous monastery at Monte Cassino and developed his Rule under the motto "Ora et labora"—work and prayer, therefore, in a spirit of brotherly understanding, contrasting in a positive manner with the violence of the social and ecclesiastical ambience of those days. On the basis of this Rule, which gathered adherents in the entire peninsula, the monastery naturally became a center of prayer, but also a nucleus of economic and cultural organization, extremely characteristic of a great part of the Middle Ages.

Felix IV died on 22 September 530, before he was able to understand the grandiose significance of monasticism.

55. BONIFACE II (530–532)

On the day of Felix IV's death, 22 September 530, a small group of priests, who had decided to respect his last wishes, hastened to elect as pope the one who had been chosen, the Roman archdeacon Boniface and consecrated him pope in the Lateran basilica. At the same time, in the Julian basilica, a larger group of priests and lay persons consecrated the Greek, Dioscuros. The two groups were in opposition, the first belonging to the Gothic party and the other to the Byzantine one. The Roman Church was thus again in the midst of battles and disputes which, fortunately, lasted for only twenty-two days. On 14 October, Dioscuros passed away and the schism came to an end with the Byzantine party rendering an act of obedience to Boniface.

We have little information about this pope and it appears that his greatest concern was the naming his own successor. Once he had been recognized as the legitimate pope, even by the priests who had supported Dioscuros, he quickly forced them to sign a document in which they admitted having disobeyed the decree of Felix IV and promised never to do such a thing again. At the same time, a judgment of condemnation was issued against Dioscuros. Then Boniface convened a council in St. Peter's basilica and presented to it a decree by which he nominated as his own successor the Roman deacon, Vigilius. This he had signed and sworn to by all the priests in the Roman community.

At this point there was presumably a reaction by the Senate and the court at Ravenna, because a short time later there was a second council, at which the Senate was also present, during which the actions of Boniface must have been discussed. It seems that the pope recognized the error of his ways, or at least admitted that he had abused his powers, since in the midst of the assembly he burned his decree and thereby avoided being judged.

The occasion served to bring to light evidence of corruption among the laymen during the election of Dioscuros. The Senate took pains to issue a law prohibiting its members from offering or accepting money to achieve the election of one or another candidate, and the decree was sent to the entire clergy of Rome for its information. This shows how common simony was in certain circumstances, and it also sounded like an invitation from the laity to the clergy to avoid behavior unworthy of an ecclesiastic.

Boniface II died on 17 October 532, and was buried in St. Peter's. He was the first pope not to be declared a "saint"— which was what his abuse of power cost him.

56. JOHN II (533—535)

The death of Boniface II in the midst of arguments and scandals arising from the method to be followed for the election of a pontiff led to a brief period of a vacant see while, presumably, a clarification took place among the parties in question (i.e., the clergy, the Senate and the court at Ravenna).

It is true that simony and illicit dealings had become, amongst the clergy, the usual way to arrange the election of a pope, and the Holy Spirit apparently had little to do with inspiration for this or that candidate, as had happened at the time of Pope Fabian. The Senate now set itself as the representative of the laity and the Roman people, using its right to vote in ecclesiastical questions. Even the deliberations of the councils had to be submitted for the Senate's approval because, in certain regards, it had replaced royal authority. Little wonder, therefore, that some ecclesiastics even sold property of the Church in order to bribe the more powerful senators.

By denouncing a situation of that kind, the decree issued by the Senate under Boniface II constituted a humiliating lesson in ethics from the civil authority to the clerical one. King Athalaric approved that senatorial edict the moment that a humble priest of San Clemente named Mercurius, or Mercurialis, was elected to the pontifical throne. But the name did not seem appropriate for the high dignity, so he became the first bishop of Rome, once nominated, to change his name. And he became John II, consecrated 2 January 533.

Athalaric sent John a letter in which he approved the decree and praised the freedom of choice of the clergy and the Roman people for the dignified election of a pontiff. Nevertheless, he stressed that he reserved the right to confirm the choice, and put at the disposal of the royal dignitaries a considerable amount of money for the purpose of securing votes for the candidate pre-selected by them. Indeed, "if disputes arose between the clergy and the laity over an election and the case were submitted to the Court, he commanded that, for the expenses of this case, as the Roman pontiff was the subject, no more than three thousand *scudi* could be spent." Which is to say that, simony aside, money always played a role in the final decisions since an "expense account" had been set up out of the royal reserves.

As a result the order sent to the prefect of Rome, Salvonzius, to engrave in marble both his edict and the senatorial decree so that they would be placed on the facade of St. Peter's basilica, did not settle the issue definitively and was purely illusionary.

Athalaric died in 534 and his mother, Amalasuntha, to save the kingdom of the Goths, married her cousin, Theodahad, who was clearly hostile to her. A climate of uncertainty enveloped Italy.

From the East, the new emperor Justinian made his voice heard on questions of religion, wanting to prove his own orthodoxy to the pope. This he did by issuing an edict in which he set forth his own doctrine on the Trinity which was in accordance with the Catholic dogma, receiving, of course, the approval of Rome. He also sent an embassy to Rome with precious gifts for the basilica of St. Peter. Rome got ready to enter the Byzantine orbit.

Then, John II died on 8 May 535.

5 7. ST. AGAPETUS I (5 3 5 — 5 3 6)

Upon the death of John II, his archdeacon Agapetus was elected. A Roman, he was the son of the priest Jordan, a follower of Symmachus, who had been killed in one of the riots in the city at the time of the schism. He belonged to the same family as Felix IV and owned a house on the Caelian, near the Church of Saints John and Paul, where he had assembled a library of works by the holy Fathers. He was consecrated on 13 May 535.

The first thing he did was to convoke a council before which he appeared with the anathema against Dioscurus, taken from the Vatican archives, and burnt it. By this gesture he proclaimed unjust the excommunication, extorted from Boniface II by his supporters. Moreover, he condemned the idea that a living pontiff could designate his own successor.

But with regard to the pontifical election, it was only a question of time before the long arm of imperial approval made itself felt. Justinian had reconquered Africa, seizing it from the Vandals, and was threatening Italy. Since Theodahad had murdered Amalsuntha, the emperor, with the excuse of avenging her death, had started a campaign against the Goths. His general, Belisarius, had conquered Sicily in 535 and was heading for the peninsula.

Unable to oppose him militarily, Theodahad tried to stop the advance by sending a mission with the pope to Constantinople to convince the emperor to desist from his plans. Agapetus reluctantly obeyed the order to set off on this mission and, since he had no money for the travel expenses, was even forced to pawn the sacred vessels and vestments of St. Peter's.

He was welcomed in Constantinople, with the same solemn honors previously reserved for John I. Yet, however well he was received, he failed to convince Justinian to give up his campaign in Italy; on the contrary, the emperor got ready for an even more decisive action.

One success the pope obtained was on the religious issues. He did not wish to communicate with the patriarch, Antimus, who was protected by the empress Theodora and secretly favorable, as she was, to Monophysitism. He succeeded in having him replaced by Menas, a monk of sure orthodox faith, whom he himself solemnly consecrated in March of 536.

But meanwhile, Agapetus fell ill and died at Constantinople on 22 April 536. His remains were sent to Rome and buried in St. Peter's.

5 8. ST. SILVERIUS (5 3 6 — 5 3 7)

News of Agapetus's death at Constantinople reached Rome where the Goth king, Theodahad, was vainly waiting for a favorable result from the delegation's mission to the emperor. He hastily arranged the election of the subdeacon from

Campania, Silverius, and even the part of the clergy which did not approve the choice was constrained to accept it. Silverius was consecrated on 1 June 536.

But the Goth king's sun was setting. Theodahad was deposed by his soldiers and assassinated while fleeing from Rome. The new king, Vitiges, decided to withdraw to Ravenna with a large part of the army to prepare a more serious attack against Belisarius who had by then reached Naples. Silverius advised the Senate not to attempt useless resistance against the Byzantine and even went so far as to invite Belisarius to come to Rome. As the latter entered the city through the Asinaria gate during the night between the 9th and 10th of December 536, the last Gothic garrison was leaving by Porta Flaminia.

So Rome fell again into the imperial orbit. As Procopius notes, "Belisarius set up camp on the Pincio whence he inspected the city, still crammed with almost all its ancient monuments, and immediately gave orders to begin stocking up supplies and to restore and fortify the walls." Vitiges soon returned and attempted to retake the city. Indeed, the Gothic king arrived, at the beginning of March 537, with 150,000 men and began a siege of the city which was to last a year. Meanwhile, within the walls a shameful injustice was being perpetrated against the pope, engineered from afar by Justinian's wife, Theodora, who wanted to have the Monophysite Antimus reelected as patriarch of Constantinople. Aware that Silverius was irremovably tied to the position of Agapetus I, the empress counted principally on the Roman deacon, Vigilius, because of his heretical leanings. He was the former apostolic nuncio to Byzantium and had been designated by Boniface II as his successor, and was indeed ready to satisfy the wishes of Theodora once he had definitively obtained the pontifical post.

He arrived in Rome with a precise program. With the assistance of Antonina, the wife of Belisarius, he succeeded in passing off as authentic certain hand-written letters to Vitiges in which the pope called for the intervention of the Gothic king to liberate Rome from the Byzantine. Sensing danger, Silverius sought refuge in the church of Santa Sabina on the Aventine, but Belisarius summoned him to his residence on the Pincio to explain himself. Arriving there, Silverius was brought with Vigilius—who pretended he was helping him out in those tragic moments— into one of the inside rooms where Antonina was stretched out on a bed with Belisarius seated at her feet. The woman covered the pope with insults, and Belisarius refused to hear his explanations. He summoned a subdeacon named John who, having led the pope into an adjoining room, removed the pope's pallium, took off his bishop's robes and had him put on a monk's tunic. In the meantime, another deacon, a certain Sirius, announced to the clergy that the pope had been found guilty and had been deposed. Belisarius sent him to Patara in Licia, reduced to the status of a simple monk, and on the 29th of the same month, the clergy, under the sway of Belisarius, elected Vigilius as the new pontiff. Theodora's plot had achieved its object.

Silverius was defended by the bishop of Patara who protested to Justinian and succeeded in getting Silverius sent back to Rome to be judged again. But Belisarius, still under siege by Vitiges, delayed and opposed his return. So Silverius was taken to the island of Palmaria in the custody of two agents of Vigilius and there he remained, a prisoner, until his death, which probably occurred on 11 November 537.

59. VIGILIUS (537–555)

The deacon Vigilius, a Roman of noble family, had longed for the episcopal seat of Rome ever since 531 when Boniface II had designated him as his successor. It had gone badly for him because, confronted with the strong opposition of the clergy, the pope had considered it wise to let the matter drop. So he had to be content with the job of pontifical envoy to Constantinople. But this had not been a waste of time since at the court of Justinian he gained powerful allies, headed by the empress Theodora and the wife of Belisarius, Antonina.

They were a group of persons very close to the heresy of Eutiches and anxious to have the orthodoxy of the Council of Chalcedon annulled. Vigilius played their game, letting them believe that, if he were to be elected pope, he would support certain of their expectations and, ambitious as he was, he apparently gave them at one point precise assurances of just that. However, a letter written by him to monophysite bishops in which he rebutted the doctrine of the two natures of Christ and recommended keeping secret some of his ideas in order to carry them out, once he had reached the Holy See, must be considered apocryphal.

The empress made her move as soon as the opportunity arose, when Belisarius arrived in Rome. The violent deposing of Pope Silverius was a true abuse of power, an intrigue prompted by debauchery and simony fomented by two unscrupulous women. Vigilius had been prepared to offer Belisarius money for a decisive and authoritarian act. The general deposed Silverius and on 29 March 537, and had the new pope consecrated by the Senate and a terrorized clergy.

Nevertheless, to be recognized as legitimate by the entire clergy, Vigilius had to wait for the death of Silverius which probably occurred on 11 November of that same year, exhausted as he would have been by the sufferings and humiliations he had undergone. Yet it is hard to avoid thinking that his death was hastened while in the custody of two agents of Vigilius on the island of Palmaria, and, according to the *Liber pontificalis,* it was on the latter's orders that Silverius was starved to death. Procopius manages to give us even the name of the assassin, Eugene, a hired killer of Antonina. In any case, Vigilius can be accused, at the very least, of "complicity in murder" and he became pope through simony and assassination. He was, according to

Gregorovius, a "felon." More simply put, he was one of those pontiffs who gave their souls to obtain the supreme ecclesiastical authority which they evidently saw as a source of power and nothing else.

During the first years of his pontificate, he appeared to repent and tried to break with those who had helped him to reach the summit of power. "At first I spoke badly and unwisely; now I cannot in any way carry out your wish by putting an end to the exile of that heretic," he is said to have replied in a letter to Theodora. She had insisted that he honor his agreement and fulfil the promise he had made that, once pope, he would recall the monophysite Antimus to be patriarch of Constantinople. "No matter how unworthy I feel myself to be, I am always the representative of the blessed apostle Peter, bearing the same dignity as my venerable predecessors, Silverius and Agapetus, who have already condemned Antimus."

It was not the reply Theodora had expected, and a woman like her was not used to being treated in that way. She had been betrayed and she would take her revenge at the first opportunity. This arose in 543 when her husband, whether urged by her or not, issued an edict which condemned the *Three Chapters*, the name given to writings of Theodorus of Mopsuesta and Theodoretus of Cirus as well as a letter from Ibas of Edessa. In effect, it was an edict countermanding the council of Chalcedony which had recognized both Theodoretus and Ibas as Orthodox.

The Eastern bishops obeyed the edict and the patriarch of Constantinople, Menas, reserved approval on the part of Rome while the apostolic nuncio Stephen condemned his action. Justinian saw that everything depended on Vigilius but he was determined to resolve the issue since his authority as ecclesiastical lawmaker was at stake. And so, probably pushed by Theodora, he ordered the pope to be brought to Constantinople to formally approve his edict. Vigilius was forced to leave his see on 22 November 545, in what was a real Byzantine blitz. The imperial troops, headed by Antimus, seized Trastevere and surrounded the church of St. Cecilia where the pope was conducting a service. Antimus strode through the crowd, arrived at the altar, and ordered Vigilius to follow him to a ship anchored in the Tiber since the emperor demanded his presence in Constantinople.

There was no resistance. The Romans were present at the sudden departure of their bishop but most of them were ignorant of the facts which brought it about. Some begged for a blessing while others, the majority, insulted him and threw stones at him viewing his departure as a flight from the danger threatening the city, that of a second siege by the new Gothic king, Totila, since Belisarius was away at Ravenna. For them Vigilius was abandoning the city, on his way to live quietly in Constantinople. Starving and mindful of his faithlessness, they cursed him with all their hatred: "May you die of hunger! May evil be at your side, you who have done us so much evil!"

Vigilius decided to answer those curses with a charitable deed which could have recuperated from afar the good will of his people. During the voyage he stopped off in Sicily and arranged to ship to Rome huge quantities of grain obtained from the rich landowners of the island. But it turned out badly for him. That "message," which would certainly have redeemed him in the eyes of his fellow citizens, never reached its destination. The Goths blocked it at the mouth of the Tiber, only too happy to seize it. Vigilius was not to have another opportunity; he would return to Rome as a corpse ten years later and certainly in no position to rehabilitate his image as a Roman pontiff.

He arrived in Constantinople in January of 547, greeted with the usual honors previously reserved for his predecessors. There was an embrace with Justinian, solemn rituals at St. Sofia and he stayed in Placidia's palace, the official residence of the pontifical nuncios. But all that was simply an act; in point of fact, he was under "house arrest" in Constantinople. "You can hold me a prisoner," he said, "but you will never be able to put the Apostle Peter in jail." This statement indicates the image of a pope, full of dignity, intent on defending the condemnation, as put forward by his envoy, Stephen, against Menas, and, at the same time, refusing to sign the imperial edict.

But the isolation in which he lived in Constantinople brought him to his senses. Without exact information about the events in the West and of the opposition of the Western bishops to the edict, and surrounded by Eastern bishops headed by Menas, all of them assiduously plying him with devious advice, singing the praises of the imperial edict, Vigilius became brainwashed and was incapable of resisting the pressures of the court. In great secrecy, he wrote to Justinian and Theodora, gave in to their insistence, and agreed to the condemnation of the Three Chapters.

For Easter, 548, he sent a letter on 11 April to the Patriarch Menas entitled *Judicatum* in which he agreed to the condemnation, even maintaining faith with the authority of Chalcedon, a compromise which satisfied the emperor and Theodora, who would die shortly afterwards. Naturally, the Occidental bishops objected. Those of Italy, of Dalmatia and of Illyricum rejected the edict and Africa even excommunicated the pope.

Vigilius had once again traded his pontifical office, but with this manoeuvring he lost all credibility. To begin with he thought it was probably more important to satisfy the imperial power rather than the episcopal. Then he reconsidered matters.

He withdrew his *Judicatum* and proposed to the emperor the convening of an ecumenical council. But Justinian had had enough of the pope's vacillations and issued a new edict of condemnation of the *Three Chapters*, which was accepted by the Eastern bishops. Vigilius had the courage to excommunicate them, and the emperor, faced with this sudden attitude of firmness, plotted his arrest and deposition.

In August of 551. Vigilius had taken refuge in the basilica of St. Peter in Ormisda together with his followers, who included the bishop of Milan, Dacius, and there the imperial guards came upon him while he was celebrating the sacred rituals. There was a slight bustle while the faithful surrounded the guards menacingly, defending the pope from this sacrilegious offense. Finally his safety was guaranteed by a solemn oath and Vigilius and Dacius were able to return to Placidia's palace, in what was really "house arrest."

On the night of 23 December 551, the two of them made a perilous escape from a window and reached Chalcedon by sea. There, on 2 February 552, the pope issued an encyclical addressed to the Christian world in which he set forth the persecutions suffered under Justinian, that new "Diocletian," and declared his strong adherence to the Orthodox faith. He showed courage, infused in him by the deacon Pelagius just returned from Rome where Narses, who had replaced Belisarius, had defeated Totila. And Justinian appeared to take a milder attitude, showing humility and sending Belisarius to him as ambassador and peacemaker, while promising guarantees.

Vigilius returned to Constantinople and proposed the convocation of the council in Italy but Justinian was adamant that it be held in Constantinople, whereupon the pope refused to participate in it. Suffering from gallstones, and given the sparse support of the Western bishops, he did not want to preside over an assembly controlled by the emperor. Nonetheless, the council met on 5 May 553, under the chairmanship of the new Patriarch Eutiche, successor of Mennas who had died the year before. The condemnation of the *Three Chapters* was adopted unanimously.

Vigilius sent Justinian a *Constitutum*, compiled in great part by the deacon Pelagius, in which he declared null and void any condemnation of the *Three Chapters* adopted by the council. The emperor rejected this and ordered the priests in the council to strike the name of Vigilius from the Dittici of all of the churches in the empire. And he did not stop there; he jailed the pope's deacons, Pelagius and Sarpatus, isolating Vigilius definitively, and forcing him once again to surrender.

Now all alone and ill, too weak to face martyrdom, aware of the possibility of his being deposed, Vigilius withdrew everything. On 8 December 553, he wrote a letter to Eutiche, the patriarch, in which he showed his adherence to the decision of the council and in a second *Constitutum* of 23 February 554, tried to explain the reasons which led him to condemn the *Three Chapters*. But it was clearly unconvincing.

Vigilius thus reached the bottom, showing how unworthy he was of his position. Seppelt's observation is correct. This pope lacked "the firmness and strength of character needed by one who holds a seat as sublime as his; firmness and strength of character which marked and made glorious many of his predecessors and successors. He did not have the stuff to be martyred for his own convictions and lacked the magnanimous spirit required of one who, as he did, carried the highest dignity, attributed to him in error."

His attitude of servility towards the emperor gained him a certain satisfaction with the *Pragmatic Sanction* issued by Justinian on 13 August 554. As a result the pope was associated with the Byzantine government of Italy, with the concession to the bishops of a sort of superintendence that strengthened their authority over the officials of the State and increased the temporal power of the papacy.

This "donation" by the emperor neither effaces nor justifies Vigilius's blameworthy conduct. Indeed, it is an indirect confirmation of the manner in which this pope sacrificed religious authority, that he should have defended to death, in favor of power in the name of which he had not hesitated to commit simony and murder.

Above all, it must be borne in mind that through this *Pragmatic Sanction* the election of the pope, by virtue of the legal-administrative context within which the pope had to act, had to be confirmed by the emperor in order to become effectively valid.

Vigilius, following this unconditional surrender, was obviously free to return to Rome. But he did not make it, as death struck him at Siracusa on 7 June 555. He was buried in the cemetery of Priscilla at Rome where his remains were later moved. However, there is no cult or ecclesiastical sign to his memory in Rome apart from an inscription in verse that he himself had engraved for the catacombs of Saints Peter and Marcellinus in which he deplored the destruction by the Goths of cemeteries and churches.

60. PELAGIUS I (556–561)

As successor to Vigilius, the Roman clergy wanted to elect a priest named Marea, but his death, in August 555, resulted in the candidature of the deacon Pelagius.

A man of unchallenged abilities, he had accompanied Agapetus to Constantinople where he had remained as the representative of Vigilius. When the latter had to leave Rome, Pelagius had acted as his vicar at the time of the siege by Totila from the autumn of 545 to 17 December 546, the date on which the Gothic king succeeded in entering the almost deserted city. Pelagius had initially attempted to negotiate an armistice, going to his camp. Then he had waited for him at the entrance of St. Peter's basilica and, when he saw him kneel in prayer at the tomb of the Prince of the Apostles, had begged him to spare the lives of the Romans. This Totila did, but the city was pillaged, even though the booty was meagre because the opulence of the pagan temples and patrician houses was, by then, no more than a memory.

Pelagius had, however, preserved the prestige of the see of Rome which Vigilius, forced by Justinian, had had to abandon to go to Byzantium. He had also remained faithful to certain principles when, back in Constantinople, he had used every means to convince Vigilius not to give in to Justinian over the orthodoxy of Chalcedon. For this he was put in prison, but even there he continued to defend his ideas, both in a work of six books on the *Three Chapters,* opposing Justinian's edict, and at the council of Constantinople in 553 which condemned them, censuring Pope Vigilius, who had approved the decisions of that council in 554, and accusing him of being unstable and corrupt.

In short, Pelagius seemed to be a man with his head on his shoulders, destined to incarnate an irreproachable sort of pope, if he could get out of prison and reach the pontifical see.

Yet, once Vigilius had died and Pelagius was released from jail and back in Rome he changed his views, condemning the *Three Chapters* and accepting the council of Constantinople. This abrupt about-face, openly criticized, guaranteed Justinian's support for his nomination as pope. He was consecrated on 16 April 556, in a Rome which had now entered the orbit of Byzantine imperial influence.

Seppelt comments: "It is difficult to state whether this change of opinion was due, in whole or in part, to his idea that, only by surrendering, could his hopes be realized."

Besides, Duchesne points out, "things had changed by then because, as Vigilius had given his approval to the synod of 553, it was ecumenical and universally binding on all Christians."

However, the rumor spread that Pelagius was, as usual, a person who preached well but did not practice what he preached. So on the very day of his consecration, faced with the objections coming from Africa and Illyricum, the new pontiff made a solemn profession of faith and declared his adherence to the four ecumenical councils, especially that of Chalcedon. As a result, since a part of the clergy and the nobility refused to take Communion with him, holding him even responsible for the death of Vigilius, Pelagius ordered a procession during the Easter week. At the side his imperial protector, General Narses, the governor of Italy, and accompanied by the hymns of the acolytes, he went from the basilica of St. Pancras to St. Peter's. When he arrived there, he stepped up to the pulpit and, with the Gospel in hand, swore solemnly to be innocent of the crime of which he was accused. But that was not the end of the story.

Persistent resentment against his election came from Gaul, now the land of the converted Franks, whose king, Childebert, explicitly demanded from the pope a declaration of faith in conformity with the principles of Chalcedon and the writings of Leo the Great. In his reply, Pelagius explained that all the disputes were generated by problems typically "eastern" and not of a nature to impinge upon the unity of the Church.

"Questions of faith," he wrote, "have not been dealt with in the East and from this point of view, since the death of Theodora, there is, thanks be to God, nothing more to fear. There were instead lively discussions on certain topics not regarding the faith, and it would be too lengthy to speak of them here." One has to say that Pelagius was telling a few lies or at least half-truths, after which he stated firmly: "We anathematise all who, even by one syllable or one word, have distanced themselves, or are so doing, from the faith of Leo the Great which was solemnly accepted by the council of Chalcedon. Your zeal for the faith and your love of humility should not be upset by malicious discourse or inappropriate writings."

But malicious criticisms continued to circulate and so, in a letter to Archbishop Sapaud of Arles, he defended himself against specific accusations of being a weathercock, trying to explain that his retraction was the result of a closer examination of facts and circumstances. In fact, he retorted, "My enemies are surely unaware how much it cost me when, on the basis of certainty, I finally agreed with that useful decree, and how much opposition I then had to suffer because of my lack of reflection. Was I supposed to harden myself forever against the truth simply because in my ignorance I had held a different opinion for a short while?" To which one can say anything except that he was convincing.

In his letter to Sapaud, he pleaded for aid rather than for his episcopal see. Rome was badly depleted, victim of the continuous sackings and incurable famine, and he needed money and clothing for the citizens, he begged, "because the poverty and the misery in the city are such that without pain and anxiety we cannot face people whom we knew once to be noble and rich."

The person speaking here is the bishop of Rome, who knows he is invested with new prerogatives by the *Pragmatic Sanction* and who, as pope, then revives that civil function carried out by him during the siege by Totila. It is a work of peace he is conducting, as Saba observes: "Pelagius I took advantage of the new Byzantine legislation in favor of Italy, eliminating the disorder in the administration of justice, recalling the courts to the urgent questions raised by the bishops regarding the clergy, using his secular authority over seditious laymen and bishops, correcting the behavior of monks, helping the episcopal sees with expert and faithful 'defenders' whom he trusted." Saba continues, "he is a capable administrator of the pontifical possessions and revenues, who gets shrewdly at Gaul's and Africa's assets, who counsels, scolds, punishes, and by his efforts restores in part the treasury, to the benefit of the poor."

And yet, notwithstanding the extreme misery of the citizens, Pelagius undertook the construction of a new church, dedicated to the apostles Philip and James, which was completed by his successor, John III, then rebuilt by Clement XI, and dedicated to the Holy Apostles.

So, in a city in ruins, yet another church. However, from then on, this kind of activity became beneficial for Rome. As noted by Gregorovius, "the construction of churches, awaited with maximum fervour, soon became the only public activity in the city, and was especially useful to the poorest who thus had work and payment." Indeed, "Rome came out of a chrysalis and was covered with cloisters; the city which had been the capital of the world became the holy city of humanity. Priests and monks built churches and monasteries incessantly and completely dominated public life." Rome was on its inexorable way to becoming a clerical city because "as all political interest was now gone, the vital energy of the Romans was turned exclusively to the service of the Church." The Church "succeeded in converting the invaders and, well rooted and protected in Italy, fought Byzantium in a theological battle which then became a political revolution and made of the Church a wealthy temporal power, mistress of Rome."

From this perspective, Pelagius I was the first pope to distinguish himself by "political" pragmatism, succeeding in keeping power despite the polemics which, as described above, arose concerning his pontificate, clearly the result of a compromise. He did not come out of it completely "cleansed." and not everybody was convinced, despite his great effort to minimize the facts. Indeed he ended in a schism with the sees of Milan and Aquileia, whose bishops were not satisfied by the pontiff's explanations.

And the schism was still going on when Pelagius I died on 4 March 561. He was buried in St. Peter's.

6 l. JOHN III (561 – 574)

Little is known about this pope. The son of Anastasius, a noble of Rome, he was also called Catelinus which, if that was his real name, would lead one to think that, as pope, he may have adopted a different one for the second time in the history of papacy. He was consecrated in fact as John III, so maybe Catelinus was just a nickname.

What is certain is that he finished the work on the basilica of Saints Philip and James, elevating the church to a cardinal's title by a papal bull which set forth its boundaries. Moreover, Lawrence, the bishop of Milan, paid him homage in 572, settling the schism with Rome, even if that with Aquileia continued.

The most important event of his pontificate was the arrival of the Lombards in Italy which began with King Alboinus in 568 and was unchallenged because Narses had been recalled to Constantinople in 567 by the new emperor, Justin II.

The *Liber pontificalis* passes on to us a different story about the old general, recorded in part by Paul the Deacon, which says that Narses fled from Rome to Campania, refusing to return to Constantinople. The Romans, fearing a siege by the Lombards, convinced John III to meet with Narses and beg him to return to Rome and defend the city. It seems that the mission was successful; Narses settled in Rome in a house near a cemetery that we cannot clearly identify and assisted in the consecration of bishops. The truth is that Rome no longer had a Byzantine army in a garrison and the legend ends by showing us a Narses "assisting the pontifical see" with military qualities no longer existing.

Meanwhile, Alboinus advanced calmly. In 569 he was in Milan and by 572 had entered Pavia, after a siege of three years, making it the capital of the Lombard kingdom in Italy. That same year, however, he was assassinated by his wife, Rosamund. The new king, Clefi, was also killed and for ten years the Lombards, without a king, were used for raids by various dukes. Faroaldus, the duke of Spoleto, descended upon Rome in 573 and set up camp around the walls to wage a strong siege. Sacred sites, monasteries and Church property all over the peninsula were now abandoned. "Like a sword withdrawn from the sheath, the savage hordes assailed us," recalls Gregory the Great, a simple deacon at that time; "men were falling everywhere like sheaves of grain, cities were deserted, castles destroyed, churches burned down, monasteries and convents razed to the ground. The fields were deserted and the countryside languished in abandon because no one tilled the land any longer; even the wealthy had disappeared, and where once had lived human beings, now wild animals were foraging in solitude."

In this dramatic situation, John III died on 13 July 574, and was buried in St. Peter's.

62. BENEDICT I (575–579)

With the Lombards camping at the gates of Rome and communication with Constantinople impossible, a Roman, Benedict I, was elected pope. His real name, or nickname, was possibly Bonosius, so it is uncertain whether he was the third bishop of Rome to assume a name different from his baptismal one. Imperial confirmation of his election was delayed in transit, so his consecration did not take place until 2 June 575.

No other information is available about this pope who, however, had his problems with the barbarians besieging Rome and the continuing famine there.

According to the *Liber pontificalis*, Emperor Justin II sent to the port shiploads of grain from Egypt.

Benedict I died on 30 July 579 and was buried in the sacristy of St. Peter's basilica.

63. PELAGIUS II (579—590)

A Roman, the son of a certain Unigildus, and a Goth by origin, Pelagius was consecrated on 26 November 579, without imperial confirmation. The state of siege in which Rome still found itself with the Lombards at the gates perpetuated the city's indigence and aid was requested from the new emperor of the East, Tiberius, but the few militiamen he sent were inadequate to resolve the problem.

Instead, a large tribute in gold was paid to the duke of Benevento, a certain Zottus, who lifted the siege and withdrew to the lands beyond the Liri, destroying instead Montecassino, whose monks took refuge in Rome and built a monastery near the Lateran.

The Lombards encircling the city allowed it temporarily a chance to breathe. Pelagius II, whose requests for assistance from Byzantium proved useless, reckoned that the Franks, faithful Christians, could fill in for the emperor. At the time it was a request destined to receive no response but, from what would happen in the space of a century, the pope showed he was a good prophet when he saw in those people the future defenders of Rome and of Italy and even of the papacy.

Indeed, in a letter to the bishop of Auxerre he wrote, "We believe that Providence has given the true faith also to your kings, like the sovereigns of the Roman empire, so that the city of Rome, where the faith originated, and all of Italy may find in you good neighbors and defenders."

The schism with the Church of Aquileia was not resolved, however, and the invasion by the Lombards of Venetian territory made contact particularly difficult. Moreover, relations with the Church at Constantinople were cool. John, the bishop there, instigated by the Emperor Maurice, called himself pompously the "ecumenical patriarch." Pelagius protested at the assumption of any such title, which implied the use of broader powers, and even though he was not heeded he prohibited its adoption.

But the disasters at Rome seemed to follow one another without a break. In 589 the Tiber burst its banks: "The riverbed was full of serpents and at one moment a gigantic one, like a dragon, was seen heading for the sea," notes Paul the Deacon giving credence to popular imagination. The next year came the plague, called *lues inguinaria*, the "Black Death" that came from Egypt and slaughtered men and animals.

Apocalyptic scenes are ascribed to this tragic scourge. "The people, infected and delirious, thought they heard the blare of trumpets, and saw on the thresholds of houses the signs of the exterminating angel, and in the streets the demon of the plague or phantasms which infected whomever they met."Rumors of the end of the world began circulating again. Victim of the plague, Pelagius II died on 7 February 590.

6 4. ST. GREGORY I, THE GREAT (590—604)

Probably born in 540, Gregory belonged to the old family of the Anici which had already given a pope to the Church in the person of Felix III. His father's name was Jordan, his mother's Sylvia and they owned a palazzo on the Aventine near San Saba. Two paternal aunts, Tarsilia and Emiliana, had become nuns.

The young nobleman was destined for a political career and received an exemplary education such as to prepare him for the top civil position. In fact in 572 he became, by appointment from Emperor Justin II, the Prefect of Rome and the highest civil servant of the old imperial capital, with specific administrative and judicial functions.

But Gregory was not satisfied with his job; he was even said to be "disgusted" with it, according to Gregorovius, because of the "political squalor of Rome." So he gave up his brilliant political career to enter monastic life under the Benedictine rule. "He who was accustomed to move about the streets of the city in bejewelled silk garments," notes Gregory of Tours, "donned the monk's habit and consecrated himself to the service of the Lord."

Indeed, he used all the family's wealth for the establishment of monasteries, the first of which was built inside his own palazzo on the Clivus Scauri, a cloister dedicated to Andrew the Apostle, next to the Church of St. Gregory and still in existence. He also founded six others in Sicily where his family had vast holdings.

Gregory led a life exclusively of prayer and solitude, under the guidance of the pious abbot, Valentine. He fasted frequently while his mother took care to send him each day a frugal meal, as recorded in the inscription at the entrance of the Cella Nova near San Saba:

HINC COTIDIE PIA MATER MITTEBAT
AD CLIVUM SCAURI SCUTELLUM LEGUMINUM

But Gregory only spent a few years in his monastery since the then pope Pelagius II decided to place at the disposition of the Church administration the monk who had acquired so much experience in the service of the State. He ordained him a deacon, making him one of the seven deacons who supervised the seven ecclesiastical regions of the city. But the ultimate aim of Pelagius was a different one since he intended to send Gregory to Constantinople to ask the emperor for substantial aid against the Lombards.

So, in 579, Gregory went to Byzantium as papal legate and remained there until 586. There he earned the friendship of certain members of the Court and of influential people such as Constantina, the daughter of the emperor Tiberius, as well as Theoctista and her brother, Maurice, who ascended the throne in August 582. Essentially, "Byzantium was for him a school of politics and theological battles," as Saba comments; "and the pale Latin monk, in the midst of luxury at the Byzantine court, appeared a strange representative of a civilization and of a faith which, in Constantinople, no longer evoked any strong fascination."

Gregory pleaded with Maurice incessantly to furnish what was necessary to Rome which now did not even have an imperial general. In 584 he managed to get a dux named Gregory and the magister militum, Castorius, be sent back to Rome, and they liberated the city and agreed with the enemy to a three-year truce. However, the truce was not respected and Pelagius II insisted that his nuncio plead again with the emperor. "We shall be condemned to extermination if God will not touch the heart of the most pious emperor," wrote the pope. But Gregory obtained no further concessions; sadly he realized that Byzantium no longer had any interest in Rome, whose salvation now had to be sought elsewhere. Understandably the pope decided that his envoy was not up to a task so beset with difficulties and recalled him to Rome, replacing him with the archdeacon Lawrence. Gregory was presumably very pleased to return to his monastic life; indeed, he went back to his cell in the monastery of St. Andrew, fulfilling his vow to live in poverty and frugality, and ready to submit to severe penances such as sleeping on the bare stone floor with a rock or a step as pillow.

Those were sad and dismal years for Italy. Besides the massacres by the Lombards, there was the devastation caused by the violence of the elements. "Torrential rains beat down on the Veneto, Liguria and other Italian regions; from the time of Noah there had not been such a deluge," wrote Paul the Deacon, "Fields and farms were turned into marshlands, people and animals died in great numbers." Even the Tiber overflowed in 589 and flooded parts of the city. "The violence of the flood," wrote Gregory of Tours, "was such that ancient buildings collapsed and even the granaries of the Church were flooded and destroyed." He was referring evidently to the ancient Annona urbis located on the *ripa graeca* of the river.

The result was a terrible plague epidemic which decimated the city and to which Pelagius II fell victim on 7 February 590. This dramatic situation required the immediate election of a new pope and the unanimous choice was Gregory, but the humble monk used every means to avoid the dignity that they wanted to thrust on him. He immediately sent a letter to Emperor Maurice urging him not to give his approval, but that letter did not reach its destination and was replaced with a letter from the prefect of Rome, Germanus, which warmly recommended the approval of such a suitable candidate.

While awaiting a reply, Gregory did not want to take on any administrative functions, which were carried out by a kind of triumvirate consisting of an arch-priest, an archdeacon and a notary and Gregory assisted the community by prayers and holy rites. In a sermon given on 29 August at Santa Sabina he exhorted the faithful to do penance and place all their hope in God and to pray wholeheartedly, and he organized a grand procession lasting three days, recorded in detail by Gregorovius and based on the chronicles of Paul the Deacon and Gregory of Tours.

"The procession was arranged in the following manner. The people were divided by age and social status into seven groups, each of which met in a different church and thence went solemnly to St. Mary Major. The altar boys left from Sts. Cosmas and Damian together with the priests from the sixth region; the abbots and their monks, from Sts. Gervasius and Protasius together with those from the fourth, and the abbesses with all the nuns and the pastors of the first region, from Sts. Marcellinus and Peter. The children departed from the church of Sts. John and Paul at the Celian, with the priests of the second region, the laymen with those of the seventh from St. Stephen at the Celian, the widows with people of the fifth from St. Eufemia, and at the end, all the married women who left from San Clemente with the priests of the third region."

It was a funeral cortege with hymns for a dying Rome in the midst of the plague which "accompanied the procession and slew people who fell down dead; but, all of a sudden, a supernatural vision put an end to the litanies and to the contagion. While Gregory at the head of the procession was crossing the bridge leading to St. Peter's, the people saw in the sky over Hadrian's Tomb the Archangel Michael who, before the astonished eyes of the faithful, sheathed his flaming sword as if to signify that the plague was over."

As a direct result of this legend, Hadrian's mausoleum was renamed Castel Sant'Angelo. In the eighth century the chapel dedicated to St. Michael was built on its summit, and still today the terrace is dominated by the beautiful bronze statue of the Angel sheathing his sword, the eighth of the series, which Benedict XIV had the German sculptor, Peter Werschaffelt, produce in 1753. Regarding this statue, Gregorovius emphasizes that "the angel replacing his sword is supposed to symbolise the noblest task of the priesthood, which is to carry on works of peace in the world. Unfortunately, however, this does not hold for the popes who often usurped even the power of the sword." This polemical observation is by a Protestant but is nonetheless true.

Once that grand procession ended, the imperial confirmation of the election of Gregory finally arrived from Constantinople. He restated his fears of the high mission which had been entrusted to him and even sought to get out of it by fleeing, according to a legend from the ninth century. Leaving Rome secretly with certain merchants, he hid in the woods of the Sabine Hill, but the Romans went out to search for him and a flaming dove, a symbol of the Holy Spirit, or rather a column of light revealed his hiding place. The chosen one was then triumphantly brought to St. Peter's where he was consecrated pope on 3 September 590.

It is extraordinary how on that occasion Gregory declared he was profoundly sad: "Desiring nothing and fearing nothing on this earth, I felt as though I were standing on the summit of a high mountain, but now this hurricane has thrown me down and I am dragged by the currents of problems and beaten about by the storm." The Church was a wreck in the storm; the "boat of Peter" had to be brought upright so that it could follow the course set by Christ, and Gregory was one of those popes who did not see "power" in the pontifical throne but the guide for a Christian redemption of mankind, convinced as he was of the imminent end of the world. Thus, as Seppelt notes, in his "reluctance to accede to the See of St. Peter one should not see simply the conventional, yet not always sincere, modesty which is noted in many elections of bishops in the Middle Ages. The sadness of Gregory and his reluctance to accept this very important position were due basically to his having to abandon definitively the life of solitude in the monastery at a time of upheavals which seemed to presage the coming end of the world; his emotions were doubtless profoundly rooted in and responded to the nature of his soul which had already once led him to renounce suddenly a brilliant civil service career."

Gregory began by cleaning up the pontifical court, ridding it of the many laymen and deacons who had always been the source of simony within the episcopal see of Rome, and giving the functions to Benedictine monks who assured him of the purity of their religious feelings. Thereafter, he devoted himself completely to his city which, according to a passage in one of his sermons, was "weighed down by unmeasurable sorrow, losing its citizens, besieged by enemies, and no more than a pile of debris." But, while he pronounced what has been called "the funeral oration of Rome," he simultaneously did something about it. In return for a promise of an annual payment of five hundred pounds of gold, Agilulfus, the Lombard king, lifted the siege in 593 and also granted an armistice.

In Byzantium it was rumored that Gregory's behavior had not been dignified, so he wrote to Empress Constance an exemplary letter justifying himself: "It has now been twenty-seven years that we live in this city surrounded by the Lombards. It is not necessary here to list the sums of money which the Church has had to pay daily so that the Romans could survive. In simple words let it suffice to say that the most pious emperors have in Ravenna, together with the first army of Italy, their little treasury that covers their daily expenses. Here in Rome I am that treasury, without taking into consideration that this Church must also maintain the altar boys, the monasteries, the poor and the population."

It is clear that through his policy the papacy was taking the place of a decadent "State" like the former Byzantine State in Italy. In a city where the Senate really no longer existed, the pope was tacitly recognized as its head, and this could be extended to the entire peninsula. Emperor Maurice accused him of diplomatic ineptitude; Gregory humbly accepted the charge against him but replied with firmness and dignity in defense of "his land," Italy. The truth is that "through necessity, Gregory had to perform tasks more important than those which were his as the bishop of Rome," notes Seppelt, and indeed "he had to resolve economic and political problems," not as a Byzantine exarch, senator or prince, but as "consul of God."

In other words, he resolved problems without the pretension of doing it with the prestige of a politician but certainly with the realistic approach of a citizen who, though still devoted to the emperor, desired peace in "his country." He achieved that peace in 598 with the aid of the new exarch, Callinicus, who probably realized that "one could not stop the development and evolution of a situation that had pushed Rome and Italy towards independence when, abandoned by the emperor in a time of compelling necessity, and without the resources sufficient for its needs." To quote Seppelt, "they had had to take this important step under the guidance of the pope."

And so Gregory, on his own initiative and in a totally evangelical spirit, took over the management of Italy's future. The Church then became an immense refuge, which put its assets at the disposal of the needy. In fact, at the beginning of each month the pope had grain, clothing and money distributed: the possessions of the Holy See, acquired from private donations, were administered not for the power of deacons and bishops but for the welfare of the people. Gregory did not want "the purse of the Church to be spoiled by shameful revenues," as he emphasized.

If it is true that the possessions "of Peter the Apostle" increased within the territory of Rome, spreading throughout the Ager romanus to the Sabina, to Tuscia and to other more distant provinces, giving substance to that temporal power which was to be the very history of the papacy, it is without doubt that "the work of Gregory I was not aimed at strengthening the political authority of the Church on the Roman duchy. This was a direct result of the inadequacy of imperial power more than that of a political program or action of the pontiff," as Rosario Villari clearly explains. Villari continues, "convinced of the coming end of the world, Gregory had no plans for power. Instead, true to his monastic calling, he aspired to separation from the world, to the conversion of as many non-believers as possible, to the reform of the Church to render it more active and capable of fully developing this urgent task."

In this sense one should remember his intense activity for the christianising of the Anglo-Saxons and of the Lombards, among whom he found the support of Theodolinda, the wife of Autari and then of Agilulfo, and already a convert to Catholicism. However, the conversion of these peoples would be only accomplished in 653 under Martin I. Through the good works of Gregory I, the evangelization of so many diverse peoples was to be realized, and the Roman Christian conception of religious and civil life, the basis of Western civilization, would be affirmed throughout Europe. It is not exaggerated to declare, as does Carmelo Bonanno, that "Gregory wanted a Europe joined and united in the faith and the law, in freedom and in the respect of human beings."

As a result of Gregory's fundamentally religious nature, he paid special attention to the organization of the cult. Proof of this are his Missal, or the *Sacramentarium Gregorianum*, which reformed the ceremony of the Mass, and the new edition of the book of hymns, the *Antiphonarius*. The so-called "Gregorian chant" personifies even today, his work in ecclesiastical music which also included the extension of the city's *Schola cantorum*.

The same evangelical spirit obviously inspired his writings, such as the *Liber Regulae Pastoralis* which laid down norms for a proper ecclesiastic life, and the *Dialoghi* in which Gregory sought to narrate the legends which would increase the glory of the Italian saints of his time, and gave rise to the literature about saints which typified then so much of Italian "culture," particularly among certain levels of the people. This work, however, was heavily criticized precisely because its style was, "extremely suited to convince the infantile minds of still very primitive people," Gregorovius notes, and decisive in confirming a whole series of superstitions under the authority of such an illustrious pontiff.

It was perhaps the only blemish on the figure of this great pope and was related to the veneration of relics which in those years was on the increase. To Empress Constantina who asked him for a fragment of the body of St. Paul, he replied that it was a mortal sin to touch the remains of saints or even to look briefly upon them and in fact, one of the workmen repairing the tomb of the Apostle who happened to touch some bones, suddenly died. He comforted her, however, by promising to send her some fragments from the miraculous cloth from the tomb of St. Lawrence that had magnetic qualities, or else a piece of St. Peter's chain if it could be detached.

"To this veneration," recalls Gregorovius, "are related all those other superstitions of that era such as apparitions of Mary and Peter, resurrections of deceased persons, fragrance of bodies, halos of saints and apparitions of devils, all beliefs deeply rooted in the souls of the faithful." It is certainly surprising "that even a man like Gregory could believe in these fantasies."

Moreover, with so many legends that this great pope had helped to circulate, he himself became the subject of one, such as when he called back to life the ashes of Trajan to purify his soul through baptism so that when he died again, Trajan could fly up to heaven with his soul. Dante recalls this popular belief in the Paradise (XX, 106–117):

> For the one from hell—where none returneth ever
> to right will, came back unto its bones, and this
> was the reward of living hope;
> the living hope which put might into the prayers made
> unto God to raise him up, that his will might have
> power to be moved.
> The glorious soul, whereof is the discourse, returning
> to the flesh where it abode short space, believed
> in him who had the power to aid it;
> and believing kindled into so great flame of very
> love, that at the second death it was worthy to come
> into this mirth.
> *(The Divine Comedy, The Carlyle-Wicksteed translation)*

Traditional iconography has pictured this pope, who possessed so many qualities as to deserve the title "the Great," with the dove as the Holy Spirit at his right ear, inspirer of his holy works. Belli recalls this in a famous sonnet, *Un papa antico* (An Ancient Pope):

> There was a certain Pope, Saint Gregory,
> who could speak Russian and Turkish,
> who knew every kind of wine,
> and how many souls there were in Purgatory.
>
> He could guess who had a roof over his head,
> and which egg had the hair or which had the chick.
> He knew about politics and could even tell you
> the latest gossip at Montecitorio
>
> He could foretell who would get warts,
> he could guess someone's confession
> and discover the ages of old women.

And guess who it was who whispered
all these lovely secrets in his ear?
Good for you! It was the dove.

A popular reputation as a miracle-worker accompanied Gregory together with the trick he used in his vocation, as satirised by Belli in two stanzas of another sonnet, *Le resie* (The Heresies):

A Freemason spread rumors through Rome
that Pope Saint Gregory was a story-teller,
a rascal and master of pretence.
That summoned the dove,
he would put
a kernel of corn in his ear.

But legends and superstitions apart, Gregory the Great really personified the image of a saintly pontiff in line with his own ideal. "The true shepherd of souls is pure in his thoughts, fearless in his deeds, wise in silence, fluent in speaking. He approaches everyone with charity and compassion, surpasses all by his relationship with God, joining humbly with those who do good works, but rises up in zealous justice against the vices of sinners. In his external functions he does not neglect matters of the soul, neither does he neglect to take care of external matters."

He was indeed *servus servorum Dei* as he liked to call himself, as his successors also liked to, though not always as worthily. According to Gregorovius, "none other than he understood the grandeur of his mission or maintained it with as much zeal and valour. A soul as sublime and generous as his never again sat on the throne of St. Peter." That is a judgment which I, however, feel must be extended to others, for example, in modern times, to Benedict XIV and John XXIII.

Gregory the Great died in Rome on 12 March 604, and was buried at St. Peter's. The inscription on his tombstone reads *consul Dei*.

6 5. SABINIANUS (604–606)

A deacon, born in Blera in Tuscia, Sabinianus had been the nuncio of Gregory the Great at Constantinople around 595 when the patriarch of that city, John, had assumed the title of "ecumenical" in open defiance of the Roman pontiff. Sabinianus had not acted with firmness when condemning the patriarch, so failing to fulfil the directives given him by the pope, who had warned him of the schismatic danger of such an attitude and had scolded him for his weakness.

"I am amazed that you have permitted your charity to be abused so much by the hypocrisy of John and his devilish threats," he wrote. "You should never have accepted it, nor sent me those letters by which the patriarch assumes the fancy title of 'ecumenical.' Do not be afraid and disdain with all your heart, out of respect for the truth, whatever you see of importance in the world which is contrary to the truth. Trust in the grace of Almighty God and in the assistance of St. Peter the Apostle, for agreeing to the usurpation of such an illegal title would be equivalent to losing one's faith." After which, he recalled him to Rome since obviously they did not have the same views.

Nonetheless, when Gregory died, Sabinianus was elected pope, although his consecration occurred only six months later, on 13 September 604, as usual because of the delay of imperial approval from Byzantium.

His brief pontificate was just the opposite of that of his predecessor, with the ecclesiastical offices of the pontifical court taken away from the monks and reassigned to the secular clergy. Moreover, while the famine intensified, Sabinianus opened the granaries of the Church to give food to the people, but made them pay for it. The reaction of the poor to such a decision was understandable. Paul the Deacon, in his Life of St. Gregory, relates that a delegation called upon the pope to protest: "Your Apostolic Highness, your sainted predecessor, Gregory, our father, saw to the feeding of his flock; will you leave us to die of hunger?"

Irritated, Sabinianus retorted that Gregory, although praised and reputed as a benefactor, would have starved the entire world. It was the reply of a jealous man, envious of the love which the people still had for his predecessor, and of the person who had scolded him and removed him from a prestigious position. Sabinianus came to hate Gregory the Great, and when the complaints against him were repeated, he went beyond justifying himself, accusing that pope, considered by the people a saint, of having wasted the assets of the church. He even tried to discredit his memory, according to the Roman, John the Deacon, by ordering the destruction of some of his writings.

But Sabinianus was bound to finish badly. A naive legend recounts that the spirit of Gregory appeared to him in a dream, scolding him gently for his behavior. The vision is supposed to have been repeated on two other nights, but Sabinianus, it seems, did not alter his behavior. So on the fourth night Gregory appeared more severe and decisive, and struck him on the head with his staff: "Some days later, Sabinianus expired amidst horrible pains."

Legend aside, Sabinianus died on 22 February 606, probably violently, victim of a popular uprising, and certainly hated by the people. It seems that even his corpse was to fear the fury of the famished population, since the funeral procession, leaving the Lateran, could only reach St. Peter's for the burial by way of hidden lanes, behind the walls, along St. John's Gate and the Milvian Bridge.

6 6. Boniface III (607)

A Roman of Greek origin, as indicated by the name of his father, John Kataandiokes, he had been a friend of Gregory the Great who had entrusted him with several delicate tasks of a diplomatic nature in Antioch, Corinth, and Corsica, until he named him his legate in Constantinople.

Gregory the Great had great confidence in his talents, as proved by the letter of credentials sent to Emperor Phocas. "The ambassador I am sending you is the first of the defenders and has lived a long time with me. His faith, his exemplary dress, his experience have been such that I selected him for this post because I deemed him worthy of the functions he will have to carry out with you. He received his ordination as a deacon from my own hands and in a few weeks he will present himself before you, who will surely appreciate his merits." Phocas thus had the opportunity to appreciate Boniface even though his election was delayed as the imperial approval was late in coming and he was only consecrated on 19 February 607. As compensation, he obtained an edict in which, according to the *Liber pontificalis*, "it was declared that the see of the Apostle Peter was the first of all the churches and any claim of primacy on the part of the see of Constantinople was without foundation."

This edict was issued chiefly because the emperor, a genuine tyrant, was in open conflict with the Byzantine Patriarch Cyriacus and wanted to discredit him with Rome. At the same time, Phocas, detested by Byzantium, was attempting to make himself well accepted by Rome.

Very little information is available on the pontificate of Boniface III. It appears that, during a council at Rome of seventy-seven bishops, he issued a decree which prohibited, so long as one bishop was alive, any electoral activity on behalf of his successor, and stated that the issue could only be faced three days following his death. However, the records of the council have been lost.

Boniface III died on 12 November 607, and he was buried at St. Peter's.

6 7. St. Boniface IV (608—6 1 5)

The election of Boniface IV, a priest born in the Marsica, was approved by Emperor Phocas ten months later with the consecration taking place on 25 August 608. It was a pontificate of almost seven years, cursed by the now chronic famine and pestilence in a Rome that showed no restraint in its own decadence. And yet, Gregorovius says, in the greyness of that period "there emerged from the obscurity in which it had been buried for many centuries one of the most beautiful of Roman monuments, the Pantheon of Agrippa," which stood "amid other marble buildings irreparably damaged by the flood of 590."

The flooding of the Tiber did not shake its foundation, "the imposing vestibule. . . stood intact with its sixteen granite columns topped by Corinthian capitals of white marble, and the statues of Augustus and Agrippa were still in the niches where Agrippa himself had had them placed. The march of time had not yet been able to break the beams of gilded bronze which held the roof together, and even the bronze tiles which covered the atrium and the cupola gleamed, still intact."

The new pope, Boniface IV "looked longingly upon that masterpiece of ancient architecture which seemed to possess all the requisites of a Christian church, and he begged Emperor Phocas to donate it to the Christian community as a token of the friendly relations between Rome and Byzantium. Phocas did not delay in agreeing, wanting to further the work already started by Boniface III of winning over the hearts of the Romans who were immediately grateful to him.

"For the numerous favors bestowed by his pious soul," they raised a column to him in the Roman forum in 608, in front of the Rostra: "A Corinthian column 78 palms high was taken from some old building and set on a large foundation in a pyramid-like form, with four steps. On the high capital was placed a statue of the emperor in gilded bronze." And so, comments Gregorovius, "the last monument that Rome, in the light of its ancient traditions, set up amid its ruins was a statue of a tyrant, Phocas, testimony to and symbol of the servitude of the city to Byzantium."

A year later, on 13 May 609, the Pantheon was consecrated as a Christian church to St. Mary ad Martyres. The temple of "all the gods" was metamorphosed into the church of "all the martyrs,"' while Boniface IV is said to have pillaged the Roman catacombs and filled twenty-eight cartloads with martyrs' bones which were reburied under the main altar of the new sanctuary.

The consecration ceremony was very solemn. "The doors of the Pantheon, countersigned with the Cross, were opened," Gregorovius recalls on the basis of chronicles of the period, "and in the huge room resounded for the first time the chants of the Christian priests who marched in procession while the pope sprinkled holy water on the remaining marble walls, now empty of any pagan traces. At the sound of the Gloria, which the great vault re-echoed sonorously, the imagination of the Romans saw in flight rows of frightened demons that sought to reach the air through the opening in the cupola. The number of these was equal to the number of pagan gods who had lived in the temple, considered since then by Romans as a truly hellish place."

According to popular fantasy, to begin with there was no opening in the cupola; it had been caused by the horns of a gigantic devil that had left the body of a crazed person. But this legend had a variation recorded by Belli in his sonnet entitled *La Ritonna*:

This church is so old my friends
that the grandfather of my grandmother knew of it.
What a shame it had to be so dirty,
without even one white column!

First it was dedicated to the Madonna
and was named in the litanies.
But later it was called the Rotunda
because of certain stories that aren't lies.

It was really a miracle, you see, because once
there were no windows, and the light
came only from a small door.

But a holy pope, who went to prison,
made the sign of the cross; and all at
once that Great Eye opened up.
And the miracle is this: the wall,
with that bugger of a void,
gives not a damn about itself or of an earthquake.

But frankly, it is not easy to determine to which "holy pope" our poet, or the tradition, was referring.

The pontificate of Boniface IV had no other particularly noteworthy events and the information about him is all rather incomplete. He died on 8 May 615, and was buried at St. Peter's.

68. ST. DEUSDEDIT I (615—618)

The Roman, Adeodatus or Deusdedit, son of the subdeacon Stephen, was consecrated pope five months after the death of Boniface IV, on 19 October 615, by which time Heraclius had been emperor for seven years, succeeding Phocas who had been slain by him. The king of the Lombards was Adaloaldus, and his subjects were relatively peaceful. In Byzantine territory, however, there were revolutions between 616 and 617, both at Ravenna, where the exarch John was killed, and in Naples. The new exarch, Eleutherius, restored order by eliminating the rebels en masse and, according to the *Liber pontificalis*, was received with full honors at Rome by the pope.

However, these uprisings were not ends in themselves but were evidence that a motivated transformation of the Italian situation was under way. As Gregorovius explains: "The Latin national conscience, reinforced thanks to the Church, was ever more consciously opposed to Byzantine domination and rose against it with increasing frequency. Those same Greek governors were showing a strong tendency towards independence, and, on its side, the Church of Rome, which had supported the nationalistic moves, was involved in a violent battle on a dogmatic terrain against the Greek conception of the State, the results of which would have grave consequences for the entire Occident."

Eleutherius, determined to become the interpreter of this "independence sentiment," would organize a proper "March on Rome" in 619 when the see became vacant at Adeodatus's death. He would be assassinated by his own soldiers.

Adeodatus had the reputation of being a healer, and legend attributes to him the cure of the most afflicted plague victims by the mere contact of his lips, as he heroically kissed their nauseating wounds. But the recent *Universal Calendar of the Church* carries none of the three names by which he may have been known: Deusdedit, Deodatus or Adeodatus.

He must have been animated by an intensely pastoral spirit, which is immortalized in his pontifical seal of lead, apparently the first in history, showing the Good Shepherd with his sheep between the Alpha and the Omega, symbols of Christ as the beginning and the end of everything. It seems that with him began the sealing of pontifical documents with this round piece of lead, like a coin or a medal, in Latin *bulla*, as a result of which the documents became known as "bulls."

He died on 8 November 618, probably of the plague, and was buried St. Peter's. He left in his will a gratuity of silver for each altar boy attending at his funeral.

69. BONIFACE V (619–625)

Boniface V, a Neapolitan, was consecrated pope on 23 December 619, after thirteen months of a vacant see, a normal event in those times. Exarch Eleutheria's "March on Rome," some months earlier, had ended disastrously. He probably had dictatorial ambitions regarding the city, more and more abandoned to itself, and the gracious reception accorded to him by Boniface IV allowed him, perhaps, to dream about the crown of Italy. However, the soldiers who killed him were more realistic, fearing a direct intervention by the emperor.

There is very little information about Boniface V. He restored the catacomb of St. Nicomede on the Via Nomentana, near what is now the Porta Pia. He also devoted particular attention to the Anglo-Saxon Church, as described in some writings preserved for us by the Venerable Bede, including a letter sent to Justus, bishop of Rochester and later of Canterbury, and another sent to the Christian Ethelberg, queen of Kent, to have her convince her husband Edwin follow her into the faith.

622 was an important year in his pontificate, the year of the Hejira. From then on the East would have to deal with the great new Moslem religion.

Boniface V died on 25 October 625, and was buried at St. Peter's.

70. HONORIUS I (625–638)

Honorius, a native of Campania and the son of Consul Petronius, was consecrated pope on 27 October 625, three days after the death of Boniface V, his election having been approved by the exarch Isaccus who was then in Rome.

This did not mean that the emperor had waived one of his rights, simply that he had delegated it to the exarch.

Honorius, educated and devout according to the *Liber pontificalis*, was inspired by Gregory the Great for the missionary work which marked his pontificate. In his desire to achieve a total conversion of the Lombards, he relied a great deal on the Catholic Adaloaldus, but the latter was dethroned by his Arian brother-in-law, Ariovaldus, so everything had to be postponed.

The missionary activity of the Anglo-Saxon church, on the other hand, made progress and the monk, Saint Birinus, sent from Rome to Wessex as a preacher was quite successful.

There were new disputes with Constantinople on the question of theological doctrine. Its patriarch, Sergius, was responsible for a Monothelitic doctrine to reconcile the contrasts, dormant but still alive in the Orient, between the Orthodox and the Monophysites on the nature of Christ. Monothelism maintained that, in the Word Incarnate, there was a single "operation," or rather there was operating only one "will," called "hypostatic," which was divine in terms of the divine nature and will of Christ, but at the same time human, in terms of the human nature and will of Jesus. In effect, will and action were considered to be attributes, not of the person but of the nature, in clear contradiction with the dogma of the dual nature of Christ.

The Palestinian monk, Sofronius, opposed the Monthelitic theory, explaining that one would have to admit "two operations" in the will of Christ. Sergius sought the support of the pope, claiming that "according to the teachings of the Fathers, in the same person there cannot exist two wills with regard to the same object" and that the term, "two operations," was scandalous.

Honorius did not realize the importance of the theological dispute and, chastising Sofronius, reassured Sergius in a letter. "We profess a single will in Our Lord Jesus Christ because there was in Him no will of the flesh, nor repugnance to the divine will. Moreover, if one were to accept the single or the dual operation, that is something to be left to the grammarians to decide; instead, one must abandon innovations through words that can give scandal, and, especially, not speak of 'one or two operations.'" He displayed the attitude of a Pilate talking to children who were simply playing with words.

Anyway, Sergius's monothelitic faction felt content and for his part, Sofronius, when he was elected Patriarch of Jerusalem, declared openly that he was in favor of the dual will of Christ and denounced the interference of Emperor Heraclius in support of Sergius's attitude.

Honorius then sent a second, clarifying letter to Sergius, but one cannot know whether it was in fact "clarifying" because it was lost. In any case, Sofronius died shortly afterwards and Sergius succeeded in having Heraclius issue an imperial edict, a "profession of faith" on the single will of Christ, called Ectesi. In short, Honorius had not realized the disaster he had created through his "clarifying" interventions, even if Saba tried to defend him by saying that: "Honorius, by professing a single will in Christ, does not do so in the heretical meaning of the Monophysites but simply wishes to exclude in Christ a duality of good and bad will, as is found in a sinful person."

Personally, I think Honorius I was totally ignorant about the subject, and in any case did not show necessary firmness. It is obvious that, precisely because of this ambiguous attitude of his, he ended up being judged a heretic. In the sixth ecumenical council at Constantinople in 680, which clearly held that to the two natures of Christ corresponded to two wills or "operations," the Monothelitic teaching was condemned as heretical, its adherents excommunicated, and Honorius I anathematised as a heretic, guilty by his letter to Sergius of having adopted the latter's ideas, even though he probably never really studied the problem. All of which, in any case, was not worthy of a pope, and furthermore the famous letter was later burnt, considered dangerous and scandalous.

Honorius I is remembered, however, for his activity in the area of public works which redeemed him at least in the eyes of those interested in the fine arts and who recognized in him an "urbanist." Suffice it to mention he ordered the reconstruction of the aqueduct of Trajan, beginning at the lake of Bracciano, which had been destroyed by Vitiges, and linked with the building of water mills on the Janiculum. His work as builder or restorer of churches was also noteworthy, on which he spent significant amounts of money, thus renewing the activity of predecessors such as Damasus and Symmachus.

The most costly refurbishing was in St. Peter's. The Confession was covered with silver weighing 187 pounds, the middle door coated with silverplate weighing 975 pounds, while on the Apostle's tomb were placed two candelabras weighing 272 pounds. The ceiling of the basilica too was embellished with gilded bronze tiles removed from the Temple of Venus, a personal gift from the Emperor Heraclius.

Utilizing another imperial donation, Honorius converted the Curia, by then deserted and abandoned, as there was no longer a Senate in Rome, into a church that he dedicated to St. Hadrian. From then on, many pagan monuments were fundamentally altered and became churches, and following on St. Hadrian's, according to Gregorovius, "other churches arose little by little in the whole area which stretched from the Campidoglio to the Forum and then along the Via Sacra to the Palatine."

Among the rebuilding of churches attributed to Honorius I are those of Ss. Quattro Coronati, which was already a titular church under Gregory the Great, and the basilica of St. Agnes on the Via Nomentana. This had a big tabernacle of gilded bronze that has since disappeared, but still visible is the 'commemorative" mosaic in the apse displaying, on a golden background, the chaste figure of the saint between Popes Symmachus and Honorius, the latter holding a model of the church.

Despite all these expenditures, which clearly made him a benefactor of the city to the extent of being recorded in an inscription on the silverplated door of St. Peter's as *dux plebis*, or "leader of the people," Honorius I kept the pontifical treasury intact. As Seppelt notes, "this pope obviously had an unusual gift for administering public funds. The management of assets must have been in perfect order under his rule since, thanks to him, they yielded such large sums as to allow him to amass a very significant treasury." This treasury was well protected in the vestiarium of the Lateran.

Honorius I died on 12 October 638, and was buried in St. Peter's.

71. SEVERINUS (640)

The Roman presbyter, Severinus, son of Labienus, was elected pope within the traditional period of three to five days following the death of Honorius I, but the imperial approval was slow to arrive, probably because the new pope refused to sign the Ectesi of Heraclius supporting Monothelism. This is to his honor since he showed clearer vision than his predecessor in assessing its heretical basis, which had escaped Honorius I.

But his attitude cost him dearly. His consecration took place only on 28 May 640, after a serious plundering of the pontifical treasury which his predecessor, by his administrative ability, had succeeded in accumulating and preserving. What happened was as follows.

The exarch Isaccus at Ravenna was in a precarious financial situation, to the extent that the Byzantine garrisons in Rome had not been paid for a long time. Maurice, a clerk whose function it was to take care of the Byzantine treasury but who was visiting Rome and acting as commander of the troops since there was no magister militum in the city, decided in agreement with some city leaders to lay his hands on the pontifical treasure, and brought both the greedy Isaccus and, as a result, the emperor himself, into the plot. Indeed, no one, in front of so much gold, would have had second thoughts.

He began by summoning the soldiers and accusing Honorius I of having seized for himself the money regularly sent in installments from Constantinople for their salaries, stating that many churches had been built with those salaries and not from private donations. The pontifical treasury had been unjustly enriched so what were they waiting for? To recover what rightfully was theirs? The garrison went wild and attacked the Lateran where the treasury was held, defended as best they could by the papal servants. The siege lasted for three days, until Maurice was able to place the imperial seals on the treasury. At which point he wanted to give an appearance of legality to his action and summoned Isaccus from Ravenna for an official review of the situation. The exarch did not hesitate to appear in the role of judge, and his administrative "inspection" lasted eight days. He set about banning from the city the cardinals in the pontifical administration, accusing them of unlawful appropriation to the detriment of the imperial State, and then carried off the entire treasury of the Lateran. The troops received their pay, but Maurice put the rest of the booty in his pockets and, of course, those of various high Roman officials. A share was sent to Emperor Heraclius who naturally did not punish the authors of the sacrilegious theft.

So Severinus was consecrated pope at the price of this pillaging, but his official pontificate had only a brief life—two months and six days. He died on 2 August 640, and was buried in St. Peter's.

72. JOHN IV (640–642)

A Dalmatian, the son of the scholastic Venanzius and deacon in the Church of Rome, John was consecrated pope, the fourth of this name, on 24 December 640. Pending imperial approval, in accordance with tradition, the see of Rome was governed by an archdeacon, an archpriest and a *primicerius* (a chief dignitary of the pontifical court).

Once confirmation by Emperor Heraclius had reached Rome, the new pope condemned Monothelitism in a council held in Rome. Moreover the emperor explained in a letter his lack of interest in the Ectesi which he himself had issued really at the insistent requests of the Patriarch Sergius. The latter's successor, Pirrus, however, sought by all means to propagandize the edict which, in fact, had not been abrogated. John IV objected to this behavior in a letter to the new emperor, Constantine III, explaining in precise terms the doctrine of the two natures and wills of Christ. But this letter ended with a defense of Pope Honorius I, so it was not very convincing.

Meanwhile, Constantine III was assassinated, and his half-brother Heraclius II met the same end in an uprising of the people which brought Constans II to the imperial throne. It was he who replied to the pope, assuring him that he would obliterate the Ectesi and defend Orthodoxy. These were false promises, however.

Beyond this, little is known about John IV who, apparently, was deeply concerned about his fellow nationals in Dalmatia, and provided them with numerous grants to ransom them from the state of slavery in which they lived under the Slavs.

Dalmatia was close to his heart. Indeed, he dedicated a chapel in the baptistery of St. John's to the Dalmatian national saint, St. Venantius, whose name his own father bore. The pope wanted to link his own country, victim of the barbarian devastation, more closely to Rome.

Still visible in the chapel are the mosaics with the figures of the four Evangelists and eight martyrs of Salonae. In this niche are portrayed, among others, the two popes, John IV, and his successor, Theodore I, who completed the construction of the chapel.

The pontificate of John IV was short and peaceful while Rome heard only the echoes of war. The Lombards of King Rotari were involved in the north with the exarch, and even the great battle on the Scultenna River (today called Panaro), which took the lives of eight thousand Greeks, seemed not to interest Rome.

John IV died on 12 October 642, and was buried in St. Peter's.

73. THEODORE I (642—649)

The election of Theodore I, son of a bishop of Jerusalem of Greek origin, was imposed by Exarch Isaccus, and his consecration took place on 24 November 642. By choosing a Greek, the Byzantine thought he had succeeded in obtaining confirmation of the imperial Ectesi. But Theodore in no way supported the illusions of the Monothelitic movement which had found in Byzantium a worthy advocate with Emperor Constans II, a close ally of the new patriarch, Paul.

Patriarch Pirrus, who had fallen into disfavor with the emperor, was forced to leave Constantinople and was replaced. But he did not give up easily and wanted, at all costs, to recover his power, hopefully with the support of the pope. At a council in Africa, whence he had fled, he pretended to renounce Monothelitism and went to Rome to the tomb of St. Peter in the garb of a penitent in order to officialise his profession of faith.

Theodore I received him with the highest honors and promised him his own support. He asked Paul for an explanation of Pirrus's removal, and requested that he transmit to the emperor his arguments in defense of Pirrus.

However the latter realized that time was going by without any progress, so he changed his tactics, figuring out that the best thing to do was to effect a reconciliation with the emperor. He left Rome, went to the exarch at Ravenna and retracted his abjuration.

When Theodore learned about this buffoonery, he convened a council at St. Peter's and condemned the apostate in a ceremony of terrible solemnity. Theophanus narrates that the pope proceeded to the tomb of the Apostle, took up the chalice and, decanting into the inkwell a drop of the "Blood of Christ," he dipped a pen into it and signed the solemn anathema. He took the occasion to excommunicate also Patriarch Paul, a partisan of the Ectesi, even though he had succeeded in concealing his true feelings at the time of his enthronement.

Emperor Constans II was aware that the theological dispute between East and West could create irreparable fractures also on a political level. A symptom of this was the series of "independentist" movements in Italy. Spokesman of the most recent one was the clerk, Maurice, who had turned the Roman militia against the exarch Isaccus, and the revolt had failed only through the initiative of the exarch and the fact that the troops at Ravenna had been faithful to Byzantium. Italy could escape from imperial domination mainly because of the increasingly significant military and political presence of the Lombards. In 643, their King Rotari had issued his famous edict which provided, as well, a legal basis for their occupation of the Italian territory.

So it was certainly time to reestablish peace on the theological level or, in any case, to change tactics. Constans II therefore abolished the Ectesi, replacing it in 648 with another edict, the Typus. This did not deal with theological questions but forbade even discussions of controversial definitions and threatened severe punishment for all who disobeyed the imperial prohibition. In effect, a gag was put in the mouth of the pope to prevent him from rendering decisions *ex cathedra*; whoever held "different" opinions had to keep them to himself. It was an absurd edict, certain to create resentment and to fail in its purpose.

Theodore I died 14 May 649, before having seen the Typus. He was buried in St. Peter's.

7 4. St. Martin I (6 4 9—6 5 5)

Born in Todi and formerly apostolic nuncio in Constantinople, Martin I was consecrated pope in July 649, before the imperial confirmation had arrived, since at that moment the exarchate was vacant. As certain rules were not followed, his election could have been considered illegal, and, in any case, the behavior of the Roman clergy sounded like an open challenge to Emperor Constans II.

Furthermore the pope immediately went into battle against the Eastern Church. He called for a council, which opened at the Lateran on 5 October 649, where 150 bishops gathered to discuss Constans II's edict, the Typus, by which he ordered all Christianity to keep silent on the issue of whether Christ's will was one or more than one. The Council condemned not only the Typus but also the Ectesi and any other writing favorable to the Monothelitic heresy, implicitly condemning the emperor who wanted to silence the Church on theological matters.

But Constans II had already counterattacked by naming Olympius the new exarch, and by sending him to Italy to have the Typus signed not only by the bishops but by the city's entire population, and to arrest the pope if he opposed it. Olympius reached Rome during the council but ran into a problem as the city's militia was not prepared to follow him. As Gregorovius observes, in this situation we discover "for the first time the existence of a proper army organized as a militia and comprised of the most distinguished and wealthiest citizens of the city. It received from time to time a subsidy from Constantinople, but essentially it was national and Roman and without its agreement, the exarch's plan was not possible."

Olympius then played another card, as the *Liber pontificalis* puts it, "he hypocritically pretended to renounce his perverse intentions. One day when the pontiff was solemnly celebrating Mass in the basilica of Santa Maria di Dio sempre Vergine, (known today as Santa Maria ad Praesepe or St. Mary Major), the exarch came forward to take Holy Communion, having ordered one of his swordsmen to stand near him and to kill the pope when he approached to give him the Sacred Host. But God Almighty, who protects his faithful servants and rescues them from every danger, blinded the soldier suddenly so that he could not see the pontiff when, holding the Eucharist in his hand, he came close to the exarch to give him the kiss of peace. Later the soldier swore under oath that his sudden blindness had avoided innocent blood being shed during the celebration of the Sacred Mysteries, as well as the horrendous crime which would have befallen the Church of God. Exarch Olympius, seeing that the hand of God was protecting the Holy Father, told him about the orders he had received, made his peace with him and left Rome with his army to fight in Sicily against the Saracens who had taken over the island." And, during that futile undertaking, he died.

The emperor sent a new exarch, Theodore Calliope, with specific orders to arrest the pope. He arrived in Rome on 15 June 653 at the head of the Ravenna troops. The pope, suffering from gout, was unable to leave the Lateran but, following protocol obligations, sent him representatives of the clergy who paid their respects in the palace of the Caesars. The exarch pretended to be distressed by the news of the pope's illness and announced that the next day he would go to him, displaying the greatest gentleness and stating that he was the bearer of a renewed friendliness on the part of the emperor. In this way he intended to avoid possible skirmishes with the Roman militia while putting into action his project. And since the next day was Sunday, anxious to protect himself against any resentment on the part of the people who would have gathered around the Lateran on a holiday, he put off the meeting until Monday.

Theodore Calliope then went into action. First, he sent word to Martin that he feared the Lateran was protected by an armed militia ready for battle, though he had come with peaceful intentions, and the pope naively allowed him to search the area. Once the exarch had done this, he surrounded the palace with his own troops and entered with his retinue. He approached the pope who was lying on a bed in front of the main altar of the basilica surrounded by the clergy, and at that moment drastically changed his attitude. He delivered to those present an imperial decree which ordered the deposition of Martin I, accused of having usurped the pontifical chair without awaiting the approval of Constans II, and his transfer to Contantinople for trial.

The clergy resisted but the troops quickly gained the upper hand, probably without bloodshed. They cut off the candles which illuminated the church with their swords, seized the pope and dragged him to the palace of the Caesars.

The exarch assured him he could take with him anyone he wished, and many in his retinue handed over their belongings for the voyage to the soldiers. The pope did not react, and his behavior was really exemplary in accepting what he guessed was awaiting him in Byzantium. He could have urged the people to revolt, call up the citizens' militia, and provoke a civil war, but he did not, evidently because Theodore Calliope's action was so rapid or, perhaps, because he wanted to avoid bloodshed.

The exarch, however, forced the pace. On the night of 19 June he had the pope put on board the ship anchored on the Tiber, allowing him the company of only six attendants. He closed the gates of the city, fearing that other trusted friends of the pope who expected to leave with him might have meanwhile mobilised the militia and the people, and sailed for the port.

From there he began the long journey which touched Cape Misenus and various islands, Nassus included, where there was a stopover of almost a year. It was a painful trip because the pope was suffering from dysentery and was never permitted to set foot on the land, travelling like a prisoner. In vain, priests and members of the faithful showed up at the various moorings to pay him homage and bring him gifts, which all wound up in the pockets of his prison guards. And this was only the beginning of his martyrdom.

When he reached Constantinople on 17 September 654, Rome already had another pope, Eugene, who had been consecrated a month earlier at the orders of Constans II. So Martin, now considered just an ordinary bishop, did not receive the honors granted to so many of his predecessors in Byzantium and was clapped into jail in solitary confinement. Only three months after his arrival he went on trial for high treason, clearly a farce, though one with tragic results.

Martin I wanted to mount his defense by examining questions of faith which he thought were the subject of baseless accusations against him, but the prefect Troilus ordered him to remain silent, pointing out that the trial was for crimes against the State. He was accused of having convinced the exarch Olympius to rebel against the emperor and of having called the Saracens to Sicily to help him in his fight against Byzantium. Martin responded: "In Olympius I embraced my former enemy who was redeemed. I gave money to the Saracens to ransom

Christians who had been abandoned by the emperor and, as the pontiff, I defended the faith against the Typus."

But the sentence had already been decided: death. Pending the capital punishment other sufferings were in store for him. Carried into a public courtyard on a chair, since his infirmity prevented him from walking or even standing, he was stripped of his papal stole and his mantle and, half naked in the piercing cold, bound in chains, he was dragged through the city to the jail.

The Monothelitic patriarch, Paul, also ill and dying, having learned from the emperor about the treatment the pope was enduring, evidently had a pang of remorse and begged Constans II to commute the sentence of death into one of exile. The emperor granted this request and did not change his mind even when, after Paul had died and the Patriarch Pirrus, a heretic, was reelected, Martin I refused to lift the anathema pronounced against Pirrus by his predecessor, Theodore I.

Martin I remained in jail until March 655, after which he was sent into exile in the Crimea, reduced to misery, abandoned by everybody and, what really saddened him, even by the clergy of Rome who, once they had had a new pope, paid no more attention to him. Martin had hoped that, following tradition, an archdeacon, an archpriest and a leading dignitary would have taken over the management of the see of Rome. But the Roman clergy were afraid and, as Saba notes, "it is difficult to excuse their weakness and lack of consideration. When Eugene was elected, the pope had not yet been barbarously deprived of his pontifical stole. He represented the Church in the misery, in the disasters, in the tortures of an exile that was nobly borne. The clergy of Rome was not up to his grandeur." And the *Annuario pontificio* considers the two of them as reigning contemporaneously!

Letters written by Martin to those few friends of his in Constantinople are moving. He regretted that the Roman Church did not provide him with even the elementary necessities of life, although it was within their power. But he nonetheless prayed God to strengthen his Church in the true faith and to guard his substitute against the heresies. He was a great pope who accepted martyrdom in defense of the orthodox religion and never compromised in politics.

On 16 September 655, Martin I died in exile, alone and friendless. His remains were buried at first in Byzantium's church of the Virgin of Blacherna, but later he was moved to Rome and probably buried in the church of Sts. Sylvester and Martin.

7 5. ST. EUGENE I (6 5 4 — 6 5 7)

A Roman presbyter from the Aventine, Eugene I was consecrated pope on 10 August 654, at the express command of the emperor, Constans II. As mentioned, the pontiff, Martin I, was still under way to Constantinople, and had yet to be put on trial and convicted, but the emperor deemed him already removed from office.

Byzantine tyranny obviously found no resistance from the Roman clergy, nor even from Eugene. The latter who could easily be charged with treason or, at the least, with a lack of respect towards a pope who had been dismissed from his duties by the emperor, but who should still have been considered the official pontiff by his bishops and priests.

Eugene should have refused the selection and respected the tradition that, in the absence of the pope, as Martin himself confided, "the archdeacon, the archpriest and the *primicerius* (the chief secretary) should rule the see." And so, for more than a year, contemporaneously, there were a pope, prisoner and dethroned yet always the vicar of Christ on earth, as well as a pope chosen by the emperor.

There is no evidence on which to judge the behavior of Eugene I. However, he had been the nuncio at Constantinople and that experience should have helped him to understand the kind of disorders with which the Church as a whole was being afflicted by imperial despotism. The sole excuse might have been that he feared, at worst, the election of a Monothelitic pontiff. But certainly the sense of "power" must have subjugated him.

Indeed, to begin with he showed himself to be accommodating. His legates in Byzantium approved a new formula invented by the patriarch, Pirrus, previously declared a heretic by Theodore I, in which one spoke of two distinct wills in the natures of Christ but added a third will as a "person." More serious was the fact that these legates readmitted Pirrus into the ecclesiastical community. Perhaps this was intended to save the life of Martin I who firmly opposed any such rehabilitation of the patriarch. But it is hard to imagine that the legates acted entirely on their own initiative. Rather, Eugene I probably revealed himself to be, in the words of the *Liber pontificalis*, even too 'benevolent, gentle, full of patience," and ended up cutting a poor figure.

Nevertheless, when Pirrus died and Peter succeeded him as patriarch and the latter sent the pope in 656 his "profession of faith," extremely ambiguous on the question of the wills of Christ, the clergy and the Romans advised the pope to reject the patriarch's document. But Eugene was not convinced immediately, and the use of force was needed in the form of a threat to prevent his celebrating Mass at St. Mary Major to get him to promise to reject the offending Synodica.

Which he did, probably aware of the risks which he was running. By that act, he redeemed a pontificate born of compromise and shabbily pursued. Death, on the other hand, saved him from the possibility of a martyrdom like that of his predecessor for which he, perhaps, did not have the mettle. He died 2 June 657, and was buried in St. Peter's.

And to imagine that the Church raised him to sainthood! Thirteen centuries after his death Rome dedicated a church to him on the Viale delle Belle Arti, near Villa Giulia, given in 1942 by the Catholic world to the then Pope Pius XII, Eugenio Pacelli, on the twenty-fifth anniversary of his consecration as bishop, and which was completed and solemnly inaugurated in 1951.

76. St. Vitalianus (657–672)

A native of Segni, Vitalianus was consecrated pope less than two months after the death of Eugene I, while Emperor Constans II was trying to reestablish friendly relations with the Latin Church. For his part, Vitalianus encouraged the emperor in this new approach and hastened to demonstrate to him his own wish for a reconciliation through the legates sent to Byzantium.

So Constans II welcomed the pontifical nuncios, confirmed the privileges of the Roman see and sent the pope a manuscript of the Bible decorated with gold and diamonds. Vitalianus was consecrated on 30 July 657.

To reinforce this link between papacy and empire, Constans II came to Rome in 663 on an official visit, accompanied by a military expedition against the Lombards in southern Italy, which was destined to fail however.

The emperor arrived from Naples along the Appian Way and the pope went to meet him six miles from the city with the entire clergy and a delegation of citizens with crosses, banners and lighted candles. Constans made his triumphal entry into Rome on 5 July 663.

"One can readily imagine the excitement in the city, so long abandoned, caused by the arrival of His Imperial Majesty. The presence of a Byzantine monarch who still had every right to be called 'Emperor of the Romans' was an extraordinary event," Gregorovius notes. As to "the relations of Constans with the Church, if not openly hostile, they were nonetheless very tense. The Church had suffered at the hands of the emperor both humiliation and insults of every kind, and had good reason therefore to be afraid of him."

Maybe this is why the pope appeared somewhat humble: "Vitalianus did not have a burning desire to face up to the Greek emperor as Bishop Ambrose had done from the steps of the church at Milan, when he resisted Theodosius the Great, staining himself with the blood of the rebels. And yet," comments Gregorovius in a reproving tone, "at the sight of the hated Constans he must have recalled even too well that the emperor had slain his brother and had sentenced Pope Martin to die of starvation." But, in fact, "Vitalianus's sad state and his obsequious manner before the emperor aroused indulgence and understanding. Many centuries would have to pass before this show of humility could be converted into the triumph of Canossa."

This demonstration of reciprocal obsequiousness with solemn ceremonies celebrated in homage of pontifical and imperial sovereignty was, in reality, only external. Indeed Constans II left Rome on 17 July, after having taken his share of booty by removing as much as it was possible to carry of the ancient "pagan" treasures. In fact, he even managed to steal the lead tiles from the roof of the Pantheon, previously consecrated as a Christian temple.

Once he had reached Syracuse, he decided to set up there his own residence, possibly to renew his attacks against the Lombards. But in reality it was to enjoy the fruits of his ill-gotten gains and to strike a blow at the prestige of the episcopal see of Rome.

He ordered by a special law that, as from 1 May 666, the Church of Ravenna would be considered independent and the archbishop of Ravenna would receive from the emperor, as an honorific ornament, the pallium. This created a sort of schism between Rome and Ravenna and the first to arrogate this authority to himself was the Archbishop Maurus who, disregarding completely the anathema which Vitalianus launched against him, excommunicated the pope.

But two years later, in 668, Constans II was assassinated at Syracuse. The military proclaimed Mesecius emperor, but the pope mobilised all the clerical forces to have Constantine IV Pagonatus, the son of Constans II and legitimate heir to the throne, recognized as emperor. And so it came about.

This action by Vitalianus, despite all the injustices done to him by Constans II, created a feeling of eternal gratitude toward the papacy, even if at that time it reaped no benefits, since the emperor was deeply involved militarily in stopping the advances of the Arabs, with whom he succeeded in reaching a peaceful settlement only by 678.

Vitalianus devoted himself in the meantime to the Anglo-Saxon church which aligned itself with Rome in the liturgy as well as in orthodox doctrine.

He died on 27 January 672, and was buried in St. Peter's.

77. ADEODATUS II (672—676)

A Roman monk from the monastery of St. Erasmus on the Caelian Hill, Adeodatus, son of Jovinianus, the second of this name, was consecrated on 11 April 672, three months after the death of Vitalianus.

He was a pontiff of little importance who made no progress on the questions regarding Byzantium and Ravenna, where the new archbishop, Reparatus, firmly held on to his autonomy, refusing to submit to the pope. Scarce is the information about him also in the *Liber pontificalis*.

He restored his own monastery on the Caelian, which was built in the sixth century but later destroyed, the ruins of which with traces of paintings could still be seen in the vicinity of St. Stephen towards the end of the sixteenth century.

Adeodatus II died on 17 June 676, and was buried in St. Peter's.

7 8. DONUS (6 7 6 — 6 7 8)

Donus, or Domnus, son of Mauritius of Rome, was consecrated as pope on 2 November 676, nearly three months after the death of Adeodatus II.

The information about him in the *Liber pontificalis* is of little interest. During his brief pontificate, however, the schism between Rome and Ravenna came to an end. The new archbishop, Theodore, submitted to the pope and renounced the autonomy of the Ravenna see. All this took place thanks to the emperor. In fact, Theodore did not have the slightest intention of giving up any privileges and even wanted to remove the name of Vitalianus from the *Dittici*, the list of bishops. The emperor indignantly rejected his request and compelled the archbishop to perform the act of submission to the pope.

Constantine Pagonatus also was determined to settle the dispute between Byzantium and Rome, intending to strengthen the latter's position in the West so that it would be the only authentic interlocutor in the dialogue with the Eastern Church.

He then began to take concrete initiatives toward this goal of re-pacification, hopefully by the convocation of an ecumenical council, Donus died on 11 April 678. He was buried in St. Peter's.

7 9. ST. AGATHO (6 7 8 — 6 8 1)

Agatho, from Palermo, was consecrated pope on 26 June 678, two and a half months after the death of Donus. According to one legend, he had reached the venerable age of 103 but could still reason well.

On 12 August he received a letter from Constantine Pagonatus in which, having now resolved the military questions, the emperor said he was ready to resume the project of ecclesiastic reunification between Rome and Byzantium. He had decided to set up an international episcopal conference in which the current problems would be discussed and all disputes settled. For this, he asked the pope to send to Constantinople representatives knowledgeable on the problems, stating that three clergymen and four monks from Rome together with twelve metropolites and bishops from his patriarchate ought to be sufficient. He assured the most complete imperial protection for the delegation through special safe-conducts.

To prepare the delegation adequately, Agatho called an Italian council in the Lateran on 27 March 680, which chose the episcopal representatives together with the papal legates to be sent to Byzantium, and approved the synodal text which was to be submitted at the conference. Set forth in it was the doctrine of the two wills and the way they acted in Christ, with express reference to what had been decided by Martin I at the Lateran Council.

The delegation from the West arrived in Constantinople on 10 September 680 where it was received by the new patriarch, George, who arranged to convene the metropolites and bishops from the Byzantine district. What had been billed as a conference, in the end, became a proper ecumenical council, the sixth to take place in the East. Indeed, representatives of all the patriarchates were present for the first session that began on 7 November 680, in a domed hall of the imperial palace, the Trullus, as a result of which it was called the Trullanus Council. The emperor was the presiding officer, flanked by two presbyters and a deacon from Rome as representatives of the pope.

Meanwhile, "strange" events were occurring in Italy, as narrated by Paul the Deacon. "A terrible pestilence broke out in Rome which lasted for three months, from July to September; great numbers of people died, and often parents and children, or brothers and sisters, were brought to a burial place together in the same box. Then, with the same violence, the disease depopulated Ticinus," that is, Pavia, "forcing all the residents to flee, some to the mountains, others elsewhere while, in the piazzas and streets of the city, grass and bushes grew. Then many people saw with their own eyes the good and the evil angel roaming the city at night and every time that at a sign from the good angel the evil angel struck with a stick he had in his hand the door of a house, within the next day a person therein died. Finally, thanks to a prophecy, it became known that the plague would stop as soon as an altar to St. Sebastian, the martyr, would be raised in the basilica of St. Peter in Chains. And so it happened: the remains of the saint, brought from Rome, were placed in an altar of that basilica, and the plague finished."

Later, the Romans adopted this legend as their own and connected the events with the church in Rome of the same name, St. Peter in Chains, where the plague was immortalized in a painting attributed to Pollaiolo. In the left nave of the same basilica can also be seen a "rough" mosaic of the period which shows an elderly St. Sebastian with a beard and completely dressed, a long shot from the image of the saint as a youth, bound naked to a tree and pierced to death by arrows!

Meanwhile, the council at Constantinople continued and after eighteen sessions a decree was issued on 16 September 681. It repeated the profession of faith established by five previous councils and unanimously approved the doctrine of the two Wills and two Energies in Christ not in conflict with each other, confirming thereby also the synodal text of the Lateran. The Monothelitic heresy was obviously condemned and, according to a legend recorded by Paul the Deacon, "an incredible number of spider-webs fell on the people, as if to signify that the abject error of the heresy had been eliminated." The anathema struck even Pope Honorius I, accused of excessive toleration of certain heretics, and his ambiguous letter to Sergius, patriarch of Byzantium, was burned as scandalous.

Gregorovius notes that "this, the only case in which a Roman pope had been accused publicly of heresy and anathematised by a part of an ecumenical council, is one of the most notable events in ecclesiastical history," so much so that, later on, "the condemnation of Honorius became a weapon in the hands of those who fought against the dogma of papal infallibility."

Finally, the council sent a document to the pope asking him to confirm the decisions. However, Agatho had already died on 10 January 681, apparently aged 107, and had been buried in St. Peter's. Rome had a vacant see again.

80. St. Leo II (682—683)

A lengthy period of vacant see followed the death of Agatho since imperial approval of the newly elected Leo II was delayed a good eighteen months. At the ecumenical council of Constantinople the official condemnation of Pope Honorius I, among other matters, took place and this was a delicate subject for which the emperor insisted on total agreement by the West. Imperial approval was therefore postponed on purpose.

The Roman delegation returned to Rome only in July 682. Leo II was consecrated on 17 August and a month later sent the emperor a letter in which he voiced his approval of all of the decisions of the council. In particular, he observed that Honorius I "made no effort to maintain the purity of this apostolic Church in the doctrine of the apostolic tradition and, by his profane condescension, allowed the spotless Roman Church to be blemished." Again, in a letter to the Metropolites of Spain, informing them about the council and inviting them to subscribe to its decisions, he wrote that Honorius was guilty "because he did not attempt to put out in the beginning, as a pope should have, the flames of heresy but rather, by his negligence, encouraged it."

During his brief pontificate Leo managed to restore two churches: Saint Bibiana and San Giorgio al Velabro, from Velabrum, as the river marshland which initially divided the Palatine from the Campidoglio was called. Located behind the Arch of Janus, the church, though rebuilt often even up to the beginning of the twentieth century, has always kept the simple structure given to it by Leo II with its interior of three naves from which issues a profound spirit of Chritian purity.

Leo II died on 3 July 683, and was buried in St. Peter's, although Paul V later moved the remains to beneath the altar of the chapel of the Madonna of the Column in the new basilica.

8 1. St. BENEDICT II (6 8 4 — 6 8 5)

The consecration of Benedict II, a Roman, took place on 26 June 684, eleven months after the death of Leo II, and imperial approval, as usual, was delayed. Constantine Pagonatus was aware that the issue of confirmation of the election of a pope cost money as well as time. So, in a letter to the newly elected pope, he renounced his personal rights, and renewed the proxy to the exarch, as he had had on other occasions, so that all would be simplified from Ravenna. Benedict II received this privilege because the emperor's relations with him were of the deepest esteem, so much so that the emperor had his own sons, Justinian and Heraclius adopted by the pope, sending to Rome as a pledge locks of hair of the two boys, which were accepted with great solemnity.

However, the confirmation of the elected pope continued not to be immediate even from the exarch, although the delay never exceeded three months. One would have to wait more than fifty years until the time of Pope Zacharias to reach the free consecration of the pontiff elected by the three classes which formed the population of Rome: clergy, army and people.

The few other items about Benedict II available from the *Liber pontificalis* are of little importance. He died on 8 May 685, and was buried in St. Peter's.

8 2. JOHN V (6 8 5 — 6 8 6)

A native of Antioch and a former apostolic nuncio, John V was consecrated pope on 23 July 685.

The little information on him in the *Liber pontificalis* does not define his personality, only that in a council he is said to have cancelled the privilege of consecrating bishops held by the archbishop of Cagliari, evidently autonomous until then, which was to return to the jurisdiction of Rome.

The new emperor, Justinian II, son of Constantine Pagonatus, gave him in a letter the title of Universalis papa. But it was his successor, Conon, who received the title because the message arrived in 687, by which time John V had already died on 2 August 686, and been buried in St. Peter's.

It should be noted that beginning with this pope as Seppelt recalls, there was "an uninterrupted series of popes who were from the East. This important fact cannot be explained by the influence or pressure exercised by the Byzantine court on papal elections, because it was precisely during these decades that the unfortunate empire was rocked by attacks from outside and by uprisings from within. Emperors succeeded one another at brief intervals, acclaimed then destituted by mutinous troops, and the change of monarchs, which took place after only a few years, was accompanied by assassinations and unheard-of cruelty. This chaotic succession therefore excluded any decisive intervention by the emperor in papal elections."

It is also true that in Rome there was a succession of pontificates of very brief duration. Gregorovius notes that "the rapidity with which, at that time, the popes reached the Chair of Peter constitutes a strange and disturbing phenomenon. Pontificates lasting thirteen years or more, like those of Gregory the Great, Honorius I and Vitalianus, are truly exceptional, since the popes in the sixth and seventh centuries never governed for more than two or three years at the most." It remains a mystery "whether the brief life of the popes was due to the fact that they were elected at an advanced age or whether there were other, more complex causes."

8 3. CONON (6 8 6 — 6 8 7)

For the election of a successor to John V, Rome was divided into two camps. The clergy supported the archpriest, Peter, and the militia the presbyter, Theodore. To prevent the consecration of Peter, the army occupied the Lateran and held meetings at S. Stefano Rotondo.

There were no battles, and negotiations took place. At a certain moment, the clergy brought forth a new candidacy, that of the presbyter, Conon, origin unknown, very elderly, who was welcomed even by the militia. The exarch, John Platina, approved and Conon was consecrated on 21 October 686.

He was very ill and his election was more than anything to gain time. One was simply waiting for him to die and the ambitious archdeacon, Paschal, put pressure on the exarch to succeed Conon on the papal throne by promising him one hundred pounds of gold. John Platina accepted this offer and gave orders to the imperial magistrates, who had some influence over the people, to have Paschal elected as soon as Conon died.

In February 687, Conon received a letter from Emperor Justinian II, really addressed to his predecessor. In it the emperor advised the pope that he had arranged the transport of the documents from the sixth ecumenical council to his palace in order to assume personal responsibility for them. By this, however, the emperor really intended to emphasize that he considered himself, as Seppelt observes, "the true master of the Church." It was not a good omen for the future.

Conon died on 21 September 687, and was buried in St. Peter's.

8 4. ST. SERGIUS I (6 8 7 — 7 0 1)

On the death of Conon, Archdeacon Paschal felt confident he would be elected because of the money he had promised to the exarch in exchange for approval. However, once again, the Roman people were divided, proposing the archpriest, Theodore, instead of the one who seemed to be the official candidate.

Both factions, installed in the Lateran palace, proceeded with the election with the result that there were two pontiffs.

The situation was untenable and, as always happens, between the two contenders appeared a third, the presbyter, Sergius, a native of Palermo and of Syrian origin, who carried on his functions in the church of Santa Susanna. He was chosen by the magistrates, the militia and a good number of the clergy.

Theodore paid him homage without objections while Paschal, who did not want to give up, sent secret messengers to the exarch, certain as a result to get him on his side. John Platina arrived in Rome completely unexpectedly and learning that Paschal was in a minority, abandoned by those very magistrates to whom he had recommended him, and verifying too the near-unanimity of the election of Sergius, gave his approval. But he did not return to Ravenna empty-handed, having demanded from Sergius the hundred pounds of gold that he had been promised by Paschal. Upon receipt of the gold, Sergius I was consecrated in St. Peter's on 15 December 687. Simony, under duress or otherwise, proved again to be the rule in papal elections.

At first, Paschal was allowed to keep his office as archdeacon but later, accused of practicing magic, he was deposed and sent to a monastery where he died in 692.

Sergius I, therefore, took his place on the pontifical throne with perfect title. He was a person of notable culture who had risen in his ecclesiastical career to the level of cardinal, developing an authoritarian character, bent above all on reaching power even at the cost of bribery as we have seen, and of concentrating this power in Rome.

Gregorovius notes that "in him the teachings of Byzantium encountered a firm opponent, worthy of those who had preceded him on the Chair of Peter. A similar determination to dominate inspired all the Roman pontiffs through a spiritual legacy transferred by Rome itself to the Church." Logically, "the city itself became accustomed to see in the pontiff its own absolute sovereign. Anyhow, to whom else could the unfortunate Roman population turn if not its own holy bishop whose acquired dignity had made him the most powerful gentleman in Italy?"

The conflict between the pope and the emperor was not long in coming. Justinian II stuck to the Caesar-Pope tendencies of so many of his predecessors and thought it opportune to give a personal touch to the Christian religion by convening a new ecumenical council in Constantinople with the support of the Eastern bishops. The pope was not even invited so it was "ecumenical" solely in the emperor's mind.

He held it in the same place as that of 680, the Trullus, but, in order to distinguish it from the Trullian, it was called the Quinisextum and should have completed the fifth and sixth councils. It took place probably in 691, and promulgated 102 laws transcribed on great parchments which were sent to Pope Sergius in Rome to have them approved and signed by him, which he understandably refused to do.

Especially dangerous for the maintenance of the ecclesiastical institutions, which were now becoming ever more important, would be the abolition of celibacy for priests and deacons. And the attribution to the see of Constantinople of the same prerogatives as ancient Rome appeared to be a direct blow at the authority of the Roman see.

The emperor felt himself animated by the spirit of Constans II and decided to proceed forthwith against this hostile behavior of the pope. First, he sent a senior Byzantine magistrate to Rome to arrest Bishop John of Portus and the priest, Boniface, an adviser to the pope. Once these two had been brought to Byzantium, Justinian II felt he was in a strong position and sent to Rome a cruel and ferocious man, Zachary, the *protospatarius*, that is the Byzantine chief of military staff, with orders to arrest the pope. Sergius I was supposed to meet with the same fate as Martin I.

But it was 692 and times had changed. This additional insult roused the populations of the Pentapolis and neighboring provinces, as well as the citizens of Rome, for the first time all indignant over a plot considered sacrilegious. There was a rush of militiamen toward Rome to save the pope, and even the army at Ravenna discovered in itself Christian feelings more important than imperial obedience.

The Chief of Staff, Zachary, was at a loss, as such a reaction had not been foreseen. He behaved in a ridiculous manner and, shedding all that ferocity of which he was so proud, fled to take refuge in the bedchamber of the pope. Meanwhile, the army from Ravenna entered the city through the Gate of St. Paul, crossed the entire city and, accompanied by a huge crowd, arrived at the Lateran.

In the pope's room, the farce got worse. Zachary hid under the bed and fainted. Sergius revived him, told him not to be afraid and asked him to have confidence in him. The tiger had become a lamb.

The gates were opened and Sergius, seated on the Apostolic Chair, received the homage of the soldiers and of the people. He interceded on behalf of Zachary, who kept his life but was thrown out of the city in disgrace.

"This was a memorable day in the history of the papacy," observes Gregorovius. "For the first time then it became clear what were the power and national importance of Rome's prestige, the product of that same centralizing energy which, working quietly, had subjected the Italian provinces to the authority of the Roman Church, and the result of the lengthy dogmatic struggles by the West against the East and the consequence of the overbearing imperial interference in the affairs of the Roman Church."

The episode had negative repercussions even in the East since the emperor had cut a very poor figure. The people felt they had been taken for a ride, and in 695, rebelled against Justinian II. The rebellion, headed by General Leonzius, led to the unseating of the emperor. Dragged into the hippodrome, his nose and ears mutilated in accordance with typical Byzantine brutality, he was sent into exile in Crimea. Leonzius then declared himself emperor.

In the West, on the other hand, the incident consolidated definitely the authority of Rome, which encouraged the development of missionary work. Relations with the Franks increased, where the famous "do-nothing kings"—the last representatives of the Merovingian dynasty—succeeded one another on the throne. Real power, in effect, was in the hands of their "mayors of the palace," governors of the individual territories which constituted the Frankish kingdom. In those days however, a single 'mayor of the palace,' Pepin, had succeeded in lording it over the others, and in consolidating his authority. Thanks to his protection, the Anglo-Saxon Willibrord began the conversion of the Frisians, who were subjects of the Franks. In order to give his mission more effectiveness and authority, Sergius consecrated him as bishop, giving him a Latin name, Clement.

Numerous penitent kings came to Rome as pilgrims and, converted, they naturally brought substantial gift offerings of gold. As Gregorovius remarks, those gifts "were used by the popes to add to the splendor of the churches" in what seemed to be a contest in detail and refinement between the Roman mosaic and bronze workers and the artists of Constantinople. "They decorated even the thuribles with columns of gold and they gave to the ciboria, that is, the tabernacles on the altars where the chalice was placed, the form of little temples of porphyry with cupolas of gold and precious stones." Sergius I himself participated in this work of embellishment of the Roman basilicas, endowing especially with numerous precious objects the Church of Santa Susanna where he had been cardinal. He also built for St. Leo the Great a new sepulcher in St. Peter's, which was the first sepulchral monument erected inside the basilica.

Sergius I died on 8 September 701, and was buried in St. Peter's.

8 5. JOHN VI (701−705)

Following the death of Sergius I and a brief period of a vacant see, a Greek was consecrated as Pope John VI on 30 October 701.

Four years earlier, Tiberius Apsimarus had become emperor, having deposed Leontius, but Apsimarus was against this pope as well, although the reasons for his hostility are not clear. In any case, it was certainly not with good intentions that he sent the exarch Theophilattus to Rome from Sicily. Again militiamen from different provinces of Italy ran to protect the city and the pope. In fact, the feeling of devoted submission to the emperor by the inhabitants of Rome and of Italy generally had disappeared, replaced by a sort of pseudo-nationalistic sentiment.

The troops set up camp outside the walls while, in the city, the people rioted and the pope behaved in the same way as his predecessor. He had the gates shut, took the exarch under his personal protection, then requested the militia to withdraw and thanking them for their attachment to him, reassured them that there was no danger.

"His balanced behavior showed how wise and prudent he was," observes Gregorovius. "The popes at that time still possessed no temporal powers, although they already exercised in Italy greater influence than the exarch. They continually professed to be subjects of the emperor and during the rebellions acted with wisdom and deliberation, showing their loyalty to the State. If Italy had freed itself too early from Constantinople, where the authority of the Roman empire then resided, that would have worked only to the advantage of the Lombards who were at that time threatening the city of Rome from nearby."

Indeed, the Lombards, who had abandoned Aryanism and were now convinced Catholics, were invading Campania, pillaging and destroying under the leadership of Gisulfus, duke of Benevento. The pope, through diplomacy but mainly by payments of cash, had succeeded in getting them to evacuate the occupied territories. So once again, the bishop of Rome had replaced a Byzantine dux, negotiating peace not as a man of arms or even a political leader but as a person with a certain realism, as Gregory the Great had demonstrated.

John VI died on 11 January 705 and was buried in St. Peter's.

86. JOHN VII (705—707)

John VII, a Greek, the son of a certain Plato, was consecrated pope on 1 March 705.

This pontiff reestablished good relations with the Lombards, and their King Aribertus even returned to the Church certain possessions along the Ligurian coast which had been seized earlier by them. The donation document was actually written in golden letters and forwarded to Rome.

In the autumn of 705, Justinian II succeeded in regaining the throne of Byzantium with the help of the Bulgarians, and he immediately took his revenge on Leontius and Tiberius Apsimarus. These two were arrested and dragged into the public circus where they were trampled on and beheaded. Heraclius, brother of Tiberius, was hanged and the Patriarch Callinicus blinded.

After which Justinian II got in touch with the pope to obtain recognition of the famous Quinisextum council, previously rejected by Sergius I, but in this case he acted with more moderation. Two Metropolites showed up in Rome with the council's canons and limited their request to having the pope accept those decisions which seemed valid to him and indicate those that he did not consider orthodox. The pope, "timid because of human frailty," as the *Liber pontificalis* puts it, did not have the courage to express his own opinion, and like a new Pilate washed his hands of it by passing the canons back to the emperor without any changes at all. He signed nothing and, in effect, he did not approve them; frightened, he simply bought time.

John VII is said to have constructed and restored various churches in Rome, decorating them with mosaics. Some still exist, such as those in Santa Maria Antiqua in the Roman Forum where, towards the center of the middle nave, stood the ambo of which remains the octagonal platform with the inscription at the ends, "John the servant of the Mother of God," referring in fact to John VII.

He also had a chapel built in St. Peter's in honor of the Virgin Mary with various mosaics, one of which represents this pope, which can still be seen in the Vatican Grottoes. In this chapel, it seems that the pontiff placed the famous shroud of Veronica, of whom there is still a commemorative inscription in the Grottoes.

Finally, his was the merit of restoring the monastery at Subiaco, destroyed by the Lombards in 601.

John VII died on 18 October 707, and was buried in St. Peter's.

8 7. SISINNIUS (708)

Sisinnius, a Syrian, was consecrated pope on 15 January 708, but his pontificate lasted only twenty-one days. The brief information about him comes from the *Liber pontificalis* which relates that he was so afflicted by gout that he had to be force-fed.

He had time only to set up quicklime kilns for the restoration of the walls of Rome, by this time in shambles, and some one else would complete the work of restoring the "defenses" of the city.

He died on 4 February 708, and was buried in St. Peter's.

8 8. CONSTANTINE (708—71 5)

Another native of Syria, Constantine, succeeded Sisinnius and was consecrated on 25 March 708.

He had to assist, helpless, at the next outburst of vengeance by Justinian II, this time against Ravenna. The militia there, in the name of a hypothetical regional "autonomy," had sabotaged Byzantine's recent initiatives by interventions in defense of the pontiffs, Sergius I, John VI, and John VII.

The patrician Theodore, at the emperor's orders, came from Sicily to Ravenna with his fleet and, once in the city, arrested nobles and ecclesiastics and dragged them in chains on board the ships anchored in the harbour. He put the city to fire and sword, slew a large number of the citizens, and then left for

Constantinople. Many death sentences were carried out and Giovannicius, the recognized leader of the revolt, was buried alive, while the archbishop of Ravenna, Felix, was blinded and sent into exile at the Black Sea. The emperor ordered this macabre punishment probably in an attempt to regain the pope's friendship, because Felix had stirred a vague sentiment of rebellion in Rome, subsequently stifled. In any case, such a punishment was an act of folly, if by it he had intended to reconcile himself with the pope and to confirm the pope's undoubted primacy.

In fact, Justinian II, after this initial show of violence, invited the pope to come to Constantinople to resolve the still pending dispute about the articles of the Quinisextum council. Constantine, energetic and courageous, accepted the summons on one condition, that he be given a safe-conduct, which was granted. He left Porto on 5 October 710, and stopped over at Naples. There he met the new exarch, John Rizocopus who, as soon as the pope left for Byzantium, moved to Rome and set himself up as a tyrant during the pontiff's absence. He condemned to death a number of ecclesiastics without the shadow of a trial, and his conduct was, in effect, a continuation of the vendetta carried out by Theodore in Ravenna.

The pope was welcomed in Constantinople with pomp and ceremony by the highest imperial staff members. His meeting with Justinian II took place at Nicomedia and the emperor went so far as to carry out the proskynesis, that is, he genuflected before the pope, kissed his feet and confirmed the privileges of the Roman Church.

The negotiations were lengthy, and the results for the emperor negligible. The pope stood his ground and accepted only that which was already in force as a result of previous councils. Early in October he left Constantinople, and this was the last visit by a pope to that city. Only after twelve and a half centuries would Pope Paul VI return, in July 1967, to meet the patriarch, Athenagora, under very different circumstances.

On his return trip, Constantine disembarked at Gaeta and arrived in Rome on 24 October 711, after a year of painful absence for the citizenry because of John Rizocopus's tyrannical actions, who in the meantime had gone to Ravenna. There the exarch died probably the victim of the open revolt that broke out in the city between 710 and 711.

The leader of the revolt was a certain George, son of the Giovannicius who had been killed in Constantinople. He was a sort of "captain of the people" and he divided the militia among the twelve gonfalons of the city, according to the damaged Cronaca of Agnello of Ravenna, which unfortunately tells us nothing else about the revolt. But it is clear that once the Armenian, Philippicus Bardane, became emperor after killing Justinian II, victory was in favor of the Byzantine.

The new emperor was also a Monothelite and felt obliged to condemn the decisions of the sixth Trullanus council, issuing a decree that there was only one will in Christ. He sent ambassadors to the pope carrying his profession of faith, which Constantine obviously rejected. He even refused to recognize Philippicus as emperor, nor did he want to have the usual procession through the streets of Rome in praise of the emperor, or to issue pontifical coins carrying the image of Bardane.

This papal opposition created a serious state of agitation in Rome with street fights in which more than thirty persons were slain. Indeed, there was an open battle along the Via Sacra between the city troops led by the dux, Christopher, previously given this post by Justinian II, and those led by a certain Peter, sent by the exarch as the new dux. A procession with banners and holy images led by Constantine passed between the combatants and brought an end to these hostilities.

The fact remained that the pope had felt strong enough to refuse to recognize an emperor, and this was an important event for the future autonomy of the papacy. "The refusal of the pope to recognize the new emperor can be interpreted as a first step towards later attempts at total detachment of the papacy from imperial influence," Walter Ullmann correctly notes. "The refusal by Pope Constantine was nothing other than the practical effect of rights of primacy reaffirmed by the papacy. On this basis, decrees issued by a synod convened by the emperor had been condemned, and the refusal to recognize an emperor who was a heretic in the eyes of the papacy had taken place." In any event, in June 713, Philippicus Bardane lost his throne, deposed by a minister who called himself the Emperor Anastasius II. This man declared his orthodoxy and his adherence to the faith of the sixth council. The authority of the pope was beginning to be felt by these emperors, for the most part unprepared and afraid of losing the throne through lack of popularity due to their authority not being recognized by pontifical Rome. The roles were being reversed.

Above all, the new exarch declared his faith in the positions taken by Anastasius II. Peter remained dux of the imperial garrison in Rome on the promise of a general amnesty, while Christopher was probably put aside for the peace of all concerned. The pope, for the first time, had stood up to the emperor. However, Constantine died shortly afterwards, on 19 April 715, and was buried in St. Peter's.

8 9. St. Gregory II (7 1 5 — 7 3 1)

Constantine was succeeded by a Roman, Gregory II. A former subdeacon and pontifical librarian, he had accompanied his predecessor as an adviser on the trip to Constantinople, where the question of the recognition of the

Trullanus council had been discussed. He was consecrated pope on 19 May 715 when Anastasius II had been the emperor for two years and Luitprand was already king of the Lombards. His immediate wish was to continue the project of Sisinnius to restore the walls of Rome, but he got no further than the stretch near the gate of San Lorenzo, since the city had grave problems as a result of "a fearsome flood of the Tiber lasting eight days; the pope ordered daily processions to calm it," according to the *Liber pontificalis*. It caused damage right up to the area of the Campus Martius.

Information is scarce on the first years of this pontificate, but it is certain that the ecclesiastical jurisdiction of the see of Rome reached to southern Italy. Indeed, when the Lombard duke of Benevento, Romualdus II, seized Cuma, the pope asked the Neapolitan dux, John, to retake the castle. His military effort was successful and Gregory II paid him with seventy pounds of gold.

In the meantime Anastasius II had been dethroned in Byzantium by Theodore, dethroned in his turn by General Leo Isauricus who became emperor on 25 March 717, informing the pope of his orthodox profession of faith. Relations between Rome and this emperor were apparently good.

In those years it seems that the reconstruction of the famous monastery of Monte Cassino was taking place. According to the account of Paul Deacon, "Petronace of Brescia, inspired by divine zeal, went to Rome and then urged by Gregory II, on to Monte Cassino. Near the holy remains of St. Benedict, he found some men in a wretched condition who had been living there for some time, and he decided to stay with them and they elected him as their head. Briefly, with the help of Divine mercy and thanks to St. Benedict, when about one hundred and ten years had passed since the place had been abandoned," destroyed by the Lombards between 581 and 589 in the days of Pelagius II, "he became the father of many monks who came to him from the nobles and the middle class. So, when the tiny cells had been repaired, they resumed living to the rules of the sacred Regola instituted by St. Benedict."

But Gregory II was not merely interested in the problems of the Christian community in Italy; he intended to continue missionary work in the countries of northern Europe.

In 716, the Bavarian duke, Theodus, had come to Rome and had spoken with the pope about ecclesiastical jurisdiction over his own territory, and the designation of German bishops. They had reached an agreement but, unfortunately, the premature death of Theodus brought matters temporarily to a halt.

Missionary work in Germany was, in any event, very disjointed. It progressed as best it could as with the Frisons, complicated by the fact that these people hated Christianity, since it was the religion of their mortal enemies, the Franks. So a more consistent effort under one person was needed and the Anglo-Saxon monk, Winfrith, was charged with this missionary work.

Arriving in Rome to pay homage to the tomb of St. Peter, who had a notable attraction for the new believers, he was questioned by the pope regarding the genuineness of his intentions, and gradually won his trust. On 15 May 719, a papal document officially conferred on Winfrith, subsequently baptised Boniface, the task of converting the Germans. The mission territory was not clearly defined, which left Boniface ample room for maneuvers, with authority to administer baptism according to the Roman rite, but with the duty to inform Rome continually about all his missionary activity.

Boniface was active first in Thuringen and later in Hesse, converting many and making his apostolate both heroic and legendary. In 723, Gregory II named him bishop.

This flourishing apostolic activity in the West, which marked the pontificate of Gregory II, was, however, overshadowed by relations with the East.

Emperor Leo III, a man of great energy, devoted himself in the early years of his long reign, which lasted from 717 to 741, to war against the Arabs, whom he pushed back from the walls of Constantinople, and then to the internal reorganization of the empire through enormous legislative activity. Taxes were raised to straighten out a bad financial situation and these applied also to the Byzantine territories in Italy, directly affecting the rich landholdings of the Church. Gregory II refused to pay a tax increase deemed excessive, considering that the earlier emperors of the East had always granted substantial reductions to the pope.

But the question of taxes was merely the beginning of more serious vexations. Indeed, when Leo III began to widen his policies toward religious matters in a Caesar-papist manner, like many of his predecessors, the empire ran into new disorders and tension between Rome and Byzantium reached an apex.

Convinced that uniformity and equality in faith was necessary for the stability of the empire, and calling himself at one and the same time "Emperor and High Priest," Leo commanded the Jews to convert to Christianity. But it seems that an insurmountable obstacle to this conversion arose from the Christian veneration of sacred images, considered by the Jews to be idolatry.

On the other hand, as Seppelt correctly observes,"the veneration of images, favored by an influential monkhood which was also financially interested because the monks produced the sacred images, enjoyed great popularity among large sections of the population. But this popularity of the cult of images caused exaggerations and abnormalities. The abuses created opposing trends, supported by existing sects, especially in the eastern part of the realm, like those of the Montanists and the Paulicians. These opponents of sacred images, who were able to recall the prohibition of images by the Old Testament and the hostile attitude of the ancient Church, had their partisans even in episcopal circles."

As soon as the caliph, Jesid, issued an edict in 723 ordering the images to be removed from the Roman churches within his jurisdiction, Leo III figured that, by imitating the caliph, he could with one stroke resolve the problem of the conversion of the Jews and achieve an improvement of relations with the neighboring Arab realm. In 726, he issued an edict against the veneration of images. As a "good example," he personally had an image of Christ, considered particularly miraculous, removed.

Facing up to the riots that this decree provoked, Leo III demanded the support of the patriarch of Constantinople, Germanus, who refused to approve it or sign it. Then the emperor turned directly to the pope, prepared probably to close his eyes to the tax issue which had been suspended, in the hoped-for but absurd case that the pontiff would accept his iconoclastic edict. Gregory II, informed in detail by Germanus on the twist taken on the issue of images in the East, instead called a council during which he rejected the edict and approved veneration of images. With a bull, he also denied that the emperor had any right to legislate in matters of faith.

Leo responded with more decrees and threatened to replace him if he did not obey the edict. However, at this point, according to the *Liber pontificalis*, the pope fended off the emperor by sending a series of "pastorals" to the Italian bishops. There was a chorus of "yesses" in favor of the crusade launched by the pope, and from Pentapolis to Calabria all the Byzantine areas were shaken by revolts against the emperor.

Leo III thought he could resolve the matter by getting rid of the pope, and he gave the task to imperial agents present in Rome where the dux Basil and the clerk Jordan, with their accomplice, Lurio, conspired to assassinate Gregory II. But the plot was foiled. The people killed Jordan and Lurio, and Basil withdrew to a monastery.

Then it was the turn of Exarch Paul who left Ravenna with the task of arresting the pope, but had to stop at the Salario bridge, blocked by the Lombards from Spoleto and Tuscia, and forced to return to Ravenna with his tail between his legs. All attempts to unite imperial authority in Italy against papal authority seemed to be doomed. The exarch, excommunicated by the pope, lost his prestige in Pentapolis, and, with the Byzantine agents expelled, local duces were elected in all central Italy.

Gregorovius observes that "Gregory saw a national feeling flame up in Italy and he needed only to give a simple sign to push the country to insurrection." But the pope himself did not give that sign, and did not join in the revolts. He not did want complete separation from the emperor but merely intended to make him understand his own strength. We can say that with this political attitude which was developing along with the very concept of the papacy, were the seeds of something highly sophisticated if not ingenious. The pope could not be in favor, for example, of a Lombard king who would perhaps name Rome as his capital because in Seppelt's words, "that would have amounted to an open threat to the role of Italy's guide, which the evolution of history had entrusted to the pope."

Political reasons were thus added to the religious motives which had caused the conflict between Church and State, resulting in the birth of clerical politics. The first crusade was launched by a pope whose standard bore the image of Christ and saints on one side but that of power on the other.

Moreover, this duality of the papacy was immortalized in two letters sent by Gregory II to Leo III, the authenticity of which has been doubted by some. These letters, according to Gregorovius, "express firmly the awareness of the supremacy of the pontiff as the archimandrite of the Christian world, which the successors of Gregory II used as models. Therein is contained, now perfect in its essentials, the concept of the papacy that was concretised later during the eras of Gregory VII and Innocent III."

While he condemned the violence and the rebellion of the provinces against the empire, Gregory II ended by threatening the emperor. "All Western peoples look with ancient devotion on him whose image you brazenly threaten to destroy, I mean St. Peter, whom the kingdoms in the West honor like God upon earth. So give up your plan; your angry violence will achieve nothing against Rome, against the city, against its coast or its ships. All of Europe venerates the holy Prince of the Apostles. Should you command that his image be destroyed, we declare ourselves as of now to be innocent of the blood that will be shed, and we affirm that it will fall completely upon your head."

And again, to Leo III who claimed to be at once "emperor and bishop," Gregory II correctly set forth the distinction between the functions: "Each of us carries out the mission for which he was destined by God." The State is to govern the things of the world by the sword, punishing by death or prison; the Church, "disarmed and undefended," is to punish by excommunication sinful souls, not to kill them but to lead them back to God.

The difference, however, was that in an Italy, which was becoming united around the Church of Rome, an emperor, regardless of his military power, risked the loss of his authority with his own subjects if he were to be excommunicated by the pope who resisting imperial abuses, was recognized as the leader of the population. In such moments, the distinction between spiritual power and temporal power in the hands of a pope vanished; he became "emperor and priest."

Besides, Gregory II was an example of duplicity. He did not excommunicate Leo III, and yet he told him, "we might have wished to impose a severe punishment upon you but, since you yourself have earned your curse, let that be enough of a punishment." Then, prudently and with moderation, he stopped the revolutionary passions of the Italians, convincing them that the emperor had been sufficiently frightened. In reality, the pope feared above all that Rome and Italy would wind up in the hands of the Lombards, whose friendship at the time appeared to be precarious.

In Italy's climate of anti-Byzantine revolt, King Luitprand indeed dreamt about conquering the peninsula, and allied himself with the exarch, advancing without difficulty towards Rome. After brief encounters, he defeated the dukes of Benevento and Spoleto, allies of the pope, and set up camp on the slopes of Monte Mario. Then Gregory II, without protectors and undefended, showed the other aspect of his personality, casting aside the role of a hypothetical head of the territory now described in official documents as the "Roman duchy."

Dressed modestly, he went to Luitprand's camp, a new Leo the Great versus his Attila, and addressed the barbarian with the same words which had been capable of arousing compassion in the hardest of hearts. The enchantment was repeated and Luitprand, prostrate at the feet of the pope, placed his sword and his crown on the ground, requested and received pardon for himself and absolution from excommunication on behalf of the exarch.

"The future of the papacy, master of the world," notes Gregorovius, "was decided in this brief moment which, in the history of the Church, shines more brightly than the legendary meeting of Leo with Attila. Three hundred years before the famous episode at Canossa, the extraordinary and mysterious power which the Roman pontiff now possessed was already apparent to the world. Humanity, confused and bewildered by ignorance, bowed before the ministry of the Church within which was venerated the only divine force existing on this earth, and gave honor to its supreme head as a holy human being of a superhuman nature."

Meanwhile, the exarch was able to reinstate imperial power in the Roman duchy while the pope showed himself willing to restore friendly relations with Byzantium, once the echoes of the iconoclastic struggle had died down. It was all so easy that he even quenched another attempted anti-imperial revolt that took place in 730 in Roman Tuscia, when Duke Tiberius Petasius, heading a straggly group of supporters, declared himself emperor. Gregory II promptly gave the exarch the task of taking care of the rebel who was beheaded and his head sent off to Constantinople. The papacy was basically convinced that the preservation of a concrete state authority was an absolute condition not only for its own also in anticipation of that one day that it could become its own ruler. Between an encounter and a re-pacification, Byzantium assured him of the objectives of this political "game" whose stake was power. The rest was rhetoric.

Gregory II died on 11 February 731, and was buried in St. Peter's.

90. St. Gregory III (731—741)

As successor to Gregory II, a priest of Syrian origin was unanimously elected by the clergy and the people. He took the pontifical seat on 18 March 731 as Gregory III.

Emperor Leo III immediately gave his approval, hoping he would be dealing with a more conciliatory pontiff than the previous one. Gregory III, however, replied to him in letters so precise about his support for Gregory II's attitude, and in such a brusque manner that the nuncio charged with delivering them, a priest named George, did not dare carry out his mission and returned to Rome with the undelivered letters. The pope made him travel back with them but he was stopped in Sicily by the imperial dux and arrested. Released after a year in jail, he was forced to return to Rome so that the pope would "understand."

Meanwhile, Gregory III had officially distanced himself from Leo III. He convened a council on 1 November 731, in St. Peter's, from whence he issued a decree of excommunication of the Iconoclasts. Constantine, the *defensor Urbis*, was charged with carrying the decisions of the council to Constantinople, but he met the same fate as George, and was arrested and detained in Sicily. Leo III wanted nothing to do with messages and messengers on religious questions, realizing that they could be a means to discredit him in the eyes of his subjects as a loyal Christian, and therefore as emperor.

As far as he was concerned, whatever was decided in Rome had to be ignored in the East, and its iconoclastic policy was not be disturbed. If it had not assured him the conversion of the Jews, it had eased his relations with the Arabs. Then there was still in suspense the issue of the Church's payment of taxes. Leo III resolved that question with a surprise move, sequestering all the ecclesiastical properties in Sicily and Calabria, which produced a yearly income of 35,000 pieces of gold.

Badly hit, the Church sought to make up for this by acquiring in Roman Tuscia the Castel Gallese which, according to the *Liber pontificalis*, was annexed to the *sancta res publica*, an equivocal expression that according to Gregorovius "can mean either the duchy, which the pope began to claim as the property of St. Peter, or the Sacrum Romanum Imperium." It is clear that, "with subtle foresight the popes left standing the structure of the Roman State, and the origins, however doubtful, of their authority in Rome, and so demonstrated convincingly their fine diplomatic art. They owed their dominion to the chaotic conditions in Italy, to the weakness of the Byzantine emperors and to their own skill and strength."

The acquisition of Gallese, which assured the connection between Rome and Ravenna, was the result of secret negotiations between Gregory III and the duke of Spoleto, Trasamund, who, just like the duke of Benevento, Godescalcus, was trying to declare his own independence from King Luitprand. Both were trying to gain advantage from the political disorder in Italy. However, it was clear that in the long run only the pope would derive any advantage.

Luitprand knew that not only had he been betrayed by the Lombard dukes but also that the pope was playing a dangerous double game and, determined not to let himself be trapped, Luitprand left Pavia in 730 for central Italy, chiefly to punish Trasimund. He took Spoleto easily, but the duke fled to Rome under the protection of the pope, who refused to hand him over to Luitprand. The Lombard king vented his wrath by pillaging the Roman countryside and conquering the important castles of Ameria, Orte, Bomarzo and Blera. There he installed military garrisons and threatened Rome with a possible attack, before returning to Pavia.

The danger over, Trasimund reconquered Spoleto but refused to help the pope free the four castles from Luitprand's military garrisons, so Rome remained under threat of siege.

Gregory III decided to turn to the Franks, where Charles Martel had inherited from Pepin, his father, the authority as the only "mayor of the palace," enhancing his position by his victory in the battle at Poitiers in 732 which had blocked the Arab advance into Europe.

In 739, the pope sent him a delegation bearing expensive gifts, the object of which was to get proper military assistance against the Lombards. The delegates were received with full honors, but their specific request was not even taken into consideration. "A coldly calculating politician, Charles Martel had personal and political reasons for not intervening in the Italian situation," Seppelt correctly observes. Aside from his precarious health, "he had no intention of renouncing his friendship with the Lombards, who were blood relatives of his." The pope and his 'duchy' thus remained under the Lombard threat, but the attempt, for that moment fruitless, had not been a false move. "Although the pope's effort with Charles Martel was not successful," observes Seppelt, "it was nonetheless forever to Gregory's honor and merit to have had the vision, heavy with consequences, of a unity between the pope and the Franks. In fact, this project would soon become reality."

Gregory III continued the missionary activity of his predecessor, entrusting Boniface with ever more specific functions, to the extent that by 738 the latter had full powers as apostolic vicar in Germany for the organization of the Bavarian Church. This was achieved through the consent of Charles Martel who assisted the work of Boniface with safe-conducts and financial aid. In this way he made clear to the pope that, even if he could not help him in a military way, he was prepared to collaborate fully in any initiative of a religious nature.

In 741, Gregory III sent him a second delegation with the keys of St. Peter and an offer to name him consul, as a result of which Rome would have passed entirely under his military authority. The pope seemed desperate, calling him again the defender of the Church, and, in effect, offering him the sovereignty of a city which was in fact under imperial jurisdiction. For Charles Martel to accept such a title would thus have meant the enmity also of Byzantium, in addition to that of the Lombards. The response could only be in the negative.

In any case, when it arrived in Rome, Gregory III had already died on 28 November 741, and Charles Martel a month later.

9 1. St. Zacharias (7 4 1 − 7 5 2)

Zacharias, a Greek born in Calabria at Santa Severina, was elected pope a few days after the death of Gregory III. A Benedictine, he had become a cardinal-deacon under his predecessor and, for the first time, no one waited for confirmation by the exarch. The consecration took place on 10 December 741.

At that time Italy was still under the scourge of Luitprand, suffered already by Gregory II and III, whose aim right then was to retake the duchy of Spoleto and punish Rome because the pope had protected Trasimund.

Zacharias was isolated since the Franks could not be expected to help for the moment. At the death of Charles Martel, his sons, Carloman and Pepin the Short, who had divided between themselves the function of "mayors of the palace" in the various regions of the kingdom, were often in disagreement with one another, though Pepin's authority seemed stronger since he had succeeded in having a favorite of his, Childericus III, named king. In any case, the two of them had no time to worry about the pope, while the new emperor, Constantine V, showed no interest in the Byzantine lands in Italy and even less of helping a pope who didn't even wait for his approval to be consecrated.

So the pope had no alternative but to initiate negotiations with Luitprand. Zacharias was eager to recover possession of those four castles in the Roman Campagna and the king promised to return them on condition that there be a joint action of the Roman army, now at the orders of the pope and no longer of the exarch, and his own troops against Trasimund, the duke of Spoleto.

Zacharias agreed, dishonoring a pledge made with Trasimund by his predecessor which he unhesitatingly disregarded in the interests of the Church. Now abandoned, the duke had his life saved by Luitprand on condition that he become a monk, which was what happened.

Luitprand also conquered Benevento but he went back to Tuscia without returning the famous castles to the pope. So Zacharias left Rome in the spring of 742 to demand what had been promised to him, and the meeting between them took place at Terni in the basilica of St. Valentine.

According to the official document, not only were Orte, Ameria, Bomarzo and Blera delivered to the pope and not to the emperor, but he also obtained other donations: the Sabine and the territories of Narni, Osimo, Ancona, Numana and Valle Magna, property of the Lombards. The Roman duchy was expanding and to seal the reconciliation at an official banquet, the duke-pope stipulated a twenty-year peace with the Lombards. It seems that Zacharias was a charming speaker and Luitprand's docility surprising. Therefore, says Gregorovius satirically, "every bite that Luitprand ate at the pope's table cost him a piece of conquered land. Yet, rising from the table the old king, smiling affably, stated that he could not remember ever having enjoyed such a delicious dinner."

The pope was by now fully convinced that he had a kingdom on this earth which was necessary to protect and have respected. Luitprand gave him the opportunity to test this. A few months after that famous dinner, the Lombard king decided to make up for his several donations by seizing Pentapoli and laying siege to Ravenna. The exarch, Eutychius, asked the pope to mediate, so the pope again left Rome to meet Luitprand, leaving the administration to the patrician, Stephen.

This time he had to meet him at Pavia on 28 June. Again the king succumbed to the oratorical gifts of the pope, giving everything back to the exarch and lifting the siege. Luitprand was probably at the end of his capacities of authority and, evidently exhausted, he no longer had the strength to react. In fact, he died in 744.

The Lombard throne passed to Ratchis, duke of Friuli, who confirmed the twenty-year armistice granted by Luitprand. But the king in question was very subservient and, realizing that politics and war were not his cup of tea, became a monk at Monte Cassino in 749.

His brother Aistulf, a much more energetic man, became king and proceeded with the plan to conquer the Pentapoli, occupying Comacchio and Ferrara, and also Ravenna in 751. Zacharias did not even think of making a "little speech" to the new king since he saw that it would be useless. He accepted the fall of the exarchate, preoccupied with the fact that the way was now open between Ravenna and Rome for a Lombard attack on his duchy. He decided to try again with the Franks where Pepin the Short, now running the kingdom by himself, had secret aspirations to take over the throne. Indeed, in 747, two years before the Lombard Ratchis became a monk, Pepin's brother Carloman had felt himself called by God. He had received his monk's tunic in Rome and retired first to Mount Soratte, where he built a monastery, then to Monte Cassino.

However, even for Zacharias it would have been extremely difficult to negotiate and "chat" with two men, the king and his mayor. But Divine Providence gave him a hand since an agonizing doubt assailed Pepin, "mayor of the palace," as to whether or not he could ignore his oath of fealty to his king, Childeric III, dethrone him to become himself the sovereign, and, thus, give birth to a new dynasty.

Pepin decided in 751 to entrust the question to a council, and sent the bishop of Wurzburg, Burcard, and the abbot of St. Denis, Folred, to Rome to ask the pope—whose moral and religious authority was recognized without question—whether it would be possible to cancel a sacred oath made to a king who was in fact—the ambassadors insisted on saying—without power. In this way, they said, the wishes of the Frankish people, who felt disoriented without the authority of a real king, could be met.

The salient points of the ambassadors's remarks seemed phrased in a way to suggest Zacharias's reply, who naturally did not need any suggestions. Ravenna had fallen, the emperor was caught up with his problems in the East, and Aistulf was breathing down the walls of Rome. The pope urgently needed military aid to defend his duchy, and Pepin would certainly not flinch from repaying a favor as big as the one that Zacharias was about to, and did, grant.

Zacharias declared, according to the *Annales Francorum*, "that it was preferable for the royal title to be in the possession of one who was effectively in power and not of one who was without power" and the pope ended his response by ordering that Pepin be crowned king.

Then and there was born in the papacy, as Saba observes, "the awareness of a high authority who could confirm a king, necessitated by the will of an entire people," so that the popes "will later affirm, at the cost of serious battles, the right to intervene in the conferring or taking away of crowns."

In this way there matured the idea of the anointing of a king as in the Bible, and his coronation became a divine consecration by which whoever had been elected king would have been chosen, as would be declared some years later, "by the grace of God." It was the beginning of a monarchic-clerical regime in the Christian sense.

I frankly think that the judgment of Walter Ullmann on this whole question is too generous when he states that, "in order to evaluate the papal initiative adequately, one must leave aside the more rigorous moral standards of the twentieth century and judge by the ideas of the mid-eighth century, according to which the kind of sanction offered without difficulty by the papacy was not to be condemned."

The truth is that Zacharias, replying in that manner, was not speaking as a man of the Church. He declared that a sacred oath was null and void for reasons strictly political and assured in this way military protection of his own duchy.

And so, Childeric III, in line with the custom, wound up in a monastery, and Pepin the Short was crowned on the fields of Soissons by Bishop Boniface between September 751 and February 752. Zacharias died shortly afterwards, on 22 March 752, having completed his masterpiece, and was buried in St. Peter's.

92. STEPHEN II (752–757)

A presbyter named Stephen had been elected as the successor to Zacharias but he died before being consecrated, so he is not included in the list of popes. In a new election, a Roman deacon of the same name was chosen, Stephen II, who was consecrated on 26 March 752.

The Lombard King Aistulf, now the possessor of the exarchate, had decided to conquer the rest of Italy and had begun his march towards the south to take over Rome. A delegation from the pope headed by his brother, the deacon Paul, succeeded in June in stopping the advance and obtaining renewal of the twenty-year armistice previously granted to the pontifical duchy by Luitprand. But later Aistulf regretted his concession and demanded an annual tribute. A second delegation led by the abbots of Monte Cassino and St. Vincent at Volturno had no success; they were not even received.

In the meantime, the new emperor, Constantine V, made himself heard from Byzantium and in several messages demanded the restitution of the territories occupied by the Lombards. Stephen sent the imperial messenger to Aistulf, again accompanied by his brother Paul, but this delegation too had no success. At this point, Aistulf requested surrender at Rome's discretion and threatened the massacre of the residents if there were a military opposition.

With all this exchange of delegations, including one from the pope to the emperor requesting military assistance, the latter, as with the others, to be ignored,the situation became ever more dramatic. The time for a peaceful resolution was rapidly diminishing in view of Aistulf's determination, but the temporising had its purpose. It was 753, and Stephen II had an ace up his sleeve, but the card was to be played at the right time and place with the situation carefully prepared. Playing for time with Aistulf was part of the game.

The population was another factor on which he gambled by spreading a justified state of alarm, but with all the frills which tradition required: a beautiful sermon in the manner of Gregory the Great to emphasize the danger which menaced the holy places in the city, and a procession through the streets behind an enormous cross upon which was fastened the document by which the perjurer Aistulf had sworn to maintain peace. All this was designed to arouse amongst the citizens a sense of deep emotion needed to swallow, once the matter was successfully concluded, the bitter pill of a foreign patricius, sworn to the Christian faith, but also with a powerful military force able to defend them. Who, then, if not the king of the Franks, Pepin? Hence, at the beginning of 753, the transmission to the sovereign, in great secrecy, by the hand of a pilgrim who was returning from Rome to his Frankish land, of a letter which unfortunately was lost, in which the pope requested a private meeting with him.

Meanwhile, during these diplomatic preparations for the meeting, the pontifical chancery was not idle. Stephen II wanted to appear before Pepin with a detailed request for military assistance against Aistulf, but not in order to rebuild an exarchate in Italy, or a glittering Byzantine power from which the papacy had so far received nothing but religious problems and military oppression. The pope wanted to claim those lands occupied by Aistulf as the property of St. Peter, stated as such an ancient imperial document, the *Constitutum Constantini*.

As is well known, this document is a fake and the merit for having first recognized the lack of authenticity belongs to Nicholas von Kues and Lorenzo Valla. As to its drafting, I am in agreement with Seppelt that "the location of its creation is to be sought in Rome" and that the time it was written was precisely "the period before the papal journey to the kingdom of the Franks." The document seems to be an edict of Emperor Constantine addressed to Pope Sylvester and his successors. In it, after the account of Constantine's illness, to which reference is made in the biography of St. Sylvester I on the cure of the emperor through the effort of the pope, it states that Constantine decided to confer on the vicar of Christ the "power," called *principatus potestas*, to raise the throne of St. Peter above the earthly one, granting it imperial dignity and honor.

The Church is recognized as an independent religious State whose sovereign is Christ, its founder and heavenly emperor, represented on earth by the pope who has the same functions as the terrestrial emperor. As a result, the imperial crown belonged to the pope who, having no wish to wear it, permitted its use by Constantine. This gave rise to numerous territorial grants by the emperor which were to give substance to the State of the Church, such as the Lateran palace together with all the symbols of imperial dignity, and *potestà* (paternal authority) over the city of Rome, the Italian provinces and the entire West. This was given because Constantine reserved for himself the East with its capital, Byzantium, where, with the consent of the pope, he took up residence deeming it unfair that a terrestrial emperor should wield his power in the very seat of the celestial emperor. Finally, the title of *patricius Romanorum*, that is, the military defender of those territories, belonged to the pope.

This false document was supposed to constitute the legal basis for the claims that Stephen II intended to present to Pepin during his visit, claiming a "right" acquired by the representative of Christ on earth.

During the summer of 753, Pepin's reply arrived through the medium of the Abbot Drottedang of Gorizia, saying he would welcome a meeting to hear what the pope's wishes were. Shortly afterwards, he sent Duke Autari and the bishop of Metz, Crodegang, to Rome to escort and accompany Stephen II during the journey.

The pope left on 14 October 753, but decided to stop in Pavia to put forward Emperor Constantine V's request for the restitution of the Byzantine territories, even though he knew that such a request was hopeless. In fact the stopover in

Pavia was meant to conceal from Byzantium the real purpose of his journey which, as an ally of the Franks, Aistulf dared not impede.

Officially, Stephen was going to France to consecrate Pepin solemnly for the second time since it was necessary to put to rest the resentment of some of the Frankish people who still saw in him a usurper. The pontiff was to resolve everything in an official, holy way and Aistulf could certainly not oppose this since he was also an ally of the Franks.

On 15 November 753, the pope left Pavia and was greeted at the border by ambassadors of the king, Folrad, the abbot of St. Denis, and Duke Rotardo. Later Prince Charles came to welcome him, while the meeting between Pepin and Stephen took place on 6 January 754, in the royal castle of Ponthion, south of Châlons-sur-Marne. The king prostrated himself and rendered homage to the pope as an equerry according to the ritual of the Byzantine court, and then the talks began.

The pope, with the *Constitutum Constantini* in hand, requested the help of Pepin to recover possession of the territories of St. Peter, obliging him to come to the defense of the Church, and the king gave him his solemn oath. But, as Seppelt observes, "the real contracting party with Pepin is St. Peter, to be considered as a single unit with his successor and representative. It was thus the very Prince of the Apostles, the Keeper of the Gate of Heaven, who had ordered Pepin to defend his own personal prerogatives and the privileges of his Church."

The pledge given by Pepin was not a small matter, chiefly because it meant breaking the alliance with the Lombards, whilst against possible Byzantine protests, the *Constitutum Constantini* could be cited. In any case, the king had to submit his decision to the Frankish nobles so Stephen II took up residence in the Abbey of St. Denis and awaited events. Pepin scheduled the negotiations in two meetings, in March at Berny-Rivière-sur-Aisne, and in April at Quierzy, where all was decided.

In fact, Aistulf had begun to smell a rat and had convinced Pepin's brother, Carloman, who had become a monk, to call on the Frankish king as his own representative and remind him to respect the alliance with the Lombards. The poor monk was the one who suffered because he was put under arrest by the pope for having illegally left the monastery, and spent the rest of his life in the prison-monastery at Vienne.

The treaty of Quierzy was contained in an official document called *Promissio Carisiaca*, or "Promise of a Donation by Pepin" which has unfortunately been lost. In any case, one may guess that in addition to confirming the promise of protection made at Ponthion, together with the defense of the Church of Rome, it would have listed in detail the territories which would enjoy this protection. According to the *Liber pontificalis*, in the biography of Pope Hadrian I, Pepin made a gift to St. Peter of "Corsica and the cities and lands south of a line which runs from Luni to Parma, Reggio, Mantua and Monselice, including the Lombard Tuscia and the exarchate of Ravenna, as well as Venice and Istria with the duchies of Spoleto and Benevento." One must say that this extremely vast territory never belonged to the pontifical State, even if, as Caspar notes, it nonetheless constituted the "sphere of interest of the Curia."

In reality, the treaty of Quierzy had determined the conquest by the Franks of the Lombard kingdom, with the handing over to St. Peter of the estates taken away from the Church of Rome and of those which used to belong to the emperor, the exarchate and Pentapolis.

The treaty received its official consecration on 28 June 754, at St. Denis when Stephen proceeded with the solemn "anointing" of Pepin, his wife Bertrade and two sons, Charles and Carloman. Pepin was recognized as "King by the grace of God;" the chrism of Divine Grace gave a charism to the "blood," sanctified by a threat of excommunication for anyone who might rashly attempt to elect a king belonging to a family other than the Carolingians. Moreover, the pope conferred on Pepin and his sons the dignity of *patricius Romanorum*, a title that sanctified the promise of Ponthion.

At this point, action had to be taken against the Lombards and Pepin tried to solve the problem peacefully, inviting Aistulf through three successive delegations to give up the occupied territories. But in August 754, when every attempt had proved vain, Pepin departed for Italy accompanied by the pope. Once the Alpine ranges had been crossed, the encounter took place at Susa, and a defeated Aistulf sought refuge in Pavia and requested peace talks.

Aistulf promised under oath the restitution of the exarchate and Pentapolis, as well as the occupied papal estates to the "Romans." Pepin escorted the pope to Rome and then returned to his own lands, convinced that he had performed his duty.

But Aistulf did not honor his oath and immediately undertook a new invasion of the Roman duchy. Stephen II sent an indignant letter to Pepin, in the name of St. Peter, accusing him of having left Rome defenseless, expressing the fear of having been betrayed and, finally, calling Pepin naive for having put faith in the promises of Aistulf. Moreover, he complained of having undertaken a dangerous journey in order to consecrate personally a king who was less than grateful, and he concluded by reminding him that on Judgment Day he would have to account to God and St. Peter about failing to live up to the promise made.

Meanwhile, Aistulf was advancing with all the military strength at his disposal, and it appeared that he wanted to conquer not merely Rome but all of Italy. On 1 June 756, the Lombards moved towards the city from three directions, Via Salaria, Via Latina and Via Trionfale. The surrounding areas were savagely pillaged and the siege lasted for fifty-six days, but Pepin did not show up. Stephen sent Abbot Vernerius to him, repeating in other letters the desperate situation at Rome. The tone was ever more inflamed and the pope said he was inspired directly by St. Peter in his complaints. He ended by threatening excommunication: "If, then, although we do not believe it, you make yourself guilty of delays or give pretexts, and you do not quickly obey our warning to liberate this city, the people who live here, the Apostolic Church given to us by God and his most high priest, know that, by the will of the Most Holy Trinity and by virtue of the grace of the apostolate granted to us by our Lord, you shall be deprived, for having disobeyed our instructions, of the Kingdom of God and of life eternal."

The risk was too great and Pepin decided to return to Italy. The mere news that the Franks were on their way convinced Aistulf to lift the siege of Rome and return north to push the enemy back from the frontier. But he was not up to facing them and he put down arms, surrendering unconditionally. He was granted only the title of Pavia and all the rest was consigned to the pope.

It should be emphasized that, meanwhile, three envoys of Emperor Constantine V had come to Rome, unaware of the Treaty of Quierzy and even less of the *Constitutum Constantini*, and had naively forwarded to Pepin the request of their sovereign to recover possession of the Byzantine territories which he had reconquered. Pepin left these messengers agape when he replied in all candor that he had made two trips to Italy for the recovery of those territories through love of St. Peter, to whom they belonged, and for the salvation of his own soul. He added that all the treasures of the world would not have sufficed to induce him to betray his word given to St. Peter, and he repeated his intention to consign all those territories to the pope.

Which territories were involved? Apart from the exarchate, the *Liber pontificalis* lists them by city in a smaller number than that presumably decided at Quierzy. St. Peter became the possessor of Ravenna, Rimini, Pesaro, Cesena, Cattolica, Fano, Senigallia, Jesi, Forlimpopoli, Forlì, Castrocaro, Montefeltro, Arcena, Monte di Lucaro, Serra dei Conti, Castello di S. Marino, Sarsina, Urbino, Cagli, Canziano, Gubbio, Comacchio, Narni, Rome and its surrounding countryside.

This time there was no way that Aistulf could disregard his engagements. Every territory was entrusted to Abbot Fulred, the plenipotentiary of Pepin, together with the keys of the cities and the delivery of hostages. The keys were deposited with the new document of the donation of Pepin at the Confession of St. Peter (in the basilica) and everything became the eternal property of the Apostle's representative and his successors. It was the summer of 756, and the Papal States were born.

Shortly thereafter, Aistulf passed away, and Stephen II informed Pepin of it by a letter truly unworthy of a pope, in view of the ignoble words with which he raged against a dead person. That "tyrant, disciple of the devil, who wanted to drink the blood of Christians and ruin the churches of God," he wrote among other things, "was stabbed by the divine dagger and cast into the depths of hell."

Desiderius, duke of Tuscia, was elected the new king of the Lombards on 7 March 757. Having seen how events were proceeding, he thought it wise to make friends with the pontiff. He therefore turned over to him some cities which were still Lombard, such as Bologna, Imola, Osimo, Ancona, Faenza, and Ferrara. Stephen II accepted them gracefully while Ratchis, the former Lombard king, who had left the monastery to reclaim his rights to the throne of his deceased brother, terrorized by the threats of excommunication, decided to put back on his monk's tunic.

Stephen II had ended by being feared by the sovereigns as the ever more fiery tone of his letters bears witness, and which helps to explain the behavior of persons such as Desiderius and Ratchis.

However, leaving aside politics, this pope managed also to do something religious in the building area. He restored the basilica of San Lorenzo and, close to the atrium of St. Peter's, erected a campanile which he had covered with gold and silver. Moreover, he built near the basilica of the Prince of the Apostles the chapel of St. Petronilla, thought to be the daughter of the fisherman of Galilee. The sanctuary was raised in honor of Pepin, adopted son of St. Peter. From this point of view, even the building work was fused with the political. Then he founded a significant number of inns for pilgrims, since religion and tourism went hand in hand in the new Pontifical State for a flourishing economy.

Stephen II died, at the acme of his political power, on 26 April 757, and was buried in St. Peter's.

9 3. ST. PAUL I (7 5 7 – 7 6 7)

With the tremendous worldly power and the prevalently political aspect that the Throne of Peter was assuming, factions competing for the election of the new pontiff now re-emerged.

Stephen II was still on his deathbed when the philo-Byzantine party, which wanted to resume good relations again between pope and emperor, proposed its candidate in the person of Theophilactus. Against him was pitted the brother of the not-yet-deceased pope, the Deacon Paul, who had been at his side during his entire pontificate. He won since two brothers succeeding each other in the papacy was supposed to assure an identity of viewpoints. Paul I was consecrated on 29 May 757.

The new pontiff informed Pepin of his election by letter, praising the *patricius Romanorum* as the "new Moses and David." The king replied with a congratulatory letter, asking him to be a godfather to his daughter, Gisella, and sending the pope a tuft of the little girl's hair to mark his favor. Pepin also wrote a letter to the nobles and to the Roman people urging them to remain faithful to St. Peter, an obvious sign that he was aware of the opposition which was fermenting within the populace and the clergy as a result of the Francophile policy which the pontiff intended to follow. The response to this letter was probably entrusted to a pontifical notary, in view of its obsequiously official tone, but in substance the Romans officially recognized the pope as their *dominus* and paid homage to the king as the pontiff's protector.

Relations with the Lombards, however, were very uncertain. The handing over of Bologna, Imola, Osimo, and Ancona, promised as a donation to Stephen II, had not yet taken place and King Desiderius wanted to settle old accounts with the dukes of Spoleto and Benevento. In fact, he attacked them and Alboinus wound up in jail while Luitprand fled from Benevento and found refuge at Otranto. Desiderius chose as duke of Benevento his vassal, Arichi, who, once he had reached Naples, met the imperial envoy, George, and began negotiations for a Lombard-Byzantine alliance which was supposed to oppose the Franco-pontifical one. But Byzantium was not really ready to break with the Franks.

Despite this situation, Desiderius came to Rome at the invitation of Paul. The pope wanted to placate the anger of the Lombard king and, at the same time, to remind him to hand over the four cities. Desiderius replied ambiguously and demanded instead the return of the hostages which Aistulf had had to send to Pepin's garrison as a guarantee of the armistice. The pope pretended to be in agreement and, once he was free of Desiderius, sent Pepin a letter in which he complained of the devastation caused by the Lombards and begged him not to release the hostages.

There seemed to be no solution. Desiderius continued to keep his cities and the property of the Church, while Paul went on sending complaints to Pepin, but without his brother's convincing force. The Lombard king confiscated more land in the territory of Senigallia and set up a garrison in a castle in Campania.

Byzantium, which had not yet abandoned its hope of reconquering imperial Italy, at the expense of the new Pontifical State, preferred to await events, avoiding any direct conflict with Pepin. Instead, it raised more and more disputes with Rome on the religious level and, at a council in Constantinople in 754, condemned again the veneration of images. Indeed, ignoring the opinions of the pope, Constantine V sent ambassadors to Pepin's court with the purpose of convincing the Frankish king to approve the decisions of that council for the West. But Pepin did not give the matter the slightest consideration and renewed with Paul I his inviolable Orthodox faith, while the veneration of images was approved at a council in 767. Two years previously, through the mediation of Frankish legates, even the differences with Desiderius had been settled by a reciprocal restitution of each one's individual rights. The exchange took place under mixed commissions and by individual cities in the frontier territories.

Like his brother, Paul I also spent time on the construction of religious buildings, linking his name in particular to the building of the convent of St. Sylvester in Capite. He died on 28 June 767 and was buried in the oratory of the Blessed Virgin which he had had built in the Vatican. He was canonized in the fourteenth century.

94. STEPHEN III (768–772)

Ambition to sit on the pontifical throne, now the unequivocal symbol of power, gave rise to heady aspirations not only among various levels of the clergy, such as presbyters, deacons and subdeacons, but within the lay circles too. The concept that even a common citizen could become pope began to make headway. Noble and popular factions, fighting over material interests, surfaced again, and while Paul I lay seriously ill in the monastery of St. Paul, they were already in dispute over who was to succeed him.

Paul I's successor was not named, however, until thirteen months after his death. This was a real case of a "vacant see," and out of the whirlpool of popular uprisings two usurpers succeeded to the throne of St. Peter, both subsequently considered antipopes.

As soon as he heard that Paul I was on the point of death, the duke of Nepi, Totone, together with three of his brothers and an armed band hastened to Rome and got involved in a series of negotiations with the nobles of the city to put his brother Constantine on the throne. The chief prelate, Christopher, who should have served as the vicar during the vacant see period, was not prepared to oppose the lay forces and had abandoned the dying pope ostensibly to set up a regular election. However, terrorized, he had hidden himself with his children. Paul I died in the presence of only Cardinal Stephen on 28 June 767 and the next day Rome already had a new pope.

Totone had gathered together the majority of the Roman patricians at his palace and, in the threatening presence of his armed troops, had his brother Constantine elected. He then led him to the Lateran. There a small problem arose as Constantine was not a priest but an ordinary layman. But this did not stop Totone. He forced the bishop of Preneste, George, to name Constantine an acolyte and then grant him, one after the other, the orders of subdeacon and deacon in the oratory of St. Lawrence. The following Sunday, 5 July, this same George was able to consecrate him pope at St. Peter's.

It was a clearly illegal election, chiefly because all the clergy had been excluded, and they had absolute precedence in the right to vote. Nevertheless, Constantine, guided by his brother Totone, had the effrontery to notify Pepin of his election, renewing the friendship of his "predecessors." The king of the Franks did not reply to that letter nor to a second one in which the new pope begged Pepin to ignore possible calumnies about him that might reach his ears.

Pepin was probably aware that something irregular had occurred, but he did not intend to interfere.

The reaction came from inside the Church itself. The chief prelate, Christopher, and his son Sergius, the pontifical sacristan, organized a conspiracy. They pretended to want to become monks, and Constantine, happy to be rid of two sworn enemies, allowed them to leave Rome and enter the monastery of the Holy Saviour. Instead, the two reached Pavia and denounced the scandalous situation to Desiderius, the Lombard king who, wishing to intervene in a papal election, agreed to provide an armed band and had them accompanied by his faithful presbyter, Waldipert. The group arrived at the Salarian bridge in Rome on 28 July 768, and the next day penetrated into Rome by the St. Pancratius gate. A series of armed conflicts took place along the streets during which Gratiosus killed Duke Totone, the brother-in-law of Sergius who, as reward, was elected dux of the Roman military district. Constantine fled to the Lateran with his other brother Passivus, but all resistance was in vain. They wound up in prison.

The rioting went on all the same and, on 31 July, Waldipert gathered together the pro-Lombard faction, went to the monastery of St. Vitus on the Esquiline and got hold of the presbyter Philip, who was taken to the Lateran and consecrated pope. An official banquet was even held for the high ecclesiastics and laymen, but by the next day his pontificate was already over. On 1 August, Christopher took charge as the chief prelate and demanded that Philip be sent away. The latter, without making any difficulties, withdrew to his monastery on the Esquiline while the pro-Lombard faction found itself surrounded by a crowd of extremely nervous clergy and laity who were determined to clean up matters in a mixture of pseudo-religious fanaticism and personal revenge.

Constantine, the usurper, dragged through the streets of Rome between curses and insults, was shut in the monastery of Cellanova on the Aventine and on 6 August, deposed. The eyes of the bishops and cardinals whom he had created were gouged out and Constantine suffered the same fate later at the personal initiative of Gratiosus. For the election of the pope agreement was reached on the candidate proposed by Christopher, that presbyter Stephen, titular of Santa Cecilia, who had stayed clear of the riots and who, moreover, had tended to Paul I during his final agony.

So Stephen III was consecrated on 7 August 768, but the tumults did not immediately die down. Even the presbyter Waldipert, who had sought to put on the papal throne a person obviously trusted by the Lombards, was the victim of the Romans' thirst for vengeance. Having fled to the Pantheon, he was discovered hiding behind the statue of a saint, thrown into jail and savagely slain. This event simply increased the open contrasts with which Stephen III began his pontificate, so he decided to write to Pepin, inviting him to send some bishops of the

Frankish church to the council which he intended to convene in Rome to clarify once again legal questions regarding pontifical elections. The sons of Pepin replied to that letter, as Pepin had died on 24 September 768 and Charles and Carloman assured the pope they would send twelve bishops to Rome, including Turpin of Reims.

The council began at the Lateran on 12 April 769, and the first meeting was a trial of Constantine, lasting two days, which ended with the beating up of the accused man who, though blinded, had defended himself ably, citing in example other bishops, such as Sergius and Stephen of Naples who also had reached the pontifical throne, although simple laymen. This was true but it aroused the resentment of certain priests who attacked Constantine in the plenary council, kicking and trampling on him and then dragging him outside. And though his end is unknown, it is easy to guess what happened. All of which hardly lent prestige or decorum to an assembly presided over by a pope. The council obviously burned the official documents of the false pope and, as far as the pontifical election was concerned, it was decided to forbid participation by lay persons, leaving to them only the right to acclamation.

However, Stephen III deluded himself if he thought that he had cleaned up the ecclesiastical milieu in Rome, since the true masters of the city remained Christopher and Sergius. Belonging to one of the noble families, they could rely on a great number of followers, and they were ready to battle to the bitter end for the supreme power, now that they had had a military force at their command. Above all, they were determined to make use of the pope for their own purposes, deeming him a puppet of theirs.

Stephen III was aware that he had fallen into a vicious circle. The sons of Pepin the Short were themselves in disagreement because of the division of the kingdom, so he had little to expect from the Franks. He did not want to be a toy in the hands of two puppet masters like Christopher and Sergius, and decided secretly upon a rapprochement with the Lombards. For the negotiations, he used as his intermediary Paul Afiarta, the head of the Lombard party in Rome.

Desiderius announced in 769 his pilgrimage to Rome with an army in tow. When Christopher and Sergius heard about this, they ordered the gates to be closed and, supported by Count Dodone, the ambassador of Carloman, they urged the people to prepare for a possible attack. The Lombard king arrived in Rome in the summer of 771 and invited the pope to a meeting outside the walls, and while Christopher and others did not oppose the meeting they were on the alert. The plan of Desiderius envisioned an uprising of the people, fostered by Afiarta, with the aim of eliminating Christopher and Sergius. The latter, however, prevented the manoeuvre and attacked the Lateran by surprise. Where, remaining very calm, Stephen III succeeded in placating the public which, with swords withdrawn, was threatening him.

He thus turned the situation to his favor and, having discredited the people's two chiefs, withdrew safely to St. Peter's under the Lombard escort of Afiarta. The population, fickle as ever, felt they had been fooled, and even Gratiosus abandoned the two and joined the pope in St. Peter's. Seeing how badly things were going, Sergius attempted to flee by scaling the walls but his and Christopher's fate were already sealed. Afiarta had no mercy: Sergius was strangled and Christopher died from the beatings he suffered.

Stephen III sent a detailed report on these events to Charles who had lamented the manner in which the defenders of the Frankish party had been treated. He recounted the armed assault by Christopher, Sergius and Dodone, those "allies of the devil" and the threat to his own sacred self, saved thanks to the intervention by Desiderius, who had finally agreed to surrender all the lands belonging to St. Peter. In other words, he had trespassed almost in order to be pardoned.

Certainly, Charles could hardly be happy with these developments. Although allied with and related to Desiderius, having married his daughter Desiderata, and his sister Giselle having married Adalgisus (the Adelchi of Manzoni), he could not tolerate that Desiderius take his place as *patricius Romanorum*. But Stephen III himself was to regret this temporary political reversal in Rome in favor of the Lombards, because Desiderius did not keep his promises and refused to return the properties of St. Peter.

Stephen III did not prove to be a clever politician, and even the administration of the provinces, which formerly belonged to the Greeks, was not going well. The pontifical officials, whether duces or magistri militum, were unsuccessful in controlling the new lands.

But at last something happened to the advantage of the pontiff. On 4 December, Carloman died and Charles (historically known as Charlemagne, or "Charles the Great") became the sole sovereign and, moreover, separated from Desiderata.

This was a marriage which the pope had always viewed in a bad light, not so much because Charles was already married, but chiefly because, as Stephen III reminded him in a letter, having sworn as *patricius* to be the friend of the friends of the popes and the enemy of their enemies (in this case, the Lombards), he had committed a sacrilege. "If anyone dares to behave in defiance of our exhortations, know that, by the power of my Lord, the holy Prince of the Apostles, he will be enchained by the edict of anathema, ejected from the Kingdom of God and condemned to burn in eternal hellfire with the devil and his terrifying infernal procession, among all the other godless people." he concluded in his letter.

That marriage lasted only one year and Charles repudiated Desiderata not out of caprice or for fear of eternal damnation, but rather for reasons of self-interest. And this was perhaps the only genial political act on the part of Stephen III. The marriage failed by virtue of the pontiff's intervention and, because of these maneuvers, the alliance between the Franks and the Lombards was dissolved, the Roman Church was again closely bound with Charles, and Desiderius was doomed to ruin.

Stephen III did not live long enough to see the triumphant results that would come from all of this. He died on 24 January 772 and was buried in St. Peter's.

95. HADRIAN I (772–795)

Pope Hadrian I was unanimously consecrated on 9 February 772. A Roman, of a noble family which owned a palace in Via Lata, he had been a deacon under Stephen III.

His first act as pontiff was to recall to Rome all the followers of the pro-Frank faction of Christopher and Sergius who had been sent into exile by Afiarta, leader of the pro-Lombard faction during the pontificate of Stephen III. He thereby showed his firm intention to continue the policy of good relations with the Franks. In fact, when the legates of Desiderius showed up to congratulate him on his election, Hadrian complained, demanding the immediate return of St. Peter's territories.

Desiderius realized that it was useless to insist on an alliance with the pope, and that strong measures were needed. In the spring of that year, Gerberg, the widow of Carloman, went with her children to Pavia to implore Desiderius's help in reclaiming her right to the lands of which her husband had been king, but appropriated by Charles. Desiderius welcomed them with open arms and took them under his protection in the hope of fomenting civil war among the Franks. For this reason, he asked Hadrian I to crown Gerberg and her children. When the pope quite logically refused, he took military action and occupied the duchy of Ferrara, placing Ravenna under siege. Ravenna naturally asked the pope for help.

The man most suited to convince the king to lift the siege appeared to be Paul Afiarta, who had every interest in strengthening his faction in Rome by a diplomatic success, and Hadrian sent him as his ambassador, while secretly intending to get rid of him.

As soon as he had left, a trial was initiated against the leaders of the pro-Lombard party who had participated in the assassination of Sergius. Some were executed, others were exiled, including Afiarta, who was sentenced in absentia. The remains of Christopher and Sergius were exhumed and buried with honors in St. Peter's, where they received posthumous rehabilitation.

The conviction of Afiarta was communicated to Leo, the archbishop of Ravenna, who was asked to arrest Afiarta upon his return from his mission to Desiderius and his arrival in the exarchate, and to exile him to some place in

Greece. But Leo went beyond the decisions of the court in Rome and had Afiarta arrested at Rimini where he had him tried, convicted and executed by the magistrates of Ravenna. Hadrian openly reproved the excessive "zeal" of the archbishop, which in reality pleased him. By eliminating the leader of the pro-Lombard party, the pope had made Desiderius lose the last possibility of exercising his own power within Rome.

However, behind this rehabilitation of Christopher and Sergius, one can recognize the first signs of papal familial favoritism. Indeed, support in Rome of the pro-Frank party really could be linked to the ascent of the family of Hadrian I. His relatives were put in charge of most important matters of state and appointed to the supreme courts, and his uncle, Theodatus, already consul and dux, became the chief prelate. Among the *iudices*, or "palace ministers" to whom were entrusted the highest administrative and judicial positions, were the pope's nephews. In short, it was the beginning of nepotism, that plague of family clientelism which was to characterize so much of the history of the pontifical State.

The transformation of the papacy from its originally spiritual nature into a political one gave birth to another negative factor; like in any monarchical state, power became a family matter.

The Lombard reaction was logical, and Senigallia, Montefeltro, Urbino and Gubbio were taken over. The delegation sent by Hadrian to Desiderius was ingenuous and ridiculous. Twenty monks from Farfa, headed by the abbot, threw themselves at the feet of the king and wept, pleading with him not to damage St. Peter's. They were not even given a reply, as Desiderius wanted a face-to-face meeting with Hadrian. The pope informed the king that he would meet with him only after the restitution of all the old and new territories occupied by the Lombards, but the king would have none of that and threatened to march on Rome.

At this point the pope felt it opportune to send a delegation to Charles, who was busy stopping border scuffles and raids from Saxony and was not really aware of was happening in Italy. The papal emissaries met with the Frankish king at Diedenfogen and declared that Desiderius had not returned the lands which belonged to St. Peter. But the Lombard king also sent a delegation to Charles, declaring that the claims of the pope were groundless as everything had been returned and that no invasion was underway.

Meanwhile, Desiderius began his march on Rome. Hadrian did prepare a defense but thought it would be more productive to rely on his personal religious authority, using methods that had worked at other times. He sent the bishops of Albano, Preneste, and Tivoli to the Lombard king to forbid him, under pain of excommunication, to cross the border of the Roman duchy. Perhaps Desiderius merely wanted to frighten the pope, or perhaps he did fear the anathema. The fact remains that he withdrew to his own territory.

Soon afterwards, a Frankish delegation arrived in Rome, which included Albinus, the king's counsellor. Charles wanted him to find out if, in fact, Desiderius had restored the cities to the pope, as he had declared, and the emissaries established that, contrary to his assurances, the Lombard king had not honored the obligations which he had undertaken, and had invaded more territories. Hadrian also informed them about the requests of Gerberg and her sons.

The Frankish ambassadors then travelled to Pavia, but Desiderius refused to return the territories and persisted in his refusal even when offered 14,000 gold florins which a new Frankish delegation proposed to give him if the pope were finally to receive complete satisfaction. In brief, Charles wanted to avoid war, but the threat arising from the claims to succession of the sons of Carloman worried him more. So a committee of the twelve nobles (Pari, whom legend later called the Paladins) selected from among the most forceful and intelligent of the Frankish lands, met in Geneva and decided that war was now the only answer.

The military campaign began in September 773, and was carried out with a new strategy, involving two fronts. A military column from the St. Bernard, along the valley of the Dora, reached Ivrea, while the main body of the army, led by Charles, passed through Mont Cenis and headed for Turin. When Desiderius, whose troops were based as always near Susa, became aware that he was surrounded and no longer had time to face the enemy on an open field, he withdrew within the fortress of Pavia, which was besieged. Desiderius counted on help from Adalgisus who had gathered troops at Verona where Gerberg and her sons were. Charles defeated the latter in open field and forced him to flee. Unable to enter Pavia, Adalgisus retreated towards Constantinople. Gerberg resignedly surrendered to her brother-in-law.

Charles, aware that the siege of Pavia would take some time, called his wife Hildegard and their children to come be with him. As the winter was over, he decided to celebrate Easter in Rome. He crossed the Tuscia with a part of the army and arrived at Rome on 2 April, Holy Saturday while the Roman authorities, judges and standard-bearers of the militia went to meet him at Novas, south of Bracciano. A large crowd waving palm and olive branches were shouting greetings at the foot of Monte Mario, in honor of the *patricius Romanorum*. At this point, Charles dismounted and, accompanied by his Pari, went on foot the rest of the way to St. Peter's basilica.

The pope was in the atrium to welcome him, where the two embraced and then entered the church hand in hand, while the clergy chanted "Benedictus qui venit in nomine Domini." Charles and his company genuflected before the tomb of the Prince of the Apostles, thanking him for the victory achieved through his intercession. Then Charles expressed his wish to perform his pious acts in the

Seven Churches, and the pope granted him permission. On 6 April, when all the solemn Easter rites and religious visits had been completed, the political discussions took place in St. Peter's.

According to the *Liber pontificalis*, Hadrian held a clear-cut discourse in which, basically, he begged the Frankish king to maintain the promises of donation made at Quierzy. Charles charged the notary Itterius to draw up a document identical to the one signed by his father with a detailed list of the territories, and signed it together with his peers. Having had the document placed upon the altar of St. Peter, they then solemnly swore that they would observe the obligations in it. Charles was supposed to donate all that had already been promised by Pepin, that is, almost all of Italy plus some provinces never really conquered at that time, such as Corsica, Venice, and Istria, as well as the duchy of Benevento. The text of this "Donation of Charlemagne" disappeared, like that of Pepin, and doubts as to its existence were raised if gradually dissipated.

However, what happened right after this treaty gave rise to a different situation, to which the pope logically objected, and so the "promise" may well have been intended as such. In fact, after departing from Rome, Charles finally succeeded in conquering Pavia, leaving Desiderius and his wife prisoners in Frankish territory and bringing to an end the Lombard kingdom in Italy. He himself then occupied the throne of the defeated dynasty. On 10 July at Pavia he donned the iron crown, assuming the title of King of the Franks and the Lombards as well as that of *patricius Romanorum*. However, this latter title was accepted only after the pope was freed from the dangers which had threatened him and, as such, it was no longer necessarily bound with that of "defender."

Indeed, Charles, as king of the Lombards, had come into the possession of prerogatives that once had been those of the exarch of Ravenna. He was thus a *patricius*-exarch and hence "the protective duty assumed by the king of the Franks and the Lombards became, by a certain iron-willed logic, a supremacy over the pope and the young pontifical State," as Seppelt observed. Tangible evidence of the change in situation was that Charles returned home without having begun to put his donation into effect. The slow and gradual restitution of the lands belonging to St. Peter resulted from Charles's conviction that "the ambition to enlarge the papal territory no longer had any logical reason to exist, due to the fundamental change in the political relations with the ex-kingdom of the Lombards."

Hadrian I was to suffer considerably for this patrimony of St. Peter, and he wrote continuously to Charles, repeating incessantly his complaints. As Gregorovius notes they were a series of letters which "one reads with the utmost distaste, so great is the cupidity for these lands and the fear that they show of losing them. While the increase of temporal power is boldly called "the elevation of the Church," the acquisition of spiritual salvation is promised in compensation for gifts of land and people, and heavenly beatitude is tied to the sacrifice of material things. Worldly desires were concealed behind a sepulcher covered with deeds of donation, letters, excommunications and oaths, and this, in the name of a holy apostle who in life had not wanted to possess anything and in death had no knowledge of and even less any desire for earthly things."

Hadrian had his first problems with Archbishop Leo of Ravenna who, as soon as Charles had left Italy, seized various cities in the exarchate, throwing out the pontifical officials and installing his own people. He wanted to create an episcopal State of Ravenna in the name of St. Apollinaris, patron of Ravenna, in opposition to the State of St. Peter. Leo personally defended his case at the court of Charles, who supported him, and at his death in 777, the exarchate remained under Frankish control.

The pope had another disappointment, this time from Spoleto, which became independent under Duke Hildebrand who recognized the supremacy of Charles. Also the Lombard Duke Reginbald of Chiusi seized Città di Castello and other areas of the Tuscia, and lastly, the Lombard Duke Arichi of Benevento incited cities of Campania to rebel against the pope. Hadrian was desperate and showered Charles with rhetorical letters: "We await Your Highness, as sweet as honey, the same way the burnt earth cries out for rain." The king, overcome by the letters, finally proposed a visit to Rome once the war in Spain was finished, and this came about at Easter in 781.

The first act at the meeting was the baptism of Charles's four-year-old son, Pepin, for whom Hadrian was the godfather and, as occurred at the time of Pepin the Short with Paul I, godfather of Giselle, this event immediately solidified relations between the pope and the Frankish sovereign. After which they went on to define the territorial possessions of the pontifical State.

The pope's ownership of the Roman duchy, the exarchate, Pentapolis and the Sabine was recognized, but Hadrian had to renounce his claims on the Tuscia and Spoleto which remained within the jurisdiction of the Franks. As for Benevento, Charles pointed out that one had to await developments because Arichus was protected by Byzantium with which Charles wanted to maintain good relations. Indeed, in Rome he received a delegation from the Empress Irene who had become regent in the name of her son Constantine, a minor, for whom she requested the hand of Charles's daughter, Rotrud. The negotiations leading to this engagement were promptly concluded, after which Charles left Italy.

However, the regency of Irene was an important event for the Church of Rome. She declared that she was in favor of the veneration of images and, in 785, she invited the pope by letter to participate personally in a council that she and her son wished to convene in Constantinople to oppose iconoclasm. The pope was enthusiastic about this initiative and sent two of his representatives. The council was inaugurated on 17 August 786, in Constantinople, but a revolt of the imperial troops, fomented by some iconoclast bishops, caused postponement of the opening of the assembly and a change of location. Once the revolt was put down, the council was reconvened at Nicaea in September 787, and this council condemned the iconoclast council of 754 and approved the veneration of images. The ecclesiastical unity between Rome and the Church of the East was thereby resumed.

But the matter did not please Charles. Offended that he had not been invited to the council, at the least as *patricius Romanorum*, he felt that he, the most powerful sovereign in the West, had been put to the sideline. Moreover, in the report of the council which was sent to him that had been translated from Greek into Latin by the pope so that Charles would understand it, the term "adoration" of images was erroneously used instead of "veneration." This mistake was seized upon by Charles who promptly went into action to avenge the insult he had suffered.

First of all, he broke the engagement of his daughter, Rotrud, with the Empress Irene's son, and then turned to, shall we say, punitive action. By the autumn of 786 he had already advanced towards Benevento and forced Arichus to pay him a tribute to keep his duchy, as well as to hand over his son, Romualdus, as hostage. Then, when an imperial army led by Adalgisus was placed at the disposal of Arichus a year later to recover the duchy in a revival of the alliance with Byzantium, Charles undertook another campaign which routed the Byzantines. Arichus and his son Romualdus died, and another son, Grimoaldus, took over the duchy. At first Grimoaldus tried to be friendly with Charles, but when the latter was beset by problems with the Saxons and showed no interest in Benevento, continually claimed in vain by Hadrian I, Grimoaldus sided with Byzantium.

But graver for Rome were the steps that Charles took in revenge for the Council of Nicaea, determined to prove clearly his supremacy in the West, not only from a political but also from a religious viewpoint.

To begin with, he claimed his right to confirm the election of the bishop of Ravenna, having recourse to his title of *patricius*, arguing that the dignity of such a title would otherwise be reduced to nothing. But Hadrian defended himself well on this particular occasion with sophisticated diplomatic ability. Even St. Peter was invested with the purple band and, as patrician, opposed the *patricius* Charles. To be an opponent of St. Peter was to run serious risks, so it was thought better to put the question aside for the time being.

As for "adoration" of images, Charles was not prepared to back down and arranged, "by the will of God," to publish a series of documents that have come down through history with the title, Libri Carolini, in which sarcasm was used to fight the decision of the Nicaean Council, and which condemned the "adoration" of images supposed to serve simply as decorations in the churches. He had a summary prepared and sent it to Hadrian to approve and recognize the nullity of the Council of Nicaea. The pope refused to and responded calmly and firmly that Nicaea had approved nothing unusual but had settled an old argument that had separated the two Churches.

Charles did not give up and quickly convened a council at Frankfurt-am-Main in 794, to which Hadrian could scarcely refuse to send two bishops as representatives. The assembly adhered to what Charles laid down during the various sessions and concluded that images were not to be "adored," and that every decision by the council of Nicaea was null and void. The papal legates had to agree, and this time the pope could do nothing other than submit to someone stronger than him. The only consolation was the condemnation by the council of adoptionism, a heresy of that era which held that Christ as Man was simply the "adoptive" Son of God. Hadrian refused, however, to go along with Charles's request to excommunicate Irene and her son.

The subject of images had begun at Frankfurt with the incorrect interpretation of the term "adoration" as "veneration." But it had become an excuse to declare how much greater the political authority of the West was compared to that of the East, enough even to lay down the law on doctrinal disputes. And this interference by Charlemagne in ecclesiastical matters was not about to stop there.

Hadrian was nearing the end of his lengthy pontificate, one during which he had also been able to take care of the Roman duchy from a social point of view by actively concerning himself with the inhabitants and renewing the very face of the city, to the extent that one can speak of a true "Hadrian's Rome." Gregorovius defines this pope as "the restorer and renewer of the city" and recalls his efforts to rebuild the banks of the Tiber following a flood in 791, as well as the restructuring of the walls that had been the fortifications of an earlier period. Also important was the restoration of various aqueducts in several areas of the city, in particular the extension of several branches of the Acqua Claudia.

The *Liber pontificalis* recalls too that what Hadrian I did for the churches surpassed considerably his predecessors's work. With him Rome began to take on that monumental image of a Christian city which was gradually replacing the pagan one. At St. Peter's he renewed the main staircase of the atrium and the two ends of the four-door portico, embellished the campanile erected by Stephen II with two bronze gates, refurbished the mosaics, laid down a sheet of silver on the floor, covered the altar with wrought gold, and replaced the silver statues on the tomb of the Apostle with ones of gold.

He rebuilt the porticos of St. John Lateran, covered the atrium of St. Paul's with marble, restored the church of San Giovanni at Porta Latina with three naves, as well as the basilica of St. Mary in Schola Graeca—so called by the

Greek community which, having escaped from the iconoclasts of the East, established itself in the area around that bank of the Tiber behind the pagan temples of Fortuna Virilis and Vesta. The appearance of this church was substantially modified through a total reconstruction with three naves, still there, and an atrium, in addition to the magnificent restorations of the interior which gave it the new name of Santa Maria in Cosmedin, that is, "well decorated."

Finally, it should be recalled that Hadrian I worked towards a more efficient organization of papal lands in the Roman countryside. Pope Zachary had undertaken the building of farms, the *domus cultae*, which where entrusted to farmers in order to repopulate the area devastated by malaria. Hadrian I established others in an intensive development of agriculture and cattle breeding, the most famous of which was that of Capracorum, in the area of Veio, on land owned by the pope's family. The farm produced grain and grapes and had a vast number of pigs, and all the produce of this farm was sent to the Lateran to be given to the poor. It was a charitable work on a grandiose scale that this pope carried out in the form of a real refectory for the poor people.

But the times were extremely difficult, and I consider Seppelt's opinion correct when he states: "One cannot deny that Hadrian knew how to adapt to the situation with intelligence, nor can one fail to recognize the special importance of the results achieved both for himself and for the pontifical State. Indeed, less than perfect diplomatic shrewdness, an imprudent attitude in situations temporarily unchangeable, and an unyielding stubbornness would only have caused irreparable damage to the papacy."

Hadrian I died on Christmas Day, 795, and was buried in St. Peter's. On his tomb was placed a marble slab sent by Charlemagne with an inscription in gold letters written by the monk, Alcuin. One can still read it, fixed to the wall in the atrium of St. Peter's basilica, to the left of the main door.

96. St. Leo III (795–816)

The day following the death of Hadrian I, Leo, a Roman priest-cardinal of Santa Susanna, was unanimously elected pope. He was consecrated on 27 December 795, and was the third with that name.

As soon as he was elected, he sent Charles a letter, not to obtain approval of his nomination but to assure him of his loyalty and obedience, as indicated by the homage gifts which he dispatched with it, namely the keys to the sepulcher of St. Peter and the flag of the city of Rome. Those gifts were intended to mean that the pope attributed to him the authority of defender of the Christian religion through the use of arms, as symbolized by the flag, and also as the custodian of the sepulcher of the Apostle at the altar of the Confession upon which Charles had taken an oath in 774 with a "promise of donations."

In fact, Leo III was reminding Charles of his hopes that he would confirm to Leo the concept of *Mater Ecclesia*, as the symbol of the temporal power of the papacy, a thesis that was being launched at that time, at least in the minds of those at the pontifical chancellery. A clear demonstration of the interpretation that the pope intended to give to the division between the two powers, religious and political, unified in the Church that Christ had founded, was in the mosaic Leo III ordered and had executed between 796 and 800 on the two sides of a vaulted ceiling in a large room in the Lateran palace, the Triclinium. On one side, Christ, seated, gives the keys to St. Peter, the symbol of the religious power, and to Constantine the flag, sign of the political power, while on the other, St. Peter, seated, gives the papal cape to Leo III and the flag to Charlemagne. Above the two holders of power sits St. Peter, signifying the *Mater Ecclesia*, giver of the "power," or the very face of "power."

But Leo III was dreaming if he thought he had found his "faithful Paladin." Charlemagne was at the pinnacle of his power, and this co-existence of ecclesiastical and political authority in the pope and the new Constantine, who ought to have recognized a single power, that of St. Peter-*Mater Ecclesia*, was the farthest thing from his mind. It contrasted with Charlemagne's evident and conscious supremacy and who, despite his great respect for St. Peter, tended to combine both political and religious authority in his own person.

All of which was clearly expressed in a letter delivered to the pope by a royal messenger, Abbot Angilbertus of St. Riquier, who had been requested by Leo III to come to Rome to receive the oath of loyalty and allegiance from the Roman populace. While the king did send the pope his advice for the good administration of the Church, he added: "It is our duty to defend everywhere the Holy Church of Christ with the help of divine love and with arms against the attacks of pagans and the devastations by infidels coming from abroad, as well as to strengthen the Catholic faith within. To you, on the other hand, Most Holy Father, as in previous times to Moses, belongs the task of assisting our army with your hands upraised, so that, with the blessing of God beseeched by your intercession, the Christian world will be forever and everywhere victorious over the enemies of the sacred name of God, and the name of our Lord Jesus Christ be glorified throughout the entire world."

Clearly, Charlemagne was convinced that the pope's actual influence had to be limited to that of being the most important metropolitan of the Church, while he, Charles, convinced of the religious aspect of his high office, assumed the responsibility of fostering and defending the Christian faith.

He assigned to Leo III the task of looking after the organization of the Church amongst the Avars whom he had conquered, but decided that the center of that mission was to be Salzburg. Indeed his interference in ecclesiastical matters had continued apace, ever since that second Council of Nicaea which had taken place without his having been involved. And it was Charles who ordered the pope to convene a council at Rome in 798 and to condemn once more the heresy which Felix of Urgel persisted in defending, despite the fact that this had been forbidden by the Council of Frankfurt in 794.

By then Charles had developed his concept that, while the pope remained the spiritual head of the Church, the king alone had to be the defender of this Church both outside and within it—a blow to the temporal aspirations of the papacy. Yet very soon it became evident to the pope of how necessary was the political supremacy of the king of the Franks.

In Rome, the faction of the nobility related to the previous Pope Hadrian I had not taken kindly to the the new pope's meek attitude towards Charlemagne, considering it a sign of weakness. The primicerius Paschal, together with the treasurer Campulus, sought to gain from the ambitions of the iudices by circulating rumors about Leo III, and accusing him of perjury and immoral conduct. Whispers of these even reached the court of Charles, but Archbishop Arno of Salzburg assured Alcuin, the trusted ecclesiastical advisor of the king, that they were lies.

Realizing that the king would not take any measures against the pope, Paschal and Campulus decided to foment a genuine conspiracy which would lead to the elimination of Leo III and to their accession to power. The opportunity arose during the traditional procession from the Lateran to San Lorenzo in Lucina, led by the pope on 25 April 799 for the feast of St. Mark. The pope was mounted on a horse and the conspirators assailed him near the monastery of St. Sylvester. They pulled him off the saddle and tried to gouge out his eyes and cut off his tongue, but the resulting turmoil was so great that they were able only to drag him into the cloister and turn him over to the Greek priests. This was a sign that the pro-Byzantine faction of the clergy was in league with the conspirators. When night came they took him to St. Erasmus on the Caelian hill, but the pope was able to escape from there thanks to the help of some of his faithful followers, among whom was the chamberlain Albinus. They lowered him from the wall by a long rope and carried him, battered but alive, to St. Peter's. At that point a large crowd of clerics and people lined up around the basilica preventing the conspirators from getting inside. The latter vented their wrath by pillaging the houses of Albinus and of the pope's relatives.

Then came the intervention of Duke Vinigi of Spoleto, by chance in Rome, who, the next day, took the pope to safety in his city. Meanwhile, the news of the attack had reached Charles who was involved with the Saxons at Paderborn. Leo wanted to go to him, but as soon as the king learned that the pope was safely under his protection, he sent a delegation with his own son Pepin under Archbishop Ildibaldus of Cologne. Leo received them with highest honors, but at the same moment a "memorandum" reached Charles from Rome from the conspirators setting forth the substance of their accusations and asking him to judge the pope's behavior.

Charles turned to his faithful Alcuin who probably had received from Archbishop Arno more reliable information, which this time partially confirmed the accusations. However, Alcuin in several letters to the king pointed out that no one could submit the see of Rome to a judicial proceeding and that he thought it would be damaging to the Church to depose the pope. It would mean discrediting him at a time when Charles himself needed an accepted pontiff. In fact he wrote, among other things: "Up until now there have been three powers in the world: the vicar of St. Peter, now insulted and rough-handled in a sacrilegious manner; the emperor, a layman, leader of the new Rome (Constantinople), who in no less barbaric a manner was toppled from the throne and replaced by a woman; and, finally, the royal dignity of Jesus Christ entrusted to you for the protection of Christians. Now this stands over all others in wisdom and power. Thus in you rests the salvation of Christianity. You therefore ought to take care of the head (Rome) first, and later you can take care of the feet (the Saxons)."

These were far-sighted words, written by a theoretician of the "theocratic" State which he found revived in Charlemagne. In fact, by referring to events in Constantinople, where Empress Irene, banned from the government by order of her son Constantine VI, had in 797 managed in her turn to overpower her son, have him arrested, blinded and immured in a monastery, and proclaim herself empress, Alcuin was reminding Charles that the imperial throne had been usurped and was to be considered a "vacant seat." Moreover, the pontifical throne would survive only by merit of Charles, authorized to act by that imperial flag which now God had assigned to him.

Certainly he had to act with great delicacy, and the negotiations at Paderborn in that autumn of 799 between the pope and the king remained secret, even if the essence of what happened is clear.

Leo III returned, accompanied by a large group of Frankish bishops and notables from France, to a triumphant welcome in Rome. Frankish diplomacy got to work amongst clergy, nobles and people of the city, put the accusers into a minority, and for the time being there was no trial. The bishops got together the documents of the judicial enquiry and sent them to Charles, along with the district chiefs of the revolt, transported to Frankish territory in order to avoid disorders. No judgment was issued since Charlemagne was to decide when he came to Rome.

And Charles, having settled the problem of the Saxons, arrived in November of 800 with his son, Charles, and an imposing escort of bishops and soldiers. He brought along with him the accusers of Leo III while his other son, Pepin, continued on south to seize the duchy of Benevento from Grimoaldus.

On 23 November, the pope went to meet Charlemagne at Nomento, twelve miles from Rome, with the clergy, the people and the militia, then returned to the city. The following day Charles entered solemnly into St. Peter's accompanied by a crowd of cheering prelates. On 1 December, the clergy, the nobles and Frankish and Roman citizens were summoned by the king to a congress, and the assembly met in St. Peter's.

Charles made a speech, saying that he had come to Rome to bring back order into the Church, that he would hear the protests of the citizens against the pope and then would decide on the innocence or guilt of Leo III. His authority was not to be challenged and the pope was to appear before the king's court like any common subject. Such was to be the procedure. But, in the course of the debates which lasted for three weeks, while the accusers failed to submit concrete evidence to the king and the figure of the pope himself was not crystal clear, the position supported by the Frankish bishops, evidently influenced by the distant Alcuin who had preferred to stay in his monastery at Tours, gained weight. They were convinced that the apostolic see could not be submitted to judgment, and declared it was "above all the Churches of God, since we ourselves are judged by Him and by his representative on earth."

Either Leo III had realized that the only way out was to submit to an oath of purgation, as Pelagius I had done before Narses, or else this move had been decided at Paderborn. So, on 23 December, in the presence of Charles and his nobles and before an immense crowd of clergy and laity, holding in his hand the Holy Scripture, the pope called God as his witness "before whose judgment everyone must appear" that he had not committed or arranged to have committed the crimes of which he stood accused. This oath of purification was deemed sufficient to establish the innocence of Leo III. His opponents were then recognized as guilty of the crime of lèse majesté and condemned to death.

However, the sentences were not carried out, due to the intercession of the pope who evidently feared that capital punishment would make some of the population even more hostile. The conspirators were instead sent into exile in Frankish territory.

Two days later, on Christmas night, the final act of the play took place. Charles, attending the ceremonies in St. Peter's, had just finished his prayers and was rising to his feet when Leo III placed on his head a splendid crown of gold, and those present shouted the triple acclamation which usually accompanies imperial coronations: "Long life and victory to Charles, the most pious Augustus, the great emperor and peacemaker, crowned by Almighty God." The crowd was certainly not "inspired by God and Blessed Peter, the Heavenly Gatekeeper," as the *Liber pontificalis* would have it. Neither had the pope, prostrating himself before Charles in order to render to him the homage given to the ancient emperors, made this historic decision on the spur of the moment, and even less can one imagine that Charles was not ready to receive that crown.

The very idea of an improvisation does not make sense with a pope who had been humiliated and who takes his revenge against a very powerful king to demonstrate the supremacy of the Church over a political leader, as a proof of the greater prestige of spiritual power as against temporal. Nor does what Eginard say ring true when he tells us about a Charles who appeared to be opposed to this action performed on him by the pope without his consent, so much so that had he had the vaguest idea of it that evening, he would probably never have entered St. Peter's. He was a great "actor" who played his part to the very end.

Even though the question was controversial and, in effect, unsolvable, I am personally of the opinion that the coronation was prepared at Paderborn, planned by a theorist like Alcuin, and that the pope had no better way both to save his throne and strengthen it. Indeed, the pope's action "conferred on the bishop of Rome an unrivalled prestige and a unique position which was later to take on an importance full of consequences," as Seppelt observes, because "only the future could reveal the very significant effects of an imperial coronation" carried out by the pontiff. For the moment, however, it was Leo III who footed the bill, since "everything fell into the hands of Charles, who remained the person who took the decisions, as he had been even before 800, and who interfered energetically and in an autonomous way even in the internal affairs of the Church. Indeed, with the imperial coronation the theocratic nature of the government was reinforced even more."

As for Byzantium, Charles did not worry initially whether or not his imperial title was recognized by that court. The official explanation which he furnished was the one reported in the *Annales Laurissenses*: "Since the Eastern throne was vacant and the Byzantine scarcely tolerated being governed by a woman, it seemed prudent to Pope Leo, supported by all the Fathers who convened in Rome, and the entire Christian world, to create emperor Charles, king of the Franks who governed Rome where the Caesars had always lived, as well as other parts of Italy, Gaul and Germany."

In substance, Charles let the pope take the responsibility for what had happened while he himself defined the attributes and limits of the title that had been assigned to him. As Ullmann noted, "to be the 'emperor' meant no more than being a king 'de luxe' who ruled over various nations," was the way Charlemagne saw it, which was why "he proposed being in the West what the emperor was in the East. His aim was to reach parity or co-existence with the empire of the East."

The ambassadors whom he sent to Constantinople in 802 had the task of conveying these views, but they found that Irene was no longer there. She had been dethroned and exiled to the island of Lesbos by a new usurper, Niceforus, who refused to recognize Charles. So the question was left in abeyance. However, in the West Charles was acting as the master, and his domination of the Pontifical State was clearly evident, overruling as he did Leo III even in strictly ecclesiastical matters. The question of papal territory was never really clarified. Charles's son, Pepin, had the title of King of Rome but he did not appear particularly responsive to the requests of the pope, and another journey by Leo III to visit Charlemagne in 804 may have defined the relationship between the kingdom of Italy and the Papal States, but there is no documentary evidence concerning the meeting.

In the theological area, a demonstration of the emperor's superiority over the pope came in connection with the symbol of the word filioque, which among the Franks and in Spain had been inserted in the "profession of faith" in the article on the procession of the Holy Spirit, which was meant to express that the Third Person descended from both the Father and the Son. The Church of Rome and the Eastern Church had never inserted this term though French monks from the monastery of the Mount of Olives in Jerusalem began to do so in the East in 808, giving rise to disorders there on Christmas night between the French and the Greek communities. The Greek monks turned to the pope for a decision on the question, but Charlemagne stepped into the picture and ordered his own theologians to draw up precise observations on the subject, to be discussed at a council convened for November 809 at Aquae Grani (now Aachen, Germany).

Insertion of the term filioque was decided upon, and Charles communicated the news to the pope through a delegation of bishops. Leo III submitted the report to an assembly which fully confirmed the Nicene-Constantinople Credo "in the Holy Spirit . . . who proceeds from the Father," but objected to the insertion of "and from the Son" in order to avoid a disagreement with the Eastern Church. The Frankish bishops who were part of the delegation did not like this and the pope could certainly not force them to give up a custom which already existed in their own country. Much later, however, the term filioque did find its way into the liturgy of the Church of Rome.

Finally, in 812, Charlemagne saw his imperial status recognized by Byzantium where a new emperor, Michael, had ascended to the throne, but it cost him dearly. In fact, it all happened at the end of a war which had been declared by Byzantium out of revenge against Pepin, king of Italy, and was waged chiefly on the Venetian lagoon and in Istria. The Byzantine put all their might into the struggle and succeeded in winning. As a result, Charlemagne ceded to Byzantium the possession of Venice, Istria, the maritime cities of the Italian south, Sicily, the Balkan peninsula and Asia Minor, while Michael acknowledged Charles as Emperor of the "Roman-Christian Western empire."

By now, however, Charlemagne was growing old. His two sons, Pepin and Charles had died, and he thought it wise to make his only remaining son, Louis, whom he himself crowned, co-emperor. Charlemagne died on 28 January 814, and was buried at what is now Aachen.

It all seemed too good to be true to Leo III who, feeling that a weight had been lifted off his back, immediately conceived a plan to free himself from imperial dominance and regain his own independence. First, he directed his energy on a vendetta against the followers of Paschal and Campulus, since he was unable to do so against them directly as they were in exile. But their supporters, having learned of the death of the emperor, set in motion a conspiracy to assassinate Leo III.

They were discovered, speedily tried for lèse majesté, condemned to death and the sentences were immediately executed. Learning about the pope's activity, Louis sent to Rome his nephew, Bernard, the new king of Italy, to make an investigation while the pope, in turn, sent his own delegation to the emperor to explain and justify the sentences.

However, the situation in Rome in 815 was chaotic. There were daily conflicts among the various factions and even farmers in Campania were in ferment. Meanwhile, the pope fell ill and Bernard succeeded in putting down the revolt, giving full powers to the duke of Spoleto who installed himself with his troops in Rome and carried out more death sentences.

Leo III died on 12 June 816, and was buried in St. Peter's.

9 7. STEPHEN IV (8 1 6 – 8 1 7)

The deacon Stephen, son of Marinus, a Roman of noble family, was elected pope only ten days after the death of Leo III, and was the fourth of this name. He was consecrated on 22 June 816.

His first act was to notify the Emperor Louis of his election, begging his pardon through his legates for the haste with which he had been consecrated, and sending him an oath of fidelity from the Roman people. The reasons for this haste were understandably linked with the tense atmosphere prevailing in Rome among the nobility, the clergy, the people and their various factions. The emperor understood this and quickly accepted the pope's desire to meet him to explain certain aspects of the local situation and of the Pontifical State.

The journey took place in September 816, and the meeting was held in Reims where Stephen IV was received with full honors. The pope and the emperor had a series of talks in which, one can be sure, the situation of the Pontifical State was discussed first, especially the privileges and immunities guaranteed to the Roman Church by the predecessors of Louis. The pope succeeded in obtaining pardon for the high prelates who were living in Frankish territory, so enabling them to return to Rome. Evidently Stephen was able to convince the emperor that this would be a good diplomatic move to win over parts of the population opposed to Frankish domination, and give hope for a return to calm.

But the fundamental event of this journey was the coronation of Louis and his wife Ermengard by Stephen IV in the cathedral of Reims. This was a second coronation, following the one of three years earlier at the specific request of his father, Charlemagne. This second coronation, however, had two important aspects.

The first was the symbolically interesting fact that the crown used was Emperor Constantine's which the pope had brought with him. Whether genuine or not, this crown was an added point of reference to the "Donation of Constantine," with all the consequences arising from the fact that the pope was transferring it to Louis.

The second element, essential for the coronation, was the "anointing," which had not been done for Charlemagne. Louis was called by Stephen IV the "second David," being "anointed by the Lord." By means of this ceremony the pope established a link between emperor and godhead; Louis was the depository of a divine intercession, of a grace obtained through the mediation of the pope. The anointing thus clearly distinguished the Western emperor from the Eastern one, never anointed because a direct descendant of the ancient Roman emperors, and making him a "favored son of the Roman Church" in a filial relationship as a result of which, as Ullmann notes, the emperor became "the military defender of the papacy, considered as the 'source' and 'mother' of the Universal Church," or even the "athlete of Christ" consecrated to "defend and protect the Church as the organized community of Christ in general, and for the papacy, as the government of the Church, in particular."

The anointment was a sacrament, which the pope had administered to a faithful believer, and as such, Louis could not fail in the obligations of a sacrament. It was a clever political move which put imperial authority into the arms of *Mater Ecclesia*, a political manoeuvre originated by Leo III which Stephen IV succeeded in bringing to fruition, even if no advantage could be derived from it at the time.

Three months after his return to Rome he died on 24 January 817. He was buried in St. Peter's.

9 8. St. Paschal I (8 1 7 — 8 2 4)

The day after the death of Stephen IV on 25 January 817, the Romans elected a new pope, unanimously choosing the abbot of St. Stephen, Paschal, the first of this name, consecrating him within twenty-four hours.

Three portraits of Paschal I have been handed down to us, a rare occurrence for popes of the Middle Ages. A long face, tonsured pate, and large eyes, he appears with practically identical features in the three mosaics still visible today in the Roman churches which were completely restored by him, namely St. Cecilia in Trastevere, St. Praxedis on the Esquiline and St. Mary in Domnica or della Navicella.

The consecration of Paschal I, even more hurried than that of his predecessor, shows how the Roman clergy tried on every occasion to block imperial interference in the election of the pope. Like Leo III, Paschal I also decided to inform the emperor immediately that the haste was only motivated by the wish to obviate the formation of other candidatures and conflicts among the factions still existing in Rome, but that nevertheless the election had been according to the rules. The ambassador was his legate, Theodore, who brought back to Rome not only the congratulations of Louis but also a *Pactum cum Paschali pontifice.*

This was a kind of diploma issued by the emperor which was like the one of the year before to Stephen IV. But with time, this "pact" had acquired a greater importance, forming part of those documents of pontifical history which had undergone clever falsification, and was comparable to the "Donation of Peppin," with all the updatings relevant to an amplification of the Pontifical State. The pope was supposed to have received as a gift from Louis the Pious not only Rome with its duchy and all those areas already donated and donated again by Peppin and Charlemagne, but also Calabria, Naples, Corsica, Sardinia, and Sicily, without taking into the slightest consideration the Byzantine empire under whose sovereignty fell Naples, Calabria, Siciliy, and Sardinia. All of which did not hold water.

Another very important point was the complete freedom granted by the emperor to the Romans in the election and ordination of the pontiff, even exempting these from imperial confirmation, which up until then had always been considered necessary. It would be sufficient, following the election or the consecration, to send the emperor some legates who, after rendering him a detailed report, would simply renew to him the old pact of allegiance.

It is precisely this last point which makes the authenticity of the *pactum* doubtful. When shortly afterwards the emperor insisted upon his right to collaborate in the papal election, the pope did not refer to any *pactum*, obviously because no such clause existed. It would be cited later at the time of Gregory VII and it is evidently to that time that one must trace the interpolation of this document, which could not have been anything but a renewal of the old promises about Frankish donations, never completely fulfilled.

In any event, Louis had more important problems to worry about, like the organization of the empire. So, in July 817, he gathered at Aachen an assembly of imperial nobles and obtained the approval of the document which has passed into history by the name of *Ordinatio imperii.* In it, imperial rank was assigned to the firstborn son, Lothar, who was immediately made co-emperor and the rank of the king was granted to the other two sons. Peppin of Aquitaine, received Gascony, the Spanish Marches, and Burgundy, and Louis of Bavaria, got Carinthia and the Eastern Marches. No mention was made of Bernard, son of Peppin, older brother of Louis the Pious, and formerly king of Italy, although he hoped to inherit at least that title; but it was an honor directly controlled by the emperor.

This *Ordinatio* most certainly would not have pleased Bernard, nor many of the lay and ecclesiastical dignitaries who saw Italy reduced to the status of an imperial province, and dignitaries urged Bernard to rebel and demand independence. Amongst these were the chamberlain, Eginardus, the king's counsellor Eggideus, Count Reginerius, the bishop of Cremona Valfoldus, and the archbishop of Milan, Anselm, who saw his position as primate being threatened. The pope merely took note of the *Ordinatio* sent to him by Louis and appeared to take little notice of the climate of rebellion which was spreading throughout Italy. In fact, Bernard expected to be supported in his resentment by his cousins Peppin and Louis but, faced with their father's huge army gathered at Châlons from all areas of the empire, they did not think it prudent to be on bad terms with him and they abandoned Bernard.

Bernard saw that he had lost and fled to Châlons to beg his uncle's pardon for himself and his accomplices. Louis had them put in prison and sent them to Aachen where in 818 took place two trials, one against the ecclesiastics and the other against Bernard. The former were judged by a council of bishops which condemned the bishops of Cremona and Milan to the loss of their ecclesiastical ranks and banishment to a monastic cloister, while Bernard was condemned by lay judges, at first to death and then to life imprisonment with the usual penalty of being blinded. This punishment was carried out, it seems, with a "technique" so barbarous that Bernard died a few days later.

Louis repented profoundly about the way he had acted and pardoned fully both the accomplices of his nephew and the bishops, and Anselm was able to return to Milan and enter the monastery of St. Ambrose. The pope does not appear to have done anything to alleviate the fate of the rebels, whether ecclesiastics or not.

In any case, the situation in Rome in those years appears somewhat wrapped in mystery. For two years the throne of Italy was unoccupied, then Louis decided to give it to Lothar, but sent him to Italy only in 822, basically to try and understand the situation there from administrative and judicial points of view. When he arrived in Pavia, Paschal begged him to come on to Rome, to be crowned and to receive the anointment, like his father.

Once Lothar had received his father's consent, he agreed to Paschal's request and was received in Rome with high honors, and on Easter Sunday of 823 at St. Peter's he was crowned emperor and acclaimed as Augustus by the people of Rome. It was an opportunity for the Pontifical Curia to reconfirm the principle that Rome was the imperial headquarters and that the anointment gave a divine character to the coronation, so putting Paschal in good light, since he performed the anointment. However, as usual the pope misdealt the cards by declaring that from that moment on Lothar could exercise authority over the Romans, a fatal mistake as Lothar promptly wanted to prove his authority by deciding on a lawsuit brought by the Monastery of Farfa against the Pontifical Court regarding the seizure of certain assets. He decided that it had been an unjust enrichment and that all of the assets in question had to be returned to the monastery.

It looked as if the temporal power of Paschal had suffered a significant blow. The Roman clergy were upset by Lothar's behavior while the Frankish nobility were so pleased that they even contemplated a revolution against the Curia. The leaders of the revolt were the chief prelate, Theodore, and Leo, the nomenclator, his son-in-law. However, the ecclesiastical reaction was immediate and violent. The two were arrested, blinded and decapitated. The news quickly reached Aachen and was received with resentment, because in 821 Theodore had been the nuncio of the pope at the imperial court, so the emperor decided to send some judges to carry out an investigation. For his part the pope, who had been openly accused of having ordered or at least suggested the assassination of the two, as well as having in fact abused power which belonged to the emperor, beat Louis to it by sending him ambassadors who declared that Paschal was innocent and was prepared to submit to an investigation.

At which the imperial judges departed and reached Rome in August 823, but were astounded to hear from the pope that he refused to submit to their jurisdiction because it was inadmissible and against all tradition to pass judgment on the primate of the see of Rome. He became the third pope to submit voluntarily to the oath of purification, but at the same time, cursing those he had condemned as guilty of high treason and declaring that their deaths were an act of justice. The judges returned to Aachen and the emperor decided it was best to suspend the investigation and drop the matter.

However, Paschal I, went to considerable lengths in his activity as a "man of the Church" with a social spirit, like when he gave shelter in the monastery of St. Prassede, built by him, to the Greek refugees from the East who were being persecuted for their anti-iconoclasm. There is also a legend that he ran to a district of Rome, inhabited by Anglo-Saxons, when this was destroyed by a fire which had also burnt the gallery attached to the basilica of St. Peter, and that he walked barefoot through the flames which suddenly died out, as if quenched by some superior force.

Also to his credit was the rediscovery of the tomb of St. Cecilia for whom he had restored the church in Trastevere. Try as he would though, Paschal I did not succeed in finding her corpse in the catacombs and he thought that perhaps the Lombards had stolen it. But then, according to the *Liber pontificalis*, he had a vision in the middle of a Sunday ceremony in the Confession of St. Peter when suddenly the angelic figure of a young girl appeared to him, in fact St. Cecilia, who urged him to continue to search in the cemetery of St. Calixtus. The search was fruitful, and the saint, wrapped in golden clothes was buried in her basilica together with her husband, Valerian, who had also been martyred.

One cannot agree with Bargellini who describes Paschal I as "a great pope who was blessed in his intentions and blessed in their achievement," just because of this social-religious side of his personality which was marginal in comparison to the political one. He behaved ambiguously in the duality of his power, or rather, as Gregorovius observes, he "was a victim of the contradiction between the two powers, temporal and spiritual, which formed part of his character." In fact, in the end he was hated by the Romans who would not permit his remains to be buried in St. Peter's deeming him unworthy of the honor. He died on 11 February 824 and was probably buried in St. Prassede's.

99. EUGENE II (824—827)

At the death of Paschal I, riots occurred during his funeral which led to real battles between the two warring factions, each of which aimed to have its own candidate elected to the throne of Peter. The clergy and the people supported a certain Sisinnius. However, the nobility, clearly on the side of the emperor, were able to enthrone Eugene, the Roman archbishop at St. Sabina on the Aventine, thanks also to the support given to this faction by Lothar's counsellor in Rome, a certain Wala.

Eugene II was consecrated in May 824, and the result of the election was transmitted to Louis by the subdeacon Quirinus, who renewed as usual the oath of allegiance and the pact of amity. However, news of the riots punctually reached Aachen where it was feared that they could continue even after the consecration of the pope. It was necessary to root out the causes of the discontent and to bring back public order in Rome with force to render the imperial claims within the Pontifical State legally binding. For this, the emperor sent Lothar again to Rome in August 824, where he arrived in the autumn.

His first act was to carry out a rigorous investigation of what went on during the pontificates of Leo III and Paschal I, followed by measures that earned the applause of the citizens when the properties confiscated from those condemned to death were returned to their families, and the authors of the penalties sent into exile.

However, the investigation brought to light especially the misfortunes afflicting the city and the bad government of the clergy. Eugene, while watching Lothar strike directly at the Pontifical Court, could not object to his forceful ways and as a result even people who had been close to him at the time of the election were sacrificed. For him the fundamental objective was to make sure that peace came back again to the Pontifical State.

To remedy the disastrous conditions of the pontifical administration in Rome, Lothar promulgated, on 11 November in the basilica of St. Peter, a famous constitution which determined the legal relations of the Pontifical State with the empire, and protected the rights of the citizens. The *Constitutio Lothari* contained nine articles and declared that all persons placed under the protection of the emperor and the pope were inviolable. It prohibited pillaging in the Roman countryside and in the lands owned by the Church, and ordered that the entire papal administration be placed under regular control through the establishment of two missi, one imperial, the other pontifical, both residents of Rome, who were to report annually to the emperor on the activities of every single State official. Finally, the procedures for papal elections were amended to readmit lay persons, with confirmation of the person elected to be obtained from the emperor before his consecration as pope, as indicated in the *Constitutio* which Lothar made the entire population of Rome swear to uphold.

These provisions represented the apex of imperial power over the Pontifical State. All the sweeping concessions granted a few years before in the *Pactum Ludovicianum* were annulled and, in effect, the Western emperor substituted the Eastern emperor in affirming complete sovereignty over the pope in the exercise of administrative and juridical powers in the Pontifical State. "I promise by Almighty God, by these four sacred Gospels, by this cross of Our Lord Jesus Christ and by the body of the Most Blessed Peter, Prince of the Apostles," the Roman people with the clergy and the nobles swore, "that from this day forward I shall be true to our Emperors Louis and Lothar for the rest of my life, with all my strength and intellect, without fraud or guile, maintaining the faith which I promised to the Apostolic Lord; and that I shall not, within my strength and intellect, permit that in this Roman see the election of a pope which is not done in accord with justice and canon law, nor shall I permit that he who shall have been elected with my approval be consecrated before he, in the presence of the imperial legate and the people, shall have taken the same oath that Pope Eugene, of his own will and for the benefit of all, has rendered in writing."

At this point, Lothar could depart from Italy satisfied, certain that he had done a good job. But this hegemony of the emperor, so clearly expressed in the constitution and so blessedly consecrated in the solemn oath, did not last very long. And the opportunity came to the pope precisely because of the wavering behavior of the emperor when the latter had to deal again with the iconoclastic issue which had broken out once more in the East.

The instigator of the iconoclastic policy was the new Emperor Michael II, the Stammerer, who after having reestablished the old laws against the cult of images, tried to involve his Western colleague, Louis, in the matter by sending to him in 824 a delegation whose purpose was to get him to bring pressure on Eugene II to spread iconoclasm in the West. Louis acted with rare diplomatic tact for an emperor, asking Eugene's permission to have the Frankish bishops prepare an opinion on the question to give to the Byzantine. Since this was already a concession, Eugene promptly gave his agreement, aware that Louis was thereby recognizing in him a certain authority on questions of exclusively ecclesiastical nature.

And so, in November 825, there was a conference in Paris of the Frankish bishops who brought forward the opinion expressed back in the days of Charlemagne, in substance contrary to the Nicene Council of 787, this time adding a declaration of the pope's accepted ignorance concerning the issue and stating that the pope should follow their version of the "truth." Louis did not want to impose on the pope the results of this conference, thereby giving further evidence of his "pious" nature and in effect acknowledging the prestige of the bishop of Rome. He merely sent Eugene an extract from the documents, deferring to him all decisions. The reply of Eugene II is unknown to us, but one may speculate on it from the council the pope convened in 826 in the Lateran at Rome in the presence of sixty-two bishops.

At this council there was no talk of iconoclasm, evidently because a precise opinion had already been expressed, but a good thirty-eight canons of ecclesiastical law were approved which in no way envisaged the eventuality of imperial approval. Amongst other questions they contained rules about the training of priests, about the tenor of life of the secular priests and monks, and about the election of bishops and their duties. The canons also called for instruction in literature and liberal arts to be provided to explain Holy Scripture in all parishes and wherever else there should be a need. This was an important development since it was the basis for the future nation-wide education of an entirely ecclesiastical type that Italy was to have for many centuries. However, this council, as Seppelt correctly notes, "also shows how the papacy energetically seized the management of ecclesiastical reform, previously carried out by Charlemagne with great zeal." It was a severe blow to the partial secularisation of the Pontifical State attempted by Lothar and also to imperial interference in ecclesiastical questions.

Eugene II died in August 827, and was buried in St. Peter's.

100. VALENTINE (827)

Valentine was a Roman, son of a certain Leontius from the Via Lata region. Very little is known about him, and his pontificate was destined to last no longer than forty days. We do not know the dates of his election, consecration or of his death, all of which however took place between August and September 827.

He had been elected a cardinal-deacon by Paschal I, but was a simple man and did not care for high office and even less for the power invested in the pontiff.

So, when in the Lateran one heard a voice from on high, who knows from whom it came, but taken as the voice of the Holy Spirit itself, which said: "The most holy Archbishop Valentine is worthy of the apostolic see!" the people, the clergy and the nobility rushed to the basilica of St. Mary Major where he was deep in prayer. He was amazed, protested that he was unworthy, declared his total lack of experience for such a high office, but was nonetheless carried in triumph to the Lateran and placed upon the throne. He was later consecrated in St. Peter's.

But poor Valentine was a weak and sickly man, and his heart probably did not stand the stress. There was not even enough time to notify the emperor of his election before he disappeared like a falling star, too "pious" for those times. He was probably buried in St. Peter's.

101. GREGORY IV (827—844)

A Roman from a noble family, presbyter of the Church of St. Mark, Gregory was unanimously elected on the death of Valentine, but his consecration, of which we do not know the precise date, took place only after imperial approval, following the rules laid down by Lothar. He was the fourth pope of this name.

During the first years of his pontificate, Lothar controlled the government of the Pontifical State. But these were the last vestiges of imperial authority because the empire was crumbling, rent by internal conflicts, and the problems of preservation of power among the sons of Louis the Pious were such that Rome took second place for him.

The *Ordinatio imperii* of 817 came up for discussion when Louis the Pious, who had remarried a certain Judith, had another son, Charles, for whom the empress wanted a kingdom. This led to rebellion against their father by the children from his first wife. Between 830 and 833 there were a series of conflicts which even brought about a temporary deposition of the emperor, and the struggle turned into a pitched battle when the troops faced each other near Colmar in Alsace.

At this point, Lothar asked Gregory IV to mediate in the dispute and restore peace. The pope accepted readily, appearing before Louis with a "factious" attitude, Gregorovius observes, as the Frankish bishops who were defending the position of the aged emperor were to realize. In fact, Gregory IV intended to exploit the situation in order to enhance his prestige before the Frankish church and later to put forward his temporal claims once the dispute had been settled. It is likely that his attitude was interpreted as a threat of excommunication, since the pope reminded the "Anointed of the Lord" of his failure to observe a deed inspired in him by God sixteen years earlier, but he had to return to Rome at the end without having achieved his aims. On their side, the Frankish bishops reminded the pope of his own oath of allegiance to the emperor, and threatened to refuse to obey him if he were to take the side of the rebellious sons.

What Gregorovius says is true: "This prince of the Church, called upon to perform the noblest mission of the priesthood, which is to placate seditious persons with talk of love and to bring peace to princes and peoples, had shown that he was thinking only about himself and aimed only at pursuing his own miserable self-interest." Back in Italy, Gregory must have begun to wonder whether he had been wise to accept Louis's invitation. Yet the latter did not abandon him despite their disagreement, since it would not have been to the emperor's advantage to have a pope who had lost prestige in front of other bishops.

Men Gregory trusted, such as Agobardus of Lyons, Wala of Corbie, and Pascasius Radbert, who advocated maintaining the kingdom of Italy, defended the rights of the pope against Louis. It was they who advised Gregory to write a letter to the Frankish bishops in a firm, authoritarian tone, but full of double meanings which underlined that papal power should always be considered by the bishops superior to imperial power because, as he explained to them, "you ought to have known that the task which falls to the pope of directing souls is higher than the earthly matters with which the emperor deals." It was in any case a diplomatic way to get the pope out of those political disputes in which he had been involved like a marionette, a symbol of a power which, at certain levels, appeared inconsistent. It should have been a lesson to the pope to be a man of the Church and nothing more, but he did not understand this and it was also because of his attitude that Colmar was nicknamed "the field of shame."

Meanwhile, the dismemberment of the empire proceeded as high politics demanded. Louis wound up isolated, betrayed even from within the ranks of his own army, and had to give in to his sons. He was imprisoned by Lothar at Soissons, in the monastery of St. Medardus, and his son Charles went into the monastery of Pruem. The empire was partitioned, but the three brothers were soon again in conflict because Louis the German took pity on his father, who had been excommunicated at Compiegne by a council of bishops loyal to Lothar, The son succeeded in freeing the father and giving him back his imperial throne.

At this point, Gregory IV became again a man of the Church and could not remain silent. He disapproved of Lothar's behavior and exhorted him to have mercy on his father, as his brother Louis had, pointing out especially that the excommunication was invalid because of the way in which it had been issued, and was only depressing for his father. Lothar replied that Gregory was not to meddle in imperial administrative matters, treated the pope with disdain and took revenge by seizing assets of the Church, pillaging and killing within territory of the Papal State.

When Louis the Pious died in 840, open warfare broke out among the three brothers, and the pope did not know which fish to hook. So he waited for the definitive outcome of the war in 843 with the famous Treaty of Verdun. Charlemagne's empire was broken up and divided among the various ethnic groups, and Germany, Italy, and France began to have their own particular national connotations. Lothar, as emperor, was assigned the entire kingdom of Italy, including even the city of Rome, and he named his son Louis II as king.

Gregory IV really played no role in these events. He had been employed as mediator in the disputes among the sovereigns, but only for their selfish ends, and every time he had tried to put forward some claims, some requests for compensation, he had only received small spiritual satisfaction. But he had remained outside the political game, and all told, as a person of importance, he had carried no weight.

Above all, his State was insecure and undefended. The Saracens, having conquered Sicily, were threatening from the south and Gregory IV feared an attack from the sea, which was why he fortified Ostia. In effect, he built a new city on top of the old one, surrounded it with thick walls and war machines on the parapets and called it Gregoriopolis, though the ancient name survived. However the question was, in the event of danger, would Lothar or Louis II have sent soldiers, or would the pope have had to make do with the scanty militia on hand?

Gregory IV rendered other services to his city by having the Acqua Traiana, that is, the Sabatine Aqueduct, reconstructed which had been restored by Hadrian I but had later fallen into ruins. He also rebuilt various country houses in the Roman Campagna destroyed during the uprisings under Leo III, including the important Galeria on the Via Portuense, as well as the farm colony called "the Dragon's" near Ostia, a beautiful villa with porticoes, which can be considered the first papal villa in Rome. And, lastly, he gave a new appearance to the Church of San Marco where he had been the presbyter. It was during that restoration that the mosaics were created in the tribune where the image of this pope appears between Christ and some saints.

Gregory IV died in January 844, and was buried in St. Peter's.

102. SERGIUS II (844—847)

At the death of Gregory IV, the majority of the clergy and the nobility elected Sergius, the archpriest holding the title of the church of Saint

Sylvester. But he was opposed by the deacon John who, supported by a large part of the populace, had himself brought into the Lateran and, having taken over the palace, set himself upon the pontifical throne. However, the nobles got together the militia and marched to the basilica of St. Martin, where Sergius had found refuge and acclaimed him as the pope, escorting him in a procession to the Lateran. John had been abandoned by his supporters and was put in jail, and, according to the *Liber pontificalis*, on that day, at the end of January of 844, a heavy snow fell in Rome, which was considered to be a good omen. John was condemned to death but, thanks to the intercession of Sergius, was instead sent into exile.

The consecration of Sergius II took place immediately in St. Peter's, without informing the emperor or awaiting his approval. The reasons for this were the chaotic situation resulting from the election and the desire to put a stop to the disruptions, as well as the awareness that imperial authority was on the decline.

However, Lothar did not accept the matter with good grace, and in the spring of 845 sent his son, Louis, king of Italy, there with a cortege of nobles and clergymen, including Drago, bishop of Metz, the imperial chief chaplain. Understandably, the pope was concerned and, wanting to be warned of any unexpected attacks sent the *iudices* and high representatives of the clergy to receive him with all the honors nine miles outside the city. He informed Louis that it would be best for the army to encamp outside the city walls, which was what happened, probably in the area of the Neronian Fields.

When Sergius II saw Louis arrive at St. Peter's basilica, he awaited him on the steps and embraced him, but he did not let him enter until the king had declared that he had come to Rome for the good of the Papal State and of the Church, forcing him to declare that he automatically recognized the sovereignty of the pope over ecclesiastical property, of which the basilica was a part. Then took place the solemn entrance to the strains of the hymn "*Benedictus qui venit in nomine Domini*" and Sergius managed to obtain all the respect due to a pope as if he had had the emperor's approval. He personally had the upper hand, even though it was quickly confirmed in the course of the discussions between him and Louis II that, in the future, no pope could be consecrated without imperial approval.

That question having been settled, the pope anointed Louis on 15 June 845 and crowned him king of Italy, after which the latter made claims to which he was not legally entitled, demanding an oath of allegiance from the leaders of the Romans. Their refusal was supported by Sergius II, who courageously declared: "I give my consent for Romans to give an oath to their supreme leader, Emperor Lothar, but neither I nor Roman patricians will ever permit the same oath to be given also to his son" who was merely the king of Italy. And Rome could not be considered merely a city of the Italian kingdom.

In other words, the attempt by Louis to put Rome and the papacy under royal authority failed.

Sergius II tried to better their relations by condescending to nominate Drago Apostolic Vicar in Gaul and Germany. He showed a certain political acumen in the wielding of his authority, which however did not exclude a brazen form of nepotism linked to a scandalous selling of bishoprics. In particular, Sergius II's brother, Benedict, bishop of Albano, was noted for very serious abuses to the detriment of the people in his diocese.

And the people ended by interpreting the invasion of Rome by the Saracens in August 846 as a divine punishment. Ten thousand of them in seventy-five ships dropped anchor at the mouth of the Tiber where the fortifications of Ostia were inadequate to stop them. On 25 August the Saracens were in Rome, where the main body of the Roman army succeeded in repelling the attack and in defending the city on the left bank of the Tiber protected by the Aurelian Walls. The horde of pirates then crossed over to the right bank of the river, and the handful of Frankish militiamen who lived in the Borgo had to surrender. The basilicas of St. Peter and St. Paul were sacked.

Lothar and Louis made no move to assist Rome. Only Marquis Guido of Spoleto ran to help and, with the local militia, managed to defeat the Saracens at Civitavecchia and push them back to the sea. But by then the precious treasures of the two basilicas were in the hands of the pirates, and many *domus cultae* of the Roman countryside had been destroyed. Certainly imperial prestige was diminished under the circumstances since the sacrosanct protection of St. Peter had not taken place. Lothar realized that the Papal State was slipping from his grasp so he sought to make up for this with a collection organized throughout the kingdom for the restoration of the damaged basilicas, and by starting a military campaign against the Saracens, who were temporarily driven from southern Italy.

Rome had suffered, but the pillage worked to the advantage of the temporal power of the popes, appearing as a condemnation of imperial disinterest, which was to have a part to play in the effective autonomy of the Papal State in the future.

Sergius II died on 27 January 847, of a "broken heart," as Gregorovius put it, over a city in the throes of famine and misery and for an ill defended power. It would be the hearts of other popes that would beat in a Rome both rich and powerful. He was buried in St. Peter's.

103. St. Leo IV (847–855)

On the death of Sergius II, the choice of a new pope fell on Leo, cardinal of Ss. Quattro Coronati, a Roman, formerly subdeacon of Gregory IV and archpriest during the period of Sergius II. The election was held in great haste and, even if the emperor was informed of it, his approval was not awaited as the Romans were afraid of more invasions by the Saracens and wanted to have a new pope as rapidly as possible.

Leo IV's consecration only took place, though, on 10 April 847, and Lothar did not voice any resentment, perhaps aware of his debt to the citizens who had been recently left to their own devices during the sacking of the city by the Saracens.

On top of that, Rome was struck, early that year, by an earthquake followed by a fire that devastated the quarter of the Anglo-Saxons which had already been damaged under Paschal, and the basilica of St. Peter, as it then existed, risked destruction when the flames reached the portico. But the miracle worked by Paschal I was repeated and, according to the popular belief, Leo IV was able to stop the spreading fire by a simple Sign of the Cross. The fire in the Borgo was later immortalized in a fresco by Raphael in one of the rooms of the Vatican, duly named the Room of the Fire.

However, there was still a threat of danger from the Saracens, who had shown up again and were besieging Gaeta. It was evident that, sooner or later, they would return to Rome, attracted by the rich booty they had seized during the previous expedition. It was necessary to hurry the overall restoration of the walls, a task that was performed between 848 and 849, making use, in part, of the funds which Lothar had ordered to be collected following the Saracens's sacking three years earlier, and the pope himself supervised and urged on the work. All the gates were fortified by reinforcements of iron bars, and fifteen towers were rebuilt, two of which near Porta Portuense were so placed that a chain could be stretched between them.

Meanwhile, the Saracens came closer and, after stopping over in Sardinia, were making for Porto. It was 849 and the pope launched an appeal to the coastal cities of Naples, Amalfi, and Gaeta to join their fleets in a league for the defense not only of Rome, but also of their own commercial trade that had been damaged by the incursions of the Arabian pirates. The treaty was duly concluded and was a memorable event in medieval history. Command was entrusted to Cesarius, son of the duke of Naples, and he ordered the united fleets to be stationed at the entrance to the port of Ostia. Leo IV gave his solemn benediction and returned to Rome full of confidence.

Victory went to the Christians but it was facilitated by a terrible and sudden storm, which destroyed a large part of the Saracens' fleet, and many of their crew members were taken prisoner. After this event, which was also immortalized by Raphael in a fresco in the same Room of the Fire in the Vatican salons, Leo IV pointed out to Lothar that a new wall was needed in Rome to protect the area of the right bank of the Tiber, that is, the Vatican, thus walling in the whole quarter.

That was the origin of the "Leonine City," a grandiose project for which all the Church's public patrimony was used, not only in Rome but also that of all the monasteries. Emperor Lothar obviously could not but increase his own contribution as a high level defender, if only in words, of St. Peter. The *Civitas Leonina* was completed in 852 and the inauguration with a grand celebration and procession along the whole wall took place on 27 June of the same year.

The fortification work was expanded to include the surroundings of the city, and the areas struck by the incursions of the Saracens were also repaired, such as Ostia, Portus, Centocelle, Tuscia, Orte, and Ameria. And of course new splendour was provided to St. Peter's and St. Paul's, as the two basilicas were refurbished with additional precious vessels and vestments, a sign that the treasury of the Church was, in fact bottomless. In particular, the main altar of St. Peter's was newly covered with layers of gold, each one weighing 206 pounds, and adorned with precious stones, while there was a beautiful display of candelabras and chalices sprinkled with jewels all over the place.

In 850 Lothar requested the pope to proceed with the coronation of his son Louis as emperor. This took place on Easter Sunday and again, because the pontiff conferred it, it became an ecclesiastical matter and an exclusive privilege of the pope, in other words a symbol of his prestige. The *Constitutio Constantini* was still in vigor and the "Pseudo-isidorian Decretals" which were being prepared in those years would confer additional privileges on the Church, such as to free it entirely from the empire and make it definitively a clerical State along the lines of the *Mater Ecclesia*.

Leo IV spent the last years of his pontificate convening two councils at Rome in 850 and 853 respectively, during which Anastasius, cardinal-priest of the titular church of St. Marcellus, was excommunicated and deposed for having abandoned his church and setting himself up in the diocese of Aquileia as the antipope to Benedict III, though he would be rehabilitated as the librarian of the Vatican under Nicholas I and John VIII.

In 855, Daniel, the *magister militum* of Rome, wanting to increase his own power in the city, personally presented to Louis an accusation about a certain Grazianus, captain of the army and pontifical counsellor, who was allegedly plotting to have the Papal State return to the Byzantine realm. Louis promptly came to Rome and was greeted with the usual splendid honors by Leo IV, who sought to calm matters by assuring him that Grazianus was not plotting anything at all. The emperor, however, wished to have the two confront each other, and as Daniel could not prove his accusations he had to acknowledge that he had made everything up. It was a pretty poor show for the imperial faction and Louis returned to Pavia, leaving the *magister militum* in the hands of Grazianus to be punished by death. The pope, however, interceded on his behalf and saved Daniel's life.

That same year Etevolvus and his son Alfred, the future king of England, arrived in Rome to be anointed by Leo IV. This symbol had become so important for kings that they all wanted recognition of their sovereignty by divine will. It was another card the pope had in hand to emphasize the notion of the supremacy of ecclesiastical authority. The English sovereign brought many gifts and a substantial contribution to the reconstruction of the Anglo-Saxon quarter which had been destroyed by the fire.

Leo IV died on 17 July 855, and was buried in St. Peter's. His name has ever since been linked to the *Civitas Leonina*, and in this sense the appellation that has been assigned to him as "Restorer of Rome" seems correct. However, apart from this edifice-building trait, his pontificate assumes fundamental importance for the future of the Papal State because of the drafting of those "Pseudo-Isidorian Decretals," which I have mentioned previously and which took place in the Diocese of Reims under Pope Leo IV himself, even though the first pontiff to take advantage of them was Nicholas I.

These were a summa of pontifical decretals, or rather a mixture of documents, altered or invented, attributed at first to Isidor of Seville, a famous doctor of the Church who died in 636, so that it might have greater authority. In fact, it was assembled between 847 and 852 by a bunch of forgers who collected all the pontifical decretals, from the oldest, artistically revised, to those of Gregory II, together with the decisions of the councils with various interpolations, and, obviously, the *Constitutum Constantini*.

The main objective of the counterfeiters was to attack the authority of the laity and the monarchy, thus giving a legal aspect to the decretals. In other words, they were a collection of "canon laws" the provisions of which, as Gregorovius observes, "put imperial power well below the dignity of the popes and even of the bishops, and raised the papacy at the same time so high over the others as to make it completely independent of the decisions of provincial synods, attributing to it instead the power of supreme judgement over the metropolitans and the bishops whose office and authority, removed from the emperor's influence, fell under the will of the pope. In a word, they conferred on the pontiff a dictatorship over the ecclesiastical world."

By virtue of such laws it was becoming ever more "difficult for a sovereign to validate accusations against bishops,"as Seppelt observes, and the pope became "the powerful protector and defender of the bishops." The basic idea of the "Pseudo-Isidorian Decretals" was, in fact, expressed in these words: "The bishops had to seek refuge with the pope as with a mother in order to be nourished, defended and liberated." All of this was connected to the image of St. Peter as the symbol of *Mater Ecclesia*, before which every religious and secular authority had to bow. And thus, as Ullmann notes, "for the papacy the false Isidore was manna from heaven, since the document contained in legal language exactly what the institution had been postulating for such a long time," constituting an irreversible and fundamental documentation for the creation of a clerical State.

It is interesting at this stage to note how a legend about a woman, the famous popess Joan, was inserted in the list of the popes, following the death of Leo IV and before Benedict III. Since this has been the subject of numerous versions, literary and historical, from Boccaccio to Platina and to Lawrence Durrell, it seems superfluous for me to recite here yet another one. Noteworthy and sufficient is to recite Belli's sonnet, appropriately entitled *La papessa Giuvanna* (in Romanesco):

> She was a real woman;
> first, she discarded her apron
> and she enlisted as a soldier;
> after that, she became a priest, then a prelate,
> and then a bishop, and finally a cardinal.
> And when the male pope fell ill
> and died, some say he was poisoned,
> she was made pope and was carried
> to Saint John's on the papal chair.
>
> But there the knot of the drama was untied,
> for suddenly she went into labour
> and gave birth to an infant, right on the chair.
>
> From then on, another chair was put into use,
> to be able to touch the baby below
> and learn if the pontiff was a pope or a popess.

It is more important to determine why this legend began. An explanation is offered, in a convincing way, by Cesare D'Onofrio in his book entitled *La papessa Giovanna*. Of the several explanations on which he focuses, the one I particularly wish to emphasize is that the story has a direct link with the concept of the *Mater Ecclesia* "inserted and 'represented' in the liturgy of papal elections by using two imperial birth chairs." generally said to be of porphyry but in fact of red marble, "on which the newly-elected, at the time of investiture by means of the evangelical keys, must assume the position of a woman giving birth," a rite which took place in the Lateran palace and was in use from the beginning of the tenth century until 1566. "It was precisely the strange liturgy of election with the two chairs with holes that give rise to the malicious idea of a woman-pope."

The legend was invented following the affirmation of the concept of the *Mater Ecclesia* with the intention of demystifying it. As to the period when it may have started, D'Onofrio is of the view that it was towards the "obscure time of the first decades of the tenth century when Rome and the popes were completely at the mercy of unscrupulous women, like Theodora and especially her daughter Marozia, 'prostitutes without shame,' a most favorable atmosphere for sowing the seed of a legend about a woman-pope."

In the final analysis this popular legend clearly bears an anti-clerical stamp. The invention of the infamous practice of putting a hand under one of the porphyry chairs, as Belli notes, to see if the pope is really a male, is an attempt to discredit the primacy of the pontiff who cannot be other than a "male," in the proper meaning of "power."

However, it fails to achieve its purpose. Papal "power" would not collapse and Urban VIII would eternalise it through Bernini's sculpture of the four marble bases of the bronze *baldacchino* (canopy) in St. Peter's. A series of six female faces in various phases of giving birth represents the concept of *Mater Ecclesia*, and the "baby" of the popess is redeemed in the smiling new-born child; a unique example of art as a joyous expression of the "face of power," to coin the term dear to Sabatino Moscati.

104. BENEDICT III (855–858)

Upon the death of Leo IV, the clergy and the population unanimously elected as pope the Roman Benedict, cardinal-bishop of St. Calixtus, but this time the emperor was sent the decree of election, duly subscribed, for approval. Nicholas, bishop of Anagni, and the *magister militum*, Mercurius, were charged with delivering the decree.

During the journey these two met at Orte Bishop Arsenius of Gubbio, one of the leaders of the imperial party, who convinced them instead to support the candidacy of his nephew, Anastasius, the cardinal who had been deposed by Leo IV and had sought refuge at Aquileia. Arsenius guaranteed that the imperial court saw Anastasius with favor and the two legates were duly persuaded, perhaps also by promises of a reward. When they reached Louis and delivered the document on the election of Benedict, they nevertheless declared themselves in favor of Anastasius.

Wanting to find out what was going on, the emperor sent Count Bernard and Count Adalbert to Rome to carry out an investigation on the election. These two met at Orte, together with the two Roman legates who had preceded them on the return journey, and bishops Rodoaldus of Portus and Agaton of Todi, as well as Anastasius with his uncle, Arsenius. This group elected Anastasius to the pontifical throne and then went on to Rome.

Five miles outside of the city, near the basilica of St. Leucius, the group encountered Benedict's messengers, Hadrian, the second highest dignitary of the papal court, Grazianus, the Captain of the Army, and Duke Gregory, who were to receive the reply of the imperial messengers. But they wound up in chains, and were dragged by the group over the Neronian Meadows to the Leonine City. While Benedict was awaiting events at the Lateran, on 21 September 855, Anastasius entered St. Peter's where he destroyed the banner which set forth the judgements of the two councils of Leo IV with his excommunication and, in a fit of wrath, damaged even the images of Christ and the Madonna. Then, still followed by his supporters, he proceeded to the Lateran where Benedict was seated upon the throne surrounded by the clergy faithful to him. There, a troop of armed men under the orders of the bishop of Bagnorea entered the church, took Benedict by force off the throne, tore off his pallium and put him in charge of two cardinals who had been deposed by Leo IV during his papacy.

The news swept the city and the people were enraged by the profanation on the part of Anastasius, as well as by the treatment meted out to Benedict. Rome was in an uproar, and the imperial representatives convened a general assembly for 25 September at the Lateran. In the plenary assembly, in fact, the people, with the bishops of Ostia and Albano at their head, declared themselves in favor of Benedict who had been elected according to canon law. The imperial legates had no alternative but to give in and remove Anastasius from the Lateran.

Benedict was immediately released and conducted on Leo IV's horse in a procession to St. Mary Major and his consecration as Benedict III took place on 29 September. Finally pope, he showed great clemency towards his adversaries, also to avoid offending the imperial party. He pardoned everyone, and Anastasius was readmitted to the ecclesiastical community with the title of abbot in the monastery of Sta. Maria in Trastevere.

This was recognized as a notable failure of Emperor Louis who, one day before the consecration of Benedict III, had become the emperor. Lothar, whose empire had been divided among his sons, had become a monk in the monastery of Pruem, near Trier, which is where he died on 28 September 855. Louis II therefore possessed Italy, Lothar II the territory that took his name, Lotharingia, and Charles, the Provence.

The pontificate of Benedict III proceeded fairly peacefully. He did not have the personality of a Leo IV, much less that of his own successor, Nicholas I. He was a mild person, although he did threaten to excommunicate the German priest, Hukbert, the brother-in-law of Lothar II, for having committed acts of violence against some abbeys. He was a simple man dedicated to the sanctity of the sacraments, evidenced when he publicly reprimanded

Ingeltrude, the wife of Count Bosone, for having fled with her lover and taken refuge in the court of Lothar II.

Basically, Benedict III did not realize that the emperor had suffered a significant loss of his influence, which he had always claimed with regard to internal matters of the Church, and that his imperial authority in itself was threatened. Either Benedict did not realize this or he was not made of the stuff to take advantage of it and dig more deeply the grave of imperial prestige in order to increase that of the pope towards definite autonomy. But the "Pseudo-Isidorian Decrees" would make sure that the task was entrusted to more energetic persons.

Benedict III died on 17 April 858, and was buried at the doors of St. Peter's basilica. His tomb, as the epitaph indicated, was indeed "worthy of tears."

105. St. Nicholas I, the Great (858–867)

Nicholas I, a descendant of a noble Roman family, and the son of a certain Theodore, was born about the year 800. A subdeacon under Sergius II, deacon with Leo IV and counsellor to Benedict III, he acceded to the pontificate after that "rite of reluctance" which, sincerely expressed in the grand personage of Gregory the Great and in that fleeting one of Valentine, seemed in this case to reflect a political purpose.

Louis II had just departed from Rome, where he had come for reasons unknown, when he learned of the death of Benedict III, and since it was a rare occasion for the emperor to be present for the election of a new pope, he went back there. When the great assembly of the electors had gathered in the monastery of St. Sylvester, he managed to swing the votes in favor of the deacon Nicholas who was absent however. "Then everyone rushed to St. Peter's where he had gone to hide," relates the *Liber pontificalis*, "because he felt unworthy of such a position. But those present forced him to leave the basilica and, among pious acclamations, took him into the Lateran palace and put him on the throne." Shortly afterwards, he was taken back to St. Peter's and crowned in the presence of Louis II. It was 24 April 858.

No doubt the election of Nicholas I met the wishes of the emperor, but the deacon had many enemies among the clergy who would have preferred Hadrian, the cardinal-priest of St. Mark's, destined to succeed him and who, faced with Louis II's clear preference, had declined to be a candidate. In this light, the "rite of reluctance" on the part of Nicholas acquires a completely "political" significance which gained general approval through this display of exaggerated modesty. In any case, the events immediately following his consecration point to a personal relationship between the emperor and the new pope.

According to the *Liber pontificalis*, after leaving Rome Louis II stopped off near St. Leucius, in the present area of Tor di Quinto, and received

Nicholas I together with the entire group of high clergymen and the nobility. The emperor went to him and, for part of the road, held the bridle of the pope's horse, accompanying him to his pavilion. There they had a conversation at the end of which the pope received numerous gifts and then remounted his horse to return to the city. Louis II, also mounted and accompanied him to the city walls where he dismounted and walked for a while to the pope's right, again holding the bridle as if he were a groom. It was an action which recalls that of Constantine depicted in the last mosaic in the church of the Ss. Quattro Coronati: "With such haughty conduct before an emperor who was himself trying to be a humble person," Gregorovius notes "did Nicholas I begin his pontificate."

While it was this was a brief pontificate of only nine years, an intense and important one since it embodied the concept of a pope whom kings, emperors, bishops and priests had to obey. The entire world was supposed to receive directives exclusively from the papacy, and though the sovereign could well be the beneficiary of political power he had to answer for it to the pope, just as the bishop or the priest in the religious context. "The entire social and religious system of the world depended on the papacy of Rome. This was how Nicholas I visualized the role of the institution, and he ruled in that spirit," stated Walter Ullmann.

Helping him in this politico-religious centralization of the world community which reflected the hegemonic mission that Rome was supposed to embody, was that Anastasius who had previously been excommunicated by Leo IV and had been the antipope to Benedict III, though later completely rehabilitated. He had become the librarian of the Vatican, so one can infer that it was he who submitted to Nicholas I those "Pseudo-Isidorian Decretals" mentioned in the biography of Leo IV. As Gregorovius has said, "Nicholas I saw in these documents the most effective weapons in his battle against the king and the synods." He made use of that ancient material, obviously aware of how much of it was false, yet integrating and giving it a coherent form for its application which can be seen from numerous extracts of his decrees which were to form part of the collections of canon law in a later period. From this joint work by Nicholas I and Anastasius while profiting from the weakness of the Carolingian dynasty, came the concept of *Mater Ecclesia* confirmed in its dual politico-religious meaning. As a result of this, Gregorovius notes, "the emperor found himself a spectator of the pope's victory." It is clear that Nicholas I did not embody what has been said, but he was certainly the creator of the medieval papacy and popes such as Gregory VII and Innocent III would be indebted to him.

According to Seppelt all of this is clarified by the fact that "as it was not possible to conceive a separation of Church and State along modern criteria, the idea of the unity of State and Church," that is of a clerical State, was maintained since one certainly cannot speak of the autonomy of a State when it "was obliged to follow in all its actions both Christian and ecclesiastical principles." So much so that "the obligations imposed by temporal laws will cease to be in force whenever they trespass into the religious area, or if they are contrary to the will of God or to ethical Christian laws."

A concrete example of this concept was provided by the condemnation of "divorce," to use a modern term, but which at that time more or less meant "repudiation" by the husband of the wife, even though cases of abandonment of the "conjugal abode" by women were not infrequent. Indeed, Benedict III had already had occasion to condemn Ingeltrude for having abandoned Count Bosone, and Nicholas I was also to assert the concept of the sacred bond of marriage with Lothar II, the emperor's grandson. But here too, Gregorovius observes, one should state immediately that the event must be put into the perspective "of an epoch of barbarous actions when there was no public opinion capable of restraining the abuses of power by princes." Which is to say, a precise secular idea of matrimony did not then exist, and hence "the conduct of Nicholas, with regard to the scandal which involved the royal family, was very noble and resolute. The power of the priesthood appears in him as the moral force which punishes vice and preserves virtue".

What happened was that Lothar II had repudiated his wife, Teuteberg, who had given him no children, in order to marry a noble lady, Gualdrad, with whom he had earlier lived, and who had given him three children he wanted to legitimize. He had convened a council at Metz with bishops who had expressed an opinion favorable to him and had justified his decision. Involved in the intrigue were two pontifical legates among whom was Rodoaldus, the bishop of Portus, who was easily bribable.

The conciliar decisions were sent to Rome with the two archbishops of Cologne and Trier. Nicholas, who was already aware of what was going on, refused to receive them for three weeks, after which he convened a synod at the Vatican and declared null and void the decisions of Metz, excommunicating Gualdrad as being a concubine and deeming Teuteberg the legitimate wife. The two archbishops, Gunther and Teutgard, were also excommunicated and deposed because they had not defended the sanctity of a sacrament, obviously motivated by who knew what promises of territorial assets from Lothar.

The archbishops requested the intervention of Emperor Louis II, openly accusing Nicholas I of abuse of power. So the emperor, convinced by the two archbishops, left for Rome with his wife, Engelberg, and an armed force, taking with him the two excommunicated prelates. He was determined to review matters with a pope who suddenly seemed to be assuming the role of an over-lord. It was February 864, and Nicholas I prepared to welcome him with a funeral "scene" ordering that Rome should be in mourning with processions and fasting. Which was how the city received its emperor, and the pope did not even go to greet him, shutting himself in the Lateran in prayer and describing Louis II as "evil and dangerous."

The processions crossed each other in the streets of Rome, and one was even attacked by certain barons of Louis, exasperated by the pope's refusal to receive their sovereign. Many priests were beaten up, crosses and banners were destroyed, and the rumour was even spread that the pope, feeling unsafe in the Lateran, had gone up the Tiber in a boat and found refuge in St. Peter's, where he had fasted for two full days. The situation was clearly intolerable, and all the tact that Empress Engelberg could bring to bear was needed to arrive at a mediation between the pope and the emperor.

She succeeded in having them meet, but obtained only a rapprochement between them and nothing else. The archbishops were still excommunicated and Lothar had to take Teuteberg back, regardless of the fact that the queen herself begged the pope to go back on his decision and give in to Lothar's wishes, because the marriage brought her only constant calumnies, the latest being that she had had an incestuous relationship with her own brother. Yet in the event of the pope's decisions not being obeyed, the threat of excommunication still hung over Lothar. As for the excommunicated Gualdrad, she was supposed to appear to be judged in a court in Rome. Louis II gave in and departed from Rome. The dispute was over, at least officially, although the whole story of this marriage, as Ullmann says, is important "in the sense that, for the first time, the papacy judged a king who unexpectedly found himself threatened with excommunication, a fate from which he was saved by the death of the pope," since he immediately resumed his relationship with Gualdrad: "Nonetheless it was a warning,"

Nicholas I was a typical manifestation of the absolutism of a pope, and under him Rome itself lived peacefully, without fights between the nobles and the ecclesiastics. Furthermore, he stood up to bishops as much as to monarchs, resolutely opposing the increasing nationalism of the Churches in various countries. For example in 861 he forced Jemar, the archbishop of Reims, to return to Rotadus, bishop of Soissons, the powers he had taken away from him in his position as metropolitan of France. Thus, bishop could not be deposed without the agreement of Rome.

He demonstrated just as much firmness with the archbishop of Ravenna, John, who sought to achieve complete autonomy within his territory acting, like a real despot, seizing property, excommunicating bishops and extorting moneys. Excommunicated by Nicholas I, he figured he could resolve the matter with the support of Louis II, but the pope automatically rejected any imperial interference and would not receive messengers from Louis, who finally abandoned the archbishop, resulting in a clear victory for Nicholas I. The excommunication of John was lifted and his functions restored to him only after he had signed a decree by which he would have to go to Rome once a year to report on his behavior. He was prohibited from any extortion of lay persons or bishops, and had to settle earlier disputes through the tribunal of Ravenna, of which would form part a pontifical legate.

Nicholas I was a truly universal sovereign even in the field of evangelization, especially in Bulgaria. The mainspring of this missionary activity was the bishop of Portus, Formosus, a future pope together with Bishop Paul of Populonia, converted masses of Bulgarians, with the support of their king who insisted on accepting only Western priests, rejecting the Greeks with the faithful themselves choosing their own archbishop. The Bulgarian king was enthusiastic about Rome's missionary activity because it brought with it the formulation of a genuine constitution which resolved many of the problems, some really puerile, of this people, and provided the basis for a true clerical State.

This constitution, entitled *Responsa*, established a code of civil laws for the education of this new nation, and was drafted on the basis of a series of questions raised by the population and their king concerning economic, legal and social issues. These ranged from how marriages should be celebrated to how one should dress in a civilized manner, how one should judge a criminal as well as even dealing with concepts of slavery and liberty. Nicholas interpreted everything from an evangelical viewpoint and thus prepared a lay constitution inspired by the Church. In effect, he managed to create a sort of "province" of the State of the Church a thousand miles from Rome. But it was difficult to keep it under control, with the result that from 870 on this ecclesiastical province fell into the orbit of Byzantium.

With Byzantium, Nicholas I's struggle was bitter and difficult, carried on honorably by him, but destined to lead, after his death, to that schism which separated definitively the Church of Rome from that of the East. Once the battle about the images was over, it appears that the two churches experienced a period of peaceful co-existence under Patriarch Methodius. When the latter died in 846, his successor Ignatius, son of Emperor Michael I, was eager to maintain good relations with Rome out of respect for the primacy of the pope, and from the decisive influence of his mother, Theodora.

The problems began when Barda, Theodora's brother, set up a conspiracy against his sister, the regent, in which he had involved his nephew, Michael III, whom he succeeded in bringing to power in 856. Michael was very young and given to unbridled high living and to drunkenness, and he let himself be dominated by his uncle, who was the real head of State. Moreover, Barda was accused by Patriarch Ignatius of incest, having taken unto himself the widow of his son, and was forced to abstain from the Eucharist during the feast of the Epiphany in 858. At that point Barda convinced his nephew to undertake a general cleansing. His mother Theodora and his sisters were forced to go into a convent, and Ignatius to agree to the decision which, in effect, was a purely ecclesiastical one. The patriarch opposed the violent deposition of the empress and her subsequent closure in a convent, so was himself relieved of his authority.

His see was entrusted to Photius, a very intelligent person who had been given various governmental functions, but who was only a lay man. Within a short space of time, he was raised to priesthood by an excommunicated bishop, Gregory Asbesta, invested with minor and major ecclesiastical dignities one after the other, and then raised to be the titular incumbent of the patriarchal see of Byzantium, all in clear violation of the most basic rules of canon law. But once he got the see, Photius had not the slightest intention of leaving it. He immediately convened a council consisting of loyal subordinates, which officially approved the deposition of Ignatius, and excommunicated him. The same fate befell all the followers of the ex-patriarch, and the resulting vacant episcopal sees were assigned to Photius's supporters. The imperial guards helped him stifle any opposition by beatings and violence.

Obviously, Ignatius appealed to the pope. Photius, however, was not idle and sent a delegation of bishops to Rome carrying many gifts, declaring that Ignatius had spontaneously renounced his office and that Photius had been forced to accept the post through pressure from the emperor and the ecclesiastical community of Byzantium, a series of false statements yet attested to even by the imperial messengers.

Nicholas I wanted to investigate the matter and sent the bishop of Anagni, Zacharias, and the bishop of Portus, Rodoaldus, —those who had previously been bribed at Metz by Lothar II, —to Byzantium to do so. Once again Rodoaldus did not hesitate to take graft, involving his colleague from Anagni in the deal. They went so far as to forge the pope's letter they had brought with them, and an assembly of bishops in 861 confirmed the deposition of Ignatius and approved the election of Photius. Strengthened by the sanctions of the synod, Photius began to persecute the monks faithful to Ignatius. He also took up relations with those Western bishops who had been chastised by Nicholas I under disciplinary rules of which the pope reminded them continually in a series of decretals. Thus Photius was fomenting a conspiracy against the see of Rome, and the pope reacted correspondingly.

He excommunicated the two treacherous legates and then, having convened a council at Rome in 863, condemned Photius, ordering him to surrender the patriarchal signs and seals. There followed a series of delegations between Byzantium and Rome. Photius appeared to be willing to do as the pope had ordered but, in fact, secretly did the opposite. Finally he showed his hand and called a council meeting in Constantinople during the summer of 867 under the chairmanship of Emperor Michael. False witnesses and paid accusers appeared before this council which had everything except the look of an ecclesiastical one, and at the conclusion of the session, Photius declared Nicholas I to be deposed as the bishop of Rome and also excommunicated.

Needless to say, the judgement was not carried out, chiefly because Emperor Michael was assassinated and the new emperor, Basil I, thought it good for the sake of peace to depose Photius and restore Ignatius to his functions as patriarch. In any event, the pope came to know about the judgement of the pseudo-council and was aware of the peril that threatened the Christian world at its very roots, menacing even the See of Peter. Although ill and aging, he set about organizing national councils in the various Churches of the East, all of which unanimously agreed on the unity of the Church under the central authority of Rome. The supporters of this charismatic affirmation of the primacy of Rome were the leading theologians of the day, such as Rathramnus of Corbie, Enea of Paris, and Scotus Eriugena, who opposed fraud and coercion, those weapons Photius had used to dismember the unity of the Christian world. It was a unanimous defense of apostolic faith and strength which, however, Nicholas I could only in part appreciate, just as he could not know of the changes which had taken place in Constantinople under the new emperor.

In fact, he died on 13 November 867, perhaps on account of these events, not convinced that he had fully achieved his objective. It is a fact that, with his death, disappeared a pope who "commanded kings and tyrants and crushed them by his imposing figure, as if he were the leader of the whole world," according to Reginone of Pruem. The evangelical mission of Peter had become politicized and this legacy would pass to his heirs. From this viewpoint, Nicholas I could rest in peace for eternity in the basilica of St. Peter, where he was buried.

106. HADRIAN II (867—872)

Even in an atmosphere of full dissent between the two opposing factions in Rome, one favorable to the emperor and the other to autonomy, which could be styled "Nicholasist" because it followed the ideas of Nicholas I, the clergy and the Roman people quickly reached an agreement on the person of the cardinal-priest of St. Mark's, Hadrian, a Roman who had been a candidate in earlier elections. Rather advanced in years and feeble, he was unanimously chosen because of his openly benvolent nature, even though it was known that he did not have the mettle of his predecessor. This election was, in fact, opposed by the imperial envoys in Rome who protested because they had not been invited to the balloting. The clergy and the people found themselves in agreement over this point, with the justification that, while the emperor had reserved his right of approval, this did not oblige them to conduct the election in the presence of his envoys. So much so that Louis II, who was then in southern Italy to fight the Saracens, advised them of his approval and Hadrian II was consecrated on 14 December 867.

His great charitable spirit was displayed immediately by the grant of amnesty for the ecclesiastics who had been punished for diverse reasons. Even certain corrupt prelates like Zachary, the bishop of Anagni, and Teutgard of Trier, previously excommunicated by Nicholas I, were readmitted into the community. This attitude of flexibility and forgiveness led, at the very beginning of his pontificate, to violence in Rome. A certain Lambert, duke of Spoleto who, entered Rome with his militia, sacking the city savagely, seizing the property of the nobility and even allowing his men to abduct and rape the daughters of the Roman nobles. The pope, as usual without any defense, sent letters of protest to the emperor and threatened excommunication on all sides. However, Lambert got away scot-free, and, when he had finished the pillaging, left Rome unpunished. Louis II meanwhile had no intention of abandoning the lands in the south to the Saracen invaders, and put off any settling of accounts. In fact, it was only in 871, and for other reasons, that he managed to depose Lambert.

The truth is that Hadrian II was weak and incapable of defending either Rome or himself and his "family." Before taking holy orders, he had married a certain Stephany, and had had a daughter who, once pope, he had promised as bride to a Roman nobleman. But Eleutherius, son of Arsenius, the bishop of Orte, had fallen in love with her and had carried her off with her mother to his own palace. The pope wrote to the emperor begging him, as a human being and as a father seeking assistance, to send his men to help him in this emergency! The emperor's men arrived in Rome and went to Eleutherius's palace but at this point the young man lost his temper and, in a blind rage, killed the pope's daughter together with her mother. The emperor's men broke down the door of the palace to find that the tragedy had already taken place. Eleutherius was captured and beheaded.

The question was whether this was simply an act of everyday life with a passionate background and a tragic ending in that Roman winter of 868, or a kidnapping within the frame of a political conspiracy against the pontifical throne, carried out by Arsenius, bishop of Orte. This was the same Arsenius who had attempted to impose his nephew Anastasius in the place of Benedict III, and had supported him as an antipope. He was probably still dying to see his nephew pope, and this time he had put the newly elected one against the wall by seizing his daughter, and getting his own son Eleutherius involved in a drama of passion as a diversion from bigger intrigues.

How can one otherwise explain his sudden flight from Rome in order to stop, or, better still, to bribe the emperor's men, which was only prevented by his own death? And then also found himself again excommunicated, accused of complicity in Eleutherius's crime, and certainly not for reasons of a love affair. A synod convened by Hadrian II on 12 October 868, sentenced Anastasius to a kind of house arrest in the basilica of St. Praxede, and the wise librarian swore his obedience to the pope, thereby gradually winning back his confidence.

A clear demonstration of the weak personality of Hadrian II can also be found in the question relating to Lothar II and his marital vicissitudes, upon which Nicholas I had pronounced authoritatively in the name of the sanctity of matrimony, obliging the sovereign to respect the Sacrament and excommunicating his mistress, Gualdrad. Her excommunication was lifted by Hadrian on condition she abstained from any relationship with Lothar, but it was clearly a concession by the pope who agreed to the request by Louis II that he meet with Lothar. They did so at Montecassino in July 868 and the sovereign swore and perjured himself once again that he would not pursue the relationship with Gualdrad and would respect the union with his wife, Teuteberg. She herself informed the pope that it would have been much more suitable to have dissolved that marriage, and to free her from the unhappy life to which she was condemned. At Montecassino the pope administered Holy Communion to Lothar and showed himself confident on the marital questions while deferring a definitive decision to a synod which would take place in Rome. But a month after this meeting, Lothar died suddenly at Piacenza, and both ladies entered a convent.

Lothar left no children and so Louis II became his legal heir, although Charles the Bald, as soon as he learned of the death, seized Lotharingia, and, on 9 September 869, crowned himself king and was anointed at Metz by the bishop of Reims, Incmarus. Charles's brother, Louis the German, was left the territory beyond the Mosel and the Rhine as far as Utrecht. The pope tried by every means to avoid this usurpation of the rights of the emperor who, otherwise occupied in southern Italy, had requested the pope to protect his legitimate claims through the bishop of Reims. But the pope obtained nothing. Incmarus even sought to justify the political conduct of Charles the Bald in a letter sent to the pope, rejecting what were called the "interferences" by the pope, and stating that the latter should busy himself only with matters of the Church and not interfere in those of the State.

Thus the pope cut a wretched figure with a person one could only term his "subaltern," who had dared remind him about the true function of a pope and who would never have replied in such a manner to a Nicholas I. But it is obvious that the bishop of Reims felt himself boss in his own home, and supported the autonomous political behavior of the Frankish sovereign in order to achieve autonomy of the Frankish Church itself. If he fired Frankish judgements at the pope he was really taking care of his own interests. As a result Charles did not hand back the Frankish territories.

Meanwhile Louis was having his own problems in the south of Italy. While his army was active in putting down various rebellions, he withdrew in 871 with his wife, senior officers, and a few soldiers to Benevento to enjoy the booty seized during his war against the Saracens. But the vexations he caused to the local population were such that the duke of Benevento, Adelchi, managed to organize a revolt which led to the arrest of the emperor and his aides as well as to the confiscation of the gold of the Saracens. His liberation came only after he had solemnly sworn to stop bothering the duke.

So Louis II, disgraced, had to leave Benevento with his tail between his legs. Rejoining his troops, he attacked Spoleto where he settled accounts with Duke Lambert and then returned to Ravenna.

The following year found him in Rome where, on Whitsun of 872, Hadrian II (a mediocre pope) and Louis II (a detested emperor) renewed the trappings of a highly prestigious and ancient ceremony of a coronation. This coronation was bestowed on Louis for the second time, probably because of the new lands granted to him by Charles the Bald from the estate left by Lothar.

More positive at the beginning of Hadrian II's pontificate was the relationship with the East. The arrival on the scene of Basil I and the return of Ignatius to the functions of the patriarch in place of the excommunicated Photius, during the final months of the life of Nicholas I, led to the great council of Constantinople which took place between 15 October 869 and 28 February 871 (the eighth ecumenical council) to eliminate disorders in the Greek Church and smoothe over, in a definitive manner, relations with Rome.

The three papal legates worked tirelessly to overcome an ever-present opposition from bishops close to Photius, and succeeded in having the decisions taken in Rome against Photius accepted unanimously. On 8 February 871, in the presence of Emperor Basil I, deputies of the king of the Bulgarians, and ambassadors from Louis II, Photius and his doctrines were condemned and all the bishops he had consecrated were deposed. The unity of the Church seemed suddenly restored. However, it was only an illusion and really the beginning of the gradual irreversible rupture, the first symptoms of which appeared three days after the end of the council.

Basil I, Ignatius, the delegates of the Eastern patriarchs and the papal legates assembled to listen to a Bulgarian delegation which had requested that the question as to whether the Church of Bulgaria should belong to Rome or to Constantinople be decided by the Eastern patriarchs and not by the pope. Despite objections by the papal legates, the patriarchs decided that the province of Bulgaria should belong to Constantinople. Rome not only lost one of its creations but was also insulted by the patriarch of Constantinople who did not react as he should have to the Bulgarian request.

Ignatius then consecrated an archbishop for the Bulgarians who, in 871, went there followed by a large number of Greek priests. But this was not all, as the Latin missionaries were evicted and the pontifical representatives barely managed to save the formats of obedience to the pope that had been signed by the Greeks and which served as proof or their betrayal of Rome.

Basil I and Ignatius tried in a way to conceal the insult by sending the pope gifts and letters full of Christian brotherliness. Hadrian II thanked them but complained about the improper behavior of Ignatius with regard to the Bulgarian question, stating again the rights of Rome in that province, and threatening to excommunicate Ignatius.

The pope, however, only verbally authoritarian, did not get that far. Death claimed him on 14 December 872, and he was buried in St. Peter's.

107. JOHN VIII (872—882)

John, son of Gundo, perhaps a descendant of a Lombard family, was born at Rome in 820, and was archdeacon of the Roman Church for more than twenty years. He was consecrated pope on 14 December 872, and was the eighth of that name. Energetic and endowed with many talents, he was a true warrior-pope who strove to maintain the papacy in the prestigious position achieved by Nicholas I.

During that turbulent period of continual depredations by the Saracens, once Louis II had died there was no Carolingian sovereign capable of protecting Italy and the Papal Estates. The situation got worse because Rome was struck by a series of local disorders that made the position of the pope difficult. The Roman nobility was divided into two factions, one pro-German, the other pro-Frank, which were carrying on an open battle to win the highest positions in the papal State.

When Louis II died without male heirs, his uncles Charles the Bald and Louis the German, both aspired to the imperial crown and the possession of Italy. In fact, Louis II had designated as his heir Carloman, oldest son of Louis the German, and the Dowager Empress Angilberg argued the case for her grandson at an assembly convened at Pavia in September 875. But her wish and that of her deceased husband conflicted with that of John VIII, who was decidedly against the German Carolingians, and he rapidly summoned Charles the Bald to Rome together with a solemn delegation in order to crown him emperor. The sovereign accepted the invitation unhesitatingly and the coronation took place at St. Peter's, with due pomp, on Christmas Day, 875.

Gregorovius underlined that "to buy the agreement of the Romans and the pope, Charles had paid out so much money that his enemies in Germany compared him to Jugurtha. He had to humble himself, like any candidate, to beg for the votes of the Roman patricians, to the point that the pope was able to state in his official speech — which had never before happened — that the Roman emperor was his creation." Following the imperial coronation, Charles the Bald had himself elected king of Italy at Pavia by the "grandees" of the kingdom, the majority of whom did not attend the ceremony. However, all of this was enough to make one understand that the papal authority was again at a peak in the peninsula, at least in the north.

But in the end Charles the Bald proved a big delusion for John VIII. He turned out not to be the right arm the pope had hoped for with regard to the Saracen raids, and the ambitious pontifical plans came to nought because of the ineptitude of the person in whom the pope had placed so much trust. The repeated and urgent appeals from the pope for help against the Saracens and the pro-German faction in Rome were in vain, and the agreements of Ponthion, which led to the revocation of Lothar's Constitution of 824, finished by being meaningless. John VIII was again forced to act alone.

The pro-German faction in Rome had persons of importance in its ranks. Among these were the nomenclator Gregory and his son-in-law, George, who, in order to marry the former's daughter Constantina, had murdered his first wife, the niece of Benedict III, but who had been acquitted by corrupt judges. There were as well the secundicerius Stephen, and the *magister militum* Sergius, who had repudiated his wife and cohabited with his mistress, the Frankish Walwisindula, while the ecclesiastical leader of the pro-German faction was Formosus, the bishop of Portus. So John VIII convened a council at the Pantheon on 19 April 876, threatening to excommunicate the bishop and the leaders of the party if they did not appear in person to explain themselves. The charge was conspiracy against the State, with the aid of Lambert of Spoleto who had repossessed his duchy, and of immoral conduct. The defendants did not appear, fled from Rome, and the excommunication was solemnly pronounced in a verdict rendered at St. Peter's on 30 June.

As for the Saracen danger, John VIII wanted to imitate Leo IV. He surrounded the basilica of St. Paul, as well as the area around Ostia, with massive walls, but the entire fortifications were later destroyed, though when and why is not known.

The pope also tried to establish a league among the various sovereigns of southern Italy, chiefly of those coastal cities of Amalfi, Salerno, and Naples in an attempt to get them to break their alliance with the Saracens, but with scant results. He only succeeded in convincing Guaifierus of Salerno and Pulcarius of Amalfi, through heavy payments, but not Sergius, the duke of Naples, who was getting important advantages from the alliance. John VIII therefore excommunicated him, had Guaifierus of Salerno attack him and, as Gregorovius reminds us, "thoughtlessly, had twenty Neapolitan prisoners beheaded."

This pope's energetic initiative resulted also in the formation of a small fleet under his personal command, pre-dating Julius II, and the warrior-pope himself directed naval operations in the area of Cape Circeo. It was the year 877, and he succeeded in capturing eighteen Saracen vessels and in freeing 600 Christian slaves, while numerous Mohammedans were slain. "This was the first time that a pontiff joined in battle as an admiral," Gregorovius notes.

After which, John carried out his revenge against the duke of Naples. The pope had him captured by Athanasius, the bishop of Naples, who, even though he was his own brother, did not hesitate to gouge out his eyes with his own hand in order to render full service to the sovereign pontiff, who then let the duke die in prison. Gregorovius recalls that "this fratricide committed by a bishop was greeted by the pontiff as a joyous event and the agreed price for the assassination was duly paid to the murderer who received a letter of congratulations. Thereby the exigencies of temporal dominion distanced the pope from apostolic virtues of priesthood which are morally totally irreconcilable with them." And this writer was certainly right.

All this bloodshed served no purpose, even though, at the same time in an isolated episode, the Byzantine fleet managed to inflict a tremendous defeat on the Saracen one in the Gulf of Naples. The league was not established, the Amalfi people mocked the pope and, having received the payoff, they continued to trade with the Saracens. Moreover, Bishop Athanasius, having inherited the ducal title from his brother, did not hesitate to make commercial deals with the infidels which insured him against attacks by the Byzantine fleet. So John VIII was forced to reach agreements with the Saracens and, by virtue of paying a heavy annual tribute, obtained a certain period of peace in his territory. "The payment of the tribute was a rather delicate matter," Seppelt remarks, "and was a profound humiliation for the pope who could, however, correctly declare that he had been forced to do so because certain Christian princes had openly sided with the enemies of Christ."

Meanwhile, in October 877, Charles the Bald passed away. Carloman immediately seized Italy, without opposition, and asked the pope for imperial coronation. John VIII attempted to gain time, as he feared a resurgence of the pro-German party in Rome. However, Carloman, stricken by apoplexy, was forced to return to Bavaria with his army which was decimated by an epidemic. The pope now found himself really on his own, and although he had settled the problem with the Saracens, he was in fact at the mercy of the first Italian sovereign who wanted to profit from the situation. Which was what happened.

Duke Lambert of Spoleto and his brother-in-law, Duke Adalbert of Tuscia, occupied Rome declaring that they were acting in the name of Carloman for the protection of the Church. In fact, the pope was held a prisoner, but the two of them failed to extort from John the promise of a future election of Carloman, although they subjected the city to every imaginable kind of violence. Lambert and Adalbert returned to their dukedoms after a month without having obtained anything other than the pope's increased antagonism to their request, which led to their solemn excommunication in yet another council at St. Peter's.

However, for the pope the situation was not a tranquil one. He abandoned Rome for France where, in August 878, he convened a council at Troyes and renewed the excommunication of Lambert and Adalbert while, on 7 September, he crowned Louis the Stammerer, the son and successor of Charles the Bald. But John VIII had placed his hopes in a half-wit who was certainly not up to helping him defend the Church and Rome. So, after a year, he returned to Italy and again switched candidates. This time, his choice fell upon Boso, count of Provence, previously named by Charles the Bald governor of the kingdom of Italy, on whom he even conferred the imperial crown in order to avoid giving it to Carloman. But Boso also deluded him, for when Louis the Stammerer died in April 879, leaving underage children, Boso had himself crowned king at Lyon by the high-ranking prelates of Provence and Burgundy.

The pope, now at a loss, was searching vainly for a protector. With Carloman ill and unable to govern, the seat of the empire was vacant, and by then the title of Emperor was but a mere symbol without any guarantee of protection for the pope. The last of the Carolingians to bear the title was Charles the Fat, and this was the final hope for John VIII who crowned him at Rome in 881, expecting that he would at least organize an expedition against the Saracens to relieve him of the shame of the tribute. But Charles simply went back north with the crown, abandoning the pope to his fate.

John VIII was still hoping for an Italian sovereign and tried to recruit Lambert of Spoleto by lifting the excommunication, but the duke died. His successor, Guido, dashed John's hopes as he simply expropriated the Church's property and imprisoned those who opposed the pro-German party, which obviously became stronger.

This pope, who cherished mainly earthly matters and viewed religious questions with scarce interest, did not hesitate, during a council in Rome, to recognize as the patriarch of Constantinople that same Photius who had previously been condemned by his predecessors, thereby showing little respect for Orthodoxy. Hoping to recover ecclesiastical authority in Bulgaria John VIII recommended, in a letter sent to Emperor Basil and to Photius, a kind of barter, yet imposing on Photius to implore pardon in front of a council. Photius translated the papal letter and the documents into Greek in his own style, modified the content so that it became a glorification of himself, and totally sidestepped the Bulgarian question. Papal legates made three trips between Rome and Constantinople to clarify various points of the dispute, but when the head of the delegation, Bishop Marinus, discovered the intrigues, Basil held him prisoner in Constantinople for thirty days, and sent the other obliging legates back to the pope. When Marinus was released at the beginning of the year 881, he returned to Rome and reported matters to John VIII, who again excommunicated Photius and his envoys.

Disillusioned and abandoned, John VIII died on 16 December 882. A chronicler recounted that a relative of his had given him a poisoned drink which was too slow in taking effect, so he fractured the pope's skull with a hammer. A terrible end but one which falls within the pattern of his behavior. "Equivocal and without a conscience, master of sophistry and knavery," Gregorovius described him, in no way a "diplomatic genius," he was incapable of "staying afloat by clever intrigues, in front of the thousand conflicting forces," of which he became the victim. It is true, Gregorovius continues, that this pope "violent and vindictive like few others, let himself be dragged along by his blind passion and thoughtless, impulsive acts, and as a result, failed in all his undertakings." I would add that he tried to defend untenable positions and failed to "master the chaotic Italian situation" as Nicholas I, his inimitable model, had been able.

108. MARINUS I (882–884)

Marinus I, a native of Gallese, was elected pope on 16 December 882. In the service of the Church since he was twelve years old, he had been ordained a subdeacon by Leo IV and deacon by Nicholas I, and had presided over the eighth ecumenical council during which his bitter enemy, Photius, was condemned. Having become an archdeacon, Marinus had been consecrated bishop of Cere in Etruria by John VIII, and had carried out the duties of treasurer of the Roman Church. More recently he had been the head of the delegation to Constantinople where he had contested the restoration of Photius to the function of the patriarch. That had led to his imprisonment by order of Emperor Basil. However, the report submitted later to John VIII had brought about the renewal of the excommunication of the unworthy patriarch.

His election to the pontifical see, about which we have no specific details, was the first instance of the transfer of a bishop to the see of Rome. This did not cause any special dissent from the clergy and the only one to resent it was Photius, who took advantage of the infraction of the rule to refuse to recognize the pope. This was simply an excuse to take revenge in some way against a permanent adversary. From Charles the Fat there were no objections, and the two met in the abbey of Nonantola near Modena where they held negotiations in a friendly fashion, since Marinus came from the pro-German faction.

In fact, a pardon was granted to Bishop Formosus and others who had joined in the plot against John VIII. Formosus was restored to his bishopric in Portus, the condemnation of Photius was reconfirmed and the emperor, in agreement with the Byzantine emperor, deposed Guido of Spoleto on the charge of high treason and ordered Count Beregarius to invade the duchy. Guido fled to the south to seek an alliance with the Saracens for a future recovery of his territory.

According to the *Annales Fuldenses*, Rome also witnessed disorders between the opposing factions, when the administrator of the papal palace, a certain Gregory, who was one of the leaders of the pro-German and pro-Formosus party, was slain.

We have no further information about Marinus I, except that during his brief pontificate the Saracens set fire to the monastery of Monte Cassino, and we know also that he had good relations with Alfred, the then king of England.

He died on 15 May 884, and was buried in the portico of St. Peter's.

109. St. Hadrian III (884—885)

A Roman from Via Lata, Hadrian III was elected pope on 17 May 884, probably while a succession of riots raged between the two leading factions in Rome. The pro-German one had the worst of it, if what Benedict of Soratte, a chronicler, stated was true. According to him, Hadrian III himself had had George, the son-in-law of the Gregory who had been assassinated under Marinus I, blinded while his wife, Mary, naked, was beaten with rods through the streets of the city.

The chronicler Martin Polonus attributes to Hadrian III two decrees which must be mentioned, although they are not necessarily authentic, because they would appear to constitute, at a critical moment for the empire, a resurgence of temporal power of the pope through a new interpretation of the "Pseudo-Isidorian Decretals." Hadrian is thought to have decided that the consecration of the pope should take place without the presence of any imperial legates, and, further, that, as Charles the Fat did not have any heirs, the crown should pass to an Italian prince.

It is true that the chaotic situation of the empire with an idiot like Charles the Fat favored the aspirations on the part of Italian dukes and marquises, particularly Berengarius and Guido who had been pardoned again by the emperor and given back his duchy at the end of 884.

When Carloman, the king of France, passed away in December of that year, Charles the Fat decided to set everything aright within the empire, and therefore convened, for the following year, a Diet at Worms to which he also invited Hadrian III. The latter started off on his journey, after having entrusted the government of the city to John, bishop of Pavia, who also played the role of an imperial legate, but when the pope reached San Cesario near Modena, in September 885, he died and was buried at the monastery of Nonantola.

1 1 O. STEPHEN V (8 8 5 — 8 9 1)

A Roman from a noble family, son of Hadrian of Via Lata, which was one of the most aristocratic areas of the Rome of that time, Stephen V was elected and consecrated in a great hurry without imperial approval as soon as news had arrived of the death of Hadrian III in September 885. Although Bishop John of Pavia was in Rome as the emperor's envoy, the election brought strong objections from Charles the Fat, who sent his chancellor Liutvard and some bishops to depose the new pontiff. But pontifical legates preceded him and conveyed to him the decree by which Stephen proved to have been elected according to the rules.

Stephen V had, in any case, the consent of thirty cardinal-priests and cardinal-deacons led by Formosus, and as the fights between the two factions continued throughout the city it became clear that the pro-German party seemed to have the better of it. Formosus himself consecrated the new pope.

Apparently, that as soon as he was chosen, Stephen V accompanied by all the bishops and deacons, went into the chamber of the Treasury in the Lateran to make the traditional gifts of money to the clergy and monasteries, and into the cellars to distribute bread and meat to the poor. To his amazement, he found instead that thieves had cleaned the place out but, wanting to carry on the tradition, he used his personal assets to do so.

Little wonder, however, that the pillaging had taken place, evidently during the period of the vacant see, since such pillages were common in the climate of anarchy existing at the election of a new pope and even during his reign. The luxury of the pontifical and episcopal courts in general was clearly not in accord with the principles of Christian doctrine, and such opulence provoked sackings by starving people who, every time a pope died, gave way to unbridled joy and simply stole whatever was supposed to be donated to the poor.

Still on the subject of pillaging, at the beginning of the pontificate of Stephen V the Saracens came out of their den on the Garigliano, and the pope called in vain for help from both the emperors of the West and of the East. He was only helped by Guido of Spoleto, who was probably hoping to obtain the imperial crown himself. He defeated the Saracens on the Liri, the victory giving a brief armistice to Rome. Meanwhile, events moved quickly at the imperial level. The Germans had deposed Charles the Fat in November 877 at an assembly in Trier, and the son of Carloman, Arnulf, was elected in his place. In January of 888, Charles finally died and Italy was once again without king or emperor. The scheming Italian dukes stirred as the

Carolingian dynasty in Germany came to an end, and pretenders to the various thrones came forward from all sides.

Oddo, count of Paris, became the king of France, Boso took over Provence, and Rudolf, Burgundy, while, in Germany, Arnulf had no opponents. In Italy there was a struggle between Berengarius, the marquis of Friuli, nephew of Louis the Pius on his mother's side, and Guido, the duke of Spoleto and Camerino, supported by numerous vassals in southern Italy. Berengarius had had himself crowned at the beginning of 888 in Pavia as the king of the Lombards, taking advantage of a temporary absence of Guido, whom Archbishop Folcus of Reims, a relative of his, had induced to dream about the crown of France. But returning hastily to Italy, Guido defeated his rival in two bloody battles and, at Pavia in 889, received the crown as king of Italy.

Basically what was important for Guido was the imperial crown since the concept of the empire was at that time superior to any form of nationalism, and Gregorovius explains this clearly. "There were various factions, those of Lombardy, Spoleto, Tuscany, which could be called nations from a certain viewpoint, but there was no nation in the political or social sense, as all of the essential elements were lacking. There was no community of interests, of language, of literature or the most essential, that of political unity." Guido did manage to obtain the imperial crown which he received at St. Peter's in February 891 from the hands of the same man who had been a vassal of the Carolingians! Perhaps Stephen imagined that the aim of his predecessors had at last been reached, as he placed the imperial crown on the head of a ward of the Church? The reality is that "the imperial majesty. . . had shrunk to a shadow," as Gregorovius notes, and the pope and the new emperor appeared to be playing with a crown larger than them, a crown made of papier-mâché in a game of political intrigues among the ambitious Italian noble families.

Stephen V died on 14 September 891, the same year as Photius, deposed about five years earlier by the new emperor of the East, Leo VI. Stephen was buried in the portico of St. Peter's.

1 1 1. FORMOSUS (8 9 1 – 8 9 6)

Born in Rome around 816, Formosus was consecrated pope on 6 October 891. He was a man linked to the Church of Rome through a long series of events, which had seen him as ecclesiastical head of the pro-German party and bound by friendship with the dukes of Spoleto from the time of his excommunication by John VIII, which had resulted in his loss of the episcopate of Portus. Released from excommunication by Marinus I and restored to his episcopal functions, he had lived peacefully under two successive pontiffs, while covertly setting his sights at the pontifical throne, the crowning of his ambitions.

It is clear that Formosus became pope thanks to the support of the pro-German party, whose chief representative was Arnulf of Germany and of his favorite, Berengarius, recently defeated by Guido in the race for the crowns of Italy and of the empire. The people of Spoleto had left that party and set up one with a definite nationalistic character. The pro-Frankish party no longer had anything to do with the affairs of the Papal State or of Italy in general, and the ecclesiastical head of this Spoletan faction was Sergius, a deacon, the opponent of Formosus in the papal election, and his unflinching enemy. Probably Formosus's election was the result of a compromise between the two factions since, in the spring of 892, the pope renewed the imperial coronation of Guido at Ravenna and at the same time crowned his son, Lambert, as the emperor. In reality, a pro-German pope was counterbalanced by an indigenous imperial dynasty, which was later to be consolidated in a hereditary form.

But Formosus quickly realized that the powerful position of the Spoletans would hardly be a guarantee for the Church of Rome of its privileges and territory, and that its temporal power was in serious danger. Guido often violated the borders of the Church's State and made raids on the lands belonging to St. Peter, while the conflict in Rome between the two parties threatened outbreaks of battles and sudden uprisings.

So, in 893, Formosus decided to send a delegation to Arnulf to beg him to come to Italy and free the Church's State from the "tyranny of the bad Christians," a generic accusation brought against all the Italian sovereigns. The king of Germany accepted the invitation and in the spring of the following year crossed the Alps. His activity against the "bad Christians" was limited to the north, where Milan and Pavia threw open their gates to him, and the Marquises Adalbert and Boniface of Tuscany declared themselves his vassals. Reckoning that his expedition was enough to restore order, Arnulf did not fire a shot or strike directly at Guido and the Spoletans, the "tyrants" against whom the pope really wanted his help. Furthermore, he returned to Germany at Easter, leaving Guido with the possibility of forming alliances with the frightened sovereigns and of planning other conquests of the Church's State. However, he died shortly afterwards as a result of a haemorrhage near the Taro, and his son, Lambert, then went to Rome to receive from the pope confirmation of his imperial rank.

Formosus found his hands tied since the Spoletan faction were applying pressure for a solemn confirmation, while the pro-German faction did not have sufficient force to oppose it. So he played for time, pretending to resign himself to the circumstances, and finally declared that he was prepared to concede to Lambert the renewal of what, in fact, he had recognized *in pectore* at Ravenna three years earlier. Meanwhile, however, he had sent another delegation to

Arnulf, who this time started marching with a strong army toward Rome from Bavaria with the intention of eliminating not only Lambert but also Berengarius, and arrogating to himself the titles of king of Italy and Emperor.

The Spoletan party felt betrayed. Formosus had done something which would cause him their eternal hatred, and they were determined that Arnulf was going to run into a well-organized defense. Lambert shut himself in Spoleto while his mother, the energetic Ageltrude, urged the Spoletan faction in Rome to revolt. The deacon Sergius with the nobles, Constantine and Stephen, captured the pope and took over the Leonine City. They were resolved to repel Arnulf's attack, bolstered by the fact that they held Formosus as a hostage in the dungeon of Sant'Angelo.

The spirit behind this bold undertaking was Guido's widow, Ageltrude, who was able to raise within the Spoletan party a hitherto unknown courage against the invading "barbarian," inspiring the people, whether Roman or not, with nationalistic and laic feelings. However, the enemy forces were greater and quickly succeeded in entering through Porta San Pancrazio and freeing the pope while Ageltrude managed to escape towards Spoleto.

Arnulf entered the city a few days after the unconditional surrender of the Spoletans and the return of the pope to his throne with all his powers. The clergy and the nobles went out to meet him at the Milvian Bridge, welcoming him like a liberator. Formosus, in line with tradition, awaited him on the steps of St. Peter's, accompanied him into the basilica and crowned him emperor, repudiating Lambert. All of this occurred in February 896.

The oath of allegiance that all Romans were supposed to give the new emperor, whether ordered or not by Formosus, sounded so full of hate for the Spoletan faction that it could be called Formosus's epitaph, or at least formed the basis for his later indictment. The *Annales Fuldenses* recite it as follows: "I swear by all the mysteries of God that, by my heart, my laws and my faithfulness to Formosus, my Lord and Pope, I am and shall be, for all of the days of my life, faithful to Emperor Arnulf, and that I shall never with any person be guilty of treason against him. Moreover, I shall never lend assistance to Lambert, the son of Ageltrude, or to his mother so that they may obtain any honor or powers, nor shall I ever, by secret deals or negotiations, consign this City to Lambert or to his mother Ageltrude or to their people."

There were no death penalties and the two noblemen, Constantine and Stephen, were simply exiled to Bavaria. Prudence and generosity inspired Arnulf and Formosus, or maybe the certainty of having the situation under control. In any event, Arnulf stayed in Rome only for fifteen days and, leaving his vassal Farlodus behind as governor of Rome, headed for Spoleto to destroy the defense prepared by Ageltrude and Lambert. But he failed to arrive there as he became paralyzed on the way and had to return to Bavaria, harmless.

This event brought about a sudden reversal of the situation in Italy since Formosus was all alone again without the protection of his German emperor. The Tuscan-Spoleto faction gained the upper hand in Rome where a whole series of riots and upheavals broke out. Pope Formosus died on 4 April 896, having probably been poisoned. He stayed buried in the area of the Vatican for only nine months, from where he is supposed to have been disinterred to undergo the famous macabre proceeding known as the "Council of the Cadaver."

1 1 2. BONIFACE VI (8 9 6)

In the chaotic atmosphere in which Rome found itself after the death of Formosus, the Tuscan-Spoleto faction seized both power and the papal throne, thus initiating an even more obscure era than previous ones in the history of the papacy, during which there was a line of popes on the See of St. Peter who were anything but religious.

As Gregorovius observes with an effective stylistic play of words, "The Ecclesiastical State fell prey to thousands of rapacious hands and even the spiritual prestige of the popes became nothing more than empty forms without any effective authority. Dark clouds shroud the Rome of that period, barely lit by timid and vague flashes which appear here and there in the ancient chronicles to throw some light on this dim epoch; a terrifying scenario to the rear of which appear the powerful barons who now are called consuls and senators; evil and violent popes who come from the ranks of the former; beautiful women, wild and lascivious; finally, imperial spectres who come forth, struggle and then disappear forever. And all of these phantoms rapidly come and go, and the new ones chase away the earlier ones, mixing everything in a precipitous tumult."

On the death of Formosus, Boniface VI, a Roman twice excommunicated by John VIII when he was a subdeacon and a priest, was elected pope. He reigned, however, only for fifteen days, from 11 April to 26 April 896, fatally stricken by gout. His pontificate is mentioned, in fact, only because it was the second shortest in the entire history of the popes.

1 1 3. STEPHEN VI (8 9 6 — 8 9 7)

When Boniface VI died, the national-Spoletan party lost no time in electing another candidate of its own, a certain Stephen, a Roman, son of a presbyter, John, who was crowned that very month of April 896. Previously the bishop of Anagni, he had been consecrated by Formosus himself, who had later become his bitterest enemy.

Clearly under the thumb of the leaders of the Spoletan party, he probably knew little of politics, even if initially he recognized Arnulf as emperor. But

Ageltrude promptly gave him to understand how he was to behave, so he recognized Lambert, who had taken the throne at Pavia as emperor, and fully submitted to the arrogance of that woman who induced him to commit one of the most infamous deeds in the history of the papacy.

It was February 897. Lambert joined his mother in Rome and made the pope start a solemn trial of Formosus. The latter had dared to repudiate the house of Spoleto, betraying Italy by inviting in a barbarian king, therefore he had to be tried and to undergo the consequent punishment. It mattered little that he had been dead and buried for eight months, and Ageltrude and her son did not hesitate even before a tomb already sealed and consecrated. The Roman clergy had to pass judgement on the evil pontiff who had betrayed a national trust! A touch of civic "fascism" was undeniably behind all this and provides a measure of the depths of ignominy to which a pope could sink as the victim of an anti-Christian hatred and the earthly interests of a perverse woman.

Liutprand and other chroniclers record this event in more or less detail, but from the many sources Gregorovius is the one who succeeds in describing what took place in the most realistic and dramatic form, and probably makes the most fascinating reading.

"Cardinals, bishops and many other ecclesiastical dignitaries gathered together in the Lateran basilica," reports the German historian. "The corpse of the pope was taken from the sepulchre in which it had rested for several months and, clothed in the papal vestments, was placed on a throne in the Council Chamber. The lawyer of Pope Stephen stood up and, turning toward that horrendous mummy at whose side stood trembling a deacon who acted as the defender, notified to him the counts of the indictment. Then the living pope demanded from the dead one, in mad fury: "How could you in your insane ambition usurp the apostolic see, you who were already bishop of Portus?" The attorney for Formosus mumbled something in his defense, as much as horror allowed him to say anything, then the cadaver was pronounced guilty and sentenced. The synod signed the act of deposition, damned the pope for eternity and decreed that all those upon whom he had conferred holy orders would have to be ordained again. The vestments were torn off the corpse, and the three fingers of the right hand, with which the Latins imparted benediction, were cut off. Then with savage shouts the corpse was dragged out of the chamber, through the streets of Rome, and finally dumped into the Tiber in the midst of the yelling of an immense throng."

But a legend lightens this macabre drama: Saba correctly notes that Gregorovius speaks of a "mummy" and he explains it as follows: "Indeed, we can wonder, without talking of a case of mummification, how on earth a corpse, some nine months old, could have remained intact for the shameful vengeance of his ferocious judges."

So that nothing would be missing from the horror of these frightful events, the ancient basilica of the Lateran collapsed: (possibly a revenge of the divine). It is probable, instead, that the "Council of the Cadaver" took place in the ruins of the basilica which had collapsed during a previous earthquake. In which case, the scenario of the ruins would have made the atmosphere still more sinister and fitting for the occasion.

In any event, despite all the variations which the sources of the chroniclers may give it, that "council" does reflect the state of barbarity in which Rome and the papacy had fallen during the tenth century. On the other hand, legendary stories, nourished also by miracles which are supposed to have occurred later near the remains of Formosus, finished by redeeming the pope from the defamation of the trial.

His body, carried along for about twenty miles by the current of the Tiber, apparently lay for three days, still in one piece, on the river bank. Then the deceased pontiff appeared in a dream to a good monk and showing him the bank of the river, begged him to bury it. Theodore II, pope in 897, is said to have actually collected his bones and placed them among the tombs of the Apostles in an imposing ceremony.

Clearly, all these legends about rehabilitation had their origin in the people's sudden anger that arose a few months after that macabre event. The spread of indignation fed a desire for the pro-German party, which all at once gained the upper hand, instigating the people to take revenge. Even Stephen VI suffered the consequences, as he wound up in jail and was strangled in August 897.

Later on, his friend, Sergius III, a lasting foe of Formosus, raised a funeral monument to Stephen bearing an inscription that reveals a deep hatred of Formosus and recounts the tragic end of Stephen VI.

114. ROMANUS (897)

Romanus, the successor of Stephen VI, reigned for only four months, from August to November 897. We know practically nothing about him, only that he was born in Gaul and probably became pope with the support of the pro-German party. In line with that faction, he condemned the behavior of his predecessor and rehabilitated the reputation of Formosus.

His fate is buried in legend but he is supposed to have been deposed and shut up in a monastery.

115. THEODORE II (897)

Theodore II, successor of Romanus, reigned for only twenty days in December 897 making his pontificate the fourth shortest in the history of the popes.

There are those who say he was born in Rome, others that he came from Greece, brought to the papal throne also by the pro-German party, which evidently had a strong following among the electorate but was unable to protect its pope.

During his brief pontificate, Theodore nonetheless convened a council which reviewed the trial of Formosus. The council documents were then the basis for a more important council convened by his successor, John IX. According to legend, Theodore II had the cadaver of Formosus, miraculously found by a monk, buried in his original sepulchre in St. Peter's.

Nothing is really known about his death.

116. JOHN IX (898—900)

John IX, son of Rampoaldus, was from Tivoli where he was born around 840, and succeeded Theodore II in January 898. A cardinal-deacon, he was a Benedictine of German origin and was probably the candidate of the pro-German party. As such, he convened a council at Rome for the definitive rehabilitation of Pope Formosus in the spring of 898.

To begin with, the "Council of the Cadaver" was annulled and all related documents burnt. The bishops of Albano, Portus, Velletri, Gaul, Orte, and Tuscany begged for pardon which they were granted after declaring that they had been forced to appear at that council under terrifying threats. Instead, the bishop of Cere, Sergius, the priests Benedict and Martin, as well as the deacons Leo, Paschal, and John, the promoters of the entire vile proceedings, were excommunicated and exiled. Moreover, all the bishops, priests and acolytes ordained by Formosus were reinstated in their duties.

It was also acknowledged that the anointing of Arnulf as emperor had been "cleverly extorted" from Formosus and, as such, was declared null and void. As a result, the earlier anointing of Lambert at Ravenna was considered valid. John IX evidently decided this ruling of the council in a shrewd diplomatic move. Even though he had come to the Pontifical Throne as the candidate of the pro-German party, he reckoned that Arnulf, still ailing, could not guarantee the defense of the Church State, nor be a danger if he were to challenge the authenticity of the imperial title. It was more opportune to patch things up with the House of Spoleto, especially since Lambert dominated Italy unchallenged, having nothing to fear from his rival, Berengar.

So Lambert and John IX met at Ravenna where the pope presided over another council of seventy-four bishops during the summer of that same year. It dealt with the ticklish problem of papal elections, which had recently brought back violence and fighting between opposing groups. Lothar's constitution of 824 was revived, with the recognition of the State of the Church renewed, together with the right of papal sovereignty over it. Officially recognized by the pope as emperor, Lambert promised the restitution of the assets illegally seized and guaranteed the defense of the property of the Church.

In other words, they renewed ancient promises, brushed up unrespected rights and guarantees, and dreamt of peace. Lambert's conduct appeared loyal, as did John IX's confirming of the imperial rank on him, even if the pope, in fact, had had no choice. However, the dream vanished in October of that year when the strong young Lambert died suddenly from a simple fall from his horse in the forest of Marengo, which, 900 years later, would become famous because of a great battle fought there. The result of Lambert's death was that matters changed radically once more both for Italy and for the pope.

Berengar, sure of himself as the only candidate, raced from Verona to Pavia, where many vassals quickly recognized him as a worthy candidate for the title of King and Emperor, and the death of Arnulf in November 899 appeared to pave the way for him. But above all, he managed to obtain the friendship of Adalbert of Tuscany and conclude a treaty with Ageltrude, the widow of Guido and the mother of Lambert. However, a new event upset Berengar's plans, namely the invasion by the Hungarians in August 899, which he tried in vain to resist. His army was decimated on 24 September near the Brenta and this defeat caused him the loss of a lot of prestige in his candidature for the crown.

At the same time, the star of a new pretender, Louis of Provence, was on the rise he claimed prestigious origins as the grandson of the famous Louis II though, in fact, he was only one of many descendants of the Carolingian dynasty. John IX unexpectedly saw all his hopes for peace and a serene co-existence between Papacy and empire flounder. Would it all be maintained by the new claimant of the imperial crown? He had no way of knowing, since death removed him in January 900. He was buried in St. Peter's.

1 1 7. BENEDICT IV (900–903)

A Roman, the son of a certain Mammolus, Benedict IV was consecrated pope between January and February of 900, and, having been ordained a priest by Formosus, he followed the policy of John IX. Failing to pursue an independent one he found himself involved in the usual problems with Saracens in the south and the new Hungarians in the north, while seeking a defender in the man whom the counts and the bishops considered the strongest and worthiest heir to the imperial crown, Louis of Provence.

The coronation of Louis III as emperor took place in Rome in February 901. From what is found in some of the decrees he issued, he exercised his imperial prerogatives in the city by nominating as *iudices* from among the most illustrious Roman nobles men such as Theophylactus and Crescenzio, important names around which the political life of Rome was to be concentrated in later years. Louis III contested Berengar's power in Italy, but then went back over the Alps, leaving the pope undefended and the State of the Church a territory of disputes and struggles among factions and families.

We know next to nothing about Benedict IV, described by the chronicler Flodoardus as "a mild man clearly of a priestly nature," perhaps not suited to live during an era destined to profane the sanctity of the Church. He died in July 903, and was buried in St. Peter's.

1 1 8. LEO V (903)

Leo V, a native of Ardea, succeeded Benedict IV, and was consecrated in July 903, at a time of overt disputes. He was on the pontifical throne for only one month because he was deposed by the Roman presbyter of the Church of St. Damasus, a certain Christopher, and it is uncertain whether or not the latter had him assassinated. In any event, Leo V died in jail in September 903, and a month later Christopher had himself consecrated, though he is considered an antipope.

His reign lasted until January 904, when the ex-bishop of Cere, Sergius, came back to Rome from the seven-year exile to which John IX had condemned him at the time of his excommunication. Sergius, with the support of Theophylactus, seized the pontifical throne by violence and forced Christopher to become a monk or, according to some, had him strangled.

1 1 9. SERGIUS III (904—9 1 1)

Sergius III, a member of a noble Roman family related to the counts of Tuscolo, had been ordained a subdeacon by Pope Marinus, a deacon by Stephen V and then bishop of Cere by Formosus. As the chief ecclesiastical instigator of the "Council of the Cadaver" he had been excommunicated and exiled by John IX. Having returned to Rome thanks to the help of Albericus, marquis of Camerino, Sergius reached the pontifical throne by violent means with the support of Theophylactus's family. In fact, Rome was a vacant see, as Leo V had died in jail in November 903, having been deposed by the presbyter, Christopher, who was consecrated pope by a portion of the clergy, but as mentioned above considered an antipope.

Sergius III was the first pope to reach the pontifical throne through the determination of a powerful Roman noble family, at the head of which was Theophylactus, dux et *magister militum* as well as *sacri palatii vesterarius*, who had combined in his hands both the military power and that of the pontifical administration. By having Sergius consecrated pope on 29 January

904, he gained control even over the pontifical throne. His worthy consort was Theodora, a forceful woman, influential in political circles and in history remembered as a high-born whore, like her two daughters, Theodora II and Marozia.

For quite a while the papacy was dependent on that family, a humiliating situation certainly not in keeping with the principles of Christianity, to the extent that, according to Baronio, this dark period of its history is usually described as that of the regime of the prostitutes and pornography.

This information, terrible for the Church but not without some foundation, comes mainly from Liutprand, bishop of Cremona, who claims that Sergius III had a relationship with the noble woman, Marozia, and that from their union was born a son who was to be the future pope, John XI. This information was believed by Baronio and Duchesne and, whether totally or only partially true, will not help us discover Apostolic virtues in this pope.

In any event, in 905 Marozia married Alberic who had followed Sergius into her bed, almost as compensation for the help he had given to her lover who was now safely on the pontifical throne. Alberic, a true *homo novus* in Rome, was climbing towards the summit of power there, for the moment in the hands of Theophylactus and Theodora, but which was to become his and Marozia's.

Sergius who, one will remember, was Formosus' arch-enemy, revoked everything that had been decided by his predecessors in the latter's favor and even declared the election of Formosus null and void, rendering as a result invalid all the ordinations which he had granted. This caused a proper crisis in the ecclesiastical community in Rome, and not a single priest or bishop felt secure about his own consecration since, at any moment they could be blackmailed by Sergius and his followers.

In the area around Rome, however, an opposition party was formed against the pontifical tyranny of Sergius III and of the family of Theophylactus. Opposition was restricted to the writing of defamatory statements which were secretly circulated, gradually engendering a spiritual resistance to the regime which, in time, could even have become a real revolution. Among the many defamations can be noted those of the Frankish acolyte, Ausilius, as well as an anonymous *Invectiva in Romam pro Formosa papa*.

But the clerical-aristocratic regime was too strong to be shaken by a few pamphlets circulating mainly at upper class cultural levels and with no populist cachet. Moreover, Sergius III was an unscrupulous man, determined to defend his own position with the same means he had acquired it.

There are those, however, like Saba, who tried to stand up for this pope, basing themselves on Gregorovius and recalling certain good works recorded by the German historian. In fact, this was not a defense or an alibi for the "monster" but rather a simple appreciation of this man of character, as stated in a papal bull in 906 which declared that "he donated a goodly amount of funds belonging to Tuscia to the bishopric of Silva Candida, whose inhabitants had been almost completely exterminated by the Saracens." And there was another bull by which "he donated to Eufemia, abbess of the Corsarum convent, substantial amounts in compensation for damages wrought by infidels upon the properties of this abbey" and, finally there was the reconstruction of the Lateran basilica, furnished with new votive offerings. Nevertheless these good works do not obliterate the stamp of ignominy which characterises the figure of Sergius III.

At this juncture, the papacy no longer had any need for imperial protection since it could protect itself. Louis III kept on making use of the title of Emperor, but his figure was of no use to the State of the Church and he must have realized this as, in an effort to recoup the prestige he had lost or never really possessed, he again crossed the Alps. However, defeated by Berengar at Verona, he was blinded by him and sent back home. Yet the unfortunate Berengar again failed to gain the crown, as he met with strong opposition in the Roman aristocracy which wanted nothing more to do with an emperor.

Sergius III died on 14 April 911 and was buried in "his" Lateran basilica.

120. ANASTASIUS III (911—913)

Anastasius III, a Roman from a noble family, succeeded Sergius III and reigned from April 911 to June 913.

We do not know much about him, only that the chronicler, Flodardo, praises his mildness and his integrity. However, it should be noted that during his pontificate the conversion of the Normans under King Rollo took place, an event that would have its influence on the future history of the papacy.

Certainly a victim of Theophylactus's regime, he must not have distanced himself a great deal from his predecessor's policies. He was buried in St. Peter's.

121. LANDO (913—914)

Lando, a native of Sabina and the son of a certain Tainus, succeeded Anastasius III, reigning from July 913, to February 914. Nothing is known about him but it is logical to conclude that he adapted himself to the regime of the lay Roman aristocracy since there was no other way out for the papacy.

As Gregorovius observes, "Theophylactus and then Alberic, or rather, their women, who held the city in their grip for a long time, signalled the arrival of a new epoch in Rome's history." And then, with a telling rhetorical comment, the German historian adds: "The history of the popes into which, just as in a cloister or a temple, only holy women should enter, received through these impudent, scheming women a clearly profane imprint." And thereby, "the Roman Church of this epoch became a bordello."

122. JOHN X (914—928)

John X, born about 860 at Tossignano near Imola, had been ordained a deacon by Bishop Peter of Bologna. He became the agent for Cailone, archbishop
of Ravenna, and often came to Rome to carry out probably secretarial missions
at the pontifical court. According to Luitprand, he (John) became the lover of
Theodora, the wife of Theophylactus. This helped his ecclesiastical career, so
much so that he was named bishop of Bologna by Sergius III and, upon the
death of Cailone—apparently by violent means—obtained the archbishopric of
Ravenna, which he held for nine years from July 905, until March 914, when
he was elected pope.

So with John X the exception of a transfer from one see to another was
renewed, which had been contested with Formosus but with John became
normal practice. His election as pope had been wanted by Theodora and by
her husband Theophylactus, even if John X had never curried favor with
them. Ambitious and unscrupulous, he was the last pope to assert his own
personality in a totally political sense, prior to a lengthy series of puppet-
popes in the power of the Roman aristocracy.

A demonstration of a last attempt to confront the city's aristocracy, in
order to defend the pope's temporal power, was the resumption of imperial
authority with an Italian sovereign, of that poor old Berengar who had
always longed for a crown. And while the blinded Louis was still alive in
Provence, his position had no significance either in Italy or for the Church.
To be in favor of a national faction therefore could mean protection for the
Pontifical State against possible uprisings from within and without.

So it was that in November 915, welcomed with the usual solemn ceremonies, Berengar arrived in Rome where he was met by Peter, the brother of the
pontiff and by the son of the consul, Theophylactus, representing the two
municipal authorities. The pope, following tradition, welcomed the prince on
the steps of St. Peter's and, after Berengar had sworn to protect the Church, the
doors of the basilica swung open and the coronation took place in the first part
of December. For the third time, by committing treason again against an
emperor still on his throne, an Italian noble had gained the imperial crown.

Berengar was a colourless, narrow-minded sovereign, who took on the
duty of protecting the Church with words only. But John X knew "his"
emperor well and it was for this reason that he had chosen Berengar. He preferred a "home-made" emperor who would not get in his way over the
recovery of the Church's assets, to a stranger full of surprises. Moreover, the
appointment was helpful for the revival of the pseudo-patriotic sentiment
John X needed to resolve once and for all the problem of the Saracens, who
were continually invading papal lands from the south and pillaging the
Roman Campagna and the Sabine area.

In the wake of this national feeling, the pope set up a league against the Saracens. Berengar did not participate directly in the military campaign but he did put at the disposal of the pope the Tuscan troops of the Marquis Adalbert, as well as the soldiers from Spoleto led by Alberic, Marozia's husband. The dukes of Gaeta and Naples were persuaded to drop their trading agreements with the infidels through gifts of lands and the still prestigious title of *Patricius*. The Saracens, expelled from the Sabine and Campania, massed together near the Garigliano where they were defeated in June 916. This episode was described by Gregorovius as "the most glorious national undertaking by the Italians in the tenth century, as the victory at Ostia had been previously." Central Italy was finally freed from the Saracen scourge.

And all of this turned into a personal triumph for John X, as Gregorovius himself notes: "The return of John X to Rome was like that of a victor in the Punic Wars. The chroniclers do not relate the banquets arranged by the city out of gratitude, or the triumphal entry of the Liberator preceded by the Saracen prisoners. Nevertheless, we can well picture his entering through one of the southern gates, marching along beside Marquis Alberic, in the midst of the public's acclaim, and at the head of the noble dukes and the consuls of Rome. And we can also imagine that Alberic, welcomed with loud applause by the city, requested and obtained from the pope the agreed prize. It is likely that John compensated him not only with material gifts but also by granting him the dignity of consul."

"Following the victory at the Garigliano," the German historian continues, "Alberic must have acquired an extremely influential position in Rome. During the years which followed, however, we do not know what he was doing or where he was living. We do not have any information even about Theophylactus. It is said that the son of Alberic was born in the palace that the family had on the Aventine, and it cannot be excluded that this was the residence of the marquis who had become consul. As long as Berengar was in power and the city docilely obeyed the administration of the pope, the emperor's friend, Alberic, had no way to achieve his ambitious projects. Indeed, for five years he was the chief supporter of the pontiff," after which, urged on by his wife, Marozia, he made his decisive move to grasp power.

One indication of the change in the situation could be noted between 921 and 924, when the nobles of Tuscia and Lombardy, led by Adalbert, marquis of Ivrea, who was also the husband of Gisella, Berengar's daughter, rebelled against the emperor and appealed to King Rudolph of Burgundy. John X then saw his dream of national unity fall apart. Indeed, Berengar, who was incapable of opposing the new pretender to his crown and now desperate, called for help from the terrible Hungarians. With the north of Italy becoming a land of pillaging and battles, Rudolph figured it was wise to return home. The Hungarians put Pavia to flames and Berengar was finally assassinated in 924.

Italy once again fell into chaos. With Berengar dead, Rudolph took over his position, but as king of Italy he did not succeed in stopping the anarchy in the country. "The cities were set aflame and the barbaric Hungarians held Bacchanalia on their ashes," records Gregorovius with his usual rhetoric, "the inhabitants fled to lonely and wild places while the king, vassals and bishops fought to seize slivers of power, and lovely women, whose faces reflected exultant insolence, seemed like maenads leading satanic dances."

It was in this atmosphere that Alberic, egged on by his wife Marozia, launched his attack. According to the chronicles, he succeeded in taking over Rome and briefly imposing his authority until John, with the support of the people, was able to retake the reins of power and throw him out. John was unable to do anything against Marozia who cleverly had stayed out of the conspiracy. Alberic is said to have fled to Orte, whence he also called the Hungarians to help him, but wound up a victim in his own castle of the same Magyar atrocities as had Berengar.

Meanwhile, the Italian nobles, antagonistic towards the inept Rudolph, called Hugo of Provence to Italy and offered him the crown. The principal plotter for this "change of the guard" was his own half-brother Guido, marquis of Tuscany. In July 926, Hugo was elected king of Italy at Pavia and received the homage of a pontifical legate in Pisa. No longer feeling secure, John X sought assistance from this new foreigner against his enemies within Rome and those opposed to the State of the Church who, after the deaths of Theophylactus, Theodora, and Alberic, were Marozia and her powerful henchmen.

John X had a meeting in Mantua with Hugo and offered him the imperial crown, but Marozia was not standing idly by. She shrewdly gave her hand to Guido of Tuscany and the marriage brought her the military strength that she probably lacked.

John X saw that now he could count only on his own forces and on his brother Peter, to whom, after Alberic died, he had entrusted the government of the city, naming him Consul of the Romans. But when it came to the battle against the troops of Guido and Marozia during the attack on the Lateran, Peter could do nothing but call to the Hungarians for help. It was clearly the end. According to the information of the chroniclers, gathered by Gregorovius, "Peter, after he had called in the Hungarians and come with them to the gates of Rome, had then joined his brother in the Lateran. He died before the pope's eyes, and Guido's soldiers dragged John away as well who, by Marozia's orders, was jailed in Castel Sant'Angelo."

It was May 928. In the inscrutable whirlpool of an inexorable destiny, John X, exalted by the love of one woman, Theodora, fell victim to the hate of another woman, Marozia, the daughter of his own mistress.

In the history of the nobles of Tossignano, one reads that it was Guido who suffocated the pope with a glove, and that this was the implacable continuation of an ancient family feud. It appears that Guido's father, Albert the Rich, had previously killed John's brother, Peter. The assassination of the pope took place between March 928, and the first months of 929.

123. Leo VI (928)

In a Rome dominated by Marozia, the real temporal first lady of the city who, with reason, had herself named *senatrix* and *patricia*, the pontiffs who followed John X on the throne of Peter were in fact men of hers. Assisting her in her maneuvers was her husband Guido, who had certainly received the title of Consul.

Leo VI, son of the senior pontifical dignitary Christopher, was consecrated while John X was still languishing in jail in May 928. Nothing is known about him except that he wrote an encyclical to the bishops of Dalmatia to induce them to obey their primate, John, the archbishop of Spalato (now Split). Platina tells us that "he was modest and holy all his life, and gave his all for the church, even though those terribly corrupt times saddened him." He died in December 928, and was buried in St. Peter's.

124. Stephen VII (928–931)

A Roman, Stephen VII, son of Teudemondus, was a creature of Marozia like his predecessor. During the year of Stephen's consecration, Marozia was widowed by her second husband, Guido, who probably died after he had done his wife the final favor of assassinating John X, if it is true that the latter was still languishing in jail when Rome already had a new pope.

Very little is known also of this pope, who was elected in December 928, and the stories about privileges he granted to certain monasteries do not form part of his biography. He was one more puppet-pope in the hands of Marozia whose only aim was to see her son, John, on the throne. Nevertheless, this woman, so criticised for her libertine behavior, has her importance.

Beyond her amorous passions, her adulteries and her several marriages, she demonstrated, as Falco has noted, a "strong will to impose her ambition in a virile way," to put a stop to the feudal anarchy in Rome and establish, in the general disorder, a strong civil authority which would eliminate the temporal power of the popes. Her mistake was to use the popes like puppets, an error which her son, Alberic, did not make. He worked with a civic, political idea in view, relegating the popes to their religious activities, which was the only reason why he maintained the institution of the papacy.

Stephen VII died in February 931, leaving the throne to Marozia's son, John, and was buried in the Vatican Grottoes.

125. JOHN XI (931—935)

Between February and March of 931, Marozia put on the pontifical throne John XI, the son whom she had borne from her relationship with Sergius III, and who was probably born around 906. There are those, like Saba, who categorically state that John XI was the son of Marozia and Alberic I, but personally, I think Seppelt's view is correct: "That gossip Liutprand is not the only source on the illegitimate origins of the new pope, so this illegitimacy can be accepted as having a factual basis."

Nothing is known about the ecclesiastical career of John XI, only that it must have been long enough to allow him to become pope. His pontificate has no history either, overshadowed by the last years of his mother's life and the beginning of his half-brother Alberic II's power.

Having been widowed, Marozia quickly planned a third marriage, this time to Hugh, king of Italy, a man of a nature very much like hers, capable of trading bishoprics and abbeys, and giving them to his impudent courtiers. In a truly libertine spirit, he was praised for these virtues by his "court poet," Liutprando, bishop of Cremona, who called him a "philosopher" for the skill with which he was able to hide his own profligacy under the cover of sophisticated manners. An unscrupulous politician, Hugh did not shy away from the opportunity offered him by Marozia to lord it over Rome, and she was dying to change her title of *patricia* and *senatrix* into the nobler one of Queen.

However, this marriage would have been a union between in-laws since Hugh was a brother of Guido, the second husband of Marozia, and canon law viewed such a marriage as incestuous. Obviously, the pope would have had no problem in overlooking this and giving his blessing to his mother's new marriage, even if it meant violating church law. But Hugh simplified matters for him by providing false documents. He invented different parents for the deceased Guido and for the other brother, Lambert, duke of Tuscany, who, in order to give credit to his true parents, underwent the "judgement of God" and came out the winner. But it went badly for him because Hugh had him blinded, after which, with the family questions resolved and being fortunately widowed, Hugh left for Rome to celebrate his marriage to Marozia. He arrived at the gates of Rome with his army in March 932, entered the city with a horse guard, and the wedding was celebrated in Castel Sant'Angelo, blessed by John XI, the bride's own son.

The imperial coronation should have followed the wedding, but what for Marozia was to have been the apex of her aspirations, the highest goal that she could have desired, turned out to be her doom. During the festivities, Hugh was arrogant and treated the nobles of the city with contempt, and capped it by insulting the young Alberic II, her son with Alberic of Camerino, slapping him in the face in front of everybody.

Alberic, already displeased by the marriage because it interfered with his plans to gain power in Rome and mortally offended by the insult, left Castel Sant'Angelo in a fury and summoned the population around him. His oration was an exhortation to the people to revolt against the unbearable tyranny of a woman like Marozia and the new lordship of Hugh, whom he called a sort of civilized barbarian and the descendant of those who had once been the slaves of the Romans.

The people were waiting for nothing better. They took up weapons, barred the gates of the city to prevent the entry of Hugh's army and attacked the Castello. The king, unable to defend himself, decided to flee. He slid down a rope from the top of Hadrian's Tomb and escaped from the city, retreating in great haste with his army. Behind him he left his wife and the much-desired crown.

The city rejoiced. In one stroke the people had got rid of a king and an emperor and they could do with the pope what they wished; they had won their independence. Alberic received the title of *Princeps atque omnium Romanorum* Senator and his first deed was to throw his mother in jail and shut his half-brother, John XI, who continued to be pope but with no temporal power, in the Lateran under strict surveillance. Marozia disappeared forever from the political scene.

Rome became a republic of dignitaries. With the donations that constituted the State of the Church, the Romans wanted to create a free state which, as Falco noted, "could have a papal aristocracy, a local dynasty and a prince who, with an iron hand would liberate Rome from the Islamic stranglehold, free it from the ambitions and the fluctuations of kings and emperors, and bring back security and grandeur to it." A sort of secular Rome was born, in which the existence of the pontiffs was tolerated but with freedom to act solely in the religious field, and who only had the political power to date their documents by the years of their pontificates.

Moreover, every legal, economic, and political action in the strict sense was underwritten by "We, Alberic, by the grace of God, the humble prince and senator of all the Romans," and his name was inscribed on all the coins issued in those years.

John XI died in December 935 and was buried in St. John Lateran.

126. LEO VII (936–939)

Leo VII, a Roman and probably a Benedictine monk, succeeded John XI and was consecrated pope on 3 January 936.

During his pontificate, Hugh, after trying to reconquer his own prestige by attacking Rome, an attempt which failed because of an epidemic that struck his army, made a treaty of peace with Alberic, mediated by Abbot Odo of Cluny, the reformer of Western monastic life. As a peace token Hugo gave the hand of his daughter, Alda, to Alberic who married her because his hopes of marrying a Greek princess had foundered.

Under Leo VII, and with Odo of Cluny as his inspiration, Alberic supported the reform of the decadent Benedictine monastic discipline, becoming, as the chronicles of the time reported, a sort of protector of monasteries by arranging their reconstruction and reforming them. As a result, the abbey of St. Paul, the monasteries of St. Agnes and St. Andrew at Rome, as well as those at Subiaco and Nepi, were revived. The palace of Alberic on the Aventine was donated to the abbot of Cluny and changed into a new abbey with the name of the Blessed Mary.

Clearly, however, Alberic was not acting solely from religious motives in this work of monastic reform and reconstruction of abbeys and monasteries. His purpose was to evict from the Roman Campagna the barons who had taken over the monastic properties, together with their vassals who occupied the farmlands of the monasteries, all of whom could some day become dangerous by opposing him with these peaceful religious communities.

Out of gratitude for all of this, Leo VII called the Prince of Rome the "merciful Alberic, his chosen spiritual son and glorious Prince of the Romans." He knew but was not able to say more. Leo VII died on 13 July 939, and was buried in St. Peter's.

127. STEPHEN VIII (939—942)

Stephen VIII, a Roman, titular priest of Saints Sylvester and Martin ai Monti, was consecrated pope on 14 July 939.

His pontificate included nothing of real importance except the continuation of the monastic reform, with related concessions of privileges to the monastery of Tolla, near Piacenza, and to the abbey of the Lorena.

According to a legend, he was a native of Germany and the victim of a popular revolt that led to his mutilation, obliging him to hide in a hermitage. This is hardly credible because it presupposes a weakening of Alberic's power, and he would never have permitted a foreigner to be elected pontiff.

Stephen VIII died in October 942 and was buried in St. Peter's.

128. MARINUS II (942—946)

Marinus II, a Roman, was consecrated pope on 30 October 942, and died in May 946.

Nothing is known about him except what a monk, Benedict, from Soracte said about him, that he blindly obeyed Alberic as a "gentle and peaceful man."

He continued the program of reformation of monastic discipline, which seems to have succeeded in keeping pontiffs such as him busy, was decidedly devout but lacking in personality. Privileges were granted to various monasteries such as those of Fulda and Montecassino.

129. AGAPETUS II (946—955)

A Roman by birth, Agapetus II was consecrated pope on 10 May 946. Under his pontificate the see of Rome gradually began to resume contact with foreign countries, partly on account of a series of changes which were taking place at a political level in Italy and in Europe.

Otto I, of the House of Saxony, had become the king of Germany, and his increasing prestige enhanced his possibilities beyond the borders of his kingdom. Calls and appeals reaching him from the confused situation in Italy were difficult to resist.

After Hugh of Provence died leaving the crown of Italy to his son, Lothar, the latter ruled under the tutelage of Berengar, Marquis of Ivrea, the nephew of Berengar I. Indeed, the sudden death of Lothar in 950 rendered Berengar suspect, especially since he had had himself immediately crowned as king. Lothar's widow, Adelaide, Berengar's prisoner in a castle on Lake Garda, found a way to send Otto a request for help together with an offer of marriage.

Otto seized the opportunity. He invaded Italy in 951, defeated Berengar and took the crown as king of Italy. The ceremonies of his marriage to Adelaide were sumptuous, but his goal was the imperial crown. So in autumn of the same year, Otto sent to Rome from Pavia Archbishop Frederick of Mainz and Bishop Arbert of Coira with an express request to Pope Agapetus II for anointment and imperial coronation. From Rome came a clear refusal, and it is obvious that Alberic was the one who replied to Otto's two ambassadors.

The new king of Italy was unable to put pressure on the pope because in the spring of 952 he had to return to Germany, called back there because of a new Hungarian invasion which he succeeded in putting down only in 955.

In the meantime, Italy went on its own uncharted course and Alberic retained power in Rome until his death in 954. As soon as he realized that his end was near, he went into St. Peter's and, in front of the Altar of the Confession, had the nobles and the clergy of Rome swear that when Agapetus II died, Alberic's son, Octavian, would be elected pope. Alberic realized that the separation of temporal from spiritual power would not last long and he feared that Otto I, who had already shown evidence of imperial ambitions, would intervene in the matter. He put his last hope in his son, at least for as long as power in Rome would remain linked to his family. Of a mild character but with a good deal of religious dignity, Agapetus was not capable of political intrigue which, in the event of pontifical elections, could easily lead to simony. He did not dare to protest or to interpose obstacles to Octavian during the period between the death of Alberic on 31 August 954, and his own in December of the following year. He was buried in St. John Lateran.

130. JOHN XII (955–964)

When Agapetus II passed away, the clergy and nobles of Rome obeyed the oath they had taken before Alberic II, and elected as pope his son Octavian, who was probably born in 937. Octavian, between the death of his father and that of his predecessor, had assumed civil authority in Rome with the titles of *princeps* and Senator. He was probably between eighteen and twenty years of age when he became regent, and, in all likelihood, he had had no ecclesiastical education whatsoever. However, in anticipation of his election as pontiff, he would have managed to complete a rapid career in a succession of appointments up to deacon or priest.

His consecration took place on 16 December 955, and he was the second pope in history, after John II, to forego his princely baptismal name of Octavian and take that of John XII. With him temporal and spiritual power were again reunited in the person of a pope. Thus the revolution of 932 had had no other result for Alberic II, its instigator, than to raise to the pontifical see another representative of the noble family which would thereafter be known as that of the counts of Tusculum.

Although he had become the pastor of Christianity, John XII had not abandoned the way of life he had led from a very tender age, and in which he would have indulged all the more as *princeps*. He continued to gratify his unbridled pleasures, and the Lateran Palace became a real bordello, with the pope surrounded by beautiful women and handsome boys in a depraved life-style completely at variance with his ecclesiastical duties.

There is a story that, in the style of Caligula who had named "Senator" a horse, a drunken John XII ordained a stable-boy deacon, and did not hesitate to consecrate as a bishop a ten-year-old boy as token of his affection, or to give sacred vessels to prostitutes, even if of distinguished lineage.

He also posed as a clever politician and tried to extend his power to southern Italy with a great military undertaking, using Roman, Tuscan, and Spoletan troops in a kind of crusade to recover properties of the patrimony of St. Peter from the lords of Benevento and Capua. However, the campaign was a disaster, and he was forced to seek a humiliating peace.

But he did not give up and, abandoning the balanced policy of his father, aimed at the reconstitution of the State of the Church within its northern boundaries by reconquering the exarchate. This involved lining himself up against Berengar and his son Adalbert, who had strengthened their power in northern Italy and were putting pressure on Emilia and Romagna. It also meant abandoning the nationalist party, thus unwisely becoming the chief of the pro-German one, something which would have earned him at Rome the antipathy of the majority of the nobility.

Having made his decision and convinced that he would find in Otto of Germany a faithful defender of Christian ideals and of the State of the Church, he offered him officially the imperial crown in 960 through a delegation which included counts from northern Italy who were opponents of Berengar. Otto accepted with pleasure and promised the papal nuncios that he would protect the possessions of the Church, renewing the ancient treaties between the Carolingian emperors and the popes. On 31 January 962, he arrived in Rome with his army and set up camp on the usual Neronian meadows. On 2 February he made his entrance into the Leonine City and was received in St. Peter's with the traditional pomp and circumstance, and on that same day Otto and his wife Adelaide were crowned. The resurrected empire thus passed into the hands of the House of Saxony.

A pact followed the coronation, the famous *Privilegium Ottonianum* of 13 February 962. In it Emperor Otto confirmed to John XII and his successors all of the rights and properties that the Church had acquired on the basis of preceding treaties. The pope, on his side, took an oath of loyalty to the emperor, promising that he would never betray the emperor and espouse the nationalistic cause represented by Berengar. The nobles and the people of Rome also took their oath of loyalty, again submitting to imperial authority. But it was evident that a people accustomed to autonomy under the leadership of Alberic would not accept any such submission. The position of John XII seemed equivocal, to say the least.

And so, once Otto had left, John XII, unable to refrain from taking the advice of the local leaders who were pressing for an immediate volte-face against the emperor, got in touch with Berengar, as though nothing had happened. However, his letters were intercepted by the imperial faction which, now alerted to what was happening in Rome, sent a delegation to Otto who was in Pavia in the spring of 963 to inform him of everything, stressing the immoral behavior of the pope and the state of abandon into which the sacred places of the city had fallen. It seems that Otto commented on the dissolute life of the pope with the mocking remark: "The pope is still a boy and he will moderate himself only through the example of noble persons." In that comment he expressed his disdain for a Church fallen into disrepute.

Otto sent two envoys to Rome to keep him informed on developments and went to San Leo to tighten the siege of Berengar. In the summer, beneath the walls of the castle, Otto received papal legates who protested and accused him of having invaded the territory of San Leo, which belonged to the Church. The emperor showed them the letters which had been intercepted and, for his part, accused the pope of betraying the pact they had agreed upon the year before. However, he declared that he was disposed to excuse the youthful indiscretions of John XII, charging his own messengers to explain to the pope that he was ready to submit to the "judgement of God" to purge himself of the accusation by the papal legates regarding the invasion, so that the good intentions of his military intervention at San Leo would not be questioned.

The emperor's messengers, treated rudely by the pope, reported to Otto that the son of Adalbert, having escaped from San Leo, had sought the assistance of the Saracens in the south and requested the intervention of the Byzantine. After which he had barricaded himself in Rome with the pope as the head of the nationalist faction.

At this point Otto delayed no longer and hurriedly left San Leo to gain Rome. The nationalist faction had taken up its position in the Leonine City and John XII, in helmet and armor, was reorganizing the ranks of the army with Adalbert, while the pro-imperial faction was barricaded within the walls of Giovannipoli. Otto joined it, ready to clash with his enemies on the other side of the Tiber, but they had suddenly disappeared. As John XII no longer felt safe, he hastily collected the Church's treasure and fled to the Roman countryside with Adalbert, first to the castle of Tivoli and thence to Corsica. It was 2 November 963, and Otto took over the city.

Four days later the emperor convened a council at St. Peter's at which certain bishops from northern Italy and followers of the emperor, as well as bishops from Tuscany and the Roman duchy, participated with the clergy and representatives of the nobles and people of Rome. The council was to judge John XII in what was in effect a trial of the pope, expressly willed by the emperor.

A summons containing the charges was sent to the pope among which the following were underlined: "Know therefore that not a few but all laymen and clerics have accused you of murder, of perjury, of sacrilege, of incest with your relatives and with two of your sisters. . . that you have made a toast to the devil and, while throwing the dice, you called upon Zeus, Venus and other demons." John XII did not appear and naturally declared, in a hurried response clearly inconsistent with the style of any pontifical letter, that he considered the trial null and void: "We have understood that you wish to change popes; if you do this, I excommunicate you in the name of Almighty God so that you will not be able to ordain priests or celebrate Mass." This message evoked hilarity on the part of the bishops who mocked the vulgar tone of the expressions used.

Undefended, John XII was found guilty of high treason and was deposed from the pontificate because of his behavior, judged unworthy of a pope. In his place, Otto imposed the election of a layman, the protoscrinario Leo, who was consecrated on 6 December with the name of Leo VIII.

Even from far away Corsica, John XII succeeded in fomenting two revolts. The first, on 3 January 964, was bloodily put down by Otto, who then had to leave the city ten days later to catch up with Adalbert at Spoleto. The second, which erupted right after Otto's departure, made Leo VIII flee to his protector in Spoleto, while John XII returned to Rome, intent upon revenge. In great haste he convened a council on 26 February at St. Peter's in which only sixteen bishops participated, eleven of whom had signed the document of his deposition. These churchmen desperately seeking to save their lives, declared that they had been forced to obey the emperor and the cardinals behaved likewise. The trial of John XII was declared null and void, and Pope Leo VIII was deposed.

For his part, John took his revenge on his most ardent adversaries, ordering their noses and tongues to be cut off, while Otto stayed in Camerino with his pope. Only after Easter had been celebrated did he move towards Rome. But now it was too late to resolve once and for all matters with John XII since, during the journey, came the news of his death which occurred on 14 May 964. According to Luitprand, and the voice of the people, he was slain by the devil while he was in bed with an adulterous woman, a certain Stefanetta. But, in this case, the role of the devil should be interpreted as the cuckolded husband who surprised him with his wife and threw him out of the window. According to others, however, John XII died of apoplexy. In any case, it was a death in line with his dissolute life as the vicar of Christ. As a politician, he lived full the dichotomy within of prince and of pope, incapable of giving a precise meaning to his power, a vacillator lacking that opportunism which ends up by justifying certain changes of party loyalty. He was buried in St. John Lateran.

1 3 1. LEO VIII (9 6 3-9 6 5)

Leo VIII was a mere layman, who lived on the clivus Argentarii, or the "incline of Marphorius." A chief clerk, he had been a member of the delegation sent by John XII to Otto to protest against the invasion of Church lands when he was attacking the castle of San Leo.

He was thrust into the limelight suddenly in the council-trial which Otto III had convened in Rome on 6 November 963. Once the deposition of John XII had been decided, even though a layman, Leo was chosen for his chaste habits and his undoubted honesty, since the emperor could not raise to the papal throne a person who was not absolutely upright.

As on other occasions, the "handicap" of his lay status was overcome in two days. Elected on 4 December, he received in a summary fashion the several orders of gatekeeper, lector, acolyte, subdeacon, deacon, and priest from the bishop-cardinal of Ostia, Sicone. He was then consecrated pope on 6 December.

His candidature did not have popular support, mainly because the emperor imposed it. So Otto decided, in the beginning, to assist his pope from nearby to prevent any popular uprisings. And indeed after the Christmas festivities, on 3 January 964, there was a genuine rebellion by the population, instigated indirectly by John XII from distant Corsica where he was hiding with the help of some of the leaders faithful to him. The Vatican was attacked but the imperial forces repelled the attackers easily, overturning the barriers raised at the Sant'Angelo bridge and giving rise to a real and proper massacre.

The carnage was halted only thanks to the intercession of Leo VIII who hoped to win over the people's obviously hostile attitude towards him. The following day the Romans begged Otto pardon and swore obedience to Leo on the tomb of St. Peter. The pope showed his good will towards the Romans and had the hostages freed. Otto stayed in Rome for another ten days and, reassured about the safety of the pope, left to attack Spoleto where Adalbert had set up camp.

In point of fact, "he left the city in a state of exasperation and the pope without any defense, like a lamb amidst the wolves," Gregorovius notes. "The blood shed on 3 January was never forgotten, fuelling the hatred for foreigners, and the Romans, whose uprising had been so severely repressed, quenched their thirst for revenge as soon as the hostages had been freed and the emperor had departed."

Indeed, the Romans recalled John XII while Leo VIII barely managed to flee and seek refuge at Camerino near the emperor. This flight saved him from almost certain death, but caused him to lose the pontifical throne because John XII took it back as soon as he had entered the city, having deposed Leo by a council on 26 February. But the death of John XII on 14 May, which rendered worthless that deposition, did not solve all the problems. The Roman people again defied the emperor, continued to refuse to recognize Leo, and in another council the clergy and Roman nobility elected on 22 May 964 Benedict V as pope.

Otto obviously had no intention of accepting a pope chosen by the Romans and besieged the city, which surrendered on 23 June 964, and on that same date a council was convened which deposed Benedict V.

At this juncture, one may ask oneself what value this council could possibly have had, as well as the council of 26 February, both convened by deposed popes. Clearly, the same validity as the one held in 963 presided over by the emperor. In the *Annuario pontificio* John XII is considered as ruling up to the day of his death, but then his deposition and the related consecration of Leo VIII, considered pope from 6 December 963, until his death on 1 March 965, should not be deemed valid. Furthermore, if the deposition of

Leo VIII is not recognized, Benedict V cannot be considered pope, although the Annuario classifies him as ruling from 22 May 964, up to the day of his death, 4 July 966, the date by which, as we shall see, his successor, John XIII, will have already been elected.

The whole matter is very confusing. I have thought it wise not to depart from the information in the *Annuario* and even less to consider Leo VIII as an antipope, as do some texts, including contemporary ones. This note may serve at least to explain to those who read these pages just how difficult it can be at times, even on an official level, to recognize a pope as opposed to an antipope, and how unfounded it may be to use one or the other term.

The council of 23 June has its own story which I felt would be better told in the biography of Benedict V, to which the reader is referred. As for Leo VIII, I shall state that, once the question of the deposition of Benedict V had been resolved, Otto issued a detailed decree on papal elections in which he ordered the Romans to surrender all elective rights. The pope gave in to this decree which, in effect, allowed no further talk of "free elections," and the papacy became "a sort of State Church annexed to the empire," as Knowles puts it, and for a certain period whoever was raised to the papal throne would have to explain his conduct to German emperors.

Strengthened by this decree, Otto left Rome on 1 July, taking with him the deposed Benedict V and leaving Leo VIII in an unenviable situation regarding his relationship with the population, from which his death fortunately freed him on 1 March 965.

1 3 2. BENEDICT V (9 6 4 — 9 6 5)

Benedict V, a cardinal-deacon, was an exceptionally well educated person, so much so as to merit the nickname of Grammaticus, and was elected pope by the clergy and people of Rome the day after the death of John XII. By this election the Romans snubbed Emperor Otto who, after John XII had been deposed by the council of 6 November 963, had imposed his own candidate, Leo VIII whom Romans did not want to recognize, considering him to have been deposed by John XII in the council of 26 February 964. They wanted "their" pope and chose Benedict, certain that he would defend the freedom of the Church and of Rome from imperial intrusions.

Very sure of themselves, the Romans sent their own envoys to Rieti to inform Otto of the election and to request his ratification. Otto's reply could only be negative, but nevertheless Benedict V was consecrated on 22 May.

Otto then besieged Rome with most of his army and starved the city into submission. On 23 June, the gates of the city were opened to him and though the population feared dire punishment, this did not occur. Instead, there was a generous pardon, along with the prompt convening of a council in the Lateran, presided over by Leo VIII, before which Benedict V appeared as the accused.

He was led into the council chamber vested as pope and the archdeacon asked him by what right he was wearing papal robes while Leo VIII was still alive. He was therefore accused of having violated his oath to the emperor by which he had sworn not to elect any pope without the emperor's consent.

Benedict V's reply was brief and apologetic: "If I have failed, have mercy on me!" Otto was apparently moved by this representative of the Church who, kneeling begged for mercy and embraced his knees, and ended defending Benedict in front of a furious Leo VIII. Leo went up to Benedict, stripped him of the pallium, grabbed the ferule from his hand and broke it. Then, as a favor to the emperor who had interceded on behalf of Benedict, he left him with the status of deacon but sentenced him to exile.

Otto took Benedict with him to Germany when he left Rome on 1 July 964, and exiled him to Hamburg where he lived under the watchful eye of Bishop Adaldagus. He died on 4 July 965, and was buried in Hamburg. However, in 999, Otto III arranged to have his remains moved to Rome with all the honors due to the reputation of holiness that he had earned.

133. JOHN XIII (965–972)

On the death of Leo VIII, the Romans did not dare attend a council to elect a new pontiff but sent a delegation to Otto I, deferring to his wishes to nominate a successor, while at the same time expressing their desire to keep Benedict V, exiled to Hamburg, on the papal throne. Thus there was a period of interregnum, or a vacant see, since the emperor found himself in a somewhat embarrassing situation, despite his desire not to give in to the pressures of the Romans. He was finally released from this delicate situation by the death of Benedict. Otto dismissed the Roman delegation and sent to Rome Bishop Otger of Spira and Bishop Liutprand of Cremona as his own representatives at the election.

The choice fell to the bishop of Narni, John, probably a son of Theodora II, the sister of Marozia. Educated in the Lateran, he had gone through all the steps of the ecclesiastical career, earning praise in the trial of John XII as a public prosecutor, but ending up by signing the deposition of Leo VIII. Moreover he had close relations with the Crescenzi family which later was to achieve great power in Rome, taking the place of Theophylactus. He was crowned on 1 October 965, with the name of John XIII.

But he was not well regarded by the populace and part of the nobility, precisely because he had been selected by the emperor. So he tried to ingratiate himself even more with the Crescenzi family to have support from within the city and the suburbs. He donated the feudal estate of Palestrina to the Senator Stefania and naming her nephew, Benedict, the husband of Theodoranda, Crescenzio's daughter, rector of the Sabine.

A tangible sign of popular dislike took place a few months after his consecration. On 15 December, a coup took place plotted by the prefect of the city, Peter, by Count Roffredus and by a vestiary named Stephen. The pope was arrested and imprisoned in Castel Sant'Angelo, and then moved out of the city into a castle belonging to Roffredus. However, John XIII managed to flee, or was helped to get away, and placed himself under the protection of Count Pandolfus of Capua.

The revolt had a decidedly democratic nature because, for the first time, leaders of the ordinary people appeared among the rebels. But even this new attempt to destroy papal power ended tragically. As soon as Otto came to Italy in 966, there was a split in the revolutionary ranks and John, the son of Crescenzio, lined up with the pope while Roffredus and Stephen were killed, and Peter escaped. In the meantime John XIII, accompanied by an escort of Capuan soldiers, passed through the Sabine and reentered Rome on 12 November 966. That ephemeral democratic republic had lasted little more than ten months.

A few days later Otto made his entrance into Rome, and he certainly did not perform acts of mercy toward the rebels. The city itself was subjected to a sacking while the captains of the people were hanged, and other of their followers blinded. Peter, the prefect, was discovered in a hiding place in the Campagna and was imprisoned in the dungeons of the Lateran where the emperor left him in the hands of the pope to be punished as he wished. John XIII had him hanged by his hair on the *Caballus Constantini*, that is, the equestrian statue of Marcus Aurelius, but his punishment did not stop there. Pulled down from the statue and stripped, Peter was put on a donkey, facing the tail, onto which was tied a little bell and placed in his hands like a bridle, while a feathered sack was fixed to his head and two attached to his legs. Thus disgraced he was made to wend his way through the city, and when this shameful spectacle was over, he was sent into exile in Germany, while the corpses of Roffredus and Stephen were exhumed and thrown outside the walls of Rome. In sum, it was a barbarous repression of which the pope alone was grateful to the emperor, and which simply increased the hatred of the Romans toward Otto and his pontiff.

But Otto did not leave Rome for six long years during which the hatred of the citizens, at whatever level, noble or plebeian, had no means of exploding and taking revenge. The next year, during a council at Ravenna, the emperor restored to the Church the exarchate and other lands on the border. This was a gift for the forthcoming imperial coronation to which John XIII was quite happy to agree. It took place in Rome on 24 December 967, and the son of the new emperor, the future Otto II, then twelve years old, who was present for the occasion, was given the title of Caesar.

Otto I wanted to give luster to his dynasty by becoming a relative of the Eastern emperor, and planned a marriage between his son and Princess Theophano, the daughter of the deceased Romanus II and niece of the then Emperor Nicephorus. The latter, however, did not like the idea of the marriage because he could not go along with Otto's policy which favored the dukes of Capua and Benevento, in open conflict with Byzantine dominion over southern Italy. John XIII complicated matters further when he sent a personal delegation to Nicephorus to facilitate the task of the imperial one, headed by Bishop Luitprand. Supporting the wish of his "chosen son." Otto I, he called Nicephorus merely "Emperor of the Greeks." As a result the latter, insulted, treated the envoys as prisoners for a while and definitively stopped all marriage negotiations. It appears that diplomacy was not John XIII's strong point.

But Otto nonetheless succeeded in arranging the love dream for his son. In 969 Nicephorus was assassinated in one of the now customary revolts at the summit of Byzantine power, and the usurper of the throne, John Tzimisces, thought it wise to please the Western emperor so as to protect himself from possible claims that the princess might later justly make against him.

The marriage of the young Theophano and the seventeen-year-old Otto was celebrated by John XIII in Rome on 14 April 972 and the now ageing Otto I thus achieved through this marriage a symbolic reconciliation between the West and the East. But the brilliant ceremony and the grandiose festivities were only a show of apparent joy and peace in the relations between the two Churches. Capua and Benevento had been elected "metropolitans" with a series of suffragan dioceses, and this amounted to a *longa manus* from Rome on the south, which was traditionally under the jurisdiction of the patriarch of Constantinople. The latter naturally responded in like vein by making the see of Otranto an archbishopric, with five attached dioceses, precisely in order to push back the influence of Rome, and managed to impose in Puglia and Calabria the Greek rite, and to prohibit the Latin one.

However, John XIII had been able to expand again the universal interests of his see by increasing the activities of the missions. The Tuscan bishop Egidius was sent to Poland, a recently converted area, to strengthen the Christian message among the Slavs and the Hungarians. Yet if this renewal of missionary activity spotlights John XIII in his religious functions, it cannot be said that his political personality had been such as to oppose the emperor and his wishes. I do not share the opinion of Seppelt who relies on the judgement of other historians, according to whom John XIII is to be "described as a precursor, if modest, of the great popes who defended the rights of the Church from the eleventh to the thirteenth centuries, struggling against imperial power." And indeed his anti-imperial activity was really less than modest, I would say non-existent. On the contrary, he proved that, without Otto I, he would not have been able to maintain the throne of Peter.

He died on 6 September 972, and was buried in St. Paul's on the Via Ostiense.

134. BENEDICT VI (973—974)

Benedict VI, a Roman and the son of a certain Hildebrand, of German origin, deacon of the sub Capitolio region, was elected immediately after the death of John XIII, but the emperor's confirmation was slow in arriving because Otto was in Germany. Thus the consecration took place only on 19 January 973.

Nominated certainly by the imperial faction, his election could only arouse resentment on the part of the people and particularly within the nationalist party whose chief at the time was a Crescenzio, son of Theodora II, and therefore probably a brother too of John XIII. As long as Otto I was alive, Benedict VI was able to assert his authority with that family, but the emperor's death on 7 May 973 caused an immediate revolt, the promoter of which was that very Crescenzio.

Benedict VI was imprisoned in Castel Sant'Angelo and deposed by the same rebels who raised to the pontifical throne one of the conspirators, the deacon Francone, son of a certain Ferruccius, who took the name of Boniface VII in June 974. Benedict VI was still alive but was strangled in jail a month later. Some chronicles report that he was assassinated by that same Boniface VII, who was apparently a real monster.

Boniface VII is considered an antipope, and the little information we have on the events of that period do not clarify whether there was a genuine consecration after his election or if it was a coup carried out with the support of a few priests as well, obviously, as that of Crescenzio. Certainly Boniface VII did not consider it was wise at that time to present himself as the true representative of the see of Rome, and in the same month of July when Benedict VI died, he ran off to Constantinople with his band of ruffians, taking with him the Church's treasury. The patriarch of Constantinople was delighted to receive him, realizing that the rebellions in Rome simply undermined the importance of that see.

Even Crescenzio disappeared from the history of Rome. The imperial legate, Count Sikko, managed in a few weeks to restore order in the city, and the rebels were punished. However, it appears that Crescenzio was able to hide away in a monastery and thereafter led a quiet life staying clear of the city's political events. He died in the monastery of St. Alessio ten years after the above events, as an inscription in that church attests.

1 3 5. BENEDICT VII (9 7 4 — 9 8 3)

Once order in Rome had been restored, it was not easy for the imperial legate and the pro-German faction to find a successor to Benedict VI. From Germany Otto II had indicated as his candidate, Maiolus of Cluny, but this holy man was not ready to get involved at certain politico-religious levels and refused. Finally, in October a candidate was found, evidently favored by the imperial faction, in the bishop of Sutri who was elected with the name of Benedict VII.

He immediately convened a council which issued a condemnation of Boniface VII, whose election was obviously not recognized as valid, and it was the beginning of a generally peaceful pontificate, which held for about nine years, notwithstanding that Otto stayed away from Italy for more than five of them. Benedict VII was a morally upright person who worked hard to bring about a monastic reform, abandoned by his recent predecessors, who had been mostly taken up with other and more worldly matters. He devoted himself also to the restoration of certain convents, such as that of Sts. Boniface and Alessio on the Aventine and, in close cooperation with the young Otto II, he increased missionary activity in the Germanic and Slavic countries. He granted new privileges to the archbishops of Mainz and Trier, and established the diocese of Prague with jurisdiction for Bohemia and Moravia.

However, it is almost certain that some popular uprising must have occurred also under Benedict VII, and he probably had to flee and call upon Otto II for help. The latter did just that in the autumn of 980 when he came down to Italy and met the pope at Ravenna where they celebrated Christmas. Otto II arrived at Rome with Benedict VII on Easter Sunday of the following year, accompanied by his mother Adelaide and his wife Theophano, as well as by Hugh Capet, duke of France, and by Corrado, king of the Burgundians.

Gregorovius notes that: "No chronicler of the period states that Otto punished those who rebelled in 974. Only certain later reports say that, following the example of Caracalla, he prepared a banquet on the steps of St. Peter's to which he treacherously invited the Romans, and after he had cut the heads off some of them, he enjoined the others to continue with the feast." Maybe this was only a legend but it indicates the climate of terror that the emperor's presence created every time among the population, and it served to calm the spirits of possible rebels. In July, Otto II departed from Rome to head south where encounters with Saracens and Byzantine awaited him.

In September 981, the emperor presided over a council at which Benedict VII pronounced a solemn condemnation of simony but which also, thanks to

Otto II's support, helped the German bishops create numerous dioceses through the partition of several areas belonging to the diocese of Merseburg that was, in effect, abolished. The incentives of a missionary nature in reality masked the private interests of Bishop Gisiler, who had been able to convince Otto of the apostolic importance of his intentions. The council did not unanimously approve the decision, which was nevertheless adopted, since such was the will of the emperor.

After which Otto left Rome for southern Italy where he planned to block the new Saracen advance and Byzantine expansionism. He failed, however, as his plans foundered with the defeat at Stilo in 982. Back in the north of Italy, the emperor seemed to have lost his former confidence. The coronation at Verona in June 983 of Otto, his three-year-old son, as king of Germany and Italy was supposed to give luster to the empire and show the German and Italian vassals that the Saxon dynasty's strength had not vanished. Having given this new breath of life in support of the imperial faction, Otto II again led an expedition into southern Italy but had to stop in Rome as the death of Benedict VII on 10 July 983 required his presence at the election of the next pontiff. Benedict VII was buried in Santa Croce in Gerusalemme.

136. JOHN XIV (983—984)

Otto II chose as Benedict VII's successor his Italian chancellor, Bishop Peter of Pavia who, in December 983, was consecrated pope under the name of John XIV, the third in the history of the papacy to take on a name different from his baptismal one. More or less contemporaneously John XIV lost his protector. Aged 28, following a brief illness, Otto II suddenly passed away at Rome in the imperial palace near St. Peter's on 7 December. He was buried in the basilica, the only emperor of German origin to have died and been buried in Rome.

It is clear that the sudden death of Otto II was fatal to the newly elected John XIV, and he probably foresaw at the emperor's bedside his own end. He certainly could not hope for much from a three-year-old child, reigning under the regency of his mother and menaced in Germany by his ambitious relative, Henry of Bavaria, who had immediately taken the title of King of Germany. Moreover, in the spring of 984, Theophano left Rome with her son and those who were faithful to her, determined to defend her rights and obviously unable also to worry about the pope.

The fall of John XIV was rapid. Boniface VII promptly returned from Constantinople, perhaps recalled by the pro-Byzantine faction in Rome, and with the agreement of the Crescenzi family was able to regain the throne of Peter. John XIV was jailed in Castel Sant'Angelo in April 984, where he was killed by poison in August. But Boniface VII was not able to keep his pontificate very long. His thirst for vengeance led him to commit a series of crimes and violent actions, like that of having the eyes of his bitter enemy, Cardinal John, gouged out., The result was that after eleven months of reign he got himself hated even by the Crescenzi now headed by Crescenzio's son, John, and he was eliminated in August 985. His corpse was torn apart during a popular uprising, dragged through the streets of Rome and finally thrown at the feet of the equestrian statue of Marcus Aurelius. The next day, his servants managed to give him a Christian burial in St. Peter's.

137. JOHN XV (985—996)

John XV, a Roman from a part of the sixth Region called Gallina Alba, and the son of a priest named Leo, was consecrated pope in August of 985 under circumstances of which we are unaware. In any case, his family was certainly an enemy of the Crescenzi, so it was an election wanted by the imperial faction against the will of the nationalist party with all the risks that that involved.

In fact, John Crescenzio had seized temporal power and assumed the title of *Patricius*, but his behavior towards the pontiff was one of complete tolerance within the strictly religious area. John wanted to be the representative of the Senate and of the Roman People and above all mistrusted imperial authority as had Albericus II. However, he had to be very clever, for times had changed and Italy was making no effort to achieve its own autonomy. Rome especially could not hope for more than the maintenance of civil power alongside the pontifical one, and certainly not the overthrow of imperial authority. The rights of that Saxon child were in fact respected, and proof of this was manifested as soon as the regent Theophano arrived in Italy in 989.

She was received with full honors with the populace paying her homage and her position as empress remained untouched. She ordered the Romans to recognize by an oath the imperial rights of her son and, on that condition, confirmed the title of *patricius* on John Crescenzio. Theophano left Rome to return to Germany once memorial masses had been celebrated for her deceased husband at Christmas of 989, and she had diplomatically resolved the issue of the relations between the Roman nobility and the pope, taking care to preserve imperial interests. However, this co-existence of authorities produced results to the detriment, if not of the pope, then of the Church of Rome which, damaged in the eyes of the Christian community, led to a decrease in the veneration of the faithful for Peter's throne.

On the one hand, the pope had established a sort of nepotism, giving away to his relatives assets of the Church and doing them as many favors as possible. On the otherside, John Crescenzio administered civil justice in accordance with family interests in a real trading of judgments. The state of profound decadence of the see of Rome seems to be documented in a sort of invective against the papacy delivered by the bishop of Orleans during a famous council of French bishops held at Reims in 991. This had been convened because of the difficulties caused by the passing of power in France to the Capetians, following the accession to the throne by Hugh Capet, through a series of circumstances connected with the election to the archbishopric of Reims of a young cleric of the Carolingian faith, a certain Arnulf.

"Oh Rome, worthy of our pity, you brought to our forebears the light of the Fathers of the Church, but our present days have been darkened by you with such terrible shadows that their memory will never vanish. Once upon a time, from this city sprang the magnificent Leos, the great Gregorys, not to speak of Gelasius and Innocent, who surpassed in eloquence and wisdom all the philosophers on earth. But what happens in our times? We saw John, surnamed Octavian, dip in the mud of passions and conspire against that very Otto who had been crowned by him. He was thrown out and a neophyte, Leo, became pope. Emperor Otto left Rome and Octavian returned; he threw Leo out, cut off Deacon John's nose, as well as the fingers of his right hand and his tongue, and in his bloodthirstiness slaughtered many leading citizens; shortly thereafter, he died. In his place the Romans raised up the grammarian Benedict, but later Leo, the neophyte, with his emperor attacked and seized him, deposed him and sent him into permanent exile in Germany. Otto II succeeded Otto as emperor and he emerged as first among all the princes for his virtues of bravery, wisdom and learning. Meanwhile, in Rome, Boniface ascended the throne of Peter, still dripping with the blood of his predecessor. He was a horrible monster whose crimes surpassed those of all mortals. Thrown out and condemned by a great synod, he returned to Rome upon the death of Otto and, violating his oath, removed from the summit of the city the pontiff Peter, an excellent person who had been the bishop of Pavia, deposed and killed him after having held him in a terrible prison. And where on earth is it written that the innumerable priests of God, scattered about the globe and having learning as well as merit, must submit to such monsters who have no human or divine wisdom and are offensive to humanity?"

The oration could be interpreted as an act of rebellion, raising once more the issue of the primacy of Rome, since the pope wound up seeming to be "the anti-Christ who was sitting on the throne in the temple of God, like a god appearing before the people." Moreover, these French bishops were able to ascertain directly the state of "tyranny" in which Rome was governed, when the council legates and those of King Hugh were not received by John XV with the reverence due to them because, as they were told, they had failed to bring gifts to *patricius* John Crescenzio. And so it was they who confirmed that in Rome one would never be listened to unless, following an adequate payment, the "tyrant" had given his consent.

Furthermore, relations between John XV and the *patricius* degenerated in 995, to the point that the pope was constrained to abandon Rome and find refuge in Tuscia with Marquis Hugo, from whence he invited young Otto to come to Italy and receive his imperial crown in Rome. Otto departed with an impressive entourage from Ratisbon (Regensburg) in February 996, and the Romans hastened to recall the pope to Rome, in an act of reconciliation. The pope was anxiously awaiting his liberator with a desire for vengeance, when he passed away in March 996 prior to Otto's arrival.

John XV was buried in St. Peter's with an epitaph which calls him "Distinguished Doctor" but rings false when claiming that he never gave in "through fear or for money or favors whatsoever."

1 3 8. Gregory V (9 9 6 — 9 9 9)

The election of the successor to John XV had to wait for a couple of months because Otto III had come to Rome and the Romans did not wish to irritate the young king and future emperor. John Crescenzio thought it wise not to trouble the waters and, satisfied with what he had succeeded in stealing for himself and his family, awaited developments. He busied himself with sending a delegation to Ravenna for the young Otto, with lofty messages that reported how eagerly the Romans were awaiting him, in order to learn his wishes regarding the election of the next pontiff.

Otto had already made his decision and chose his cousin Bruno, his chaplain, a young priest 24 years old, well educated and of a decisive character. Accompanied to Rome by the archbishop of Mainz and the bishop of Worms, Bruno was received with high honors, obviously not spontaneous. For the first time, a man of German blood occupied the throne of Peter. Since the days of the Syrian Zacharias, Romans had been used to seeing mostly pontiffs of Roman birth, apart from seven popes whose origins were, in any case, in the immediate vicinities of the city. Both their parochial sentiments and their pride were hurt.

The consecration of Bruno took place on 3 May 996, and he took the name of Gregory V, and from then on, all popes changed their baptismal names to signify that the supreme election to the pontificate was basically a kind of second birth.

Only after his cousin had been enthroned did Otto III arrive in Rome to be crowned emperor, an event which took place at St. Peter's on 21 May. However, four days later, Otto and Gregory convened in the old basilica a council specifically to clarify the situation in the city once and for all. It was a council which, in effect, had the character of a judicial tribunal.

Those rebellious Romans who had thrown out John XV were summoned to it, but their submissiveness served to lighten the judges' sentences. There was no death penalty and the chief leaders such as John Crescenzio, initially condemned to exile were later pardoned by the express wish of the pope who, in his attempt to win over the populace, obtained a full amnesty for the defendants from Otto. John Crescenzio tendered his oath of loyalty and Otto and Gregory were sure they had the situation sufficiently under control to be able to grant the acts of clemency, which turned out to be a real political mistake.

When Otto III left and returned to Germany in June, a plot was organized in Rome against the German pope, the instigator being John Crescenzio. Gregory V was publicly accused of having bribed high civil officials favorable to the emperor with the intent of imposing a despotic regime. The revolt broke out on 29 September 996 and the pope fled. John Crescenzio well knew that Otto III would immediately come to Rome to put down the revolt, so he set himself up with a large army in Castel Sant'Angelo and fortified its defenses, fully determined not to surrender.

Meanwhile, Gregory reached Pavia where he convened a council at the beginning of 997. He issued a number of decrees regarding the German church and, sure of the support of his cousin, displayed great dignity and fearlessness. As far as the situation in Rome was concerned, he simply urged the German bishops to confirm the excommunication which he had pronounced against John Crescenzio, and to continue to recognize the supremacy of the See of Peter. Among other things, he announced that, as the bishop of Rome, he would have forcefully supported, against decisions of the provincial councils, the "Isidorian Decrees" or the Pseudoisidorian, as they were more conveniently called, of which we spoke in the pontificate of Leo IV. From the time of Nicholas I no pope had been capable of making full use of their vast possibilities in the struggle for power.

In other words, Gregory V was confident in his functions and considered the rebellion a temporary event, reckoning that it was only a matter of a few months and relying on the intervention of Otto which would not be long in coming, once he had repulsed the attack of the Slavs against Germany.

In the meantime, Crescenzio had again assumed the title of *patricius* and had managed also to give the Romans another pope in the person of John Philagathus. A Calabrian and a favorite of the empress Theophano, elected bishop of Piacenza, he had joined the rebels betraying the imperial faction. Eager for power, he immediately seized the opportunity John Crescenzio offered him and assumed the dignity of pontiff with the name of John XVI in April 997. He was clearly an antipope.

Leaving temporal matters to Crescenzio, he was supposed to represent religious authority and sought support from the emperor of the East and the patriarch of Constantinople. But, basically he was on his own as the East did not want to risk a hopeless war against Otto III who, once he had rid himself of the Slavs, went to Italy at the end of 997. He met his cousin at Pavia where they celebrated Christmas together, after which they moved calmly towards Rome, arriving there in February of 998. They found the gates open and the walls undefended. Only Castel Sant'Angelo was occupied by Crescenzio, determined to resist to the last drop of blood. The antipope, John XVI, had fled in terror to Campagna, but was discovered by the imperial cavalry, and dragged off to Rome with his head looking like a sieve. By Otto's orders, his nose had been cut off along with his tongue and his ears, and his eyes were gouged out. Thus maimed, he was thrown in chains into a monastery where his wounds were supposed to be tended to while he awaited a final judgment. This came about in March when Gregory convened a council in the Lateran. With the terrifying appearance he must have had, Philagathus was summoned there, mutilated and wearing the pontifical vestments. In the plenary council he was stripped of the pallium and, pilloried, was led through the streets facing backwards on a donkey, as had happened to the prefect, Peter, under John XIII.

Meanwhile the assault on Castel Sant'Angelo was proceeding and on 29 April 998 the Marquis Eckard of Meissen, in charge of all operations, succeeded in conquering the fortress. John Crescenzio was beheaded on the battlements of the castle and his corpse, thrown from the top of the walls, was hung on gallows raised at the foot of Monte Mario.

Some reports say that first his eyes were gouged out, then his limbs torn off and finally his tortured body, wrapped in a cowskin, was carried pilloried through the streets of Rome. Monte Mario was renamed by the Germans as Mons Gaudii, but for the Romans it remained Mons Malus, and their "hero" was later buried at Saint Pancratius on the Janiculum.

Gregory V and Otto III then used strong methods to impose their authority in Rome and fought energetically the arrogance of the Sabine nobles, most of whom were related to the Crescenzi, by reinforcing the monastery of Farfa which was favorable to the empire.

After the council of 998, however, Otto was assailed by remorse and made a pilgrimage in southern Italy to various monasteries and abbeys in search of internal peace.

Gregory V probably had no problems of this kind and always maintained a firm dignity despite his youth. What Seppelt wrote about him seems substantially correct: "The first German pope in the Middle Ages demonstrated by his way of life and by his actions, that he fully supported ecclesiastical reformation and, even more important, that he was filled with the spirit of a Gregory the Great and a Nicholas I, even if his family relationship and obligations of gratitude kept him in close connection to the emperor. Gregory had decided to protect with all his energy, indeed with his youthful zeal, the rights of the apostolic see within the sphere of the universal Church. As when he took care of the ecclesiastical controversy of Reims during which the conduct of the

French bishops had seriously threatened the prestige of the apostolic see. Furthermore, during a Roman synod (end of May 996) the pope publicly declared that Arnulf was the legitimate titular of the archbishopric see of Reims and did not hesitate to call Gerbert, who was protected by the emperor and who would be his own successor to the throne of Peter, an intruder."

Gregory V died on 18 February 999 at the age of only 27 and was buried in St. Peter's.

139. SYLVESTER II (999–1003)

After the death of Gregory V, the Romans did not dare raise to the pontifical see a candidate of their own, but awaited the emperor's arrival in Rome at the end of March of 999 with his own candidate, Gerbert, who was one of his counsellors. He was "a genius who shed a bright light on his epoch," Gregorovius justly states. Indeed, his great erudition, especially in the scientific field, was so disconcerting for the ignorant and superstitious masses that they presumed he did not acquire his knowledge in a natural way. He came into folklore with the nickname of "the wizard pope," who had reached the papal throne thanks to a "pact with the devil," and legends about him grew.

Born between 940 and 945 at Belliac in Auvergne, he was probably accepted as a monk into the nearby abbey of Aurillac in 952. But all of a sudden, weary of the monastic life, he left the monastery and went to Spain, attracted by the mysteries of Arab religious culture.

In the school of the monk Atto of Vich in Catalonia, he learned the first rudiments of Islam, filtered by Christian instruction, but he was not above frequenting also the circles of Mohammedan wise men in the region to delve into the secrets of genuine magic.

"Now, one approaches these masters only by abjuring the faith," observes Mario Bacchiega in his recent biography of Sylvester II. "The Arab sages required a disciple to undergo an initiation before revealing to him their secrets, hermetic researches and formulas for spells. And only a very few well-prepared and initiated persons could accede to them. Gerbert was an apostate. Obviously he would never have revealed to anyone during his lifetime this unique and important experience, because in the tenth century no one would have understood him," and he would have been judged a heretic. Instead, he completed that mysterious experience consciously in order to have a "lucid proof of moral and religious freedom" and "to draw free gnosis."

While visiting one of those learned men, Gerbert had an adventure, which smacks of a fable, as recounted by an English chronicler, William de Malmesbury: "He was conversing with the philosopher and received from him books which he was copying. He made notes . . . ardently wanting to obtain . . . prayers, pleas, names of gods, protections . . . used by his teacher."

The wise man happened to have a daughter and the two young people fell in love. Gerbert was especially anxious to obtain a book that the wizard kept under his pillow, so "one evening the girl he loved got her father drunk" and the young aspiring wizard took the book and fled. It was an interminable flight with the teacher, once awake, chasing the thieving pupil, and a mutual consultation of the stars to find the trail for the one, and to hide for the other, until Gerbert finally reached the sea and *"ibi per incantationes diabolo accersito, perpetuum paciscitur dominium."* He makes a "pact with the devil," swears eternal gratitude if he succeeds in escaping safely to the other side of the sea, and indeed is saved. "There is no doubt about his sacrilege," pontificates Malmesbury. But here the devil turns up in the medieval chronicle while in reality it is his own subconscious. As Bacchiega notes, the fact is that Gerbert "loves the flames like a salamander" and this pact "is only a firm pledge with himself. . . a transient moment needed to proceed further in his evolution, which will then dissolve itself in the bones of his personality."

Thus fortified, he succeeds 'in seeing the stars again' and commences his ecclesiastical career. By 970 he is in the company of Atto in Rome where he finds a way to have himself appreciated by John XIII and by Otto I, who entrusts him with the education of his son. Some years later he is in Reims, summoned by Archbishop Adalberone as a teacher of philosophy, his reputation having already reached European levels. Between Christmas 980 and January 981, on another trip to Rome with his archbishop, he competes with a monk named Otrik in a public scientific debate at Ravenna. The latter was another emerging philosopher at the school of Magdeburg, who was in the entourage of Otto II during his foray into Italy where he would find his death. Gerbert won the philosophical disputation, and, while Otrik lost all hope of obtaining the bishopric of Magdeburg, Gerbert was called to direct the abbey of Bobbio near Piacenza in 983.

But that did not last long. He was continuously persecuted and when Otto II died, he fled to Pavia, taking refuge with the empress mother, Adelaide. Here he also met Theophano, the young widow, shortly to be the regent for the little son, Otto III. It is an important meeting for the future of Gerbert who, thanks to Theophano, will attain success.

For the moment Italy did not interest him, so he returned to his friend the Archbishop Adalbert at Reims where he campaigned politically for the Ottos, held the chair of philosophy, collected rare manuscripts in the library and, according to the chronicler, Raoul de Longchamps, had a Golem built. Gerbert had captured a demon in a head of gold to whom he posed particularly difficult questions. The Golem responded by a nod of the head. *"Inde est quod locus ille inexpositus, saltus Gerbertus appellatur:"* the answer that the demon gave him was called "Gerbert's leap."

As Bacchiega clearly explained, "the Golem became the real ritual nucleus of a magical and mystical initiation which was carried out so that the initiate perceive secret knowledge," but specifically it was "the actual human figure manifesting itself by means of magical powers of a vocal nature." It is Gerbert's conscience which speaks and replies in a kind of autohypnosis. And as the monk Elgard of Fleury wrote, "by questioning the Golem he probably held the key to his own destiny: *scandit ad R Gerberus in R post papa viget R.*" With this R, indeed, begin the names of three basic seats of his ecclesiastical career: Reims, Ravenna, Rome.

In 991 he became archbishop of Reims thanks to Hugh Capet who, in a council convened there, deposed the reigning bishop, Arnulf, without waiting for a response from Pope John XV. However, in a subsequent council at Monson in 995 the pontifical legate forced him to submit to a suspension of the nomination pending the final decisions of the pope. These confirmed the suspension and relative excommunication and the following year Arnulf was restored to his position.

Gerbert escaped to Magdeburg with Otto III and became his teacher and counsellor, from whence comes his total rehabilitation. In 998 he was appointed the archbishop of Ravenna, and, a year later, he acceded to the throne of Peter. Gerbert was consecrated pope with the name of Sylvester II on 2 April 999 and, as of that date, his apostasy and excommunication vanished into thin air.

A new configuration for the world, an historical turning point awaited his pontifical work. Otto III dreamt about a *renovatio imperii Romanorum* in which he would embrace the world in an ecumenical concept of love and power in the light of divine justice. Rome was the capital of the world, as the Roman Church was the mother of all the Churches. The emperor and the pope, the representatives of the supreme powers united in an agreed action would bring peace back to the world and lead the peoples along the path of God. Otto III would sit on his throne on the Aventine contemplating the ancient imperial city and taking on the task of being the protector of the pope while holding a tight rein on the Church in order to guarantee the dignity of the apostolic see.

The year 1000 would thus not be the end of the world, but a period of massive changes in which the Church, and, as a result, humanity itself would recover its original purity. That meant the annulling of the imperial donations from Constantine onwards, in other words the end of the old temporal power, but all replaced by new donations, a symbolic "stripping" to be followed by a new grant of lands in an authentic *renovatio.*

In this ecumenical atmosphere, Sylvester II gave a new slant to the Christian message, particularly in Poland and Hungary. Otto III freed the duke of Poland from the bonds of vassalage that united him with the empire and the pope then established the diocese of Gnesen. Furthermore, the emperor sent the royal crown to the Hungarian duke, Waik, who, having converted to Christianity, assumed the name of Stephen and Hungary, where the diocese of Gran was founded, became independent and was donated to the apostolic see of Rome. Finally, Sylvester II launched an appeal, the first pope in history to do so, for the liberation of the Holy Sepulcher from the Moslems who often blocked Christian pilgrimages and visits to the Holy Land. But Europe was not yet ready for a crusade.

With the year 1000 over, however, the dreams began to crumble. Once the terror of the end of the world at the millennium had vanished, the usual problems were back. Germany called for its emperor, and the pope had to stand alone. Sabina revolted as in the old times and Sylvester, who was at Orte and directly threatened, was forced to go back to Rome where the atmosphere was no better.

Otto returned, spoke kindly to the population and succeeded briefly in soothing the most inflamed souls, but his words achieved little. Subversion spread again, and the emperor was persuaded by Henry of Bavaria to leave Rome together with the pope in February of 1001. It was, in fact, a flight and Gregory of Tusculum (Frascati) took command of the revolt which had spread also to the Roman Campagna.

Otto moved further away. He celebrated Easter at Ravenna with the pope and the new abbot of Cluny, Odilon, who sought to revive in the emperor those ideals of a mystical renewal which had temporarily been shelved. Otto III, though, was now driven by a spirit of revenge against southern Italy and Rome. He captured Benevento, but in his drive towards Rome he got no further than Paterno, near Civitacastellana. Sylvester followed him like a shadow, though perhaps by then it was apparent to him that the ideal of a *renovatio* had vanished. On 23 January 1002, Otto III died and was buried at Aachen next to Charlemagne.

In the chaotic climate which arose after his death, Arduin of Ivrea managed to have himself named King of Italy while in Germany, Henry II of Bavaria ascended the throne in June and, though he shared Otto III's ideals, it was impossible for him to re-establish imperial authority in Italy right then.

Sylvester II lived on only briefly after his emperor, and legend did not leave the "wizard pope" even in the last days of his life. To the precise question he posed to the Golem about his death, "will I die before singing Mass in Jerusalem?" the Golem is supposed to have replied in the negative. So Sylvester thought that he could sleep tranquilly because it would be up to him alone whether or not to make a pilgrimage to Jerusalem. However, he frequently went to the church of Santa Croce in Gerusalemme to celebrate Mass. On 12 May 1003, a fateful day mentioned by the Golem, Sylvester II was taken ill following the Mass, and realized it was his end and that the Golem had answered correctly.

He summoned the clergy to him and ordered that his body be put on an oxcart and buried wherever it stopped. His wish was respected. The oxcart with his bier halted in the atrium of the church of the Lateran where, in fact, he was buried. Notwithstanding this story, it is probable that Sylvester II was murdered.

However, the tales about him do not end here. It was said that when a pope was about to die, water would come from his tomb, but when it was a cardinal the sarcophagus would only be damp. In 1684 when the sepulcher was opened, and the body of Sylvester was discovered still intact, dressed in pontifical vestments, his arms crossed on his breast, and the tiara on his head. It was the glimpse of an instant, for upon contact with the air it all turned to ashes, while all around the fragrance of embalming could be sensed. That was the final evidence of his wizardry.

140. JOHN XVII (1003)

Chaos reigned in Rome during the final months of the pontificate of Sylvester II. At his death, the noble families struggled with each other over the pontifical throne, but in reality power rested with John Crescenzio, the son of that Crescenzio who had passed into popular tradition as a "hero" because of his horrendous death on the battlements of Castel Sant'Angelo.

John's authority as *patricius* lasted about ten years and probably extended as far as Spoleto and Camerino, while his relatives ruled over the Sabine. Very little is known about the popes who succeeded Sylvester II, and were elected at the wish of this new master of the city.

The first one was the Roman, Siccone, from the Siccone family, who was consecrated in June 1003, with the name of John XVII. He died in the first days of December and his burial place is unknown.

141. JOHN XVIII (1004—1009)

Again very little is known about this pope. A Roman named Fasanus was elected toward the end of December 1003, and was consecrated in January of the following year under the name of John XVIII.

It seems that he perceived his episcopate in a completely religious manner, encouraging missionary activity among the Slavs and sending St. Bruno to convert Russia. Relations with the Church in the East were momentarily peaceful, and the patriarch, Sergius, included the name of John XVIII in the sacred *Dittici*.

Henry II of Bavaria came to Italy during his pontificate, routed Arduinus and was crowned king of Italy at Verona by the archbishop of Milan on 14 May 1004. A revolt of the people broke out in Pavia against Henry who put it down by setting fire to the city.

John XVIII may have hoped for Henry's intervention in Rome, but in vain, for he was recalled to Germany because of domestic problems, and Italy remained in chaos while the Crescenzi continued to control Rome.

John XVIII died in July 1009, in the abbey of St. Paul where he had apparently retired to a monastic life, and it was there that he was buried.

142. SERGIUS IV (1009–1012)

Information about this pope is also scarce. His name was Peter and his surname Bocca di Porco (Bucca porca or Os porci) and he was the bishop of Albano. He was consecrated pope on 31 July 1009, with the name of Sergius IV.

At the beginning of his pontificate, on 23 September 1009, an event occurred, the consequences of which were to determine the future of European history in relation to the East; namely the Moslem profanation of the Holy Sepulcher which Sylvester II had dreamt of defending, having perhaps as a "wizard" foreseen its destruction.

The caliph of Egypt, Hakim, had pillaged the Holy Places and persecuted Christians and pilgrims. This led Sergius IV to become the promoter, following Sylvester II, of a crusade, and to send letters in 1010 to all Christian nations in which he urged the various sovereigns to revenge the Holy Sepulcher and in particular the maritime republics to get together a great fleet which would sail to Syria. Directly interested in this appeal should have been France, which had had a kind of protectorate over the Holy Sepulcher ever since the times of Charlemagne.

But his appeal produced no response. Sergius IV died on 12 May 1012, and was buried at St. John Lateran. That spring John Crescenzio also passed away and with his death the domination of the city by his family virtually ceased.

143. BENEDICT VIII (1012–1024)

On the death of Sergius IV, the indomitable Crescenzi, with the support of the clergy, tried to raise to the papal throne a Roman, a certain Gregory. However, the counts of Tusculum (Frascati) put up as a candidate one of their own, Theophylactus, son of Count Gregory and brother of Romanus (who was later to become pope with the name of John XIX).

There followed a real armed conflict from which Theophylactus emerged victorious. He was consecrated by a layman on 18 May 1012, with the name Benedict VIII.

Gregory felt he had been deposed and travelled to Germany to assert his rights before the king. Henry accepted the papal emblems and assured him of his support.

However, Benedict VIII had also sent his legates to Henry, who ended up in favoring Benedict since he promised him the imperial crown. So Gregory was abandoned to his fate as anti-pope without further ado. Henry II, in fact, came to Italy with a large entourage of bishops, nobles and high clergymen and in 1014 was at Ravenna, after having spent Christmas of 1013 at Pavia with his wife, Cunegond.

On 14 February Benedict crowned Henry II emperor at St. Peter's. So began a very cordial relationship with the pope, with Henry II giving Benedict a document which repeated in effect what had already been granted by Otto to John XII, and contained the right of the emperor to verify that the pontifical election was performed according to canon laws. This was a measure directed against the Roman nobility, especially against the Crescenzi and the counts of Tusculum, to whom the pope himself belonged.

Eight days after the coronation, a violent riot disturbed the serenity of that period and was certainly fomented by Arduinus, eager to get back the crown of Italy. The emperor punished those who were guilty but he was aware that his situation in Rome was somewhat unpleasant since he was always considered a foreigner. He returned to Germany, remaining however on friendly terms with the pope and the Tusculan family, who showed themselves to be allies of the imperialist faction, even if only to protect their own interests.

Benedict installed his brother Romanus as the head of the city, giving him the title of Consul and Senator of the Romans, and his father was named Naval Prefect. The domination of the counts of Tusculum was now complete. The Crescenzi were forced to submit to the pope, while Arduinus, who had supported the Crescenzi, realized that his hope of recovering the crown of Italy had now vanished and became a monk in the abbey of Fruttuaria where he died in 1015.

An external peril for the State of the Church came from the Saracens, who were threatening Salerno and had landed in Tuscany, putting Pisa to fire and sword. In 1016 Benedict VIII got together a fleet commanded by his father, while he himself set off with an army and won a great victory over the Saracens who fled to Sardinia, and the fleet, in league with the maritime cities of Pisa and Genoa, succeeded in driving the infidels out of Sardinia and in liberating the island, which became a colony of Pisa.

Another danger in the south was the advance of the Greeks. In 1020 the pope went to Bamberg and pleaded with the emperor to repel the Greek peril. Henry promised to do so and kept his word. He came to Italy in 1022, appeared suddenly in the Marches and then broke up the Greek resistance in their redoubts in Campania and in Puglia. The Normans of Duke Melo were repaid for their aid with lands in Campania, and nephews of Melo were named counts and vassals of the empire. The pope himself made an alliance with that scanty group of Normans which, in the future, would prove effective for the State of the Church.

Notwithstanding these tasks of a military and temporal nature, Benedict VIII dedicated himself fervently to the reform of the Church. In 1018, having failed to convene an ecumenical council, he arranged a provincial one at Ravenna. It was significant because he promulgated a series of canons that were fundamentally important for the reform of the clergy's way of life, and particularly for the observance of celibacy and the open struggle against simony.

Unfortunately, many of these rules remained only in writing, despite the efforts of Benedict VIII and Henry II who sought to convert some of the canons into State laws. The papacy was still destined to have its "demons" within it and, after Benedict VIII, to fall again into the darkest barbarism, in thrall to the noble Roman families amongst which was emerging that of the counts of Tusculum.

The grandiose project of universal peace which Benedict VIII and Henry II had projected with King Robert of France and King Rudolph III of Burgundy, along with the dreams of Sylvester II and Otto III, ended in nothing with the pope's death on 9 April 1024, and the emperor's in July of the same year. Benedict VIII was buried in St. Peter's.

144. JOHN XIX (1024–1032)

In spite of the holiness of the ecclesiastical institutions so vigorously defended by Benedict VIII, it was his brother, Romanus, a layman, who ascended to the papal throne after his death. A consul and Roman senator through bribery or extortion, he was consecrated pope between April and May of 1024 after receiving, with the usual speed, the various sacred orders. He kept the position of senator, while his brother Albericus was nominated consul.

Believing that the pontifical throne was a throne like any other, he was apparently tempted to sell it to the patriarch of Constantinople. But the Italian bishops and the Cluny's community openly rebelled at this prospect, so John XIX, however reluctantly, had to inform the claimant Eustachius that there was nothing doing. From that moment on, the definitive split took place between the Churches of the East and the West and the names of the popes disappeared from the Eastern *Dittici*.

When Henry II died in July, the uncertainty which existed in Germany over his successor led to the reawakening of hope among the sovereigns and nobles of Italy. The opposing parties naturally impeded any united national interest so that when Conrad II, the Salian successor, was elected king of Germany in September, the powerful bishop of Milan, Aribertus, hastened to offer him homage which signified protection for the prelates from the ill-disposed nobles of Lombardy. Moreover, Conrad maintained that the king of Germany was automatically king of Italy, and Aribertus did not hesitate to recognize him as such, inviting him to receive from him the iron crown, an event which took place in the spring of 1026.

Even John XIX paid homage to the newly elected king, and all the cities of northern and central Italy, including the most hostile ones, ended by submitting to him. Continuing on his voyage, Conrad arrived at Rome with his wife, Gisela, where the pope solemnly crowned them at St. Peter's on 26 March 1027, in the presence of the king of Burgundy, Rudolph III, and the king of England and Denmark, Canute. The festivities which followed the coronation were as usual disturbed by fights between certain prominent Roman and German citizens and the chronicles speak of a "horrendous slaughter of Romans," following which the people had to beg for mercy from the new emperor.

During his stay in Rome, in addition to granting the usual privileges to convents and monasteries, Conrad issued a decree by which, in view of the disputes which continually took place between the Lombard judges and those of Rome in respect to the application of Lombard law or Roman law, he ordered the adoption of Roman law in Rome and its territory thus became, thereby, the symbol of law and of a thousand-year tradition.

Early in April the emperor moved to southern Italy to reinforce certain possessions, after which he went back up north.

John XIX governed Rome quietly but, in reality, he had no authority on an international level, and he was able to use his power only inside the walls of Rome, beyond which any decision of his was blocked by the emperor. A tangible proof of the disdain in which Conrad II held him was when the pope renewed to the abbot of Reichenau the privilege which had been granted him by Gregory V to use pontifical vestments during a sung Mass. The emperor publicly burned the papal document during a council recognizing the claim of the bishop of Constance to have that privilege.

A Maecenas-like gesture did occur during John XIX's pontificate when he gave protection to Guido d'Arezzo, the inventor of the new system of musical notation. Otherwise, the Church did not lose much when he died in the last months of 1032. He was buried in St. Peter's.

145. BENEDICT IX (1032–1044)

On the death of John XIX, the papacy, like the city, seemed to be a matter which concerned solely the family of the counts of Tusculum. They possessed all the power and, with a tolerant emperor like Conrad II, Albericus III, the new head of family, had nothing to fear. Bribing the group of clergymen who still counted in Rome, it was not difficult for him to place on the throne of Peter his son Theophylactus, who took the name of Benedict IX. The see of Rome could be purchased, it seems, just like any other bishopric, having completely lost that apostolic character which was traditionally attached to the See of Peter.

Benedict IX was consecrated at the end of 1032, though some sources say it was in January of the following year. He was very young, if not a twelve-year-old as many have maintained, and certainly without any experience or an ecclesiastical background that might have partly justified his election. He was merely the second son of the consul, Albericus III of the counts of Tusculum, and that sufficed. His older brother, Gregory, was at the same time given the title of Senator, thus diplomatically avoiding the title of *Patricius* which might have irritated the emperor who was already only too complying.

According to one of his successors, Victor III, Benedict IX was a thief and an assassin, and he actually expressed his shame in having to recall the base, evil life of this predecessor of his. Desiderius of Monte Cassino manifested the same horror when recounting the iniquities perpetrated by this pope. It is clear, as Gregorovius notes, "that with Benedict IX the papacy reached the bottom of moral decadence. The conditions in Rome at that time appeared even worse than with John XIII, and perhaps surpassed in horror those of the Borgias, if we were able to compare these periods with each other."

The abuse of power by the Tusculans in Rome was well known and the news that in June 1036 the people rose up and tried to kill this pope whom they considered unworthy of his position, was probably not unfounded. Benedict IX is supposed to have escaped to the protection of the emperor who had just come to Italy to resolve a problem that had become delicate for the empire, namely the claims of the lesser suzerains in Northern Italy. These overlords had rebelled against the despotic regime of the archbishop of Milan, Aribertus, who wanted to turn his archdiocese into a kind of Milanese pontifical state. The pope did meet with the emperor but only to put an end to matters with Aribertus.

To begin with Conrad thought he would act on his own, and in 1037 he decided to side with the overlords, conceding to them the heredity of feudal estates. Aribertus refused to obey and Conrad vainly laid siege to Milan. When he failed by force of arms, he convened a council at Piacenza on his own initiative without the support of the pope or other ecclesiastics, and declared Aribertus deposed, naming a successor whom the Milanese population obviously did not accept.

At that point the emperor turned to Benedict IX who appeared strong enough in his position to be able to leave his see whenever he wished without worrying about possible coups. Their meeting took place at Spello in March of 1038, while Aribertus from his see in Milan claimed to be the reformer of the Church and criticized the scandalous life of the pontiff. Conrad II needed the intervention of the pope, so he made him understand that it was best to excommunicate the archbishop in both their interests, and Benedict happily issued the anathema against the stubborn Aribertus.

Conrad proceeded with his expedition in Italy, going to the south to set up garrisons and fortresses in what was still a dangerous situation for the State of the Church, and in which the only new element was the strengthening of the

Normans who were establishing themselves throughout. In this situation, the emperor assigned the county of Aversa to Rainulf.

When the plague suddenly broke out in his army, Conrad was forced to return to Germany where he caught it himself and died in 1039, after having ensured that the throne would be inherited by his son, Henry.

However, years passed before the new German king came to Italy, not only to take possession of his territory but also to restore, one may say, a certain moral order within the Church. Henry III, unlike his father, felt inspired by God to undertake a reformation in keeping with the moral awakening already under-way in many ecclesiastical circles, but which had not received support from higher levels. Aribertus had been one of the last to suffer the consequences.

Benedict IX calmly continued to govern from his papal throne, smearing it with infamy, even if from time to time he shamelessly went about showing a new pontifical dignity. In 1040 he was in Marseilles to consecrate the church of St. Victor and to participate in a council which championed a philanthropic law about the Peace of God, the *Tregua Dei*, but was certainly in conflict with the behavior of the pontiff who did not show any sense of divine justice at all.

However, between the end of 1044 and the beginning of the next year, Benedict IX received his first lessons. A popular uprising threw him out of Rome and replaced him with a new pope, Sylvester III. At this point ended the first pontificate of Benedict IX who is the only pope in history, as attested by the *Annuario pontificio*, considered to have been elected three different times, thereby reviving a series of inconsistencies in the listing of the Roman pontiffs, as I have already observed with regard to John XII, Benedict V and Leo VIII in the latter's biography.

Indeed, Benedict IX succeeded in coming back to Rome in 1045, evicting Sylvester III (deemed by many to be an antipope, but recognized as a legitimate pope, instead, by the *Annuario pontificio*), and simply continuing his pontifi-cate, since he had not been deposed by a council. But during the same year he did not hesitate to sell the papal throne to the archpriest John Gratian who, a month later, took the name of Gregory VI, with Benedict IX abdicating of his own will. That was his second pontificate.

While Benedict IX retired to continue his adventurous life in his Tusculan castles, Henry III arrived in Italy in 1046, inspired to reform the Roman Church. The council, which he convened at Sutri on 20 December 1046, deposed all the popes on the scene and elected Clement II.

The Tusculans had no wish to retaliate and remained calm when Henry III came to Rome and installed his own pope. They concealed in that way the absence of Benedict IX who watched developments from Tusculum, where he waited for the propitious moment to take back the pontificate.

The moment came when Henry II had returned to Germany and Clement II had died in October of 1047. Benedict fell like a falcon on the throne again and stayed there until July of the following year, only to be kicked off it by the imperial legates who installed Damasus II. And that was Benedict's third pontificate, officially recognized by the *Annuario pontificio*. The matter seems pretty confused even in this case, since in some sources the qualification of "antipope" is ventured for the second and third pontificates of Benedict IX.

Once he finally abandoned the pontifical throne, this amazing pontiff withdrew to his castles in Tusculum. Some think he entered the monastery of Grottaferrata near Frascati, where in fact he was buried. It is frankly difficult to imagine the transformation of a person like him and it is easier to picture a pleasure-loving pope reduced to a pleasure-loving monk. His death around 1050 coincided with the end of the tyranny of the counts of Tusculum over the pontifical throne to which they had succeeded in raising no less than five popes, although they continued to be important to the history of Rome for most of the twelfth century.

1 4 6. SYLVESTER III (1 O4 5)

As mentioned in the biography of Benedict IX, a popular uprising between the end of 1044 and the beginning of the next year put this pope to flight. His supporters had sought shelter in the Leonine City and the attack by the population lasted three days. However, information about all of this is rather confusing, and there is mention of an earthquake which is thought to have caused a large number of deaths among the rebels, headed by Count Gerard of Galeria.

In the end the Romans declared openly that they had had enough of Benedict IX and wanted to replace him with the bishop of the Sabina, John. This suggests that the Crescenzi, masters of the Sabin, had something to do with the rebellion. John was consecrated pope on 20 January 1045, but his election cost him a good deal of money to compensate the rebels, particularly Gerard of Galeria. Sylvester III, however, had no military support and Benedict IX managed to get rid of him as soon as calm was restored in the city, which happened on 10 February of that year. After a pontificate of only twenty-two days, Sylvester took refuge in a mountain of the Sabina while continuing to claim the title of Pope, and the *Annuario pontificio* considers him to have reigned until the above date. Officially deposed at the council of Sutri on 20 December 1046, he was probably authorized to maintain his diocese, but nothing further is known about his life.

1 4 7. BENEDICT IX (1 O4 5)

When Sylvester III had been ousted, Benedict IX resumed his functions as pope but this, his second pontificate, lasted from 10 April 1045 for only twenty-one days. Enough time to excommunicate Sylvester and to unload the throne itself which had probably become a burden for him. The sale took place on 1 May in exchange for a sizeable income, Peter's English pence collection, along with a formal contract in which he declared his abdication in favor of John Gratian, archpriest of the Church of St. John at Porta Latina.

The broker in this contract must have been Gerard of Galeria, who had already purchased the pontifical throne for Sylvester III. He appears to have promised Benedict IX the hand of his daughter but later wisely reneged on his promise.

148. GREGORY VI (1045−1046)

John Gratian, probably a descendant of the Pierleoni family, archpriest of St. John at Porta Latina, who was reputed to be a pious churchman, purchased the papal throne from Benedict IX and was consecrated pope on 5 May 1045, with the name of Gregory VI.

His election, outside Rome, was greeted as an exceptional event. Pier Damiani, the famous monk who had called for a general reform of the Church and a return to the original ideals of the papacy, and was evidently unaware of the commercial transaction which had brought Gregory VI to the See of Peter, wrote to him that finally "the dove had returned to the ark with the olive branch." Perhaps Gregory VI had resorted to simony, deeming it the only means of eliminating so unworthy a pope, but he really did have the best of intentions to bring the papacy back to the position of prestige and honor that it had lost a long time before. A guarantee of this were his reputation for piety and, indirectly, the fact that his chaplain, Hildebrand of Soana, was destined to bring historic changes in the papacy and in Christianity in the course of the years to come.

However, in more than one occasion, this pope personally had to lead armed forces to restore order in a city which was in complete chaos, as Gregorovius records, basing himself on chronicles of the period: "The streets were alive with brigands; pilgrims were regularly assaulted and robbed; in the city the churches were falling into ruins and the priests wined and dined. Every day there were murders which made the streets unsafe, even in St. Peter's, Roman nobility dared to come with sword in hand to pillage the gifts which devout hands had placed on the altars." When Henry III came to Italy in the autumn of 1046, preceded by his fame as a reformer of the church and was promptly crowned king of Lombardy, he convened a council at Pavia of Germans, Burgundians and Italians to discuss the basis of a real reform of the ecclesiastical world. Gregory VI was eager to meet him at Piacenza, to have Henry on his side, so as to discredit as much as possible Benedict IX and Sylvester III. However, while treating him with all the honors appropriate for a pope, Henry II appeared diffident and left decisions about those whom Gregory VI had judged antipopes to the council he had convened at Sutri.

This council met on 20 December and summoned the three popes. Sylvester III, who had been deposed but was very probably authorized to retain his diocese as bishop, and Gregory VI appeared. The latter, held guilty of simony upon his own statement, was considered unworthy of the position and was invited to abdicate. Condemned to exile in Germany by order of the king, he was entrusted to the supervision of the archbishop of Cologne, Herman, and he died in 1047 "on the banks of the Rhine," attended to the very end by his chaplain, Hildebrand. His burial place is unknown.

149. CLEMENT II (1046—1047)

On 23 December, Henry III convened another council in Rome at which Benedict IX was tried in his absence, since he had not appeared at Sutri, and was, of course, deposed. The following day the king, in agreement with the clergy and the people, chose a Saxon, the bishop of Bamberg, Suidger of the nobles of Morsleben and Honburg, as the new pope. He was consecrated on 25 December 1046, with the name of Clement II.

A few days later in St. Peter's, probably as the first official act of his pontificate, this German pope crowned Henry III emperor with the usual pomp and splendor, together with many mutual oaths of fidelity and defense of the Church. What is certain is that the new emperor thus assured for himself power over the pontifical throne. He was to elect three German popes successively and, in principle, limited himself to defending the State of the Church, adding to his title of Emperor that of *Patricius Romanorum*, together with the privilege of designating his own candidate in future papal elections who would be voted on by the clergy and the population.

However, with the help of Henry, Clement II succeeded in organizing a major council at Rome in January 1047, at which it was decided that whoever conferred ecclesiastical orders based on simony would be excommunicated. The reformist spirit appeared to be on the march. But the pope did not feel secure in Rome and, as long as Henry III was there, followed him like a shadow. The emperor sought above all to bend the Tusculans to obedience, but they resisted from within their well-fortified castles, so he went as far south as Capua and Benevento to shore up imperial authority. In the spring, Henry III returned to Germany followed by the pope, as they wanted to plan together the introduction of ecclesiastical reforms also in those areas.

Clement II returned to Italy in the autumn, determined to confront alone the possible enemies of his pontificate, knowing he had a real ally to support him, but he died at Pesaro on 9 October 1047, probably poisoned by agents of Benedict IX.

He is the only pope in history to have been buried in Germany at the cathedral of Bamberg, seat of his diocese.

150. BENEDICT IX (1047–1048)

Benedict IX took possession again of the pontifical throne as soon as he was notified of the death of Clement II and installed himself there on 8 November 1047, in his third pontificate, officially recognized as of that date in the *Annuario pontificio*.

Helping him to regain power was Boniface II of Tuscany, a champion of independence from the emperor, who looked with suspicion at this powerful vassal who was married to Beatrice, daughter of the duke of Lotharingia, and as such linked in a way to Germany. He aspired to the position of Roman *patricius*, a position which Henry III had himself assumed along with his title of Emperor, relegating Boniface to the role of an imperial *missus*. But Boniface supported and tolerated the new election of Benedict IX precisely in order to show Henry III his own power, and he succeeded for eight months in opposing Henry's will. The pro-German party in Rome informed the emperor of this, proposing as an alternative the candidature of Alinard, the archbishop of Lyons, who was popular with the Romans.

But Henry had the bishop of Brixen, Poppone, elected at Pöhlde on 25 December and sent him to Italy to Boniface, instructing the latter to accompany the papal designate to Rome and to remove Benedict IX.

The marquis refused, resolved to make Henry understand how important he was, and Poppone returned to Henry in Germany. At this point, the emperor threatened his vassal, and made clear what would happen to him if he did not carry out his orders. Boniface was thus forced to take the German pope to Rome, and Benedict IX was finally thrown out by the imperial legates on 17 July 1048. It was the end of his third pontificate.

151. DAMASUS II (1048)

Poppone, a native of Bavaria and bishop of Brixen, who had been elected at Pöhlde on 25 December 1047, was consecrated pope with the name of Damasus II, on 17 July 1048, the date from which the *Annuario pontificio* considers he was reigning.

His very brief pontificate of only 23 days did not allow him to do very much and he probably did not feel at home in Rome, a big city with a lot of problems to resolve. Perhaps he missed the town in the Tyrol where he was bishop, so he moved to Palestrina, a feudal estate of the Church, run by the Crescenzi, enemies of the counts of Tusculum, where he could pass the summer in peace, far from the heat which beat down upon Rome that year, and from the malaria.

But he suddenly died on 9 August, probably a victim even there of malaria, or, as others believe, poisoned by Benedict IX, who though had, by then, lost any hope of regaining the throne.

Damasus II was buried in the basilica of St. Lawrence outside the Walls.

1 5 2. ST. LEO IX (1 0 4 9 – 1 0 5 4)

Between the death of Damasus II and the election of his successor, there was a short vacant see period because Henry III could not find a person he liked nor one who would accept the burdens of such a position, all the more exacting with the climate of reformation within the Church, now desired by so many and even by the emperor himself.

Ultimately his choice fell on the bishop of Toul, an Alsatian named Brunone of the noble family of Egisheim-Dagsburg, born around 1002, and who had a pious desire for reform. Some biographers report that he accepted on condition that his election be confirmed by the clergy and people in Rome to protect him from any charge that he had illegally occupied the pontifical throne. Whether this information is true or false, it is significant that he arrived in Rome in February of 1049 dressed so simply that the condition in question was achieved, as he was acclaimed by a population which of late had been only too prone to revolt against its bishop.

Thus Brunone was welcomed as a holy man by the population which gathered as a crowd in a procession at Porta Latina and unanimously acclaimed the confirmation of his election. On 12 February 1049, Brunone was consecrated pope with the name of Leo IX.

For the great reformation to which he intended to devote his pontificate, he gathered around him the most outstanding men of the ecclesiastical world of the time, beginning with Hildebrand of Soana who had become a monk at Cluny at the death of Gregory VI and had been called by Leo IX to accompany him on his journey to Rome. He was ordained a subdeacon and entrusted with the administration of the abbey of St. Paul. He can be considered the authentic renovator of the Church with the office, one can say, of "minister plenipotentiary" for four other popes, or "secretary of State" according to the more modern term.

Other collaborators called to Rome by the new pope were Humbert, a monk from the abbey of Moyenmontier, who was his travelling companion and often his ambassador, Archdeacon Frederick of Lorena as librarian, who would later be pope with the name of Stephen IX, and Abbot Hugo Candido, all these men were free of political ties and eager to work together for the reform of the clergy and the papacy. They were men with whom Leo IX laid the groundwork for what would be the "College of Cardinals," something like a governing board that supported the pope obediently in the administration of ecclesiastical matters.

This is without counting the support of other figures such as Abbott Hugo of Cluny, Archbishop Alinard of Lyons, and Pier Damian, Prior of Fonte Avellana near Gubbio. Although far from Rome, these persons held continuous exchanges of views with Leo IX, who was destined to bring about the pre-arranged objectives through repeated journeys, so many in fact that in the five years of his pontificate he only managed to reside in Rome for a few months, because he wanted to be present in person wherever the apostolic function required the bishop of Rome to hold councils in Italy, France or Germany. He was history's very first "travelling pope."

In his first council, held in Rome a few weeks after his consecration, after renewing Clement II's decrees against simony, he deposed several bishops who were known to practice simony and paid particular attention to the rules against concubinage of priests. He then visited the north of Italy where, in another council at Pavia, he recited the Roman decrees, and from there he went to Germany and met Henry III at Cologne, and pronounced an anathema against Duke Godfrey of Lorraine and Count Baldwin of Flanders for having rebelled against the emperor.

In October 1049 he went to Reims to consecrate the church of St. Remigius and to convene a council during which he laid down twelve canons purporting to do away with simony and the concubinage of priests in the French territory. There followed a council at Mainz, held with Henry III, in which the laws against simony and concubinage were renewed in the German dioceses. And there followed still other councils, also bent on verifying and correcting the situations in various areas, as if to establish a sort of continual inspection of the morality of the ecclesiastical world and, by reflex, of the public one as well.

Leo IX also had to concern himself with the heresy of the canon of Tours, Berengarius, who was denying the presence of Christ in the Eucharist. Excommunicated already once in a Roman council in April 1050, he was condemned in several following councils, until he appeared before one held in Tours in 1054 under the chairmanship of Hildebrand of Soana, and signed the Catholic formula, renouncing his heretical theories.

Under the pontificate of Leo IX, the discussions about the schism with the Eastern Church were renewed, initiated by Michael Cerularius, the new patriarch, who accused those Christians using the Roman liturgy of heresy, and ordered the closing of the monasteries and Latin churches in Constantinople. Leo IX protested in January 1054, pointing out the tolerance which existed in Italy for Greek monasteries and their liturgy. Emperor Constantine IX showed himself more conciliatory than his patriarch and more respectful of the dignity of the pope, who thereupon sent a mission to Constantinople to negotiate the dispute. His legates were, however, received coldly by Cerularius and the monks, although the emperor himself treated them with the respect due to them. Leo IX had already died when his ambassadors excommunicated Cerularius at a council in the church of Santa Sofia on 16 July. The patriarch responded by excommunicating the pope. The schism therefore persisted and was indeed reinforced.

However, Leo IX did not concern himself only with ecclesiastical reform and even he, a man so fervently devoted to the religious nature of his pontifical position, became involved with temporal power. Henry III who, at Worms in 1052, made a donation to the Church of Rome of the city of Benevento and other towns in southern Italy indirectly offered the opportunity to him. It was an attempt to support papal claims in the south where, while Byzantine sovereignty had weakened, that of the Normans was being strengthened.

The Normans no doubt represented a permanent danger to a city like Benevento, because Henry III had ceded part of the duchy to them as well. The people of Benevento felt defenseless and feared that sooner or later they would fall under Norman sovereignty, so they invoked the intervention of the pope.

In fact, the Normans were pillaging near the city but basically to defend land they had conquered at the cost of battles and sacrifice, as opposed to the popes who showed documents of imperial concessions, considered by the Normans to be nothing but usurpation.

Leo IX was thus constrained to ask for military assistance from the emperor who returned to Italy in February of 1053 with an army, albeit small, made up of Germans and soldiers of fortune, even though accompanied by a military leader, Godfrey of Lotharingia. Confident, he recruited other militiamen in Italy, since the Normans had been excommunicated meanwhile for having seized lands of the Church, and wanted to avoid a battle and settle the dispute by a treaty of peace, bearing in mind the alliance set up years earlier with Pope Benedict VIII. In fact, Richard of Aversa and Robert Guiscard were ready to swear obedience to the pope and to pay tribute to the Church as the Christians they deeply felt themselves to be, and they wanted to obviate a fight against him whom they considered above all the vicar of Christ.

Sure of victory the pope refused to negotiate, but, instead, encountered a memorable defeat on 18 June 1053, at Civitate in the Capitanata, south of the Gargano, where he was taken prisoner. Five days after the battle, the Normans took him to Benevento and kept him in their custody for the entire winter. It was a defeat which seriously damaged the reputation which Leo IX had built up of a holy and venerated pope, for the father of all Christians had taken the sword against zealous followers of Christ, and popular opinion could easily see in that defeat the punishment of God.

Hildebrand of Soana was unable to be near him in those unhappy days, being busy presiding over the council at Tours which succeeded in bringing the heretic, Berengarius, to more orthodox views. On 12 March 1054, Leo IX was finally released by his jailers. He lifted their excommunication and, in effect, the Normans obtained recognition of their territorial conquests, even if under conditions which are not clear to us from the sources available.

On 3 April, the pope arrived in Rome, a deluded, sick man who, sensing his end near, had himself carried to the Lateran where he died on 19 April 1054. He was buried in St. Peter's.

153. VICTOR II (1055–1057)

Hildebrand received news of the death of Leo IX while still in France, and hastened to Germany for the nomination of a successor. At the same time, the Roman nobles also sent a delegation to Mainz in an attempt to have an anti-reformist chosen. But Hildebrand got the upper hand, and managed to persuade Henry III to choose a relative of his, Gebhard of the counts of Dollnstein-Hirschberg and bishop of Eichstätt, who accepted the tiara on condition that the emperor commit himself to help the Holy See regain its property and not abandon him, as had happened to Leo IX. Once he had obtained this promise, which Henry could in no way have honored because he died the following year, Gebhard departed for Rome.

On 16 April he was consecrated pope with the name of Victor II, and in June, at a council held in Florence Henry III gave him the title of Imperial Vicar. It was a means like any other for the emperor to rid himself of responsibility, while at the same time bolstering what temporal power the pontiff could have had.

Victor II gave Hildebrand the job of pursuing the reform, especially in France, where various nominations of bishops unworthy of the distinction were taking place. For his part Victor was looking in Italy for a counterpart to the military defense that was apparently not forthcoming from Henry III. He found it in Godfrey of Lorraine, "the Bearded," brother of Archdeacon Frederick.

Godfrey had at one time rebelled against Henry and, as a result, had had the duchy of Lower Lorraine taken from him. He had married Beatrice, the widow of Boniface of Tuscany, who had died in 1052 in a hunting accident, becoming by this marriage the most powerful lord of Italy. The emperor had tried to dispossess him but without success; in revenge, though, he had taken the widow Beatrice and stepdaughter Matilda as hostages to Germany. When Henry III died in October 1056, Victor II found himself regent and, on the advice of Hildebrand, first of all resolved the problem of Godfrey, and convinced the empress, Agnes, to make peace with him and to return his wife and step-daughter to him, as well as the Lorraine.

Once these exchanges had been carried out and the rehabilitation had been completed, Victor left Germany, turning the regency over to Archbishop Annon of Cologne, yet making Agnes responsible for her son Henry who was barely six years old. Victor II returned to Italy and, at a council in Florence, designated Godfrey as *patricius* and his brother, Frederick, already the abbot of Monte Cassino, as cardinal-priest of St. Chrysogonus in Trastevere.

The stresses of his journeys and his responsibilities at the imperial level prob-ably hastened Victor II's death, and on the return trip to Rome on 28 July 1057 he died at Arezzo where had stopped over to settle a dispute between the bish-ops of Arezzo and Siena. His remains, which should have been transported to Eichstätt were blocked by the residents of Ravenna and he was therefore buried in Rome, probably in the church of St. Mary in Cosmedin.

1 5 4. STEPHEN IX (1 0 5 7 — 1 0 5 8)

The death of Victor II coincided with the rise in Italy of the house of Lotharingia, capable of combating the imperial hold over the papal throne. Nobles, clergy and people all agreed to elect Cardinal Frederick as pope. It was the spontaneous choice of a person in whom these groups indirectly recognized a man who had been persecuted by the emperor, and he was consecrated on 3 August 1057, with the name of Stephen IX.

The news was received at the imperial court with anger because the imperial rights to choose the candidate had, in this case, been totally disregarded. However, Empress Agnes did not have the strength to affirm herself, and she accepted the election of the man from Lorraine with good grace after hearing the explanations and excuses given with diplomatic tact by the Apostolic Nuncio, Hildebrand, who was the real operator in the "new papal regime," both on a religious level and on the strictly political one. Stephen IX relied blindly on him, since he and his family were indebted to him for what they had achieved. And Stephen also put Pier Damiani to help Hildebrand in the work of strengthening of the Church, nominating him as cardinal-bishop of Ostia.

Stephen IX, therefore, continued the reform movement but did not hesitate also to make bold projects in the temporal field. Maybe it was purely his, and not Hildebrand's, scheme of creating an Italian kingdom for his brother, Godfrey, to the detriment of the Normans. Perhaps it was to raise an army that he demanded that the monks of Monte Cassino transfer the abbey's treasure to Rome, after which he decided to meet his brother at Florence, to carry out cer-tain projects of a temporal nature. He contemplated reaching an agreement with the Byzantine to put the Normans between crossfires, and it is not sure that he didn't actually dream of the imperial crown for Godfrey. These projects, none of which were completed because of his sudden death, were certainly overshad-owed by the activities of Hildebrand and Pier Damiani, and of all the other men working from the time of Leo IX for the spiritual cleansing of the Church and the papacy, but they were ones which tended to cast a blur on his personality as the vicar of Christ.

He died on 29 March 1058, upon his arrival in Florence, and he was buried in the cathedral of that city.

155. NICHOLAS II (1059–1061)

As soon as the news of Stephen IX's death reached Rome, the nobles attempted to regain their authority in the papal election by a coup, under the leadership of Gregory of Tusculum, brother of Benedict IX. Invading Rome with troops on 5 April 1058, they raised to the pontifical throne a Roman named John, bishop of Velletri, nicknamed "Mincio" by the people, or "Stupid," on account of, let us say, his lack of personality. As bishop of Ostia, Pier Damiani was supposed to have carried out his consecration but he refused to, so the nobles assigned the task to a simple priest from Ostia, and John was consecrated pope with the name of Benedict X. It was a clear case of an illegal election and consecration, and indeed he is still considered an antipope. All those who were part of the reformist clergy, with Pier Damiani at their head, refused to recognize him and were forced to flee from Rome to wait for the return from Germany of Hildebrand of Soana to decide on a new candidate.

The reformists gathered at Siena and there, on 18 April, with the support of Godfrey of Tuscany, they elected as candidate for the pontifical throne the bishop of Florence, Gerard of Burgundy, born at Chevron in the Savoy around 980. A delegation was sent immediately to the Empress Regent Agnes who confirmed the choice of Gerard, and authorized Godfrey to accompany the newly elected pope to Rome for the crowning ceremony. The matter was not a simple one because the Roman nobility had control of the city and the people themselves, although they had little sympathy for the "Mincio," did not seem disposed to tolerate a pope indirectly chosen by the imperial court. It was necessary to proceed with tact and, if necessary, to use the same means as the enemy, that is, bribery. Gerard was thereupon duly elected and took the name of Nicholas II. He quickly summoned a synod at Sutri by which Benedict X was deposed and excommunicated. Meanwhile, in Rome, through a wealthy man, Leo Baruch, the son of a Jew who had converted and was a relative on his mother's side, Hildebrand spread a lot of money around and succeeded in provoking a popular uprising in which some of the nobility took part. Benedict X was forced to flee under the protection of Gerard of Galeria while Nicholas II was able finally to enter Rome accompanied by Duke Godfrey, and was consecrated in St. Peter's on 24 January 1059. All of these events again had shown how urgent it was to control the election of popes so as to eliminate all irregularity and outside interference in the ecclesiastical world. The reformists were more than convinced of this and convened a council in the Lateran in April 1059, in which 113 bishops, almost exclusively Italians, participated. The council renewed the condemnation of Benedict X as well as the prohibition of concubinage by the priests and of simony. Finally, a new decree on the election of the pontiff was promulgated. All this was issued by Nicholas II in the bull *In nomine Domini* of 13 April 1059, which was probably, both in form and in substance, the work of Cardinal Humbert, even if one must also recognize that Hildebrand of Soana exercised considerable influence on it.

In substance, the decree restricted the electoral body to cardinal-bishops only, while the cardinals who were not bishops could merely give their loyalty to the newly elected, with the simple clergy and the laity limited to giving solely their consent. This, in the final analysis, meant they no longer had any special weight since the determining vote was that of the cardinal-bishops. Furthermore, the decree took into consideration the possibility that the election could take place outside Rome, in any other location which the cardinal-bishops might deem necessary, thereby involving a smaller number of clergy and laity. However, the Roman people were excluded and all that remained for the Romans was a sort of right to express a preference for a candidate from among those born in Rome who might be "worthy and capable;" otherwise the choice was from among "the personnel of the entire Church." The emperor was assigned the last place in the election procedure, with merely a general right out of consideration and respect. Nicholas II notified all Christianity of the council's provisions, and gave his bull the widest possible distribution.

Foreseeing a fight to the last drop of blood, first of all with the emperor and then his various vassals, as well as with the Roman nobility, the new men of the Church reached a brave decision to change the course of the entire papal policy and, facing the triple threat against the decisions of the Lateran council, pinned their last hope on the Normans. Hildebrand was the first to realize that these would sooner or later found a strong dynasty in southern Italy which, once recognized by the pope under certain conditions, would become a powerful and faithful defender of the Church.

With this in mind, Nicholas II himself travelled to southern Italy to make an alliance in a solemn form with the Normans at Melfi, where he also held a council in August 1059, at which Richard of Aversa and Robert Guiscard, the victors of Civitate, were present. As a feudal estate from the Church they received all the lands they had conquered, except for Benevento. Apulia and Calabria were assigned to Robert, along with the title of Duke, while Richard was acknowledged as the prince of Capua. On their side, the Normans swore the oath of vassalage to the pontiff and solemnly promised to help the Church keep its patrimony and to come to the military aid of duly elected popes to protect their dignity.

As Gregorovius observes, one is certainly struck by "the boldness of the pope who ceded foreign provinces to foreigners as if they belonged to him and assured them even the possession of lands not yet conquered." A valid hypothesis is cleverly offered by Seppelt when, in searching for "the juridical basis on which the investiture rested," declares that "it can be found in the Donation of Constantine, the authenticity of which was not then in doubt and that, with the reinforcement brought to it through the Pseudo-Isidore forgeries, was at that time still to be considered valid." In sum, the reformists, who were very careful to insist on the legality and the purity of their ideals, ended up supporting illegal and historically false institutions.

As the first result of the Alliance of Melfi, the Normans accompanied the pope to Rome with an army to squash the pretensions of the Roman nobles who continued to recognize Benedict X as the pope. The latter besieged in his castle in Galeria, had to surrender immediately. His life was spared and he was able to return to the city to live, thanks to the guarantee given by the Roman nobles, but a council with precise instructions from Hildebrand defrocked him from the priesthood, and he was confined like a prisoner in the church of St. Agnes. Gregory VII is supposed to have freed the by now powerless Benedict, readmitting him to the community and accepting him in St. Mary Major.

Shortly after having concluded the agreement with the Normans, the pope planned to gain the additional support in southern Italy of the "Patarini," a political movement among the common people which for several years under the deacon, Harold, and the subdeacon, Landulf, had been supporting the reform faction in the Church. They had provoked the "little people" to complain about married priests, and this revolt of the ragpickers, the name of the movement, had led to looting and cleavages among the clergy which Archbishop Guido was evidently unable to control. The papal emissaries, Pier Damiani and Anselm, bishop of Lucca, managed to resolve the dispute (it was especially the former who took control of the situation through a splendid speech in the cathedral), and made Archbishop Guido and the entire clergy of Milan take an oath to renounce simony and concubinage.

The official intervention of Nicholas II with the "Pataria" in the reform movement in the Church was a historically important moment. "By joining with this mass movement, the papacy took a truly revolutionary step," Walter Ullmann noted. The original social obligations of the church's apostolic mission, now reappear in contact with "the lower lay and clerical strata arrayed against the powerful conservative forces centered in the nobility."

As far as the relations with the imperial court were concerned, the pope sent Cardinal Stephen as his legate to Germany to justify Rome's behavior with the Normans and with Milan, but he was not even received by the empress. Certain German bishops close to the court went so far as to declare the decisions of the pope null and void and the new decree on papal elections illegal, even rejecting the bull of Nicholas II. It was open revolt, which could lead to schism. However, before he could do anything, Nicholas II died in Florence on 27 July 1061. He was buried in the cathedral of that city.

156. ALEXANDER II (1061—1073)

At the death of Nicholas II, a delegation of the Roman nobility, led by Count Gerard of Galeria, went to the imperial court to obtain the nomination of a new pope. At the same time, representatives of the Lombard bishops presented themselves officially, requesting the election of the chancellor, Guibert. But before any decision could be taken, Hildebrand, in open defiance of the imperial court and applying the decree of 1059, convened the cardinals in Rome and they elected pope Bishop Anselm of Lucca. He was someone who was favorably looked upon by the imperial court and who was elected according to the new electoral system. By this move Hildebrand had hoped to protect the position of the reformers. The opposing factions in Rome went immediately into action but the newly-elected pope, under the protection of the troops of Richard of Capua, was rapidly and peacefully crowned on the spot on 1 October 1061, at St. Peter in Chains, taking the name of Alexander II.

In response, the German bishops and some of the Lombards, under the leadership of Guibert, convened a council at Basel on 28 October 1061, which recognized the title of *patricius* for the ten-year-old Henry IV and declared illegal the election of Alexander II. The council raised to the papacy Bishop Cadalus of Parma who took the name of Honorius II. As a result there was a full-blown schism.

Nonetheless, a general recognition of Honorius II was indispensable which meant he had to go to Rome for the coronation. Protected by the Lombard troops however, he only succeeded in arriving near Rome in March of 1062 where there was a battle with the Roman troops, mustered by Hildebrand in April, which ended with Honorius II occupying the Leonine City including St. Peter's. Yet he stayed there only a few days since he had to go out into the Roman countryside to seek reinforcements while awaiting the arrival of the Normans.

In the beginning of May, Duke Godfrey of Tuscany, who was a friend of both sides, stepped into the fray wanting to reach a settlement. He managed to persuade the two contenders for the papal throne to withdraw to their bishoprics and leave the decision to the parliament of Augsburg. In the meantime, a sort of coup d'état had taken place in Germany, led by Archbishop Annon of Cologne who had taken the regency from the empress and put the young king under his "protection."

Annon convened parliament for the end of October and entrusted the proceedings to his nephew, Bishop Burcard of Halberstadt, who declared that the election of Alexander II had been completely in order. Once this pope learned the result of the proceedings, and without waiting for the decision by parliament, he immediately expressed his gratitude by conferring on Burcard the archbishopric of Pallium and on Annon the archchancellorship of the Church of

Rome. In April 1063, escorted by Duke Godfrey's troops, Alexander II took his seat in Rome and convened a council at the Lateran, where he issued the excommunication decree against Honorius II and renewed the canon laws against simony and the marriage of priests.

However, Honorius was not prepared to give in and called a council in Parma, which, in turn, launched an excommunication of Alexander II. Moreover, after receiving substantial financial aid from some of the Roman nobles, he managed to raise a small army, invade Rome again and seize the Leonine City once more while Alexander II, defended by the Norman troops, barricaded himself within the Lateran. Honorius hoped for help from the German court, but in vain, in view of Annon's and Burcard's now clearly hostile stance towards him.

Notwithstanding this, Cadalus's call for help did not go unheard, and there were those who wanted to resolve the matter once and for all, especially through the intervention of Adalbert of Bremen, an opponent of Annon. So a council of Italian and German bishops met in Mantua on 31 May 1064, as a result of which Alexander II was definitively and unanimously recognized as the legitimate pope. Honorius II, however, still would not give up and continued to assert his claims until his death in 1072. But he no longer had sufficient support, and the schism within the Western Church finally came to an end.

The pontificate of Alexander II brought the Church of Rome into the European context. In 1066 England, which was dominated by a faction against reform, was conquered by the Norman duke, William, and the pope hastened to approve his military action by sending him the banner of St. Peter, a symbol of his solemn blessing. At the same time, a similar standard was waving before the troops of Roger I, brother of Robert Guiscard, who were busy with the conquest of Arabian Sicily in a war that was by then more than thirty years old. Close relations were established with the Christian kingdom of Spain where Cardinal Hugh Candido was sent in 1065 as legate to hold a number of councils against simony and the marriage of priests.

Especially exacting was the continuation of the reform in the archdiocese of Milan where the "Pataria" had suffered setbacks in its struggle. Here, unfortunately, the contribution of Pier Damiani who, under Nicholas II, had brought about a kind of submission of Milan to Rome, was missing. He had died in 1072 and the see of Milan now risked falling into the imperial orbit.

Alexander II sent the papal banner to the new head of the "Patarini," the knight Erlembald who was an opponent of Archbishop Guido, accused of having violated the oath against simony and concubinage which he had sworn in 1060. By so doing, the pope officially imparted his blessing and support to the "Patarini" in the riots which they fomented, after the abdication of Guido, against the followers of the Lombard bishops who had elected as archbishop the priest, Godfrey, at the behest of Henry IV.

The "Patarini," on the suggestion of the pope and with the military assistance of Erlembard had, in the presence of a papal legate, elected Atton as archbishop on 6 January 1072. He was definitively recognized by the Lateran council of 1073 that condemned both the election of Godfrey and the conduct of the Lombard bishops. The conciliar decree seemed clearly formulated to annul the authority of Henry IV, though without mentioning his name, and to put a stop to the right of ecclesiastical investiture which was to remain the chief motive of the struggle between Henry IV and the Church. Claimed by the king of Germany and exercised until then without being challenged, it was now incompatible with the new course forced on the Church by the reformists. The parcelling out of bishoprics and abbeys to unworthy persons and even to lay persons, more often than not by simony, could not but cause firm opposition from the see of Rome. Hildebrand of Soana, next on the papal throne, was to be the most tenacious defender of this renewed politico-ecclesiastical policy.

The struggles for the reform disturbed even the situation in Rome, where a truce reigned among the factions within the city, but which were always ready to battle in the Roman Campagna where the papacy appeared still powerless. The election of the prefect, by now the most important civil post in Rome, continued to be the only weapon in the hands of the nobles to oppose papal authority. A Roman, Cencius, probably from the family of the Crescenzi, held this power under Alexander II and, wanting to rule over the city, was prepared to make the most of any opportunity. Furthermore the pope was, since 1069, without the strong support of Godfrey of Tuscany who had died in Lotharingia. His patrimony had passed entirely to his son by his first wife, Godfrey the Hunchback, husband of Matilda, the only daughter of Beatrice, and this lady was to have great sway as protectress of the Roman Church under the new pope, Gregory VII.

Alexander II died 21 April 1073, and was buried in the Lateran basilica.

1 5 7. St. Gregory VII (1073—1085)

When Alexander II died, the archdeacon, Hildebrand of Soana, was acclaimed pope on 22 April 1073 right in the middle of the funeral rite in the Lateran basilica. It was the common people, urged on by Cardinal Hugh Candido in a kind of selection "*per quasi inspirationem*," who wanted him as pope. This Hildebrand tried to get out of, since the Nicholas decree was not being respected with the cardinal-bishops not given priority. But despite his reluctance, Hildebrand was practically dragged to the church of St. Peter in Chains where he was enthroned with the name of Gregory VII.

Hildebrand was born at Soana, now Sovana, a part of the commune of Sorano in the province of Grosseto, between 1014 and 1028, and was son of an artisan named Bonitio and his wife Bertha. Thanks to a maternal uncle,

Lawrence, abbot of the monastery at St. Mary's on the Aventine, he was able to come to Rome as a young boy and be given a religious education in which he early showed interest. However, his guide towards a future career in scholarship was the archpriest at St. John's at Porta Latina, John Gratian, whose chaplain he became when John was elected pope with the name of Gregory VI.

Following on the papacy of Leo IX, who had wanted him at his side and had recalled him from Cluny where he had withdrawn on the death of Gregory VI, Hildebrand had been the direct collaborator of four other popes. And after he had helped in their elections, he had given them advice on every political and religious move, carrying forward that reformation of the Church which, when finally pope, he was to continue with unusual energy. He received his solemn consecration on 30 June 1073.

The first actions of his pontificate are reflected in the many letters, which he sent to friends, seeking their support in the great task that had been entrusted to him. He wrote to Abbot Desiderius at Monte Cassino, to Abbot Hugo of Cluny, to Beatrice of Lorraine, to the king of Denmark, to everyone, proclaiming his firm intention to fight for the liberty of the Church. To Henry IV, then twenty-three, he had probably already written to tell him of his election, making it immediately clear that he would not be a weak pope, resolved as he was to bring order in the Church by excommunicating those who practiced simony as well as the concubine priests. Indirect evidence of this is his letter to Godfrey the Hunchback, husband of Matilda of Tuscany, expressing his wish for coopera-tion from the king of Germany to control the properties of the Church and to regulate ecclesiastical investitures. If he would work with justice and honor his throne, so much the better, otherwise, the prophecy of Isaiah, "accursed be the person who pulls out of the blood the Lord's sword," would fall on him and not on the pope.

However Henry IV did ratify the election of Gregory VII, with a show of humility, if convinced of the imperial supremacy with which he was invested. Meanwhile, the pope started convening his first council which began the first Sunday of Lent in March 1074. In it was clearly decided that all clergymen who obtained orders by means of simony were to be considered excluded from the Church and those bishops who had obtained benefices by money had to sur-render them immediately under pain of excommunication. Henry IV, to whom a delegation was sent with the decisions of the council, of which his mother, Agnes, formed part, pledged to restore the usurped properties and gave his con-sent to a council which could verify the situation in his kingdom.

But it took a long time to convene this council since the senior German cler-gymen were in an uproar, and there was a general reaction with death threats by married clergymen against bishops and abbots who wanted to have the rules issued by Rome honored. Even slanders concerning the pope circulated.

Gregory VII responded forcefully with another council in February 1075, in which he suspended five bishops, advisers of Henry, who had overtly interposed obstacles to the implementation of pontifical legislation in Germany, and to the convening of the council for controlling ecclesiastical investitures. According to the Milanese chronicler, Arnulf, Gregory VII issued a further instruction regarding the ban on investiture, forbidding Henry IV to grant bishoprics, as he had done up to then, threatening him with excommunication. It was the beginning of the "struggle about investitures" between pope and emperor that severed relations between the two powers. The conditions for a peaceful settlement were clearly set forth by Gregory VII in a series of canons assembled in the famous *Dictatus papae* which was issued in March of that year.

The basic premise of the *Dictatus papae* was the supremacy of the Church of Rome and of its bishop over other churches and over the empire, a politico-ecclesiastical affirmation based in effect upon the Donation of Constantine. Only the pope could bestow the imperial symbols and only he had the right to depose emperors and to release subjects "from the oath of loyalty made to unjust persons." And, of course, the pope alone had the right to make ecclesiastical appointments and to condemn unworthy bishops as the representative of Christ on earth and the successor of St. Peter, with the unlimited power to "loose and bin" which was granted by Christ himself to the apostle. In effect the relationship between State and Church was completely reversed: it was no longer the emperor who elected the pope but the pope who named and deposed the emperor.

If on one hand the *Dictatus* constituted the definitive conception of the bishop of Rome as the sole and infallible primate in the ecclesiastical Christian world, on the other, "it shook to the roots the social realities of the times by attacking the system of lay property owned by the church, that is, the ascendancy of the laity over the clergy." By declaring the supremacy of clerical authority over lay, it was an act of defiance against the very conception of the State.

Henry IV accepted the challenge since his prestige and the vitality of the empire were seriously endangered. So he continued to grant investitures upon payments received and, ignoring the threats of the pope, he even interfered in the internal matters of the Italian clergy. He put his chaplain, Thedald, in the see of the archbishop of Milan, in opposition to Annon who had already been the titular of the archdiocese for two years. Then he openly supported the archbishop of Ravenna, Gilbert, around whom was forming a kind of opposition party within the Italian clergy against Gregory VII, and which was finding adherents even in Rome.

This brought about a conspiracy at top ecclesiastic levels led by Gilbert and by Hugh Candido—the very person who got Hildebrand elected so hurriedly by the people but suddenly an enemy of Gregory VII now,—and put into action by the prefect Cencius. On Christmas night, 1075, the prefect entered St. Mary Major while the pope was celebrating Mass, went up to the altar, threw Gregory to the ground and wounded him. Then, opening a way through the crowd with the help of an armed guard, managed to carry him off and shut him in a tower. However the population was furious and, after the first few hours of disorder and terror, managed to free their bishop. The following day, as he left the tower, Gregory calmed the mob that wanted to kill Cencius and asked them to pardon him. He returned to St. Mary Major and resumed his celebration of the Mass at the point where he had been interrupted. Cencius fled to the Roman countryside, followed by Cardinal Hugh Candido who had been deposed, and together they sought refuge with Henry IV in Germany.

In the beginning of January 1076, the pope invited Henry IV to appear in Rome to exonerate himself under pain of excommunication. Instead of replying, the king convened an assembly of princes and bishops at Worms on 24 January. The chief accuser of Gregory VII was Hugh Candido according to whom the pope was simply an arrogant man who wished to take Italy away from Henry, conspiring with Matilda of Canossa in a plot based on witchcraft and sinful relations. Many bishops did not believe him but Henry felt himself authorized to judge Gregory unworthy of the papal throne, and sent him a declaration of disobedience signed by the German bishops which was also approved by the Lombard ones in Pavia and Piacenza. The pope responded by a solemn excommunication of Henry in another council convened at the Lateran on 22 February in the presence of Empress Agnes and Matilda of Canossa. The excommunication applied not only to the king but also to the rebellious bishops of Germany and Italy.

The sentence was naturally received with anger by Henry's court, though public opinion was on the side of the pope. Moreover, a kind of divine wrath seemed to punish the guilty ones as many of the pope's opponents were suddenly dying, including the archbishop of Utrecht and the Roman, Cencius. The princes who opposed Henry took advantage to revolt, and there was danger of a civil war. The only way out would be a pardon by the pope, and the princes gathered at Tribur in October proposed this to him, promising to recognize him still as king if he obtained the revocation of his excommunication from the pope within one year. They agreed to meet him at Augsburg and to confirm their allegiance or depose him on 2 February of the following year. Henry did not know what to do, as he did not want to give in. However, when he learned that by December Gregory was already on his way to Augsburg, he decided to cross the Alps with an army and head for Rome.

Gregory was not sure how the king intended to appear before him and, learning of his departure when he was at Mantua, sought refuge with Countess Matilda of Canossa at her castle in the Emilian Apennines.

Henry IV arrived in the morning of 25 January 1077 and asked to be received. Gregory did not allow him to enter and received only his wife and son in the castle. Fruitlessly, Matilda, Abbot Hugo of Cluny and his mother-in-law, Adelaide, interceded on his behalf. The king had to wait three days and nights in the snow and the tramontana, a freezing north wind, and only on the third day did Gregory decide to receive him in the chapel and listen to his plea to be pardoned. Then, in a solemn ceremony the pope readmitted him into the community of the faithful and gave him Holy Communion. Thus humbled, the king agreed to accept the conditions imposed by the pope without argument, swore to confess his misdeeds before the parliament of Augsburg, and to submit royal authority to that of the pope. However, in his heart Henry IV was already meditating his revenge.

Back in Germany, he set about recuperating his throne since, by then, most of the population was against him and the majority of the princes, notwithstanding the pope's revocation, no longer wanted him as king. Indeed, with the parliament in Augsburg dissolved, they met at Forchheim on 15 March and elected King Henry's brother-in-law, Rudolph, duke of Swabia, who was crowned at Mainz by Archbishop Siegfried. Germany was thus divided in two, and Gregory tried his best to reunite it. Unfortunately, he now lacked the effective mediation of Empress Agnes, who had passed away at Christmas 1077, so his efforts were fruitless. Henry defeated Rudolph in two battles, but as Gregory VII maintained that Henry had earlier prevented the convening of the assembly at Augsburg and had violated his oath of fidelity taken at Canossa, he excommunicated him again at a council in Rome on 7 March 1080 and reaffirmed Rudolph as king.

However, this second excommunication did not have the results of the first. Henry IV immediately reacted by convening, on 25 June 1080, a council of German bishops at Brixen and making accusations against the pope. Hugh Candido was again in the limelight, this time describing him as an assassin, guilty of simony and a heretic. Gregory VII was deposed and in his place the archbishop of Ravenna, Wibert, was elected with the name of Clement III. He was clearly an antipope.

The situation had taken a dramatic turn for Gregory who, in northern Italy, could count only upon Matilda of Canossa. He finally had to resort to the only recourse left to him, the perfidious Normans, for some time now vassals of the Church. Robert Guiscard, excommunicated during the council of 1074 for having invaded Benevento, which belonged to the papal state, was contacted through Desiderius, abbot of Monte Cassino. A meeting took place on 29 June 1080 at Ceprano, where Robert was readmitted into the community of the faithful and ceded the land that he had already conquered. It was a definitive renunciation by the Church of southern Italy but at the same time the acquisition of a mighty ally, at least theoretically. Robert renewed the oath of fidelity to the pope, as did Prince Giordano of Capua, Richard's son.

On 15 October, in another battle on the banks of the Elster, Henry defeated Rudolph who died on the battlefield. But despite that victory the population and the princes still remained opposed to him and to his antipope who had excommunicated Gregory. Henry had to get to Rome, conquer it and eliminate his enemy if he were to win once and for all. And that was what he tried to do in a first attempt in February 1081, when he reached the walls of the city. He succeeded in isolating the pope, bribing Giordano of Capua and indirectly neutralising any intervention by Robert Guiscard. Only Matilda of Canossa came to Gregory's aid, giving even the treasury of her own chapel to help the economic situation of a besieged Rome. The Romans, virtually alone with their bishop, succeeded in making Henry retreat after a one-month siege.

But, two years later, the king was again in Rome. He seized the Leonine City and Gregory had to seek refuge in Castel Sant'Angelo. Assistance from Robert did not arrive and many Lombard bishops acknowledged Clement III as pope. On 21 April 1082, Henry IV solemnly entered Rome. The Roman nobility had more or less opened the gates to him and then, with a vague promise to have Gregory crown him as emperor by the following year, they managed to get him to leave the city in December. But, at the beginning of the new year, Henry was back, and this time he easily entered Rome at Porta San Giovanni. Completely ignoring Gregory VII in his retreat at Castel Sant'Angelo, he had Clement III solemnly consecrated as pope at the Lateran on 24 March 1084, and himself crowned emperor ten days later by Clement.

At this point Robert Guiscard appeared. In fact, the pope's request for help had reached him two years earlier, but at the time he was engaged in stopping a Byzantine insurrection, and only now was able to march toward Rome with a huge army. Advised of this by Desiderius of Monte Cassino, permanent intermediary between the two forces in those years, Henry IV realized that he could not face the Norman forces and, on 21 May, he abandoned Rome, moving northward. Clement III stopped at Tivoli awaiting developments, still considering himself the real pope.

On 27 May the Normans entered through Porta San Giovanni and sacked the city, the price Gregory VII had to pay for his ransom. The Romans tried to fight back but were massacred. On the night of 30 May, a terrible fire raging from the Colosseum to the Lateran destroyed churches, monuments and houses. The wrath of Christians avenging their pope had fallen on the city and only a third of it remained standing. Gregory begged Robert to end the massacre but when the Norman king finally did, the pope could not expect to be reinstated by him in Rome amongst citizens who naturally hated his liberators. And if Robert had to withdraw his troops, he was convinced he would have to take "his" pope with him, so as to be sure no harm befell him. In reality, Gregory became the king's prisoner, even though he was his "guest" in Salerno.

Gregory VII no longer had any supporters having, in effect, lost his battle in the name of divine justice. The Romans, feeling betrayed, abandoned him completely and welcomed joyously the return of Clement III from Tivoli. The great pontiff, with his imposing personality which had "a pinch of devilish determination," to use Ullmann's phrase finished up defeated and alone, as even Matilda was far away.

He died on 25 May 1085, in the church of St. Matthew at Salerno. His last words were "I have loved justice and hated iniquity; that is why I am dying in exile." He was buried where he died, vested in pontifical robes, in a sarcophagus from the third century. In 1953 his mortal remains were transferred to a new urn in the church of St. Matthew.

It is likely that his death was the result of his having aimed too high in his theocratic dream. The pope who, according to the canons of his *Dictatus*, wanted to reduce Europe to an ecclesiastical Roman State in which individual countries were to be considered feudal estates of the Church in the service of the papacy, and all sovereigns on earth docile subjects of the pontiff, died in the hands of a vassal. Certainly his zealous struggle against simony and clerical immorality, his great achievement, did not deserve such an end. But in the final analysis, he was not understood by the people to whom he had sought to give an awareness of themselves. As De Stefano has observed, "thanks to Gregory VII, the laity called upon to judge the conduct of the clergy was developing a more independent and informed religious conscience. And it was from this that soon would germinate the popular heresy of evangelical inspiration. One should find here, in this grand religious and social experience, the seeds of the future development of a civil conscience among the populace, the first signs of a new social class." Gregory VII could not possibly have imagined the consequences which his affiliation with the masses would bring about in the future formation of a lay conscience in Italy. The empire was born from his invitation to civil disobedience of lay authority of the time, in an impossible theocratic dream. It was the same conscience which, while Gregory VII was still alive, exalted an antipope in Rome.

1 5 8. VICTOR III (1 0 8 6 – 1 0 8 7)

Whether or not he was designated by Gregory VII as a probable successor, according to contradictory information handed down to us by his contemporaries, the abbot of Monte Cassino, Desiderius, a native of Benevento, was proposed by Prince Giordano of Capua as candidate for the papal throne. At first he categorically refused, and even went as far as to protest formally to his own supporters, amongst whom was Mathilda of Tuscany, stating that it should be a council to elect the new pope. But, under extreme pressure he went to Rome during the Easter season of 1086 and finally gave in to the pleas of the cardinals. He was elected on 24 May of that year, and took the name of Victor III.

The *Annuario pontificio* gives that date as the beginning of his pontificate, but, in truth, a full year passed between his election and his enthronement since validity of his election was contested by Roger, son of Robert Guiscard, with a conspiracy in Rome four days after his election which led to an armed battle between the opposing factions. Desiderius, however, was not the type to fight to keep a throne which he had taken against his will. If anyone had something to say against him, so much the better. Without delay he left Rome and reached Terracina by the sea where he divested himself of the papal insignia and returned to his abbey, resolved not to go back on his decision. In the meantime, Clement III resurfaced in Rome and installed himself in the Lateran.

Because of pressure from Prince Giordano, Desiderius convened a council in March of 1087 at Capua, not as pope but as vicar of the Roman see in southern Italy, to discuss the election of a pontiff. The Norman chiefs were all present, now in agreement for his candidacy and this time the old abbot was not able to remove from his head the tiara that he did not want. In effect he was re-elected and agreed, as a result of the Normans's support, to oust Clement III from the Vatican. This took place on 9 May 1087, the day on which Desiderius, or rather Victor III, was at last consecrated in St. Peter's.

His pontificate, however, began under an evil star, as often happens to undertakings assumed against one's will. Rome continued to be menaced daily by fights between opposing factions, because Clement III had managed to barricade himself inside the Pantheon and Victor III did not have the soul of a warrior. So eight days after his consecration he returned to Monte Cassino. He had satisfied his supporters and had become pope, but he was unable to give up the peace which only the monastery could give him. Once again, however, Matilda came back to take him away from there, and convinced him to return, reminding him that it was his duty not to move from the See of Peter.

So Victor III followed the countess, only to remain peacefully on the Tiberine Island while Clement III lorded it over at St. Peter's and Castel Sant'Angelo, having at his side an imperial legate sent by Henry IV still tied up in Germany, to support "his" pope. Victor III himself fell ill and returned to his abbey at the end of July, where he convened a council at Benevento for the end of August. There he decided to take an official position, as Gregory VII had, against Clement III by renewing the excommunication, in addition to approving new rules against simony. It was probably at that time that he launched an appeal to the sovereigns and to the cities of Italy for a kind of crusade against the Saracens in Africa. This undertaking, in which Pisa, Genoa and Amalfi participated, led to the conquest of certain cities, including Mehedia.

But Victor III now felt he was close to the end and returned for the last time to Monte Cassino where he died on 16 September 1087, after an actual pontificate of little more than four months. Desiderius did not possess the spirit of the pontiff, which the times required, as he was born a monk and wanted to remain a monk. Forced by circumstances to high office, he turned out to be the pope with the least personality of those years. He was buried in his abbey; beatified by the Church, he was canonized in 1887.

159. URBAN II (1088–1099)

On the death of Victor III, Rome was still under the control of the antipope, Clement III. As occurred after the pontificate of Gregory VII, there was again a period for several months of vacant see prior to a new election, which was particularly wanted by the reformists.

But it was not until 8 March 1088 that a meeting of about forty clergymen including cardinals, bishops and abbots could take place at Terracina. John of Porto represented the Roman clergy, whereas the prefect, Benedict, represented the populace. The terms of the decree of 1059 concerning papal elections were fully respected, even taking place outside of Rome, and the election was therefore held which led to the choice by acclamation on 12 March of Eudes de Lagery, bishop of Ostia. He was consecrated that same day with the name of Urban II. French, born around 1042 at Chatillon-sur-Marne in a family of knights, he had been archdeacon of the cathedral of Reims, before entering the Abbey of Cluny. Gregory VII, who had held him in great esteem because of his ideas about reform, had elevated him to the dignity of cardinal, assigning him the bishopric of Ostia. He had been frequently sent to Germany as a legate.

Indeed, in a letter written on the very day of his election to the princes and bishops in Germany who had supported his candidacy, he stressed his intention to follow the line laid out by Gregory: "I reject what he rejected, I condemn what he condemned, and I embrace what he loved. I confirm and approve what he considered just and Catholic, and I think as he thought; I am in complete agreement with him." So, from the beginning of his pontificate, he could not but encounter enormous difficulties.

Escorted by the Norman army, he was only able to reach Rome in November 1088, where he stayed, as if in prison, on the Tiberine Island, in a city completely in the hands of Clement III. However, unlike Victor III and certain of the legality of his election, he did not leave his see, convinced of the correctness of his position, even when the antipope excommunicated him in a council held at St. Peter's at the beginning of 1089. Urban knew well, however, that everything depended on Germany, and he entrusted his defense there to Gebhard, the bishop of Constance, conferring on him the post of Apostolic Legate in April 1089, with precise instructions included in the letter of appointment. These were the renewal of the excommunication of Henry IV, of Clement III and all those who supported them, together with penalties related to their guilt in strictly legal terms. The letter shows the prudence of Urban, not wanting simply to repress but also to develop a sense of Christian life under the banner of justice.

However, the position of Henry in Germany had improved so much that, once the armed resistance had been put down, most of the bishops were, in fact, on his side and he was preparing to invade Italy. Urban requested assistance from the Normans but received only vague promises and was forced to flee to them when Henry advanced towards Rome in 1090, determined before all to eliminate the only person who was able to oppose him in northern Italy, Countess Matilda.

The latter, the widow of Godfrey the Hunchback, at the suggestion of the pope had a year earlier married the young Welf V, son of the duke of Bavaria, in the hope that Bavaria and Tuscany together would be a bastion of defense of the papacy. But Welf left his wife as soon as he found out that Matilda had donated her property to the Church two years before their marriage. So a union which was supposed to be an advantage for the pope brought him nothing but Henry's anger.

To begin with the battles were favorable to the emperor, who conquered Mantua and various fortresses beyond the Po. But then Matilda managed to get the better of him at Montebello and Canossa and this victory created enthusiasm around her in many Lombard cities which revived their campaign against Henry. Her reputation reached beyond the Alps and Conrad, the son of Henry IV, and his second wife, Praxedes, both of whom were disgusted by his politics, took refuge with her. A genuine league of the north arose around these figures, which included Milan, Cremona, Lodi and Piacenza, headed by Matilda herself, who personally took command of the troops.

Henry IV, with his inglorious title of emperor assigned to him by an antipope, suddenly lost ground and barricaded himself in Verona. Meanwhile, Urban II succeeded in returning to Rome and finally occupying his seat at the Lateran in 1094. The Normans did not help him as much as the money amassed by Abbot Godfrey of Vendôme in French territory through a "crusading" spirit which was spreading about. That money furnished an army led by Hugo, count of Vermandois, who succeeded in liberating Rome completely in a series of battles that lasted until 1096. Clement III remained alone in Castel Sant'Angelo, conquered two years later by Pierleone who had continued to head the citizens' militia faithful to the pope. So for the moment Urban II was able to pursue his project of reformation without worrying about his see.

This reform movement was manifesting itself in all Europe though encountering difficulties in England and in the pope's homeland, where King Philip I was in favor of simony and had deserted his wife, Berta, to take up with

Bertrada, countess of Anjou. He had had this second marriage blessed by the bishop of Senlis, but in October 1094, Yves, bishop of Chartres, obtained from the papal legate the excommunication of the king at the council of Autun. Nevertheless, Philip and Bertrada did not submit to the pope until 1104.

In England, King William II was particularly hostile to Anselm, bishop of Canterbury, because of his closeness to the pope and his intransigence on the question of lay investiture. Anselm came to Italy and denounced the behavior of the king. However, at a council in Bari in 1098 he managed to avoid having William excommunicated so as to keep open a possibility of compromise, which, it was hoped, would lead sooner or later to a positive conclusion for the Church without necessarily making an enemy of the king.

Apart from reform, Urban II was destined to link his name to the first crusade. Alongside the struggle over lay investiture, another motivation was needed to bring the Church to a genuine unification, something that would involve the entire Christian community in a universal religious mission. And what greater incentive than that of liberating the Holy Sepulcher from Moslem infidels?

This presented itself opportunely in a memorable council held at Piacenza between the 1st and 7th of March 1095, before 200 bishops and 5000 ecclesiastics from Italy and France. Also present were the ambassadors of the emperor of the East, Alexius, who, threatened by the Turks at Constaninople, begged the pope to send help "for the defense of the Holy Church against the infidels." It was a real chance to finish with the schism, but the pope insisted on the liberation of all the Churches of the East from the Moslem danger, with the Holy Sepulcher as the beginning of this grand enterprise.

In such an emergency the theocratic idea of Gregory VII, carried on by Urban II, became a truly missionary activity based upon mass psychology fuelled by renewed religious fervour. So it was necessary to give substance to the movement through a specific organization which would transform ordinary soldiers into soldiers of Christ in a "holy war" for the Christian conquest of the world. For this purpose, Urban II departed for France in August 1095.

From Piacenza the pope went to Cremona, where Conrad, recently crowned king of Italy by the archbishop of Milan, paid homage to him. From there to Le-Puy-en-Velay where he met with the bishop of Monteil and organized a great council at Clermont for 18 November. In a fascinating speech, the pope described the disasters suffered by Jerusalem, and the profanation of the Holy Places in Palestine by the Turks. With a sweeping oration full of images taken from the Bible, he exhorted the Christian world to take up arms against the Turks. The Christian world had sinned and would redeem itself by paying this price because "God wishes it!." And such was the battle cry of the crusade.

The enterprise was to be carried out by Christian princes and knights in an army called the "militia Christi" which, in a way, represented the release of a mass of repressed energy placed at the service of a religious ideal with many compensations and privileges. These would become, once the first wave of enthusiasm was over, the incentive for the crusade's departure. Besides the granting of a plenary indulgence for sins committed, since the crusade was to be chiefly a pilgrimage, the crusaders were granted immunity from taxes and levies, as well as a moratorium on debt repayments. The "Truce of God" became a universal ecclesiastical law by which the protection of the crusaders's assets was guaranteed.

The rest is part of the history of Europe and of its economic reconquest of the Mediterranean, in which the dream of Urban II of the union of the two Churches and the retaking of the Holy Places was doomed to dash itself on the rocks of commercial imperialism in the Levant.

Urban II died on 29 July 1099, before he could learn of the success of the first Crusade, in a Rome again suffering from internal struggles with the ever-present Clement III who, once more, forced him to live in the fortified palace of Pierleone. He was buried in the crypt in St. Peter's next to Hadrian I; beatified by the Church, he was canonized in 1881.

160. PASCHAL II (1099—1118)

The successor to Urban II was Cardinal Raniero, a priest at the church of San Clemente in Rome but born in Blera (Viterbo) around 1050. Formerly a monk at Cluny, he had been a papal legate in Spain under Urban II. His election on 13 August 1099 in his titular church was followed the next day by his consecration in St. Peter's. He probably was helped in his election by the military and financial assistance provided by the Norman Duke Roger. It is a fact that Roger succeeded in ousting the antipope Clement III from Albano, where he had fled, and in pushing him as far as Civitacastellana, where he died on 8 September 1100, having been the antipope of four different popes, but abandoned by Henry IV because the royal authority in Italy, acquired by his son, Conrad, supported the pope.

However, the nobles of the city, amongst whom Peter Colonna, the representative of the most famous family of medieval Rome appears for the first time, had not given in. Openly accusing the pope of simony, they elected another antipope, the cardinal of St. Rufina, who took the name of Theodoric. But he was immediately taken prisoner by the Normans and interned in the abbey at Cava dei Tirreni where he died in 1102. A second antipope was elected, Bishop Albert of the Sabine, who was interned by the Normans in the monastery of S. Lorenzo in Aversa where he also soon ended his days.

In fact, Paschal had sufficient support to abort the claims of these antipopes without imperial help. Yet his pontificate was fated, like those of his predecessors and immediate successors, to have to steer through many obstacles in order to survive in a chaotic Rome "where occur continually outbreaks of rebellions by the people, flights and exiles of the popes, their triumphal returns, their tragic subsequent collapses and, once more, their unfailing resurrections," to cite a description of the city by Gregorovius.

Following these events, which had served to strengthen momentarily his own power, Paschal II renewed the excommunication of Henry IV in the Lenten council of 1102, with an assembly which swore obedience to him. Conrad died in July and Henry IV, in an effort to regain his status within and outside of Germany, announced in 1103 to the parliament at Mainz his intention to under-take a crusade which, reflecting the religious spirit of the time, was expected to bring a period of peace throughout the empire for a period of four years. The pope, however, did not change his position, realizing that the crusade of Henry IV was only a stratagem. At the same time Henry IV had to experience a bitter disappointment. His second son, Henry, raised by him to the dignity of king of Germany so as to set him against his own brother, Conrad, but with an oath of loyalty in which he recognized his father as emperor, at Conrad's death in 1104 suddenly rebelled against him, taking the side of the princes opposed to him. There followed a civil war in which Henry IV was defeated, made a prisoner and forced by his son to renounce his title of Emperor. He died in 1106 at Liège where he had gone after being freed by those faithful to him and with whom, in vain, he had plotted his revenge.

Meanwhile, Paschal had had his problems with the new king of England, Henry I, as a result of a contest between the king and the archbishop of Canterbury, Anselm on the question of the investitures. Each one had sent his representatives to Paschal, in Rome, who naturally refused to grant the king per-mission to make investitures. The result was that the king exiled Anselm in 1104 and confiscated the assets of the Church.

A third antipope also appeared on the scene, proposed as usual by the Roman nobles, this time supported by Henry IV's son, who was shortly to take over his father's claims against the Church of Rome after an initial conciliatory policy which had evidently served only to get the German princes and bishops on his side.

On 18 November 1105, the imperial party succeeded in electing as antipope the Archpriest Maginulf who took the name of Sylvester IV. This person, however, was unable to hold his position in Rome and withdrew to Tivoli with Marquis Guarniero of Ancona, a former comrade in arms of his, to await developments.

Having consolidated his power in Rome, Paschal II was able to resume diplo-matic relations with Henry V, who had gone on proclaiming his devotion to the Church. At a council in Nordhausen in May 1105, he had hypocritically claimed that he had rebelled against his father not out of any desire for power, but really to reconcile all of Germany with Rome and to be himself the pope's first faithful subject. However, at the council of Guastalla in October 1106, where envoys of Henry V were present and a general amnesty was proclaimed for all those who had been found guilty by the religious authorities in the preceding struggles between Henry IV and the Church, no agreement was reached and Henry V continued to confer investitures.

Paschal II then sought a supporter in France against the young king of Germany and tried to resolve the dispute with King Philip I over his second marriage with Bertrada, both of them still under excommunication. However, the ensuing negotiations between the parties in the spring of 1107 at Châlons-sur-Marne had no result, and the projected meeting between the pope and the king did not take place.

On the other hand, the problem with England was resolved, following lengthy negotiations between Henry I, Anselm and a papal delegation, and thanks to the mediation by Queen Matilda, countess of Blois, who was an admirer of the saintly archbishop of Canterbury. Paschal agreed to recognize the homage of bishops as vassals of the king on condition that Henry I would renounce investitures. So a concordat was concluded on 1 August 1107 between the king and the archbishop in an assembly of barons and bishops at London. By its provisions no clergyman could any longer receive investiture with the pastoral staff and the ring, but in return no clergyman could be consecrated without first having taken an oath to the king.

However, Henry V still went on granting investitures while stating that he wished to reach an agreement with the pope, suggesting that the best way would be to meet him in Italy. So, in August 1110, he began his journey toward Rome with a large army. Given the apparent good will of the king, an agreement was in fact reached at Sutri on 9 February 1111, whereby the king would renounce investitures and the pope would order the bishops to return the items and the regalia conceded to them, and following the execution of these agreements, Henry V's coronation would take place at St. Peter's on 12 February.

The bishops, however, protested because they had no intention of losing their position as princes of the empire, and a fight ensued between the parties, which almost resulted in a blood bath. The king seized control of the situation by force of arms and put the pope and the cardinals in prison, fully intending to take back his right of investiture and to have his coronation as well.

The pope waited two months for help from the Normans that did not arrive, then decided to give in. This led to the infamous agreement of the Mammolo Bridge on 11 April 1111, by which the pope agreed that the king would have the right of investiture of bishops and abbots before their consecration with ring and staff in the regalia, provided that they were elected without simony but with the agreement of the king. Sixteen cardinals validated the pope's promise under oath while, for his part, Henry V released the pope and arranged to have the antipope, Sylvester IV, also render homage to the pope and renounce his own position. So on 13 April, the pope crowned Henry V as emperor in St. Peter's.

This privilege of investiture was heavily contested, especially in Italy and France where the pope's action was condemned so thoroughly that, at a certain point, he thought about abdicating. But at the Lateran council in March 1112, he was caught up in the climate of reaction in which an appeal was made for a renewal of the dignity of the papal see, now clearly compromised, and he admitted that he had given in only because he had been forced to do so. But the assembly imposed on him a formal "act of faith" in which he denied the privilege he had granted and declared that he would follow the principles of Gregory VII and Urban II, as a result of which the agreement of 1111 was deemed null and void.

In other councils, a firm position was maintained and in several instances the pope was criticized. In the one of September 1112, held by Archbishop Guido of Vienna, an anathema was declared against the emperor, and confirmation by Paschal was called for in a menacing tone. He, however, declared that he could not violate his oath and did not pronounce the excommunication. His attitude was contradictory for, while he left his envoys free to do as they wished, he personally did not expose himself. But when Bishop Conon of Palestrina, the papal legate at a council in Jerusalem, again declared in favor of excommunication of the emperor, the pope was inevitably involved because, at the subsequent Lateran council in March 1116, Conon demanded from the pope approval for his action.

The pope and the council sanctioned the excommunication, though without the name of the emperor being specifically mentioned, and the imperial privilege of investiture was condemned. This was happening while Henry V was coming into Italy. Mathilda of Tuscany had died, and he was on his way to claim possession of her riches, by right of inheritance as the most important relative, regardless of the fact that the countess had previously left her property to the Church. The pope did not object, as he had other problems. In fact, as soon as the arrival of Henry V became known, bloody riots broke out in Rome over the position of prefect which the pope wished to assign to one of the Pierleones. Instead, he had to give it to Peter, son of the previous prefect, who was supported by the majority of the nobles close to the emperor.

As Henry V was nearing Rome, Paschal II went to hide at Monte Cassino, demonstrating once again his inability to defend the decisions of councils and thus disappointing the cardinals, since he had clearly fled through fear. The nobles welcomed Henry V and his wife, Matilda with great honor at Easter of 1117. Maurice Bourdin, archbishop of Braga, as was the custom for the more important religious feast days, placed the imperial crown on their heads while the cardinals refused to attend the ceremony.

At this moment Paschal II recovered a little of his dignity, and excommunicated the archbishop of Braga at a council in Benevento. But this was of little import and, in general, his personality was equivocal and weak. Justly, no mausoleum recalls his pontificate.

Nonetheless, Paschal II must be praised for having taken up the work of repairing buildings and restoring various churches, in particular the rebuilding of the basilica of the Ss. Quattro Coronati which was destroyed in the fire caused by Robert Guiscard, and which he consecrated a few days prior to his last flight from Rome.

He was able to return only at the beginning of 1118, taking possession of Castel Sant'Angelo, but, while riots broke out once more, he died on 21 January 1118. He was buried in the Lateran.

1 6 1. GELASIUS II (1 1 1 8 – 1 1 1 9)

Only three days after the death of Paschal II, on 24 January 1118, his successor was named. He was cardinal-deacon John Caetani, a member of a noble family of Gaeta, the Anagni branch of which, according to some sources, would provide a pontiff in the person of Boniface VIII. John had been a monk at Monte Cassino but had been called to Rome by Urban II as a secretary of the Church, and had been a faithful colleague of Paschal II, defending him against charges of weakness and simony.

While riots raged in Rome, his election took place with great secrecy in a monastery on the Palatine, the first to have taken place almost in the form of "conclave," this is, *cum clavi*, under lock and key. John Caetani barely had time to choose the name of Gelasius II before the factions opposed to his selection, headed by Cencius Frangipane, stormed into the church. Frangipane dragged the aged pope outside as soon as he had been elected, maltreated him brutally while his men attacked the cardinals in a punitive raid. Gelasius II was shut up in chains in the tower of the Frangipane until, with the riots over, the supporters of the pope finally got the upper hand and a truce was reached between the prefect, Peter, and Pierleone, a claimant to the office. The pope was freed and was able to take possession of the Lateran, but only briefly.

News of these happenings naturally reached Henry V in northern Italy and he hastened to Rome on 3 March. Gelasius wisely fled to Gaeta, declining the perfidious emperor's invitation to return to Rome, and there he was consecrated on 10 March. Meanwhile, Henry, considering the pope as having abandoned his see, and egged on by the Frangipanes, had arranged the election two days earlier of an antipope Archbishop Maurice Bourdin, already excommunicated by Paschal II, who assumed the name of Gregory VIII. Gelasius responded to the election of the antipope by excommunicating on April 9, both the emperor and Gregory VIII from Gaeta.

In fact, the aging Gelasius II defended himself well, and as soon as Henry V had left Rome, he returned hastily to his see, determined to fight back against the Frangipane. They did not make him wait long, invading the church of St. Praxedes with armed men on 21 July while the pope was celebrating Mass. But they did not succeed in reaching him. In a farcical escape, old Gelasius, still wearing his priestly vestments, managed to jump on a horse and flee from Rome.

But he certainly could not go on mounting horses and fleeing all the time like a young lad. So, tired and ill, he decided to go to France accompanied by part of the College of Cardinals to hold a council at Vienne, which would define once and for all the internal situation of Rome, and guarantee the person and the dignity of the pope. He did not make it, however, because death caught up with him on 28 January 1119 at Cluny, where he was buried.

162. CALIXTUS II (1119–1124)

It seems that on his deathbed Gelasius II had designated to the cardinals who had accompanied him to France his successor, Conon, the bishop of Palestrina. But Conon declined the position and proposed the candidacy of Archbishop Guy of Vienne, who was elected with unanimous consent by the cardinals present at Cluny on 2 February 1119, and consecrated in the city of his bishopric with the name of Calixtus II seven days later, on 9 February.

The cardinals who had remained in Rome, as well as the Roman populace and clergy, sent their agreement. The new pope, a descendant of a family of counts from Upper Burgundy, appeared to be the kind of man who could squarely face the problems of the church. He was not a monk, and had broad views with evident diplomatic and political skills with which he felt confident he could put an end to the battle with the emperor over investitures. There were immediately good omens at the imperial diet convened at Mainz in 1119, which recognized Calixtus as the legitimate pope and abandoned the antipope, Gregory VIII, to his fate. Moreover, the German bishops promised to attend the council convened at Reims by the pope.

Calixtus II was in no hurry to get to in Rome where Gregory VIII continued to occupy the papal throne, a puppet pope, kept on it as a result of internal squabbles amongst the nobles, and Calixtus concentrated his energy on the council at Reims, which began on 20 October 1119.

However, following his enthronement, the pope wanted an immediate meeting with the king to find out personally Henry V's real intentions. He sent two emissaries to him to test the ground, who reported back on the mutual distrust existing between the parties, so Calixtus decided it was useless to have the meeting. The council continued its work and, after having been advised that the emperor was responsible for the failure of negotiations, unanimously approved a canon that prohibited investiture by a layman of bishops and abbots. When

the council was over and he had visited various episcopal sees in France to promote his image in the eyes of Europe, Calixtus II decided to go on to Rome
where he arrived on 3 June 1120 and was welcomed in triumph, while Gregory
VIII fled to Sutri.

Satisfied about the good intentions of the Roman nobles, Calixtus decided to
finish with the antipope's opposition. After eight days of siege, pontifical soldiers, led by Cardinal John of Crema, succeeded in convincing the citizens of
Sutri to hand over the antipope. Brought to Rome in chains, he was then sent
to the monastery in Cava dei Tirreni where he died without ever having
renounced his rank.

Calixtus II devoted his energy again to reaching an agreement with Henry V.
He intensified the negotiations which resulted, in the autumn of 1121, in twelve
important principles favorable to the pontifical cause that, in the presence of the
two German factions, were drafted in Würzburg and formed the basis of an
agreement. The draft was presented to the pontifical delegation headed by cardinal-bishop Lambert of Ostia. The negotiations took place at Worms and
finally on 23 September 1122, the agreement, which was called the Concordat
of Worms, was proclaimed.

In it the ruling was determined that the investiture of spiritual authority in
the bishop with the pastoral staff and the ring belonged exclusively to the pope,
the emperor retaining the feudal investiture. In Germany, this preceded the consecration of a bishop, in contrast to Italy where the bishop was first consecrated.
The treaty, moreover, permitted the emperor to be present at the election of a
bishop. This was the principal point in dispute by the most intransigent representatives of the Church, but they were forced to reach a compromise which, in
fact, reflected a flexible attitude by both parties. However, what had been one
of the aims of the Gregorian reform had been attained with the elimination of
the right to ecclesiastical ownership attached to the office.

A noteworthy consequence of the concordat was the convening of the ninth
ecumenical council at the Lateran in March 1123, the first to take place in the
West. No new dogma was promulgated, but all the canons issued by previous
councils were definitively approved. Simony was condemned as well as concubinage of priests and the employment of lay persons in the management of
ecclesiastical matters. The sacred bond of matrimony, the "Truce of God" and
all the privileges of the Crusades were confirmed, while relations between
monks and bishops were also regulated in legal terms.

In conclusion, the Concordat and the ninth ecumenical council solemnly, and
finally, asserted the primacy of the Church of Rome, represented by the pope,
against any attempt at autonomy by the great national churches and by the episcopate. The entire Christian world was submitted, *ratione peccati*, to the
supreme guidance of the pontiff in questions concerning religion or morals. In

this sense, the theocratic vision of Gregory VII had triumphed, since every civil authority had to account for itself to the pope. It was a blow, albeit not mortal, to the lay spirit which would be given new life in its search for an independent religious conscience only with the reformation.

Calixtus II survived the council briefly but did not have time to enjoy fully the important triumph. He died on 13 December 1124, and was buried in the Lateran next to Paschal II.

1 6 3. HONORIUS II (1 1 2 4 — 1 1 3 0)

During the last period of the pontificate of Calixtus II, the two Roman families of the Frangipane and the Pierleone, which were contending for the civil dignity of the prefecture, had managed to infiltrate the College of Cardinals with agents, thereby making their influence felt in the election of a pontiff. Thus the electoral decree of 1059 revealed its inadequacy as well as its ineffectivess in eliminating the lay element.

On the death of Calixtus II, the Pierleoni faction succeeded in getting their own candidate elected, the cardinal-priest, Theobald Boccadipecora, who took the name of Celestine II. He had barely accepted the dignity, however, when a group from the Frangipane faction, led by Cardinal Aimerico, entered the Lateran and forcibly removed the new pope. He resigned immediately, as he had suffered injuries in the fight that had followed, and, indeed, died a few days later. The cardinals took note of his resignation and on 15 December 1124 recognized as pope the Frangipane candidate, Lambert, bishop of Ostia.

Born in Fiagnano, a tiny suburb on the outskirts of Imola, cardinal from the time of Paschal II and companion in exile of Gelasius II, he had been the executor of the Concordat of Worms, therefore one of the ablest counsellors in the papal diplomatic corps under Calixtus II. He was consecrated on 21 December 1124, with the name of Honorius II.

The five years of his pontificate passed peacefully in a Rome under the control of the Frangipane, and Honorius gave all his attention to international issues, ignoring domestic matters. Practically speaking the Curia itself was in the hands of Cardinal Aimerico who was influential in the nomination of new cardinals favorable to the Frangipane family.

In Germany, after Henry V had died early in 1124 and the House of Franconia had become extinct, the throne was taken by Lotharius of Saxony who showed himself to be accommodating to the papacy, as opposed to the other pretender to the crown, Conrad of the Hohenstaufen. And in a genuine change in relations between the papacy and the empire, which implied a promise of the imperial crown, Honorius gave his consent to the German delegation, which came to Rome to obtain his approval. The Hohenstaufen were excommunicated by the bishops of Germany at Christmas 1127, and the pope confirmed the excommunication the following year. Many northern cities, instead, recognized Conrad who came to Italy and was even crowned by the archbishop of Milan, Anselm. As a result he was excommunicated in a council in Pavia held by the pontifical legate for Lombardy, John of Crema, so the crowning of Conrad lost all its validity.

The situation in southern Italy became problematic when William, duke of Apulia, died in July 1127. Count Roger II of Sicily, who had inherited from his father, Roger I, a Sicily completely free of Arabs, pounced on the territory, deeming himself to be the natural heir and knowing that the only challenger could be Boemon II, who was fighting in a crusade in Palestine where he died a year later. Honorius excommunicated Roger II for this illegal appropriation, in the name of pontifical feudal sovereignty, since the territories in question should have returned into the Church's possession.

Then the pope organized a military operation against him, which was badly handled and led to the defeat of Honorius and his allies. In the end the pope had to recognize the feudal estate as Roger's and, in 1128, Roger II, became duke of Apulia, Calabria and Sicily.

For Honorius II, as for other popes of his type, it was a bitter lesson of how burdensome the possession of temporal property was, since he also became involved, with the help of the Frangipane, in numerous battles against the nobles at the castles in the Roman countryside.

When he sensed he was close to death, he had himself carried to the comfortable monastery of St. Gregory at the Clivus Scauri, where he died during the night of the 13–14 February 1130. Meanwhile the two factions, the Pierleoni and the Frangipanes, were fighting over the candidates for the papal throne and on the very day of his burial in the Lateran, his successor was enthroned there.

164. INNOCENT II (1130—1143)

At the death of Honorius II the fight between the Pierleoni and the Frangipane was resumed and pandemonium broke out the nights of the 13th and 14th of February 1130. A pope was dying and sixteen cardinals who belonged to the Frangipane faction, headed by Cardinal Aimerico, precipitously elected Cardinal Gregory Papareschi as pope in a sort of "conclave" inside the fortress of the Frangipane. He took the name of Innocent II.

The other fourteen cardinals, faced with a "fait accompli," refused to recognize the validity of the election, and a few hours later, gathered in the church of St. Mark, proceeded to elect Cardinal Peter Pierleoni, who took the name of Anacletus II. His election got the consent shortly afterwards of some of the cardinals in the group which had elected Innocent II, so Anacletus wound up having a majority in the College of Cardinals, as well as the agreement of the representatives of the populace and of all the nobles, from the Tebaldi to the Stefani.

However, neither of the two popes was prepared to give up his nomination, and both received the consecration on the same day, 23 February. Innocent was invested at the Lateran, after which he sought refuge in the fortress of the Frangipane on the Palatine, and Anacletus acclaimed at St. Peter's with full honors and the support of the population which acknowledged him as its pope. In brief, thanks to the power which the Pierleoni enjoyed in the administration of the city, Rome apparently put its faith in Anacletus II. Its pope could feel secure, sit on all the papal thrones of the city's basilicas, and get his hands on the treasury of the Church, whereas Innocent II could only flee.

In this schism, which had inexorably opened within the Church of Rome, are apparent the defects of an electoral process which allowed non-ecclesiastical interests to enter into play through the College of Cardinals being directed from the outside by lay elements. It also remained to be seen to which of the two contenders the Christian world would give its consent, since it was no longer up to Rome alone to decide, but to the States of Europe as well, and unfortunately not on strictly religious grounds either, but on political ones. And it was not Christian ideals that guided the conflict of the two contenders so that, as Ullmann observes, "the public speeches of each pope focussed on an exchange of insults and disgraceful verbal abuses, in which the Innocentian faction was especially virulent, attacking, in an unchristian spirit, the Jewish origins of Anacletus II."

In fact, Germany, England, France, much of Italy and all the monastic orders recognized Innocent II, and the poor "pope from the Ghetto" found support only from the fickle Normans. Anacletus II indeed offered to give the royal crown to Roger II to show his appreciation, and the Norman duke did not let this opportunity go by. In September 1130, a mutual defensive-offensive alliance was concluded between the two, and a cardinal-legate anointed Roger I at Palermo as king of Sicily, Apulia and Calabria on Christmas Day of that year.

Meanwhile, Innocent II was in France where he had found as counsellor the Abbot Bernard of Clairvaux, thanks to whom he had managed to obtain the support of Louis VI of France and of Lothar, king of Germany, whom he visited at Liège in March of 1131. At the council of Reims, held in October, Innocent II was recognized by England and Spain, and a solemn excommunication was pronounced against Anacletus II. In a subsequent council at Piacenza in April 1132, Innocent was acknowledged by all the bishops and nobles of Lombardy, with the exception of the archbishop of Milan, and the following year Lothar came to Italy to place Innocent on the papal throne in Rome and to receive in return the imperial crown. A delegation from Anacletus was received at Viterbo by Lothar but with no result as the German bishops stifled the king's hesitancy by reminding him of the obligations taken at Reims.

Lothar arrived in Rome in April, but Anacletus II, barricaded in Castel Sant'Angelo, did not give in while the king and Innocent made their entrance into the city where, if they were warmly received by the Frangipanes, they were not by the populace who did not welcome the newcomers. The pope installed himself at the Lateran while Lothar took up residence on the Aventine for the imperial coronation. But the grandiose procession from the Aventine to St. John's did not have the solemnity of other ceremonies, and the coronation itself, which took place on 4 June 1133, was celebrated modestly.

Having achieved his aim, Lothar returned to Germany and left Innocent abandoned to himself in a Rome that was totally committed to Anacletus. It did not matter that from the Tiber northward Innocent had the undisputed recognition of the nobles and bishops of Italy, who had also been joined by the archbishop of Milan in the council at Pisa in 1135. Rome, the Roman countryside and southern Italy ruled by Roger, supported Anacletus as a block, and were ready to take up arms. So it was vital for Innocent II to convince Lothar of the necessity of a military expedition which would reduce the power of the Norman king. An appeal was sent to him both by Innocent and by the princes of Apulia who opposed Roger's domination, and once again the intervention of Bernard of Clairvaux proved fruitful since he convinced the emperor that it was his duty to seize southern Italy from a usurper and to reunite it with the empire.

And Lothar fell on Italy like a hurricane, laying waste the areas where the Norman armies were hiding and finally reached Bari which he drowned in a bloodbath while, Innocent II, at his side, blessed the expedition. Roger escaped to Sicily where the Norman nobles suddenly found glory and undreamed riches, and Innocent was able to return safely to Rome where Bishop Peter of Porto and Bernard had prepared the way for him within the Curia and in the College of Cardinals. Although Lothar died in December 1137, the pope did not have to fear a new battle with Anacletus II, shut away in Castel Sant'Angelo, since Roger had the problem of recovering his kingdom, so was unable to worry about him. Finally, Anacletus died on 25 January 1138, thereby ridding Innocent of an embarrassing situation. The new antipope, Cardinal Gregory, quickly elected by the Pierleoni, under the name of Victor IV, has no history. Elected in March, he was convinced by Bernard to renounce the nomination and repent on 29 April, recognizing Pope Innocent II, to whom even the Pierleoni paid homage in May.

Innocent was thus finally able to devote himself to the religious reformation and to convene in April 1139 the tenth ecumenical council, the Lateran II. It was the end of the schism. Anacletus's acts were abrogated with the excommunication of Roger and the condemnation of the doctrines of the monk, Arnold of Brescia. The latter was expelled from Italy, found refuge and understanding in France with Abelard, the proponent of a faith based exclusively upon a careful and critical examination of what was being affirmed. His ideas constituted an attack on the "revealed truth," challenging the traditional concept of faith, and were condemned as heretical. This censure took place at a council in Sens in 1140 with an inquisition held by Bernard of Clairvaux. In vain Abelard appealed to the pope, who confirmed the verdict and ordered permanent silence about him.

Meanwhile Roger pressed on from the south for the reconquest of his lost lands and the recognition of his monarchy. It was a war without truce, against which the nobles created by Innocent, with little military or political experience, were unable to oppose. In July 1139, the pope had to give in and confirm on "the august and famous sovereign" and his heirs, the kingdom of Sicily, Apulia, and Calabria, including also the territory of Capua which was thus removed from its Norman duke notwithstanding his protests. When the Byzantine duke of Naples also surrendered to Roger, the kingdom of southern Italy was constituted entirely under the domination of the Norman bloodline.

The last period of the pontificate of Innocent II was troubled by the revolt by the city of Tivoli which wanted a municipal administration independent of Rome. This was a civil problem in which lay forces of Rome felt themselves involved and wanted to punish Tivoli by destroying the town. The siege took place in 1142 and the people of Tivoli surrendered, not to the Romans, but to the pope, swearing loyalty to him. So the pope opposed the vendetta wanted by his subjects, with the result that there was a violent uprising of the Roman populace who, recovering the democratic spirit that had inspired the revolt headed in his time by Alberic, managed to reestablish the ancient Senate at the capitol and to decree again the end, albeit temporary, of papal authority. A proper republic was declared in that communal spirit which was spreading from Lombardy throughout the whole of Italy. It was a historic moment of laic reawakening in a papal Rome.

In the midst of these riots, Innocent II died on 24 September 1143. He was buried in the Lateran, but seven years later his remains were interred at Santa Maria in Trastevere, a basilica which he had restored and embellished with mosaics.

1 6 5. CELESTINE II (1 1 4 3 — 1 1 4 4)

In a republican Rome run by the middle class and the lesser nobles and defended by the common people, the election of the new pope seems to have been considered a minor matter. It was followed only by the higher nobles, and still had value solely because of its religious significance. But this depended entirely on whom was to have the position.

The new pontiff was elected two days after the death of Innocent II, and there were no arguments within the College of Cardinals. He was Cardinal Guido, born in Città di Castello, a former disciple of Abelard but who had later abandoned Abelard's ideas when they were deemed heretical. He was consecrated on 3 December 1143, with the name of Celestine II.

This pontificate did not produce any particular events, given both the situation in Rome and its duration of only three months. One should remember, however, that it was with this pope that began the famous prophecy of Malachy, the Irish archbishop of Armagh, who died in 1148. Celestine II died on 8 March 1144, in the monastery near St. Caesarius on the Palatine where he had probably taken refuge under the protection of the Frangipane against a possible attack by some hotheaded "revolutionary." He was buried in the Lateran.

166. LUCIUS II (1144—1145)

As successor to Celestine II, the cardinal from Bologna, Gerard Caccianemici, former chancellor of Innocent II and legate in Germany to King Lothar, was elected with the name of Lucius II and consecrated on 12 March 1144.

Determined to get rid of the Commune, he asked Roger for help, at the same time urging the higher Roman nobility to assist him so that they could reconquer their feudal estates controlled by the democratic republic headed by Giordano Pierleoni, the brother of the antipope Anacletus II. Already in 1144 a municipal constitution had been adopted and the idea had been broached to exclude the pope definitively from any function whatsoever of a temporal nature, thereby dethroning him.

Finding that his request to Roger for help went unheeded, Lucius II turned to Conrad III of Germany who had brought the Hohenstaufen dynasty to the throne but who had already been excommunicated by Honorius II. It is clear that the sovereign, while welcoming the papal delegation, did not want to go to Rome to support a perfidious papacy. And he was just as cordial to a republican delegation which came to ask him simply for official recognition of the Commune of Rome and nothing more, as if to say that the Romans could manage their internal affairs by themselves.

So Lucius II decided to attack the Capitol with a few faithful militiamen and lead his troops himself, like a good warrior-pope. However, a stone thrown from the top of the hill hit him on the head and he died a few days later on 15 February 1145, in the monastery of St. Gregory where he had been taken by the Frangipane. He was buried in the Lateran.

167. EUGENE III (1145—1153)

In the midst of riots and the very day that Lucius II died (15 February 1145), the cardinals hastily gathered in secret in the monastery near the church of Saint Caesarius on the Palatine to elect a new pope. Once more it was a kind of "conclave," an almost hidden election, this time *"propter metus senatorum et populi romani consurgentis ad arma."* The choice fell on the abbot of the monastery of

Sts. Vincent and Anastasius at the Three Fountains (ad aquas Salvias), a man from Pisa, perhaps from the family of the Paganelli of Montemagno, who took the name of Eugene III.

He was able to take his throne without difficulty in the Lateran, but the senators barred the street to St. Peter's for the consecration because he refused to acknowledge the new republican constitution of the city. Eugene III was in fact constrained to leave Rome and go into the Sabine to the old abbey of Farfa where he was consecrated on 18 February 1145. While awaiting events, he transferred his see to Viterbo.

Meanwhile in Rome the populace vented its continuing wrath by pillaging towers and palaces belonging to nobles and cardinals, abolishing the prefecture, the representative of imperial authority, and then electing a *patricius*, John Pierleone, with wide powers to represent the Senate and the people. From Viterbo, Eugene III issued an excommunication of the *patricius* and set up a kind of league among the nobles of the Roman countryside in order to isolate the city. The Romans then reached an agreement with the pope early in December by which they would restore the prefecture, depose the *patricius,* and give homage to the pontiff, who in turn would allow the Commune to continue with pontifical investiture. On these conditions, Eugene III was allowed to come back to Rome at Christmas, 1145.

It was a compromise that would not last long. It meant that the Commune would in reality be subject to the Church, and the most ardent republicans would not permit that to happen. Who provoked the conflict were the people of Tivoli, once again in rebellion against Rome's administration. The Romans demanded the town's destruction, but the pope went only so far as to permit the demolition of its walls.

However, Eugene III was not able to live in a city which was continually hostile to him, and in March 1146, he returned to Viterbo, then a year later he moved to France, from whence King Louis VII was preparing to leave on the second Crusade. The pope had called for it two years earlier, granting to the participants the usual plenary indulgence in the renewing of the "Truce of God." Yet, despite the use of imposing manpower, this Crusade would end in complete failure in 1148.

Meanwhile, in Rome, the Commune remained very active, with Giordano Pierleoni as the *gonfaloniere* of the city's militia, who got new support when Arnold of Brescia arrived in Rome unexpectedly from his exile. At Viterbo Eugene had released him from his excommunication on the understanding that he would render obedience and promise to live in a state of atonement. This meant asking too much of him and, once the pope had reached France, Arnold addressed the population full of enthusiasm for the republic.

He harangued the people with his great oratorical gifts in public gatherings, attacking the wealth and good living of the cardinals and of the papacy, and calling the pope "no apostolic man, but a man of blood." Following his speeches, the latent animosity of the Roman populace towards Eugene III turned into real hostility. Arnold, the rabble-rouser of the masses, showed himself to be a leader with a following both in the ranks of the lower clergy, more open to the purifying reforms of the Church in a revolutionary manner, and in the middle class which was slowly coming into existence. The Commune took this new class officially into its own service, so giving birth to the idea of a Roman Republic as leader of the world and independent of both the pope and the emperor.

Toward the end of 1148, Eugene III returned to Italy and went to Viterbo. From there, at the beginning of the new year, he ventured into the neighborhood of Rome, and was received at Tusculum (Frascati) by Count Tolomeus. He gathered around him faithful vassals of the Church and mercenaries, distributing large sums of money which he had been collecting in France. Finally, he made an alliance with the Norman king, Roger, with whose troops he tried to reenter Rome, but the republicans managed to repulse the attack.

At that point, Eugene III asked for help from Conrad III, back from the Crusade, even if it was absurd to hope for his intervention, albeit with the mirage of the imperial crown, since the pope had made an alliance, however unproductive, with King Roger who had, in turn, allied himself with Conrad's enemy, Welf VI. More sensible was the request made to him by the Romans to come to the aid of a republic prepared to submit to imperial protection if only to get rid of the temporal dominion by the popes. This was a unique occasion that Conrad's ancestors had never had and, when he had defeated Welf in 1150, he started getting ready to descend into Italy in September 1151. Eugene III who was touring in upper Lazio, between Segni and Ferentino, immediately sent him messengers and reached an accord with the German king at Segni in January 1152. Completely betraying Roger's cause, he managed to bring to his advantage Conrad's expedition, even inviting the German princes and bishops to support it with the obvious aim of the imperial anointment. However, on 15 February Conrad III passed away.

After less than a month, on 5 March, his nephew, the famous Frederick Barbarossa, was enthroned and both Eugene and the Romans hastened to curry his favor, both of them offering him the crown. But the German king preferred anointment "by the grace of God" and, in March 1153, arrived at a treaty with the pope which was signed and sealed at Constance. Barbarossa bound himself not to conclude any peace with Rome and the Normans without the pope's consent, and promised to bring papal power back to Rome, including temporal power, and to get rid of the republic. In exchange, the pope promised him the imperial crown.

Learning about the negotiations which would lead to the Pact of Constance, the Roman republic declared null and void the constitution previously agreed upon with the pope, decreeing a new one which foresaw an emperor, two consuls and a hundred senators. However, this could not be actuated due to Frederick's lack of support for it. The democratic faction then split in two, with some thinking about a different emperor, while the position of the moderates favorable to an agreement gained ground. Which meant that Eugene III was able to reenter Rome towards the end of 1152 in order to delay as long as possible the arrival of Frederick, now apparently intent on destroying the republic. Hoping that the Pact of Constance would not be executed, Arnold of Brescia allowed the return of his enemy into the city.

However, Eugene III was not to witness the actual implementation of the Pact. He died at Tivoli on 8 July 1153, but was buried in St. Peter's. Beatified by the Church, he was canonized in 1872.

1 6 8. ANASTASIUS IV (1 1 5 3—1 1 5 4)

The successor to Eugene III, elected on 12 July 1153, was the cardinal of the Suburra, an aging Roman named Conrad, formerly the prior of St. Anastasius and bishop of Santa Sabina. He was consecrated that same day with the name of Anastasius IV.

The Senate, while still presiding over the voting, did not cause any riots or interfere in the election. Anastasius never dreamed of attacking the constitution and calmly carried on a pontificate devoted exclusively to religious matters, not even putting pressure on Frederick to carry out the Pact of Constance.

He agreed to the nomination of Viemann as archbishop of Magdeburg which had been made by Frederick though not in accordance with the rules in the Concordat of Worms, but the appointment of a cardinal as legate to Germany was vetoed, all of which probably cooled relations between Frederick and the papacy.

In sum, the republic had perhaps found in Anastasius IV its ideal pope, but this peaceful co-existence did not last long as death claimed him on 3 December 1154. He was buried in the Lateran.

1 6 9. HADRIAN IV (1 1 5 4—1 1 5 9)

The day after the death of Anastasius IV, an Englishman, Nicholas Breakspear, former cardinal of Albano and papal legate in Norway, was elected pope and consecrated on 5 December 1154 in St. Peter's with the name of Hadrian IV. He was the only Englishman in history to rise to the pontificate.

According to the direct testimony of the chronicler, John of Salisbury, an excessive avarice leading to a craving for power was to characterize his life as a priest prior to accession to the pontifical see. Once pope, he seems to have redeemed himself, conscious of the duties his new office imposed on him. Dante erroneously attributed this avaricious lifestyle of the English cardinal to Hadrian

V, pope in 1267, putting him into his *Purgatory* (XIX, 97–145). This was as a result of a confusion between the two pontiffs, one into which Petrarch also fell in the *Rerum memorandumarum liber* (III, 95) but later corrected in an epistle (*Rerum familiarium*, IX, 25–28). In any event, Hadrian IV, whether repentant or not about his earlier life, as pope did not fall short of those notions of grandeur which had guided him until then. As Gregorovius notes, Hadrian had as his role model Gregory VII and "wanted to apply the principle of the universal dominion of the papacy."

Hadrian IV came immediately into conflict with the Roman republic, the Senate denied him its approval, and he denied his to the Senate. Intending to overthrow the Commune by putting into practice the Pact of Constance set up by Eugene III, he awaited Frederick's intervention. Meanwhile the Romans made contact with William I who had succeeded Roger on the Norman throne in southern Italy. Hadrian was barricaded in St. Peter's, while hostility against the Church and the priests increased in the city and a cardinal was beaten up on the Via Sacra. Hadrian viewed this act as a crime against the majesty of the Church and issued an interdiction against Rome.

This was a sort of divine curse upon the city through which all religious ceremonies automatically ceased, sacraments were not administered, and the deceased were no longer buried in consecrated ground. The populace, faithful at heart, could not last long under these conditions. The idea of an Easter in 1155 without Mass was torture. They marched threateningly towards the Senate, which was forced to accede to the pope's request. The exile of Arnold of Brescia was the price to free Rome from the interdiction. This monk, who for nine years had put his enthusiasm and talent to work on behalf of the freedom of the citizens, would have to leave Rome. He would have to wander about the Roman countryside, from one castle to the other, finally finding a welcome with the viscounts of Campagnano who "honored him as a prophet" in their castle.

Hadrian absolved Rome of the interdiction and celebrated Easter at the Lateran, afterwards going to Viterbo. He had another impending problem regarding the city: the arrival of Frederick Barbarossa who had come to Italy for the first time in October of the previous year. How would he act? Would he go directly to Rome and support the republic, placing it under his protection, or would he respect the Pact of Constance and restore to the pope his temporal power?

By June 1155, Frederick was already in Tuscany after having restored imperial authority in the Lombard cities, and, to sound out his intentions, Hadrian asked him to hand over Arnold of Brescia. The king did not hesitate to content him; he sent troops to Campagnano, arrested one of the viscounts and, thanks to this hostage, obtained the delivery of Arnold. Turned over to the papal legates, the monk was condemned by the prefect of the city to death by hanging. His corpse was then burned and the ashes thrown into the Tiber.

With the pope's diffidence overcome, Frederick was able to do something about Rome. Hadrian was afraid of the Normans and wanted peace, while on his part, Frederick wanted the crown and, with this purpose in mind, he entered the city on 18 June without using military force. The citizens did not rejoice at his arrival but neither did they find the strength to oppose him. On that same day, the pope crowned Frederick emperor at St. Peter's.

Then all of a sudden the Romans recovered their pride and organized a mad, impossible revolt, more a guerrilla movement than anything, assaulting isolated imperial soldiers and the odd priest or cardinal supporting the imperial cause. The result was a bloody repression, although the Romans did manage to shut themselves behind their walls and finally defeat him. Frederick was without supplies and they refused to furnish him any. So, the day after his coronation, the emperor had to move out of Rome, taking with him the pope and the cardinals.

He stayed in the Alban hills with the high prelates until the end of July, pretending he wanted to resume hostilities and to install the pope in a peaceful Rome, but his German vassals were opposed to a continuation of the expedition in Italy and a probable conflict with the Normans. So Frederick returned to Germany with his crown, leaving Hadrian IV to himself.

Meanwhile, William the Norman was pressing from the south and had put Benevento to fire and sword, but his purpose was not to arrive at Rome and defend a republic which was of no interest to him. He simply wanted to be released from the excommunication, which the pope had issued against him when he had taken possession of his father's estates and had given silent support to the Commune of Rome. He achieved his purpose in June 1156 when the excommunication was lifted and he was recognized king to all effects by the pope, who thereby freed himself from this headache at his borders.

However, Frederick was not pleased with this agreement even though in the end it guaranteed Hadrian IV's reentry to Rome in November 1156. In fact, William, with money and threats, managed to bring to obedience the Romans who, also out of hatred of Frederick, came to an understanding with the pope. Thereafter a serious disagreement was to separate the emperor from Hadrian IV and his successor. And useless was the proclamation which the emperor issued to all his subjects with the intent to discredit papal authority and confirm the idea that his imperial authority came to him directly from God, and that whoever had followed him would reach independent power, whether duke, count or commune.

On the basis of this proclamation, Frederick came to Italy a second time, in 1158. After having forced the powerful city of Milan to swear fidelity and to deliver hostages to him, he held a parliament near Roncaglia to which were summoned the great feudal lords, the bishops, and the representatives of the Communes. It was decreed at this parliament that none of the rights of the State could be asserted in any location in any part of the empire, including in Rome, without imperial consent.

Although the pope responded to the parliament by solemnly affirming the right of St. Peter to nominate magistrates and denying Frederick any right to deal directly with the Romans, who were to be considered exclusively the subjects of the pontiff, negotiations were initiated in the spring of 1159 with the emperor for the recognition of the Senate and, possibly, to conclude an agreement with the pope on Church matters. But the imperial delegation, which had come expressly to Rome, did not reach an accord with the Commune.

To complicate matters was the death of the pope at Anagni on 1 September 1159, who was buried in the crypt of St. Peter's. Hadrian IV died while in complete disagreement with the emperor, demonstrating to the end his extraordinary ability, as Gregorovius points out, to face up to "the most powerful monarchs as if he were not only their equal but much superior to them. To the talents given him by nature were added breadth of thought and experience of life that he acquired thanks to an unusual strength of character in which, in addition to pride, even moderation was not lacking in due course." He was, in any event, essentially a politician, "a capable, practical and resolute man," and for this reason did not hesitate to abandon his apostolic see to look after the reinforcement of temporal power around the city. Although he found it impossible in fact to dominate Rome, he nonetheless was able to "weaken the aristocracy in the countryside and to bend it to his own purposes."

170. ALEXANDER III (1159—1181)

On the death of Hadrian IV, the College of Cardinals was apparently split into two factions, one on the side of the emperor and headed by Cardinal Ottaviano, and the other decidedly independent, led by Bosone, a nephew of Hadrian IV. After three days of meetings at St. Peter's they had not reached unanimity, so on 7 September the stronger faction elected a man from Siena, Roland Bandinelli, a distinguished theologian and canonist, trained at the Bologna law school under the monk Gratian. He had been made cardinal-deacon of Sts. Cosmas and Damian by Eugene III and later cardinal-priest at St. Mark's.

But his election was not accepted by Cardinal Ottaviano. The cardinal supported by two other cardinal-priests, and while the newly-elected was putting on the papal mantle, tore it off him and put it over his own shoulders. An irate senator grabbed it, but Ottaviano managed to get it back with the help of his chaplain. In the mêlée he put it on his shoulders inside out, making himself look ridiculous to the College, but after the laughter came the rioting.

Armed soldiers entered St. Peter's and acclaimed Ottaviano as pope with the minor clerics, the people and the majority of the senators giving their assent. Roland Bandinelli and his supporters retreated into a tower in Trastevere while a long procession accompanied Ottaviano toward the Lateran. Thanks to the Frangipane, Roland fled to Ninfa where the bishop of Ostia, Cardinal Ubaldo, consecrated him as pope with the name of Alexander III on 20 September 1159. From there the new pontiff went to Terracina, placing himself under the protection of the Norman King William.

Still in command of a large part of Rome thanks to the support of many of the noble families, including the Monticelli who descended from the Crescenzi and of which he was a member, Ottaviano acted calmly expecting the support of the emperor. To begin with he thought it best to leave Rome, which was in the midst of rioting, and go to Farfa, where he was consecrated on 4 October with the name of Victor IV, the same name with which the preceding antipope had been called in 1138. And there he awaited the decision of the emperor to give his nomination recognition at a European level.

The emperor did indeed take the side of Victor IV, disregarding both the fact that he had been excommunicated by Alexander III and the letter which his elector cardinals had sent him. He went so far as to prohibit the bishops in the empire to recognize either of the pretenders and summoned a council to meet in January 1160, at Pavia to decide on the dispute.

For this reason the emperor came to Italy for the third time, but the opening of the council was delayed, as Barbarossa was taken up with the siege of Crema which was stubbornly defending itself. Once that was over, the emperor opened the council on 5 February but Alexander III did not appear, citing the rule according to which the Roman Church was not to be judged by anyone. An accomplished jurist, Alexander thought it best to stick to his legal rights, confirming to the Christian world that he was right to do so. He also declared that it was contrary to church law for the emperor to have convened a council. Victor IV, however, did appear at this gathering of only fifty German and Lombard bishops, and was duly declared the legitimate pope by the will of Barbarossa, while Alexander was excommunicated as a schismatic.

The reaction to the scandalous interference of the emperor in ecclesiastical matters was heavy in consequences. The archbishop of Salzburg opposed the schism, and numerous bishops in northern Italy lined up behind Alexander III. The religious controversies in many Italian cities were tinted with political aversion to the emperor, of which Alexander became the symbol. In February, the archbishop of Milan excommunicated Frederick and his antipope, and on 24 March the pope confirmed the excommunication from Anagni, absolving all subjects in the empire of their oath of fidelity to Barbarossa. The sovereigns of all the European States declared themselves in favor of Alexander III.

Barbarossa spent his anger and disappointment over the disapproval by the European leaders for his political opposition to Alexander III by directing his military forces against Milan. Barbarossa was determined to conquer and punish the city, considering it to be mainly responsible for the revolt of the Communes of northern Italy against imperial authority. And after two years of resistance, in 1162 Milan had to open its gates and witness the destruction of its walls and many of its houses.

In the meantime, Alexander had convened a great council at Tours for May 1163. An impressive number of bishops from France and England turned up, and his pontifical sovereignty was unanimously recognized while Victor IV, the imperial chancellor Rainald of Dassel and the abbot of Cluny were expelled from the Christian community. The excommunication of Frederick was not renewed because the pope hoped secretly for a reconciliation with him, sooner or later.

Meanwhile, Victor IV withdrew to Germany and called a council at Trier to revive his wavering papal dignity. Alexander was able to return to Rome, though he realized that his responsibilities would not be limited to his see as bishop. He sensed within himself a pontifical spirit of a universal nature because of the recognition he received, and took to heart especially the destinies of the Italian Communes in the north.

On 20 April 1164, Victor IV died at Lucca. The imperial faction immediately arranged to replace him with a faithful friend, Cardinal Guido of Crema, whom the bishop of Liège consecrated on 26 April with the name of Paschal III. He canonized Charlemagne at Frederick's behest to exalt that sovereign as the supreme symbol of the German empire.

Lombard cities meanwhile formed a league in Verona. Milan rebuilt its walls, and Frederick came to Italy for a fourth time, his destination Rome, where Alexander III had regained his throne and was sending appeals to all the Christian peoples, while arousing the Normans in the south from the isolation in which they had been peacefully living.

Frederick entered Rome on 22 July 1167 and there were terrible battles between the invaders and the besieged, while the Germans slowly conquered the various areas of the city. Finally, Barbarossa was able to occupy St. Peter's by force of arms and there his antipope, Paschal III, placed the imperial crown on his head. After which followed devastation, fires, and death in many quarters in the fruitless search for Alexander III, who had escaped to the Normans in Benevento. Barbarossa had triumphed in a Rome he considered his, the city of the empire, but soon came the first warnings, seen by the populace as a sign of divine punishment. A terrible plague laid low the German army and one of the victims was the imperial chancellor Rainald of Dassel. At the same time a resistance movement was formed in the city, headed by the Pierleones and the Frangipanes, now united against a common enemy. And Barbarossa once again had to head for home.

From then on, without pause, Alexander III's star began its bright ascent into the heavens not only of Rome but also of all Italy. The league of the Communes grew quickly in the north with Padua and Bologna joining it. Then came the famous oath of Pontida when Alexander III was acclaimed Protector of the League and the city of Alessandria was founded in his honor between the Tanaro and the Bormida rivers.

On 20 September 1168, the second antipope, Paschal III, died and the imperial faction immediately furnished a successor, Abbot John of Strumi near Arezzo, who had been appointed cardinal-bishop of Albano by Victor IV, and who took the name of Calixtus III. Barbarossa quickly recognized him and came to Italy for the fifth time, having tried in every possible way, through international diplomatic channels, to isolate Alexander III again and, above all, to separate him from the League of the Communes.

The emperor was determined first and foremost to destroy Alessandria, nicknamed by him "the city of straw," which he hated because it was the symbol of the pope. But despite a siege of six months, he failed to conquer it and then, without the military assistance of his most powerful vassal, Henry the Lion, who was engaged against the Slavs and the Danes, Frederick was confronted by the army of the League at Legnano on the Olona 29 May 1176, while trying to rejoin his allies. The citizens' infantry, closely flanking the Carroccio (the Oxcart) was able to defeat the cavalry and Frederick, beaten in a bloody battle, saved himself only with difficulty.

The emperor then had to come to terms directly with Alexander III at Anagni in October 1176, who defended not only his own rights but also those of the Communes and of William II. These negotiations found concrete application at Venice in May 1177, where the Sicilian plenipotentiaries, the representatives of the Communes, and the imperial dignitaries, including Archbishop Christian of Mainz, met.

Alexander III was recognized as the legitimate pope by Frederick who abandoned the antipope and promised to defend the Church, while the question of the lands of Matilda of Canossa, seized by Frederick but donated by the countess earlier to the pope, was put on ice.

William II concluded a treaty of peace for fifteen years with the emperor, though with the Communes there was a truce for only six years that would lead, in 1183, to the peace treaty of Constance as a result of which they would obtain complete independence.

From Venice, Alexander III headed for Rome to take definitive possession of his see, protected by the imperial vicar, Christian of Mainz. On 12 March 1178, he entered the city and was welcomed joyously by the citizens who pledged loyalty to him, perhaps hoping that the ideals of communal liberty defended in the north by the pope would also be respected in Rome. Calixtus III, who had no intention of giving up his position, withdrew to Viterbo where Christian of Mainz found him after besieging the city and brought him to Alexander at Tusculum. There the antipope admitted his guilt and on 29 August finally renounced his appointment. Alexander pardoned him and appointed him ecclesiastical governor of Benevento.

Certain barons from the Roman Campagna, bent on their own interests, went on looking for an antipope with which to oppose Alexander, and found him a year later in the person of Lando of Sezze, who took the name of Innocent III. He would find no supporters among the clergy, however, and in 1180 would be sent off to the monastery at Cava dei Tirreni where he would end his days.

It was the last insignificant link in the long chain of attempts by the emperor, including the three antipopes, to confound the legitimacy of a pope who had succeeded in defending himself through untiring activity and in stirring once again in Italy a pseudo-patriotic enthusiasm.

Religion and politics had fused with dignity, and in the same fashion Alexander III sought to conduct himself with Henry II of England who, while acknowledging him as the legitimate pontiff, had engaged him in a conflict over ecclesiastical privileges on a question of criminal jurisdiction which had arisen between the sovereign and the archbishop of Canterbury, Thomas Becket. But events became tragically bitter and, in final analysis, seemed like a slap in the face for the Church of Rome.

Since 1164, with the constitutions of Clarendon, the king had reaffirmed the supremacy of lay authority over the ecclesiastical, and this had encountered the firm opposition of Becket, obviously with papal support. After an apparent reconciliation, however, the archbishop was assassinated in 1170 in the cathedral of Canterbury. In a council in March 1171, the pope excommunicated the assassins and ordered the king to perform a public penance, requiring in addition the revocation of the decrees of Clarendon. The tone of the pope's statements was, however, not such as to provoke a break with the English sovereign, and the negotiations led to an agreement which appeared more like a compromise, and basically did not redeem the mortal offense suffered by a high prelate of the Church.

In May 1172, in the cathedral of Avranches, the king swore that he had not provoked and had not wanted the murder of the archbishop, while acknowledging that he had caused it indirectly through the constitutions of Clarendon, unwittingly predisposing some ruffian to commit the criminal act. Moreover, he promised to be faithful to Alexander and his successors and to return the assets of the Church of Canterbury.

It was only a compromise though. While the bishops were released from their vows given to the Clarendon decrees, these decrees continued to be in force. Also the assassins of Thomas Becket went unpunished and even remained in the king's employment. The Church would canonize the archbishop of Canterbury as an ultimate reward for a noble person whom the papacy had not been able to protect adequately, either alive or dead.

Moreover, when Henry II performed his penance before the tomb of the martyr in July 1174, allowing himself even to be scourged by the monks who were present, this humiliating act which should have been a moral triumph for the archbishop, actually freed the king from any feelings of guilt and allowed him to win over his subjects who, until then, had probably been devoted only to their saintly archbishop.

However, Alexander III, after the agreements of Venice, sailed with the wind in prow and prepared to celebrate his glory officially by convening in September 1178, an ecumenical council at Rome, the eleventh in all, and the third in the West, to be known as the Third Lateran. It took place in March 1179.

More than three hundred bishops were present and there were about a thousand speakers. Once all the ordinations and deposings effected by the antipopes had been declared null and void, special decrees were promulgated, like those against duelling and dangerous mounted tourneys, usury and, once more, simony and incontinence amongst the clergy. But the most important decision was the one on papal elections, of which the defects of the decree in force since 1059 had become evident.

In this regard, the constitution, *Licet de vitanda discordia*, established that "if, for any reason, complete agreement among the cardinals for the election cannot be achieved, he who has been elected by a two-thirds vote is without any exception to be considered the Roman pontiff of the Universal Church." So the question of the number of votes, left in abeyance since Nicholas II, was defined and the two-thirds rule, still in force today, was established.

However, the fundamental matter was that the right to elect was recognized to be exclusively that of the College of Cardinals in its entirety, without distinction between cardinal-bishops, cardinal-priests and cardinal-deacons. The College did not gain importance merely for elections of popes, but became a new order around the pope at the summit of the universal Church.

This was the last important deed in the pontificate of Alexander III, who was unable to reside in Rome without interruptions because of repeated rioting. Honored all over Europe, it was only in his city that he continued to be unpopular. A city where nobles did not find it in their interest to support a pope who had sided with the Communes, which were opposed during their initial years to any sort of aristocracy, and the Senate, though protected by the militia, which was not able to have its laws obeyed, much less those relating to protection of the pope.

Alexander III was in exile in various locations in Latium during the last years of his pontificate and in June 1181 he was in Viterbo, possibly to

request his protector, Christian of Mainz, to intervene in Rome. Shortly afterwards, on 30 August, he died at Civitacastellana.

Carried to Rome to be buried in the Lateran, he had no floral offerings from
the common people and his bier was stoned, a final proof of their undiminished
hatred. Yet, perhaps, he did not deserve so much scorn. He was a "mediocre
pope completely without originality," as Walter Ullmann observed, "but with a
huge capacity for tolerance" which led him to compromise, as in the notorious
case of the assassination of Thomas Becket, though "the papacy emerged at the
end of his long pontificate stronger, more respected and more alive than when
he rose to the throne of St. Peter."

He probably got involved despite himself in the League of the Communes,
the standard-bearer of a freedom he was certainly not prepared to tolerate in
Rome, which may explain why the Romans replaced the flowers with which
they welcomed him after the Pact of Venice to the stones they used to pelt his
funeral bier. He was "the first pope equipped with a proper legal education,"
gained at the school of Gratian at Bologna, and "as pope, his first task had been
that of applying the theory of canon law."

Thus, thanks to his decrees, the "consolidation of papal administration
was reached, in other words, the effective mechanism of government and its
organization were in large measure developed," putting to rest, once and for all,
the democratic spirit of the Commune.

For which there remained still only a stone or two to throw.

1 7 1. Lucius III (1 1 8 1 − 1 1 8 5)

As successor to Alexander III, Ubaldo Allucingoli of Lucca was elected pope
at Velletri on 1 September 1181. Formally cardinal-bishop of Ostia and papal
legate on various occasions, he had accomplished numerous missions for
Alexander III to Frederick Barbarossa who had considerable esteem for him.
He was consecrated pope at Velletri on September 6 and took the name of
Lucius III.

During his pontificate he was only able to reside in Rome for the winter of
1181–82, due to continual conflicts with the population which wanted to reach
a definite agreement to make communal freedom a reality, whereas the pope was
opposed to and would not recognize this new structure of the Commune. There
was also the old dispute with Tusculum, which the Romans wanted to incorporate into their municipality. Faced with the siege to which the fortified castle was
being subjected, Lucius, who had sought refuge at Segni, called in from Tuscia
Christian of Mainz who was able to disperse the Romans with his troops. But
when, on 25 August 1183, the archbishop died at Tusculum of a fatal fever,
the Romans returned threateningly to the walls of the castle and pillaged the
nearby territory, pursuing their looting into Latium. "Their hatred of the

clergy was savage and barbaric," writes Gregorovius: "Once they captured a
number of priests in the Campagna and put out the eyes of all but one of them.
Then, forcing them to ride on donkeys and capping them with parchment mitres
on which were written the names of cardinals, they ordered the one who had
not been blinded to lead this macabre cortège to the pope."

Lucius III fled to Verona where he met with the emperor just back from having made peace with the Communes at Constance. In November 1184, a general
decree was issued against the heretics of that period, the Cathari and the
Waldensians, who were banned both by the Church and the empire. Disputes
arose, instead, regarding the investiture of the archbishopric of Trier, to which
Rudolph of Wied, well esteemed by the emperor, had been elected by majority
vote, whereas a minority favored Volkmar who had appealed to the pope. The
archbishopric remained vacant pending study of the issues, but the dispute
between the parties was sharpened over the problem of Matilda of Canossa's
legacy, which Barbarossa had no intention of giving up, and over the emperor's
formal request for the anointment of his son, Henry, which the pope refused.
This led to a breach between the parties.

Frederick returned to Germany, consoled by the official betrothal between
his son and Constance, the daughter of Roger II of Sicily, a bond between the
empire and the Normans which spelt danger for the State of the Church. Lucius
III vented his spleen by excommunicating the Roman rebels.

He died on 25 November 1185, at Verona and was buried in the cathedral
of that city.

172. URBAN III (1185–1187)

On the same day that Lucius III died, the archbishop of Milan Uberto
Crivelli, from the family of the counts of Dorno and Lomello and once cardinal-
priest of San Lorenzo in Damaso then bishop of Vercelli at Verona, was elected
as pope. He was consecrated in the cathedral of Verona on 1 December with the
name of Urban III, and decided to retain also the archbishopric of Milan.

Under his pontificate the disputes between the papacy and the empire continued, and notwithstanding numerous negotiations, the pending issues of
Matilda's property and that of the archbishopric of Trier were not resolved.
Furthermore, in Germany Frederick failed to observe the Concordat of Worms
by interfering in religious matters and giving to lay persons the tithes of
churches, all of which was worsened by Urban III's forced isolation in Verona.

But the greatest insult the pope received was on 27 January 1186 when, without the presence of the pope who was also the archbishop of that city, the
marriage of Constance of Altavilla and the son of Frederick, Henry, was celebrated in the cathedral of Milan followed by the triple coronation of Henry with
the crown of Arles by the archbishop of Vienna, the Italian patriarch of Aquileia

and a German bishop. It was an insult that Urban III at first decided to avenge with excommunications but then changed his mind. Towards the end of his pontificate, seeking to come closer diplomatically to Barbarossa he had resumed negotiations. He told the imperial envoys that he was convinced the best way to settle the problem of Trier would be to hold a new election, and the emperor was pleased by this idea.

However, there seemed to be no solution to the issue of Matilda's property. Henry VI had taken over her lands as regent and from there encroached into Latium, finding Romans as allies in his ventures, so all hope of returning to Rome was dashed for the pope.

Urban III never took residence in Rome and, a few weeks before his death, the authorities of Verona, faithful to Barbarossa, forced him to move to Ferrara where on 20 October 1187, he died. He was buried in the cathedral of Ferrara.

1 7 3. Gregory VIII (1 1 8 7)

The day after Urban III's death and in the same city of Ferrara, Albert de Morra from Benevento was elected to succeed him. A papal legate in various European countries, he had been a teacher in the Studio of Bologna and had entered the College of Cardinals under Hadrian IV. He was a legal expert and had therefore been called to the papal chancery where he had compiled a treatise on the style to be used in papal documents. He was consecrated pope at Ferrara on 25 October 1187, with the name of Gregory VIII.

His brief pontificate lasted less than two months and was marked by his wish for constructive commitments beginning with that of freeing the pope from the isolation in which he risked ending up. For this reason, Gregory declared that he was prepared to resolve his disputes with the emperor. He demanded that Volkmar desist from his bitter attitude towards his adversary in the competition for the archbishopric of Trier, and also indicated that he was ready to confer on Henry VI the imperial coronation which his predecessor had refused. As a result, Barbarossa realized that the new pope was in fact well intentioned.

A reformative spirit certainly inspired his actions, such as the rigorous decree he issued against the foppish way of dressing of priests and the unbridled passion for gambling and other practices not exactly suitable to the life of a churchman. But more than all Gregory wanted to launch a new Crusade, and, with this in mind, in December of 1187 he went to Pisa as a peace mediator between that maritime city and Genoa, whose alliance would be useful in a crusade.

Passing through Lucca, before arriving in Pisa, he had the tomb of Cardinal Ottaviano, the antipope Victor IV, opened and his bones thrown out of the church: a reprehensible act which also proved the extremely severe spirit of this pope.

Gregory VIII died at Pisa on 17 December 1187, without having managed, like his predecessor, to reside as pope for even one day among the Romans he had regularly excommunicated. He was buried in the cathedral of Pisa.

174. CLEMENT III (1187–1191)

Two days after the death of Gregory VIII, the College of Cardinals at Pisa elected a Roman, Paolo Scolari, cardinal-bishop of Palestrina, who was consecrated in the cathedral of Pisa on 20 December 1187.

The first objective which Clement III set himself was to achieve peace with the Romans in order to be able to get to Rome, his native city and the true see of a Roman pontiff, as soon as possible. Indeed, following speedy negotiations, it became possible from the beginning of February 1188 for Clement to go to there, and for a sworn agreement between the pope and the Commune, drafted by the Roman Senate in the forty-fourth year of its establishment, to be concluded on May 31.

In this treaty the sovereignty of the pope over Rome was recognized and the Senate took an oath of loyalty to him and restored his right to coin money, although one-third of the incomes went to the Senate to pay off ecclesiastical mortgages. For his part, the pope agreed to compensate the Romans for the damages caused by the war and to make donations of money to the senators, also that he could use the Roman militia in defense of his assets, but only upon adequate compensation in cash. The Roman nobility was clearly obliged to recognize the Senate, and, as a result, the nobles, in order not to be left out of the political game in Rome, were forced to get their members into the Commune, mainly to give it an aristocratic slant. This naturally ended up betraying the republic's democratic origins. If the constitution of 31 May 1188 proved a noteworthy success for the Commune of Rome, now recognized just like the other Italian Communes, it gave the nobles new possibilities to have the upper hand and to appropriate as theirs the liberal conquests of the common people and the middle class.

Having thus resolved the problem with the Romans, Clement III turned to his relationship with the empire. The Third Crusade having been solemnly proclaimed in April 1188 with the direct participation of Frederick Barbarossa, who had rediscovered his responsibility as protector of Christianity and had left the regency to his son, Clement III declared that he was prepared for the immediate imperial coronation of Henry VI. The pope wrote of his intention in a letter to Henry sent in the summer of 1188, in which he succeeded also in solving the question of the archbishopric of Trier which was still a vacant see. The pretenders, Volkmar and Rudolph, were cast aside and John, the imperial chancellor, was elected.

At Strasbourg in April 1189, the emperor promised to return to the pope all lands of the Papal State without mentioning specifically the properties belonging to Matilda of Canossa. Then, in November of that year, William II died leaving no heirs and Henry VI, as the husband of Constance of Altavilla, decided to take over southern Italy and Sicily.

However, to complicate matters, a natural son of Roger II, Tancred, suddenly appeared claiming Sicily, and the archbishop of Palermo immediately crowned him king, obviously with the approval of Clement III.

A military intervention was needed in order to resolve the question, but it had to be done under the emperor's guise, and since Barbarossa had died during the crusade in June 1190, Henry VI sent messengers to the pope and the Senate to receive him in Rome during the spring of the following year in order to celebrate his coronation at Easter. In January, he was on the march towards Rome. Clement III feared that Henry VI would somehow seek revenge for the Church's concession of the feudal estate in Sicily to Tancred, but death freed him from the dreaded meeting in March 1191, and he was buried in the Lateran before the German king's arrival in Rome.

1 7 5. CELESTINE III (1 1 9 1 — 1 1 9 8)

As Henry VI was nearing Rome, the College of Cardinals quickly decided on the election of the successor to Clement III, an eighty-five-year-old Roman, Hyacinth Boboni, from the Orsini family. Since he was only a deacon, it was necessary to complete his ordination as priest before he could be consecrated, which took place on 14 April 1191.

Henry VI was already in Rome and wanted his imperial crown, but the Senate stated that it would oppose the coronation unless he removed the military garrison posted three years previously in defense of Tusculum, which the Romans definitely wanted to take over. Henry had to give in and on 15 April was crowned together with his wife, Constance, while on the following day the Germans withdrew from Tusculum. The Romans then attacked and destroyed the hated city.

After which Henry VI departed from Rome to conquer his wife's inheritance, but he was not to do it by force of arms. Tancred's death in February 1194 allowed him to put on the crown of the Norman king at Christmas of that same year. The very next day Constance gave him an heir, the famous Frederick II.

Celestine III, meanwhile, carried on his pontificate quietly in Rome, irrespective of the feuds of the factions which were inflaming the city, not against him but for the conquest of seats in the Senate. The common people had the courage and the strength but not the funds to impose their will, and the middle class was "weak, due to the almost total lack of corporations among the various arts," as Gregorovius put it. With the result that the nobles won, "eminent spongers who lived at the expense of the pope, of the bishops and of the pious places in Rome" for sure, but who could always count on having the money. So the aristocracy no longer obstructed a Commune which it now was beginning to support and which it planned to take over.

Gregorovius notes: "The consuls became part of the Roman government with the precise intention of giving it an aristocratic imprint, while the nobility sent its members to fill the ranks of senators, and it was not difficult to get them elected. As from 1143, the Senate had been primarily plebeian, but little by little the patricians had managed to infiltrate it to the extent that, by the time of Clement III and Celestine III, the patricians of ancient lineage were more numerous in it than the middle class and the knights."

The pope himself indirectly helped this insertion of his "god-children," the nobles, and the Senate became a civil institution with a clerical bent. The Pontifical State was thus able to reorganize its finances and keep an itemized account of its incomes, as attested by the *Liber Censuum* of the chamberlain, Cencio Savelli, the future Honorius III, who recorded lists of the moneys which the numberless taxpayers owed the Church of Rome among them castles, monasteries, hospitals and villages of the Roman Campagna.

In March 1195, Henry VI decided to go on a new Crusade, almost as a vindication of his father's death during the third unfortunate expedition, and Celestine III could not play second fiddle in such a holy initiative. So, in a series of messages to the various sovereigns of Europe, he proclaimed what would be the fourth Crusade. At the same time, however, he wanted to resolve the problem of the lands that had belonged to Matilda of Tuscany over which Henry VI had placed his brother, Philip, as governor. As the latter was making continual raids into Latium, it was clear that the dream of the emperor was to join the whole of Italy to the empire, to the detriment of the State of the Church.

Despite his old age, Celestine III was not the sort to be pushed aside. Moreover, the Curia was right then shaking the dust off the principles, never shelved, of the *Mater Ecclesia*. Indeed Cencio Savelli, the chamberlain, obviously at the suggestion of the pope, had installed two bronze portals in the Patriarchius of the Lateran, one of which showed in the upper part two statuettes representing a seated *Mater Ecclesia*.

Henry VI, however, did not intend to break relations with the papacy. He came up with more credible explanations regarding what his brother, excommunicated by Celestine, was doing and again promised his fidelity to the vicar of Christ. Above all, he made a concrete offer to repay the Church for the territories of the Countess Matilda with the income from the benefices of the wealthiest presbyteries of all the churches in the archbishoprics of the empire, which would mean substantial economic support for the Curia. The pope was undecided whether to accept or not, since by doing so he risked exposing himself to criticism which might turn into accusations of simony. According to some, the emperor is supposed to have made a more attractive offer, which was the investiture of the empire by means of a golden globe, which would signify that the empire had been declared a feudal estate conferred by the pope. All at once the forged Donation of Constantine would lose its illegality, the Pseudo-Isidore would take form in an effective juridical context, and the *Mater Ecclesia* would discover a legitimate son.

Seppelt believed in this revolutionary offer from Henry VI, which Barbarossa, as the emperor himself emphasized in writing to the pope, would never have dreamed of doing. It was therefore an insane proposal, and "at first glance it seems amazing that Henry VI could have gone so far as to make such an offer. . . But it was a fact known for a long time that the ecclesiastical party had promoted the concept that it was the pope who granted the empire because at that time a feudal grant from the Church and especially from the pope who was the representative on earth of Christ, would not seem out of place or humiliating." On the other hand, Seppelt adds, "a lasting recognition made by the pope under the guise of a feudal estate had a purely theoretical significance. It changed nothing in the emperor's dominant situation vis à vis the pope."

The offer was not accepted. Celestine III requested a postponement for the investiture with the golden globe, but it was clear that the Church had made its choice. Better to go ahead on a series of decrees which only the Church knew to be false, to carry on a dirty policy which would in time prove him right. It was also the symbol of a faith, and whether it were truly Christian or not, mattered little.

Henry VI took it badly, but while he was conducting these negotiations, he suddenly died in September 1197, at only 32 years of age. Shortly afterwards, Celestine III also passed away, on 8 January 1198 and was buried in the Lateran.

176. INNOCENT III (1198–1216)

The election of the successor to Celestine III took place in Rome in a chamber dug out of the ruins of the ancient Septizonium, transformed into a fortress and a prison, owned by the Frangipane. According to some, it is considered the first conclave in history and in fact, as indicated by Giancarlo Zizola, "for the first time in this election the *oratio de eligendo pontifice* was held, and for the first time ballots were distributed. It was also the first clear application of the distinction between the electoral process and the liturgical process in the selection of a pope, the election being clearly a lay action, political in nature, which is followed elsewhere by the sacred rites."

It was 8 January 1198, and cardinal-deacon Lothario from the Conti family of Segni was elected. Born in 1160 at Gavignano near Rome, as a youth he had studied theology at Paris and law at Bologna. When he returned to Rome, he was ordained a sub-deacon and later made a cardinal-deacon of the church of Saints Sergius and Bacchus in the Forum by his uncle, Clement III. Under Celestine III he had been put on the shelf because of an ancient rivalry between the Orsini family, to which the pope belonged, and the Contis.

Although very young at thirty-eight years, the newly-elected pope, who assumed the name of Innocent III, was mature and full of energy and conscientiously prepared to take on papal dignity as the vicar of Christ. He was also convinced that, more than any other man on earth, he held total power in his hands. In reality, when he was elected, the sovereignty of the pope in Rome no longer existed and very little remained of the State of the Church. It was a situation not to his liking and so, even before his consecration, which took place 22 February in St. Peter's, he busied himself with restoring papal authority in Rome. Blocking his way, principally, were the Senate, the representative assembly of the people and protector of their rights, and the prefect, representative of the imperial claims.

As for the Senate, in a Commune now decidedly aristocratic, with an executive power which oscillated between a form of oligarchy and a monarchy (of the fifty-six senators who had been nominated in 1197 there was only one in office when Innocent III was elected.) This one senator was removed and replaced by a person who took an oath of loyalty to the pope.

This was a genuine coup to which the population did not know how, or better, did not wish to react. Through the distribution of large amounts of money the people were convinced to give up suddenly the democratic achievement of free elections for the Senate, which the new pope was claiming again as a pontifical privilege. The *golpe* was completed by the substitution of *justitiarii*, or judges, until then elected by the Capitol, with pontifical employees. As for the prefect, Innocent III forced him to submit to him the day after the coronation and to swear an oath of vassalage, becoming also a kind of employee of his.

In fact, in the six weeks before his coronation, Innocent III managed to take control of the city's civil administration, and lay the basis for an effective reorganization of authority by taking advantage of his extended and influential circle of relatives. Thanks to them, he was able to bring into a kind of oligarchy many noble Roman families who controlled the situation authoritatively until May 1203, when a sudden uprising of the people took place which forced Innocent III to flee from Rome and seek refuge in Palestrina.

It was basically a return on the scene of the Orsini family which, under Celestine III, had achieved prestige and wealth but now saw themselves cast aside. This was accompanied by deeper contrasts between the nobles who supported the pope and the fallen family of the Poli. In this difficult situation the right of the populace to elect the senators directly surfaced again, together with the republican ideals promoted by John Capocci. He was aware, however, that he was only a tool in the hands of the noble 'patricians' and, after a series of battles, which he even won, he settled for money and surrendered all his rights to the pope who had returned to Rome in 1204. Peace among the various factions was reached in 1205 with the executive authority remaining in the hands of a single senator, or *podestà*, appointed directly by the pope.

The restructuring of papal power within the city was part of a broader project to give the papacy a secure base outside the walls of Rome, as far as possible reforming entirely the State of the Church through the so-called "policy of the recoveries," that is, the recovery of lands considered to belong to the papacy but which had been unjustly usurped. In this matter, Innocent III was helped by the sudden collapse of German sovereignty in Italy following the death of Henry VI, and his astuteness in knowing how to put to good use the innate antipathy of the Italians for the Germans by fostering the renewal of a budding nationalistic sentiment.

So the duchy of Spoleto and the March of Ancona were returned to the State of the Church without much difficulty through a personal homage of their residents, who wanted to submit to papal sovereignty as subjects of the vicar of Christ. However an attempt to incorporate in it Romagna, taking into account both Christian and pseudo-patriotic sentiments, failed mainly because of the behavior of the archbishop of Ravenna who wanted autonomy, and so Innocent III was not able to recover possession of the patrimony of Matilda of Canossa.

Basically, therefore, the grandiose project to increase the State of the Church was only partially realized, but certainly the restructuring of pontifical sovereignty in the reconquered territories was sound, and definitively served to remove the papacy and its property from the clutches of the empire.

Fundamentally, it was with Innocent III that the precise formulation of Gregory VII's theocratic ideal took substance. According to this, absolute dominion over all the powers on earth belonged to the papacy, a theory that then became a practical conviction with broader horizons. The terms of reference were still the same, from the *Constitutum Constantini* to the Pseudo-Isidore, but now the concept of *Mater Ecclesia* seemed to base its desire for power through essentially religious and philosophical ideals.

Starting with the concept that the soul is superior to the body, that the spiritual must dominate the material, and, as a result, the management of spiritual matters must be superior to the management of the things of this earth, the papacy had to be considered superior to the empire, with the emperor receiving his authority only from the pope, just as the moon receives its light from the sun. Thus the Christian spirit ends by being still more at the service of political issues and, in the final analysis, theocracy turns out to be the mask of power.

Based on these principles, Innocent III set about dealing with the question of the succession in the empire. The wife of the deceased Henry VI, Constance, had managed to have her three-year-old son, Frederick, crowned king of Sicily in May 1198 at Palermo. However, she had died in November, leaving a provision in her will that Innocent III should take on the guardianship of her son and the regency of the kingdom of Sicily while Frederick was a minor. This was a powerful weapon in the hands of the pope who accepted the task with pleasure, since he could consider himself the arbiter of the power vacuum in Germany, for which his ward, Frederick, was considered the legitimate heir. In the meantime, however, the majority in the Hohenstaufen faction had decided to offer Germany's crown to Henry VI's brother, Philip of Swabia, whereas the Guelph minority backed Duke Otto of Brunswick.

The pope did not enter into this dispute immediately, also because the civil war worked to the advantage of his ward. He issued his verdict only when he understood it was time to use papal prestige to make clear, in unambiguous terms, the Church's basic principles on the government of Christian society. Even if the majority of the princes and the king of France were on Philip's side, Innocent III could not forgive him for having been crowned in September 1198 at Mainz by the Burgundian archbishop of Tarantasia, a foreign prelate without authority. Nor could the pope forget that Celestine III had excommunicated Philip and that the anathema was still in force, not to mention Philip's stubborn claim to the imperial crown as "king of the Romans" on the strength of which he had declared his intention of coming to Rome to be crowned by the pope. Instead Otto, although supported only by the minority, had been crowned in the right place, at Aachen, by the archbishop of Cologne, who had been authorized to do so, and was, moreover, protected by his uncle, the king of England. Even more important, he had declared that he practically renounced German rights in Italy. Taking his side meant increasing the territorial "recoveries" with the acquisition of the properties of Matilda of Canossa, as well as having a safeguard against the feared union of Sicily with the empire. So Innocent recognized Otto IV as the legitimate king and promised him the imperial crown.

Notwithstanding the intervention of the pope, criticized obviously in different ways by not only the princes but also the bishops of Germany, the civil war continued. Philip gained ground gradually and Otto was isolated, abandoned even by the archbishop of Cologne who, in 1205, placed the imperial crown on Philip's head at Aachen. That anointment, made with all of the chrisms recognized by the pope, put Innocent III into a difficult position—he could see the ever-increasing precariousness of Otto's situation, and, as a result, was forced to take heed of the changed circumstances and reach an accord with Philip. However, in the midst of negotiations, Philip was assassinated at Bamberg in June 1208, probably by hired killers of Otto's. It looked as if the situation had resolved itself and Innocent III began dreaming about the triumph of his policy. Otto renewed his own promises and, in August 1209, met with the pope at

Viterbo, falsely swearing to the renunciation of Matilda's property and to his rights over the former exarchate. On 4 October 1209, he was solemnly crowned at St. Peter's by Innocent III, trustful as ever. After which, Otto IV betrayed all the pope's expectations. The next year, he seized areas in southern Italy, sent troops into Sicily, granted feudal estates to German officials in the territories recovered by the pope. Innocent then had no other defense except excommunication, which automatically freed the German princes from obedience to Otto.

It was a defeat of the papal policy at the imperial level, and it became vital to obviate the damage. Frederick, the son of the late Henry VI and the ward of the pope was only sixteen years old but he was the only card still in the pope's hand. Innocent openly supported the candidature of the lad and in 1211 the German princes formally elected him as king.

Frederick was crowned "king of the Romans" in 1212 at Mainz and a year later, in the Golden Bull of Eger, he renewed the promise made ten years earlier by the Guelph, Otto, on the separation of Sicily from the empire and the famous "recoveries" of lands belonging to the State of the Church. Frederick was still a boy, but a strengthening of the position of this pontifical ward came in 1214 with the defeat of Otto in the Battle of Bouvines by the combined forces of Frederick and Philip II of France.

For more than ten years, Innocent III had been involved at the vertex of the empire and, regardless of the betrayal by Otto IV, the pope's brilliant strategy and his perfect mastery of the theocratic ideology had resulted in an assertion of this pope's personality at a European level. He had become the incarnation of law and order, and this meant that the papacy was able to interfere in the politics of several kingdoms, precisely to protect this revived image of its power.

In fact, Innocent had forced the king of France, Philip Auguste, through an interdiction, to take back his wife, Ingeborg, whom he had rejected, and the king of England, John Lackland, to acknowledge himself as a vassal of the Church of Rome. He had received feudal homage from Peter II of Aragon, from Otto of Bohemia, from Alphonso IX of Leon, and from Sancio I of Portugal, and in 1212 the armies of the kings of Spain, encouraged by the Christian spirit, had finally stopped the expanding Arab power at Las Navas of Tolosa. But the feudal lordship of Innocent over the European monarchies, as Falco observed, was "a power in great part illusory, based on a diminishing faith" which had to give way to new national and communal organizations. His theocracy became an instrument for order and conservation in the Europe it had created, but which every day was becoming less tolerant of tutelage.

In such a Europe, crusades and struggles against heretics no longer had the significance of earlier times, but these were still two issues close to Innocent's heart and he was one of the most active promoters of the Fourth Crusade which ended in 1204. However, the crusaders, who had decided to reach the Holy

Land by sea and had made a contract with the Republic of Venice to supply transportation, were not in a position to pay the huge price requested, and wound up being an instrument in the Venetians' ambitious designs in the Levant. As for the heretics, Innocent III started out on the wrong foot by considering them the same as the heretics of the first centuries of the Church. In reality, they preached a Christian way of life as in the Gospel and should have been seen as a logical outcome of popular movements, once defended by the Church, such as the "Pataria." The Humiliated, the Spirituals and the Jacobites did not put in doubt dogmas, but instead condemned the outright immorality of the clergy and the laity, they accused bishops and sovereigns, and even the very summit of the papacy itself for a decline of the religious spirit and domination by politics (even though of a theocratic nature)which was a basic betrayal of the evangelical message. Naturally, to a theocratic pope like Innocent, these movements were displeasing and were, for the most part, banned by the Church. Thus, under the banner of Orthodoxy, which, in fact, concealed an anxiety about, and desire to stifle this secret, unquenchable, ever-threatening fire, the heretics were persecuted from then on with proper exterminating expeditions, in support of which, through an enormous political and religious mistake, the solidarity of the nation-states was sought.

An example was the sadly famous expedition against the Albigenses between 1208 and 1209 brazenly called by Innocent a crusade, encouraged by him, and during which the minds of the crusaders were inflamed with the burning words of St. Dominic of Guzman. It was a crusade of pitiless ferocity against the Christian heretic whom the crusader thought he was fighting as if he were an infidel. Even if the Albigenses had denied the most sacred truths of the Christian religion, such as the use of the sacraments, where the pope's condemnation was obviously sacrosanct, it was wrong to involve the political world in a clearly religious issue. Without a doubt, the vassals of the king of France viewed the crusade simply as an excuse to go to war against the flourishing state of the counts of Toulouse and the pope, when the strictly heretical resistance had been crushed, was unable to restrain the voracious greed of the crusaders Thus even the religious meaning of the expedition vanished. But above all, once Toulouse fell, the Church of Rome would find itself owner of the county of Avignon.

In resisting the religious movements of his times, Innocent was certainly inspired by respect for Orthodoxy while, at the same time, seeking to come to terms with the spirit of poverty and evangelical justice in the name of which the "heretics" were denouncing the Church. His reforms within the Curia and the government of Rome at the beginning of his pontificate may have aimed at ridding the See of Peter the Apostle of its corruption and restoring its former dignity, but it is a fact that in all this Innocent was guided by political necessities which perverted the spirit of purification when he himself used money to reach his aims. He was inexorably trapped by the very ideals to which he was devoted by virtue of the non-evangelical means that were used to attain papal universalism.

In such a program, very little room was left for certain poverty-related factions. Only those were spared who could keep within the limits of the idealisation of a virtuous Christian life, without getting involved in the condemnation of their leaders, and who could adopt a Rule as well as obtain the recognition of their group as a proper religious order within the Church, as it was for the Humiliates, the Poor Catholics and the Penitent Brothers of St. Francis of Assisi. The permission granted to St. Francis to practice penance and to preach, however, "was a decision the significance of which no one at that time could foresee the importance," as Seppelt observes. "Indeed, who could have foretold then that, through the 'Poverello' of Assisi and his foundation, one would see come true what, according to the legend of Thomas of Celano, Innocent III had seen in a dream—a simple, scorned man supporting on his shoulders the collapsing Lateran basilica."

How much more comprehensible, instead, for Innocent was the attitude of St. Dominic. In him the pope found "a positive intellect, determined to apply practical measures to uproot heresy," as Gregorovius notes, "who took advice from the gloomiest heroes of the war against the Albigenses. . . and was a witness to the massacre of a noble people." And, "in the midst of these horrors, faced with which a trembling Francis would have retreated, the Spanish fanatic felt only deep love for the Church, only heartfelt humility, since the sole passion which inspired him was the unshakeable impulse to separate men from beliefs which he considered criminal." For this reason he could only be considered a kind of right hand of the theocratic policy of Innocent III.

In conclusion, this pope was a great man of power who concealed his own intentions through a Christian conquest of the world, celebrating his triumph with the twelfth ecumenical council, the fourth Lateran, which began on 11 November 1215. It included an extraordinary number of participants with more than 70 patriarchs and archbishops, about 400 bishops and 800 abbots, the various ambassadors from European sovereigns, as well as the presence of Frederick II in person. The outcome of the conciliar discussions, published in seventy canon rules which became in their entirety part of the *Corpus iuris canonici*, began with the approval of the term, "transubstantiation," to indicate the transformation of substance in the Eucharist. It went on to impose on Christians to go to confession and receive the Eucharist at least once a year, and to condemn various heretical movements, including the Florensian Congregation of Joachim of Flora who died in 1202 and whose relics were venerated by the faithful in the monastery of St. John in Flora. His prophecy about a third age of the human race, without any Church or State, for a community of believers destined finally to live in an egalitarian and modest society, an indictment chiefly of the hierarchical set-up of the Church, was condemned as heretical.

Finally, the council laid down rules for a new Crusade against the Turks to begin on 1 June 1217. It was to be conducted under the direction of the Church in order to avoid the usual political digressions. Indeed, when the council was over, Innocent III went to northern Italy in the spring of 1216 to settle the disputes between the seaports of Pisa and Genoa and to inculcate in their citizens a strictly religious spirit, so as to avoid the commercial exploitation which had been enacted by Venice during the fourth Crusade.

He died, while on this missionary undertaking, at Perugia on 16 July 1216 and was buried in the cathedral at Perugia. However, in 1890 Leo XIII had his remains transported to the Lateran basilica where a monument was erected to him.

177. HONORIUS III (1216—1227)

Only two days after the death of Innocent III, on 18 July 1216, the College of Cardinals elected at Perugia a new pope, Cardinal Cencio Savelli. A Roman, formerly a canon at St. Mary Major, he had been an administrator of the Holy Roman Church, or more properly a *camerarius*, that is, a chamberlain under Clement III and Celestine III, linking his name to the *Liber Censuum* which we spoke about in the biography of the latter.

Cencio Savelli was consecrated at Perugia on 24 July, the same month as his election, taking the name of Honorius III, but was enthroned in the Lateran only in September, when he was joyously welcomed by the Romans who finally saw a fellow citizen as pope. Cencio Savelli reached the see of Rome at an already advanced age, and maybe had used up the best of himself as a chamberlain. He did not have the energy of his predecessor and did not appear capable of confronting the young Frederick II. A single, impassioned purpose seemed to guide him during his pontificate, the Crusade called for by Innocent III, which he entrusted to Frederick II to carry out.

Excited by this project and aware of the imperial ambitions of the young Hohenstaufen, Honorius thought the best way to involve him in the enterprise would be to confer upon him the imperial crown. However, before the coronation of Innocent III's ward, Honorius consecrated on 9 April 1217, the emperor of the East. It was an unusual occurrence since a pope had never crowned a Byzantine emperor and it took place quite by accident. The French count, Pierre de Courtenay, had been called to the throne of Constantinople as he had married Yolanda, sister of Emperor Henry who had died without heirs. However, the count was crowned in St. Lawrence outside the Walls and not at St. Peter's to distinguish the procedure from that reserved for the emperor of the West. He left Rome with his wife and children on their way to Constantinople, but never made it to the throne as, trying to conquer Durazzo for the Venetians, he ended up in the dungeons of Theodore Angelo, the despot of Epiros, and died there the following year.

Meanwhile, Honorius was urging Frederick to take the initiative for a Crusade. In fact, the grand undertaking that could reunite the whole of Western Christendom, as planned by Innocent III, seemed to be blocked before it started because of the persistent quarrels between France and England. For his part, Frederick had obtained a postponement of the expedition, and while he was alive, Otto IV would not dream of leaving Germany to the mercy of his foe. However, even after the death of the latter in 1218, Frederick again managed to defer the Crusade, while renewing his pledge to the Church, which he never really intended to keep. The Crusade was the last thing on his mind, but Honorius continued to be fooled. Frederick's only concern was to get his hands on Sicily and the empire and this, of course, was going against all the pope's plans.

Indeed, at the Diet of Frankfurt in 1220, unbeknown to Honorius, Frederick had his young son, Henry, elected king of Germany by the German princes. He then hastened to assure the pope that the election had been a decision of the Diet on the spur of the moment and without his knowledge, and only because the German princes did not want anything bad to happen to the succession when he, Frederick, was absent on the Crusade. He also stated that he would soon travel to Rome, and from there go on the Crusade. He reassured the pope that Sicily was unquestionably not part of the empire and, as evidence of his good intentions, he forced the nobles of Tuscany to take the oath of vassalage to the pope in respect of the properties of Countess Matilda.

Persuaded by the crafty Frederick, Honorius offered him the imperial crown, although the situation at Rome was again turbulent, forcing the pope to leave and seek refuge at Viterbo in June 1219, when the Commune took advantage of the new pope's mild ways and tried to regain its former liberty. Frederick, however, intervened with force, making the most of this opportunity to demonstrate his talents as protector of the Church. He sent Abbot Conon of Fulda to Rome as his envoy, to read in public certain letters from the king at the Capitol which ordered the Romans to obey the pope. Senator Parenzo gave assurances that the city would renew its fidelity to Honorius, and eliminated all disputes so that Frederick could be crowned in a peaceful city. The Commune did not have the strength to go against the will of the king, with the result that in October of 1220 Honorius was able to regain his see.

Frederick reached Rome in November, accompanied by his wife, Constance, and pitched camp on Monte Mario. There was a meeting with papal legates and the king sent the pope a written documentation in which he excluded any union of Sicily with the empire, recognizing Sicily as being still a feudal estate of the Church, and also confirming the rights of the Church over the territory of Radicofani at Ceprano, and over Spoleto and Ancona. Thus reassured, Honorius proceeded on 22 November with the solemn imperial coronation of Frederick and his wife.

Three days later, Frederick got round the pope again and obtained a further delay for the Crusade until August 1221, as he wanted to go to Sicily. But since this upset Honorius, the emperor humored him by stopping over at Capua where, in addition to issuing immediately new laws for southern Italy, he reconfirmed to the pope his possession of the lands of Countess Matilda.

However, 1221 also passed without Frederick leaving for that blessed Crusade, as the kingdom of Sicily was in such administrative and military chaos that he had to restructure the government and recoup the royal authority. The task was evidently so difficult that a year would not have been enough. So, in a series of meetings almost annually with the pope, Frederick continued to put off the expedition, charming Honorius with his repeated territorial promises, to which he never fully lived up, so much so that at Spoleto the imperial faction had even thrown out the papal representatives.

In the meantime, Frederick had succeeded in putting a new face to his Italian kingdom, turning it into a well-ordered country where the will of the king was absolute. In 1224 he founded the University of Naples as a purely secular institution for the lay education of the imperial employees. The whole structure of the kingdom was based on a civil concentration of power to the extent that Frederick even took over the assets of five vacant bishoprics and dismissed the papal legates who wanted to install new bishops. His policy was clearly opposed to the Church's, and this way of governing was inevitably destined to go beyond the borders of the southern kingdom, and infiltrate the territory of the Church, creating a following there which would take protective measures against claims from the Lombard cities which refused to respect the rights of the empire as recognized by the Treaty of Constance.

Honorius was, in fact, much too kind a pope and there reigned in the Curia an atmosphere of mistrust not only of Frederick, who kept on making false promises, but also of the pope himself. Frederick, widowed in 1225, had married Isabella who, as the daughter of John of Brienne, was the heiress of the kingdom of Jerusalem. By that marriage the Curia hoped to get the emperor to leave finally with the prospect at least of recovering a kingdom of his overseas. But through his father-in-law, Frederick once again obtained a postponement of the Crusade, on grounds of the hostile attitude of the Lombard Communes which had organized their league. Then, at the Treaty of Saint-Germain in July of that year, in the presence of the papal legates, the emperor swore under pain of excommunication and of the loss of the kingdom of Sicily, which the pope could then dispose of as he wished, that he would depart for the Crusade in August 1227.

It seemed a definite promise this time since it involved terms which otherwise could be fatal for the prestige of the emperor. Moreover, Frederick answered the complaints of the pope about anticlerical behavior in the south by calling a great Diet at Cremona for April 1226 through which, by skirting around the issue, he proposed to make detailed preparations for the crusade, to uproot the heresy that despite all the pope's pressuring continued to spread through northern Italy, and to assert there the rights of the empire.

In the meantime, the pope again had to move out of Rome. Richard Conti had been defrauded by Frederick of the city of Sora and had gone to Rome hoping to obtain the support of a pontiff who could think of nothing but the Crusade. He found support, however, among many of the nobles and from Senator Parenzo, so once again the populace was instigated to riot and the pope fled to Rieti. The emperor, who had just concluded the Treaty of St. Germain with the pope, succeeded in getting him to return to Rome in February 1226 by replacing the anticlerical Parenzo with Angelo de Benincasa, certainly closer to the Savelli family. The pope then entrusted John of Brienne with the government of the papal territory from Viterbo to Rome, thereby assuring himself protection against further revolts and riots.

Meanwhile, the Diet of Cremona did not take place because the Lombard League had blockaded the entrance to Verona, thus preventing the German troops under the command of the emperor's son, Henry, from advancing. Since those troops at Frederick's disposal were not sufficient to change the situation, he returned, disappointed, to the south. From there he issued a ban against the federations and even found complaisant bishops to issue excommunications on his behalf. However all this showed the pope's lack of authority, and Frederick did not want to lose complete contact with Honorius. So he begged him to act as mediator in the dispute with the Lombard Communes and, to show his good will, recalled to Sicily the bishops previously exiled.

Fooled once again by the emperor's behavior, Honorius probably felt he had been finally invested with an authority conversant with his pontifical dignity. He had been called to be the umpire in a dispute between the empire and the Communes and maybe he secretly dreamt of walking in Alexander III's footsteps. So he ordered the Lombards to recognize the supremacy of the emperor by pledging 400 knights who were to serve for two years in the Holy Land, a decree which, in view of its vagueness, carried no weight, and the dispute went on.

Moreover, Honorius III was not the right pope to take on certain political obligations. He was really one dedicated to the religious purpose of his position, and this is to his credit. He zealously supported the rapid diffusion of

Christianity in the countries of northern Europe, such as Denmark, Sweden and Norway, through missionary work that also spread to Poland and Russia. He also exhorted the king of Castille to combat the Arabs, continuing the work of Reconquest.

St. Dominic of Guzmàn obtained the approval of his Order of Preachers in December 1216 and stayed in Rome to carry out the high function of "Master of the Sacred Palace." Francis of Assisi, whose followers had increased substantially, had to renew the Rule which, when submitted to Honorius with the support of Cardinal Ugolino, the future Pope Gergory IX, protector of the Order, received solemn approval in a bull in November 1223. Francis died three years later.

Honorius did not long survive the saint of Assisi. Busy until the end preaching to everyone to participate in the then imminent Crusade, he failed to see the result of his efforts and died on 18 March 1227. He was buried in St. Mary Major.

178. GREGORY IX (1227–1241)

As the successor to the peaceful Honorius III, the College of Cardinals gathered at St. Gregory's elected on 19 March 1227, Cardinal Ugolino, bishop of Ostia. He came from the family of the counts of Segni and was born at Anagni between 1145 and 1150. He had lived through the rule of several popes, and had been able to gain experience at different levels.

Innocent III, a relative of his, had consecrated him a cardinal and he had been a legate in Germany numerous times, becoming a friend of Frederick II. Under Honorius III he had been again a papal legate in northern Italy where, thanks more to his intervention than to that of the pope, he had succeeded in settling many disputes between Guelph and Ghibelline Communes with an energy which led the Curia to hope that it had finally found an authoritarian pope to stand up to the emperor, even if one who was eighty years old. His political talents were accompanied by a great spiritual faith which had led him to emerge as the protector of the Franciscan Order, helping Francis obtain in 1223 Honorius III's approval of the Second Rule.

Consecrated on 21 March 1227 in St. Peter's with the name of Gregory IX, he had written to Frederick three days later to announce his election, reminding him that the deadline for his departure on the Crusade would expire in August without possibility of extension. Gregory's tone was firm but cordial as befits an old friendship. Frederick well knew, however, with whom he was now dealing and had begun serious preparations. Troops had arrived from Germany, but with all the armed forces gathered in July at Brindisi for the embarkation, there were so many that there were too few ships to transport them and the catering was inadequate. An epidemic broke out and Frederick himself was taken ill.

Nevertheless, he sailed off but then had to stop at Otranto and temporarily give up the Crusade because his conditions of health had worsened. He finally withdrew to the baths of Pozzuoli to recover.

He had immediately notified Gregory by messenger of what had happened, but, given the precedents, it was difficult for the pope to believe the story of the illness. Indeed, he was convinced that the emperor had simply found another excuse. So Gregory denounced the non-performance of the Treaty of St. Germain and excommunicated Frederick on 29 September, setting out in an encyclical to all Christendom the lies, the dissolute life and the tyranny of the emperor.

But for once Frederick was not guilty. Let us say that things had gone wrong for him this time and Gregory had perhaps acted too impulsively. In a communication of 6 December, the emperor repeated in a calm tone his "innocence" and announced that he intended to leave in May of the following year. Gregory still did not believe him and repeated the excommunication on 23 March 1228, this time on grounds of his oppression of the Church in Sicily. Faced with the pope's intransigence, some of the nobles, headed by the Frangipane who had been won over by the emperor to his cause, organized a riot five days later in St. Peter's during the Mass while Gregory was preaching a homily against Frederick. The rioters insulted him and forced him to leave the church. There were fights in the streets, and the pope fled first to Viterbo and then to Perugia, where he announced the excommunication of the rebels.

At this point, just to put Gregory in the wrong, Frederick finally embarked on the Crusade, leaving the management of the kingdom to Rinaldo, the former duke of Spoleto. Sailing from Brindisi in June, he recovered Jerusalem and the Holy Places peacefully, and concluded a treaty with the Sultan of Egypt in February of the following year. Crowned king of Jerusalem in the Church of the Holy Sepulcher, he was back in Italy in June 1229.

During his absence, his subjects in the kingdom of Sicily and in the empire had been released from their oath of loyalty but, while in Germany his son Henry had succeeded in stifling an attempt to create an anti-king in the person of the nephew of Otto IV. However, in Italy, Rinaldo had been defeated by papal troops in his attempt to recover his own duchy.

Frederick immediately set about putting down the insurrections in the kingdom with an army which included a lot of Germans who had been on the Crusade, and advanced to the border of the State of the Church. There he stopped, planning to make peace with the pope at a meeting, which, he hoped, would clear the air. Gregory had managed to return to Rome by February 1230, recalled by the population, who seeing the city struck by a flood of the Tiber and prey to starvation, had superstitiously thought it was a sign of divine punishment.

The pope was reluctant to meet Frederick but, because of the latter's successes in the Holy Land, he finally had to agree to the negotiations which produced the Peace Treaty of Ceprano on 23 July 1230. The emperor agreed to submit to the Church on all the points that had provoked the excommunication, to return the property of monasteries and churches, and to recognize the bond of vassalage between Sicily and Rome. On August 28, Frederick was released from the excommunication and on September 1, meeting the pope at Anagni, a friendly relationship between the papacy and the empire was restored.

In fact, it was only a truce. Frederick had not given up his dream of restoring a kind of new Roman empire, the precondition of which was effective control of all Italy. With this in mind he increased the attacks against the Lombard cities to ensure imperial rights in the north, renewed the incursions into the papal State, and promulgated a code of laws for the south, compiled by Piero delle Vigne, which aimed at the establishment of the king's absolute dominion over ecclesiastical property.

The pope could not combat those actions by excommunication since the emperor did not act openly, and the anticlerical moves were always concealed beneath other apparent ones. As an example, in November 1231, at Ravenna, Frederick had issued laws against heretics even more drastic than the existing ones, which Gregory could certainly not complain about, but at the same time the emperor permitted his allies, the Saracens, to devastate a church at Lucera. In these matters he acted from behind the scenes, never in the open. And, when in May 1234, a new uprising of the Romans forced Gregory to escape to Umbria, Frederick ran to help in his role as protector of the Church of Rome. Once the rebels were defeated in October at Viterbo, he was able to put them down definitively and allow the return of Gregory to his see in October 1237.

Indeed, the temporal power of the Church was preserved in Rome only through the help of the emperor and Gregory could only be grateful, compensating the favor as best he could. When Henry, the emperor's son aged 16, rebelled against his father, threatening the imperial throne, Gregory excommunicated him, so his father was able to have him arrested, dethroned and kept in prison until he died in 1242.

After all this, Frederick felt fully justified to do what he felt like and inflicted on the Lombard League a devastating defeat at Cortenuova in 1237. However, no matter how much he cried victory and sent the Cart to Rome as a war trophy, there was no unconditional surrender by the Communes. It simply gave the imperial faction a feeling of euphoria while Gregory fled again to Anagni in July of 1238. However, the former quickly won the battle between the Guelphs and the Ghibellines and the pope was able to return to his see already by October.

At this point, Frederick had thrown off his mask, and the shipment of the Cart to Rome seemed like a declaration of war. Disregarding the Treaty of

Ceprano, he openly instigated the Romans against the pope, imprisoned the papal legates sent to his lands and blocked the appointment of bishops. Obviously, his intention was to destroy the temporal power of the Church when he bestowed on his son, Enzo (who had married the widow of the judge of Torres and Gallura), the title of King of Sardinia, a territory claimed by the papacy on the basis of the Donation of Constantine. The serious danger to the very existence of the State of the Church prompted Gregory to excommunicate Frederick II again in a solemn form on Palm Sunday of 1239.

This new excommunication sparked off a war between the papacy and the empire with a series of invectives from both sides. The one called Gregory a madman, a two-bit prophet, an infidel, a profaner of the temple, the seed of Babylon. The other saw in Frederick the Beast of the *Apocalypse* and a heretic who considered Christ an impostor. As Walter Ullmann notes, "on both fronts, the pamphlets, the manifestos and the encyclicals were masterpieces of style, of substance and of literature. They were no longer learned and pedantic treatises but articles intended to inflame people and to create the appropriate atmosphere for later actions."

This ideological war was accompanied, naturally, by armed battles. Frederick occupied vast areas of the Papal State in order to isolate Rome, while Gregory pushed the Venetians to invade Apulia in a vain effort to block the advance of the enemy from the south, and convened an ecumenical council at Rome for Easter of 1241. Frederick managed to make that impossible, barricading the roads to Rome, hunting out the assembled clergy and taking more than a hundred of them prisoners, including two cardinals and many bishops and archbishops.

The pope did not give up, even under these circumstances. He urged the prisoners to bear their burden with patience, because other dangers were coming for the Church from the East. In those days, in fact, hordes of Mongols had descended upon Europe. Gregory sought to turn the attention of the Christian world to the common peril in front of which everyone had to put aside personal problems and unite in a real crusade. Conrad, king of Germany since 1237, proclaimed in a Diet in May a general peace, accepting the plea of the pope, but the crusade did not take place, while the Mongols, fortunately, halted their advance and returned to their country in December.

Meanwhile, in August the emperor pitched camp at Grottaferrata, having been invited there by Cardinal John Colonna who had openly broken with Gregory. That was a betrayal from within the College of Cardinals, a real blow to the pope, now almost a hundred years old, but still undaunted. Occupation of the city seemed near when, on 22 August 1241, Gregory IX died like "a general who falls into the breach in front of the enemy," according to Gregorovius. "Then messengers flew to Frederick; the pope was dead!" For him this was good news and to show that his enemy was not the Church but only Gregory IX, he lifted the siege of Rome and returned to his own kingdom while the pope was being buried in St. Peter's.

What Seppelt wrote was true. "As pope, Gregory proved to have a dominating nature, was a fearless champion of liberty and of the rights of the Church, had a distinguished bearing, and was outstanding for his unusual energy, persistent and consistent to the point of extreme severity. He was not to be shaken from his faith in God, and was undaunted by difficulties and even peril," as prove the courts of the Inquisition which he set up in 1232 for the repression of heretics, entrusted to the Dominicans by a bull issued on 20 April of that year. The organization of these ill-famed and gloomy courts were probably the result of Gregory's juridical mentality, as was the task given to Raymond of Penafort to collect in a "summa" of five volumes all the papal decrees, commonly called *Liber extra*, which constituted the basis for the *Corpus juris canonici* of Pius X and Benedict XV.

"Nonetheless, this proud leader with his passionate temperament was not unmoved by tender impulses of his heart," Seppelt adds. "There can be no doubt about the sincerity and the depth of his piety, tainted by mysticism. He was linked through admirable veneration and sincere friendship to the major religious figures of his epoch," as for example Francis of Assisi whom he himself canonized in 1228, as well as Anthony of Padua and Dominic of Guzmàn, later raised, again by him, to the honors of the altar.

In his double-sided, energetic personality lies perhaps the keystone of his capacity to oppose Frederick on an equal footing with a Machiavellian ambiguity in keeping with the genial statesman that he was.

179. CELESTINE IV (1241)

The College of Cardinals, which met in the monastery of the Septizonium at Rome to elect a successor to Gregory IX on the day after his death on 22 August 1241, consisted of only twelve members, two of whom had been taken prisoners by Frederick II when he had lifted the siege of the city. The remaining ten were unable to reach agreement on a two-thirds majority, which led to endless bickering between the Gregorians and the moderates.

The senator in charge, Matteo Rosso, who had shut them in the Septizonium determined not to let them out until they had elected a new pope, made them come to an agreement and, in a technical sense, this gave birth to the first conclave in history. The unforeseen situation in which the cardinals found themselves had not allowed them to prepare the room for a "retreat" that could have lasted a long time. The hygienic conditions soon became intolerable because of the odor of excrement, and one of the cardinals died. Nevertheless, the nine survivors still could not find an agreement on a suitable new pope, and it was only when the senator threatened to exhume the corpse of Gregory IX and show it to the Romans dressed in papal vestments, that the decision was finally made, although it was simply a solution to escape from the forced seclusion.

On 25 October 1241, they unanimously elected Geoffrey Castiglioni, bishop of Sabina, a sickly old man from Milan, who was nephew of Urban III and formerly a monk at the monastery of Altacomba, where he had written a history of the kingdom of Scotland before being elevated to cardinal with St. Mark's as his titular church.

The other eight cardinals, aware that the newly-elected pope would certainly not live long and terrified at the idea of having to return there soon under lock and key, departed from Rome without waiting for his consecration.

Castiglioni took his seat in the Lateran on 28 October, assuming the name of Celestine IV, but he passed away seventeen days after his election, on November 10 without ever having been consecrated. The *Annuario pontificio* nonetheless lists him as pope.

180. INNOCENT IV (1243–1254)

Following the death of Celestine IV there were two years of vacant see, which was understandable with the lack of security in Rome, menaced with a siege by Frederick II, and with the attempts by the cardinals to obtain the release of their two colleagues, still the emperor's prisoners, for whose liberation severe conditions had been imposed. The eight veterans of the conclave of 1241, meeting at Anagni beginning in February 1242, after much negotiating eventually succeeded in coming to an agreement with Frederick. In other words, he showed his magnanimity by releasing the two cardinals who were able in June to join the Sacred College and proceed with a new election.

On 25 June 1243, they unanimously elected Sinibaldo Fieschi. Born in Genoa around 1195, formerly a magistrate in the Curia at the time of Honorius III and later the vice-chancellor of the Church, he had been made cardinal by Gregory IX, with a titular church San Lorenzo in Lucina. He was consecrated at Anagni on June 28 and took the name of Innocent IV.

Frederick II wrote to him from Melfi to congratulate him, embellishing the letter with praise of his Genoese family, traditionally devoted to the empire. Innocent was not fooled by these words and showed his determination by immediately sending the emperor a delegation headed by Cardinal Otto with a peremptory demand for the release of all the prelates who were still prisoners.

Furthermore, Frederick was informed that the excommunication against him was still in force and was invited to show his good will in order to be readmitted to the bosom of the Church, the pope reserving himself the right to look into the question during a council. For his part, Frederick put forward a series of justifications and complaints but had no intention of including the problem of the Lombard Communes in the negotiations. An understanding was possible regarding the respect of papal rights on its own lands, in order, amongst other things, to allow a peaceful enthroning of Innocent in Rome.

Notwithstanding their disagreements, the negotiations were not broken off, though to threaten their conclusion was an incident provoked by Cardinal Ranieri, a battling enemy of the Swabians. He fomented a revolt in Viterbo, a city faithful to Frederick and controlled by a garrison of his which had to barricade itself in the castle while the majority of the citizens and the pontifical troops led by Ranieri occupied the rest of the city.

Frederick immediately set siege to Viterbo but was not able to conquer it. Cardinal Otto convinced him to desist by personally guaranteeing the safety of the garrison, but Ranieri, wanting to get to the root of the matter, attacked and ill-treated the imperial troops. Innocent himself condemned the cardinal's shameful conduct and threatened Viterbo with ecclesiastic censure, but the prisoners were not released. To the emperor's renewed protests, the pope pointed out that in fact Viterbo was a city that still formed part of the State of the Church. So the negotiations ended in an agreement that was signed and sworn to by the imperial plenipotentiaries at the Lateran to which Innocent had been able to return on 31 March 1244. By this agreement Frederick II guaranteed the immunity of the pope's supporters and the restitution of the Church's assets, the essential condition for lifting the excommunication. But the issue of the emperor's rights in Lombardy had not been settled, and that was the precarious element in the conditions, which shortly led to a breakdown of peace negotiations.

In fact, when Frederick's ambassadors came to the pope to learn the penance which the emperor had to do to obtain the lifting of the excommunication, the reply was that the first and decisive condition was the immediate restitution of the State of the Church. The imperial delegation obviously refused that, but Frederick himself sought to resolve it by proposing to the pope the immediate return of a part of the lands, begging him, however, to settle the matter in a personal meeting with him.

Innocent accepted and journeyed to Narni, since the emperor had taken up residence at Terni, then went on to Civitacastellana, preferring to send Cardinal Otto to Terni to test the ground. In reality, the crux of the problem was the restoration of imperial power in Lombardy, to which Frederick would not renounce but which appeared to the pope a mortal peril in terms of the liberty of the Church and to his own security, caught between two fires in a mainly "imperial" Italy.

So, Innocent IV suddenly decided to break off all talks and to declare war against Frederick, seeking allies beyond the Alps. On 27 June he left

Civitacastellana and, in disguise, reached Civitavecchia where Genoese ships were waiting for him. Sailing on June 30, he reached Genoa but illness kept him there until the beginning of October, after which he continued on to Lyon where he had decided to convene an ecumenical council for June 1245 to put Frederick II on trial.

Meanwhile, in August 1244, Jerusalem had fallen again into the hands of the Turks. The patriarch, Albert of Antioch, hoping to bring peace between the pope and the emperor with whom he was on friendly terms, and to produce a climate favorable to another crusade, became the mediator for a resumption of negotiations. However, Frederick ruined everything when his troops invaded the State of the Church and again besieged Viterbo. The patriarch of Antioch, who had successfully obtained from Innocent a promise to remove the excommunication, put pressure on Frederick to lift the siege. Frederick did so but Cardinal Ranieri, who acted in Italy as the pontifical governor of the State of the Church, immediately denounced what had happened to the pope who then backed down and left the whole matter to the council to sort out. The thirteenth ecumenical council opened at Lyons on 28 June 1245, but the attending prelates were mainly Spanish and French, with a few Englishmen. The principal item on the agenda was Frederick II's position, represented and defended by Judge Thaddeus of Suessa. On July 17, Frederick was excommunicated and deposed as emperor, condemned as a heretic for having violated his oath of vassalage to the pope, and for holding as prisoners the prelates who were on their way to Rome for the council convened by Gregory IX. Frederick's German and Italian subjects were absolved from their oaths of loyalty, and the electoral college of Germans received orders to proceed to a new election.

The deposing of Frederick made a tremendous impression on the Europe of that period, and the ex-emperor's Chancellery was extremely busy in sending edicts and appeals to all Christendom to rise up against the Anti-Christ represented by Innocent IV. The atmosphere of ideological and military warfare, which had characterized the struggle between Frederick and Gregory IX, was back again, while the king of France vainly sought to mediate.

In Germany, the new king, Henry Raspe, managed to defeat Frederick's son, Conrad, but he died in February 1247, while chaos reigned in Sicily, with continual plots and uprisings. The emperor was roving around northern Italy where he could count upon Ezzelino da Romano and his son, Enzo, but his life was always at risk what with the Communes in constant ferment. He was able to lay siege to Parma, but on 18 February 1248 the besieged people managed to come out of the city and destroy the enormous tent city of Vittoria erected by the emperor near the town. In the skirmishes, Thaddeus of Suessa died and Frederick only saved himself with difficulty, finding refuge near Cremona. In May of the following year, he also lost the help of Enzo, who was defeated and taken prisoner during the battle of Fossalta by the citizens of Bologna. At that point, he left for the south where, distrusting everyone, he even had the chancellor, Pier delle Vigne, blinded because he thought him guilty of secret dealings with the pope, and imprisoned the guiltless jurist who then killed himself. Dante Alighieri recalls the story in his *Inferno* (XIII, 58–78).

Frederick was now all alone and even the news of Ezzelino's victories in the north did not excite him. On 13 December 1250 he died at Fiorentino in Apulia at the age of 56. Just as he had rejoiced at the death of Gregory IX, now it was the pope who showed his own happiness over the death of the "sworn enemy of the Christian Church" in letters to European monarchs which became famous for their contemptuous tone concerning the deceased emperor, not very dignified for the vicar of Christ on Earth.

Innocent IV departed from Lyons after Easter 1251, and by the beginning of November he was in Perugia where he remained for a year and a half. Now he had to prepare for the struggle with the heirs of Frederick II, Conrad IV in Germany, and in Apulia, Manfred, the son born from the relationship of the emperor with Countess Bianca Lancia, who was acting as his half-brother's representative in Italy. The pope was determined to take over the kingdom of Sicily as part of the State of the Church (hereinafter, Papal State), and to squash any Swabian claim. When King Conrad came down from Germany to Sicily in October 1251 and received sovereign power over the kingdom of southern Italy, without encountering any resistance from his half-brother Manfred to whom he conceded merely the princedom of Taranto, the pope clearly refused Conrad's ambassadors any recognition of him either as king of Sicily or as emperor.

It was then that Innocent, realizing that he could not stand up to Swabian power with his own military and financial resources, thought of entrusting the conquest of the kingdom of Sicily to a foreign prince. As earlier dealings with Charles of Anjou had not worked out, Cardinal Ottobono Fieschi, his nephew and future pope Hadrian V, reached an agreement in 1253 with Henry III of England for the investiture of Sicily in his nine-year-old-son, Prince Edward.

Conrad IV, accused of committing abuses against the Church, was excommunicated in April 1254, and Innocent IV then officially conferred the investiture of the feudal estate of Sicily upon the English prince on May 14. But Conrad IV suddenly died eleven days later at the age of only twenty-six so the agreement was put aside pending developments, since by his will Conrad had put his two-year-old son, Conrad, in the custody of the Church, entrusting the pope personally with his care as presumptive heir to the throne of Sicily. Innocent IV needed to learn the reaction of Manfred to this, so he travelled to Anagni near the border of the Papal States where he received a German delegation led by Manfred himself who officially requested the recognition of little Conrad. The pope declared that he would take the possible rights of the

Swabian infant into consideration when he would reach majority, but that for the moment he insisted on the immediate handover of the kingdom, based on the guardianship which had been bestowed on him by Conrad. Manfred, who submitted to the pope's wishes without any reservations, probably in order to gain time and to avoid the danger of investiture of Prince Edward, was named Papal Vicar in the south and given the feudal estate of Taranto.

Innocent IV had finally reached the objective of his policies. He was to all effects the sovereign of southern Italy and did not hesitate to leave for the South to take possession of it. Suddenly, but only briefly, the Papal States had become very large, larger than it would ever be, stretching from Tuscany to Sicily. During his journey toward Naples, Innocent passed through exultant crowds, and he received splendid tributes when he arrived in the city of Parthenope on 27 October 1254. He had already issued instructions for the installation of papal administration, including grants of independence to certain cities, while distributing privileges and favors for the prompt setting up of papal sovereignty, when he learned that Manfred was scheming behind his back in Apulia. He was organizing riots but, more important, he had taken into his own service the militia of Saracens, still faithful to his father. The papal army set up resistance at Foggia, but there it was defeated on 2 December.

The bad news reached Innocent while sick in his bed in the palace of Pier delle Vigne at Naples. He died five days later on 7 December 1254. At first he was buried in the church of St. Restituta, but his remains were finally moved into an impressive funeral monument erected for him in 1318 in the cathedral of St. Gennaro.

He was essentially a politician and, even if for only a few days, he did witness the realization of the dream of some of his predecessors. Clearly, though, his behavior toward the last of the Swabians appears imprudent, and the decision to abandon a pro-German policy needed more cohesiveness in order to handle the complexity of the many kingdoms and princedoms with which the pope, by then alone and without the emperor, was getting entangled.

Along with the empire, the political power of the papacy was beginning to decline within the European context and with it the universal significance of the Church's Christian message risked being compromised. Evidence of this was the appeal addressed from Lyons in 1243 to all nations for a new crusade, but accepted only by the French king, Louis IX, with an expedition which turned into a disaster, while the cry for a crusade against the Mongols was entirely ignored. More productive was the missionary activity of the two great Orders, the Franciscans and the Dominicans from eastern Europe to the Caracorum through a series of evangelically motivated initiatives. An indelible black mark remains, however, in the bull *Ad extirpanda*, issued in 1252, in which Innocent IV allowed the Inquisition to use methods of torture.

1 8 1. ALEXANDER IV (1 2 5 4 – 1 2 6 1)

The cardinals gathered to elect a successor in Naples, the very city where Innocent IV had died, and after only seven days unanimously chose Rinaldo from the Conti family of Segni, a native of Jenne near Anagni and the son of a sister of Gregory IX. His own uncle had made him a cardinal-deacon and later bishop of Ostia. He was consecrated on 20 December 1254, with the name of Alexander IV.

From the earliest days of his pontificate, it was clear that he was not capable of dealing with the political situation. Gregorovius's portrait of him is probably correct: "A pope who did not care about wars, a paunchy and good-natured fellow, equitable and God-fearing, but also weak and greedy." One can well understand how complex the political picture must have appeared to him and, "endowed with mediocre intelligence, the new pope tried to move ahead on the perilous path laid out by Innocent IV," entering into this labyrinth without Ariadne's string to help him escape.

Not knowing how to handle Manfred, whom he excommunicated, he made proposals to half of Europe in the space of one year. On the one hand he tried to set aside the inheritance rights of little Conrad, assigning in February 1255 the duchy of Swabia to Alphonso X of Castille, the nephew of the deceased king of Germany, Philip, and favoring as candidates for the kingdom of Germany, first William of Holland then, when he died in January 1256, Richard of Cornwall. On the other, on 9 April 1255, he revalidated the contract previously signed by Innocent IV and Henry III, king of England, and temporarily set aside, which invested Prince Edward with the kingdom of Sicily. This contract which carried with it a down payment on the feudal estate, for which Henry III used the tithes of the English Church, gave the pope the necessary funds to pursue a futile war against Manfred, one that turned into another disaster for the papal army.

This defeat led to open opposition in England to the agreement with the pope and, faced with a revolt instigated by ecclesiastical circles, the king had to give up any thought of a military conquest of the kingdom of Sicily. The contract was broken and Manfred was free to undertake vaster projects without objections on the part of the pope.

Indeed, Alexander IV assisted helplessly at the failure of the anti-Swabian policy which the papacy had until then pursued, letting loose territories of the Papal States and the pope's sovereignty in Rome. Senator Brancaleone of the Andalo family from Bologna governed the city alone, supported by the middle class in a revival of republicanism. It was only in November of 1255 that the Roman nobility managed to do away with his sole governorship and resume that of having two senators. Then, for a brief period, the pope was able to return to Rome. But new bloody battles broke out in which the senator elected by the nobles was also killed and Brancaleone, on the people's side, restored his power by strong measures. The pope fled again from Rome to Anagni and from there to Viterbo, while Brancaleone took his revenge against the nobles by destroying about 140 of the city's fine towers.

Meanwhile Manfred, who had consolidated his power over a united Sicily and in southern Italy, had no intention to act as the regent for the little Conrad who lived far away in Germany, and apparently repudiated by the pope as his "godchild." Manfred even spread a rumor that the child had died and, on 10 August 1258, getting himself elected king by the Parliament of Palermo, was both crowned and anointed by various archbishops.

Alexander IV declared Manfred's coronation null and void because he had been excommunicated, and issued the anathema against the archbishops in question. However, the Ghibelline reaction throughout Italy was so strong that the pope had no idea how to get out of the situation. The Guelph Communes were left to their own devices, and in Tuscany they were defeated at the famous battle of Montaperti in 1260. Vast areas of the Papal States came under the control of Manfred, from the Marches of Ancona to the duchy of Spoleto and Romagna, and even the anti-Swabian northern Italy bowed before his lordship.

At Rome, with Brancaleone dead and his uncle's temporary senatorship terminated, the nobles who appointed two senators from their own faction did not look with favor on a return of the pope, and the elections of 1261 were the scene of an open battle between the Guelphs and the Ghibellines. The former, with the support of the College of Cardinals, succeeded in electing a senator for life, Richard of Cornwall, previously elected king of Germany, while to oppose him the Ghibellines chose Manfred. Once again, the pope showed his ineptitude and decided to leave his see and return to Viterbo. There he would end his not very edifying pontificate, notable on a strictly religious level for the recognition in a bull of the reality of the stigmata of St. Francis of Assisi and threatening to excommunicate those who might deny it, and also for the canonization of St. Clare.

He died in Viterbo on 25 May 1261, and was buried in the church of San Lorenzo in the same city.

182. Urban IV (1261–1264)

Meeting in Viterbo after the death of Alexander IV, the cardinals took three months to find a successor, and since they could not reach a majority in favor of one of their own members, they finally agreed, on 20 August 1261, upon someone not from the Sacred College, a Frenchman named Jacques Pantaleon, patriarch of Jerusalem, who happened to be at the Curia for discussions regarding the Holy Land.

He came from humble origins and was the son of a shoemaker from Troyes, where he was born around 1200. He had studied in Paris, been a canon at Lyons and an archdeacon at Liège. Innocent IV had appointed him bishop of Verdun and papal legate in Germany, where he was esteemed for his notable activity on religious and diplomatic levels, and he was sufficiently capable and trustworthy for Alexander IV to have made him the patriarch of Jerusalem in the Holy Land. He was consecrated as pope on September 4 at Viterbo and took the name of Urban IV. He was never to set foot in Rome.

The election of a Frenchman signified new political relationships for the papacy, as already foreseen with Alexander IV. However, the most urgent problem came from Rome, where the Guelphs had proposed Richard of Cornwall for the post of senator and the Ghibellines, Manfred. There were, of course, public skirmishes of armed men between the two factions which the pope was able to control only from a distance, and, while there was a kind of "vacant see" in the Senate, a mixed committee governed the Commune for more than a year. Meanwhile, Manfred officially proposed his own candidacy as king of Sicily with an attractive proposal, both financially with an annual feudal tribute and politically by territorial recognitions and concrete support for a new crusade in the Holy Land. But by then, quite apart from the doubts concerning the sincerity of Manfred's proposals, the Curia had political designs which went far beyond the Swabian dynasty. Urban IV again contacted the brother of the king of France, Charles of Anjou, with a view to granting the crown of Sicily to him. As a result, the Guelphs in Rome abandoned the candidacy of Richard and supported that of the French count, succeeding in having him appointed senator for life in the summer of 1263, though without communicating the election results officially to the pope.

Urban IV was at Orvieto but, in any case, he had no civil authority in Rome, having lost the Senate's investiture at the time of Brancaleone. However, it was all a double game by Charles who, while dealing with the Romans, had at the same time accepted the feudal investiture of Sicily. The pope was upset but, faced with the danger of Manfred's enthronement, accepted the "fait accompli" and annulled the clause which precluded the count of Anjou from assuming the position of Senator in the agreements being negotiated regarding the investiture. However, he did successfully insist that this would be for no more than five years, and would cease the moment Charles conquered the kingdom of Sicily, after which, the pope would again have the power to assign the senatorial nomination. Non-fulfilment of these engagements would bring excommunication, interdiction and the loss of the feudal estate. Moreover, the feudal tribute would be reduced to 2,000 ounces of gold per year and consideration would be given to the possibility of full or partial remission of the 50,000 pounds sterling requested by the Church after the conquest. The contract was signed on 15 August 1264.

Charles of Anjou accepted the appointment as senator but did not immediately take up the position. As his representative, he sent to Rome Jacques
Gaucelin, with a contingent of horsemen from Provence who installed himself in the Capitol as from May 1264. When Gaucelin died shortly thereafter,
Jacques Gantelme, with the backing of John Savelli, took his post, and a last
minute attempt by the Ghibellines to take over the Commune failed. Manfred
himself plotted an attack on the pope at Orvieto but had to pull up short
before blockades, installed by Guelph bishops and barons at strategic points
throughout Latium.

All the same, Urban, felt insecure since the contract for the payment of the
tithes which would finance the Sicilian enterprise for three years had yet to
receive the approval of the French bishops. Moreover, the German situation
appeared chaotic and the pope could not make up his mind between the two
pretenders to the crown, Alphonso of Castille and Richard of Cornwall. So he
put off any decision until November 1265, simply recognizing both of them as
"pre-selected kings of the Romans," even if Richard had already been crowned
as king of Germany at Aachen in 1257.

Urban spent the final months of his pontificate fruitlessly awaiting the ratification of the contract by Charles of Anjou and, above all, his arrival in Rome to
take up the position of senator which would assure the pope of his enthronement in the Lateran. So he continued to urge the count to hasten his arrival,
while he pursued the strictly religious task of introducing into the liturgy the
Feast of Corpus Domini, already the subject of a special cult at Liège because of
visions seen there by the Augustinian nun, Juliana. Thomas Aquinas received the
assignment to draw up the religious function with a series of hymns, but the full
liturgical installation of Corpus Domini did not take place because of the pope's
death. This installation would happen at the council of Vienne in 1311 with the
renewal of the Bull of Introduction by Urban IV.

And so this pope died without seeing any of his initiatives come to fruition.
On 9 September 1264 he left Orvieto for fear of a Ghibelline invasion and, dur-
ing the journey to Perugia, fell seriously ill and died there on October 2. Like
Innocent III, he was buried in the cathedral of Perugia.

1 8 3. CLEMENT IV (1 2 6 5 — 1 2 6 8)

After the death of Urban IV there was a four-month period of vacant see, the
time it took the College of Cardinals meeting in Perugia to find a successor. The
choice fell again on a Frenchman, Guy Foulques, born in St. Gilles near Nimes
in Provence, so in effect a subject of Charles of Anjou, which showed the strictly
political slant of the election.

Before becoming a Carthusian monk he had been married, and he was the
father of two children. A famous lawyer and a secret counsellor to the king of

France and renowned for his diplomatic skills, he had withdrawn to a monastery to show his contempt for the world when his wife had died. However, his political and executive gifts could not be ignored by the Church, so he was first appointed bishop of Le Puy, then archbishop of Narbonne and finally raised to the cardinalate by Urban IV as the bishop of Santa Sabina. Urban also put him in charge of several legations. When he was elected on 5 February 1265, he was in France returning from a mission in England and, given the perilous situation for high French prelates in Italy, he was only able to reach Perugia disguised as a monk. There he was consecrated on 15 February with the name of Clement IV.

To this pope fell the task of concluding the final contract of the Church with Charles of Anjou. In fact, a few days after his coronation, he gave new instructions to Cardinal Simon de Brion, who meanwhile had obtained the French bishops's approval of the grant of the tithes to finance the Sicilian undertaking. He insisted that the count of Anjou intervene immediately in Rome, but since the whole expedition involved substantial costs, Charles wanted to be able to rely on a solid financial base before arriving in Italy. The pope was therefore forced to request contributions also from the bishops of England and Scotland who had already given funds for the investiture of Prince Edward, subsequently postponed. In Rome, moreover, the situation was growing more dangerous for the Guelphs because the Ghibellines, who had left the city, were secretly returning to stir up trouble. So the Guelph nobility begged Clement IV to put pressure on Charles since further delay could well endanger their situation in Rome.

In April 1265, Charles finally decided to leave by sea to avoid a battle against the Ghibellines in northern Italy and a storm, fortunately for him, pushed Manfred's fleet out to sea. The French count moored his ship at Ostia where the Guelphs joyously welcomed him on May 21. He entered Rome two days later through Porta San Paolo and took his residence in the Lateran rather than in the Capitol. That was slap in the face that Clement, even though away in Perugia, could not take lying down. He wrote a letter pointing out that it would be a good idea to make up for the discourtesy by immediately vacating the papal palace, and reminding Charles that he was always a "creature" in the hands of the pope who knew him well, and that he should move to the palace of the Quattro Coronati on the Celian hill, as it would be undignified for him to go to the Capitol where his representative was in residence.

Once these residential problems had been resolved, significant only in terms of their respective dignities, on 21 June 1265, Charles received the symbols of a senator in the monastery of Aracoeli and, on the 28th of the same month, the investiture of the crown of Sicily. The ceremony took place in the Lateran basilica and was celebrated by four cardinals authorized by the pope. The senator took the oath of vassalage to the Church and received the banner of St. Peter as the symbol of the investiture. He was to return the senatorial authority to the pope as soon as the conquest of all southern Italy had been completed.

But he still had to have an army, and to get one more money was needed. So Clement undertook to raise it by preaching for a kind of crusade against the heretic and excommunicated Manfred, since the Swabian was being supported by the Saracens. The funds for the conquest of Sicily, as Gregorovius puts it, were "scraped together, in the real sense of the term, from alms and loans from usurers." So much so that the pope wrote to Charles, who was bombarding him with requests for money: "How can a pope, other than through unworthy methods, raise troops and money for both himself and others?" Indeed, to get a loan of 30,000 pounds from Roman merchants, Clement had to take out a mortgage on the Church's assets in Rome. An "Institute for Religious Works," something yet to come, would have spared the Holy see this sort of humiliation, even if involving it in a capitalistic system no less embarrassing to its evangelical dignity.

At the end of December 1265, an army of 30,000 men, made up for the most part of adventurers seeking booty but decorated by the pope himself with the sign of the crusaders, arrived in Rome from France. The Lombard cities had helped their advance, which the Ghibellines in Tuscany had been unable to oppose, since the troops had circled around them by passing through the Marches of Ancona and Umbria. On 6 January 1266, in St. Peter's, Charles was crowned king of Sicily with his wife Beatrice by five cardinals duly empowered by the pope, and on the twentieth of the same month he left Rome at the head of his army.

By the 26 February the outcome of the war had already been decided. Manfred was defeated at Benevento, and died on the battlefield. Charles of Anjou had him buried under a cairn near the bridge at Benevento. However, the archbishop of Potenza, Bartholomew Pignatelli, by order of the pope, had his remains exhumed and carried outside the kingdom to the banks of the Liri, leaving them to the mercy of the elements, as Dante himself records in his *Purgatory*, because he died while excommunicated. The poet imagines, in lines which are still famous, that the Swabian king repented at the last moment, asserting a divine mercy considerably more valid than any condemnation by the pope (III, 121–135):

> Horrible were my transgressions;
> but infinite goodness hath such wide arms
> that it accepteth all that turn to it.
> If Cosenza's Pastor, who to chase me was sent by Clement,
> then had well read that page in God,
> the bones of my body would yet be at the bridgehead near
> Benevento,
> under the guard of the heavy cairn.
> Now the rain washes them, and the wind stirs them, beyond
> the Realm,

Hard by the Verde, whither he translated them with tapers
quenched.
By curse of theirs man is not so lost that eternal love
may not return,
so long as hope retaineth aught of green.
(The Carlyle-Wicksteed translation)

Charles of Anjou entered Naples triumphantly, acclaimed by the populace
and the nobles. Clement IV heard the news with great pleasure but was to learn
quickly that Charles was not a docile man ready to submit to his every wish, In
fact, Charles began by retaining the dignity of senator in Rome, which he was
to renounce only at the end of May, and by not helping the pope in the slightest
way to enter Rome and install himself in the Lateran.

The Romans elected two senators and requested back the funds advanced to
Clement for the military campaign, while Charles thought only about collecting
as much as he could and burdening with taxes all his new subjects, pillaging even
the lands belonging to the Church. Deaf to all papal remonstrations and paying
no attention to the contract, he showed a thirst for ownership even greater than
the Swabian, and the Curia began to think it had gone from the frying pan into
the fire. However, they had to make the best of a bad situation, as the struggle
against the Swabians appeared in no way finished when out of Germany
appeared Conradin, who had just reached his majority.

He had himself proclaimed king of Sicily, and many German princes took
his side. In particular, Prince Henry of Castille, brother of Alphonso of
Castille who was the pretender to the throne of Germany, offered to be his
ally. A personal enemy of his cousin, Charles of Anjou, Henry had been
elected sole senator in Rome in June 1267 in a restored democratic republic
which represented a return of Ghibelline spirit in the city. The young Swabian
thus planned a new expedition to take back the Italian kingdom, the rights
to which he was asserting even though, in October 1266, Clement had
already brought a legal action against him in Viterbo, issuing at the same time
a bull in which he forbade the princes of Germany to elect Conradin king,
and threatening to excommunicate his followers.

In the spring of 1267, the Ghibellines of Tuscany called for the intervention
in Italy by the young prince, to whom the pope, on the other hand, sent a summons ordering him to appear in court. The excommunication issued against him
had no apparent effect. The danger began to take on alarming proportions, and
Charles decided on a military move outside his own kingdom. He attacked
Tuscany and conquered Florence. The pope reluctantly entrusted him with the
government of Tuscany for six years with the title of Restorer of Peace, and at
the same time confirmed him as reinstituted in the position of Roman Senator,
which he had abandoned two years earlier, even if, for Charles, it was absurd to
hope to re-enter Rome where his cousin, Henry, ruled without opposition.

A series of rebellions broke out in Sicily and Apulia, and Conradin was acclaimed king. It appeared that the focal point for a possible military attack against the Angevin kingdom would be Rome, so Charles advised the pope to stir up disorder in the city to overthrow Henry, but Clement could not find sufficient support for his schemes. Conradin was already at Verona in October 1267, and by mid-January of the following year he left for Rome in forced marches. Charles left Tuscany and decided to return to the south and wait for the battle there.

But first, he met with the pope in Viterbo, where the latter renewed the excommunication of the Swabian, extending it to all the Ghibelline leaders. He also threatened Rome with interdiction if Henry did not leave his position to Charles of Anjou within one month. But these were all last minute attempts by the pope and his vassal, destined to vanish into nothing.

The Ghibellines woke up in a Tuscany abandoned by Charles, and Conradin arrived in Pisa in April. A month later he continued towards Rome, undisturbed, and reached it in July, greeted with joy by the population. With Henry he organized the assembly of their troops, the main body of which was to be at Alba Fucezia near the Salto River close to Lake Fucino. And that was where the decisive battle against the army of Charles of Anjou took place on 23 August 1268, in the area near Tagliacozzo.

Defeated, Conradin fled towards Rome with Frederick of Austria and the rest of those faithful to him, but did not find the welcome he had expected. The Ghibellines were terrified, and the Guelphs were getting the upper hand. The Swabian prince continued his flight toward the coast, embarking at Astura near Nettuno. However, John Frangipane, the local lord, stopped him out at sea and brought him back to the mainland, imprisoning him and his followers in the castle of Astura. Then he delivered him to Charles of Anjou who summarily tried him for "lèse majesté" and had him executed in the Market Square in Naples. The only one of his followers who was spared was Henry of Castille, out of respect for the royal house of Spain, but he remained in jail until 1291. Although they were absolved of the excommunication, the pope denied Conradin and his companions a religious funeral.

Clement IV died in Viterbo a month later, on 29 November 1268, without having resolved the ten-year-old papal uncertainty concerning the choice between the two pretenders to the crown of Germany, Richard of Cornwall and Alphonso of Castille, and without ever having been able to occupy the see of Rome. As of 15 September Charles had resumed his senatorial position, placing his faithful officials in the Capitol, totally unconcerned about putting the pope back on the throne of Peter. With his ten-year tenure as senator, he dreamed about a future in which there was no room for a pope.

Clement IV, who, as a layman and a Frenchman, had served the king of France, now as pope supported the brother of his former sovereign. His illusion, ingenuous but sincere, that Charles would be able to act in the interest of the Church seemed to indicate that, as pope, he was motivated by an unquestioning patriotic attitude since the pro-French policy of the papacy had reached its apex with him. The Papal State was in a situation of desolate abandonment, and now there was a false vassal(Charles)was running Rome who was, possibly, even thinking of inflicting the insult of three years earlier by taking up residence at the Lateran. In this way he could savor once more the pleasure of the offense he had caused the Roman pontiff.

Clement IV was buried at Viterbo in the church of St. Francis.

184. GREGORY X (1271—1276)

The death of Clement IV led to a vacant see period of nearly three years, the longest ever. The eighteen cardinals gathered in the Papal Palace at Viterbo could not reach an agreement to counterbalance the influence of Charles of Anjou's partisans. This majority faction, though without the prescribed two-thirds majority, wanted to restore the empire, still without an emperor, so as to cut down the Angevin pretensions that had proved of little good for the papacy still forced to reside elsewhere than in Rome.

The sessions went on while rioting continued within the city. The one group, led by the Franciscan Bonaventure from Bagnoregio, decided in January 1270 to sequester the cardinals in the bishop's palace. All the exits were walled up and the Savelli nobles organized a guard service which would become traditional and known as "marshals of the conclave," an honor to be inherited subsequently by the Chigi family.

The cardinals gave no indication of ending their dispute, so the people of Viterbo took the roof off the palace at the end of May. As Giancarlo Zizola notes, "it was a stroke of genius, the definitive sign of the people's timeless revolt against every palace which asserted a monopoly over truth, the running of history, the imprisonment of the conscience, the possession of God. The palace was roofless. It rained inside. The sun shone inside only at noon. The masses complained loudly. The fresh air and the breeze disturbed the discussions of the cardinals, undermining the diplomacy. There was no more extra-territoriality, no more 'summit.' Only bread and water arrived from outside. Two cardinals felt sick, while the others delegated the election to six of their brethren." But it was not merely their contingent precariousness which induced the College of Cardinals to reach a compromise.

To resolve the situation was the news from the whole peninsula that Charles of Anjou was acting as the master of Rome, coining money and enacting laws for his personal advantage and to the detriment of ecclesiastical benefices. In addition, his tyrannical activity carried on throughout central Italy had brought on a Ghibelline reaction in Lombardy. In Genoa, the Guelph government fell, and William of Monferrat, a friend of Charles up to that point, became the leader of a group of Ghibellines supporting the claims of Frederick of Thuringia in opposition to Alphonso of Castille.

On 1 September 1271, the six designated cardinals who could also choose someone from outside the Sacred College finally gave their verdict. In spite of Charles, they elected an Italian, Teobaldo Visconti, born in Piacenza around 1210, an archdeacon at Liège and an expert on the secular affairs of the Church. However, the new pope was at Acre in Syria following the English crusade of Edward, and it would take him four months to return after he had received the news. In fact, it was only on 1 January 1272, that he disembarked at Brindisi, from whence he was transported to Viterbo and, on 13 March, arrived in Rome accompanied by King Charles, who was evidently unwilling to give up his position. Finally after twenty years, a pope had returned to his own see.

Teobaldo was consecrated in St. Peter's on 27 March 1272, with the name of Gregory X.

When the new pope ascended the throne it seemed that the aim pursued by his predecessors had been attained, with Sicily again a papal fief under a new dynasty, and a symbol of that authority both civil and religious through which the papacy wanted to express its own universal character. Yet, Gregory X was aware that he was alone. Charles had not turned out to be exactly the good vassal that the Church had hoped for, but a dangerous and bothersome protector. So the idea took shape in the pope's thoughts that the empire should arise again, as, without it, the Church no longer had an alter ego to support the restructuring of its State and upon whose shoulders it could at the same time unload its own power.

Gregory therefore immediately took on the task of making the Holy Roman empire arise from the ruins. Indeed, following Richard of Cornwall's death a few days after his consecration, Alphonso of Castille had expected to get the imperial crown, but Gregory let him know that his claims were unfounded and rejected them. At the same time, he ordered the German electoral college to proceed with an election within a determined period, threatening otherwise to transfer the empire to the French. So the assembly of the German nobles met at Frankfurt on 23 September 1273, and elected Count Rudolph of Habsburg, who was crowned at Aachen on 24 October by the archbishop of Cologne.

The new king hastened to send his chancellor, Otto of Speyr, to the Curia to assure it both of his devotion to the Church and his intention to work for peace in the world. But Gregory deferred any decision about the emperor's coronation until the ecumenical council of Lyons, announced for May 1274.

Gregory had already set out for Lyons in the spring of 1273 accompanied by Charles. In June he reached Florence which he found in an uproar because of violent fights between the Guelphs and the Ghibellines. After attempting to make them come to an agreement, he had left the city in great frustration, issuing an interdiction on it as well as the whole of Tuscany, where Charles was his representative.

The fourteenth ecumenical council began at Lyons on 7 May 1274, and lasted until 17 July. It was the second such council held in that city and was of unusual importance. While the main topic discussed was the reunification of the Western and Eastern Churches, which would put an end to the schism for only a brief period, thirty-one other canons established numerous decrees of a fundamental nature, such as that which reserved to the bishop alone the power to confer the Sacrament of Confirmation, and that which condemned the view that Christ prohibited ecclesiastical orders from owning property, thus protecting the Church from accusations, I would say correct, in the name of a sacrosanct evangelical poverty.

Since the chancellor of Rudolph of Habsburg was present at the Council, Otto of Speyr, in a consistory on 6 June, swore an oath in the name of his own sovereign that the possessions of the Church of Rome would remain undisturbed, renounced any claim on Sicily and confirmed that he was ready to state again these promises after the coronation of the emperor. Finally on 16 July, the Constitution *Ubi periculum*, wanted by Gregory X, was promulgated. It dealt with papal elections and declared the necessity of a conclave for the Sacred College of Cardinals. It was laid down too that the cardinals present in the Curia would wait only ten days in the city where the pope had died for those who were absent, after which they would be segregated from the outside world. It was up to the senator, or the mayor, to keep watch over the conclave. Moreover, rules restricting the meals of the cardinals were prescribed in case they had not arrived at an agreement within three days, reducing them to bread and water after eight days, and also that these high prelates were not to receive any income for the entire length of the conclave. The cardinals protested, especially about the latter provision, while the minor clergy unanimously approved. Apart from some later temporary suspensions and amendments, especially regarding the meals and the cessation of income, the decree has remained substantially in vigor ever since, although it never succeeded in reaching its basic goal, which was to speed up papal elections.

Gregory immediately left for Italy, stopping off on the way in Lausanne to meet Rudolph, who confirmed to him the promises made by his chancellor, and consented to the marriage of Rudolph's daughter Clemenza, to Charles Martel, nephew of Charles of Anjou. Peace between the papacy and the empire was officially declared and the date of the imperial coronation was fixed for 2 February 1276, in Rome. However, the pope was not to survive until then.

In December he reached Florence where, before entering the city, Gregory lifted the interdiction and conducted some religious ceremonies. But, after seeing that the city had still not achieved peace and calm, he departed, renewing the interdiction.

He arrived in Arezzo, fell ill and died on 10 January 1276 and was buried in Arezzo's cathedral.

The description of Gregory by Gregorovius that: "He shined like a Titus of his epoch" sounds rhetorical. But it is undisputed that, even during a brief pontificate rich in initiatives both on the political and on the religious levels, Gregory's personality reflected sureness and prestige. He kept faith with his engagements, denounced the errors of his predecessors, correcting them where possible, and to those of his successors who might wish to follow his example left a clear indication of how to operate wisely at the summits of power.

Beatified by the Church, he was canonized in 1713.

1 8 5. INNOCENT V (1 2 7 6)

As decreed by the *Ubi periculum Constitution*, the Sacred College of Cardinals opened its conclave at Assisi on the eleventh day after the death of Gregory X, on 21 January 1276, and the same day elected the Savoyard Pierre de Tarantaise. He was the first Dominican to become pope.

Born around 1225 in a family of nobles, at a tender age he had entered the Dominican Order of which he became provincial and then general, succeeding St. Thomas as rector of the University of Paris where he held also the chair of theology. Consecrated by Gregory X as archbishop of Lyons and later cardinal-bishop of Ostia, he did not however pursue Gregory's policy as pontiff. For once crowned in Rome on 22 February with the name of Innocent V, he immediately confirmed Charles of Anjou as Senator and as the imperial vicar in Tuscany.

Rudolph of Habsburg resented this and wrote to him requesting the imperial crown, but at the same time he sent his envoys in Rome to receive the oath of vassalage from the Angevin king, as Tuscany was a province which had belonged to the empire since the time of the Ottos, always promised but never effectively handed over to the Church of Rome. Rudolph wanted to assert his own rights there, not to keep possession of it but to have a territory from which to threaten the dominion of Charles of Anjou, who clearly enjoyed the pope's favor.

Proof of this lay in the fact that Innocent lifted the interdiction of Tuscan cities imposed by Gregory X and excommunicated the Ghibellines of Verona and Pavia in an obvious anti-imperial move. Innocent did not have the foresight of his predecessor nor his authority and independence. The strong influence of Charles of Anjou, who wanted to convince the pope to adopt an inflexible attitude towards Constantinople because he was planning to attack the Eastern empire, limited the policy of rapprochement with the Eastern Church begun by the Council of Lyons. Had his delegation to Emperor Michael VIII, charged with establishing the truce in precise terms, ever reached Byzantium, it would have been totally unproductive. But the legates were about the embark at Ancona when the news reached them of the death of Innocent on 22 June 1276, so they returned to Rome.

Innocent V was buried in the Lateran. Beatified by the Church, he was canonized in 1898.

186. HADRIAN V (1276)

At the death of Innocent V, Charles of Anjou was in Rome, and the *Ubi periculum* Constitution provided that he, as senator, had to supervise the conclave, so he could manoeuvre it as he wished. He insisted on the strict observance of the rules laid down by Gregory X and, since the conclave lasted more than eight days, the restriction to bread and water for meals came into force. It was applied, however, only to the Italian cardinals since the Frenchmen continued to receive their usual meals. This severe, discriminatory treatment exasperated the group of Italian cardinals, and their leader, Giovanni Gaetano Orsini, the future Pope Nicholas III, was never to forget it and would take his revenge.

Ottobono Fieschi, from Genoa, was elected pope on 11 July 1276. He was from the family of the counts of Lavigna, and though he was an Italian, he met the requirements of Charles of Anjou as he was an upholder of the anti-imperial policy, like his uncle, Innocent IV, whose envoy to England he had been. However, his election was a delusion because he was very old and unwell, so the king could not count on him. Indeed, thirty-eight days later, he was already dead.

Dante places him among the avaricious in his *Purgatory*, with exact details about his family, accusing him of greed for material goods, a sin for which he is thought to have repented during his brief pontificate (XIX, 100–108):

> Between Sestri and Chiavari flows down a fair river,
> And from its name the title of my name takes origin.
> One month, and little more, I learned how the great mantle
> Weighs on him who keeps it from the mire,
> So that all other burdens seem feathers.
> My conversion, ah me! was late, but when I was made Pastor
> Of Rome, so I discovered the life which is false.
> *(The Carlyle-Wicksteed translation)*

Yet it does not appear from the sources that he had ever been avaricious or greedy for power, and even less that he had repented during the few days that he was pope. Dante simply confused him with Hadrian IV, as noted above in the biography of the English pope.

He had been made a cardinal-deacon by his uncle, Innocent IV, and was supposed to have been ordained a priest and become a bishop before being crowned as pope. Instead, after assuming the name of Hadrian V, on the very day of his election he summoned the cardinals to a consistory at the Lateran and caused the Gregorian Constitution on the conclave, so severely applied by Charles of Anjou, to be abrogated because of its "unbearable and even obscure deliberations." Then he quickly moved to Viterbo to escape the oppressive heat of Rome. At Viterbo he died on 18 August 1276, without having been crowned, and was buried in the church of St. Francis in that city.

187. JOHN XXI (1276–1277)

Ten days had passed since the death of Hadrian V and the cardinals gathered in Viterbo had still not come to agreement on the election of a new pope, so the mayor of the city decided to close them up in the conclave pursuant to the *Ubi periculum* Constitution. However, the cardinals protested and drew attention to the abrogation of that decree, while Charles of Anjou, who was in the neighborhood of Viterbo to stir up trouble among the unhappy inhabitants and get them to segregate the cardinals, spread the rumor that Hadrian V had, on the point of death, suspended the abrogation. The cardinals immediately issued an official declaration which caused rioting in the streets, and only when order was restored did the Sacred College reconvene on 15 September 1276, to elect a successor to Hadrian V. On that same day it selected a Portuguese, Pietro Juliani, cardinal-bishop of Tusculum.

Known as Pietro Ispano, he should have been called Pietro Portoghese since he was born in Lisbon around 1220. A well-known humanist, he had written a treatise on logic in Paris which was to be the basis for the teaching of this discipline for two centuries. Interested also in medicine and natural science, like so many working in this field at that time, he was constantly classified as a "magician" by contemporary chroniclers who "treating him either as a scholar or as an ignoramus," as Gregorovius notes, "called him a wise fool sitting on the holy chair, a person without scruples or dignity, a lover of science and disdainful of monasticism." In effect, with him returned the legendary figure of a "wizard pope," reminding us of Sylvester II. The people's ignorance had not changed and science, even almost three centuries later, was still considered as having to do with witchcraft and devilry.

Pietro Ispano was consecrated pope on 20 September 1276, under the name John XXI, skipping number XX who had never sat on Peter's throne. He was extraneous to the politico-ecclesiastical world, totally immersed in that of science and literature and without any experience whatsoever in papal matters. He relied, therefore, on Cardinal Giovanni Gaetano Orsini, who in effect paved the way for his own pontificate. Orsini began by getting him to renew the abrogation of the *Ubi periculum*, declaring that that Constitution would be replaced by a more appropriate one. This decision was strongly criticized by many bishoprics, and the question was raised as to whether the Curia in fact had the authority to abolish a decree of a council. At the same time, John XXI established a committee to investigate the riots in Viterbo prior to his election, and to identify those responsible.

Charles of Anjou wanted to renew his feudal oath to the pope, but John XXI made no explicit declaration that he would confirm his positions of senator in Rome and vicar in Tuscany as had preceding pontiffs, even if there was no decree of abrogation. In any event, it was the sign of a change in the course of pontifical politics.

Furthermore, Rudolph did not have the time to enter into negotiations with the pope before his death, and the same fate befell the new delegation to Constantinople. The patriarch there swore in a council at which were present the papal legates that the primacy of Rome and the Catholic religion was recognized, and an agreement was reached between the two Churches on a strictly religious level. However, Michael VIII was not able to obtain a reply from the pope on his requests for guarantees against the expansionist aims of Charles of Anjou concerning his empire. When the papal legates reached Rome, John XXI had already died on 20 May 1277, in Viterbo. He was buried in the cathedral in that city.

1 8 8. NICHOLAS III (1 2 7 7 – 1 2 8 0)

After the death of John XXI, there were six months of vacant see since the seven cardinals who comprised the electoral college needed that much time. They were a small number as there had been no elevations since the time of Gregory X, and because the eighth cardinal, Simon de Brion, had remained in his legation in France. On 25 November 1277, they finally elected the one that Charles of Anjou distinctly did not want, the Roman Giovanni Gaetano Orsini.

Born about 1210, he was the son of Senator Matteo Rosso, famous at the time of Frederick II. Archpriest at St. Peter's, he had been elevated to the cardinal's purple by Innocent IV with the titular church S. Niccolò in Carcere, and serving as protector of the Order of Friars Minor and as Inquisitor General. He had been in the service of eight popes, had assisted at seven councils, including the one 'in jail' of 1276 which had elected Hadrian V, and he had an account pending with Charles of Anjou.

He was consecrated in Rome on 26 December 1277, under the name of Nicholas III: "With him came a pontiff whose dominant nature had been compared," according to Seppelt, "to that of an Innocent III. He, too, profoundly understood and was aware of the dignity flowing from his high office as the vicar of Christ and the successor of the Prince of the Apostles." It is true, however, that, as a member of a famous Roman family, he basically had "a princely idea of his own self" in terms of power, as Gregorovius observes, and as pope he came "to practice a nepotism which surpassed all limits. He was indeed a 'grand' Roman, energetic and regal, avid in amassing treasure, completely dedicated to worldly interests." It is clear that, though the representative of the vicar of Christ, he ended by being blinded by material concerns. And, if Nicholas III wanted first of all to ensure the liberty and independence of the Church of Rome, he fashioned papal sovereignty for personal advantage, the first of the popes to do so in such a manner as to become a model for many of his successors.

The first goal that Nicholas III set himself was that of challenging the power of Charles of Anjou. For this purpose, he quickly established good relations with Rudolph of Habsburg, inviting him to ratify the agreements made with Gregory X at Lausanne in 1275, insisting though that the extension of the Papal States be detailed in a document, city by city, on the basis of the ancient donation certificates.

On 4 May 1278, an envoy from Rudolph, the Franciscan friar Conrad, subscribed to the document in Rome, which referred back to the privilege of Louis the Pious and included decrees of Otto I and Henry II. Rudolph accepted without any argument, but he had some hesitation regarding the cession of Romagna. Nicholas III informed him that this was a sine qua non for the ceding, as a counterpart to the imperial rights over Tuscany, of which up to that point Charles of Anjou had been the vicar by papal nomination. So the documents concerning the oath of loyalty imposed on Romagna two years earlier having been cancelled in May, Nicholas III took possession of the territory on 30 June, immediately putting in control members of his own family who arranged for the cities to pay homage to the Church.

Named as the papal legate was his nephew, Latino Malabranca, cardinal-bishop of Ostia, and, as the count of Romagna, another nephew, Bertoldo Orsini. Moreover, for military defense Latino called into service some Neapolitan troops, which Charles was required to furnish him as a vassal of the Church, so Romagna passed legally into the pope's hands.

The treaty with Rudolph had as a result the weakening of the power of Charles of Anjou. First, he lost the vicariate of Tuscany, correctly claimed by the king of Germany, and then he was forced to give up the position of senator. But as he would have, in any case, reached the end of his ten-year term on 16 September 1278, Charles went to Rome in mid-June and declared that he would give up the position so as to avoid a conflict with the pope who, with time, would have been able to pit him against Rudolph.

On 11 July 1278, Nicholas issued the Constitution *Fundamenta militantis ecclesiae* by which the appointment of senators in Rome had to be in the hands of the pope, yet preserving the voting rights of the Roman citizens. The sovereignty over the city was entrusted to the pope, assisted by the cardinals, and it was restated that the papal election, as well as the appointment of cardinals, had to take place in complete freedom without any influence by laymen. Also forbidden was the election in future of any emperor, king, prince, marquis, duke, count, or baron to a post of senator, captain of the people, or patrician, either for life or for a limited period. Such positions were to be filled only by Roman citizens and for the maximum duration of one year.

This edict of Nicholas III served simply to strengthen the ambitions of the noble Roman families. The Orsini, the Colonna, and the Savelli acquired additional influence and from then on fought for power in the Senate and over the whole city. The pope, himself a member of the powerful Orsini family, was elected senator by the citizens but, with their consent, he turned the office over to his brother, Matteo Rosso, who was followed, in October 1279, by Giovanni Colonna and Pandolfo Savelli.

Charles of Anjou found some compensation for the loss of his posts in the peace treaty that, with the pope acting as intermediary, was concluded in 1280 with Rudolph of Habsburg in a reciprocal recognition of their royal sovereignties. Nicholas III thus succeeded in achieving peace with the empire, recognition of the sovereignty of the Church and the submission of the Capitol, as well as a limitation of the power of Charles of Anjou. As for relations with the East, he did not agree to the requests of Michael VIII who tried to get the pope to have Charles of Anjou break his alliance with the princes of Epirus and Thessaly, but at the same time would prohibit his vassal from going ahead with his plan to attack the Byzantine empire. In short, he avoided taking one or the other side in order not to compromise the union of the Churches.

Nicholas III managed to achieve a brief but memorable pontificate, succeeding in building up, in the words of Gregorovius, "a Zion for his relatives." It is a fact that "as a true Roman, he was fond of luxury and ostentation and he did not hesitate to obtain them even at the expense of the Church and of the Christian world," to the point of deserving a place among those guilty of simony in Dante's *Inferno*, where the poet has him saying (XIX, 70–72):

> . . . and verily I was a son of the She-bear, so eager
> to advance the Whelps
> that I pursued wealth above and here, myself.
> *(The Carlyle-Wicksteed translation)*

However, the Rome with which Nicholas was closely linked benefited itself from his immoderate love for luxury. Spending enormous amounts of money, he restorated St. Peter's basilica, even placing in it portraits of the popes up to his own time. He was also responsible for the expansion of the Vatican palace, and for laying out the famous gardens. In effect, he was the real founder of the Vatican as the papal residence.

He also restructured the Lateran basilica, by rebuilding the San Lorenzo chapel, the famous Sancta Sanctorum that had been destroyed in 1207 by an earthquake. In addition, he built at Soriano, near Viterbo, a splendid palace that he then donated to his nephew, Orso, where he died struck down by an apoplectic stroke, on 22 August 1280. He was buried in the Orsini Chapel in St. Peter's.

189. MARTIN IV (1281–1285)

Bloody riots erupted in Rome on the death of Nicholas III, fomented by the Annibaldi family against the Orsini, and the senators in function were ousted and replaced by members of the two opposing families. The riots had repercussions at Viterbo where the College of Cardinals had gathered for the election of a new pope, with the usual disagreements between the Italian and the pro-French factions. Charles had gone to Viterbo to try and get a pope elected who could assure him additional prestige. By agreement with him, Riccardo Annibaldi had managed to wrest from Orso Orsini the post of mayor in order personally to control the conclave, and under his guidance the people of Viterbo, by then used to certain ventures, attacked the Bishop's Palace, seized the Orsini cardinals, Matteo Rosso and Giordano, and imprisoned them in a room preventing them from participating in the election. Faced with this violence on 22 February 1281, the remaining cardinals elected as the new pope, a Frenchman named Simon de Brion, Cardinal of St. Cecilia's. Charles of Anjou had achieved his goal.

The newly-elected pope was none other than the legate charged by Urban IV with the lengthy negotiations which had brought the papacy to the contract of feudal investiture with Charles of Anjou. So he was certainly one upon whom the king could rely, and not belie his expectations, having pursued an ecclesiastical career entirely at the service of France. Archdeacon and chancellor at Tours, then the treasurer of the church of St. Martin in that city, he had been taken on by King Louis IX, the brother of Charles, as his counsellor, then as chancellor and guardian of the Seals. In fact, Simon de Brion, perhaps realizing that he could well become a tool in the hands of the Angevin king and recognizing that he would not be able to stand up to him, tried to avoid his own consecration. He was probably sincere, and his was not the usual "rite of reluctance," a show of false modesty as with so many of his predecessors. But he was evidently induced or constrained by Charles to accept, and wound up putting himself entirely in his hands though an unworthy form of submissiveness, and by allowing Charles to take advantage of him during four years of his pontificate, causing the Church to lose all that had been achieved by Nicholas III.

The new pope wanted to be crowned in Rome, but the Romans refused to grant him this. After issuing an interdiction against Viterbo for the riots which had taken place during his election, he moved to Orvieto where he was consecrated on 23 March 1281, taking the name of Martin IV. He was in fact only the second pontiff of that name, but in the weird cataloguing of the popes in those days, Martin I and II had been erroneously listed as Martin II and III.

Charles took care to smooth the path for a return of "his" pope to Rome through the Annibaldi, or better said, the road was opened for his own grand, personal return to the apex of power in the city. Suddenly the Romans wanted Martin among them and they offered him the post of senator for life, as had been the case with Nicholas III. At first he wavered and shied from the senatorship, until he decided to accept the honor in order to pass it on to Charles of Anjou. So in one fell stroke he gave up the sovereignty over the city of Rome and the victory gained by his predecessor's forceful policy.

From that time on, the power of Charles of Anjou and the Guelph party was on the increase again all over Italy. The most important offices from Sicily to the Po were taken over by the French. The sole exception was Romagna where the Ghibelline, Guido of Montefeltro, became the sovereign, and the Church temporarily lost even that territory.

Martin IV gave Charles a free hand in Byzantine policy as well, ruining the temporary union achieved between the Churches of the East and the West, and showing himself especially stupid on this matter. To facilitate the expedition which the king was preparing, in alliance with the sovereigns of Epirus and Thessaly, he granted the Angevin the tithes from the bishoprics of Sardinia and Hungary for six years to finance the crusade. He also excommunicated Michael VIII as the promoter of heresy and of schism, the very person who, right up to his death in December 1282, had done all he could to fulfil the pacts made with Nicholas III. His only reaction had been to forbid the mention of the pope in the common prayers in the churches, for which he found support from the patriarch, John Beccos, like himself a steadfast defender of the union. When Andronicus II, Michael VIII's son, ascended the throne, there was a final rupture of relations and an anti-unionist, a certain John, replaced the patriarch. The schism was back in place, and all the fault of Martin IV.

Suddenly, however, a very serious event blocked Charles of Anjou's plans for hegemony—the Vespri Siciliani (Sicilian Vespers). On 31 March 1282, the island rose up against the French king, invoking the protection of the Church and proposing to Martin the sovereignty of the kingdom. This was something which would have made Innocent IV jump for joy, having done everything he could to lay his hands on the island. Instead Martin IV, to whom it was offered on a silver platter, turned it down, fooled by the relaxed reliance of Charles of Anjou and believing that the latter's interests coincided with those of the Church. His only response was to condemn severely the revolt and to excommunicate the Sicilians.

But it did not stop there. When, by a unanimous vote, the rebels offered the crown of Sicily to Peter of Aragon who happily accepted it, disembarking in August at Trapani to take possession of the island, Martin IV excommunicated him as well. And he issued a series of bulls against the Aragons, even calling for a crusade to reconquer Sicily, determined to have all the Italian Communes participate in the venture. By then the behavior of the pope had become so absurd that the Curia began to criticize him openly.

But he persisted in his foolhardy policy. He considered the throne of Aragon vacant and offered it as a fiefdom to the son of the king of France, Charles of Valois. The act of cession was decreed by Martin on 5 May 1284. In any event, the attempted conquest of that kingdom was to flounder the following year with the destruction of the French fleet by the Aragons under the command of Roger of Lauria, the same admiral who, in June 1284, had defeated the Angevin fleet in the Gulf of Naples and had taken prisoner the young son of the king, the prince of the same name, Charles. So, when Charles of Anjou died on 7 January 1285, he could only view the void behind him after such a sudden and easy climb to the summits of triumph.

Martin IV had by now committed so many blunders that all he could do was try to avoid others. He therefore notified Rudolph that it would be wise to postpone the imperial coronation because of the riots that were constantly breaking out in Rome, and in this way kept alive his intent to restore the empire. Moreover, while in Orvieto, he managed to make known his irritation when the people elected Giovanni di Cinzio Malabranca as Tribune of the Republic. No longer able to count upon Charles of Anjou, he did conserve a minimum of dignity by complaining that not only papal rights but also those of a senator for life had been trampled upon, rights which he had passed on to the Angevin. He was listened to, so he magnanimously confirmed Giovanni di Cinzio as "prefect but only for a year" and also agreed to recognize the Council of Priors, elected by the artisans's guilds. As for the senatorial posts, he would personally appoint two of his representatives.

The people made no protest, reckoning their rights protected, and Richard Annibaldi, the tyrant of the Viterbo conclave, paid for everyone. He was forced to make an act of submission by order of the pope, going on foot, with a rope at his collar to the palace of Cardinal Matteo Orsini to beg his pardon. And the constitution of Nicholas III was thereby applied again, so at least something was left of his policy.

Martin IV died in Perugia on 28 March 1285, and was buried in the cathedral there.

190. HONORIUS IV (1285—1287)

Martin IV's successor was elected with surprising speed by the College of Cardinals sitting in Perugia, and the liberation of the Church from the lengthy protectorate of Charles of Anjou made itself immediately felt. On 2 April 1285, a Roman, Jacopo Savelli, was elected. He was the Cardinal at S. Maria in Cosmedin and was consecrated in Rome on 20 May under the name of Honorius IV.

The new pope, born about 1210, was the son of Luca Savelli and Giovanna Aldobrandeschi of the counts of Santafiora, and the brother of Pandolfo Savelli who, during the election, was senator along with Annibaldo. As soon as Honorius was elected, the Romans made him a senator for life, an office that he transferred to his brother, Pandolfo. Two brothers thus held the highest positions in Rome, both of them aged and not in good health, to the point that it was said about Honorius that he could no longer stand and that, when he was saying Mass, he used a mechanical device to raise the Host. His mind, however, was still alert and sufficient to assure the Savelli family a period of unchallenged domination while, as pope, he devoted himself to bringing peace to the Papal State and to resolving the Sicilian problem.

To achieve the first objective, Honorius began by lifting the interdiction against Viterbo by which Martin IV had punished the city after his election because of the riots during the conclave. Moreover, he succeeded in pacifying Romagna, the province that, since 1286, Guido of Montefeltro had voluntarily given up and which returned to form part of the Church's territory. Honorius chose his cousin, Pietro Stefaneschi, to be the count there.

In southern Italy, as Charles II was a prisoner of the Aragonese, he entrusted the government to Robert d'Artois. Sicily seemed already lost. When Peter of Aragon died in 1285, his son James succeeded to the throne and was crowned in Palermo in the presence of his mother, Constance. The bulls of excommunication against both of them were completely ignored.

A new situation suddenly arose when Charles II, to free himself from the Aragon prison, declared that he was prepared to renounce his claim to Sicily by a treaty in Barcelona in February 1287, in favor of James of Aragon. However, Honorius declared that the treaty was null and void, insisting that the House of Aragon should bow to the Church. And, like Martin IV, he promised to provide for the collection of tithes everywhere in order to organize an expedition to free the prisoner.

Honorius established friendly relations with Rudolph of Habsburg who kept requesting his imperial coronation in Rome. The pope promised it to him and even fixed a date, but it was fated that the crown of Charlemagne was never to circle Rudolph's head. On 3 April 1287, Honorius IV died in his residence on the Aventine where he had had a palace built.

He had not finished various tasks and, in fact, he had managed simply to set up an absolute sovereignty for his own family, as well as increasing its wealth. The Savelli, already the owners of the hills of Latium and the territory of Civitacastellana, inherited from the pope the palace and the fortress on the Aventine, together with another palace with several towers in the Parione quarter. Honorius IV was buried in the Vatican, but Paul III had his remains removed to the church on the Aracoeli near those of his mother.

191. NICHOLAS IV (1288—1292)

On Honorius IV's death, the cardinals met in a conclave in the residence of the deceased pope, but could not reach an agreement. Summer came and, with it, a malaria epidemic as a result of which six of the cardinals died while the others left to avoid contagion. The only one to stay there in the church of Santa Sabina, defying death, was Cardinal Girolamo Masci. Perhaps to reward him for his constance, the College of Cardinals meeting again after a year of vacant see, elected him pope on 22 February 1288. He was consecrated the same day under the name of Nicholas IV.

Born about 1230 at Lisciano near Ascoli Piceno, of humble origin, Nicholas was a Franciscan and General of the Order, who had distinguished himself as a legate of Gregory X. He was appointed a cardinal by Nicholas III and was bishop of Palestrina under Martin IV. He was the first Franciscan pope, disinterested in personal matters, and intent upon bringing peace to the world.

As with Honorius IV, the Romans awarded him the senatorship for life, but he quickly passed that on to two Senators of the Orsini family, first Orso and then Bertold. During the first year of his pontificate the situation in Rome was somewhat chaotic, with fighting among the factions of the nobles who were contending for primacy once the domination by the Savelli had disappeared with the death of Honorius IV. He withdrew to Rieti but, when he saw that the Orsini were unable to control the situation and restore peace, he ended by resorting to the Colonna family with whom he was already linked by bonds of friendship.

He began by assigning the March of Ancona to Giovanni Colonna, naming his oldest son, Pietro, Cardinal of S. Eustachio, and the youngest, Stefano, count of Romagna. The latter, a very violent man earned the enmity of the Communes and the nobles. There was an uprising, led by the sons of Guido of Polenta, and the count was taken prisoner in November 1290. All the tenacity and diplomacy of the bishop of Arezzo, Hildebrand of Romena, sent immediately by the pope, were needed to put down the revolt and to free Stefano from jail.

Meanwhile in Rome, Giovanni Colonna, named sole Senator, had been triumphantly seated in the Capitol. To this true "padrone" of the Roman countryside, Nicholas IV entrusted the entire government of the city, since he preferred to live in Viterbo, Sabina, or in Umbria. An illustration of the sovereign power which Giovanni Colonna wielded was provided when the Romans started a bloody war against Viterbo which was refusing to carry out its obligations in its vassalage relationship with Rome. The pope became the mediator of a peace treaty that was concluded and signed in May 1291 by Senator Colonna. This led to a renewal of the oath of loyalty by the people of Viterbo, together with compensation for war damages, delivered to the senator acting as the papal regent.

On the other hand, Nicholas personally saw to the problem of southern Italy and Sicily. Charles II, in order to be freed from the Aragon prison, had again in 1288 renounced Sicily by another treaty signed at Oléron through the mediation of King Edward I of England. But again the treaty was rejected by the pope, in line with the policy of Honorius IV, who insisted on an unconditional release of the Angevin. This demand was obviously not granted, and Nicholas IV found himself forced again to collect tithes on the property of the clergy for three years since he sincerely wanted Charles to regain the Sicilian feudal estate from James of Aragon. There followed a third treaty at Champfranc with the immediate release of Charles, this time presented to the pope as a "fait accompli." Nicholas rejected the usual conditions, though sworn to by his vassal, but nevertheless crowned Charles II at Rieti in May 1289.

However, until James could find support from his brother, King Alphonso III of Aragon, hope of regaining Sicily was not great. Moreover, the plan adopted by the Curia to separate Aragon from Sicily was useless. The Curia had organized a grand coalition with France and Castille as a result of which Alphonso, in view of the fact that the Cortes were not in favor of supporting the Sicilian campaign, decided to abandon his brother. But all came to nothing when King Alphonso died in June 1291. James of Sicily, as his brother's heir, received two kingdoms, and appointed his younger brother, Frederick, as the governor of the island. The threats from the pope to give Sicily back to the Angevins were not heeded, and James calmly accepted his excommunication. The problem was only to be resolved later with Boniface VIII.

Meanwhile, the domination by the Colonnas in Rome began to bring violent reactions from the other nobles. As Gregorovius notes, "the pope was ridiculed for having given himself body and soul to a single family, and satires were written against him." In a defamatory writing, *Initium malorum*, "he was pictured nailed to a column, the emblem of the Colonna family, from which appeared only his head with the tiara while on the sides were two other columns representing the two Cardinals Colonna." A compromise was reached with the Orsini family which wanted to regain senatorial dignity. In 1291, Pandolfo Savelli was elected and, in the following year, the function was shared between Stefano Colonna, formerly the count of Romagna, and Matteo Rinaldo Orsini.

Nicholas IV wanted to continue the work of beautifying the city started by Nicholas III, and he really took it to heart. He could therefore be called a genuine Maecenas (generous patron of the arts and literature) of the thirteenth century. Indeed, thanks to him, artists such as Arnolfo di Cambio, Pietro Cavallini, and Giacomo Torrito carried on their work in Rome. To the latter, in particular, was entrusted the restoration of the apse of San Giovanni with the vast mosaic created by using, in part, the ancient mosaics, as well as the construction of a huge new apse at St. Mary Major. Also to be credited to this pope was the increase in missionary activity, especially by the Franciscans, among these Giovanni of Monte Corvino spread the Christian message in Asia and, travelling to India and China, would become the first archbishop of Cambaluc (Beijing) in 1307.

Nicholas IV died on 4 April 1292, in the palace he had had built near St. Mary Major, the church in which he was buried. A year earlier, Rudolph of Habsburg had died, without having been able to be crowned emperor in Rome. In the East, Acre fell, the last Christian possession in Syria, thus bringing to a miserable end the chapter of the crusades. The Church had witnessed the relentless disappearance of that mystical spirit which had inspired them and, in a changing world, would be wise enough to imbue the missions with the breath of faith, hope and charity, even if dictated at times by the powerful machinery of papal politics, and the *longa manus* of an imperialistic power.

192. St. Celestine V (1294)

After the death of Nicholas IV, as of April 1292, the College of twelve cardinals met several times at St. Mary Major, on the Aventine and at S. Maria sopra Minerva but without reaching an agreement, and the matter had to be further postponed due to a plague epidemic. The French Cardinal Cholet died but, after the danger of contagion had passed, the eleven survivors could not even agree on a location for their meetings.

The Colonnas and their supporters remained in Rome, the others went to Rieti; threatened with schism, they agreed on Perugia. They met there on 18 October 1293, but the conflicts were not resolved and months went by before they could elect a new pope. Nor did the news from Rome about disorders which had broken out there, and the resulting election of two neutral senators, serve to conciliate the cardinals or stifle protests from ecclesiastical circles about the serious inconveniences caused by the long period of vacant see.

At the end of March 1294, Charles II and his son, Charles Martel, went to Perugia, and personally entered the meeting chamber which was supposed to be inaccessible, even if it was not truly a segregated room. The king urged a prompt election because new negotiations with James of Aragon were going on which could lead to a renunciation of Sicily by James, and he needed the approval by a pope. As a reply to this demand, at the specific insistence of Cardinal Benedetto Caetani, he and his son were ejected from the meeting hall.

But the cardinals realized that a decision had to be taken and they were saved from embarrassment by cardinal-deacon Latino Malabranca who brought to the attention of his colleagues the preaching of the hermit, Pietro of Morrone, who had prophesied that the Church would be threatened by serious misfortunes if a pope had not been elected by 1 November. Charles II, returning to his kingdom, probably went to visit Pietro on Mt. Morrone and, counting on the hermit's deep desire to have a pope elected, convinced him to write a letter to Cardinal Latino who had long admired his ascetic life. And Cardinal Latino, praising the miracles attributed to this saintly man, proposed his candidature and defended it with courage in the face of the cardinals' understandable perplexity, by citing the untainted piety of the hermit which made him the most worthy person to fill the high office of the vicar of Christ on earth.

So, after twenty-seven months, on 5 July 1294, the College of Cardinals unanimously elected the monk, Pietro Angeleri, setting forth in the decree of election that the agreement finally achieved had only been possible because of a prodigy, or prophetic sign, "almost an inspiration." However, as Seppelt notes, "one must not exclude that for some cardinals, like Benedetto Caetani, a cool political thinker, the agreement had been facilitated by the knowledge that it meant their having a decisive influence in the business of the Curia, given the lack of experience of the hermit and his complete alienation from worldly matters." Nonetheless, a basic disagreement remained among the cardinals since not one of them wanted to take the news to the new pope in his hermitage on the Maiella. So they deputized three bishops, who did not form part of the College to do so.

Pietro Angeleri was born in 1215 at Isernia to a peasant family, the eleventh of twelve children. At a tender age he had become a Benedictine monk and, once ordained a priest in Rome, he had withdrawn to a hermitage on the slopes of Mount Morrone above Sulmona. His life as a hermit interrupted for a while, he had organized his followers into a community and had obtained from Gregory X recognition of it as a branch of the Benedictine Order. The congregation was called simply "Monks of Pietro of Morrone," although later they called themselves "Celestines" after the papal name of their founder.

Great enthusiasm filled the spirit of the congregation as soon as they learned of the election of Pietro to the papal throne, and the fact that a humble anchorite could become the pope appeared to prove the prophecies of Gioacchino of Fiore. Jacopo Stefaneschi, son of the senator, gave an eyewitness description in poetry of those moments of popular frenzy which accompanied the announcement to the aging hermit, in a cave, of his elevation to the highest dignity. At first, he refused it, but later accepted with extreme reluctance after a real internal struggle, as described with intensity by Ignazio Silone in his book, *The Adventure of a Poor Christian.*

"If I refuse, I said to myself, how can we continue to complain that the Holy See, instead of being a center of peace and brotherly love, permits itself to be dragged into conflicts between States and even blesses fratricidal weapons?" the saintly monk asks himself in a monologue in Silone's drama. He continues: "How can we complain that the yet so recent teachings of St. Francis are wilfully ignored, and that his most faithful followers are remitted to ecclesiastical courts? But, no sooner was I leaning toward acceptance and thought about my imminent obligations, than I again felt my resolve failing me. I would ask myself: where shall I find the knowledge, the wisdom, the experience which I lack? Whom shall I be able to trust within the Curia of Rome?"

Indeed, even then a certain perplexity could be heard voiced above the hymns of praise of humble people, and Jacopone of Todi did not share the illusions of his own spiritual brethren when he addressed the newly-elected in his famous warning, beginning:

> What will you do, Pier of Morrone?
> You have reached the summit.

Then followed the justification of his own diffidence:

> The purpled group is in a low state, each intending
> to enrich his family.
> Beware of the benefices you will always find famished,
> such is their drought they need no pruning.
> Watch out for their tricks making black seem white,
> if you aren't careful, your will sing out of tune.

The cardinals had called Pietro to Perugia but he convened them in Aquila, because that was the wish of Charles II to whom the new pope had quickly turned for advice when he saw him arrive at the cave with his son Charles Martel. The papal cortège travelled to the city dressed so humbly with the hermit-pope wrapped in his poor tunic astride the back of a donkey, being led by the bridle by a king and a prince in the midst of a crowd of people, that for the populace it was like the entry of Jesus into Jerusalem.

On 29 April 1294, Pietro was consecrated in the church of S. Maria di Collemaggio outside the walls of Aquila with the name of Celestine V.

As pope, this "poor Christian" fell completely under the sway of King Charles, following whose advice he immediately revived the Constitution of Gregory X regarding papal elections, raising the Angevin to the rank of "Marshal" of future conclaves. He also appointed twelve cardinals, six of whom were Frenchmen, four from southern Italy and two from the congregation of

Celestine. He made Charles happy too by ratifying his treaty with James II of Aragon, on the strength of which Sicily became again an Angevin kingdom. The peace treaty would be signed the following year under Boniface VIII.

In the autumn, the pope was planning to go to Rome, but Charles convinced him to move the papal Curia to Naples because that would help him finalise the negotiations on the treaty of peace with Aragon. So Celestine V took up residence at Castelnuovo in a small room that he had had built of wood where he could find refuge to pray. The idea of renouncing the papal honor was already maturing in his mind and, once his project of entrusting the government of the Church to three cardinals acting as his regents had come to naught, he confided his plan to Cardinal Benedetto Caetani, an expert in canon law. He asked him about the legality of a renunciation of the papal position and, once he knew that it was technically legal, he decided to take the great step.

Charles sought in vain to dissuade him. In a consistory on 13 December 1294, after a bull prepared for the purpose was read out in which the abdication of a pope for serious reasons was authorized, he read the act of his own abdication. Clearly the bull and the act had been drafted by Caetani who, in view of his own candidacy at the next conclave, gave subtle assistance to the poor pope crushed under the weight of his own power.

His renunciation was certainly not proof of cowardice as Dante had called it if, in fact, the poet was referring to him in his *Inferno* (III, 59–60) for Celestine V did not "make his great refusal out of cowardice" but, as Petrarch explained, it is more just to consider "his action as that of the highest type of free soul which did not recognize any imposition, that of a truly divine spirit." In reality, he shed the papal honor when he realized that it was impossible to wield power without violating the most basic principles of Christian morality, because "the exercise of command subjugates others" as Silone has Celestine say in another passage of his book. "The desire to command, the obsession of power at all levels is a form of madness. It consumes the soul, it tramples upon it, it makes it false, even if one wants power 'for a good purpose,' especially if one seeks power 'for a good purpose.' The temptation of power is the most diabolical that can be offered to a person, if Satan dared to offer it even to Christ. He did not succeed but his agents do."

In the final analysis, the renunciation by Celestine V, proved rather that, as Seppelt has observed, "the supreme head of the Church on earth, beyond leading a holy and blameless life, should not lack the necessary culture and capacity for his high office" in the contradictory aspects of Church-political vs. Church-mystical, which is the keystone to the interpretation of the papacy, and the most difficult power on this earth in view of the contradictions to which it is subjected.

"The adventure" of this hermit-pope, however, did not end with the renunciation. He would have wished to return to his hermitage, but his shrewd friend of the last days of his pontificate, Benedetto Caetani, would not let him. Once elected pope with the name of Boniface VIII, he was afraid that his enemies might bring back the old Celestine to confront him in a schism. So he had him arrested on 16 May 1295 by the constable of the kingdom, William of Estendard, after his attempt to flee to the East had failed. Brought first to Capua and then to Anagni to the residence of Boniface VII, Pietro was shut up by him in the fortress of Fumone above Ferentino where he died on 19 May 1296.

Rumor spread quickly that Boniface had assassinated him. In any event, the reputation of martyrdom remained, as testified by a series of iconographs including the relief on the great bell of the abbey of S. Spirito at Sulmona, and a fresco of the fourteenth century in the hermitage of S. Onofrio. Celestine V was at first buried in the monastery of St. Anthony in Ferentino but his remains were later removed to the church of S. Maria of Collemaggio where he had been consecrated as pope. Clement V, at the instance of Philip the Fair, canonized him as a "holy confessor" rather than a martyr.

193. BONIFACE VIII (1294—1303)

Ten days after the abdication of Celestine V, the conclave, pursuant to the instructions of Gregory reestablished by the hermit-pope, gathered at Castelnuovo at Naples on 23 December 1294. It was a very brief one since, already on the 24th, it had reached a two-thirds majority, and Cardinal Benedetto Caetani was elected assuming the name of Boniface VIII.

Simony was probably involved. Dante was certain of that, as he placed Boniface in the company of the simonists with Nicholas III (*Inferno*, XIX, 52–57) and put in the mouth of Guido of Montefeltro the expression "the prince of the nine Pharisees" (*Inferno*, XXVII, 85). Caetani had clearly made his arrangements with his electors when he had "advised" Celestine V to abdicate.

Born in 1235 at Anagni, he came from the noble family of the Caetani, descended from Gelasius II (Giovanni Caetani), which under this pope was destined to achieve enormous importance within the Papal State by the acquisition of vast real estate and financial means. A legal expert, thanks to his advanced studies at Todi and Bologna, he had made a rapid ecclesiastical career with confidential missions to the Courts of France and England. In 1287 he had become a member of the College of Cardinals.

As the first action of his pontificate, he immediately moved the papal residence from Naples to Rome so as to get the Curia away from the sway of Charles II, who had certainly influenced his inexperienced predecessor. For this reason, Boniface VIII declared null and void the decisions taken hastily by Celestine V, while at the same time going ahead with the negotiations already underway between the Angevin and James of Aragon for the recovery of Sicily.

Boniface VIII was crowned in St. Peter's on 23 January 1295 with grandiose pomp, surrounded by all the Roman nobles and in the presence of King Charles and his son, Charles Martel. But over that sumptuous ceremony hung the threatening shadow of Celestine V despite his humility, and Boniface probably did not feel safe while he was free in the hermitage on the Morrone, for someone could always insinuate that Cardinal Caetani had put pressure on the "poor Christian" to abdicate. Rumors to that effect would have spread around quickly, and be given weight by the French cardinals opposed to Boniface VIII, who could even maintain that the abdication bull was invalid. It was better to stifle any suspicion and to inform the simple hermit that "an abdicated pope had no further right to freedom," making clear to him, in the hypothesis of Gregorovius, "that the obligations of religious devotion required him, after renouncing the tiara, to give up his freedom."

Charles II, in a courteous act of vassalage, delivered the message from which Pietro of Morrone sought vainly to escape, obviously unwilling to carry out certain final duties invented and perversely imposed on him by Boniface VIII. As I have already recorded in his biography, he was captured on 16 May 1295 by the constable of the kingdom, William of Estendard, and handed over to the pope. He is thought to have died in the dungeon of Fumone. The suspicion that he was assassinated by order of Boniface remained, and has been discussed at length without reaching any definite conclusion, in circumstances resembling those which had occurred more than seven centuries earlier between the popes Silverius and Vigilius. In any case, the imprisonment of Celestine V, clearly at the orders of the Caetani pope, was undeniably a very serious crime which was enough to indict this pontiff.

With Celestine V in jail, Boniface felt more secure on his throne and hastened to repay Charles's favor. On 20 June 1295, through the peace treaty of Anagni, James II of Aragon renounced his rights over Sicily in favor of the Church, which reassigned it to Charles II. However, none of this took place because the Sicilians did not want to give up their autonomy and recognized as their only sovereign, Frederick, who had been governor of the island from when his brother James II had ruled over Aragon, and on 25 March 1296, he was crowned king in the cathedral of Palermo. In practice, the papal policy was heading towards a defeat, which was officially sanctioned by the treaty signed in 1302 at Caltabellotta between Robert, the son of Charles II, and Frederick who obtained Sicily from the Church as a fiefdom for his lifetime, by which he bore the title of King of Trinacria. However, the island was never actually returned to the Angevins, but remained bound to the Aragonese, an advance post for future Spanish expansion in the Mediterranean, something the papacy would never be able to stop.

The Sicilian episode is certainly not the only such case in the history of relations between the Church and other States, nor is it the only defeat suffered by Boniface VIII in Europe. He was destined to close the account of such relations in a humiliating way for both himself and the Church, not from weakness or lack of personal ability but rather as a result of the anachronistic ideology that he pursued. Through a series of bulls it appears clear how, according to Boniface VIII, the sphere of ecclesiastical power had to be enlarged by absorbing the sovereigns's temporal power on the grounds that papal sovereignty could have no limits, being *"plenitudo potestatis"* by virtue of its divine origin. That was a medieval concept pushed to its extreme in an epoch when, however, the Middle Ages were coming to an end and the age of the great nations was emerging.

This all began with the publication of the bull *Clericis laicos* on 25 February 1296 by which lay persons were prohibited, under pain of excommunication and interdiction, from imposing any taxes or levies on ecclesiastics without the consent of the Church of Rome, and ecclesiastics were prohibited under similar punishments from paying such taxes. The bull branded on an historic level the hostility between the laity and the clergy and "raised the important question," in Seppelt's words, "of whether, in addition to the papacy, as absolute owner of the assets of the Church by virtue of its jurisdictional authority, the State also had the autonomous right to levy taxes on its churches and monasteries." For the State, this put its very existence in question.

In Germany, the new king, Adolph of Nassau, fearing opposition by various princes and bishops to his own imperial candidacy, did not object to the application of the bull, while in England Edward III would have preferred to ignore it but had to give in to the bishops's strong opposition to the payment of any new taxes.

In France, matters took a different turn. King Philip the Fair replied to the bull in two edicts by which he prohibited both clergymen and lay persons from exporting gold, silver, and jewellery, and prohibited aliens from taking up residence in his kingdom, which precluded the Curia's sending legates beyond the Alps to collect tributes. The pope began to be seen in a bad light in France where there were defamatory declarations circulating against him. Also the bishops, like the cardinals in the conclave, were hostile to his attitude, and this could touch off feelings of autonomy within the French church. As a result, Boniface realized that he would have to come to some accommodation on the rules promulgated in *Clericis laicos*. So he authorized Philip the Fair to collect taxes from the clergy in case of dire necessity even without consultation with the papacy while, on his part, the king revoked his edicts. Peace between France and the papacy was further strengthened by the solemn canonization of Louis IX, Philip's grandfather, on 17 August 1297.

This sudden change in relations with France, through a concession in effect humiliating for the Church versus a State, can be explained by the precarious situation the pope found himself in at Rome as a result of his despotic way of ruling.

In fact, he had made enemies of many members of the Roman aristocracy, particularly the Colonnas, and the two Colonna cardinals, Giacomo and Pietro openly criticized him in the Curia, claiming that his election was unlawful, because, in turn, the abdication by Celestine V was invalid. They had become the leaders of a bitter opposition on the part of the clergy and populace of Rome and of the surrounding countryside, which found support also among the Franciscan Spirituals. The spokesman for these was Jacopone of Todi who, in one of his vehement sermons, called the pope "a new anti-Christ." The conflict came to a head on 10 May 1297, with the signing of a memorandum, the so-called "Manifesto di Lunghezza," by which the Colonnas and various Spirituals declared the pope deposed and suggested that the faithful refuse to obey him.

The reaction of Boniface was stormy and violent. The two cardinals were deposed in a bull which underlined the insults from their "damned family and their damned blood" which he would have wanted to exterminate "because it always reared its head full of pride and disdain."

To this bull, the two cardinals reacted with a new memorandum, protesting against the pope's unfair conduct while, for his part, Boniface VIII ordered the confiscation of their property. In fact, the Colonnas were hoping for an intervention by Philip the Fair, but the king did not wish to complicate his relations with Rome since the pope had resisted him successfully on the issue of ecclesiastical tributes.

One after the other the forts of the Colonnas fell. Zagarolo and Palestrina were destroyed. Jacopone was imprisoned in a monastery and excommunicated, to be rehabilitated only after Boniface's death. The two Colonna cardinals were excommunicated, expelled from the Papal State and took refuge with Philip at whose court they continued to plot against the pope while their confiscated properties were divided between the Caetani and their traditional enemies, the Orsini. An apparent peace descended on Rome and, in this climate of armistice, Boniface VIII decided to celebrate the first Jubilee in history.

The bull, which declared the Holy Year *Antiquorum habet fidem*, is dated 22 February 1300. It granted a plenary indulgence for all those who, during that year or any future hundredth year, would visit the basilicas of Saints Peter and Paul in Rome. This was truly an exceptional event and all the chroniclers of the time agree in reporting the influx into Rome of an enormous number of pilgrims, which Villani calculated at two hundred thousand.

Even Dante mentions these masses of pilgrims in Rome, the first time for the Veronica and the second for the Jubilee, in a sonnet of the *Vita Nova* (XL, 24) which begins:

Hey there, pilgrims who go pensively,
thinking of unseen things,
You come from far away people, as your appearance shows.

And in the *Inferno*, recalling the influx of a "huge army," meaning the continual procession of people entering and leaving the city (XVIII, 28 and 31–33):

... so that, on the one side, all have their faces towards the Castle
and go to St. Peter's; at the other side,
they go towards the Mount.
(The Carlyle-Wicksteed translation)

For Boniface VIII the event represented, aside from the abundant income
from the offerings and from increased tourism, a strengthening of his own prestige, shaken by the recent fights with the Colonnas as well as by the mortifying
insinuations about the legitimacy of his pontificate. The Jubilee Year in this sense
helped to restore in him the awareness of his primacy among the sovereigns of
the world. "In those days he could taste to the full the meaning of his nearly
divine power," Gregorovius notes, "by watching the flow of thousands of people from all parts of the world, pilgrims who reached his throne and prostrated
themselves before him as if before a supernatural being." Actually, there were no
great sovereigns among the pilgrims except for Prince Charles Martel, but
Boniface did not mind and recited his role to the full, even appearing many times
before the "Romans" with the splendid imperial emblems, exclaiming "I am
Caesar, I am the Emperor." Seppelt comments, "he wanted to hold in his hands
the twin swords of spiritual and temporal power, but did not want to admit that
his power in fact was illusory." However, all of that became clear, as soon as the
Holy Year was over, in the struggle which began again with France.

Philip the Fair too personified a new concept of sovereignty. "He did not
recognize anyone superior to him," as the chronicler, Pierre Dubois, notes,
"and he aspired to a position of prominence in Europe, without saying that
in his kingdom, he considered himself the emperor." Not by chance had he
created in 1299 an alliance of friendship and peace with Albert of Habsburg,
the new king of Germany, accused openly by the pope of having assassinated
Adolph of Nassau, and invited to appear in Rome to explain his act of lèse
majesté. A sovereign so aware of his own power and so clearly anticlerical as
Philip, had to act as the *padrone* even towards the French Church, which
included the usurpation of ecclesiastical property, and this led to a new conflict between him and Boniface VIII.

On 4 December 1301, the pope abolished the privileges granted to the
king in the bull *Salvator Mundi* and on the following day in another bull,

Ausculta fili, called for a meeting on 10 November of the following year in Rome of the French bishops together with Philip in a council which was supposed to define once and for all the relations between State and Church. In the second bull, Boniface set forth explicitly the notion that only the pope had been placed by God over all sovereigns, and hence Philip could not presume that there was no one superior to him; he was subordinate to the pope and had to apologise to him.

Philip had circulated in France a summary of the two bulls, which deviated considerably from the originals and, in order to embitter public opinion against the pope even more, he also circulated a letter of his in reply, which was never sent to Rome, wherein he declared that, with regard to temporal matters, the king was not subject to anyone. In April 1302, Philip convened the Estates-General in Paris which supported his attitude and, on that occasion, a letter to the pope was prepared and unanimously approved, including by the clergy, in which they protested against the pope's offensive behavior toward the king of France who, for his part, prohibited the French clergy from participating in the council at Rome.

Nevertheless, thirty-nine French bishops did go to Rome and were later punished by Philip, who confiscated their property. The result of the council was the famous bull *Unam Sanctam,* issued on 18 November 1302. It reiterated in dogmatic terms that "there are two swords in the power of the Church, the spiritual and the temporal: the first is wielded by the Church, the second on behalf of the Church, the first by the priest, the second by the king but upon instructions of the priest" because "the spiritual power must command and judge the temporal power." Therefore, "whoever opposes this supreme spiritual power, exercised by a man but derived from God through his promise to Peter, opposes God Himself. It is therefore mandatory for everyone who desires salvation to be subject to the bishop of Rome."

As his only reply Philip convened his Council of State at the Louvre on 12 March 1303, at which for the first time William of Nogaret set forth detailed accusations against the pope, confirmed by a memorandum of the Colonna cardinals in Paris. Boniface was deemed an illegitimate pope, a heretic and a simonist, so the king felt empowered to convene a general council in Paris, which would in effect have been a proper trial of the pope. However, the pope's presence in Paris for the meeting was necessary, and William of Nogaret received secret orders from the king to arrest him and bring him there.

Boniface VIII was aware that the situation was deteriorating rapidly and wrote to Philip explaining that he had been excommunicated because he had prevented French clergy from travelling to Rome for the council. This was simply a means to buy time while awaiting developments which achieved nothing as the bearer of the letter was arrested at the king's order. Then the pope tried to win the support of Albert of Habsburg and, in a consistory on 30 April, recognized him as the king of Germany as well as the sovereign monarch of all the kings on earth while awaiting his imperial coronation. It was an effective way to split the Franco-German alliance and, indeed, Albert solemnly promised the pope his protection and defense against all his enemies, though when the moment came the promise was not fulfilled.

In mid-June there was another assembly of the Estates-General at the Louvre, with a kind of pre-trial of Boniface VIII where Nogaret, as prosecutor, was replaced by his friend William of Plasian since Nogaret had left for Rome on his secret mission. The pope was accused of being a sodomite and the murderer of Celestine V, of denying the immortality of the soul, and of having forced certain priests to violate the secrecy of the confessional. The king said that he was convinced of the need to convene an ecumenical council which could depose the pope and, despite the opposition of numerous members of the minor Orders who landed in prison, the main part of the French clergy and common people unitedly supported the king's decision.

When the pope heard the news of these events he was at Anagni from where he rejected all of the accusations. He prepared a bull for the king's excommunication, the *Super Petri solio*, which was to be proclaimed on 8 September 1303, but the day before that the conspiracy erupted preventing its publication.

William of Nogaret, in Italy since the spring of that year, had been in touch with the Colonna family, mortal enemies of the pope, whose head at that time was Sciarra. A conspiracy was organized which included the Anagni bourgeoisie and some of the members of the College of Cardinals. On the morning of 7 September the conspirators burst into the town to shouts of "Long live the King of France and the Colonnas!" and forced the inhabitants to storm the Papal Palace which, by evening, had fallen into the hands of the conspirators. Boniface VIII, abandoned even by his own servants, donned the symbols of his office and, wearing his tiara, sat on his throne awaiting the aggressors.

When Nogaret and Sciarra Colonna entered the hall, they ordered him to restore the two Colonna cardinals to their positions, to abdicate and become their prisoner if he wanted to save his life. "Here is my neck, here is my head!" the pope shouted, rejecting indignantly these conditions. That Nogaret slapped the pope with his nailed glove was maybe a figment of collective imagination, but Boniface was certainly maltreated and hurt, especially by Sciarra Colonna who wanted to kill him. The affront filled even many of his political foes with indignation, such as Dante, who considered the attack as aimed at Christ Himself (*Purgatory*, XX, 86–90):

> . . . I see the fleur-de-lys enter Alagna, and in his vicar
> Christ made captive.

A second time I see him mocked, I see the vinegar
and the gall renewed . . .
(The Carlyle-Wicksteed translation)

Contrary to Colonna, Nogaret did not want Boniface dead and was determined to bring the pope to the king. And their opposing views saved the
pope's life. After three days of prison, the bourgeoisie of Anagni suddenly did
an about face and came to the aid of their fellow citizen while, in another
assault on the Papal Palace on 9 September, they put the conspirators to flight
and liberated Boniface.

On the evening of that same day, the pope blessed the populace and pardoned them, though he certainly did not feel safe in his hometown. Under the
protection of the Orsinis, he returned to Rome on 25 September, crushed physically and morally, by now but a shadow of the great pope he thought himself
to be. He died on 11 October 1303, and was buried in St. Peter's in the Caetani
Chapel which he had had especially erected by Arnolfo di Cambio. However, it
was later torn down when the new basilica was built, and his remains were then
moved into the Vatican Grottoes.

It is beyond doubt that that tomb "is a monument to the medieval papacy
which the powers of that epoch buried with him," as Gregorovius observes. "He
was the last pope to conceive the idea of a hierarchical Church, ruler of the
world." His megalomania could be seen also in his support of the arts. Behind
the foundation of the University of the Sapienza in Rome and the cathedrals of
Orvieto and Perugia bloomed a "Caesarian" madness which became a narcis-
sistic adoration.

No pope before him had himself immortalized while still alive in such a
number of marble and bronze statues, still visible in Orvieto, Bologna,
Florence, Anagni, and the Lateran, not counting the fresco of Giotto which
handed him down to posterity reading the bull proclaiming the Jubilee Year
from the loggia of San Giovanni. His mania was not merely a sin of weakness, a sign of unfettered ambition for his posthumous reputation, it was
vainglorious pride in a true apotheosis of his own person, the most serious
sin a man could commit especially when he should have been, in the words
of St. Gregory the Great, "servus servorum Dei."

194. Benedict XI (1303–1304)

Riots and street fights between supporters of opposing factions accompanied
the bier of Boniface VIII. The city was an armed camp. Charles II with his sons
Robert and Philip, as well as troops, had arrived from Naples and even
Frederick had sent ships from Sicily which were anchored in the port of Ostia.

The worst was feared when the cardinals, gathered in a conclave at St. Peter's ten days after the death of Boniface VIII, found a successor on 22 October 1303, in a certain Nicholas Boccassini, cardinal-bishop of Ostia, who was crowned in St. Peter's on 27 October with the name of Benedict XI.

Born in 1240 at Treviso, he had been a tutor at the home of a Venetian nobleman and then, having become a Dominican, had followed an ecclesiastical career, being elevated to the purple by Boniface VIII. A mild-mannered man, he became responsible for the definitive surrender by the papacy to the lay forces of the State against which his predecessor had fought.

In fact, he had no allies against the king of France, as he could not even count on support from Germany. And yet he was constrained to do something about the mortification the Church had suffered with the attack at Anagni, so he began with a trial of the conspirators on 6 November that ended on 23 December. But this turned into a farce because the Colonnas were able to defend themselves so effectively that they claimed indemnity for the wrongs done to them by Boniface VIII. Except for Sciarra, they were absolved from the excommunication and received back some of the land that had been confiscated, though had to wait for special permission from the pope to reconstruct their fortresses.

Cardinals Giacomo and Pietro also asked to be restored to their positions, but Benedict refused this, and they then invoked the protection of Philip the Fair. The latter, basically looking after his own interests and by repeatedly declaring his intention to convene a council which would condemn all the actions of Boniface VIII, made Benedict bend to his will.

Indeed, without waiting for a delegation from the king, the pope spontaneously abrogated all the decrees issued against Philip by his predecessor through the special bulls promulgated on 13 May 1304. There was thus a reconciliation between France and the Church, but these bulls, as Gregorovius noted, meant "the death sentence of the papacy as a political body. They signalled its withdrawal from the dominant position which it had boasted in the universe and was the solstice of its history." From this would arise the totally denigrating operation against the Caetani pope under Clement V.

However, the situation in Rome continued to be chaotic in a fight to the finish between the Caetani and the Colonnas, with the latter managing to make themselves heard once again in the Capitol where Gentile Orsini and Luca Savelli were Senators. Benedict deemed it wise to leave Rome and take refuge at Montefiascone, then at Orvieto, and finally at Perugia. Here new proceedings were opened on the happenings at Anagni and a firm verdict was reached leading to the excommunication of William of Nogaret, Sciarra Colonna, and other leaders. In the bull which sanctioned the verdict was tacitly included Philip the Fair as the person who ordered the attack. The bull was courageously published on 7 June but, precisely one month later, on 7 July 1304, Benedict XI died, perhaps poisoned.

According to the account of Villani, "while he was seated at the dining table, a young man dressed and veiled like a woman came toward him, appearing like a serving girl from the nuns of Santa Petronilla in Perugia, carrying a silver bowl containing some beautiful ripe figs, and presented it with devotion to the pope as a gift from the abbess of that convent. The pope took it joyfully because he loved figs, and since a girl brought them, he ate many of them. Suddenly he fell ill and, a few days later, died."

His death is said to have been caused by diamond dust injected into the figs, and even if Castiglioni observes that this was a "strange method of poisoning" and Gregorovius says that "it was clearly an invented story," there is no reason not to think it was an assassination committed by Nogaret and Sciarra Colonna, who had been excommunicated a month earlier.

Benedict XI was buried in the church of St. Dominic at Perugia. He was beatified by the Church and canonized in 1736.

195. CLEMENT V (1305–1314)

Only three days after the death of Benedict XI, ignoring the Gregorian decree on conclaves, the cardinals met in the Archbishop's Palace of Perugia in the hopes of a speedy election which would avoid any external interference. The College of Cardinals, however, was sharply divided into two factions: the pro-Italian under Cardinals Matteo Orsini and Francesco Caetani, and the pro-French one headed by Napoleon Orsini and Nicholas of Prato, upon which lay the *longa manus* of Philip the Fair.

The arguments between the cardinals went on for a full year, accompanied by armed fights between the supporters of the two sides both in Rome and throughout the Papal State, but finally a compromise was reached. The pro-Italians would propose a list of three candidates from which the pro-French faction would choose the new pope. It happened that all three, although French, were opponents of Philip the Fair, who was immediately notified, together with the counterproposal of the archbishop of Bordeaux, Bertrand de Got. The king quickly summoned the French candidate to Paris and made an agreement with him. According to Villani, the Archbishop is said to have promised the king massive concessions, in the event he was elected, including the use of "all of the tithes in the kingdom for five years" (VIII, 80). Dante was also convinced that Bertrand de Got, "the lawless Shepherd," had become pope "by buying" the powerful aid of Philip, and for this assigned him a place in his *Inferno* among the simonists (XIX, 83 & 85–87):

A new Jason will it be, of whom we read in Maccabees;
And as to that high priest his king was pliant, so to this

Shall be he who governs France.
(The Carlyle-Wicksteed translation)

Bertrand de Got, a native of Villandraut in Gironde, was thus elected on 5 July 1305. A Gascon, he had studied at Orléans and Bologna and had been chosen archbishop of Bordeaux by Boniface VIII. He was on friendly terms with the king of France and, eager to become pope, he surrendered unconditionally to his requests. His first act, and as such a significant one, was to send a message to those who had elected him to move to France because he wished to be crowned in his own country.

This took place on 14 November 1305, at Lyons in the church of St. Just in the presence of Philip the Fair, Charles of Valois, Duke John of Brittany and numerous nobles of France. Bertrand de Got took the name of Clement V.

During the procession, which followed the ceremony, certain incidents occurred which the common folk immediately took for omens of bad luck and disasters in the near future. A wall collapsed on the pope, who fell off his horse, while his crown rolled in the dust and a beautiful diamond was lost. Charles of Valois was seriously injured, the duke of Brittany died of his wounds, and twelve barons were killed on the spot.

But these fatalities, which foretold dark days for the Church, did not influence the king and the pope on what they had decided at their meeting. The Holy See was moved from Rome to France, first to Lyons, then to Cluny, Bordeaux, Poitiers, and, finally to Avignon in Provence. In this city the papacy was to remain for about seventy years, a period which passed into history under the name of the "Avignon Captivity." The popes, official guests of the king of Naples in his role as the count of Provence, were, in the popular view, subjects of the king of France, even though the Church already owned the Venaissin county near Avignon. It is a fact that the popes of Avignon were all Frenchmen, and because of their national feeling they were closely bound to their native land.

And then there was the absurdity of the bishop of Rome being so far away from his diocese, and of the Apostolic and Roman Church being run from Avignon where no apostle had ever been. For this entire period Rome was left to itself amidst battles between factions, and the Papal State escaped almost completely from pontifical sovereignty, in a decadence such that any return of the Curia to Rome became strictly out of the question in a foreseeable future.

Already with Clement V, the subordination of the papacy to the king of France was evident. Just a few weeks after his election he showed his compliance to the wishes of Philip the Fair by nominating nine new French cardinals, relatives or friends of the king, so as to permit a clear majority of the French within the College of Cardinals who had full control over the policies of the Curia. Even Cardinals Giacomo and Pietro Colonna were restored to their positions.

But what interested Philip and the majority of the cardinals most were the proceedings against Boniface VIII. Clement V tried as best he could to gain time and did manage to avoid an official condemnation of the late pope, but it cost him numerous concessions always damaging to the image of Boniface VIII. These began in February 1306, when the pope revoked all the measures taken against the Colonna family, who recovered possession of everything they had lost to the Caetani and the Orsini. Philip also received the church tithes, promised to him by the pope before his election. Moreover the bull, *Clericis laicos*, was abrogated and as a result the relations of the king of France with the Church were to remain the same as those enjoyed by him prior to the issuance of that bull.

Clement V thought he had adequately compensated his king for having supported him in the election to the pontificate, but he was wrong. At a meeting at Poitiers in May 1308, the two of them got into a bitter row because of some claims made by Philip. He wanted a condemnation of Boniface VIII by a proper proceeding and the cancellation of the excommunication of Nogaret, as well as the convocation of an ecumenical council in France and the dissolution of the Order of the Templars, an Order of Knights which had received an ecclesiastical Rule from Bernard of Chiaravalle because of an activity related to the Holy Land. With the twilight of the Crusades, the Order had lost any practical importance, but had continued to prosper especially in France with the opening of numerous monasteries, which were depositories of the treasures collected by these ecclesiastics. Indeed, as Ullmann notes, "with the development of commerce between the Levant and western Europe, the Templars began to serve as merchant bankers. Moreover, as there were many who had deposited jewellery and other personal assets with the Templars in France, the Order was on the way to becoming a great economic power enjoying many privileges and immunities." In reality, Philip wanted to lay his hands on this immense fortune by pushing the pope to dissolve the Order of the Templars, even at the price of giving up the trial of Boniface VIII, which was what occurred.

Clement V promptly gave his consent to the holding of a council, whereas on the other matters he was more reluctant, giving in gradually, so as to save as far as it was possible, the memory of pope Caetani.

As for the Templars, the pope thought he could manage that problem by giving full power to the bishops and to the Inquisition so that the committees in the individual dioceses could examine the situation of the monasteries on a case-by-case basis. But the truth was he did not have a free hand even in the formation of the committees, more or less all of which were directly managed by Philip. And these committees, by applying torture, managed to extort from the most eminent representatives of the Order of the Templars confessions to the heresies which the Inquisition considered true and, therefore, sent them to the funeral pyre, their retractions not deemed valid, while the guilty ones were considered heretical "recidivists." No heed was paid to their appeals to the pope, and Clement V succeeded only in postponing a decision condemning the Order until the council at Vienne, convened for October 1310. But this was further delayed for a year because Philip and his court, pressed by the Colonnas, wanted the trial of Boniface VIII, continually put off by the pope, but which finally started in March 1310 at Avignon.

The prosecution was maintained by William of Nogaret and William of Plasian, who were members of the King's Council of State and authors of all those murky manuevers which had led to the "insult at Anagni," while the two Colonna cardinals, personal enemies of the Caetani pope, served as prosecution witnesses. At this point, however, the king knew that he would have to concede something to poor Clement V and, faced with still another delaying tactic, decided not to inflict another humiliation on the papacy. Naturally this was not through piety but rather to get definitively the consent of the pope for the dissolution of the Order of the Templars during the council. So, on 27 April 1311, in the bull *Rex gloriae*, Clement V recognized expressly the innocence and the *bonus zelus* of the king in his proceeding against Boniface VIII and lifted the excommunication of Nogaret. And, it should be noted, in every one of the bulls issued by that pope all passages containing any reproaches of the king were literally "scratched out."

So the council of Vienne, the fifteenth ecumenical council, began in the presence of Philip on 16 October 1311. It was meant to deal essentially of the Templars case and it did so in a unilateral way, on the basis of the trials already held by the Inquisition and of the report of a French episcopal committee. By his bull *Vox in excelso* of 3 April 1312, unanimously approved by the Council, the pope decreed the dissolution of the Order by the simple explanation that the Order no longer dealt with the tasks for which it had been created, connected as they were to the Holy Land and with the Crusades which were now over, and noting that many of its adherents had been recognized as heretics. All the wealth and the property of the Templars were divided between the Hospitalers and the Johnites, but most of the riches fell into the hands of Philip the Fair who was imaginative enough to dream up expedients which gave him the last word in every circumstance. He transformed the tower of the Temple in Paris into his residential castle, which, during the French Revolution, would be the prison of Louis XVI and Marie Antoinette.

As for Boniface VIII, his trial was considered over or cancelled, but by then the figure of the Caetani pope had finished in ignominy. The Council declared his faith orthodox and all allegations of heresy unfounded; so the name of Boniface was not removed from the list of Roman pontiffs. As Walter Ullmann observes, "the price paid by the papacy to avoid the trial of the deceased

Boniface was very high; there is no doubt that his reputation suffered a great deal from this whole story." Above all, the canonization of Celestine V, which took place in Avignon on 5 May 1313, and strongly backed by Philip the Fair, was indirectly the condemnation of another deed by Boniface VIII, that is, the imprisonment of the hermit-pope. In effect the memory of Benedict Caetani was saved in form but not in substance.

Clement V was, by then, very ill and incapable of any action even of a diplomatic nature. He had placed the last vague hopes of restoring some semblance of a Papal State in the new king of Germany, Henry VII. Then, urged by Philip and heeding the appeals of the Blacks from Florence, who had opposed his entry into the Tuscan city and had suffered a siege and looting, he ended by lining up against him, and arrogating imperial power to himself through Robert of Anjou, the king of Naples. So when Henry VII died in 1313, the dreams of the last of the Italian Ghibellines and of idealists such as Dante, who had seen him as the saviour of an Italy on the verge of anarchy, vanished into thin air. The pope had appointed Robert of Anjou, dedicated solely to his own personal interests, as the imperial vicar in Italy, That was the final act of weakness on the part of a pope who had been suffering, probably from the very beginning of his pontificate, from an illness by then incurable. As his last days , he moved to Carpentras. He died at Roquemaure on 20 April 1314 and was buried at Uzès, where his tomb was later destroyed. A few months later, Philip the Fair also died.

The severe judgments pronounced against Clement V have been somewhat attenuated by modern critics, who have tended to excuse his weakness of character because of his illness. Ullmann talks, however, about his "lack of diplomacy, experience, training and intuitive ability which explains the headlong fall of the papacy." Above all, if he was not in perfect physical health when he was elected, even more serious appear his murky manuevers in becoming the pontiff, a position that he would not have been able in all conscience to exercise freely with a wasting physique.

In the final analysis all justifications of this kind are useless when confronted with the serious nepotism which marked his pontificate. As Seppelt recalls, "no fewer than five members of his large family were brought into the College of Cardinals, many others were installed in bishoprics, and certain ones obtained rich benefices, while he granted his lay relatives lucrative jobs in the Papal State. And even in his will he bequeathed them such large amounts that, under his successor, there was an unpleasant trial." So, it is difficult to defend a pope of this kind, whether as a political person or as a man of the Church and, in the light of certain observations, all the accusations made by contemporaries against this "lawless pope" would seem to ring true.

196. JOHN XXII (1316—1334)

After the death of Clement V, the College of Cardinals gathered at Carpentras, where the pope had recently moved his court, for the election of the new vicar of Christ. There were twenty-three cardinals but only six were Italians, all the others being either Frenchmen or linked to the king of France, so the election of a candidate like William, bishop of Palestrina, was unthinkable and the efforts of the Italian cardinals, who wanted above all to return the papal see to Rome, proved in vain. Poignant and impassioned was the appeal sent to them by Dante, who exhorted them to labor for the Bride of Christ, the Church, on behalf of Rome and Italy; it was a message from the last prophet of a Christian world now shrouded in darkness.

The conclave continued in an atmosphere of intrigue, bribery and violence in which there was no place for such a message, and matters came to a head at the end of July 1314, with the invasion of the episcopal palace by armed bands of Gascons, led by Bertrand de Got, nephew of the deceased pontiff, who forced the Italians to flee with, as result, the temporary suspension of the assembly.

Two years of parleys passed before the two factions got together again. Louis X, first-born of Philip the Fair and his successor, failed to bring them to an agreement but when he died, his brother, Philip V, used force and on 28 June 1316 shut the cardinals up in a Dominican monastery at Lyons. Nevertheless, another month was to pass before a new pope was elected. On 7 August, the choice fell once more on a Gascon, Jacques-Arnaud d'Euse, born in Cahors.

This man clearly enjoyed the protection of Robert of Anjou, thanks to whom he had become the bishop of Fréjus and later of Avignon, before being appointed Cardinal of Porto by Clement V. He was consecrated pope on 25 September 1316, under the name of John XXII and took up residence at Avignon.

His pontificate was marked by two interlocked problems, the dispute with Emperor Ludwig of Bavaria and the controversies within the Franciscan Order. On the death of Henry VII, a serious crisis had erupted in Germany because of disagreements among the Electors which had led to the election of both Frederick of Austria and Ludwig of Bavaria, while the pope, ignoring the expectations of the two contenders, supported Robert of Anjou as the imperial vicar in Italy.

As regards the Franciscans, the pope had to deal with the headaches which the rebellious Spirituals were causing the Order by their arbitrariness and disobedience pertaining to their dress and food, in the name of a rigid application of their Rule both in Tuscany and Provence. In 1317, he issued a Constitution which in effect banned the Spirituals and, although most of them obeyed the pope, the few who did not went before the Inquisition which defined them as heretics, and condemned them to the funeral pyre. Their brethren obviously viewed them as martyrs and saw in this pope, who continued to issue bulls against their ideas and called them disdainfully "little brothers," a kind of anti-Christ.

Dante thought the same and accused him of ruining the vineyard of the Church (Paradise, XVIII, 130–132):

> ... but thou, who but to cancel, dost record, reflect that Peter and
> Paul who died for the vineyard thou layest waste, are living yet.
> *(The Carlyle-Wicksteed translation)*

This was a clear reference to the simplicity and poverty of the Apostles which should constitute the true life of Christianity. It was precisely John XXII's rigid attitude towards the Spirituals which brought about, among the various factions of the Order, a consensus of opposition to him. The conflict is generally described as the "polemic on theoretical poverty," as a result of which the theological question as to "whether Christ and his Apostles had possessed anything, either individually or as a community" surfaced again. In fact, through the words of their General Michael of Cesena in a circular addressed to Christendom, the Franciscans declared that their stand on the poverty of Christ corresponded to Catholic doctrine. The pope then issued a bull in 1323 in which he declared such a stand heretical. The Order resented this and many Friars Minor went so far as to accuse the pope of heresy, censuring even the canonization of Thomas Aquinas, on the occasion of which John XXII had defined as apostolic the modification of the doctrine on the poverty of the Dominicans.

All this was going on while Ludwig of Bavaria, who had defeated his rival Frederick of Austria and considered himself the only contender for the imperial crown, indicated his intention of descending to Italy and establishing his own power there. The pope continued to oppose his imperial ambitions and to defend the position of the imperial vicar, Robert of Anjou, and, on 23 March 1324, he excommunicated Ludwig, accusing him of having exercised authority without the pope's approval.

At this point, Ludwig endorsed the accusation of heresy made by the Minors against the pope and, in the famous Manifesto of Sachsenhausen of May 1324, requested the convocation of an ecumenical council to try John XXII for abuse of ecclesiastical censures in pursuit of his own interests. Ludwig's position was very strong in this open war against the pope, not only because of the support of the German laity and clergy, but also because a large proportion of the Minors were arrayed on his side. A famous professor from the University of Paris, Marsilius of Padua, even offered to help the king as a consultant in the conflict. In his *Defensor pacis*, among other things, he denied the primacy of Peter and declared that the Apostle had never been in Rome so that the primacy of the bishop of Rome was not of divine origin; moreover that the pope had no right to choose or to depose an emperor. Such ideas fitted perfectly into the scheme of the king of Germany who decided to come to Italy to take over the imperial lands and to be crowned emperor. The expedition took place in 1327 and was obviously greeted enthusiastically by the Ghibellines.

Ludwig arrived in Rome on 7 January 1328 when the rebels had already ousted the partisans of Robert of Anjou. Ten days later, elected by the Romans as Senator and Captain of the People, Sciarra Colonna crowned him in St. Peter's "in the name of the Roman people." It was a revolutionary coronation, based on lay principles of imperial thought.

The response of the pope was immediate with the excommunication renewed and no recognition of the title of Emperor to Ludwig, together with an interdiction for all of his followers, both lay and ecclesiastical. However, John XXII was now alone. Even the General of the Franciscans, Michael of Cesena, summoned to Avignon to defend his attitude deemed critical of the pontifical decrees against the orthodox wing of the Order, abandoned the pope and sought refuge at Ludwig's court together with William of Occam. He too was promptly excommunicated.

At this point, the emperor felt sufficiently strong to allow himself to be brought into Rome by the people's leaders. Arriving on 14 April 1328, he initiated a trial for heresy against the pope, which was followed four days later by an imperial decree which deposed John XXII as being guilty of the crime of *lèse majesté*, and passed his case to the ordinary secular tribunal with the accusation of being a heretic.

With the deposing of John, there followed the election of a new pope on 12 May 1328 by a committee of thirteen representatives of the Roman clergy, and a Franciscan named Pietro Rainalducci from Corvara was confirmed pope by an imperial decree. This was obviously not a legal election, and the one chosen could only be considered an antipope, but Ludwig and his followers considered him the pontiff to all intents and purposes. He took the name of Nicholas V and, as his first act, repeated the coronation of Ludwig with due observance of the traditional rite and its related anointment.

All this was somewhat of a farce, especially as the great anti-John theoreticians had not produced an emperor or an anti-pope of impressive prestige. Nicholas V was a nullity with no supporters amongst the ecclesiastics and mainly the Minors and those excommunicated on his side. He finally realized the weakness of his own position, and in August 1330, he repented and supposedly went to see John XXII at Avignon who is said to have pardoned him. Forgotten, he died in October 1333.

Ludwig's luck in Rome was also minimal. The heavy taxes he imposed in Rome caused such resentment that he had to flee the city, which returned to the power of Robert of Anjou, and by December 1329 Ludwig was back in Germany.

It is true that even John XXII showed the paucity of his own culture on a purely theological level. In various sermons, and in particular in one he gave on All Saints Day in 1331, talking about the length of time it took to have the "beatific vision" for those who die in the state of grace, he declared that this would be achieved not immediately after death but at the time of the resurrection of the body which would happen at the Universal Judgment "under the altar," that is, with the comfort of the human nature of Christ.

This was a thesis in conflict with traditional Orthodoxy which provoked a scandal and lent credence to the accusations of heresy which had been voiced by his political opponents. But this time even competent theologians near him openly clashed with him. John took the trouble to explain in writing that it was merely a personal opinion and one that was open to discussion, but it was only a way out. On his deathbed he had to withdraw his declaration before the College of Cardinals, thus probably saving the Church's doctrine but not the prestige of a now personally discredited authority.

A further accusation can be levelled at this pope on his financial policy. If it was clearly necessary to clean up in a systematic fashion the administration of the universal Church, the means used by the pope appeared to be a particularly scandalous way of increasing the income of the apostolic see. It was to his merit that he organized the chancery and established the *Sacra Rota* (Ecclesiastical Court), so called because of the rotation of the jurists on the bench by turns. However, the pressure to accumulate huge sums gave rise to a chorus of protests to the point of his being accused of having reduced to misery numerous churches by the fiscal system of *commende* (the assignment of ecclesiastical advantages).

However, as Castiglioni also remarks, "the institution of the *commende* developed rapidly and widely since all offices and dignities of chapters became subject to *commende*. Not only ecclesiastics but also lay persons could be given *commende* which, with the passing of time, became attractive sinecures sought by unworthy persons, and objects of commerce and merchandising. Once the road of abuses was opened, it was not simple or possible to limit or even put a brake on the scandals."

As a result the papal bureaucracy flourished with hundreds of notaries, archivists, and compilers of bulls in a very efficient organization which culminated in the Registry of the Apostolic Chamber, part of the financial department of the Curia, in an intricate mechanism of income and expense entries. It was the beginning of a "system" that would be perfected over the centuries. John XXII set it up but did not benefit personally from it. In brief, he was not the "Midas of Avignon," as Gregorovius called him, and it was a pure invention of Villani that he had left an inheritance of 25 million florins. However, John XXII did use this "system" with its centralization to reward relatives and countrymen with jobs and gifts, in a wave of nepotism *ante litteram* which certainly did him no honor.

He died at Avignon on 4 December 1334, and was buried in the church of Notre-Dame-des-Doms.

197. BENEDICT XII (1334—1342)

The conclave to elect the successor of John XXII met in Avignon ten days later, and by 20 December 1334 had completed its task. The French Cardinal Jacques Fournier was elected, consecrated on 8 January 1335, and took the name of Benedict XII.

The son of a miller of Savardin in the county of Foix, he had been a Cistercian monk, then bishop of Palmiers and of Mirepoix, and subsequently made a cardinal by John XXII. Blessed with a notable theological background, he stood fast on orthodoxy and opposed any heresy. He was, however, very different from his predecessor and, while he inherited the financial system installed by John XXII, he sought to get rid of the abuses which had taken place. A stranger to nepotism and scrupulous with appointments, he never placed any relative in either lay or ecclesiastical jobs in the Curia during his pontificate, apart from a nephew named archbishop of Arles, but then only after the intervention of the cardinals.

As soon as he was elected, he received a delegation of Romans who begged him to return the apostolic see to their city. He tried to agree to this just request but the College of Cardinals, controlled by the king of France, was against the return to Rome, even though Benedict wrote personally to Philip VI a letter full of heartfelt pleas. So he had to resign himself to starting the construction of the magnificent buildings which were to assure the papacy of a worthy see in Avignon.

In fact, the oldest part of the Papal Palace, called the Old Palace, goes back to his time. As Pastor observes: "This ponderous structure, a strange mixture of fortress and cloister, of dungeon and palace, reflects the circumstances of the Holy See at that time," or rather it reflected the austerity of the ex-monk who disdained worldly luxury. Later buildings in the complex are said to have given a more luxurious and courtly aspect to the palace of the popes.

The Romans lost any hope of seeing their bishop again, after their offer of the position of senator, and subsequently, the lifetime lordship, was turned down. Benedict had but kindness and good words for his distant subjects in the letters transmitted by his nuncio, thanks to whom he succeeded in temporarily restoring order in republican Rome, still the victim of abuses by the nobility. So the Papal State found a moment of peace, and several cities accepted the sovereignty of pontifical authority or that of vicars appointed by Benedict, who personally did not stir from Avignon.

Negotiations for a rapprochement between the papacy and Ludwig the Bavarian were hindered by Philip VI, who saw in a possible peace treaty between the pope and the emperor the likelihood of a return of the papal see to Rome. The French sovereign, therefore, forestalled matters by forming an alliance with the emperor, brushing aside any problems about religion, since Ludwig, being excommunicated, was not supposed to have any standing in the eyes of other Christian sovereigns. Benedict criticized the behavior of Philip, which evoked the indignation of the German princes faithful to the Bavarian, and who declared that he had the right to the title of Emperor even without the approval of the pope.

On the basis of these principles, Ludwig issued in August 1338, the constitution *Licet juris*, which affirmed that the emperor could not be judged by the pope because imperial power came directly from God. Furthermore, supported at court by a learned group of theologians, he dissolved the marriage of Margherita Maultasch, heiress to Tyrol and Carinthia, to give her as bride to his son in 1342. In his essay, *Del potere imperiale in materia di matrimonio*, William of Occam justified this action. In vain Benedict XII intervened in defense of the marriage bond, but he was not able to follow the developments in the dispute which reached a conclusion durign the time of his successor, Clement VI. Death came to Benedict on 25 April 1342 in Avignon where he was buried in the cathedral in a splendid mausoleum which was destroyed, however, in the eighteenth century as it was unstable.

The maxim attributed to him, "the pope must be like Melchizedech who had no father, no mother, nor even a family tree," gives an exact picture of Benedict XII, who was shy of personal power and was devoted exclusively to the restoration of the authority of the Church. Although occupied with the construction of Avignon, he was the only pope of this period seriously interested in the see of Rome, and he allocated huge sums of money for the restorations of the Lateran and St. Peter's. This "love" from a distance for the apostolic see was recorded in an inscription at the base of a bust erected by the Romans in his honor at the main entrance to the Vatican basilica, later moved to the underground grottoes.

198. CLEMENT VI (1342—1352)

Thirteen days after the death of Benedict XII at Avignon, on 7 May 1342, the cardinals elected as pope Pierre Roger de Beaufort. Born in Malmont in 1291 and a Benedictine monk at a very young age, he had been a teacher of theology at Paris and bishop of Arras, as well as a chancellor for Philip the Fair. Thereafter bishop of Sens and Rouen, and raised to the cardinal purple by Benedict XII, he was consecrated as pope on 19 May with the name of Clement VI.

Closely linked to his motherland, he gave no thought of going to Rome and, instead, worked on the expansion of the residence at Avignon, annexing to the severe Old Palace the more elegant and attractive New Palace which gave to the whole complex a splendor worthy of the later popes of the Renaissance. Prestige and prosperity then characterized Avignon which, from being a small provincial town, became the capital of Christendom. However, with the growth of traffic and population as well as increased wealth, it took on the look also of a huge commercial center.

Avignon had in effect two faces. It was a second Rome, with the offices of the Curia all running at top efficiency as a result of the improvements made by John XXII, and, for that very reason, it also became a financial center. No fewer than four thousand people gravitated around the papal court, including commercial representatives and branches of the great Florentine and Sienese banks in Avignon.

The Church was involved in more or less legitimate transactions, sufficient to earn its definition as the New Babylon in the *Rhymes* of Petrarch (CXIV, 1–4):

> From impious Babylon whence every shame has fled,
> and all good things have left, inn of sorrow,
> mother of errors, I fled from it to survive.

And the poet of Arezzo appeared still more nauseated about the papal residence: "ever . . . terrible . . . that place seemed to me . . . for its collection of the iniquities and the garbage of the entire world," he noted in a letter to the archbishop of Genoa (Seniles,X,2), adding that "so much so that, not to speak of the rest, faith and charity would never find a home there, and about that place one may say what was earlier said about Hannibal, there is nothing true in it, nothing sacred, no fear of God, no sanctity of oaths, no religion . . ."

Petrarch, of course, used such invectives in order to convince the pope to return to Rome. But, however exaggerated by the heat of argument, the image reflected a basic reality.

As Castiglione himself observes, "the spendthrift megalomania of Clement VI had already evidenced itself when he was a cardinal, and it was good for his creditors that Pierre Roger became pope since he wanted to recompense them all with large gifts. The officials of his court, whether clerics or not, received huge salaries and the expenses of government were enormous. Moreover, around his court could be found every kind of adventurer including alchemists, and sellers of stolen goods and contraband, who certainly gave Avignon an appearance which would have horrified Dante into seeing the Church, more than ever, as 'a woman of the streets.'"

As for the return to Rome, for Clement VI it was a subject not to be discussed and, in a deed dated 9 June 1384, he purchased the city of Avignon from Queen Joan of Naples who had feudal sovereignty over it. In Rome he took pains to make the populace happy by entrusting Cola di Rienzo, sent to him as ambassador in 1343, with the office of notary to the city's Chamber. It was a title which gave the young man the opportunity to capture the admiration of his fellow citizens, when he fired them with republican ideals in his orations from the Capitol even if at the beginning, he was respectful of the Avignon pope. Cola thus became chief of the democratic leaders in Rome and, in 1347, was duly appointed "by authority of Our Lord Jesus Christ, the strong and awe-inspiring Tribune of liberty, peace and justice, and Liberator of the Holy Roman Republic."

On the imperial scene, Ludwig the Bavarian, at loggerheads with the papacy, pretended to want peace with Clement, but the latter influenced certain German princes to elect a kind of anti-king in the person of Karl of Moravia, a loyal subject of the pope and his guest at Avignon, with enough oaths of loyalty to suffice until his coronation, which took place in 1346 at Bonn. In September of the following year, Ludwig died and Karl IV was recognized by all the princes of Germany. William of Occam and a large number of the theologians gathered at the court of the Bavarian and paid homage to the pope who pardoned them and annulled their excommunication.

"Pontifical" Rome was experiencing meanwhile the mad and wonderful communal adventure of Cola di Rienzo in a mixture of megalomania and democracy which was to become fatal to the Tribune. Displeasing to both Clement VI and Karl IV was the incident when Cola was crowned as Knight at St. Mary Major with seven crowns signifying the seven gifts of the Holy Spirit, and the silver orb as a symbol of the empire. Power had gone to his head and probably distanced him from the democratic spirit with which he had conquered the Roman plebeians. So it was easy for the papal vicar, Raymond, bishop of Orvieto, to portray him in a bad light and then to declare him deposed from every position and to excommunicate him in December 1348.

The ex-tribune fleeing north attempted to convince Karl IV in 1350 to become the promoter of a renewal of both humanity and of the Church, making him a participant in the prophetic visions of a hermit friend of his, Brother Angelo. However, a papal sovereign like Karl did not waste much time listening to Cola, and the archbishop of Prague had him imprisoned, shipping him off to Avignon to have him tried for heresy. In August 1352, a tribunal of three cardinals condemned him to death although the verdict was not final. Between appeals from Petrarch, his great admirer, and from the Romans who wanted him back to restore justice in a city which was prey to anarchy, notwithstanding the Jubilee of 1350, Cola spent the final months of the pontificate of Clement VI as a well-behaved and benevolent prisoner, despite the death sentence hanging over his head.

The Jubilee Year 1350 was announced by Clement VI, so reducing to 50 years the interval between one Holy Year and the next one, in accord with the Jewish custom, and with the addition of a visit to the basilica of San Giovanni. Officially the pope wanted to bring a little spiritual serenity to Italy and to Christian Europe, so tortured by the plague of two years earlier. Villani notes though that the real purpose was economic because "from the offerings given by the pilgrims, the Church would gain a great deal of money, and the Romans would all get rich through providing services." In essence, if the Holy Year gave Rome the chance to become again the center of Christianity, also the prospect of good business for the citizens left to their own devices was very real. As Villani again points out, some vendors profited from the occasion, for example, by "fraud on the part of the butcher who sold bad meat mixed with good," while the innkeepers speculated with the beds by assigning one to two or three persons and then "made as many as six or seven lie in them."

So in certain aspects, Avignon had a "branch office" in Rome, and the fact that Clement increased the number of basilicas to be visited to three, adding to St. Peter's and St. Paul's also St. John Lateran, caused a greater flow of pilgrims and thereby of "alms." These went directly into the hands of two cardinals sent to Rome by the pope with full powers, Guido of Boulogne-sur-Mer and Pietro Ciriaco of Limoges, as well as into those of the papal vicar, Cardinal Annibaldo Gaetani of Ceccano, who was resident in the Vatican.

This man set up a traffic in absolutions for the pilgrims who had been excommunicated, where the concept of "alms" went up in smoke because of a genuine "under the counter" market. Annibaldo roused the wrath of the pilgrims, suffered an assault and reacted with arrests and torture, even inflicting an interdiction on Rome in the middle of the Holy Year. Clement understood then that it would be wise to replace him and sent him to Naples, but this did not save Cardinal Annibaldo from being killed as he was poisoned on the way there. Everything seemed symptomatic of the manner in which the religious meaning of the Jubilee had been distorted, precisely because the pontifical mini-court in Rome mirrored the habits and attitudes of the big, official one at Avignon.

Indeed, Clement VI was enjoying himself in his Babylon, entrenched in a luxurious and, in no way, apostolic court. Castiglioni himself had to give credit to the Masons who "judged Clement very harshly and did not spare him from the charge of avidity for money, of a spendthrift living, and even of a suspicion of immorality," echoing what Matteo Villani had written about this pope who "knew no limits in elevating and enriching his relatives, and provided the Church with so many young and dishonest cardinals, all his relatives, and lived with them such a vile, dissolute life that it was an abomination" (Annals, 1352).

Clement VI died at Avignon on 6 December 1352, and was buried in the abbey of Chaise Dieu in the Upper Loire.

199. INNOCENT VI (1352–1362)

Twelve days after his death, Clement already had a successor as, on 18 December 1352, the cardinals elected a Frenchman, Etienne Aubert, born in Mont near Beyssac in the Limoges diocese. A learned canonist, formerly bishop of Noyon and Clermont, he had been Cardinal of Ostia since 1342. He was consecrated pope on 30 December and took the name of Innocent VI.

Aware of the absolute nature of his power, he fully restored the *plenitudo potestatis*, and, as the first act of his pontificate, refused to put into practice an agreement that the cardinals had adopted under oath during the conclave. Among other things, it contained clauses stating that the newly elected pope would not increase the number cardinals in the College to over twenty, that the Curial income would be divided equally among the cardinals, and that it was forbidden to give important positions to one's relatives. The College wanted to introduce an oligarchical form of government within the Church, to the detriment of the absolute primacy of the pontiff, and Innocent VI was careful not to fall into this trap by issuing on 5 July 1353 a bull, *Sollicitudo pastoralis*, which annulled that agreement.

He simplified the administration of the Curia along the ideas of Benedict XII as opposed to what had been done by Clement VI. Decidedly against all worldliness and wisely counselled by the General of the Dominicans, he revoked many investitures granted by his predecessor, and toughened the obligation of residence at their sees for prelates under threat of dire punishment. Avignon thus rid itself of many seekers of prebends and regained an appearance more in keeping with religious dignity. But he was also rigid about the maintenance of the Franciscan Rule in terms of its orthodoxy. So the Spirituals continued to be subject to trials by the Inquisition, and this led to very severe judgments against Innocent even by the devout Catholic Princess Bridget of Sweden, who had taken up residence in Rome since the Holy Year. At first, she had praised this pope because of his moderate spirit.

Yet even Innocent's management proved in the long run to have lapses, like the numerous concessions granted to his countrymen and certain nepotistic tendencies from which he could not escape completely, despite the rigorous spirit that appeared to mark him at the time of his enthronement. So Innocent VI wound up being a delusion for those who had praised him and Petrarch, who had described him as *"magnus vir et juris cultissimus,"* revised his judgment to the point of refusing the post of special assistant which the pope had offered him.

The task to which Innocent IV was particularly dedicated and which did him honor was the restoration of pontifical authority at Rome, its real see and age-old seat of power. Innocent's constant preoccupation was the uncontrolled situation there and in the Papal State, where the local gentry dictated the law.

For this important question he decided to put his trust in Cardinal Gil Alvarez de Albornoz, who was both a military officer, a diplomat and a legal expert. He also sent Cola di Rienzo to the Cardinal, deciding that it was time to free him from prison in Avignon, having pardoned him and lifted his excommunication. A man like Cola, he reckoned, could well be helpful to Albornoz who could use the knowledge that the ex-tribune possessed on the Italian situation, as well as the prestige that he still had among the Romans.

The idea of returning some day to Rome if Albornoz could make it possible did pass though Innocent's mind. And Albornoz did succeed with the help of a small army in repossessing the Papal State, after drafting soldiers from the Roman populace thanks to a new constitution, the so-called "Egidian Constitution." This provided for the appointment of a single "foreign'"senator for a period of six months, assisted in the government by a democratic college of seven members, real heads of the Commune, elected by the people. The government of Rome was taken away from the nobility in the Capitol and given to the common people from whom, in due course, would come the new noblemen. Cola partially contributed to the success of this reformation, but they were the dying moments of a republican dream. Albornoz used him without yielding to compromises, ready to discredit him in the eyes of the people when he began to get in the way, and to make him a victim of plebeian fury on 8 October 1354.

With Rome again under the control of the pope, it was now even possible to think of an imperial coronation. Karl IV received this on 5 April 1355, as "Emperor of the Romans," after which, though, he went back to Germany. In any case, the figure of traditional emperor no longer made any sense. The sworn promises of protection of the papacy had not been kept for a long time, and the emperor, crowned by a cardinal in the absence of the pope, deemed it sufficient to leave Albornoz a contingent of five hundred German cavalry to help him in the military operation then underway. In reality, Karl felt the crown was his by right of blood, and he hastened to say exactly that in 1356 in the "Golden Bull" which referred to the *Licet juris* of Ludwig the Bavarian. The right of the pope to share in creating the emperor was in fact annulled. It was the end of an epoch.

Meanwhile, Albernoz was finishing his task with a series of lengthy battles from the Campagna to the border regions, costing the Curia enormous amounts of money. Yet Innocent VI put all his energy into this military operation convinced that behind it lay the salvation of the prestige of the Church. All the ancient provinces came back under his scepter, except for that of Bernabò Visconti who put up resistance in his native Bologna, while nobles like the Este, the Ordelaffi and the Manfredi returned to the service of the pope as his vassals. And Rome, freed from domination by the nobles, wanted the pope back again within her walls.

Innocent VI was not deaf to their repeated prayers and was on the point of giving in to the urgent exhortations for the great return sent to him by Bridget of Sweden and by Petrarch. The emperor himself, notwithstanding the "Golden Bull," offered to accompany him in person, but old age and ill health prevented him from bringing the matter to fruition.

He died on 12 September 1362, at Avignon and was buried in the Carthusian monastery at Villeneuve-les-Avignon, founded by him.

200. URBAN V (1362—1370)

The successor of Innocent VI was Guillaume Grimoard of the noble family of Grisac, where he was born in 1310. A Benedictine monk and professor of canon law at Montpellier, he had been abbot of S. Vittore at Marseilles but had not been made a cardinal. He was elected on 28 October 1362, while in Naples as papal legate, so his consecration in Avignon could not take place until 6 November. He took the name of Urban V.

With him the possibility of a return to Rome of the pontifical see became rapidly a reality. Urban knew Italy and he was not opposed, like the French cardinals, to leaving his fatherland, in view of the fact also that the situation in France was not all that stable due to the disastrous Hundred Years War. Obviously the pope could not seriously consider the matter until Albornoz had finished the job of restoring the Papal State, even if he could not defeat Bernabò Visconti, the last bastion of an extreme Ghibellinism in Bologna. The latter did not recognize the pope as a temporal sovereign and confiscated ecclesiastical property, while Albornoz was unable to overcome him militarily. Urban did excommunicate him, but considerably more was needed to overpower him.

In any event, the Romans immediately conferred on the new pope the government of the city, while he confirmed the democratic constitution issued by Albornoz. However, if Rome was peaceful, the nobles of the Campagna were in rebellion and would only stop if the pope would present himself in person. So, in the spring of 1363, a Roman delegation went to Avignon to invite officially Urban V to return, but the pope wanted first of all to have the matter of Bernabò Visconti settled. Thanks to the mediation of Karl IV, it was resolved in March 1364; Visconti demanded a large amount of money to leave Bologna free, and Albornoz was constrained to agree. However, this great statesman who had succeeded masterfully in completing the restoration was not able to perform this final step and, put in a bad light at the court in Avignon, he was replaced by Cardinal Arduino. In order to assuage the resentment of his ex-vicar, the pope asked him to remain in Italy as his legate in the kingdom of Naples.

Meanwhile, Urban V was receiving repeated invitations to return from Bridget of Sweden and from Petrarch. The latter wrote him a letter from Venice on 28 June 1366 (*Seniles*, IX, 1), in which the religious importance of the

Roman see was emphasized in unusual rhetoric: "Consider that the Church of Rome is your bride. Some might argue that the bride of the Roman pontiff is not one particular Church but the universal Church. I know that, Most Holy Father, and heaven forbid that I should restrict your see when, in fact, I would extend it further if I could and would not give it borders other than the ocean itself. I admit that your see is wherever Jesus Christ has worshippers, but that does not change the fact that Rome has special relations with you. All other cities have their bishop but only you are the bishop of Rome."

However, as Maria Luisa Rizzatti noted in a story about Avignon, the letter is also "a document of great interest to understand the dispute for and against Rome. A significant part of it concerns, in all seriousness, the advantages of Italian wines. It seems that one of the strongest objections of the French cardinals (in private discussions, of course) consisted in their concern about having to do without the fine wines of Burgundy and Beaune." On this question, the poet of Arezzo pointed out: "Nobody wishes to deprive you of anything; if you really do not want to adapt to Italian wines, please remember that the Tiber is still navigable and thus you can easily import all the casks of Burgundy wine you desire."

Peter, the son of James II of Aragon, who had renounced the privileges of his nobility and entered the Franciscan Order, came to Avignon to plead with the pope. The three Italian cardinals also tried every day to get the pope to move, as did the French prelate Philippe de Cabassoles, friend of Petrarch, while Charles V, king of France, attempted to dissuade him in every way he could. He sent to Avignon his old teacher, Nicholas Oresme, who, in a proud speech, tried to convince the pope that this city of Provence should remain the papal see because it is the center of the world. The French cardinals even applauded the absurd homily.

By then Urban had decided to make the "great return." He ordered his vicar in Rome to prepare a suitable residence for him in the city and on 30 April 1367, he set off for Marseilles where a fleet of twenty-three galleys offered by the queen of Naples and the Venetians, Pisans, and Genoans, was waiting for him. Eight cardinals accompanied him, seven others were to come overland to Rome, while the other three refused to leave France.

The fleet reached Corneto on 3 June. Among those waiting for him was Cardinal Albornoz who wanted to be the first to welcome the pope back to his own State. The cortège progressed slowly and triumphantly, reaching Viterbo where the pope was forced to stop because of the epidemic of fever which was infecting the Latium, and of which Aegidio Albornoz himself was a victim, dying before he could see Urban enthroned at the See of Peter.

The pope entered Rome on 16 October, and this was, of course, an event of exceptional solemnity. On the vigil of All Saints a pontiff celebrated Mass again in St. Peter's, something which had not happened since the time of Boniface VII, with the gentlemen of the Papal State and many Italian nobles present, such as the Marquis d'Este, Amadeus VI of Savoy, and Rudolph of Camerino. Urban V took up residence in the Vatican, which had had to be restored hastily for his arrival since the whole city seemed to be in a state of decay and abandon. Urban was certainly aware of this through his vicar and from the descriptions of poets and chroniclers of that period. As Gregorovius observes, "the city's decay appeared even sorrier amongst ruins and marshes . . . towers without stones and houses consumed by flames and every kind of devastation."

The first thing Urban did was to arrange for restoration of the churches, supplying them with the necessary furnishings. He especially rebuilt the Lateran, and had the beautiful marble Gothic tabernacle placed on the main altar. He also reformed the city's government, abolishing the college of seven elected by the people and replacing it with three conservators completely under the Holy See. In other words, the people instantly lost what they had achieved and communal democracy disappeared.

This created malcontents who disturbed the pope, upon whom also landed the immediate reproaches of all the French cardinals as they did not feel at home in Rome. In addition, Rizzatti mentions, "the Italian wine must have made a bad impression since, a few months after the return of the papal court, Urban V ordered from France: 'LX casks of wines from Beaune and Grurejo and as many from Neumas or Lunello, for the use of our guests." But it was not simply a question of wine, "they complained about everything, even the music and the singing. The Italians, according to them, could not sing in church but only quaver, making noises like goats." The pope stayed in Rome all winter and in March 1368 received a visit from Joan of Naples and then one from the king of Cyprus. In May, he moved to Montefiascone for healthier air, which was the first sign that Rome was not ideal even for him, and in October he met with Emperor Karl IV in Viterbo and returned to Rome with him, a return which vaguely recalled the happy times of other famous papal-imperial couples, but this time did not enthuse anyone.

Urban repeated the coronation of Karl IV and of his wife in St. Peter's, and the emperor and the empress then left Rome. The pope was hoping for some military assistance against the gangs of adventurers infesting Italy, but "Karl behaved like a vulgar ringleader," according to Gregorovius. He avoided quarrels, bribed various leaders whom he encountered just to secure free passage to return to his own country, leaving the Papal State and its sovereign to fend for themselves. The Papal bull issued in 1366 against certain groups of mercenaries who were invading land of the Church had no effect whatsoever.

In October 1368, the emperor of the East, John Paleologus, came to Rome to pay homage to the pope and to abjure the schism, but especially to beg the pope to call for a crusade among the Christian sovereigns to help him save his threatened empire from the attacks of the Turks. Nobody listened to the pope's appeal and revolts broke out in Viterbo, Perugia, and other cities of the Papal State. Louis, the king of Hungary, offered to come to the pope's aid with 10,000 men, but Urban declined the offer. Living in Rome under these circumstances, shedding blood, and ending up being hated, did not constitute a part of his plan. He was sick of it all, and when he revealed his intention to return to Avignon, the French raised a chorus of approval.

The new pleas of the Romans and even the tragic prophecy of Bridget of Sweden to whom a "voice" had revealed that Urban would die if he returned to Avignon had no effect. She recounted her vision to Cardinal Roger de Beaufort who refused to report it to the pope. So she herself went to Montefiascone to pass it personally to Urban, but he was deaf to the words of this prophetess, who was later canonized.

On 5 September 1370, the pope set sail from Corneto towards Marseilles and by the 24th he was already at Avignon. A few days later he fell ill and died on 19 September 1370. The visionary Bridget had foretold the truth. He was buried in the monastery of St. Vittore in Marseilles and, beatified by the Church, he was canonized by Pius IX in 1870.

201. GREGORY XI (1370–1378)

On the death of Urban V, the College of Cardinals consisted of three Italians and one Englishman, all the others being French. So only one day was needed for the conclave, and on 30 December 1370, Pierre Roger de Beaufort, a nephew of Clement VI who had made him a cardinal at the age of eighteen, was elected. Born in Rosier d'Egletons in 1329, he was still only a deacon and therefore had to be ordained a priest and a bishop before he could be crowned pope on 5 January 1371, when he assumed the name of Gregory XI.

On the whole, like his predecessors at Avignon, Gregory elevated exclusively Frenchman to the cardinal's purple, and he particularly favored relatives, resuscitating a shameless nepotism, none of which facilitated a return of the Curia to Rome. And yet, from the beginning of his pontificate, he had announced his imminent transfer to the see of Rome, even fixing the date for May 1372.

Bringing this project about was delayed, however, because of both the constant pestering of the French cardinals trying to dissuade the pope and pressure from the king of France to keep Gregory in his realm as he wanted to use the pope to mediate an acceptable peace with England. However, the pope's attempt to do this was fruitless, as was the appeal for a crusade to give aid to the threatened Byzantine empire.

On the political front, Gregory XI's action was in effect a failure, just as the Curia suffered a defeat from Emperor Karl IV who, on the basis of the Golden

Bull, had managed to obtain from the German princes the election of his fifteen-year-old son, Wenceslaus, as king of Germany. The Curia had informed Karl that the coronation would only take place after the pope's approval, but all the same, the princes crowned Wenceslaus on 6 July 1367 at Aachen. However, the emperor, a shrewd and cunning man, did not want to break off relations with the papacy, and succeeded in sending the pope a letter dated before the coronation in which he begged the pope to ratify the election but made no mention of approval. And Gregory XI, satisfied by what was really subterfuge, issued a document with his consent.

Precisely because of these political defeats, Gregory XI probably saw that a return to Rome would be a way to recoup his own dignity, a matter that he took very seriously. Timorous by nature, he turned over and over in his mind the menacing prophecy of Bridget of Sweden a few months before her death in 1373 by which, according to a message to her from the Madonna, if he did not return immediately to Rome, he would lose not only his temporal, but also his spiritual, power.

The bad news which reached Avignon from Rome made a strong impression on the pope, for the papal vicar, Philip de Cabassoles, cardinal-bishop of Sabina, did not have the wisdom or the determination of an Albornoz. His work within the Papal State appeared ineffectual, since from 1375 in almost all the cities revolts had suddenly broken out, instigated by Bernabò Visconti, which showed just how despotic and inefficient the pontifical administration was. Only Rome was free of rebellion, while Florence went wild.

Gregory XI put into force strong prescriptions, placing an interdiction upon the city in March 1376 and excommunicating all the Florentines. Moreover, he recruited about 10,000 mercenaries from Brittany under Captain Jean de Malestroit, camped near Avignon, and sent them to Italy in the retinue of his new legate, Cardinal Robert of the counts of Geneva, the future antipope, Clement VII. He was a violent man, totally without scruples, and his mission must have been to annihilate every revolt from Bologna southwards so as to prepare a "peaceful" return to Rome for the pope.

Faced with the dangers which threatened mainly its prosperous commerce, Florence decided to send to Avignon as its ambassador the Dominican nun, Catherine of Siena, a very prestigious person, who was to carry on the mission of Bridget of Sweden. She was received by the pope on 18 June 1376, and held a series of conversations with him for which her confessor, Father Raymond of Capua, acted as her interpreter, translating into Latin the Sienese dialect of that extraordinary woman, destined to become a very popular saint. According to the numerous letters which Catherine sent to the pope at various times, in which she set forth the reality of things by virtue of a "providential" enlightenment, she called Gregory XI "my dear Daddy," a Tuscan expression, very familial but at the same time respectful, to which she also put strength and feeling by insisting upon his return to Rome ("Up, be a man! You must come!"). In invoking forgiveness and clemency in imitation of Christ, "his vicar," when dealing with his rebellious subjects because, she pointed out to him, "I do not see any other way nor any other remedy to get your lambs back."

But her efforts with Florence were wrecked because, at the same time, another Florentine delegation exacerbated the negotiations for an agreement. "Although Catherine's work as an intermediary for peace failed in this case, her success under other aspects was tremendous," Seppelt indicates, "since we owe to the untiring remonstrances, whether written or oral, of this blessed and spirited woman who spoke to the pope with the same quiet frankness with which she pushed him towards a reform of the clergy, that Gregory XI, regardless of all resistance and opposition, decided on the return to Rome, till then always procrastinated." Others tend to minimize this effort, claiming that the urgings of Catherine were of little importance and that the motivation for the return was exclusively political, echoing the prophecy of Bridget. As Seppelt again notes, however, "the transfer of the Church to the city of the Prince of the Apostles was essential unless one wished to witness the final collapse of papal authority."

On 13 September 1376, Gregory XI left Avignon. It was said that the horse he mounted would not obey his command to go, as if refusing to carry him, and this incident was immediately interpreted in a negative way. The duke of Anjou had been sent in great hurry by his brother, the king of France, to dissuade the pope from leaving, while the mother and four sisters of the count de Beaufort were weeping near their aged father who, stretched out in front of the entry to the palace, sought to bar his departure. Gregory jumped over him and all attempts to stop him were in vain. Six French cardinals remained in the palace at Avignon, custodians of the bastion of the future schism of the West.

From Marseilles the pope arrived by sea at Genoa where Catherine met him, and this time her voice was determinant since Gregory seemed to want to turn back, but embarked again, and on 6 November he was in Pisa and by 5 December at Corneto. There the Curia stayed for more than a month before concluding the negotiations with the Romans about the recognition of papal sovereignty over the city. Indeed, the situation in the entire Papal State continued to be chaotic as the mercenaries from Brittany had only succeeded in re-establishing order in a few places. In this turbulent atmosphere Gregory XI made his solemn entry into Rome on 17 January 1377, taking up residence in the Vatican where his predecessor, Urban V, had settled for that brief period of his return to the See of Peter. And from then on, the Vatican would replace the Lateran.

The rebellion within the Papal State became ever more dramatic and indeed, as Castiglioni himself admits, "the abuses and disorders were too imbedded for all to grow peaceful in one moment." Further negotiations with Florence came to naught, and Cardinal Robert, wandering from one area to another, decided on his own to teach the rebels a lesson when the inhabitants of Cesena, in desperation because of the oppression by the Breton garrison, rose up in February and slaughtered many of them. The vicar ordered a bloody vendetta and four thousand people of Cesena were massacred, a deed which earned him the name of "Butcher of Cesena."

The situation in Rome also worsened and Gregory fled to Anagni, only able to return to his own see in November when, under the regency of Gomez Albornoz, pontifical sovereignty was again recognized. However, the real change came thanks to a peace treaty with Bologna and the coming into Gregory's service of Rudolph of Varano, the captain of the Florentines. In March 1378, it was finally agreed that a congress of the many representatives of papal cities would be held at Sarzana, under the chairmanship of Bernabò Visconti, to restore order in the Papal State. One cardinal and two archbishops represented the pope, but the discussions were interrupted by the sudden death of Gregory on 27 March 1378.

Eight days earlier, sick and aware that he was dying, he had issued a bull, following the numerous disputes within the College, which was to facilitate the election of a successor. It authorized the cardinals present in Rome to proceed in the shortest possible time with the election of a pope without waiting for those who were absent.

Gregory XI was buried in S. Francesca Romana at the Forum. In 1584 the Roman people erected a monument there in gratitude for his having returned the see from Avignon to Rome, as pictured in the bas-relief showing the return of the pope with St. Catherine between the fallen walls at Porta San Paolo and Minerva, the city's symbol.

202. URBAN VI (1378–1389)

When Gregory XI died in Rome, sixteen cardinals were present, nine French, four Italian and one from Aragon, while six French cardinals had stayed in Avignon and a seventh was in Tuscany for the peace negotiations with Florence. When ten days had passed, the College began its conclave in the Vatican on 7 April 1378. The atmosphere in Rome was not peaceful, despite the fact that the Capitol's delegation had given the Curia guarantees on the maintenance of public order in the Borgo quarter, with a presidium of various citizens under the command of the captains of the Regions who had sworn to do their duty. The common people also made themselves heard and, when the procession was passing to go to the conclave chamber, cried: "We demand a Roman or an Italian!" The shouting continued during the brief period that the cardinals were meeting, and they decided to choose an Italian but not a Roman, and not even one of their own. In fact, this was to be the last time that a person from outside the College of Cardinals became pope. On 8 April, they chose Bartolomeo Prignano, archbishop of Bari, a learned canonist, born in Naples in 1318.

The name of the man elected was not immediately made known because he was not at the Vatican, and the rumor spread that a Frenchman instead had been elected. So the populace invaded the conclave chamber and the terrified cardinals, to gain time and to calm the rebels, said that the old Roman Cardinal Francesco Tebaldeschi had been elected. The people wanted to see him on the throne immediately, but the old cleric objected, revealing the name of the new pope. Many of the cardinals fled fearing the worst, but ten days later, on 18 April, the twelve cardinals who had remained gathered in St. Peter's with Bartolomeo Prignano who was crowned and assumed the name of Urban VI.

Certainly the cardinals in the conclave did not feel free in their selection and their behavior at the invasion by the populace shows it. They were threatened and intimidated and the events following Prignano's election might well have led to a declaration that the conclave was invalid, but that did not occur. Instead, the cardinals announced officially to all Christendom the news of the coronation, and in the following week took part in consistories presided over by Urban VI to issue new regulations on the management of the Church. They recognized him as the legitimate pope and accepted the many privileges which he immediately offered them to gain their favor. The cardinals who had remained in Avignon even sent an order to the captain of Castel Sant'Angelo to give Urban VI the keys of the city.

Everything appeared to be in order, but all of a sudden the first signs of discord appeared when the French cardinals proposed to transfer the papal see back to Avignon. Urban said, firmly, no. The atmosphere became tense and at the beginning of summer the French cardinals and the one from Aragon, Pedro de Luna, left the Curia and went to Anagni. Urban remained in Rome with the four Italian cardinals, to whom the "secessionists" wrote in July inviting them officially to come and join them, saying that the election of Urban VI was in danger of being declared null and void because it was carried out under the threat of a people's movement. However, the Italian cardinals stood by the pope while the arguments between the parties grew more and more bitter. Admonitions and invitations to moderation, such as those that Catherine of Siena frequently sent to the pope, came to nothing. On 2 August the cardinals at Anagni signed an official statement which considered Rome to be a vacant see and on the ninth of that same month proclaimed to all of Christendom the annulment of the election of Urban because of apostasy.

On the international level, Emperor Karl IV favored Urban, but the king of France, Charles V and Queen Joan of Naples took the side of the rebel cardinals who, for more security, moved to Fondi under the protection of Count Onorato Caetani.

There, on 20 September, they elected as pope Cardinal Robert of Geneva, the "Butcher of Cesena," who was crowned in the cathedral of Fondi, taking the name of Clement VII.

The cardinals in Avignon immediately acknowledged him as the legitimate pope and invited him to take possession of the see of Provence while the Christian world was divided. Following Karl IV, Hungary, Poland, Sweden, Denmark, England, Flanders, and Italy, apart for Naples, lined up in favor of Urban, while Castille, Aragon, and Portugal hesitated on giving their preference. Charles V and Joan were strenuous defenders of Clement VII who, according to the *Annuario pontificio*, is officially considered an antipope. The great schism of the West was underway, to be settled only in 1415 by the Council of Constance.

Before moving to Avignon, Clement attempted to take over Rome by force and the battle between his mercenaries from Brittany and the Italians in the service of Urban led by Alberico from Barbiano took place at Marino in the Alban Hills on 28 April 1379. Clement VII was defeated, left Italy and on 20 June took his seat in Avignon amidst the splendors of a court which recalled the worldliness of Clement VI.

Urban VI did not feel safe, however, and planned to strengthen his position in Italy with the support of a faithful sovereign who could prevent any possibility of Clement returning. He therefore declared Joan of Naples to be a heretic and a schismatic because she backed the antipope, and invited Carlo of Durazzo with his numerous warriors to take over the kingdom. Carlo accepted promptly and Urban made him a Roman senator and crowned him king with the name of Carlo III, after which he immediately departed on his mission. Joan was strangled in 1328 and Carlo succeeded in stopping the advance of Louis of Anjou, who had earlier been adopted by Joan as her heir and given the kingdom of Naples in fiefdom by Clement VII. But Louis died in 1384.

Carlo of Durazzo had the kingdom fully under his control and was able to receive Urban VI solemnly at Naples even if tension had developed between them because the king no longer wanted to be the pope's vassal. Urban stayed in Naples until May 1384, almost like a prisoner, then moved to Nocera where the Curia was, which he proceeded to enlarge by nominating twenty-nine cardinals. These were quickly angered by the haughty and despotic manner of the pope who had asserted absolute power in the running of the Church, effectively in order to prevent any possible coups. But this distrust led many cardinals to plot against him with King Carlo III.

Someone plotted even to kill him, but the pope, sensing revolt in the air, inveighed against the cardinals in a consistory on 12 January 1385 and had six of them arrested. He also summoned the king to appear in court to plead his innocence, but since he did not appear, he was excommunicated and his kingdom put under interdiction. The king replied by putting Nocera under siege for six months.

Freed by Count Raymond of Nola at the head of the mercenaries from Brittany, Urban remained in effect prisoner of his rescuer who forced him to pay enormous sums of money under pain of being transferred to Avignon to the court of Clement VII. In the end he was liberated at Genoa where he was able to install himself, but was still in open disagreement with the Curia. He had the cardinals believed guilty of the conspiracy brought to him, and they ended their days in prison and were probably slain at his orders.

The harshness of this absolute monarch, certainly not appropriate for the vicar of Christ who was supposed to be apostolically ready to forgive, lost him the support of many cardinals, who abandoned him to seek refuge with Clement VII. Always insecure, neurotic, and without adequate support, Urban VI continually changed his residence going from Lucca to Perugia until he could once again reach Rome. There he succeeded in getting the affection of the citizens with the bull *Dominus noster* of 8 April 1389, which reduced the period till the next Jubilee Year to 33 years, in memory of the earthly life of Christ, and consequently setting the next Holy Year in 1390.

In effect, this was the only "religious" deed that he carried out, if one can term it such. However, he did not live to see its "fruits" because he died in Rome on 15 October 1389. He was buried in St. Peter's and his sarcophagus is at present in the Vatican Grottoes.

203. BONIFACE IX (1389—1404)

On the death of Urban VI, Clement VII expected to obtain official recognition as the sole pope, but the fourteen cardinals in Rome, decidedly hostile to him, continued to consider him an intruder and proceeded with a new election. On 2 November 1389, they chose a Neapolitan, Pietro Tomacelli, cardinal of S. Anastasia, who was consecrated on 9 November with the name of Boniface IX.

His first pontifical acts dealt with repairing the damage resulting from disputes within the Curia caused by Urban VI, which had brought the Roman see into disgrace on a political level. He pardoned many who had been condemned by his predecessor, restored cardinal rank to four who had been stripped of it, and came to a reconciliation with the kingdom of Naples, recognizing as king, Ladislas, son of the deceased Carlo III. Ladislas swore to help him against the antipope and, as a reward for this sign of devotion, Boniface IX had him crowned at Gaeta by his legate and later helped him financially, until he was able defeat Louis II of Anjou who was supported by Clement VII. In this way, the pope ensured the obedience to Rome of the kingdom of southern Italy.

This was a clever move which was followed by another one, no whit less happy, which led him to give the title of Pontifical Vicar to the lords of the various cities who were stealing property from the Papal State, such as the Estes at

Ferrara, the Montefeltros at Urbino, the Malatesta at Rimini, and the Ordelaffi at Forlì. The office meant that they had jurisdiction over various communal lands against payment of an annual tribute and recognition of the pope's sovereignty. "To break down the Papal State into a number of little hereditary states meant hastening the process of dissolution," Gregorovius correctly observes, "but in such a manner Boniface IX not only acquired substantial assets but also witnessed the recognition of his control over the patrimony of the Church, something which no pope had for a long time been able to claim."

Boniface IX could thus sit on his throne calmly and enjoy the fruits of his power as he wished, and in that sense the celebration of two Jubilees was a big plus. In fact, after the one announced by Urban VI for 1390, there followed another in 1400, proclaimed by him since the institution of a Holy Year every 33 years in honor of Christ's life on earth did not eliminate the Holy Year of every 50 years, and visits to the basilicas were definitively increased to four with the inclusion of St. Mary Major. As again Gregorovius notes, there is no doubt that "the holy celebration of the Jubilee had by now been transformed into a speculative manuevers by the pope who, through emissaries going to the most remote countries, was auctioning off indulgences for what a trip to Rome would cost." So began the "traffic" that would produce the reactions among the clergy and the faithful which would bring about the Reformation. Up until then, the papacy would carry on financial operations on a grand scale including simony and other unscrupulous financial deals.

That the Jubilee Year of 1400 was a show of collective asceticism with scads of "scourgers" who poured into Rome from various areas of Italy in a renewed wish for peace, did not disguise the true face of Boniface IX, who was an unworthy vicar of Christ and sought only to enrich himself by taking advantage of his position as a temporal sovereign. In fact, he always had a great need for money, importuned not only by a greedy mother and by two brothers who, of course, got the most important and lucrative papal assignments, but also by several nephews to whom were given significant ecclesiastical benefices. And, to satisfy this ensemble of nepotism, he gave away ecclesiastical positions to whoever paid for them, accepting any petition if it was sufficiently compensated.

Relationships with the Romans were good in the period following the Jubilee Year of 1390, since the wealth brought by the pilgrims meant profitable business for the local population, although disputes and attempted rebellions kept cropping up. Only in 1398 did the pope manage to obtain full sovereignty over Rome by eliminating the republican system and renewing the senatorial one on the basis of his own selection. Then the Holy Year of 1400 brought prosperity to all once more, despite the discomforts of still another plague. In any event, to strengthen his own power, Boniface IX had Castel Sant'Angelo restored and turned into a fortress, as happened with the Vatican palace and the Capitol.

From there he used his temporal sovereignty solely to squeeze every possible source of money and to consolidate his throne.

On an international level, his thirst for money brought with it a lessening of the prestige of the apostolic Roman see, and in Germany the resentment caused by the preachers on indulgences, sent by him with exaggerated demands for money, forced him in 1402 to withdraw numerous plenary indulgences.

But he did not worry too much about the criticism, confident that his actions could not be questioned and did nothing at all about the schism. When Clement VII died in 1394 and the cardinals at Avignon chose the Aragon cardinal Pedro de Luna to succeed him, who took the name of Benedict XIII, he did not even make much of an effort to be recognized as the only pope, aware that he was despised because of his scandalous simony practices. Indeed, when the Assembly held in Paris in 1398 at the proposal of the University and the French clergy, which did not appreciate Benedict XIII's imposition of tributes, voted with learned theologians, bishops and abbots, for a "subtraction" of obedience to the Avignon pope, it did not discuss joining the Roman pontiff.

The king of France, who did not care for an Aragon pope at Avignon, approved the decree of the Assembly and decided to besiege the city of Provence, simultaneously opening negotiations with Boniface IX, but the latter wanted to maintain the status quo which was so profitable for him. Moreover, the idea was gaining ground among European sovereigns to depose both pontiffs at an ecumenical council.

At this point, Boniface IX tried to strengthen his position in Germany, in the very country where his financial policies had taken a beating. He told Wenceslaus that he wanted to crown him emperor in Rome, and granted him the collection of the tithes from the assets of the churches in Germany and Bohemia. Obtaining the support of the emperor meant for the Curia prolonging the schism while awaiting better moments. When in 1400 Wenceslaus was deposed by the majority of the German princes whose candidate was Robert of the Palatinate, the pope initially stepped aside only to reappear in 1403 when Robert had definitively strengthened his position and was considered the legitimate sovereign by all the princes. He issued then a ridiculous bull in which he claimed that the deposition of Wenceslaus and the appointment of the new king had taken place by his explicit wish.

Meanwhile, Benedict XIII, escaping the siege of Avignon, had succeeded in 1403 in reaching Château Reynard and reacquiring a certain prestige. Suddenly the French clergy seemed to be again favorable to him, so much so that the entire nation, by royal decree, returned to his obedience. The same University of Paris which had so violently fought against him appeared to back him, and the ecclesiastical contributions owed to him were paid, even with the arrears. This latest ascent by Benedict to the summits of power was clearly due to Boniface IX's behavior in the money market, which had disgusted all Europe. The pope of Avignon began to feel so exalted in international opinion that he sought a meeting with the Roman pontiff in order to settle the schism, and to this purpose sent a delegation to Rome in the summer of 1404.

Boniface was not well and, according to the chroniclers, the envoys were so irritating that they worsened his condition. The Curia actually held them responsible for his death on 1 October 1404, and imprisoned them in Castel Sant'Angelo, releasing them only upon the payment of bail.

In this way Boniface IX's greed for money had a codicil, almost a "posthumous work," and what Gregorovius says does not appear simply rhetorical: "Even on his deathbed, the desire for money tormented him." He was buried in St. Peter's, "modestly," Castiglione reports, and his adding "only later was a mausoleum erected for him in the basilica of St. Peter" sounds somewhat ridiculous.

204. INNOCENT VII (1404—1406)

At the death of Boniface IX, Rome quickly became torn by rioting, fomented mainly by the Orsini and the Colonna families back in the limelight at the head of opposing factions. The first was protecting the Capitol which was under the control of a brother of the deceased pope, while the second was heralding a return to democratic ideals and invoked the intervention of Ladislas of Naples to resolve the dispute in a democratic way. Amid these disturbances the cardinals met in conclave and, frightened by the approach of the king of Naples, hastened to elect the new pope, Cosimo Migliorati, on 17 October 1404. Born in Sulmona around 1336, he had been the archbishop of Ravenna, later the bishop of Bologna, and since 1389 the cardinal of Santa Croce.

The newly elected pope took the name of Innocent VII, but had to wait almost a month to be crowned. In fact, although elected pontifical sovereign, he was in possession of neither the Vatican, nor Castel Sant'Angelo, nor the Capitol, all of which were controlled by the rebels. Moreover, the people refused to take the oath of loyalty to him so, as the vassal of the pope, Ladislas felt obliged to restore order and papal authority.

By 19 October he and his troops were already in Rome, warmly welcomed by the populace to which he announced that he had come to render service to the pope and he did, in fact, manoeuvre cleverly between the two factions, yet mainly taking care of his own interests. In the space of one week he succeeded in getting signed an agreement between the parties, and the people breathed again the air of republican freedom which had preceded the enthronement of Boniface IX. With the installation of ten governors in the Capitol alongside the senator, Innocent VII was able to mount the throne at the Lateran. His coronation took place in St. Peter's on 11 November and Ladislas, apart from obtaining several remunerative appointments, such as that of rector of the Campagna, got the pope to promise not to work for the unification of the Western Church unless he were to be recognized universally as the king of Naples.

Once Ladislas had departed, Benedict XIII made himself heard again, repeating the idea of a meeting with the Roman pontiff, and he started out for Italy without delay, reaching Genoa at Easter of 1405. Innocent declined the invitation, however, also because he was again having problems with the troublesome Romans and was unable to install himself in the Vatican in peace.

The situation precipitated in August when a delegation of fourteen citizens called on the pope and, in strong words and insults, accused him of doing nothing to settle the schism. His nephew, Luigi Migliorati, a violent sort of man who acted imprudently in defense of his uncle stepped in, and, on his own initiative but, evidently, having a free hand, had eleven members of the delegation killed and their corpses thrown into the street. The resulting reaction in Rome was chaotic and the pope and cardinals fled to safety at Viterbo.

Only in August a year later was the pope able to return to his see. But faced with the disputes between the factions, the mediation attempts by the nobles of the Papal State and the new intervention by Ladislas, Innocent experienced a miserable pontificate. He issued excommunications right and left which were later withdrawn, together with bulls against and for Ladislas, at first declared deposed as king of Naples and then rehabilitated as the true standard-bearer of the Church.

All of which goes to show the absence of policy with Innocent, as well as an obvious lack of seriousness in the use of his religious authority. Gregorovius correctly asks: "How could the power to loose and to bind preserve any religious meaning if a solemn curse by the Church was changed in an instant into an equally solemn blessing? Was it perhaps sublime Christian morality that inspired the pope's condemnation? Or was it not the customary art of politics which caused his judgment to waver like a flag in the wind?"

On 1 September 1406, once back in Rome, Innocent ordered a restructuring of the University of the Sapienza with the creation of a chair of the Greek language, and he welcomed to the service of the Curia certain humanists such as Leonardo Bruni and Pietro Paolo Vergerio. It might have been the symptom of a new direction in the cultural horizon of the Church, but these initiatives were fated to be the only positive marks of this pope. He could, or would, do nothing more, being of an almost too peaceful a nature, to the point of being accused of hypocrisy for failing to do anything, however vague, to attempt to settle the schism.

He died on 6 November 1406, and was buried in St. Peter's.

205. GREGORY XII (1406—1415)

When Innocent VII died, before entering the conclave the fourteen cardinals present in Rome signed an agreement requiring the new pope to renounce his pontificate as soon as the Avignon antipope would do likewise, and Benedict XIII received notice of this within one month. A delegation was to be sent to Avignon to begin negotiations for settling the schism within three months, which meant that the new pope was to have a limitation on his sovereignty, conditioned by developments. He was to be in reality a caretaker of the interests of the Church, in itself something positive, although that of the College of Cardinals potentially limited his authority for at least fifteen months. This was the period of time granted to the new pope to reach an agreement, after which he would be free to act on his own initiative.

The conclave sat on 18 November 1406, and on 30 November, elected the Venetian cardinal, Angelo Correr, Latin patriarch of Constantinople, who was crowned on 19 December with the name of Gregory XII. Eighty years old, very tall and thin, all "skin and bones," according to a chronicler of that time, he was both ascetic in appearance and in character. This was shown by the "biblical" tone of the expressions he used in the communication sent to Benedict XIII and to all Christendom concerning his strong desire for peace, even at the cost of abdication. He declared he was ready to imitate the mother who before Solomon preferred to hand her own child over to strangers rather than see him killed, and he decided to seek again the unity of the Church "on a fishing boat and carrying a pilgrim's staff."

These were sublime words which touched the international clergy and the sovereigns, putting Benedict XIII with his back to the wall since he could not go back on his word. So he responded evasively, saying that he favored a meeting with the Roman pontiff at Savona. The University of Paris, through its esteemed theologians, considered such a meeting useful and favored a simultaneous abdication. Due to certain declarations, and realizing that meeting with Benedict would mean basically recognizing him as a legitimate pope, Gregory rethought his position. Simultaneously, his relatives brainwashed the old pope, because they could see they would lose all their advantages if he abdicated. So it was nepotism which stifled the unionist initiatives of Gregory, too old to react and quickly becoming the target of atrocious insults in the public opinion through a series of defamatory writings such as the "letter from Satan" addressed to Archbishop Giovanni Dominici of Ragusa which was highly ironic about the methods used by Gregory's relatives to restrict his authority.

However, the first to pay was Benedict who was again besieged in Avignon by order of the king of France; yet he succeeded once more in fleeing to Aragon in 1408 where he issued a bull calling a council in Perpignan. At this point, the king of France proposed to ignore the two pontifical personages and, instead, arrange a meeting with the cardinals of the two factions. The idea was approved by various sovereigns and was carried out by the convening of a council at Pisa in March 1409. This was promulgated by seven cardinals who had rebelled against Gregory for having appointed two of his nephews as cardinals, and by seven others from the Avignon faction who met at Leghorn as a result of a compromise between the two sides. In effect, the prelates of the entire Christian world were invited to a synod that was to force the two contenders either to abdicate or to be deposed.

Gregory XII reacted forcefully but also in a magnanimous spirit, recalling the seven rebel cardinals to obedience and making a promise to call an ecumenical council in a city in Veneto. He then appointed ten new cardinals and, since the rebels did not change their attitude, he excommunicated them. However, he sought a safe place in which to continue his mission of peace, which he certainly could not do in Rome. Thus, in the beginning of March 1409 he moved to Rimini under the protection of the Malatesta. From there he sent a letter to Florence, complaining about the support given by Tuscany to the secessionists and declaring any council called by cardinals and not by the pope, illegal.

By now the council, opened at Perpignan by Benedict XIII in November of 1408, was gaining in importance with 120 prelates gathered there, and the confusion was considerable. Sovereigns were opting for one or the other of the two popes without knowing really why, and while Robert of the Palatinate was backing Gregory because he sensed behind the council at Pisa the *longa manus* of the king of France, Ladislas of Naples, acting as the defender of the Church of Rome, took advantage of it to occupy the city abandoned by Gregory and protested against those cardinals gathered at Pisa.

In this chaotic atmosphere the council in Pisa was opened on 25 March 1409. In the end it was worth it because every sovereign sent a personal representative, so one could count on the presence of 10 cardinals on Benedict's side and 14 on Gregory's, together with 4 patriarchs, 80 bishops, 27 abbots, several doctors in theology and canon law, as well as conciliar prelates who had abandoned Perpignan. The aged cardinal of Poitiers, Guy de Maillesec, presided over the council.

On the first day the two absent popes were summoned to the council, vainly awaited until 30 March and then held in contempt by the council. Gregory's position was defended by the king of Germany, Robert, who again raised the point that a council not convened by the pope was null and void, and declared that the deposition of the pope was illegal. Carlo Malatesta also defended Gregory and tried to convince the assembly to move its operations to a location more acceptable to the Roman pontiff. They went unheeded. The council was declared to be ecumenical, and the fusion of the two groups of cardinals into one College of Cardinals took place, which refused to obey either Benedict or Gregory.

On 5 June, the patriarch of Alexandria read out the verdict which decreed that both Pedro de Luna and Angelo Correr were deposed from their pontifical positions as schismatics and excluded from the community of the Church, whereupon the Holy See was deemed vacant. Ten days later, the twenty-four cardinals went into conclave and on 26 June unanimously elected the archbishop of Milan, Pietro Filargo of Crete, to be pope. He was consecrated on 7 July in the cathedral of Pisa and took the name of Alexander V.

It was the intention of the new pope who, according to the *Annuario pontificio*, is considered to be an antipope like Benedict XIII, to continue the work of the council in order to take up the problem of a reform of the Church, but the prelates were worn out. The assembly was adjourned and everything was put off to a new council that was supposed to take place in 1412.

At this point the situation within the Christian world had worsened. On the international level, the decisions of the council at Pisa did not receive the general approval its most enthusiastic promoters had hoped and canonists and theologians began to find that assembly was without any juridical basis, nicknaming it a "would-be council." Now there were three popes, each with his own supporters both within the clergy and amongst the sovereigns. Gregory XII had Italy, Germany and northern Europe on his side; Benedict XIII had Spain, Scotland, Sardinia, Corsica and part of France on his; while Alexander V had most of France and numerous religious Orders favorable to the reform, which would now have to wait.

However, Gregory XII did not sit idly by and, at the same time as the council in Pisa, held his own council, as he had promised, at Cividale in Friuli near Aquileia. During the session on 22 July he declared that only the Roman popes were legitimate from Urban VI to Boniface IX and himself, whereas those of Avignon were antipopes, including Clement VII, Benedict XIII as well as the recently elected Alexander V. He was still prepared to abdicate but insisted that his two competitors do the same and be ready to recognize a new pontiff who would be elected by at least two-thirds of the cardinals from among all three allegiances gathered together in a single College. He therefore recommended to the sovereigns, Robert of Germany, Ladislas of Naples and Sigismund of Hungary, to act together and make a peace plan to achieve this. But events preempted this call in the Venetian republic, where the patriarchs of Aquileia and Venice proclaimed their loyalty to Alexander V and attempted to take Gregory prisoner. He managed to escape in disguise, while his valet in his papal vestments was beaten by the soldiers sent to arrest him, and he reached Gaeta under the protection of Ladislas of Naples.

Rome was under the control of Louis II of Anjou whom the council of Pisa had recognized as the new king of Naples, in opposition to Ladislas. So, Alexander V was able to enter Rome in the spring of 1410 where he was acclaimed by the populace as the Roman pontiff. But his glory was brief for the one who was weaving the web of the "Pisan" papal politics was the Neapolitan Cardinal Baldassarre Cossa, the legate of Alexander V at Bologna, who plotted openly to succeed him at the summit. It was easy to lure him to Bologna where on 3 May Alexander V passed away, probably poisoned by Cossa who had himself elected the successor in a hasty conclave on 17 May. He was consecrated on 25 May under the name of John XXIII and the following year took the throne at the Vatican.

For Gregory XII, Rome was only a mirage by now, since in the meantime he had lost two of his supporters. Robert, king of Germany, had died suddenly the day after the coronation of John XXIII, while Ladislas, having become aware of Cossa's ability for political intrigue, had begun negotiations with him, as the spokesman for the council of Pisa, to have him cease support by Louis II of Anjou. The two agreed by means of a mutual declaration of their respective sovereignty and Ladislas forsook Gregory and recognized John as having been elected "by divine inspiration." The latter appointed him "gonfaloniere" (chief defender) of the Church in Rome and conferred several benefices on him. Gregory was forced to flee from Gaeta on a Venetian vessel which, eluding Cossa's fleet, bore him safely to Rimini and Carlo Malatesta, the only noble upon whom he now could count.

In Rome, John XXIII further fortified the Vatican by constructing, according to Gregorovius, a long raised corridor, the famous "passage," probably rebuilt by Alexander VI, which allowed him to reach Castel Sant'Angelo. He also took up the work of the Curia again until the new pretender in Germany to the imperial crown, King Sigismund, made himself heard in the name of Christianity and declared intolerable the existing situation with three pontiffs lacking real authority. Whereupon, Ladislas broke off also with John XXIII, who fled to Florence while the king of Naples reached Rome and subjected it to a lengthy sacking.

On 30 October 1413, Sigismund officially convoked sovereigns, cardinals, bishops, abbots and patriarchs to an ecumenical council which was to begin at Constance on 1 November 1414. An invitation was also sent to the three pontiffs with, as the main proposal, the settlement of the schism, but also in order to condemn the new heresies and to plan the reformation of the Church. John XXIII adopted as his the initiative of Sigismund, gave it his blessing, and on 9 December 1413, convoked the council with an encyclical, explaining that it would be a continuation of the council of Pisa. Gregory XII refused to recognize the validity of such a convocation, and Benedict XIII did likewise.

John was delighted with the attitude of his two rivals and, when he had received Sigismund's assurance of his safe passage, started his journey to Constance which he entered triumphantly with an imposing retinue on 28 October 1414. Representatives from all over Christian Europe gradually joined him with a total of 1800 clergymen, including theologians, bishops, archbishops, patriarchs and 29 cardinals in addition to the envoys of various sovereigns. The council was declared open on 5 November, but the work began only after ten days to allow time for all the participants to reach Constance. The first sessions were held under the chairmanship of John XXIII. Sigismund, who had been crowned as Emperor at Aachen on 8 November, arrived only on Christmas Eve, and as a result of his presence the council assumed a certain character due to particular innovations.

The main innovation, a revolutionary one, was to divide the assembly by nation, (Italy, France, Germany, England and Spain), each of them with its own president. Another change, equally unusual, consisted in granting voting privileges to all those present, clerical and lay, in a sort of democratization of the Church. This meant that the authority to decide matters was given to the council as a whole and not to one of the three popes, whose primacy was in effect set aside, so that in the early sessions the principle of pontifical sovereignty was ignored. This was a hard blow for the see of Rome and at that point the future of the papacy was in real jeopardy.

Nevertheless, Gregory XII sent his legate, Cardinal Giovanni Dominici of Ragusa, to Constance and informed the assembly of his readiness to resign if the other two pontiffs did likewise, requesting only that John XXIII be removed as chairman of the council. That request seemed fair to the assembly and the "Pisan" pope played his role masterfully. On 2 March 1415, he read his "withdrawal," knelt before the altar and swore that his only aim was the peace of the Church and the settlement of the schism. It was a theatrical and electrifying performance as scandalous rumors had begun to circulate in the council about him, and he no longer felt very safe. The duke of Austria helped him flee to Schaffhausen, and from there, John denounced the intrigues and prejudices of the participants in a council which had violated papal prerogatives.

This provoked a crisis and all Sigismund's diplomacy as well as the religious authority of Cardinal Pierre d'Ailly were needed to prevent the council from being dissolved. Indeed, at the meeting on 29 March 1415, everyone was reminded that all clergymen, including the pope, had to obey an ecumenical council. The idea that the three pontiffs ought to abdicate simultaneously or be deposed was gaining ground. It began with John XXIII whom the count of Nuremberg managed to bring back from Schaffhausen to be closer to Constance. On 29 May he was declared deposed because of the practice of simony and was condemned to prison. Cossa pleaded for a pardon but Sigismund turned him over to the Palatine count to be kept in custody until the end of the council. He was to be passed as prisoner from one German prince to another until the new pope, Martin V, freed him, bringing him back into the Church as cardinal-bishop of Tusculum. He was to pass away in 1420.

The council then took up the case of the pontiff of Rome, and Gregory XII behaved with great dignity. On 15 June 1416, he asked his friend and protector, Carlo Malatesta, to notify the assembly that he was abdicating of his own will. Moreover, to give an official ecumenical aura to the council. Gregory, as sole true pope, convoked the council as of that date in the name of his legate, Cardinal Dominici, and thus legitimized the later actions of the assembly. From that date the Church considered the council of Constance to be truly ecumenical.

On 4 July, Carlo Malatesta presented the written renunciation of Gregory XII and, in recognition of his dignified comportment, the council invited this resigning pope to become the bishop of Portus and the papal legate to the Marches. Gregory thanked the assembly in a letter which he signed simply "Angelo, cardinal-bishop." He died at Recanati on 18 October 1417, and was buried in the cathedral there.

Walter Ullmann speaks about a "victory for conciliarism" through which "the power was no longer lodged in the papal monarch but in the Church represented by the general council" and "from being the master, the pope was now the servant of the Church, an ordinary official" within a collective sovereignty. That is not wholly exact, or rather it is only a temporary affirmation of that concept to which Gregory XII voluntarily submitted for the good of the unity of the Church, and this was completely to his merit. On the other hand, the fact that he felt obliged to convene a council again which was already functioning, but null and void in the strict terms of canon law, and that he resigned only after that act, explains that basically, in his heart, he never recognized that he was inferior to the council.

Furthermore, the legitimate pontiff who succeeded him at the see of Rome, Martin V, was to confirm the work of Gregory by abstaining from approving the council as a whole and by denying decrees which were contrary to the divine primacy of the pope. Eugene IV took the same position, confirming decisions taken at Constance but preserving "the dignity and the primacy of the Holy See" of Rome.

Thanks to the noble conduct of Gregory XII, therefore, the concept of the pope as the descendant of Peter survived, consolidated in the image of a pope-king determined not to give in even to the Lutheran reformation, and ready to strengthen his position with the "counter-reformation."

206. Martin V (1417−1431)

After the abdication of Gregory XII, the council of Constance tried to reach an amicable settlement with Benedict XIII through the mediation of Emperor Sigismund himself at a meeting in Perpignan, but the Avignon pope remained "impenitent,"' resolved to assert his sovereignty even when the Spanish nobles themselves had abandoned him. He left France and, out of fear of becoming a prisoner like John XXIII, took up residence in the castle-fortress of Peñíscola in Valencia The assembly, having noted his refusal to abdicate, on 26 July 1417 declared him deposed from papal dignity as a schismatic and a heretic. And even though Benedict XIII continued to consider himself as the official pontiff, the council of Constance viewed the schism as terminated and turned to preparations for the conclave during which the new legitimate pope would be elected. As an exception, in addition to the twenty-three cardinals, six representatives of each of the five nations would also have the right to vote. However, Gregory XII's recommendation that the majority of two-thirds of those present was necessary for election carried the day.

On the evening of 8 November 1417, the fifty-three electors went into the conclave in the Chamber of Commerce at Constance, and three days later had completed their task. On 11 November, cardinal-deacon Oddone Colonna, born at Genazzano in 1368, was elected. He had been elevated to the cardinalate purple by Innocent VII, had been present at the council of Pisa, later favoring John XXIII, until the latter's flight to Schaffhausen. Immediately ordained a priest and consecrated bishop, he was crowned on 21 November in the cathedral of Constance, assuming the name of Martin V. After thirty-nine years, the Western Church rediscovered unity under one sovereign pontiff.

Martin V promptly took over the chairmanship of the council which now was supposed to tackle the question of the reformation. On this matter, various complications arose, particularly because of the right which the Roman Church asserted to impose taxes, justifying them on the basis of serious needs caused by the condition of abandonment to which it had sunk since the times of Avignon and then with the schism. A compromise was reached involving three different concordats: one with Germany to which Poland, Hungary and the countries of Scandinavia adhered, a second with France, Spain and Italy and the third with England. In general, these pacts established rules for the composition of the College of Cardinals, set limits on the papal rights regarding benefices and the levying of tribute, and provided for the judicial immunity of the Curia. In compensation, submission to the dogmatic definitions of the pope was to be viewed as precepts for all the faithful, and this was an important face-saver for the Roman pontiff.

Moreover, during the closing moments of the council, all the decrees were officially sanctioned. Regarding heresy, the council had previously expressed its opinion during the first sessions in 1415, condemning the writings of the Englishman, John Wyclif, and of his pupil, John Hus. When Hus refused to retract his "errors," he was delivered to the secular branch of the law as a heretic and condemned to be burned at the stake on 16 July 1415. The same fate befell his follower, Jerôme of Prague, but their ideas took root, especially in Bohemia, and were to be responsible for Luther's irremediable stands.

The council ended on 22 April 1418, with a promise by Martin V to convene a synod in 1423 at Pavia. Martin remained in Constance for a while and Sigismund invited him to take up residence in Germany, offering him the cities of Basel, Mainz and Strasbourg while Charles VI was urging him to visit Avignon. The pope courteously declined, fully aware that Rome was the true see from which the vicar of Christ was to guide the Church, feeling really free and sovereign there.

In May 1418, he departed from Constance en route for Italy, passing through Bern and Geneva. On 12 October he was in Milan where he consecrated the main altar of the cathedral which was under construction. He then went through Brescia and reached Mantua where he stayed for three months. The anarchical situation in Rome and the Papal State made his return to the apostolic see problematic. However, in February 1419, he moved closer, arriving in Florence where he remained for a year and a half. There he came to an agreement with the powerful military chief, Braccio of Montone, who was in control of a large part of the papal lands in central Italy.

Martin V had to consign to him as feudal estates the cities of Perugia and Assisi with the surrounding Umbrian countryside, and to give him the title of vicar of the Church. As a counterpart, Bologna came back to the Papal State and accepted a legate from Martin. Peace also returned between the papacy and the Angevins when Joan II, queen of Naples, made an agreement with Martin, and the Neapolitan troops left Rome. On 30 September 1420, the pope entered the city from the Porta del Popolo, enthusiastically received by the Roman populace, which after 135 years, was finally seeing a pope who was a fellow Roman.

Rome was in a pitiful state with its partially ruined houses and churches, widespread famine and epidemics. Platina mentions "houses in shards, collapsing temples, muddy streets, a sadly abandoned city" which "was faceless, without a sign of urban life" in a state of terrifying decadence. Martin V rolled up his sleeves to put a face on the city, first and foremost by providing open streets in Rome and establishing the "*magistri viarum*" (street inspectors), who like real policemen cleaned up the streets of thieves and criminals. He tried also to gentrify the citizenry by introducing the custom on the Sunday before Easter of distributing "golden roses" to famous citizens and noble ladies as well as hats and swords to senior officials at the beginning of each year.

Above all, however, he saw to the restoration of churches, decorating them with works by Gentile da Fabriano and the young Masaccio, from whom came the frescoes in San Giovanni, St. Mary Major and S. Clemente. He also laid the grounds for the reconstruction of the entire city, thanks to an urban planning by his administration which was to be vastly extended by his successors. Of course, he took pains to return to the Papal State a strong monarchy, trying gradually to centralize in Rome that complex of towns and provinces governed by special and heterogeneous rights and laws. However, these were arduous tasks and their solutions were only to be found a century later.

Not knowing in whom to trust in this work of political reconstruction, he used on the whole his relatives, the only ones in whom he had confidence, making them powerful through marriages that linked them to various noblemen from the provinces of the Papal State. It was obviously a nepotistic action, reprehensible but no doubt technically necessary for the city's organization. Besides, one must emphasize, as Gregorovius notes, that "for economic reasons, he avoided pomp and splendor" to the extent of "holding court cheaply in the palace of the Holy Apostles." "Still a product of the uncouth fourteenth century" he tended to the restoration of ecclesiastical affairs without surrounding himself "with theatrical magnificence," and this was certainly praiseworthy. And it should not be forgotten that he was the one who opened the papal chancellery to other humanists, continuing the cultural renewal begun earlier by Innocent VII. The most important of these was Poggio Bracciolini, the fortunate discoverer of ancient manuscripts.

In 1423, he announced the fifth Jubilee, in deference to the thirty-three years of Christ's life on earth and to the Jubilee Year of 1390. Perhaps more than its predecessors, this Jubilee preserved a religious aspect, thanks also to the sermons of Bernardino of Siena which called for a kind of "reevangelization" of Rome, abandoned to itself in a decrease of the Faith, betrayed by a misery without hope on the one side and by an unrestrained pagan life on the other. Martin V, on his part, revived devotion to the Eucharist and approved the establishment of several religious congregations, like that of the Donors of Santa Maria, founded by the Roman matron, Francesca Buzzi, later to be canonized as Santa Francesca Romana.

That same year the pope issued instructions for the opening of the council at Pavia, as he had promised in Constance. But when it was declared open on 23 April 1423, few of the bishops were in the city because of the plague, so the papal legates moved it to Siena, postponing the opening until 21 July.

Disputes arose among the participants and work went on slowly, and the prelates wound up abandoning the assembly that was dissolved by the papal legates on 7 March 1424. It had been a failure. Martin V notified them that he would convene a new council at Basel in 1431 and approved the few decrees issued at Siena. These amounted to a confirmation of some that had been already defined in Constance, such as those against the heresies of Hus and the excommunication of the followers of Benedict XIII, who had died in his castle at Peñiscola on 23 May of the preceding year, and who had nominated four cardinals.

After his death and with the consent of the king of Aragon, three of them had elected a successor, a certain Gil Muñoz, canon in Barcelona, who assumed the name of Clement VIII. However, he resigned in 1429, asking his three electors to recognize Martin V as pope. Martin pardoned him and generously named him bishop of the Balearic Islands, where he died in 1446. The fourth cardinal, Jean Carrière, had created in 1425 his own personal pope, Bernard Garnier de Rodez, who took the name of Benedict XIV but passed away in 1430. The story of these two was so ridiculous that the *Annuario pontificio* does not even list them among the antipopes.

More serious attacks on the papal supremacy of Martin V came instead from France where, despite the war still going on with England, Charles VII did not want to recognize the concordat signed at Genazzano because of its restrictions on many Gallic freedoms regarding ancient rights to benefices and jurisdictions. Martin resisted the strong pressures from Charles, just as he reacted firmly to the disobedience that had again begun to circulate among the French clergy. In provision for the council at Basel, on 1 January 1431, the pope named Cardinal Cesarini to preside over the assembly, conferring on him as well the authority to transfer the council elsewhere if he thought it wise in order to assure a tranquil conduct of the sessions.

That was his final important decision as on 20 February 1431, he died of a stroke. He was buried at St. John Lateran. A splendid bas-relief in bronze depicts him on the front of the monument with an epigraph which calls him "*temporum suorum felicitas,*" a rhetorical eulogy "not completely without basis," as Gregorovius concedes, mainly because under him Rome and the Papal State entered a new and, under some aspects, more humane era.

207. EUGENE IV (1431—1447)

The fourteen cardinals present in Rome at the time of the death of Martin V met in conclave in the monastery of Santa Maria sopra Minerva on 1 March 1431 and by the 3rd they had already made their choice in the person of Cardinal Gabriele Condulmer. Born in Venice in 1383, he was a nephew of Gregory XII, who had named him bishop of Siena and later Cardinal at San Clemente. He assumed the name of Eugene IV.

The day after his coronation in St. Peter's on 11 March, he issued a bull in which he confirmed a convention which the College of Cardinals had sworn to before proceeding with the election. According to it a limit was placed on papal authority, in that the pope could take no important decision without agreement of the cardinals. He promised also to reform the pontifical court and, in any event, to move it out of Rome.

The renewal of the court, the first act of his pontificate, earned him the open opposition of the relatives of Martin V, the Colonnas, who wanted to keep for themselves Castel Sant'Angelo, Ostia and other lands. They rebelled against Eugene who excommunicated them on 18 May 1431, depriving them of their positions. With the assistance of Joan of Naples, he managed to handle the situation, but he had clearly made enemies of the Colonnas.

He then confirmed that Cardinal Cesarini would preside over the council about to begin in Basel, although in his heart he would have liked to convoke it in an Italian city and thereby favor the intervention of the emperor of Constantinople, John VII Paleologus, with whose help he intended to reach a settlement of the schism with the Eastern Church. The council was opened on 23 July in the cathedral of Basel. At the beginning, those present were mainly abbots and canons but very few bishops, but the attendance had increased by 14 December for the solemn opening under the chairmanship of Cesarini. He was only able to arrive then having been delayed in Germany by the problem of the Hussites, who in the end were invited to the assembly to discuss their beliefs.

Eugene IV, concerned over this attitude towards the heretics, declared the council dissolved in a bull of 18 December and moved it to Bologna. Those who had gathered at Basil, offended by Eugene's action, left the meeting on the day when the bull was read out and continued their work under a new chairman. Cesarini himself sent a letter of protest to the pope about the order of dissolution, openly rebelling against his authority. The council prelates found support for their action from the University of Paris and from the sovereigns of Spain and France, as well as from Sigismund and the princes of Germany.

Strengthened by this support, the assembly announced, on 15 February 1432, in firmer tones than that of Constance, that the authority of the council came directly from Christ and that even the pope had to submit to it. It proclaimed that this "ecumenical" council could not be dissolved and moved elsewhere without a reason recognized as valid by the assembly itself. Gradually, as further bishops began to arrive, the assembly grew more and more convinced about the work it had completed till then and, on 20 June, deliberated that the papal election was to be reserved to the council rather than to the College of Cardinals. The result was that the see of Rome was considered to be vacant, the nuncio, Giovanni of Prato, was held prisoner, and Eugene IV was summoned to appear in person before the council.

Sigismund understood that matters had taken a turn for the worse and, since he planned to be crowned in Rome by Eugene, instigated negotiations which led to a papal document on 14 February 1433, wherein the pope declared, in order to avoid a new schism, that he was prepared to reconvene the council at Basel on condition that what had been so far decided would be annulled. There were lengthy discussions while Sigismund was crowned by the pope in St. Peter's on 31 May, and on 1 August he convinced Eugene to publish a bull in which he recognized the council, provided that the chairmanship be conferred on his representative, and that the decree adverse to papal sovereignty be annulled. In

December, the pope made further concessions, acknowledging the ecumenical character of the council.

However, Eugene now had other problems. Once Sigismund had been crowned and had received in substance approval of the council's work he had returned to Basel, but meanwhile the papal territories were being invaded by Francesco Sforza and Nicholas Fortebraccio, in the pay of the duke of Milan, Filippo Maria Visconti. Many cardinals fled from Rome as the danger approached, and the Roman nobility was arrayed against Eugene who tried to pit Sforza against Fortebraccio by granting Sforza the vicariate of Ancona and the rank of standard-bearer of the Church. Obviously the pope did not know which way to turn.

The Colonnas incited the population against him, accusing him of treason, and Eugene thought it best to leave town. On the night of 4 June, dressed as a Benedictine monk, he and a friend boarded the boat of a certain Vitellio, which was anchored at the Ripa Grande, and put his fate in the hands of a robust sailor named Valentino. It was an eventful escape, since some Romans saw it all and sounded the alarm. When the boat passed near St. Paul's, the crowds threw stones and arrows at it, but Eugene lay stretched out on the bottom covered by a shield. Valentino manuevered cleverly, managing to evade a boat that tried to block the way near Ostia, and once he reached the high seas, Eugene boarded a ship. He disembarked at Pisa a few days later and reached safety in Florence on 23 June, lodging in the Dominican monastery at Santa Maria Novella. But Rome was not lost. Leone Sforza, Francesco's brother, managed to gain control of the situation and place the city under the sovereignty of the pope, who appointed Giovanni Vitelleschi, bishop of Recanati, as well as a famous soldier, as his vicar.

From Florence, Eugene resumed communications with Basel, sending two cardinals there with conciliatory proposals. But faced with renewed demonstrations of revolt, the pope issued another decree dissolving the council, and dispatched letters to the European sovereigns requesting them to recall their subjects from Basel. Within the assembly there was a split, where certain prelates abandoned it and others, once again, summoned the pope to appear before the court.

By this time, Eugene had had enough and considered the council de facto dissolved. Another council was convened at Ferrara, which began on 8 January 1438, under the chairmanship of Cardinal Albergati and in the presence of the pope who, on 15 February with approval of the assembly, proclaimed the council at Ferrara to be ecumenical, excommunicating the one of Basel which in reality had the support only of Charles VII, king of France.

The two councils continued their labors contemporaneously while Basel suspended Eugene from his duties on 24 January. Unfortunately, he could no longer rely on the support of Sigismund who died suddenly in December 1437, leaving Germany divided on obedience to the two councils. Meanwhile, in March John VII Paleologus arrived in Ferrara with a large company of bishops from the Eastern Church. But all of a sudden the plague appeared, and in January 1439 the council had to move to Florence. Meetings resumed in February and focussed on religious issues which separated the two Churches, reaching a "formula" for union on 8 June, two days before Patriarch Joseph of Constantinople passed away in the plenary council in Florence. The universal primacy of the Roman pontiff was recognized, an important declaration for the West, especially for the secessionists of Basel, and in August the Eastern delegation returned to Constantinople with the emperor.

The council continued its work, and, on 4 September, condemned as heretical all the "truths of the faith" which had been agreed upon in Basel. A limit was reached there on 5 November 1439 when, in a parody of a conclave consisting of one cardinal, eleven bishops, seven abbots and nine canonists, including Eneo Silvio Piccolomini, the future Pius II, Prince Amedeo VIII of Savoy, was elected pope. He was a layman who, upon the death of his wife, had renounced the administration of his lands in favor of his son, Ludovico, and had withdrawn to the solitude of Ripaglia, near Lake Geneva, where he lived as a hermit. He was flattered and accepted the nomination, wishing above all to take Holy Orders, and after he had received these, he was crowned on 24 July 1440, taking the name of Felix V.

Meanwhile, on 23 March, the council at Florence had excommunicated him, and even Charles VII of France, close as he was to the Baselians, could not bring himself to recognize him as the pope, and ordered his subjects to be obedient to Eugene IV. The duke of Burgundy and the kings of Castille, Aragon, and Poland all did the same. Evidently the settlement of the schism of the Eastern Church was bearing its fruit, especially with the recognition even there of the primacy of the bishop of Rome. The poor prince of Savoy, the last antipope to be listed as such in the *Annuario pontificio*, was of course completely dependent upon his electors at Basel who had given him as Secretary Enea Silvio Piccolomini. His position lasted for only as long as the council itself, that is until 1449, by which time it had become an insignificant function supported by no sovereign and relying solely on the neutrality of Frederick III of Habsburg and the German princes.

Eugene IV had substantially reinforced his own standing with an undisputed prestige in Italy. Recognized by the duke of Milan and having reached peace with the new king of Naples, Alphonso of Aragon, the pope saw the way open for his return to Rome. He left Florence and reached his see on 23 September, and even the council continued with its work at Rome, dealing exclusively with problems of a religious nature, while Syrians, Maronites and Chaldeans returned to the Church of Rome, abandoning their various heretical beliefs.

Eugene IV expressed his joy over these victories of the apostolic faith in his bull *Benedictus sit Deus*, of 7 April 1445, which is deemed a sort of final consecration of the Ecumenical Council XVII, the only one in history to have had three separate seats, Ferrara, Florence, and Rome, and declared closed by the pope.

Unfortunately, the joy of Eugene IV was dampened by disputes that suddenly arose within the Eastern Church. The patriarchs of Antioch, Alexandria, and Jerusalem did not accept the union agreement approved by their colleague from Constantinople who had died in Florence. The emperor himself was threatened with excommunication and the unionists were persecuted. After only a year of impassioned expressions of universal faith, the schism of the East was back again, more forcefully than ever.

On the other hand, in the West, the situation was more and more favorable for the pope. Frederick III of Habsburg, to whose service Enea Silvio Piccolomini had come in 1442, abandoning the cause of the antipope, recognized Eugene IV as the legitimate pontiff, thanks to the conferment of certain episcopal appointments on Austrian territory and the promise of the imperial crown. The neutrality of the German princes was concluded in Rome on 7 February 1447, with a concordat in which the decree from Constance concerning the obligation of holding regular ecumenical councils was accepted. The sponsors of the agreement were Piccolomini for the German princes, and the legates Carvajal and Parentucelli for the pope, the latter being rewarded by elevation to the cardinals' purple.

A few days later, on 23 February 1447, Eugene IV died and was buried in St. Peter's, as he had wanted, beside Eugene III. During the works on the new Vatican basilica, his remains were moved into the monumental tomb erected by Pisanello in the church of San Salvatore in Lauro where they have remained. "He was a grand and glorious pope; he disdained money, he loved virtue; he was not proud in fortunate times and in unfortunate times he was not disappointed; he knew no fear; his tranquil soul was reflected in his ever calm face," Piccolomini said about him, although he had earlier lined up on the side of the Baselians against him as secretary to the antipope, Felix V.

One must add that Eugene was certainly not nepotistic, and this ended by giving him the headaches of a turbulent residence in Rome. Almost too diplomatic, he managed to get his way precisely because of his mildness. A man of modest background, he continued to introduce Humanism to Rome, by surrounding himself with learned men, some of whom were his secretaries, such as Poggio, Aurispa, and Biondo, and summoning artists like Donatello, Pisanello and Fra Angelico to restore the churches. Finally, he commissioned Filarete to create the bronze doors of St. Peter's, in great part inspired by the council of Florence, which constituted the first realization of Renaissance art in Rome.

208. NICHOLAS V (1447–1455)

The conclave to choose a successor to Eugene IV took place for the second time in the monastery of the Dominicans at S. Maria sopra Minerva. The eighteen cardinals present in Rome entered there in the evening of 4 March 1447, and two days later, by the morning of 6 March, had already completed their task. Cardinal Tommaso Parentucelli, archbishop of Bologna, was elected. Born in Sarzana, he had been raised to the cardinal's purple just three months earlier because of his labors in concluding the concordat with the princes of Germany. He was only 49 years old.

This was an unexpected choice, so much so that the Romans, convinced that the choice would fall to Prospero Colonna, had already followed tradition by pillaging his richly furnished dwelling. When they learned who was in fact elected, they repeated the attack on the home of the new pontiff, but their booty was not much. After losing his father, Parentucelli had studied at Bologna where he had been the secretary to cardinal-archbishop Albergati in whose retinue he had acquired considerable political experience through several missions, but he had not enriched himself. He was more than anything a passionate bibliophile, but books still did not interest the general public.

He was crowned on 19 March and took the name of Nicholas V. During the first years of his pontificate, he simply reaped the fruits of his predecessor's policy. Felix V abdicated his phantom role of antipope on 15 April 1449, recognizing Nicholas V as the legitimate pope, who generously appointed him cardinal and gave him charge of the bishoprics of Lausanne and Geneva, where he died two years later.

Instead with Frederick III and the princes of Germany, the pope reached a new concordat, more detailed than the two separate ones concluded by Eugene IV. It was signed in Vienna on 17 February 1448, thanks to the ability of Cardinal Carvajal, his colleague in the negotiations a year earlier. This concordat was to govern ecclesiastical questions in the German states for several centuries and granted considerable rights to the Holy See. It put an end to the ambiguity about the relations within Germany between the pope and the council, and the recognition of the sovereignty of the Roman pontiff was a great victory for Nicholas V.

He believed that the unity of the Church in the West had been established by this concordat, as it evidently was. So, putting aside any idea of reformation, he thought only about solemnly blessing this event, and on 14 September 1449, announced a Jubilee for the following year. The crowds for that Holy Year were immense and pilgrims came from all over Europe to earn the indulgences. The crush of people, however, had some fatal results, as happened one day in December when some two hundred were suffocated by the crowd on the S. Angelo bridge and died, either drowned in the Tiber or under the hooves of the horses.

Even worse disasters were caused by the customary plague that spread through Rome and Italy, and Nicholas V did not cut much of a figure by leaving the city, from 18 June to 25 October, in the middle of the Holy Year to avoid contagion. "The court of Rome ran off deplorably as if there usually was no court or Curia here," criticized a representative of the Teutonic Order. "Cardinals, bishops, abbots, monks, without exception, all escaped from Rome just like Our Lord's Apostles on Good Friday. Even our Holy Father the Pope has departed from Rome . . . His Holiness has gone to a castle called Fabriano and, it is said, has forbidden anyone who has been in Rome either secretly or openly to approach Fabriano, under pain of excommunication and the loss of benefices and the pope's good graces, whatever his position might be." But the financial side of the Jubilee proceeded as usual, even without the presence of the vicar of Christ, since it was not necessary to come to Rome to receive the indulgences. It sufficed to have the money, as Seppelt recalls, because "during the Jubilee year it was given to numerous princes, through special papal dispensations, to receive the Jubilee indulgences without having to make the difficult journey to Rome. And the possibility of earning the indulgences was offered to all the faithful who were unable to make the pilgrimage to Rome. This was set forth in special bulls for individual countries in the year following the Jubilee Year. The price of the indulgences was, in addition to the usual conditions, a cash offering amounting to about half the cost of a trip to Rome."

All this contributed to consolidating the authority of the pope in Rome. Nicholas managed to restore good relations with both the Colonnas and the Orsinis and appointed a number of his faithful followers as cardinals. The ever-rebellious Bologna recognized his sovereignty and other cities followed suit, all thanks to the work of the legates and vicars, among whom excelled Cardinal Bessarione, who could all rely upon significant military and financial means.

In fact, the temporal power of the popes began to have a modern and precise structure, mainly because of the use of ecclesiastical incomes for political purposes. In this way the Christian ideal of the papal institution was betrayed and, regardless of all the good intentions, Nicholas V "in the eyes of the Apostles," according to Gregorovius, "committed an error by mistaking the papacy for the Church and the affairs of the clerical State for those of the republic of Christ."

The emperor was now destined to remain outside the organization of the Papal State. In effect the concordat of Vienna was an immutable point of reference, and the imperial coronation which, Frederick III wanted and received in Rome on 16 March 1452, took on the flavor of a worldly ceremony, combining it as he did with his marriage to Princess Eleonora of Portugal, the last marriage celebrated by a pope in his city. It did not have the weight of former times, even if the proud Habsburg wanted to immortalize it in his motto by the vowels AEIOU, presumably meaning "Austriae Est Imperare Orbi Universo." But, above all, on 9 May 1453, Constantinople fell to the Turks and thus the Eastern empire ceased to exist, and with it the last trace of the ancient Roman empire.

In Rome, papal authority was enforced by a vigilant police force, the first victim of which was Stefano Porcari, who had plotted to reinstall the republican constitution. The insurrection, which was to break out in early January 1453, planned the seizure of the pope, possibly his assassination, as well as the elimination of certain cardinals. Word of it reached Cardinal Bessarione on 5 January and the plot was discovered in time. Porcari was arrested and, after a summary proceeding, executed together with the other plotters, Francesco Gabadeo, Pietro de Monterotondo, Battista Sciarra, and Angiolo Ronconi. The pope was accused by the populace of reneging on his promise, not to have Sciarra and Ronconi executed and to have been so drunk at the moment of the execution that he was unable to sign the pardon.

With that began the first *Pasquinade*, even though the bust of Pasquino had not yet seen the light, with the anonymous one that referred to Porcari's plot:

> Ever since Nicholas has been pope and assassin,
> blood abounds in Rome but wine is scarce.

and the one written by Antonio Tebaldeo against the Curia:

> Your arrogance grows ever greater;
> God is no longer honored, only Bacchus and Venus;
> perforce Heaven will send you over the precipice.

And the epigram was in no way too caustic. The pomp of the ceremonies at the court of Nicholas V began to put Rome on the same level as that at Avignon under Clements V and VI. With this pope, indeed, worldly splendor acquired new meaning, coinciding with the emerging force of the Renaissance, which found in him a great Maecenas. The papal court was enriched by even more humanists, which included the bookdealer, Vespasiano of Bisticci and the great Lorenzo Valla, and with their help Nicholas was able to indulge fully in his hobby as a bibliophile.

He acquired manuscripts from their countries of origin, which he had copied and researched, and founded the Vatican Library, which during his reign already had about 1200 manuscripts, mainly of a theological nature. For the library he spared no expense, convinced that in time it would serve a vital function in the progress of culture, not to be reserved simply for ecclesiastics but *"pro communi doctorum commodo."*

As a genuine man of the Renaissance he devoted himself to a patronage of the arts, which obviously brought him fame but also assured Rome of some badly needed reconstruction. These included the restoration of the city walls ruined by repeated attacks, the new fortification of Castel Sant' Angelo, and the restoration work done by Alberti for the Trevi Fountain with a pool built against the wall dating from the Roman era to which battlements were added.

But the point of departure for the renewal of the city was to be the project submitted to Nicholas V by Leon Battista Alberti for the restructuring of the Leonine City with the construction of a new basilica of St. Peter and of the Vatican itself as a single complex. The pope did not have in mind any such gigantic project but he approved it enthusiastically, even if the grandiose works were to remain in their initial stages due to his premature death.

However, he was so taken by the fantastic architectural undertaking that it seems he decided to obtain the construction materials from ancient monuments, winding up in the proverbial situation of 'stripping one altar to adorn another.' In fact, he had marble and travertine removed from the Colosseum and from the Circo Massimo, and also demolished the surrounding Servian walls at the foot of the Aventine. The justified complaints that arose came from those very humanists he patronized. Piccolomini was their spokesman through an epigram which was in Latin but can be translated thus:

> Rome, I like to gaze at your ruins,
> from the collapse of which blossom antique glories.
> But your inhabitants, in deference to quicklime,
> fire the hard marble wrenched from the ancient walls.
> Impious people, continue this way for a further
> three hundred years, and you'll see
> that not a trace of nobility will remain!

But when, on 24 March 1455, Nicholas V died, the future pope, Pius II, did praise him in the epitaph engraved on his funeral monument, erected in St. Peter's and later moved to the Vatican Grottoes, as the one who had caused Rome to recover its golden age.

209. CALIXTUS III (1455–1458)

On 4 April 1455, the fifteen cardinals present in Rome went into conclave in St. Peter's and as a result of a split of the Italian cardinals into two factions, between the Orsinis and the Colonnas, the Spanish succeeded in electing one of their own. On 8 April the Spanish Cardinal of the Ss. Quattro Coronati, Alonso de Borja, was acclaimed pope. His name was commonly italianised as Borgia.

Born in Játiva, Valencia, he had been a canon with Benedict XIII but when Martin V was recognized as the legitimate pope, he had appointed him bishop of Valencia. Alfonse V later called him to Naples as adviser, but he had not agreed with the anticlerical policy of that king. Eugene IV raised him to the cardinal purple and, on being crowned pope, on 20 April, he took on the name of Calixtus III.

In contrast to his predecessors, he was not interested in culture, leaving half-finished the building projects and allowing the manuscripts in the recently built library to collect mildew. His sole aim was to maintain public order, but this he did by going back to the scandalous nepotism which had characterized Martin V. To excuse this, as Castiglioni does, by the "need of the popes to surround themselves with devoted and interested people to help them protect the State against the turbulent louts who were usurping positions and lands of the State" is utter nonsense.

The only exception of a religious nature to his dedication to relatives was his active promotion of a crusade against the Turks by a number of bulls which called upon Christianity to sign up for this sacred mission. For this he contributed enough from the treasury to provide a fleet of sixteen triremes which, in fact, did not accomplish much. More important was the victory in July 1456, of the brave Hungarian, John Hunyadi, who stopped the advance of the Turks when they reached Belgrade. But the rest of the Christian sovereigns did not even reply to the pope's appeal.

So the brief pontificate of Calixtus III brought advantages only to his relatives, who would attain the peak of their ambitions through Alexander VI and his children. Everything began with the appointment as cardinals of two sons of his two sisters, Luis Juan de Mila, formerly bishop of Segovia, and Rodrigo de Borja y Doms. Luis Juan was appointed papal legate to Bologna, and Rodrigo, at the age of twenty-five, became the vice-chancellor of the Church, captain of the papal militia and bishop of Valencia. A third nephew, Don Pedro Luis, Rodrigo's brother, remained a layman but nevertheless reached the highest posts in the Papal State as Captain General of the Church with the ownership of Castel Sant'Angelo and other fortresses, and Prefect of Rome. He was in all likelihood his uncle's favorite and, with such support, he managed to give various friends of his a number of "ministerial" jobs so that "Rome underwent a real Spanish invasion," or rather a Catalan one, in view of the fact that "relatives and partisans of his family, adventurers seeking their fortune, flooded the city in droves," Gregorovius observed.

There were clearly a lot of them since a biographer of Calixtus wrote, "Calixtus corrupted the Curia offices creating room servants, prothonotaries, judges of first instance, subdeacons, and chamber acolytes, even forming a Pretorian court. He appointed about fifty secretaries and filled their posts with notaries, laborers, and a large number of ignorant people. He fired all the incumbents of the Curia, and passed the honor to unworthy persons." Disappointed nobles and clergymen had their say about this nepotistic pope and the Borgia invasion of their city. What is generally considered the first real "Pasquinade" in history goes back to that period, though it is not dated:

> Christ left his Church to his poor apostles;
> The good Calixtus today leaves it
> as prey to his rich nephews.

However, the dominion of Don Pedro Luis ended with the death of his uncle and, having heard that Calixtus was dying, he feared for his own life. He sold Castel Sant'Angelo on the night of 5 August for 20,000 ducats to the group of cardinals including his brother, Rodrigo, who were protecting him, and fled from Rome to Civitavecchia where he fell victim to malaria.

Calixtus III died on 6 August 1458, certainly not mourned by the Romans who, instigated by the Orsinis, avenged their hatred on the Catalans by pillaging the homes of the Borgias. The pope was buried in St. Peter's, and his remains, together with those of his nephew, Alexander VI, are said to have been transferred later to the Spanish church, S. Maria of Monserrat.

210. Pius II (1458–1464)

The nepotism of Calixtus III had made the College of Cardinals apprehensive and so, from the moment that the pope was on his deathbed, they began to think about coming to an agreement for the election, which took effect the moment they entered the conclave. They decided what the program of the new pope should be, from the crusade against the Turks to the reformation of the Curia, but chiefly they wanted to strengthen the function of the members of the Sacred College with regard to the appointment of new cardinals and the assignment of dioceses and abbeys. The conclave began on 16 August 1458, in the Vatican, and by the 19th Cardinal Aeneas Silvius Piccolomini was elected.

To trace the lines of his biography means to refer mainly to his autobiography in his *Commentarii*, a work which Piccolomini ambitiously intended to "leave to posterity," as Falconi notes, as the "neo-pagan pope" he was, thereby "making the most perfect and fullest image of himself" since "he himself and no one else was his only idol, his true divinity."

Born in Corsignano, later called Pienza, near Siena on 18 October 1405, in a noble but poor family, he had studied law at the University of Siena, spending a happy youth, happy also because of his love of a certain Angela, praised in his first poems under the name of Cynthia. Following a journey to various Italian cities, he returned to Siena where he had the good fortune to meet Bishop Capranica who took him on as his secretary, and with him Enea attended the council at Basel and thus began the most exciting period of his life.

He carried out important diplomatic missions for various prelates, but became involved in the attempted capture of Eugene IV in Florence, although he is careful not to mention this in his *Commentarii*. Withdrawing from that venture, he again was lucky with Cardinal Albergati who sent him on a mission to the court of James I in Scotland. This was a heady experience for the young man, and included some spicy adventures that produced two children, one with a Scottish woman, the other with a Breton "whom he later cynically saddled the father with," as Falconi observes. It is a fact that, as a true child of his times, "he never claimed a blameless past," and so, if Aeneas Silvius depicted the journey to Scotland as a period of "abstinence" despite temptations galore, he did so because, again as Falconi states, "he wished to declare in his own defense that he could, when necessary, master his own penchants."

In any event, those adventures also were part of his formation as a diplomat, so that when he returned to the fortress of Basel, ready to take advantage of every chance to show himself off in a favorable light, he succeeded in obtaining high positions thanks to his oratorical ability and his political acumen. When Eugene IV ordered the transfer of the council to Ferrara, he stayed behind with the dissidents of Basel and took part in the council-farce which led to the election of Amedeo VIII of Savoy as pope, the antipope, Felix V. He became his secretary and, in his defense, he wrote *Libellus dialogorum de generalis concilii authoritate*. Later, however, aware that Felix V was a pope without a flock, he agreed to enter the service of Frederick of Habsburg.

Then he began a period of intense literary activity, culminating with the unprejudiced *Historia de duobus amantibus*, but also of diplomatic activity with several missions, during one of which he came to terms with Eugene IV, becoming an ardent defender of papal authority. Astutely, he realized that that was the path for an ambitious person and, whether or not through opportunism, he then took Holy Orders becoming, in the space of one year, subdeacon, deacon, priest and, in April 1447, bishop of Trieste.

His was a meteoric career, much talked about, which constrained him publicly to repudiate his mundane writings and interests, but brought him to the height of his aspirations. At first he continued to carry on his activities with Frederick III taking a major role in the peace negotiations between Nicholas V and the emperor, which were sealed with the Concordat of Vienna. Then he enthusiastically accepted the appointment in 1450 as bishop of Siena, returning after many years to his native land, until 1456, when Calixtus III raised him to the rank of the cardinal as a reward for his work on behalf of a crusade against the Turks. His election on 19 August 1458 to the pontificate was certainly the result of a series of circumstances which made him appear to the College of Cardinals as a mirror of modern times, and also because he did not come from a cloister or from a clerical background. He had behind him a prestigious political and cultural career and would be a vicar of Christ with a "secular touch," according to Gregorovius, "in a world which had become freer and more humane in all its manifestations."

When his election was announced, Aeneas Silvius Piccolomini burst into tears and the finishing touch to the image of this "neo-pagan pope" came with his words after the tears: "We do not deserve to be elevated to this honor; instead we would declare our total unworthiness and we would not accept it if we did not fear the judgment of the One who has called us." In all of this, there is a "cynicism which borders on sacrilege when," as Falconi intelligently puts it, "he brings God Himself into the picture, citing Him, and only Him, as the true author of his election, the pedestal of his glorification."

He was crowned on 3 September and, with obvious reference to the pius Aeneas, he decided to take the name of Pius II. His election was welcomed enthusiastically by the humanists who were certain of a return to the days of Nicholas V, but they were fooled. The new pope did not sponsor any artist and many, like Filelfo, resented that, accusing him of greed. Filelfo declaimed: "Repudiate Aeneas; bid Pius welcome," but Pius II clearly did not want to give substance to rumors of his past life by an excessive patronage of the arts. He did, however, assign various jobs to the humanists in the restructured College of Letter Writers (Abbreviatori) at the papal chancery, where they had to make extracts of petitions and drafts of replies—always a dignified position for literate persons.

The fact is that Pius II devoted himself chiefly to improving his own image for posterity through a genuine neo-pagan cult. His own *Commentarii*, as has been noted, had precisely that in aim so that, in his own words, Aeneas Silvius Piccolomini "shall be praised and mourned, so that at his death he cannot return. Envy of him after his death will cease, and once the emotions which distort judgment have been forgotten, his true and unsullied fame will emerge again to include him among the illustrious popes."

This then was his program, clearly a personal one, as can be seen from the magnificent improvements he made in his hometown with the construction of that jewel, fashioned by Bernardo Rossellino between the cathedral and the surrounding majestic palaces, and calling the town with his own pontifical name, Pienza. Other examples are the archaeological diggings at Tivoli and the start of construction of the castle in 1461. Further evidence of the personalization of his power lies in his nepotism shown by his appointment as cardinals of two nephews one of whom, Francesco Todeschini, was to become pope Pius III and both of whom supported him in opposing the authority of the College of

Cardinals. And this does not include the relatives and townsmen whom he had placed in key positions in the Curia and in the Papal State in a manipulation of power not much different from that of Calixtus III.

But no matter how nepotistic, Pius II had the significant merit of drawing the broad lines of the "new" concept of the Papal State. These were the years when Lorenzo Valla had denounced to the whole world the falsity of the *Constitutum Constantini*, and a humanist like Piccolomini could scarcely challenge that declaration. At the same time he felt somehow obliged to oppose what Valla called the "new papal tyranny," that is, the bad administration of the lands which, Constantine apart, were the property of the Church, including donations from the Frankish kings and other sovereigns up to the properties of Matilda of Canossa. He became the ideologist of a Papal State within the context of other nation-States, breaking away from outdated theocratic ideas.

In a *Tractatus*, untitled and in the form of a conversation between Aeneas Silvius, Bernardino of Siena, and Pietro of Noceto, the pope-king idea is set forth: "Government by a good priest is superior to and holier than that of a good layman" because the former combines in himself priestly *instructio* and royal *praeceptio*, guaranteeing maximum concentration of authority which "cannot be self-contradictory." It thereby avoids any conflict caused by fragmentation of power and, while delegating to laymen certain functions, leads in practice to a clericalism of the entire administration.

As a pope-king, Pius II had to affirm himself on the one hand by getting rid, as far possible, of the military power of the lords in the several cities of the Papal State and, on the other, by doing away with any form of constitutionalism, whether of the cardinalate or the conciliar type. The famous bull *Execrabilis* of 1460 refers to the latter, and condemns any appeals to councils against papal decisions. As for the struggle with restive vassals, military action would be applied, like the shelling in 1461 of the Savelli in the Roman countryside. Also excommunication and interdiction would be used in a manner which tended to identify the political enemy with the enemies of the faith, as was true in the case of the Malatestas who were defined as "perfidious rebels against God and the Apostolic Faith."

This political concept of the absolute pope-king would slowly produce its fruits for the "pontifical sovereign," but Pius II did not have time to wait. He wanted to leave signs of his presence in the earth itself and, almost deliriously seeking that immortal glory to be achieved in the pages of the *Commentarii*, he threw himself head first into what seemed to him to be the only worthwhile and timely opportunity to consecrate his sovereignty, the crusade against the Turks. So, substituting himself for the emperor, now without power or interest, he called for a Diet of all the Christian sovereigns to be held at Mantua in June 1459. However, his efforts came to naught faced with the conflicting interests of various States. The Diet was a failure.

He did not lose courage. In a frantic missionary mood, he thought about skipping the crusade and simply converting all the Turks. So he wrote a letter to Mohammed II, stressing the strength of his culture, and to impress the Sultan even more, he went so far as to promise him the imperial crown, like a new Constantine. A mixture of genius and pagan-Christian irregularity must have inspired in him this idea of converting the Moslems, which certainly would have been the biggest coup that any pope could achieve. However, as one could obviously have expected, the letter brought no response.

Pius II went back to the idea of the crusade and decided to head personally the expedition. He preached it with all available means and, in a blend of hypocrisy and religious fanaticism, decided to inflame the participants in the crusade by parading around Rome a precious relic, the head of the Apostle Andrew, which the last of the Palaeologus had brought from the East in 1462. It had come from Patras, the presumed location of Andrew's martyrdom.

There was a huge influx of pilgrims to Rome for the veneration of that relic, with continuous triduums and novenas for the expedition against the infidels. By coincidence, the war cry of Godfrey of Boulogne during the first crusade had been "St. Andrew of Patras!" On 22 October 1463, the prayers were followed by the publication of the bull which promulgated the Holy War. The freeing of the East from the infidels in the name of Christ could, as Pius II saw it, even be the sacrifice of his own life in martyrdom and the source of eternal glory.

And so, ill as he was, and thinking that, like a new Godfrey, he could draw with him a group of indifferent sovereigns sustained by purely idealistic enthusiasm and devoid of military and financial means, he set off for Ancona, which had been chosen as the meeting place for the fleets of all of Christendom. However, when he arrived there on 12 July and did not see the ships and the armies which he had expected, he realized that it was all a dream, a castle in the air, created by his own illusions or perhaps he went towards that which, in his heart, he had always desired and, in his pagan way, "experienced" the collapse of every heroic effort.

With his death, which he sensed was imminent, he attained the essential purpose of his entire existence, his achievement of glory in posterity. Pius II, "pagan to his very marrow," as Falconi wonderfully noted, "lived to a point of delirium the pagan ideal of the warrior, especially for his relationship to the cult of the 'beautiful death' . . . the creed which from his youth had nourished and raised him through his constant reading of the classics" and which, "when he became pope, was the leitmotiv of all his orations . . . the mirage from which, especially in his last years of life, nothing could distract him." And, on the hill of St. Ciriacus he greeted that "beautiful death" on 15 August 1464, just as a dozen Venetian ships appeared on the horizon, not enough for the venture but a fitting setting in their uncertainty for the end of Pius's life.

His remains were brought to Rome and he was buried in St. Peter's in a tomb which was transferred in 1614 to S. Andrea della Valle, the church of the apostle in whose name Pius II had spurred Christians, in vain, to join in "his" impossible crusade.

211 PAUL II (1464—1471)

The conclave to elect the successor to Pius II gathered in the Vatican on 27 August 1464. The election was not contested and already at the first ballot on 30 August the Cardinal of S. Marco, the Venetian, Pietro Barbo, was elected. He was the son of a sister of Eugene IV, born on 26 February 1418, to a wealthy family of businessmen and was set to go into business himself had his uncle not put him on an ecclesiastical career. He had already been made a cardinal when only twenty years old.

After the election, he expressed his wish to be called Formoso, but the cardinals dissuaded him from that ridiculous idea which reminded them of the dark times of the medieval papacy, and they also discouraged him from taking the name of Mark, because it recalled the battle cry of the Venetians: "San Marco!" So he finally took the name of Paul II and was consecrated on 16 September 1464.

However, as pope, he conceded little to the College of Cardinals. During the conclave the cardinals had sworn to an electoral agreement which, in a series of conventions, tended to diminish considerably papal sovereignty and to give more weight to the Sacred College.

Paul II should have confirmed that in a bull three days after his coronation, which didn't happen. Instead, he presented the cardinals with a bull for signature which, in substance, annulled what had been established in the conclave, thereby blocking any attempt toward "constitutional monarchy" or oligarchical power. He compensated the cardinals by increasing their emoluments, granting no more judgeships to lay persons, by a total clericalism of the administrative structure and the appointment of a clergyman to the post of governor of Castel Sant'Angelo. That was accomplished in the same year as his coronation, by naming Rodrigo de Arévalo to that position.

He thereby reaffirmed fully the absolute sovereignty of the pope, already evidenced by Pius II. Even the tiara, the symbol of the universal power of the papacy in the form of the three realms, which since the fourteenth century had taken over from the mitre, a simple symbol of spiritual and episcopal authority, assumed greater splendor. Paul II desired for himself a tiara of gold studded with jewels, recorded by an anonymous humanist in two verses that ridiculed the sovereign:

> Pope Paul's head is empty. It is then right
> that it be loaded with jewels and gold.

Indeed, the humanists had reason to be unhappy with this pope, since the elimination of the laity from the papal administration meant as well the abolition of the College of the Letter Writers (*Abbreviatori*) established by Pius II. This resulted in an outcry by the numerous groups of literate men without an income. Their complaints were not heeded, even if one of the loudest voices was that of Platina, the future librarian of the Vatican under Sixtus IV. He proposed appealing to the Sacra Rota, but in vain. Paul II's reply was "I am the pope and I can do what I wish with people."

When Platina then wrote a letter, a little arrogantly, directly to Paul II threatening to convene a council before which the pope would have to account for his conduct, orders were issued for him to be "seized and put into the stocks." After four months of prison and torture in Castel Sant'Angelo, the humanist was only saved through the intercession of Cardinal Gonzaga. Platina did not forget, however, later writing maliciously about Paul II with all the rancour in his soul in his *Vitae pontificum*. Among other things, he declared: "He so hated studies of humanism, disdained and reviled them so much, that he called those who were working in this field 'heretics.' And he urged the Romans not to let their children waste time in studying these writings; it was enough if they learned how to read and write."

That this was true was confirmed in a passage from the letter of Lorenzo of Pesaro to Duke Francesco Sforza, quoted by Pastor: "The pope has prohibited all school teachers from reading Latin poets because His Holiness does not like the heresy which certain teachers who admire those poets have learned from them." In reality, it was precisely because Paul II was such a profound student of art, as bear witness the many precious items he collected in the treasury of Castel Sant'Angelo, and the splendid palazzo of St. Mark (future palazzo of Venice), that he knew well the value of culture. He invoked the policy, typical of absolutist regimes, of leaving the people in their ignorance. To keep the people away from talking about municipal matters, "he fed them bread and circuses." as Gregorovius noted, correctly reading in the chronicles of that period certain facts about life at Rome under Paul II.

"In the city he built granaries and slaughterhouses, and in a truly mundane sense he welcomed the pre-Lenten celebrations of '*carnevale*' in 1468, in accordance with the ancient tradition of '*panem et circenses*.' For the occasion, as the German historian records, "Bacchanalian parades were formed, with mythological images of gods, heroes, nymphs and spirits. And as the pope wanted to watch the races from the balcony of his palace, he ordered that the starting point be fixed at the Arch of Domitian and the finishing line under his windows. He was thus the first pope to revive in Rome the pagan character of the carnival games. Very few people questioned whether what was all right for a Pompey or a Domitian was suitable for a pope. Even Cardinal Ammannati, who raised his voice against these excesses probably heard in reply only the laughs of those around him. When the games were over, the pope invited the populace to gather in front of the palace where he spent most of his time, while eminent citizens sat at richly decorated tables and the vice-chamberlain Vianesio of the Albergati family and other Curia members watched over the crowd to avoid any disorders. Meanwhile, Paul II stood on his balcony, forgetful of his papal dignity, and threw coins down to the simple folk who fought to carry off the remains of the banquet. Gazing at the senators, conservators and citizens busily devouring the food he offered them, the pope might well tell himself that neither the Senate nor the people were worthy of the freedom they had." A bitter statement, but one which found a verification in the events that accompanied the now traditional celebration of 1468. That year, a sort of conspiracy against the pope was discovered within the group of humanists from the Accademia Romana founded by Pomponio Leto. At least Paul II was convinced that those educated persons, "drunk with ideas and customs of the ancient Romans," as D'Onofrio sees them, "focussed upon an archetypical, idealistic republican liberty," had plotted against his sovereign person, so they all wound up in Castel Sant'Angelo.

"It has never been clear what this plot was or what aims it had," D'Onofrio goes on, "also because the man who was said to have been the leader of it, the Florentine Filippo Bonaccorsi . . . tipped off in time, fled from Rome to find comfortable hospitality with King Casimir of Poland." All the others were finally released and the only sad result was that the Accademia Romana was dissolved. The incident in fact was, as D'Onofrio correctly concludes, "the final bloodless and even anti-historical attempt at lay freedom for Rome from pontifical authority. From then on one may say that protesters would no longer be heard of. Everything would move within the narrow, ever more orthodox and severe tracks."

The pontificate of Paul II holds nothing more for us, even if one mentions again the strengthening of the Papal State by his elimination of the Anguillara family of "brigands." His international prestige involved him in a new crusade against the Turks in support of Hungary, but which was doomed by the superior forces of the enemy which extended its sway into Albania upon the death of that country's great defender, Skanderbeg, who had personally sought the aid of the pope.

By the bull *Ineffabilis Providentia*, Paul II definitively established, in 1470, that the Holy Year would be celebrated every twenty-five years and he was already preparing to reap the benefits from the Jubilee of 1475, when he died suddenly of a stroke in his palace of St. Mark on 26 July 1471. Platina, however, raised the suspicion that he had been poisoned, "because the day before the night when he died, he consumed two enormous melons," apart from the joke that he was strangled by a spirit enclosed in one of his many rings.

A splendid tomb was erected to him in St. Peter's, the work of the sculptors Mino da Fiesole and Giovanni Dalmata, which was praised by Vasari as the most exceptional funeral monument ever erected for a pope. However, when the new basilica was built, it was broken up and only the sarcophagus came to rest in the Vatican Grottoes.

212. SIXTUS IV (1471–1484)

Eighteen cardinals participated at the conclave in Rome in August 1471. First of all, they drafted and approved an electoral treaty which repeated that of the previous conclaves, recommending reforms and a crusade against the Turks, but had an objective to strengthen the power of the College of Cardinals against the increasingly absolute sovereignty of the pope. And this time, too, it went badly for the Sacred College when Cardinal Francesco della Rovere was elected on 9 August 1471, and consecrated on 25 August with the name of Sixtus IV.

Born in Celle at Savona on 21 July 1414, a student and later a teacher in the universities of Pavia and Bologna, and cardinal in 1467, he had been the Superior General of the Franciscans. But if as such he had been engaged in reforms he did not take a similar role as pope, except for strictly political and financial reasons.

That crusade, for which he had worked zealously at the beginning of his pontificate by sending cardinals as envoys to various European sovereigns to ask for their intervention, was a total failure. The fleet, armed with the help of Venice and Naples under the command of Cardinal Oliviero Caraffa obtained negligible results in Asia Minor. The lack of success in organizing the crusade was due to intrigues of nepotism, which under Sixtus IV reached heights never before recorded. As a result of which he was involved in chaotic politics which caused grave damage to the Papal State.

The benefices granted to the numerous relatives who came to him from two brothers and four sisters, a group of fifteen nephews and nieces through various degrees of relationship, was enormous. The Franciscans, Giuliano della Rovere, the future pope Giulio II and Pietro Riario, were immediately made cardinals. The latter, loaded with lucrative incomes from abbeys and bishoprics of Split, Seville, and Valencia, wasted his wealth in dissolute living which led to his early death at the age of twenty-eight. But another Riario, Raffaele, barely sixteen years old, was available to take his place in the College, while a third one, Girolamo, a former businessman in Savona, raised to the rank of Count and after marrying Caterina Sforza, the daughter of the duke of Milan, received the fiefdom of Imola.

It was Girolamo Riario, who knew nothing about politics, who dragged the pope into wars and intrigues which proved disastrous for the Papal State, since Sixtus IV's ambition to create a grand principality for this idiotic nephew led him to threaten the very stability of the Italian political equilibrium. The greatest opposition to the project came from Florence where Lorenzo de' Medici, angry with the pope because he had not raised his brother, Giuliano, to the cardinalate, backed various papal vassals in their insubordination and tried to isolate the pope economically. To manage the financial affairs of the Curia and eventual investments by the Vatican, Sixtus IV retained the Florentine bank of the Pazzi. The result was a series of lawsuits and verdicts out of which the papacy emerged sullied.

Then on 26 April 1478, as is well known, two acolytes actuated the conspiracy of the Pazzi in the cathedral of Florence. Lorenzo was saved, but Giuliano was killed. The people's uprising against the Medici did not break out as the Pazzi had hoped and, instead, there was a vendetta against the conspirators and their families.

Members of the Pazzi family and Archbishop Salviati of Pisa were hanged from the windows of the Palazzo della Signoria, and Cardinal Raffaele Riario, who was in Florence as the guest of the Pazzi, was imprisoned but later released as he had had nothing to do with the conspiracy. It has long been discussed how much Sixtus IV had to do with any of this, but it is difficult to imagine he was left in the dark about it all, and it is certain that he was indirectly involved.

Nevertheless, his reaction to the condemnation of Archbishop Salviati and to the imprisonment of Cardinal Riario, which included a demand for satisfaction obviously rejected, were understandable. Lorenzo de' Medici was excommunicated and Florence interdicted, resulting in an armed conflict with Sixtus IV frighteningly alone. Indirectly, it was the Turks who saved him when in 1480 they crossed the Adriatic and conquered Otranto. The whole of Italy was suddenly terrorized and reunited around the pope, who removed the interdiction on Florence and launched again the idea of the crusade. This never got off the ground and all it did was to throw the Turks back into the sea and free Otranto.

But Girolamo Riario got his uncle involved in further politico-military misadventures. He allied himself with Venice, promising it Ferrara where he would eliminate Ercole d'Este, his personal enemy. But the latter found support from his father-in-law, King Ferdinand of Naples, whose army, however, was defeated by the Venetian Papal troops in 1482 at Campo Morto in the Pontine Marshes. Clearly, however, Venice was becoming too powerful, and would have ended by being a big danger to the principality of his beloved nephew, so Sixtus IV changed policy and joined his enemies, abandoning the Republic of the Lagoon.

In this struggle, carried on imprudently from a political viewpoint, the pope naturally used his ecclesiastical weapons and issued an interdiction against

Venice. But this proved of little use. In the constantly changing world of diplomacy the great republic regained the support of the allies of the pope, who again found himself isolated, and was forced into the humiliating peace treaty of Bagnolo in 1484.

The situation in Rome in those years was no less chaotic, always because of Girolamo Riario. To support the Orsinis, he made open warfare against the Colonnas who, together with the Savellis, pillaged the Roman Campagna in 1482. The cardinals from the two families paid the price, being hostages in Castel Sant'Angelo for a year, until the Orsinis managed to conquer Albano, ousting Antonio Savelli, and seizing the major representative of the Colonnas, Oddone, who, despite having barricaded himself in the cardinal's home, was captured and beheaded. Then the palace was set on fire.

Sixtus IV added to this disastrous political situation a financial one in deficit. It was inevitable that with limitless payments to his relatives, the wars and the intrigues, the finances would be in a terrible state, especially when the Pazzi bank failed as a result of the conspiracy. To handle this situation, he naturally resorted to abuses by granting benefices, which led to the practice of simony, not counting the proceeds of the indulgences during the Jubilee of 1475. There were also new taxes and speculation that led to an unpopular rise in the price of bread.

The collection of tribute was assigned to the Permit Office (*Dataria*) which, with the Apostolic Chamber, came to be the other important financial center of the Holy See. In other words, any means of amassing money seemed good to him, and there was a common saying that, "The pope needs only pen and ink to raise the amount he wants."

Despite the increased price of bread, he managed to keep the Romans happy with semi-pagan celebrations including dinner on Easter Thursday in the Capitol, and traditional games in Agone and Testaccio, the costs of which were borne by the Jewish communities in the city. The Carnival of 1473 in honor of Cardinal Caraffa for the minor victories over the Turks was particularly memorable, surpassing in splendor the Venetian Carnival.

But fortunately not all the money spent by Sixtus IV was wasted on the vanity of the nephews or on amusements for the common folk. Some of it was used in construction work in Rome to beautify the city. He understood that for this he needed the collaboration of true artists and, therefore, established good relations with humanists at the very beginning of his pontificate. The Accademia Romana was reopened, and the College of the Letter Writers (*Abbreviatori*) reorganized. People like Pomponio Leto and Platina could breathe again an unhoped air of culture.

Platina, who was commissioned officially to edit the *Vite dei romani pontefici*, was appointed "*custos et gubernator*" of the Vatican Library then under construction, whose librarian was Bishop Giannandrea Bussi of Vigevano. The work began in 1471 and consisted in the redesigning of three great halls on the ground floor in the complex of buildings restructured thirty years before by Nicholas V, and embellished by paintings of Ghirlandaio and Antoniazzo Romano. When Bussi died in February 1475 and the work was completed, Platina became the librarian and the Library was officially instituted with the bull of 15 June 1475. This event was immortalized by the famous fresco of Melozzo of Forlì in 1477 that adorned the first hall of the Library. Sixtus IV is pictured on the throne there with his two nephews, Cardinals Raffaele Riario, and Giulio della Rovere, as well as Platina who, on his knees, points to the inscription below which praises the pope's many construction projects.

Then there were the restoration of ancient churches and the completion of new ones, among which is to be remembered S. Maria del Popolo which became in a way the burial church of the della Rovere, and the repairing of the closed Acqua Vergine aqueduct that was extended from the Quirinal to the Trevi Fountain. In addition, there was the rebuilding of the S. Spirito hospital, the paving of the principal streets, and the bridge named after him, Sisto, all with a view to renewing Rome for the Holy Year.

Finally, one cannot forget the Sistine Chapel, built in the Vatican palace expressly for the pope's religious ceremonies. The greatest artists of that time were invited to paint in it, from Mino da Fiesole to Sandro Botticelli, Domenico Ghirlandaio, Pietro Perugino, Luca Signorelli and Pinturicchio, and where Michelangelo's masterpieces then completed it all.

On the strictly religious level, Sixtus IV did not accomplish very much. Aside from the Jubilee, which brought the now habitual economic benefit and the splendor of the new structures, the pope was especially concerned with the spread of devotion to the Madonna, with financial donations for the sanctuaries of Genazzano and Loreto. And he also dedicated the Sistine Chapel to the Immaculate Conception, creating an appropriate liturgy for the feast on 8 December, whose dogma would later be proclaimed by Pope Pius IX.

However, the name of Sixtus IV is linked as well to the infamous Spanish Inquisition authorized by the bull of 1 November 1478. Authority was granted to Ferdinand of Aragon and Isabelle of Castile to appoint as inquisitors the clerics they considered valid both in doctrine and wisdom. As Castiglioni records, "the procedure of the inquisitors soon degenerated, and religious motives were often no more than pretexts for political vendettas." The age of the auto-da-fé had begun and vain were the attempts to put an end to its cruelty and injustice. In all this one name stands out, that of the first great Inquisitor General, Thomas Torquemada.

Sixtus IV died on 12 August 1484. He was buried in a monumental tomb, considered to be the best work of Antonio del Pollaiolo, later transferred to the

Vatican Grottoes. With him died the first truly Renaissance pope, or, to use Gregorovius's term, the first pope-king.

The anonymous *Pasquinades* were numerous on the occasion of the death of Sixtus IV, but the most poisonous is certainly the following one:

> Sixtus, at last you're dead: unjust, untrue, you rest now,
> you who hated peace so much, in eternal peace.
> Sixtus, at last you're dead: and Rome is happy,
> for, when you reigned, so did famine, slaughter and sin.
> Sixtus, at last you're dead, eternal engine of discord,
> even against God Himself, now go to dark Hell.
> Sixtus, at last you're dead: in every clever deceit,
> in fraud, betrayal the best of teachers.
> Sixtus, at last you're dead: ruffians, knaves,
> Bacchantes, Maenads
> give you an orgy of filthy deeds.
> Sixtus, at last you're dead: opprobrium and vituperation
> of the papacy, have you really died, Sixtus?
> Sixtus, you're finally dead: rise up and feed your damned
> limbs to the wolves and the dogs.

213. INNOCENT VIII (1484—1492)

The conclave which began on 26 August 1484 to elect the successor to Sixtus IV was a real nest of simonists, run by the heads of the two opposing factions of cardinals, Rodrigo Borgia and Giuliano della Rovere who, through promises and bribes, were fighting over the tiara either for themselves or for a candidate of theirs.

Everyone was trying to get personal advantage from the future pope and, in the conclave, the man most prone to granting favors right and left was Giovanni Battista Cibo. According to the report of the famous master of ceremonies, Giovanni Burcardo, who was at the conclave during the night before his election, Cibo signed a whole batch of petitions that he was to grant once he became the pope. As a result, he was elected on 29 August, and on 12 September he was crowned in St. Peter's with the name of Innocent VIII.

Giovanni Battista Cibo was born in Genoa in 1432. His father had been senator in Rome under Calixtus III and then viceroy of Naples under Ferrante, at whose court Giovanni Battista had had jobs while living a worldly life. He was converted from libertinage through the good offices of Cardinal Calandrini, archbishop of Bologna, who started him on his ecclesiastical career, but his past had left its mark. Appointed bishop of Savona by Paul II and Cardinal by Sixtus

IV, Innocent VIII never concealed his numerous children, born to a Neapolitan woman. But seven were too many, so except for the two better known ones whom he recognized officially, Franceschetto and Teodorina, the others were passed off at Court as nieces and nephews. However, the *Pasquinades* increased the number of children:

> One must give praise, my fellow Romans, to Innocent
> as his progeny in the tired motherland grew in number.
> Eight bastards and eight maidens did he father;
> Innocent will be called Father of his country.

It is certain that such a pope, elected the way he had been and with such a licentious past, could not be expected to show immediately those qualities of moral and spiritual rectitude needed in his exalted position. Let us say that he had a family to think about and, ignoring the reformation of the Church, he busied himself exclusively with accumulating money by any means to take care of his domestic problems.

But the fact was that before him had come Sixtus IV, and the financial situation of the Curia was very precarious because of that pope's administration. Innocent VIII did not lose courage and, to begin with, pledged his tiara and part of the Treasury to a Roman bank to cover immediate necessities. Then, to garner additional income, he created new jobs in the papal secretariat, even though they were not needed, and sold them. Apart from an abuse of power, this led to trusting a large part of the administrative offices of the Curia to incapable persons who, in their greed, sought only personal profit, and this became an everyday rule in the Holy See. All the employees were corrupt, and the most blatant case was the foundation of the College of *Plumbatores* of papal bulls, fifty-two persons in all, many of whom set up a business of their own and, being clever forgers opened a shop which issued forged bulls, an active and lucrative trade until it was discovered in 1489 and they were all hanged.

Like Sixtus IV, Innocent VIII was also involved in the Papal State's messy politics which resulted mainly in problems with Naples, where armed conflicts alternated with periods of peace. In the war of the barons that broke out as a result of the tyrannical government of Ferrante and his son Alphonso of Calabria, the pope opposed the Aragons. This did not do him much good since the enemy arrived at the gates of Rome, which was only saved through the military ability of Cardinal Giuliano della Rovere, and resulted in an armistice in 1486.

Meanwhile, Innocent also managed to convince the Orsinis and the Colonnas to reach an armistice for the good of the city and, contrary to Sixtus IV, created good relations with Lorenzo de' Medici by the marriage of the daughter of the ruler of Florence with his own son, Franceschetto, which was celebrated in grand solemnity in the Vatican on 20 January 1488.

Unlike the Riarios and the Borgias, the Cibos were interested only in amassing fortunes and living luxuriously, and had neither the ambition nor the ingenuity to aspire to princely positions. For example, Franceschetto lost 60,000 *scudi* gambling with Cardinal Raffaele Riario which were used by Sixtus IV's nephew for work on his palazzo, started in 1483 and one of the masterpieces of early Renaissance architecture, which became the Palazzo della Cancelleria. When Innocent VIII died, Franceschetto did not think twice about selling Cerveteri and Anguillara, that his father had granted to him in fief in 1490 with the title of Count, to the Orsini. Theodorina, another daughter of Innocent, had also assured a good position for herself by marrying the merchant, Gherardo Usodimare, who had been raised to the post of Papal Treasurer.

If the prestige of the apostolic see under Innocent went downhill in terms of morality, it was more due to him than to his children. It was he who immersed himself in worldly matters, while his relatives simply created situations he never tried to avoid. In the same year when he opened the Vatican for the marriage of his own son, he did the same for the marriage of his granddaughter, Peretta, Theodorina's daughter, to Alfonso del Carretto, marquis of Finale. A chronicler of the period commented on how "grave scandal it was to see the Holy Father seated at a banquet in the company of beautiful ladies."

Moreover, the College of Cardinals itself was a crowd of prelates who for the most part were anything but priests and bishops in the religious meaning of the word. It could not have been otherwise, with a pope who appointed the illegitimate son of his brother a cardinal and, under pressure from Lorenzo il Magnifico, assigned the purple to a thirteen-year-old, Giovanni de' Medici, who at the age of seven was already an apostolic prothonotary with corresponding benefices and *commende*. This latter appointment formed part of the negotiations leading to the marriage of Maddalena de' Medici to the son of the pope, and which was satirised in a *Pasquinade*:

> To join the Medici girl to his son Franceschetti,
> Innocent made a little boy a cardinal.
> If it's true that the Holy Spirit
> makes the pope superhuman,
> in this case the Holy Spirit
> made him a matchmaker.

Meanwhile, Innocent reached an understanding also with Ferrante of Naples who, seeing danger loom on the horizon in the form of Charles VIII of France eyeing his throne, wanted to turn the pope away from his pro-French policy.

This alliance was sanctioned with another marriage, this one also celebrated in the Vatican at the beginning of 1492, between the very young Battistina Cibo, the second daughter of Theodorina, and Don Luis of Aragon, Ferrante's nephew. But, it was a marriage never consummated as Battistina died shortly afterwards while Don Luis became a priest and later a cardinal.

However, what with all these marriages and worldly duties Innocent VIII clearly could not be bothered with the crusade against the Turks or any religious issues. When he did get involved with the latter, he did so incompetently, as proven by the infamous bulls against witches, issued at the request of two Dominican inquisitors, Enrico Institore and Giovanni Sprenger, who had encountered opposition in Germany with their "witch hunting." These bulls authorized the two to carry out their police activity and to send to the stake numerous women accused of being possessed by demons and of causing harm to men with their witchcraft. "It was sad enough that the pope listened to the fantastic descriptions of the witches' crimes through the accounts of the two inquisitors," Seppelt bitterly notes, "but his bulls also stimulated a vast litera-ture on the subject which was inserted in Christian teaching at that time. Sprenger and Institore produced a copious work of libel with their *Malleus maleficarum*, or the "Bewitched Hammer," and as Seppelt states, "this infamous work, rightly recognized as one of the most pernicious works of the entire world's literary output, explains in repugnantly fullness the action of witches, dwelling particularly on the evil doings and diabolical sex, and concludes with instructions on the procedure against witchcraft."

One can say that Innocent VIII was not interested in anything more or less religious and the "crusader spirit" in Europe over the fall of the last bastion of the Moors in Granada, Spain, which happened under his pontificate on 2 January 1492, was certainly not due to anything he did. Nevertheless, he cele-brated it as a symbol of a triumph of Christian arms over the infidel. In Rome bells rang, rites of thanksgiving and nocturnal candlelit processions took place coinciding with that year's Carnival. That was enough of a reason to make those festivities, by now traditionally beloved by the people, the occasion of events such as the games in Piazza Navona, masquerades along the Corso, Spanish bull hunts and ancient scenic performances, all arranged by Cardinal Raffaele Riario.

Innocent did not do much else for Rome and the patronage for the arts declined. It was true that churches were restored, including work at S. Maria della Pace and the rebuilding of S. Maria in via Lata, and artists such as Pinturicchio and Mantegna decorated the Vatican residence with their frescoes that were later, unfortunately, destroyed. But no doubt most of the money wound up in the pockets of the children and grandchildren of the pope, caught up with feasts and hunts for which the Villa Magliana, erected on the via di Porto, began to be a splendid theater.

Innocent VIII died on 25 July 1492, and was buried in the basilica of St. Peter in a sumptuous bronze monument by Antonio Pollaiolo.

214. ALEXANDER VI (1492–1503)

After the funeral of Innocent VIII, twenty-three cardinals met in conclave in the Sistine Chapel at St. Peter's on 6 August 1492. By the ballot held during the night between the 10th and 11th of August, Cardinal Rodrigo Borgia was elected, but rumors of simony overshadowed his election. For Pastor, "there is no doubt that manuvers involving simony contributed to it," and most historians support that statement. Those few who tried to uphold that his was an "uncorrupt" choice were trying to defend an untenable position and even if they did not go as far as to attribute it as the work of the Holy Spirit, they adduced political motives. Ferrara states: "He was elected because it had to be a strong candidate . . . who knew best the needs of the Holy See," following the theory of La Torre who maintains that "the requests and the promises which were advanced in this conclave . . . were not considered simony by the cardinals."

It is absurd to limit an election based on simony simply to cold cash, since the various benefices promised by Borgia in the conclave have the same weight as those he distributed as soon as he was elected such as the vice-chancellorship, and his own palazzo to Cardinal Ascanio Sforza, his chief supporter, the ownership of Monticelli and Soriano to Cardinal Orsini, Subiaco and its nearby castles to Colonna, and Civitacastellana to Savelli.

Born on 1 January 1431 at Játiva, the same hometown as that of his uncle, Calixtus III, who had made him a cardinal at the age of only twenty-five, he had been vice-chancellor of the Roman Church, and had enriched himself with lucrative benefices so that he had at his disposal a princely income. Pius II had officially reprimanded him by a "brief" for his wayward life, which Rodrigo did not even bother to conceal. He had had a relationship with Vannozza de' Cattanei, married three times, who had given him four children, and he had three others by unknown women. He continued this libertine behavior while he was pope and had two more children, the last one towards the end of his pontificate, if not after his death. His official mistress as pontiff was the wife of Orsino Orsini, the beautiful Giulia Farnese whom her contemporaries referred to as the *concubina papae*, or, in blasphemous words, "the bride of Christ" and whose brother Alexander was made a cardinal.

From this point of view, "Alexander VI seems so enigmatic a figure as to remain a mystery in the eyes of the smartest psychologist," Gregorovius observed, and it is beyond question "that his boundless sensuality was pathological," as Seppelt emphasizes, even if he was not the first pontifical sovereign to behave this way. Rivers of ink have been written about this consecration of eroticism, but what we have already said is sufficient without dwelling on any other particulars. We can take as true, in any case, what Franco Molinari said that in effect the Borgia pope "was only a man, in the sense of a poor fellow" and we shall conclude with him that from this point of view, "perhaps never did the tiara rest on a more unworthy vicar of Christ."

That took place in St. Peter's with unusual pomp on 26 August 1492, when Borgia assumed the name of Alexander VI. As his earlier life was well known, he was the object of a *Pasquinade* that stressed the simony and deals, linking his number, the sixth, with a less than glorious tradition. The Latin verses can be translated thus:

> Alexander sells keys, altars and Christ;
> he is entitled to sell what he previously bought.
> From vice to vice, from a spark is born a blaze,
> and Rome perishes under Spanish dominion.
> Tarquinius the Sixth, Nero the Sixth and this one too.
> Rome under the Sixths has always gone to ruin.

On the other hand, there was a humanist ready to extol about the splendor that Rome might have under such a sovereign pontiff, although with pagan qualities, unsuited to a vicar of Christ, hence presumably ironic.

> Under Caesar, Rome was great, now it is the greatest;
> Alexander the Sixth reigns.
> The former was a man, but this one is God.

And to think that at the beginning of his pontificate, apart from the donations necessary for his election, Alexander VI gave reason to hope there would be a cleansing of principles as a result of the restoration of law and order in a city like Rome where, during the brief period of the vacant see, 220 murders were committed, as well as a wise economic policy coupled with one to preserve peace in Italy. It seemed like repentance, but only for an instant. As Molinari observes, "the weight of sinning humanness then strangled any hope of moral improvement," recalling that destiny offered him the opportunity for redemption and dedication to the Church as its father, "when the ceiling fell on him wrapping him in a cloud of dust and an avalanche of debris, and then when an assassin slew his son, Giovanni, whom he dearly loved. Both times he said he was going to change his life, but his promises were not kept." And even Girolamo Savonarola could not put him on the right road, since Savonarola was fated to die at the stake, a victim of his own sermons and of political events larger than even his exalted figure.

For Alexander VI, the papacy and the Church were simply a means to enrich and elevate his family, assuring to each of his children a dominant position.

Caesar was the one destined to reap the most benefit and from the most tender age. Appointed apostolic prothonotary at only six years old, he had been elevated to be bishop of Pamplona by Innocent VIII, and his father, as soon as he was elected, made him archbishop of Valencia, bringing him into the College of Cardinals in 1493. His favorite, Giovanni, duke of Candia, was enfieffed in 1497 with the duchies of Benevento, Terracina and Pontecorvo, taking over in effect a portion of the Papal State. However, he did not have long to enjoy it since he was killed that same year under mysterious circumstances.

Lucrezia, immortalized also in "serialised novels," was better than people said, and her alleged incestuous relations with her father and her brother Caesar, for example, have never been proved. She married three times; first was Count Giovanni Sforza, lord of Pesaro and a relative of Cardinal Ascanio Sforza, as a kind of codicil of gratitude to the latter from Rodrigo Borgia for help in his pontifical election. Celebrated with great pomp in the Vatican and blessed by the pope-daddy in accordance with the custom established by Innocent VIII, it was declared null and void because "not consummated' after several years. Lucrezia could thus marry in 1498, for political reasons but happily this time, Prince Alphonso of Bisceglie, natural son of Alphonso II of Naples. And Lucrezia was widowed two years later because her brother, Caesar, killed her husband, again for political reasons. The third marriage, still on a political level, to Alfonso d'Este, heir to the duchy of Ferrara, celebrated by proxy on 30 December 1501, with true Bacchanalian orgies which lasted until the Epiphany, was to take her away from Rome to live as a duchess until her death in 1519. It should not be forgotten that her father, who temporarily had to leave Rome twice, gave her authority to run the city, thereby raising her to the level of vice-pope, or a genuine "popess."

For his children, Alexander VI used the pontificate in an exclusively political way, and he displayed extraordinary talents when dealing with Charles VIII of France concluding, between 1492 and 1493, a series of treaties which assured the support of England, Spain and Emperor Maximilian, as well as of the lord of Milan, Ludovico the Moor, to gain possession of the kingdom of Naples, as the heir of the Angevins. Although initially hostile to the house of Aragon, he was reconciled with Ferrante in 1493, cementing the alliance by the marriage of his son Godfrey with Sancha, the natural daughter of Alphonso of Calabria. When Ferrante died the following January, he hastened to feoff Alphonso II as king of Naples and the coronation was celebrated in Naples by Cardinal Giovanni Borgia. This was a challenge to the claims of Charles VIII who immediately invaded Italy. Florence surrendered, ousting the Medicis and, faced with danger, Alphonso II ceded the crown to his son, Ferdinand II, and fled to Sicily. The Aragons in effect were not liked by the people and the pope suddenly found himself in a prickly situation, worsened by the rebellion which the Colonnas and other noble Roman families, helped by Cardinal Giuliano della Rovere, quickly fomented in the Papal State. They even came to the point of talking about deposing the pope.

On 31 December 1494, Charles VIII entered Rome with no resistance. Alexander VI, closed in Castel Sant'Angelo which had been transformed into a new fortress by Antonio of Sangallo, meditated on a novel approach to the king. On 15 January 1495, he officially conceded free passage to the French troops within the State of the Church, offering his son Caesar as Cardinal Legate to lead the French troops to the border of the kingdom of Naples. It was a clever move that fully redeemed Alexander VI and there was no more talk about deposition; on the contrary, Charles VIII swore obedience to the pope in a consistory.

On 22 February the French king entered Naples without a fight. Ferdinand II, finding himself abandoned by the pope, fled to Sicily by way of Ischia. However, the ease with which Charles VIII had conquered the kingdom in southern Italy immediately showed all Italian states the grave threat posed to their very existence. As a result, on the 31 March Venice set up an anti-French coalition in the presence of the pope who again changed position. Charles VIII thought it wise to retreat. He recrossed the Papal State, without Alexander VI trying to stop him, but the army of the League blocked him at Fornovo where, however, the king managed to pass through just the same. With the return of Ferdinand II the Aragons were back in charge.

After Louis XII had mounted the throne of France, Alexander VI again changed his policy and made an alliance with the new king. When the latter succeeded in ousting Ludovico the Moor from the duchy of Milan, joining his territory with France, the pope saw ample horizons opening for his son Caesar. The latter had renounced in 1498 the dignity of cardinal but, with his marriage with an Aragon lady up in thin air, and the prospect of the principality of Taranto having vanished, he married Princess Charlotte d'Albert, sister of the king of Navarre, through the good offices of Louis XII, who gave him the duchy of Valentinois, and promised him help to conquer a state in Romagna.

In this manner, Louis XII assured himself the neutrality of the Papal State for the new expedition which he planned for the recapture of the kingdom of Naples, and during the French campaigns in Italy between 1500 and 1503, Valentinois's activity in Romagna also went ahead. Alexander VI started searching for funds to finance it, resorting to simony with the appointment of twelve cardinals who had to pay heftily for their purple mantle, and to the sale of indulgences for the Jubilee of 1500. The military expedition was mainly the work of Caesar who, as a real "prince" in the style of Machiavelli's, did not shrink from any means to gain his ends and successively occupied Pesaro, Cesena, Rimini, Faenza, Urbino, and Senigallia, receiving from his father the title of Duke of

Romagna. The Papal State thereby lost a large province which became a hereditary principality of the Borgia.

But the plans of Alexander VI and his son did not stop there. The ultimate objective was the secularisation of the entire Papal State under the regime of the Borgia. They threw themselves into this grandiose project without respite, confiscating possessions of the Colonna, Savelli and Caetani families, all powerless before the Italian situation so favorable to the aims of the two Borgias. The duchy of Sermoneta was assigned to the son of Lucrezia, Roderico, barely two years old, thus gaining a fiefdom from his pope-grandfather. The duchy of Nepi went to the smallest of the sons of Alexander VII, Giovanni, he too only two years old. Caesar seized the duchy of Urbino and Camerino and, with diabolical ability, pitilessly exterminated at Senigallia some of its leaders who were plotting against him.

Once they had dispossessed the Orsinis as well, by eliminating Cardinal Giovanni Battista and banning all the others, Alexander VI and Caesar planned to complete the project by conquering Tuscany. Additional funds were still necessary and the pope obtained them by more cardinal appointments and the sale of new jobs in the Curia. The fundamental flaw of this grandiose political edifice was that it was not supported by any effective governing body. It was all based upon rapidity of action by a prince equipped with Machiavellian "virtues," poised to take advantage of the "fortune" of his father, but it was obvious that the scaffolding would collapse as soon as one of the two bearing pillars was no longer there. So, when Alexander VI died suddenly on 18 August 1503, Caesar continued to defend his own prestige through the short pontificate of Pius III, even coming to an initial understanding with the next pope, Julius II. But later, left to himself, he would lose everything, down to being arrested by Consalvo of Cordova, the captain of Spanish troops in Naples. As a prisoner in Spain, he found a haven with his brother-in-law, the king of Navarre, but he also found death in 1507 during his final adventure under the castle of Viana.

During the riots, which broke out at his death, Alexander VI was initially buried in St. Peter's without any special funeral rites and his remains were then moved to the basement of the Vatican to await a worthy burial. His bones were again removed to the church of S. Maria of Monserrat, the Roman Church of the Spanish, where they remained abandoned for a long time, finding their definitive resting place only in 1889.

Concerning the cause of death of the Borgia pope, officially ascribed to malaria, there have always been serious doubts, confirmed by famous historians such as Guicciardini. The pope is supposed to have been poisoned in error, during the course of one more plot organized by him and his son Caesar against Cardinal Adriano Castellesi of Corneto to get hold of the cardinal's wealth. The cardinal had invited them to dinner in his villa on the Janiculum and they bribed the sommelier to put Spanish fly, a poison with a base of arsenic, in a glass of wine which was to have been passed to the host, but by a fatal mistake was drunk by Alexander VI.

That is scarcely credible as other sources indicate that Castellesi on that same day was also stricken by malaria, without counting Caesar who was infected as well. But such a pope, according to the voice of Pasquino, would have to suffer a death which was in line with his life, as recorded in one of those anonymous epitaphs that were written in Latin, and went like this in the vulgate:

> Torture, treason, violence, frenzy, wrath, turpitude,
> you are the horrendous sponge full of blood and cruelty!
> Here lies Alexander VI; now, O Rome, enjoy your freedom,
> because my death gives life back to you.

One thing is certain: Alexander VI was not a saint, as his few apologists like Ferrara and Fusero would have us believe. For the former, he was "a priest in a very exclusive meaning of that word: indulgent in all human matters, but rigid when it came to the secular privileges of his religion," and for the latter, "the efforts of Alexander VI tended to safeguard the unity of the Christian world . . . and to defend its doctrinal purity."

Those are unfounded statements. The sole deed of his pontificate which had any religious importance was born from the hands of an artist, the *Pietà* of Michelangelo, while the very apartment of the Borgias in the Vatican with its splendid frescoes of Pinturicchio seems to evoke an atmosphere of secret crimes.

The fact remains that Alexander VI was "without scruples, without faith, without morals," according to the categorical judgment of Gervaso, who nonetheless fairly acknowledges his "exceptional energy and an impeccable political sense" for which he is deemed "a terrible pope" but at the same time "a very great monarch."

And "in a society in which, according to a chronicler, even the stones were shouting for 'reform,' Borgia starred by virtue of his absenteeism and his lack of interest," as Molinari notes. But in a Church which was Renaissance-humanistic to the limits of the credibility of the Faith itself, "Alexander VI by himself was clearly not the determining factor of such a widespread moral deterioration." As evidence of all that, there is the statement"that God was no longer in fashion even in the College of Cardinals, since a contemporary could write that in Rome the god was not trinitarian but rather quatrinitarian." (Note the play on the word *quattrini* meaning cash money).

215. PIUS III (1503)

On the death of Alexander VI, his son Caesar, though in bed with malaria and surrounded by soldiers, kept the Vatican under his power, and seized the pontifical treasury, determined to control the outcome of the next conclave. With the return of Orsini and Colonna, riots did erupt in Rome but without achieving anything. The College of Cardinals was afraid of a coup by Valentinois or, in any case, of his decisive influence over the next pontiff. So they came to an arrangement with him which assured him of safe passage within the Papal State and guaranteed that he could retain his possessions in Romagna and the title of Standard-Bearer (*gonfaloniere*) of the Church, provided that he would leave Rome and that the conclave could proceed calmly. Caesar accepted and moved to Nepi for his convalescence.

So the conclave began on 16 September 1503 at the Vatican with thirty-eight cardinals. Because of the considerable disputes, a transitional candidate was needed while events matured. On 22 September, Cardinal Francesco Todeschini Piccolomini was elected. A man with already a foot in the grave, he suffered from gout and was in such bad condition that, following his coronation in St. Peter's on 8 October, he was not even up to taking over the Lateran basilica. He assumed the name of Pius III.

Born in Siena in 1439, he was the son of a sister of Pius II who had made him a cardinal when only twenty-two years old. During his long cardinalate he had been famous for his dignified behavior and his piety, in stark contrast to the rest of the College.

He had been a patron of the arts in his own Siena and had embellished the cathedral with a splendid library frescoed by Pinturicchio, among others. He was not involved in politics, and that fact helped him in his election to the pontifical throne.

His candidature had been strongly supported by Giuliano della Rovere who was sure he could do as he wished with this sickly pope during the short period of his reign. However, this lover of peace had no intention of confronting Caesar Borgia, as perhaps della Rovere would have liked, and he even came to the point in his naive kindness of accepting Valentinois's request to return to Rome.

"I would never have believed that I would feel compassion for the Duke, but I feel it strongly," he stated. "The Spanish cardinals interceded for him and told me that he was seriously ill and will not get better. He desperately wishes to return to Rome for his last breath, and I have granted him this favor." But Caesar did get better and, once back in Rome, he took over as if he were the owner of the Castel Sant'Angelo. The Orsinis and the Colonnas insisted with the pope that he arrest him. The pope responded: "I wish the Duke no ill, since it is the duty of the pope to be merciful to everyone. But I see that it will not go well for him before the judgment of God." And he condemned any action that might be taken against "our dear son, Caesar Borgia of France, duke of Romagna and Valence, standard-bearer of the Church."

When Pius III finally took to his bed, the Orsinis and the Colonnas engineered a coup to get rid of Borgia, but in vain. On 18 October 1503, the pope died, murdered, according to a chronicler of that time, with a poison given to him apparently by a lord of Siena, Pandolfo Petrucci, who was considered by the pope a usurper and a tyrant in his native city. He was buried in St. Peter's in a tomb which was moved in 1614 to the church of S. Andrea della Valle, together with that of his uncle Pius II.

216. JULIUS II (1503–1513)

The death of Pius III did not catch the College of Cardinals unprepared in their choice of a new pope. In effect, during the pontificate of Piccolomini, which was known would be brief because of his incurable illness, the various groups had already begun negotiations to reach an agreement in the conclave which began on 31 October 1503, and elected Cardinal Giuliano della Rovere in a few hours.

A man of prestige, two days after the death of Pius III he had brought together, in a pre-conclave in the Vatican, the Spanish cardinals and Caesar Borgia, ensuring their support with the promise (which he would not keep) that he would name Valentinois Captain General of the Church, confirm his lands in Romagna while promising the cardinals various benefices. At the same time, in a separate meeting, he managed to obtain support from the other group of cardinals, obviously through bribes. In fact, Cardinal della Rovere "went into the conclave already pope," Castiglioni notes, as shown by the almost unanimous vote which he had from the first ballot. And to think that on 14 January 1506, he would declare in the bull *Cum tam divino* that the election of a pope based on simony would be considered null and void, imposing the most severe ecclesiastical penalties on those electors guilty of simony!

Giuliano della Rovere was born in Albisola near Savona in 1443. A Franciscan, while still a very young man he had been elevated to cardinal by his uncle, Sixtus IV, with the titular church of St. Peter in Chains and had displayed even then his military ability. He had put down a revolt in Umbria and subdued the tyrant of Città di Castello, Niccolò Vitelli, giving a little light to that dark period in which the papacy found itself politically involved through the fault of Girolamo Riario. Under Innocent VIII, who owed him his election through simony, he had again figured as a warrior by repelling the assault brought to the gates of Rome by the Aragons in 1486, while under Alexander VI, after the failed attempt to support Charles VIII against the pope, he had remained on the defensive. When he was elected pope, despite his sixty years of age, he still had a strong temperament and extraordinary physical power. The nickname of 'the Terrible,' which his contemporaries gave him, referred to his undeniably tempestuous and dominating nature.

During his cardinalate he had shown military and political talents but not those of a religious person. His simonist intrigues and his libertine ways—he was the happy father of three daughters — were proof of that. As pope, however, he is supposed to have put aside these pleasurable adventures and to have avoided nepotism in general, except in the case of one nephew, Galeotto della Rovere, whom he made a cardinal but who died in 1508 before he did. Crowned pope on 26 November 1503, he assumed the name of Julius II.

The Papal State was in complete disorder. The consolidation begun by Pius II had foundered upon the rocks of the power of the Borgias, so it was necessary to begin all over again, sword in hand, and rebuild the State. With Julius II, the warrior-pope, as with some of his predecessors, "Christianity found a golden age (not in the abstract meaning, but historically and politically)," as Paolo Prodi observed, because "there was no difference between religion and politics, indeed, the restoration of the Church took place through political action." In effect, the reformation could wait, and the duty of the pope-king, like any other prince of his time, Cardinal Bellarmino was to point out, was to preserve power, resorting to war if necessary. How very far off seems the evangelical admonition: "He who lives by the sword will perish by the sword!"

And let us recall those worthy wars, including the one with Venice which, taking advantage of the revolt in Romagna against Caesar Borgia, had occupied Faenza and Rimini. While Valentinois, who had fallen out with the pope and gone to Naples, by then a Spanish possession, hoping to find help to recover his duchy, wound up as a prisoner in Spain where he is said to have died, (as already mentioned in the biography of his father), Julius II began by simply sending warnings to the powerful Lagoon City. When later Perugia and Bologna were liberated respectively by the Baglioni and the Bentivoglio families, his tone became firmer. However, faced with the tenacious resistance of Venice, and not being able to obtain recognition of his rights through peaceful negotiations, he became the promoter of the international League set up at Cambrai in 1508, with Emperor Maximilian, Louis XII, the king of Spain, and the duke of Ferrara.

Seriously defeated at Agnadello the following year, Venice realized that its very existence was in grave danger. It managed to break the alliance, returning to the pope the cities of Romagna and reaching a peace agreement that amounted in effect to an alliance. Julius II could scarcely ignore the importance that the Venetian Republic had as a defensive bastion against the Turkish peril, and at the same time he was convinced that a fundamental requirement for the Papal State's independence was, in fact, the ending of French domination over Italy. In this matter, his political strategy was not especially brilliant. In fact, the events, which led to the ousting of the French, had as a consequence their substitution by other foreigners, the Spanish.

And it was the Holy League with its battle cry, "Out with the barbarians!," against which Louis XII countered by alliances with Florence, with the marquis of Mantua and the duke of Ferrara, the third husband of Lucrezia Borgia, but more importantly by the convocation of a council at Pisa in September 1511, which included nine dissident cardinals, headed by Carvajal and Sanseverino. The king of France intended to create a schism and, in brief, to depose Julius II. Emperor Maximilian, though angry with the pope for the change in his political bent, appeared to support him by continuing the war against Venice. Julius II responded by convening an ecumenical council in Rome for 19 April 1512, declaring the one in Pisa null and void, and its adherents schismatics, who were all excommunicated and deposed.

The rebellious cardinals stuck to their position while Louis XII supported them, but when the French position weakened, they moved their mini-assembly first to Milan, where they went so far as to decree the suspension of the pope from his functions, then to Asti and finally to Lyons, where the "rump council" was dissolved. The cardinals are supposed to have finished up begging the next pope, Leo X, pardon and by being restored to their position.

Meanwhile the Holy League was defeated at Ravenna on 11 April 1512 by the great Gaston de Foix, and the pope witnessed the end of his projects. Nevertheless, the death of the French commander and the opening of the Ecumenical Council XVIII at the Lateran on 3 May coincided with a sudden turn of events in favor of the Holy League. The emperor decided to recognize the council opened in Rome and abandoned Louis XII, while at Mantua in June the allies divided up the fruits of their unexpected victory. Julius II got Modena, Reggio, Parma, and Piacenza which were taken from the duke of Ferrara.

In the light of all this, the Lateran ecumenical council V had a clearly political significance, and the only religious aspect of note was the approval of the bull against simony issued by the pope in 1506, which only God knew to what degree it was to be respected! That council was the last opportunity Rome had to avoid the split which shortly afterwards was to take place between the western Christian world and Luther, but instead "it resulted in a farce." Molinari notes bitterly, nor was it to be any different under Leo X who closed it in 1517. It was simply further evidence that Julius II with his wars had really forgotten the main functions of a pope who was supposed to inspire peace and love among men, and reconcile them firmly in a faith in God.

The other aspect which marked the pontificate of Julius II was his notable patronage of the arts and especially his wish to embellish Rome through a precise urban plan, which began with the opening of the splendid Via Giulia, the first street in the city laid out in rectilinear form. Three Renaissance artists left the indelible imprint of their genius: Bramante, with his grandiose plan for reconstruction of the Vatican, using funds raised by the granting of indulgences, the source of permanent scandal; Raphael, with his frescoes in the rooms of the palazzo of Nicholas V, rooms which then took his name, and Michelangelo; with his outstanding masterpieces in the Sistine Chapel, as well as the funeral monument for the pope which Julius himself commissioned. This mausoleum, originally in St. Peter's, was moved to the church of the della Rovere family, S. Maria del Popolo, and finally to the titular church of the pontiff, St. Peter in Chains. The famous statue of Moses, in which Julius II himself is represented, was part of the monument.

That monument was completed after the death of the pope on 22 February 1513, and had more modest proportions than the original design, but nevertheless has a grandiose aspect. Was this perhaps the "paradise" which St. Peter, in the anonymous pamphlet, *Julius exclusus a coelo*, advised Julius II to have erected by a "vigorous builder?" In that *Pasquinade*, the apostle does not open the gates of heaven for him, recognizing him guilty of having made the Church a "slave of earthly powers," and bitterly concludes that "with such a pest ruling it, it is no wonder that there are so few people up there in paradise."

217. LEO X (1513–1521)

The conclave which resulted in the election of Cardinal Giovanni de' Medici on 9 March 1513, was brief. He was only thirty-eight years old, but the fact that he was the son of the "Magnifico" had led him to be named by Innocent VIII, for obvious political reasons, apostolic prothonotary when he was only seven years old and cardinal when he was thirteen. When elected pope, he was still only a deacon. However, even though young, his pontificate was not expected to be lengthy because of his delicate health—he was confined to his bed even during the conclave and had to undergo surgery. It is likely that the College readily accepted his election because it would place a Medici on the throne only for a short period. It was not an election based upon simony but the candidature of Giovanni de' Medici was the fruit of clever planning by his private secretary, Bernardo Dovizzi of Bibbiena, through compromises and alliances that were nonetheless far from being "divinely inspired."

The coronation of Giovanni de' Medici had to be postponed for about ten days, the time needed to ordain the newly elected pope to priest and bishop, with the result that he was consecrated pope on 19 March under the name of Leo X.

Even his first actions showed he did not have the warrior spirit of his predecessor. This was evident from the pardon granted to the cardinals who had organized the "rump council" at Pisa, to the official reconciliation with Pompeo Colonna who had attempted to instigate the common people to establish a republic, as well as to the successful mediation in Florence, after discovering the conspiracy of Boscoli and Capponi against the Medici, to save the life of Machiavelli. He was not constant in his politics, vacillating from anti-French to pro-French and, finally, to pro-emperor. Basically he had at heart only his family. He made both his cousin Giulio, the future Pope Clement VII, and his nephew, Innocenzo Cibo, cardinals.

When the new king of France, Francis I, the ally of the Venetians, reconquered the duchy of Milan in 1515 as well as Parma and Piacenza which had been assigned to the Papal State three years earlier, the pope let it pass in order to begin secret negotiations to settle matters between him and the king. This took place in Bologna where the basis was set up for a concordat that was supposed to determine once and for all the religious issue in France. It was signed in 1516 and was the only positive note to be confirmed by that Lateran Ecumenical Council V which went on slowly until it was closed by Leo X on 16 March 1517.

That same year the pontiff's life was at risk through a conspiracy against him within the Sacred College instigated by Cardinal Alfonso Petrucci, son of Pandolfo, lord of Siena. Some suspected him of having eliminated Pius III, who had died leaving his authority to his other son, Borghese. But in 1516 Leo X had ousted him from Siena, giving the lordship to another Petrucci, Raffaello, bishop of Grosseto, who had the advantage of being a friend of his.

Blinded by hatred and thirsting for vengeance, Cardinal Petrucci wanted to kill Leo X, but, aware that the strict security surrounding the pope would prevent an attack, he decided to use poison. He bribed the physician of the pope, Pietro Vercelli, and induced him to poison the medication he was administering for a fistula that Leo X had been suffering from for some time. However, a letter addressed to his secretary, Antonio de Nini, was intercepted and the plot was discovered. Cardinal Petrucci, after being arrested and prosecuted, was strangled in Castel Sant'Angelo on 6 July 1517, while de Nini and Vercelli were drawn and quartered. During the prosecution, it came out that four cardinals were involved, Riario, dean of the Sacred College, Sauli, Volterrano, and Castellanese. They were all deposed and managed to avoid imprisonment only by paying huge sums of money. Riario also lost his palazzo which was thereupon made the head office of the Chancery.

In view of the fact that the thirteen cardinals in the Sacred College had shown so clearly their hostility to him, and in order to surround himself with people devoted to him, Leo X appointed at one fell swoop thirty-one new cardinals, something which had never happened before and was not to be repeated after him. However, those death sentences obliterated the previous generous deeds and the pardon of the pope, and the pardons granted *sub condicione* to the four cardinals were severely criticized in Italy and Germany, where there were mounting expressions of discontent over the scandalous sale of indulgences.

As is well known, in order to amass money needed for the construction of the great Vatican basilica, Leo X had ordered, back in 1514, the proclamation of an indulgence throughout Europe, by which, whoever in a state of grace made an offering would earn an indulgence, more or less ample according to the amount of the offering, applicable also to the deceased. Speculation in indulgences involved even bankers such as the Fuggers in the collection of money, and especially scandalous was the behavior of the Dominican, Giovanni Tetzel, who promised the immediate release of deceased persons from the pains of purgatory upon payment of one florin by a living relative!

And so on the vigil of All Saints, in what was to be that horrendous year of 1517 for Leo X, Luther affixed to the door of All Saints church in Wittenberg his ninety-five theses. The pope thought it was one of those usual disputes between monks and university professors and simply summoned Luther to Rome. When this Augustinian friar refused to obey the summons and went on expounding his doctrine of "free conscience" between 1518 and 1520, Leo X condemned those expressions of faith in the famous bull *Exurge Domine* of 1520, which was burned by Luther in the square of Wittenberg in front of an exultant and applauding crowd. The pope then excommunicated him and invited the newly elected Emperor Charles V to give his sanction to the condemnation. Charles summoned Luther to the Diet at Worms in March 1521, where the reformer asserted his doctrine and refused to retract it, so was proscribed by the empire. He was to find hospitality with the elector of Saxony, and his reformation would proceed.

Recalling these events, it becomes apparent that Leo X was totally unfit to tackle the enormous problem he was facing, and Seppelt's stated it truly by saying "for the Church, it was indescribably unfortunate and a disaster that he was seated on the chair of Peter. He was not aware of the gravity of the impending disaster and did nothing to eliminate it, his common sense lost in frivolity and in political intrigues," is absolutely correct.

In fact, Leo X, while going up to the Vatican apartments, is known to have said to his brother, Giuliano: "Let us enjoy the papacy, because God has given it to us." And it was a continual celebration, as Gregorovius records it, "in the strangest mixture of paganism and Christianity with masked balls, performances of ancient mythology, Roman tales acted against magnificent scenery and, on the other hand, processions and splendid church feasts, with performances of the Passion in the Colosseum, classic orations in the Capitol, and more feasts and speeches on the anniversary of the founding of Rome. There were daily parades of cardinals, ceremonies for the arrival of ambassadors and princes with groups so large they looked like armies. Retinues, too, of the pope when he went off to hunt at Magliana, at Palo, at Viterbo, with the falcons at his wrist, with packs of dogs, heavy baggage, flocks of servants, the suites of the cardinals and of foreign preachers, the happy crowd of the poets of Rome, and a mob of barons and princes, all in such a clamour as to seem a company of Bacchantes."

The vicar of Christ took part in the shows and appeared to enjoy the stupidities of the court buffoons that his valet, Serafica, had the job of bringing to Court. Among these was a certain Querno who, dressed like Venus, as a chronicler of that time tells us, "sang poems and drank a lot." There was also Mariano Fetti, Apostolic Sealer in the Chancery, better known as the court clown. A formidable glutton and drinker, he amused the pope with his "caprices" and his buffoonery, inviting him to enjoy life, saying: "Let's live it up, Holy Father, for everything is a joke." Leo X, who enjoyed writing verses himself in the midst of so many poetasters and clowns, had dictated in advance an epitaph for Fetti:

> A friar white below and black above,
> big eater and drinker,
> while alive a pig on the outside and smelly inside;
> now he infests a cemetery.
> Don't bring holy water or a harp, traveller.
> If you wish to remember him in his way,
> bring good wine to sprinkle and no thoughts.
> Although he pretended piety, he had little religion,
> and performed to escape the sadder game.
> He was a clown among his brothers, for he was
> more like a pal, and clung more to the cook than the sacristy
> while he joked with his tummy.
> And at the end, with his soul in flames, his fame gone,
> if you don't want to drop dead, beware of your steps

And then there were the *hetaerae*, or the courtesans, of that period, for whom the term "whores" would have been out of line, as Georgina Masson observes, since their "idea of pleasure was not limited to the sexual aspect, trained as they were in the arts, especially in music . . . for their allure, for the taste they showed in dressing, for the smart and lively conversation they could carry on, they were much sought after as guests at the many banquets." At the court of Leo X, the most charming were Beatrice Ferrarese, possibly immortalized by Raffaele in the Fornarina, and Lucrezia of Clarice, nicknamed "Mommy does not want it," the answer she would give her ardent wooers in order to sell dearly her own "flesh."

There is no doubt that lasciviousness and moral corruption reached the highest levels with Leo X and *Pasquinades* like the following ring true in this respect.

> Do you want to be rich and give me your favors?
> Then give me for my pleasure little boys and virgins.

> MARFORIO: How is business?
> PASQUINO: Excellent, Marforio;
> The jesters are in command.

The second is an exchange of phrases between the two "talking statues" of Rome, Marforio and Pasquino, and with this atmosphere of worldliness certainly not of art, came the taste for theatrical performances, seen as the typical expressions of pleasure. The comedies of Plautus, the Mandragola of Machiavelli, and the Calandra of Cardinal Bibbiena, performed entirely in the Vatican, created a sensation, not so much for their cultural significance as for their spicy and scandalous content. This was "the Rome of Leo X," because "the reputation which Leo had as the greatest patron of the arts is exaggerated," as even Castiglioni is forced to admit. "He had risen to the pontificate when Rome had already become the mother land of all of the intellectuals of that period" and, "even if the literary and artistic atmosphere of the city had a certain driving force, it was not as a result of any cultural effort by the pope, nor because he was a likeable, intelligent and cultured person," but rather through his dilettantism, as a gluttonous bon vivant, so to speak.

Otherwise one cannot understand how a lowly poetaster like Baraballo, a priest from Gaeta, could be acclaimed in the Capitol as a new Petrarch while Ariosto received no such recognition. Let us say that Rome became the stage for many "one-armed poets" like Camillo Querna, "the archpoet laureate," Giovanni Gazzoldo and Girolamo Britonio, who were able to make the pope laugh at table between one glass and another, at par with the buffoons mentioned above. And thank goodness Leo X at least had Britonio whipped once for having recited "lousy" verses! So, writers more famous like Bembo, Castiglione and Aretino, although present in the papal court, were not able to get rid of that "histrionic" facade which, in effect, was the only one their patron wanted.

But Leo X was clever enough to take advantage of the numerous artists working on the beautification of the city inherited from Julius II. Among these he preferred Raphael, who continued his frescoes in the Rooms, designed the ten tapestries for the Sistine Chapel, brought to completion the Vatican *Logge*, and even found time to immortalize the pope in a famous portrait, though the unfinished *Transfiguration* was completed by Giulio Romano.

Leo X died on 1 December 1521. Just a few days earlier, he had reaped the harvest of his new anti-French policy by the elevation of Charles V to Defender of the Catholic Faith against the spread of Lutheranism. The return of Milan to the Sforza assured the Papal State the reacquisition of Parma and Piacenza, for which grand festivities were being prepared.

The sudden death of Leo X at only 46 years of age gave rise to a rumor that he had been poisoned, and indeed his wine steward, Bernabò Malatesta, was arrested. The court master of ceremonies, Paride de Grassis insisted on an autopsy but nothing was done, and everything was hushed up. It was Pasquino again who spoke in a series of satires on the death, among which the following is perhaps the most meaningful:

Weep, you merry musicians; weep, tuner of violins;
Weep, Florentine jesters beating on plates, dishes and trays
Weep, you skinny clowns, or civets;
Weep, you mimes and ham actors; you gluttonous friars,
Weep with your throats full.
Weep for your lord and master, you tyrants;
Weep, Florence, for all your bankers and idiotic officials;
Weep, servant of God, weep for Peter; you evils ones,
Weep, now that Leo Tenth is dead.
That fellow who loved the clowns and villains,
That dirty tyrant, dishonest and corrupt.
To make what I say clear, Florence, the Church and Piero
Pledged to follow his ideas.
And I am sure that, were he still alive,
He would sell Rome, Christ and himself.
But the sorriest of all are those wretches
Whose money failed to bring them the cardinal's hat.

Temporarily buried in St. Peter's, he was later transferred to his mausoleum in S. Maria sopra Minerva.

218. HADRIAN VI (1522–1523)

A full two weeks of conclave, from 27 December 1521, to 9 January 1522, were needed to find a successor for Leo X. There was a considerable divergency between the major factions, one pro-Charles V and the other pro-Francis I. Giulio de' Medici was the emperor's choice, but the king of France sent a message to the thirty-nine cardinals that there would be a schism if the emperor's candidate were to be elected. Henry VIII of England pressed instead for his minister, Cardinal Wolsey.

If there were no deals involving simony, there were certainly some of a Machiavellian nature, and there is no doubt that the choice was limited. To resolve the problem, Cardinal de' Medici proposed an apparently neutral candidate in the person of Adriaan Florensz, bishop of Tortosa. In fact, this cardinal, who was not present at the conclave and not well known to the Curia, had been a teacher of Charles V, who welcomed his election.

At the proclamation of a foreign pope, the Romans got angry and greeted the cardinals coming out of the conclave at the Vatican with catcalls, insults and stones. In reality, the lengthy conclave had been followed with great enthusiasm by the populace, who laid bets on the various candidates, among whom was the one chosen by the courtesan "Mommy doesn't want to." According to Masson "she would have slept with anyone who would give her one hundred ducats to hold in the event that the cardinal she named before the election would be elected pope, while if someone else was elected, 'Mommy' would have slept three nights for nothing with the man who had accepted her bet." But no one had expected that the Dutchman would be chosen, so that the hoax was a double one: a foreigner as pope and a totalizator who kept all the bets.

Pasquinades poured out at full speed, the most famous of which were those of Aretino who wrote more than forty. The following one sets forth clearly the indignation of those excluded:

> O, traitor to the Blood of Christ,
> College of thieves, you have given the Vatican
> To the German anger.
> Is your heart not broken by sadness?
> O world destroyed, o century full of mistakes,
> O false hope, O futile thoughts,
> The great name of Rome has fallen and
> Been given as a victim to barbarian furor.
> And if no one moves to take revenge,
> Our wounds will disappear
> Unfair, O Peter, is he who honors you.
> What indignity, old or new,
> Has stained the ancient and modern maps?
> The sun thus shines by mistake today.

The newly elected pope was at Vittoria in Biscay when the unexpected news reached him. There was rejoicing in the city but the new pontiff quickly stated that he had "many reasons to be saddened" by such an election, aware of the great responsibility to which he had been called. He knew of the disorders that existed in the Papal State and was convinced of the need for a reformation to cure the Church's ills. When, on 9 February, Antonio d'Estudillo, secretary to Cardinal Carvajal and dean of the Sacred College, arrived in Vittoria to give him the official notice of his election, Florensz did accept it but stated that he did it to obey the will of God and not out of desire for power. This was an unusual response, which mirrored his integrity.

Adriaan Florensz was born in Utrecht in 1459 into a working class family but had turned his studies at the University of Louvain to good use, becoming a professor there until Emperor Maximilian chose him to be the teacher of his son, Charles. After being appointed bishop of Tortosa, he had been made cardinal by Leo X. He delayed going to Rome and stayed in Saragossa until Pentecost while waiting for a ship which would take him to Italy. Meanwhile, one by one, Henry VIII, Francis I, and Charles V tried to curry favor with him, inviting him to come to their court before going to Rome, but he was not be fooled by anyone and, on 8 July, he sailed to Tarragon avoiding a further attempt by the emperor to win him over. He then went on to Barcelona and from there to Leghorn.

On the 27th, his fleet reached the port of Civitavecchia. Rome was in the midst of the plague and no arrangements had been made to welcome the pope since everyone thought he would not wish to expose himself to the risk of contagion. Instead, the new pope headed directly for the city and was welcomed only by the cardinals at St. Paul's outside the Walls to whom he immediately made a speech which showed the severity of his intentions. Aware that gangs of brigands coming from the south had invaded Rome, he warned the cardinals not to allow anyone into their palaces so that justice could take its course.

Once in the city, and hearing that a triumphal arch was being built in his honor, which would cost 500 ducats, he ordered the construction to be immediately stopped. This action and the courage shown while risking his own life during the spreading epidemic suddenly changed the people's feelings, and they ran enthusiastically to his coronation which took place on 31 August 1522 on the steps of St. Peter in a simple ceremony. He took the name of Hadrian VI.

But the enthusiasm lasted only a short while. The day after the coronation he revoked the cardinals's general pardons, imposed a severe economy, which provoked discontent in the Curia. He made it clear that he intended to carry out the reform seriously, and requested all the cardinals to give definite assistance in this undertaking. The very life of the court had to change and be consistent with an ecclesiastic atmosphere. So, out with all the parasites and the pretty ladies, and out with the poets or clowns, or whatever they were. But through them, the resentment filtered down to the common people, with new *Pasquinades* which were to torment him throughout his brief pontificate.

From the moment in 1501 when, near the Orsini palazzo, now Braschi, the torso of Parione saw the light of day and became the "talking statue," anonymous satires, critical of the pope or of whoever were in high positions, were affixed to it in order to discredit them. In fact they were written by poets hired by cardinals, prelates, and nobles who had been excluded from power, and were the voice of the Curia, not that of the people. The story goes that poor Hadrian VI wanted to destroy the statue to which the Romans attached the verses against him, and throw it into the Tiber, but was dissuaded by the duke of Sessa who, according to Giovio, "by polite and clever ingenuity, told him not to, adding that Pasquino, even at the bottom of the river, like the frogs would not stop chattering."

And yet, Hadrian did not deserve all that hatred, evidently fuelled by those excluded from power rather than by circumstances linked to the pope's person. Perhaps he was "wrong" to be too severe and too conscious about his obligations, with people accustomed to carefree, pagan-like celebrations, and who did not appreciate his moral integrity.

He was deeply conscious of the tremendous task of reform that he intended to undertake, but his reign was too brief, even if, as Seppelt notes, "perhaps not even a longer pontificate would have sufficed to change radically the corruption that had existed for decades and decades." Being suspicious and especially not trusting the Italian clergy, he relied chiefly on his compatriot, Wilhelm Enkenvoert, whom he named bishop of Tortosa in his place, and cardinal a few days before his death. This would worsen the tense atmosphere within the Curia through a series of misunderstandings that served only to augment the lamentations of the population.

However, Hadrian VI did not use his power for personal interests and was completely immune from nepotism. In fact, the story is told that once some relatives of his came to Rome hoping to find undreamt riches and that he "ordered them to carry on their usual business because he had not become the pope in order to give away the property of the Church to his relatives." And to the clerics who complained that they were deprived of so many benefits he customarily said, "The pope is supposed to adorn churches with prelates, not prelates with churches."

On the international level, he concentrated all his energy in trying to stop the spread of heresy in Germany and, through his legate at the Diet of Nuremberg, he urged the German princes to be united in respecting the empire's ban against Luther, trying also to involve them in a crusade against the Turks, who had conquered Belgrade and were threatening Hungary. But his request was not heeded, and the papal legate was insulted. Among the princes there were also numerous Lutherans, and the apparent neutrality of the pope was considered a ploy which, in reality, showed that he favored the empire.

Events moved on and in March 1523, the pope learned from correspondence seized from Cardinal Soderini that Francis I was plotting to take over the kingdom of Naples. So Hadrian accused him of high treason, and Soderini was shut up in Castel Sant'Angelo. The king of France broke off diplomatic relations with the pope, who at this point, decided in favor of open adherence to the Imperial League with Henry VIII and Venice. But Francis I invaded Italy just as Hadrian VI suddenly fell ill and died, on 14 September 1523.

For the Romans, his death was a day of rejoicing. On the door of his personal physician, Giovanni Antracino, appeared this inscription *"Libertori Patriae S.P.Q.R."* or "To the Liberator of the Fatherland, the Senate and the Roman People." Cardinals, court staffers, courtesans, clowns, and parasites joined in ridiculous merriment, expecting to regain what they had lost with the new pope.

He was temporarily buried in St. Peter's between Pius II and Pius III, and the *Pasquinade* reached even there: *"Hic jacet impius inter Pios,"* or "here lies an impious one among the pious." The simple but nasty inscription received a worthy and noble response, "here lies Hadrian VI who had the greatest misfortune of all, to reign," written by his only faithful friend, Wilhelm Enkenvoert, upon whom even dead he could count, and who in August 1533, saw to the removal of his remains to a splendid mausoleum in S. Maria dell'Anima, the Germans' church in Rome.

219. CLEMENT VII (1523–1534)

More than fifty days were needed for the cardinals in conclave to choose a successor to Hadrian VI. The main candidate was Giulio de' Medici, backed by Emperor Charles V in the preceding conclave, whereas the crowd of French cardinals supported Alessandro Farnese. But the decisive votes were those controlled by Pompeo Colonna whose family was traditionally hostile to the Medici, so when the two cardinals put aside their personal rancours, the election of Giulio de' Medici was ensured on 19 November 1523.

The newly elected pope was born in Florence in 1478, and was the son of Giuliano who had been killed in the Pazzi conspiracy. Leo X, his cousin, had first made him archbishop of Florence and then cardinal. Although very young, he had demonstrated excellent diplomatic and financial abilities as vice-chancellor of the Church of Rome, was serious and evidently not corrupt as compared with the worldly and dissolute behavior of the pope, his cousin. His election was therefore warmly greeted, although certain hopes were quickly dashed because Giulio de' Medici proved incapable of resolving in a decisive and practical manner the difficult problems which he had to face. He was crowned on 26 November 1523, and took on the name of Clement VII.

The new pope started off grandly as the promoter of universal peace, and sent the archbishop of Capua, Nicholas of Schomberg, as his ambassador to the kings of France, Spain and England, but his mission was a failure. And so when, in October 1524, Francis I conquered Milan, Clement VII backed down from his pro-empire position and made an alliance with France and Venice in January 1525. This treaty assured the Church the prospect of possessing Parma and Piacenza, and guaranteed to the Medicis the control of Florence, while the pope provided free passage through the Papal State for the French troops heading for Naples.

But a month later, Francis I was defeated at Pavia and taken prisoner and, faced with the misfortunes of his ally, Clement felt lost. He reversed his policy and in April formed an alliance with the viceroy of Naples which assured the rights of the Papal State, and of the Medici family over Florence, in exchange for upholding Spanish claims over the duchy of Milan. The pact was to have been ratified within four months by Charles V who, at this point, obviously could not rely blindly on such an unstable ally. In fact, while the pope was following his path, a strong anti-imperial alliance was gaining ground within the Curia. This was consolidated when Francis I, in order to be released, had to accept the severe terms of the peace treaty in Madrid in January 1526, by which he gave up all rights in Italy.

In May, the pope joined the "holy" League of Cognac and, after a few hesitations found himself the ally of Francis I and Venice, as well as of Francesco Sforza. And still Charles V tried to get Clement onto his side, sending a delegation to Rome in June, which was unfortunately unsuccessful. In reply the pope set forth in a "brief" a kind of justification for his change of position in the complex web of international politics that ended with an abusive attack on the emperor. The latter, by then, had had enough and, in September, made violent accusations against the pope in an official document calling him a "wolf" who was no "shepherd." He also threatened to convoke an ecumenical council on the Lutheran issue.

During that same month, Cardinal Pompeo Colonna, heading the resentment of the Curia over the pope's doings and supporting the imperial position, unleashed his soldiers on Rome. The Vatican quarter was sacked and the entire city fell under the cardinal's control. The pope had to give in and humiliatingly request an armistice which should have precluded a realignment of the Papal State with the empire. Pompeo Colonna retreated calmly toward Naples but, once the siege of the city had been lifted, Clement VII resumed hostilities, retaking some strongholds of the Colonnas and deposing the cardinal from all of his functions.

At this point the pope could no longer abstain from a pro-French policy, and when he found himself alone without military assistance a year later, with even the duke of Ferrara on the side of Charles V, he suffered the dramatic consequences with the German Lancers on the march towards Rome. The undisciplined German troops, which their commander Charles of the Bourbons could not restrain, proceeded in the first days of May to enter the city, eager for booty. Even the funds obtained from the appointment of six cardinals, who paid well for their titles, and promptly transferred to the Bourbon, Charles, failed to get the imperial troops to change their mind and they attacked Rome on 6 May 1527.

Charles the Bourbon fell during the siege, and the Lancers, without any guide, went about their terrible pillaging provoking a memorable calamity. Murders, rapes and all kinds of vandalism brought catastrophe to Renaissance Rome, where numerous works of art were also destroyed. Many people interpreted this devastation as a punishment by God for the scandalous life led by the popes and the clerics at the center of Christianity. For the See of Peter it was a very bitter warning to return to the good principles of the Gospels, as the now widespread Lutheran reformation firmly requested. The pope's defenses in Castel Sant'Angelo collapsed on 5 June when an imperial garrison entered and held Clement prisoner for seven months. After lengthy negotiations the evacuation of the fortress began on 6 December. The pope had to produce huge sums of money and, thanks to the cooperation of a few officials, succeeded a day later in fleeing from the city by using the passage called the "Passetto" disguised as a street vendor. He went to Orvieto and from there to Viterbo. Only in October 1528 was he able to return to Rome, but he found a city in ruins and empty. It would take a long time to repair the damages and, above all, careful financial planning as well as an immediate reconciliation with Charles V.

In June 1529, a peace treaty was signed in Barcelona. The famous "peace of the two ladies" established a truce between Charles V and Francis I and provided for the return of the Medici to Florence, as well as the restitution to the Papal State of several cities lost during the sacking of Rome and as a result of the defeats suffered by the Cognac League. The revived alliance between the papacy and the empire was blessed by a marriage of two "bastards," the infante Margherita, natural daughter of Charles V, and Alessandro de' Medici, natural son of Lorenzo, duke of Urbino, but publicly known as "the son of the pope," who received the title of Duke of Florence. On 24 February 1530 Clement crowned Charles Roman Emperor in the church of S. Petronio at Bologna, in what was to be the last coronation by a pope.

But, regardless of the peace accord and appearances, the relations between Clement VII and Charles V were never ones of mutual trust. In fact, during the last period of his pontificate Clement seemed to get closer to France. In October 1553, he travelled to Marseilles to bless the union of his grandniece Catherine with Henri d'Orléans, second son of the king of France, and the wedding was an opportunity to start secret negotiations with Francis I, secret up to a point since word reached the ears of Charles V, who was naturally angry.

This ambiguous behavior of Clement was unpardonable, and Berni criticized it in an epigram:

> A papacy made up of greetings, considerations and speeches,
> of more, of then, of but, of yes, of perhaps,
> of yet, of many words without meaning.

Clement was clearly deleterious for the good of the Church of Rome, mainly because the very devout Charles V could have been the only real means to curb the Lutheran Reformation, proof of which was the first Diet of Speyer in 1526 when Charles V, in a dispute with the pope, allowed Lutheranism to spread in Germany and permitted, among other things, the marriage of priests. And the second Diet in 1529, when relationships were better between Clement and the emperor, although annulling what had been decided three years earlier, he certainly did not stop the development of the revolt against Rome. On the contrary, the Lutheran princes, "protesting" against certain decisions, triumphed definitively through the organization of the Lutheran Church as a State Church in 1530 with the Confession of Augsburg.

If one adds the fact that, shortly after the death of Clement VII, England also separated from Rome and established the Anglican Church, one can well understand how this pope demonstrated his total incapacity to shore up a situation that had become catastrophic on a religious level. Even the proclamation of a Jubilee Year for 1525 made no sense with those now infamous and little blessed indulgences. Nevertheless, with unbelievable impudence Clement VII took steps to renew certain practices even while Martin Luther's just protests were still being echoed. It was burlesque as Francesco Berni let it be understood.

> So whoever needs to understand about immortality
> and eternal life, do come to Florence to my tavern.

From this religious point of view, Ranke's affirmation that Giulio de' Medici "was the most unfortunate of all the popes who rose to the Roman throne leaving it at his death, infinitely degraded in reputation, with neither spiritual nor earthly authority" was well to the point. The Romans of the period shared his judgment as the *Pasquinade* below confirms:

> With you reigning over this poor Rome,
> floods, flames, ruin and plagues abounded
> while drunkenness took over.
> And yet I shall not call you a god of clemency or cruelty
> as in you the Hell of the Furies gathered all power.
> Shall I name you? Ah well, in you I see
> plunder, fire, flood and plague in Rome:
> May you live in eternal shame!

With the devastation caused by the sacking, the Romans saw the worst of the consequences of the disastrous policies of this pope, and they naturally grumbled, just as they did not happily accept the heavy new taxes which Clement VII had to impose to improve the situation. And he was certainly an expert in high finance, as was shown when in 1526, he established the Mountain of Faith (*Monte della Fede*), "the first public debt which placed the Church in the avantgarde of the European world from a point of view of exceptional financing!" to quote Mario Caravale.

More an economic expert than a political one in the broad sense of the term, he was obviously incapable of exercising all of the functions of a sovereign. However, it should be remembered that, in conformity with the tradition of his family, he continued to be a patron of the arts and channelled part of the revenues that way whenever it was possible. He made significant additions to the Vatican Library, went on with the construction of St. Peter's basilica, finished the courtyard of S. Damaso and, just prior to his death, commissioned Michelangelo to fresco the end wall of the Sistine Chapel with *The Last Judgment*, which was to be terminated under Paul III.

Clement VII died on 25 September 1534 and was buried at S. Maria sopra Minerva, in a mausoleum designed by Antonio Sangallo, across from that of Leo X.

220. PAUL III (1534—1549)

The conclave took only two days to select a successor to Clement VII and on 12 October 1534, Cardinal Alessandro Farnese was elected. His candidature imposed itself quickly through his independence of both the French and the imperial factions, and also for the prestige he had within the Sacred College by virtue of his forty years of seniority.

He was born in 1468 at Canino near Viterbo where the illustrious Farnese family owned a lot of land. He was crowned on 3 November and took the name of Paul III. His background reflected the Renaissance imprint of many of his colleagues. He owed his elevation to cardinal to his sister, the beautiful Giulia, favorite of Alexander VI, after which he had his share of dissolute living, fathering many children though only three were legitimized, Pier Luigi, Paolo, and Costanza. The year 1513 is indicated by all of his biographers as basic to his change of life-style, marked from then on by a greater degree of maturity which was reflected in his priestly work in the diocese of Parma.

But he had an innate worldly attitude that he never lost even as pontiff, so the Curia was able to go on happily with its frivolities. Masked balls, shows with clowns and singers, and lewd comedies continued to abound at court, to the pope's great pleasure.

Of course he was involved in unrestrained nepotism, and his greatest concern in the administration of power was to make the Farnese dynasty as influential as possible. He began this by naming two of his grandsons cardinals: Alessandro, the fifteen-year-old son of Pier Luigi, and Ascanio, aged sixteen and son of Costanza, who was married to Bosio Sforza, count of Santa Fiora. With the passing of the years the first one became a great patron of the arts, completing the work on the Farnese palazzi in Rome and in Caprarola begun by his grandfather, entrusting both of them first to Antonio Sangallo and then to Vignola. He also had the church of the Gesù constructed while the second, commonly known as the Cardinal of Santa Fiora, did no less for the arts than his cousin, and arranged for the building of the Chapel of the Assumption at St. Mary Major on a design of Buonarroti.

Also raised to the purple were Alessandro's younger brother, Ranuzio, and the half-brother of Costanza. But the one who made the most of Paul III was naturally Pier Luigi, probably his first-born, for whom the pope pursued the abuses carried out by Alexander VI for the Valentinois, to the detriment of the Papal State.

First of all, Paul III named him standard-bearer of the Church and supreme commander of the papal troops, then he created just for him a little duchy with Castro as its capital, granting it to him as a hereditary fiefdom, in addition to the permanent government of Nepi and the county of Ronciglione and Caprarola. Finally, in 1545, he entrusted to him the cities of Parma and Piacenza, separating these as well from the Papal State, which had only recently acquired them. Thus was born the duchy that would belong to the Farnese family for about two centuries.

But Pier Luigi did not have the Machiavellian ability of a Caesar Borgia, and his tyrannical government gave rise to discontent among the subjects of the duchy. In 1547, he became the victim of a conspiracy engineered by Giovanni Anguissola but ordered by the Gonzaga and approved by the emperor, since Pier Luigi was carrying on a pro-French policy. Riddled with stab wounds, he was thrown from the window of his palazzo to incite the population to rebel. Piacenza finished in the hands of the Gonzagas, but the son of Pier Luigi, Ottavio, quickly went from Rome to Parma and was able to keep control of that city.

Ottavio was the other Farnese who Paul III, as his grandfather, favored. At barely fourteen, he was married to the nineteen-year-old Margherita of Austria, widow of Alessandro de' Medici, forced into a second marriage for political reasons at the will of her father, Charles V, who wanted to link himself to the pope, who in turn planned to raise his dynasty to the highest ranks of the nobility. Margherita "did not like Ottavio Farnese and considered him unworthy of her background," Castiglioni notes, "regardless of the fact that Paul III showered him with honors, positions and wealth. To content her father, the bride had to whisper her sacramental "I do" on 4 November, but later denied having done so. She disliked her bridegroom so much that she did not even want to live maritally with him. The discord between the two spouses who, according to Cardinal Lenoncourt, stared at each other like cat and dog, became common knowledge among the Romans who made witty jokes about it.

The following *Pasquinade* in Latin, which reads like this in vernacular, is an example:

O you poor girl who wed a fellow too young,
what do you do in the silence of night in your lonely bed?
I think you are sad because your crop is in the hay
with that little thing that distresses your heart.

Paul III was deeply saddened by this and did his utmost with the emperor through negotiations, which were gossiped about by Pasquino as affairs between Margherita and a senile pontiff. Below is what the famous talking statue says to his colleague Marforio who asks him to help find a mule to "mount like a doctor:"

> Don't fool around with mares; they cost a lot:
> The Holy Father bought one and had to pay
> three hundred thousand.
> Then they always kick and this one
> Without a good rider with difficulty
> lets itself be mounted

And yet this pope, "for whom love goes about his house devouring his heart,"according to another verse of Pasquino, because he was "a slave to his personal life, to his nepotism and to the lay and secular customs of the Renaissance," using the words of Seppelt, had the Reformation at "heart." He was aware of the needs of the Church and was determined to do something about them even if he ultimately dashed so many hopes during the last years of his pontificate, involved as he was in a series of political intrigues by his son Pier Luigi and his grandson Ottavio, both of whom alienated him from his ally, Charles V.

Points of reference to his work in favor of reform were, first of all, the support he gave to the old religious Orders and the approval of new ones like the Theatines, the Somaschians, the Barnabites, the Capuchins and, especially the Jesuits of Ignatius Loyola. The latter were to have decisive impact in modern and contemporary Catholicism, becoming a kind of right arm for papal ecclesiastical policy. Another good deed of Paul III was to convene the Council of Trent, officially opened on 15 December 1545, with the task of eliminating the schism of the Western Church and of activating a common struggle of Christian peoples against the Turks. This Ecumenical Council XIX was of unprecedented importance. However, though it firmly clarified dogmatic points of Catholic doctrine, necessary to root out habitual corruption, it was unable to recuperate the followers of Lutheranism and of the Anglican Church, thereby leaving a permanent fracture within the Christian world.

The important decisions taken in the first phase of the Council were regarding faith and ecclesiastical discipline. Starting from the decree on the obligation of interpreting Holy Scripture in conformity with the teaching of the Church, and therefore opposed to the "free conscience" of the Lutherans, the concepts of divine grace and human freedom, as well as the doctrine of the sacraments (particularly baptism and confirmation) were defined in detail. At the same time, in the field of reform, the qualifications of candidates to the episcopate were enumerated, and the conferral of benefices was subjected to regulation.

Then, suddenly, war broke out between Charles V and the Schmalkaldic League, threatening to compromise the continuation of the council. The pope, who opposed the emperor also on account of his son Pier Luigi, began to think about moving the assembly from the German and "imperial" city of Trent to a city within the Papal State. Italian prelates showed great weariness for conciliar activity, and the envoys of Paul III proposed to the assembly that it be moved to Bologna, justifying this by the outbreak in Trent of some cases of petechial typhus. This was clearly an excuse, yet the proposal was approved on 11 March 1547. It was a serious error which compromised in a decisive way any general reform to which the Lutherans might have subscribed by augmenting the basic reasons of the schism.

Charles V rightly protested against the decision on the council's move. His victory over the Schmalkaldic League might have led the Protestants to soften their attitude and given rise to their return to the Church of Rome. But the hope of the emperor to have the Protestants participate in the Council was dashed because they would certainly not have attended an assembly in a city belonging to the Papal State.

Paul III seemed disinterested in the matter, devastated as he was by the death of Pier Luigi. In 1548 he suspended the Council and then dissolved it completely on 14 September 1549, almost as if to acknowledge the collapse of the good work that it was conducting. When it reopened, it was to assume a different significance in the conservative sense of the "Counter-Reformation," which brought about the definite rupture of the Church of Rome with the Protestant Christian world in its various forms.

An initiative which preceded this stiffening of the pontifical position was the establishment in 1542 of the Holy Roman and Universal Inquisition, the purpose of which was to maintain, uncontaminated by errors, the Catholic religion and to punish severely any who persisted in heresy. Presided over by a committee of six cardinals that subsequently had the title of Holy Office, this institution found its first fervent promoters in Ignatius Loyola and Gian Pietro Caraffa, the future Pope Paul IV. "In principle, this tribunal was moderate and merciful, true to the nature of Paul III," as Cardinal Girolamo Seripando noted, although he had to admit at the time, very objectively, that "later, however, when the number of cardinals running it augmented and the power of the judges increased, but especially because of the hardness of Caraffa, this tribunal acquired a renown such that it was said nowhere on earth were so awful and horrible verdicts pronounced."

Under Paul III, however, Rome was not associated only with the Inquisition, since it was also thanks to the good work of this pontiff that the face to the city was restored following the damages from the sacking of 1527. Aside from what his grandchildren accomplished, he entrusted the fortification of the walls to Antonio Sangallo, even though the original project was reduced and limited to the Leonine City. Sangallo also built the Pauline Chapel and the Royal Hall (Sala Regia) in the Vatican palace. Michelangelo, instead, who had completed the frescoes in the Sistine Chapel of his *Last Judgment* and restored the Capitol with its piazza and the positioning in it of the equestrian statue of Marcus Aurelius, received the management of the Workshop of St. Peter's. The earlier plans were thereby modified, including that of Bramante, and the structure of the basilica with its grandiose cupola was defined.

Paul III died on 10 November 1549, and was buried in St. Peter's in a mausoleum, the work of Guglielmo della Porta, which was quickly attacked by Pasquino:

> In this tomb lies a greedy, rapacious vulture.
> He was Paul Farnese, who gave nothing and took everything.
> Pray for him: he died of indigestion.

221. JULIUS III (1550–1555)

That there was no atmosphere of reform and that the inspiration of the Holy Spirit was lost in an intrigue of politico-clerical deals became immediately clear in the conclave for the election of a successor to Paul III. The forty-seven participating cardinals, divided into two basic factions, pro-imperial and pro-French, together with a cohort of other venal ones, were certainly not guided by spiritual motives while raking in votes for one or another candidate. Above all, it was not a true "conclave" because contact with the outside world was continuous, with door locks forced, and everything going on more or less with "open doors."

The vacant see lasted from 29 November 1549 to 8 February 1550, and Rome enjoyed a sense of freedom such that the citizens gave themselves to masked processions that were blatant satires about the cardinals in conclave. In St. Peter's Square itself, "they made a fine battle pulling arquebuses behind them and a fine carousel," according to Cola Coleine of Trastevere, so that the governor of the city banned masquerades "dressed as cardinals, bishops or prelates" on pain of a corporal punishment of "three lashes administered in public at the time and place of arrest without asking nor knowing who they are."

Then, all of a sudden came the announcement. On 8 February Cardinal Giovanni Maria Ciocchi del Monte, a Roman, was elected, and this time there was a grand celebration which lasted until the day of the coronation. The authorities interposed no objection to the rowdy festivities organized by the

Romans, who were delighted to see one of their fellow citizens on the pontifical throne after more than a century.

On 18 February, as Coleine remarks, "the Romans organized a hunt at the Capitol with 6 bulls, and they staged a lovely comedy, as well as a splendid supper for the relatives of the pope and many gentlemen and ladies who made a grand parade; they also set up a carousel for 40 or 50 children with 42 trumpets and drums; the banner was turquoise and gold." And the pope who had taken the name of Julius III presided over these celebrations which had nothing to do with religion. Moreover, under him, Rome would return to the glitter of the Renaissance and would welcome in a pagan manner the pilgrims to the Jubilee that started shortly after the coronation.

Julius III was sixty-three years old, and if until then he had shown himself to be brusque and somewhat severe in his conception of ecclesiastical life, in line with his scholarly studies of civil and canon law and in a correct execution of tasks in the administrative offices of Rome entrusted to him by Paul III, as pope he apparently intended to enjoy his power.

In the teeth of the reform and the spirit of Christian renewal, and in the midst of the crisis over the half-finished council, as well as in defiance of the "Counter-Reformation," Julius III devoted himself to splendid banquets highlighted by troops of clowns, as during the time of Leo X. He attended the bull hunts organized in the square from the loggia of the basilica of St. Peter and was not ashamed to renew the spicy theater performances in the Vatican. As far as religion was concerned, papal dignity was cast aside. It was not for evangelical, spiritual peace that this pope had a magnificent country villa built outside Porta del Popolo in an imposing park, named Villa Giulia.

Needless to say, he was an unscrupulous nepotist and all his relatives found well-paid positions and considerable sources of income in Rome, even though they did not reach the level of international political intrigues of the Farneses. However, his older brother, Baldovino, was appointed governor of Spoleto and obtained the county of Monte S. Savino from Cosimo de' Medici. Baldovino's son, Giovanni Battista, was appointed standard-bearer of the Church but he died in war in 1552. As a result, the male line of the del Monte family became extinct, so Julius III told his brother to adopt a certain Fabiano, a depraved fifteen-year-old custodian of monkeys, who assumed the name Innocenzo del Monte. It is very probable that he was a son of the pope because so much affection and attention for such an abject human being like him would be otherwise inexplicable. Julius III elevated him to cardinal, making a farce of the Sacred College, and went as far as to appoint him to the Secretariat of State, even if only in name as he was totally incapable of handling its business.

The *Pasquinades* about this shameful, adoptive son-nephew, designated with the nickname "Monkey," multiplied, and naturally the dignity of the Curia was affected, as the following shows:

Del Monte loves with equal ardour his monkey and its keeper.
He sent the purple hat to the empty and feminine boy.
For equal treatment, why can't he make the monkey
cardinal too?

As pope-uncle Julius III would have allowed Fabiano to get away with any-thing, but not his successors. Pius IV imprisoned him in Castel Sant'Angelo for having killed two people at a banquet and, once liberated, took away his source of income, exiling him to Tivoli; subsequently Pius V was to take away his car-dinalate. This bandit, Fabiano-Innocenzo del Monte, is said to have met a frightful end at only 46, although he was even shamefully buried in the church of S. Pietro in Montorio.

However, Julius III, despite his dishonorable personal conduct, did resume and continue the Council of Trent. Charles V was pleased with the pope's deci-sion because he found him receptive on various questions which had been reasons for disputes with Paul III. Hence, he urged the Protestant princes of the empire to attend the council, still thinking he could settle the schism.

The assembly met on 1 May 1551 and established the doctrines of the Eucharist, Confession, and Extreme Unction as dogma, but when the Protestants arrived the situation became difficult and, after various discussions, the hopes for reconciliation were shattered. So, on 28 April 1552, there was another suspension of the Council for two years, but the hostilities which had broken out in European politics were such that the idea of reconvening the assembly was temporarily shelved.

The cause of friction between Charles V and the pope was again a Farnese, Ottavio, to whom Julius III had officially given the duchy of Parma, while the emperor had still no intention of returning Piacenza to him. Ottavio allied him-self with Henry II of France so the pope declared him deposed. A war ensued and Julius III gave in to the French king's threats to convene a national council, and recognized Ottavio once again as duke of Parma and, as well, of Castro.

In contrast, the situation for the Catholic Church in England became rosier when the first daughter of Henry VIII, Mary, ascended the throne in 1553. The dream of reuniting that country with the Church of Rome did not last long because, in 1558, under Elizabeth, everything would be back to what it was before, and definitively so. However, on 23 March 1555, the pope died still under the illusion that, despite the crisis of the Council of Trent, the schism would be resolved favorably.

Although suffering from gout, Julius III so loved the pleasurable life he was leading, especially at his villa outside the walls, that he thought he would never die and only at the last moment did he agree to receive Extreme Unction. He was buried in a simple sarcophagus in the Vatican Grottoes, as his contemporaries evidently did not deem him worthy of a mausoleum. And this was right, considering that, in the words of Ranke, "his administration left no profound trace."

222. MARCELLUS II (1 5 5 5)

The successor to Julius III was elected by acclamation, confirmed by a secret ballot, on 9 April 1555, during a fairly short conclave. This was because, as a logical reaction to the crisis in the reform, a man was needed who possessed the gifts to get it going. That man was Cardinal Marcello Cervini. Born in Montepulciano near Siena in 1501, he was a prelate of great distinction with a blameless past and wholly marked by spiritual gifts which were brought to light while he was Secretary of State and during his presidency of the Council of Trent.

He was crowned on 10 April and he did not change his name, "to let it be understood that this new position made him change nothing at all," said Paolo Sarpi. He was therefore called Marcellus II.

The authentic contemporary reformists expected great things from him, one of whom was his spokesman, Cardinal Girolamo Seripando, who expressed congratulations for the choice of the new pope as follows: "I had prayed that a pope would come who might be able to remove from the degradation into which had fallen the beautiful words: Church, Council, Reform. By this election, I find my wish has been satisfied and it seems that my prayer has been answered."

But the joy did not last long because Marcello's papacy was one of the shortest in history. Twenty days of illusion, this anti-nepotist pope *ante litteram*, forbade his own relatives to come to Rome and intended to stay out of politics in order to affirm the exclusively spiritual significance of the vicar of Christ, and to bring peace to all peoples as the common father of Christianity.

His coronation itself bore witness to the simplicity of his spirit, free of any celebration as he had wished, with the distribution of the money provided for the occasion to the benefit of the poor. Moreover he immediately gave orders to bring moderation into court life, forbidding any luxuries and removing from the table any gold or silver tableware. For the Holy Week rites, he went on foot to St. Peter's, despite being "rather infirm, especially since he had a hidden sore in one leg," as a chronicler of that time noted. He suffered in silence, hoping to get better, but it was not to be.

It seemed that the popes who were inspired to reform the Church according to the spirit of the Gospels were destined to reign only for a short time, for the same fate had befallen Pius III and Hadrian VI. Marcellus II died on 1 May 1555, and was buried in the Vatican Grottoes in a simple old Christian sarcophagus, as he would have wished. The memory of this exemplary pope is recorded in one of the most famous musical creations of the Church, the Messa for six voices by Giovanni Pierluigi of Palestrina that was sung in St. Peter's on Easter Sunday. It was the only luxury that Marcellus II conceded to himself, a hymn in praise of God.

223. PAUL IV (1555–1559)

The successor to Marcellus II emerged from a two weeks conclave overshadowed by a dispute between the pro-imperial and the pro-French factions. On 23 May 1555, Cardinal Gian Pietro Caraffa, was elected in spite of Charles V who was known to be against this choice. But his personal veto, conveyed by his ambassador to the conclave participants, was ignored. It is said that Caraffa replied to the Spanish Cardinal Francisco Mendoza who suggested he not be upset because Charles did not want him: "The emperor cannot prevent me from being pope if God so wishes; indeed, I shall be happier because I shall owe my position to God alone." He was elected by general acclaim.

Gian Pietro Caraffa, born in S. Angelo della Scala near Avellino, in 1476 was notoriously inimical to Spain, perhaps because as a young man he had lived at the court of King Ferdinand as the chief chaplain and member of the King's Council, and had come to know the domineering attitude native to the people. Julius II had appointed him bishop of Chieti but, according to the Venetian ambassador, Navagero, he showed his own antipathy to Spanish domination when he defined them as "heretics, schismatics, accursed by God, half Jewish and half Moorish, dregs of the earth," and by deploring the wretchedness of Italy which was constrained to bow down to such "vile, abject people." The bitter experience of the sacking of Rome and the ostentatious Catholicism of Charles V, which seemed suspect to him, weighed heavily in his harsh judgment.

In him was a pseudo-nationalistic Renaissance spirit which he was never to lose, linked to an inflexible toughness of character and severity in his conception of Christianity. He had founded, together with Gaetano of Thiene, the Order of the Theatines, and once Paul III had raised him to the cardinal rank, he had been the spirit behind the Roman Inquisition, giving it the imprint of inflexibility that his pontificate was to emphasize.

His nomination was greeted enthusiastically by the reform party, which saw in him the ideal person to achieve unitary faith in the western world through the reopening of the council, but it had to think again. As pope, Caraffa was to let himself be caught up in a blind political passion and to ignore the idea of the unity of Europe in Christ.

The coronation of Paul IV, which was the name adopted by Caraffa, took place on 26 May and restored the pomp of many years earlier. The court resumed the elegance of the princes, the gold and silver returned to the papal table, despite the fact that the pope, an ascetic, was personally given to long periods of fasting. What he wanted was formality, its external manifestation, the style which demanded immediate respect for the person of the sovereign pontiff. As he used to say, kings and emperors had to sit at his feet and listen to his opinions, much as students before a professor.

This aspect of the pope-king emerged especially as of one who cannot make a mistake, with the self-assurance and gravity of a duce "who has in sight a grand and noble idea, that of freeing Italy and the papacy from the oppressive weight of the Spanish." Castiglioni wrote this referring to Paul IV during the twenty years of Fascism, emphasizing with pride that he "was trying to bring together in one *fascio* all the princes of Italy against Spain" and recalling that, faced with the absence of any hoped-for patriotic coalition of the Italian sovereigns, "with his head high he protested, but did not lose spirit. 'Whatever may be the feeling of others, I wish to serve my country. If my voice is not heeded, the idea of having raised it for such a noble cause will at least console me, and I believe that people will say that an Italian, an old man with one foot in the grave, who should be doing nothing but resting and regretting his faults, had his heart filled with this glorious project.'"

It all began when Charles V abdicated, leaving the throne of Spain to his son, Philip II, and imperial authority to his brother, Ferdinand I. The latter was promptly recognized emperor by the electors, obviously without having consulted the pope, as he would have wished, thus brushing aside outmoded and disputed papal right to approve the nomination. Paul IV seized on this, as well as the fact that Ferdinand had given his word to the Protestants that he would hold fast to the decisions on religious peace taken at Augsburg by Charles V before he left the throne. This meant the renouncement of a single religion within the empire and, therefore, the collapse of any possible further attempt at union through a resumption of the Council of Trent.

In a consistory, Paul IV declared that the abdication of Charles V was invalid and, therefore, the succession of Ferdinand I non-existent. However, he did not ask for the support of the cardinals in this anti-imperial struggle, convinced that he was the sole liberator of Italy. He trusted only his relatives, who would not cloud his image as a duce, and so even he, acknowledged as the spirit of rigorous reform, fell into a marass of unscrupulous nepotism.

It seems useless to excuse this nepotism of Paul IV by pointing to motives of a patriotic nature, because the fact that he gave his nephews ecclesiastical lands, that he set a soldier to manage religious matters, that he committed acts of war and bloodshed, is far from the pure spirit of Christianity. The label of patriotism is a mask to cover ecclesiastic and personal motives.

So, thoughtlessly, he followed the advice of his favorite relative, his nephew, Carlo Caraffa, an unscrupulous captain raised to the purple a few days after the coronation, who had his pope-uncle under his thumb and could make him do whatever he wanted. Paul IV knew well what kind of person he was because, *motu proprio*, he pardoned him, once he was a cardinal, for all the crimes of his loose life as a layman, and made him Secretary of State. It was he who exacerbated the tensions with Ferdinand I and Philip II, taking as an excuse the capture of two French galleys in the port of Civitavecchia by Carlo Sforza, envoy to the emperor. He led his uncle to believe that this blitz was part of a conspiracy against him organized in Rome and supported by the "imperials" which had been engineered by the Cardinal of Santa Fiora, Ascanio Sforza. As evidence, Carlo Caraffa produced intercepted letters addressed to the emperor in which the cardinal apologized for not having been able to prevent the election of Paul IV. He was immediately imprisoned in Castel Sant'Angelo with his secretary and, at the same time, lands of the Colonna "imperials" were confiscated and assigned to Carlo's brother, Giovanni, who received the title of Duke of Paliano.

On 15 December 1555, the pope signed a treaty of military alliance with the French who promised to put an army of 12,000 men at the disposal of the Church.

Paul IV, who was very talkative and never learned how to hold his tongue, said in statements devoid of strategy, that he had turned to France through expedience because the French and the Spanish "are both barbarians and it would be better if they stayed home and that there be in Italy no language other than our own; however, the Spaniards hold on like creeping grass to whatever they attack, whereas the French would not stay unless they were bound." In other words, in due course he could get rid even of the French.

But Spain blocked the papal initiative when, in September 1556, the duke of Alba entered the Papal State from Naples. The Franco-Papal army did not win the victories they expected and the French forces were recalled home since they were needed for the great battle of Saint Quentin. The duke arrived at the gates of Rome where a new sacking was feared but, thanks to mediation by Venice, a treaty of peace was reached at Cave on 12 September 1557. Paul IV was forced to recognize Philip II as an obedient Catholic king and had to retract his earlier accusations about the king and his father, Charles V, being schismatic and heretical. He also had to renounce his alliance with France and declare the neutrality of the Church.

Such was the result, scarce indeed, of nepotism and the pseudo-nationalist policy of Paul IV, without considering the rumors about the immoral behavior of Cardinal Carlo that continued to circulate in the Curia. The cardinal of Lorena actually accused relatives of the pope of homosexuality, "that abominable sin in which one makes no distinction between masculine and feminine sexes."

For Paul IV it was a blow. Disgust and bitterness filled his soul and, as Ranke notes, "his eyes were gradually opened to the blameworthy behavior of his relatives whom he got rid of in an impetuous spirit of justice following an inner conflict. From then on, he went back to his old proposals for reform and began to rule as one supposed he would have from the beginning, promoting a reform of the State and, above all of the Church, with the same passion with which he had promoted hostility and war." In the consistory of 27 January 1559, he publicly condemned the behavior of his nephews, calling upon God as his witness that he never had known anything, and that he had been deceived by them: "*Nunc dicendum et scribendum*," and concluded, "*Pontificatus anno primo*" from the expulsion of his nephews. That year of his pontificate was also to be his last year. Carlo kept his cardinal's hat but was sent into exile.

Since the peace accord of Cave, Paul IV had devoted all his energy again to the reform, but a pope-leader like him could not believe in the council and he gave its reopening no serious thought. The reform had to come directly from Rome, beginning with the uprooting of the "heresy of simony" within the Curia, and by giving broader authority to the Inquisition, whose jurisdiction was originally limited to questions of faith. This tribunal then worked with merciless severity following the directives of the pope who often presided over the hearings. As Ranke notes, Paul IV "gave it the cruel privilege of applying torture, called by the doubtful term of 'rigorous examination,' solely 'to force out the names of accomplices. He paid no attention to the social status of persons, dragging before the tribunal the most famous barons. He threw into jail cardinals like Morone and Foscherari, whom he had earlier used to examine the content of important books, like the spiritual exercises of Ignatius, because he had come to doubt their orthodoxy.'"

The increasing diffidence of the pope was becoming pathological, as proven by these latest measures, which later would be abrogated by his successor. Through his deep concern to preserve the purity of the faith, even the strict measures he took against the Jews can be explained, but not justified. The Jews of Rome and in other cities in the Papal State were kept in ghettos and had to wear yellow caps as distinctive markers. In 1559 the first *Index Librorum Prohibitorum* was published, so strict that Pius IV would have "reformed" it.

From this severity, born of the blindest fanaticism was to come the "Counter-Reformation." In this sense, Paul IV had, through his unbalanced character which had drawn him into misadventures with his relatives, provided a merited lesson for the strengthening of the Church of Rome from inside, a lesson which Pius V would adopt.

And so Paul deluded himself that he could put things right in respect of the conclaves which had been in fact "open," with simony hidden under various forms of gifts and political pressures. The bull *Cum secundum Apostolorum* of 16 December 1558, prohibited every sort of deal outside the conclave to do with the election of a pope, but was of no avail.

His final months of life, after the shocking discovery of the perverted behavior of his nephews, were seen by Paul IV as expiation for those faults. It is said that he went from one altar to another in St. Peter's, lost in prayer. Even in the days preceding his death he maintained the strictest penitential diet possible and refused that small amount of food advised by his doctors to keep him alive. This the Romans did not believe. In line with the slander of a contemporary chronicler who assured people that the pope might not be eating but was drinking a lot of wine which was "potent and robust, dark in color and so thick you could cut it with a knife," they mocked him with these quips between the two famous "talking statues" in Rome:

> PASQUINO:
> Goodness me, what strong wine in this Carafe!
> MARFORIO:
> You're wrong; it's vinegar.

He died on 18 August 1559, and Rome went chaotic. The pent-up resentment to the pope's tough administration exploded in a fury of destruction. The Inquisition building was set afire, and the marble statue of Paul IV in the Capitol was demolished and, with the head broken off, dragged through the streets finishing in the Tiber. The *Pasquinades* were numerous, such as the following:

> Caraffa, hated in Hell and Heaven, is buried here
> in his stinking corpse; the Devil has received his soul.
> He hated peace on Earth; his prayer denied,
> he ruined the Church and the people, offended man and God;
> faithless friend, a beggar of the host ill-omened to him.
> You wish to know more? He was pope and that's all.

The corpse of Paul IV was secretly buried in the basement of the Vatican to keep it away from the wrath of the people, until Pius V gave him a decent burial in S. Maria sopra Minerva.

224. Pius IV (1559–1565)

The disturbances in Rome on Paul IV's death delayed the opening of the conclave, which took place only on 5 September 1559. It was to last for nearly four months with forty-eight cardinals taking part, including Morone, released from Castel Sant'Angelo, and Carlo Caraffa, recalled from exile by the Sacred College.

Under these circumstances, the conclave's seclusion was not really observed since intrigues and political deals took place through a hole bored in the wall of the Sistine Chapel. The waters were calmed only when Philip II, through his ambassador, notified the conclave that he would no longer veto any candidate. As a result there was agreement between the French and the Spanish cardinals in respect to Cardinal Giovan Angelo de' Medici, who was elected by acclamation on Christmas Day 1559.

Under the impression they were returning to the golden era of Leo X, the Romans greeted his election with enthusiasm, but Giovan Angelo was not even a distant relative of that pope's family. He was born in Milan on 31 March 1499, in a family of humble status which had acquired a certain position and wealth because the older brother of Giovan Angelo, Gian Giacomo, had had a brilliant career earning the title of Marquis of Marignano, and had married an Orsini, sister-in-law of Cardinal Farnese. Thanks to him, Giovan Angelo had become apostolic prothonotary in the service of the Farnese and carried out the duties of Commissioner General of the papal troops which had helped the imperial ones in the war against the Schmalkaldic League. Paul III had made him cardinal, but he had not agreed with the rigid stance of Paul IV and his opposition to the reopening of the Council of Trent. Giovan Angelo had therefore left the Curia, returning to Rome only for the conclave. He was crowned on 6 January 1560, and took the name of Pius IV.

The enthusiasm of the Romans would be reciprocated by the mild character of the new pope who, among his first decrees, granted pardon for the sacrilegious excesses of the populace at the death of Paul IV. At the same time, he limited the jurisdiction of the Inquisition to what it had been, candidly condemning the severity of the verdicts. He was almost never to preside over a session of that tribunal and was convinced that the true reform had to come from the Council of Trent, which he intended to reopen with the agreement of all of the Christian States.

With this in mind, he resumed relations with Emperor Ferdinand I, recognizing his election, and with the king of Spain, Philip II, by deciding to ignore former disputes. He announced to the world the continuation of the Council for Easter of the following year with a bull of 29 November 1560, though the first session of the assembly took place only on 18 January 1562.

Its work proceeded despite obstacles and difficulties mainly due to a proposal of reform by Ferdinand I who, while insisting on discussing this before tackling the problems of dogma, urgently recommended the concession of receiving Communion under both forms, as well as the marriage of priests, viewing the latter as a fundamental issue to avoid a conclusive break with the Protestants. When Ferdinand then proposed moving his court to Innsbruck to be closer to Trent, surrounding himself with a large number of theologians to serve as his consultants on the issues before the Council, a full crisis appeared to be imminent. Above all, the fact that the Cardinal de Guise presented a series of French requests quite like those of Ferdinand I, and the count de Luna, representative of Philip II, joined the "imperial" theologians, gave the impression that those consultations might develop into a separate council alongside that of Trent. The danger of another schism reared its head.

The pope responded to the situation by sending the capable Cardinal Morone to Trent as president with the task of shortening the sessions and reaching conclusions on the points of dogma. Morone managed to convince the emperor of the loyal behavior of the pope and to approve the dogmas as basic points for the development of the reform about which the discussion would be more complex. As a result came the decrees on the order of priesthood, on matrimony, on purgatory, on the veneration of saints, and on indulgences which only the Church of Rome could grant. Finally, the supremacy of the pope over the conciliar assembly was recognized. Nothing else was discussed about an "opening" towards the Protestants. On 4 December 1563, the Council of Trent was closed. If it had been born from some reformists's idea to place limits on the power of the Roman pontiff, in that respect, it had absolutely failed. Indeed, that power was reinforced since all the decisions of the Council had to be approved by Pius IV if they were to come into force, as with the bull *Benedictus Deus* on 26 January 1564.

European sovereigns accepted the decrees without difficulty but that did not mean they would apply them. On the other hand there was no longer any alternative for the Protestants who had either to accept or reject them, and stay either within or outside the Church of Rome.

And with this Council, undoubtedly important for its future in terms of prestige and discipline, the Church of Rome simply recognized its limits, and "rejected with infinite anathemas, Protestantism," as Ranke notes, for if "in the Catholicism which had preceded the Council there was an element of Protestantism, that was now definitively expelled." It was an irreversible choice, since unity of religion was renounced, and Christianity was divided into a series of Churches separated from Rome, which would but multiply over the centuries. However, the Church of Rome and the papacy came out of it strengthened, and that was a great political victory. The conclusion which had to be drawn, however, was a bitter one, as Pasquino opined in a dialogue with his "colleague" Marforio:

> MARFORIO:
> After all that noise from Trento,
> Pasquino, what came of it?
> PASQUINO:
> May it please the Lord,
> we stayed at year one thousand one hundred,
> as usual.

MARFORIO:
But then, how about the Reform?
PASQUINO:
Be quiet, it seems to be asleep.

Perhaps the pontificate of Pius IV was born under an evil star for, during the long period of vacant see, the brother of Carlo Caraffa, Duke Giovanni of Paliano, had had his wife strangled because of her adultery, and had personally slain her presumed lover. Once pope, Pius IV decided to take action against his predecessor's nephews so as to get rid of that corrupt family once and for all. To begin with he had them all arrested and appointed a committee of cardinals, all enemies of the Caraffas with the exception of Ghislieri, the future Pius V who, for that reason, was appointed bishop of Mondovi. So the trial was rigged and resulted in death sentences for the chief defendants, including Cardinal Carlo and Duke Giovanni, though the young Cardinal Alfonso was pardoned in the end. Subsequently, Pius V ordered a review of the trial, cancelled the verdict and restored their property to the Caraffas.

One must not think that with that trial Pius IV had indirectly condemned nepotism. He himself followed the same path despite the call for reform and raised the numerous nephews who came to him from other related families, like the Serbellonis, the Hohenems, and the Borromeos, to senior lay and clerical positions within the Papal State. The greatest favors went to the latter, amongst whom excelled Carlo, the great saint of the Diocese of Milan, who was raised to the cardinalate and became the pope's trusted confident.

Carlo Borromeo was the proponent of the Catholic restoration, and Pius IV was convinced, despite the princely life with which he wanted to identify the papacy, that the strict line of conduct required by the council should from then on be the banner of the Church of Rome, beginning with the election of its leader. Remembering that "hole in the wall" at the conclave, and the easy talks between the sovereign's ambassadors and the cardinals, he became convinced that the electors had to be trained in conclave discipline and refuse any contact with the outside. So he ordered the compilation, in an organic whole, of all the existing legislative documents concerning papal elections which became the *De eligendis* constitution of 1562.

After their initial enthusiasm, the Romans did not find great satisfaction from his administration since Pius IV's mildness and magnanimity did not provide them with much. The princely splendor he put into effect benefited indirectly his own person and was all to the advantage of his relatives and the court. And given the usual difficult financial situation, he had to impose new taxes, which obviously increased the ill humor of the population. This led to demonstrations in the public squares and the pope thought about abandoning

Rome and moving to Bologna. But he did not do so, even if he had reason to fear death by assassination.

In 1564 another conspiracy was discovered, planned by a madman, Benedetto Accolti, son of a cardinal who had been exiled by Pius III. Obsessed, he went about preaching ideas full of religious fanaticism, including his dream of unifying all the Churches under a kind of angelic pope, himself, of course, with a mad plan which, first of all, called for the elimination of the worldly Pius IV. He managed to attract a few followers who wound up at the gallows with him in January of 1565.

Pius IV, however, did not skimp on expenses to renew the tradition of a pope as patron of the arts. From that point of view, Rome received numerous benefits through the construction of a lot of public works. Michelangelo transformed the Baths of Diocletian into the basilica of S. Maria degli Angeli, and opened a new gate along the walls called Porta Pia. The quarter between the Vatican and Castel Sant'Angelo became Borgo Pio, and Villa Pia or the Casino of Pius IV was built in the Vatican gardens by Pirro Ligorio.

The most worldly event in Rome under this pontiff was certainly the marriage between Ortensia Borromeo, niece of Carlo, and Annibale Altemps, named a Count by the emperor and Lord of Gallarate by Philip II. The pope could not be outdone and gave Ortensia a dowry of 100,000 *scudi* that his successor, Pius V, was able to cut in half, as the full amount had not been paid over when Pius IV died. The celebrations reached their apex with a famous tourney waged in the arena of the Belvedere on 5 March 1565, in which about twenty of the most famous Italian and Spanish knights took part in front of some 6,000 spectators and was recorded by chroniclers of that period, like Alveri and Crescimbeni.

The main event took place in the evening when "at a given moment the many lights of the numerous chandeliers, placed in the various arches, went on and, after a brief pause, the trumpets began to sound." The celebration ended with a banquet for over a thousand persons, right in front of the poor people of the city, and at the end "after much dancing and all kinds of music, the decision of the judges was announced" and the bride gave out prizes to the knights.

Although he loved elegance, Pius IV kept nothing for himself, and in his last months he regained somewhat the populace's admiration by giving a lot away to the poor. He always led an exemplary life from the viewpoint of clerical morals and was profoundly "pious." Carlo Borromeo was close to him in the last days of his pontificate, also in administrative matters, when he began to suffer from the hard and severe self-inflicted penances. Carlo was at his bedside when he died on 9 December 1565. He was buried in S. Maria degli Angeli.

225. ST. PIUS V (1566–1572)

Carlo Borromeo had control of the conclave which began on 19 December 1565. Fifty-three cardinal electors respected the closure and theoretically avoided political pressures, in accordance with Pius IV's revived constitution. The atmosphere of the Catholic restoration was being felt and in this sense the great nations stayed out of it for the time being, divided as they were by internal religious disputes. The cardinals in Rome were more or less in agreement on the Counter-Reformation, but the burning question was how to achieve it? By full restoration or by a conciliatory approach? Advocates of the former won and on 7 January 1566, Borromeo saw elected his candidate, Michele Ghislieri, commonly known as Cardinal Alessandrino because he was born in Bosco Marengo near Alessandria on 17 January 1504. He was crowned on his birthday and took the name of Pius V.

Of humble origin, as a boy he had been a shepherd. Later, the usual wealthy friend of the family had noted his talent and had had him enter the Dominican monastery at Voghera when he was fourteen years old. He observed all the rules with exemplary, religious zeal, particularly in respect to poverty. From the alms collected, he kept only what he needed, studied, became a theologian and was ordained a priest at the age of twenty-four.

Although he became the confessor of the governor of Milan, he permitted himself no luxuries and travelled on foot with a sack over his shoulder. He displayed his severity as the prior in a monastery, taking a stand in favor of the old doctrine. He was a tough priest and as soon as the Inquisition was established, Rome named him first Inquisitor for Pavia and then for Como. Those were hot spots on the border of Protestant Switzerland, and Michele Ghislieri applied the law zealously and visibly. He was stoned but did not give up. At night he felt safer in the homes of peasants, where he tried to escape from those who hated his "inquisition." A count threatened to throw him into a well, but he replied that God's will would be done.

In 1557 Paul IV appointed him a cardinal and the Grand Inquisitor at Rome. He was not happy to take on that job and, even though he condemned people severely, he would then pray and fast for long periods. His severity seemed suspect and, under Pius IV, the Curia was against him. He was relieved from his position and transferred to the bishopric of Mondovi, though he never reached his see. Brigands robbed him of his baggage so he was allowed to remain in Rome. Ill, suffering from gallstones, and drinking only mare's milk, he lived like a refugee until Carlo Borromeo rescued him from isolation. The papacy, however, was not to change his nature: papal restoration of Catholic severity was with him a fact of life.

The coronation was done in a minor key with the money for a celebration given to the poor. Under his pontifical vestments Pius V wore his hairshirt, and slept his few hours of sleep on a straw bed. He would continue to observe his fasting with the same strictness as in all his pious exercises, such as walking very often to the Seven Churches of Rome. "The people were fascinated when they saw him in processions, barefoot and bareheaded, his face a pure picture of true devotion, his beard long and as white as snow," Ranke writes, relaying information from the chroniclers of that time, adding "they thought there had never been such a devout pope and said that his glance alone would convert Protestants."

In short, he was a "vigorous" pope, as one of his biographers put it, and he seemed to personify the ideal religious pope, who banned any military engagement and, full of faith in the supernatural, used to say that the Church had no need for cannons and soldiers, and that its weapons should be prayer, fasting, and Holy Scripture. It is clear that political considerations did not matter to him, that he was really not versed in affairs of State, and that he was completely foreign to nepotism. He had to be begged at length by the Sacred College, since he always said he did not trust anyone, to make at least his nephew, the Dominican Michele Borelli, a cardinal. This nephew was close to him and did not abuse his power, very different from another appointed commander of the palace guard and governor of the quarter who was a braggart. So the pope degraded him and banished him from the Papal State.

His religious severity led him to a general "cleansing" of the Curia and of Rome as a true man of the Counter-Reformation. Having abolished the opulence of the papal court, having got rid of the buffoons still there under Pius IV, he did not simply issue instructions to the Curia and the populace, but insisted upon immediate action. Cardinals and bishops were obliged to reside in the city, where he did not want them wandering aimlessly around town, and for both the clergy and the laity there were severe sanctions for violating Sundays and feast-days, as well as for swearing and concubinage. No begging was allowed, but large donations were made to the really poor. There was no pre-Lenten carnival and he insisted on the protection of the sacred bond of marriage, with public whippings for adulterers.

At first prostitutes and courtesans were supposed to move out of Rome and the lower level ones did so. But, alone and unprotected they were attacked and robbed of their belongings as soon as they were out of the city. Some were thrown into the Tiber and were drowned while others died of hunger on the street. So the pope had second thoughts and, agreeing to the pleas of the ambassadors and the nobles, permitted those who had not yet left to stay, on condition that they would live in a special area. Otherwise, the whipping and the ban were applicable.

It looked as if Rome would become a monastery, but it was logical that it should if the restoration was to come about. And the Inquisition got its palazzo—since the common people had destroyed its temporary headquarters at the death of Paul IV—with its offices, archives and, of course, its dungeons. The first stone was laid on 2 September 1566, and work was finished three years later when Pius V could proudly have the following inscription incised on the great iron door of the building: "*Haereticae pravitatis sectatores cautius coercerentur a fundamentis in augmentum catholicae religionis.*"

Very soon though the people were no longer "fascinated" by that "pious" pope who punished evildoing with the whip; they were terrified because nonbelievers were "lost" and those who did not obey or who argued were as good as dead. If Pius V was to be canonized by Clement XI in May 1712, there were those who did not agree and, according to Giovagnoli, they "placed him between Tamerlane and Domenico Guzmàn as one of the most frenetic and bloodiest monsters who have ever dishonored the human race." Pasquino spits poison in an epigraph affixed to a latrine in the Vatican which the pope had built:

> Pius V, having compassion for everything in one's stomach,
> erected this shithouse as a noble piece of work.

Niccolò Franco was accused of being the author of it and, although Cardinal Morone defended him, he was hanged. And the Latin poet, Antonio Paleario, suspected of having written the following verses against the Inquisition, ended up at the stake:

> As if it were already winter,
> Pius burns Christians like sticks,
> to get used to hellfire himself.

The pope's example encouraged bishops and cardinals to follow this trail of blood in various Italian dioceses, with Carlo Borromeo in the lead, and the sovereigns leant a hand in the carnage, Cosimo de' Medici receiving as a recompense the title of Grand Duke. The representative of the House of Habsburg, a faithful tool of the Counter-Reformation, upset even as he felt superior, would be compensated with a new title of Archduke.

But Pius V did not stop at Italy and addressed appeals beyond the Alps for crusades and Inquisitions against heresy. Writing to Philip II he recommended, as regards heresy, that he should "never give in; never show mercy; get rid of the heretics; get rid of those who resist; persecute to the very end; slaughter, burn, put everything to the torch and draw blood, for the Lord to be revenged; much more than his enemies, they are your enemies."

And again he, the pacifist, sent troops to help French Catholics and gave the order to their commander, the count of Santa Fiora, to "take no Huguenot prisoners and kill immediately whoever falls into your hands," and he "feels sorry for the Count who does not follow his orders to kill immediately any heretic who falls into his hands." As Giovagnoli says, "he got drunk" on the massacres of Cahors, Tours, Amiens, Tolosa, and he sent the duke of Alba a cape and sword which he had blessed as a reward. Something pathological was possessing him and it was not the God of mercy, nor the Christ through St. Paul, but the vengeful biblical God who was guiding his hand and his mind. And no one more than he would throw himself into the struggle against the infidel Turks, overcoming every obstacle to see the Venetians and the Spaniards united, giving them also ships and money. When he heard the news of the victory at Lepanto in 1571, he burst into tears and exclaimed: "Now, Lord, dismiss your servant in peace!" For a permanent record of this event, he established the Feast of Our Lady of Victory on 7 October, the very day of the battle, which Gregory XIII would move to the first Sunday of that same month, as the Feast of the Our Lady of the Rosary.

However, unbridled fury and persecution of Protestants in Catholic countries had tragic consequences in England. Elizabeth did her part against whoever opposed the Anglican Church, and Mary Stuart was put in prison. The excommunication of the English queen would have no other result than a still more violent persecution. Blood calls for blood, hate begets hate, and this provoked Pius V to make a choice which would be good for the future of the Church of Rome but damaging to the unity in Christ for which he prayed very much.

This pope, a saint for the Catholic Church, carried out his religious despotism conscientiously and one can only marvel with Ranke, "at the contradiction in the fact that those in a religion of innocence and humility, of true mercy, become persecutors!" From this contradiction, death freed Pius V on 1 May 1572. He was first buried in St. Peter's but later moved by Sixtus V to a mausoleum in St. Mary Major.

226. GREGORY XIII (1572–1585)

They had been in conclave only a few hours when Alessandro Farnese, who was busy trying to get the tiara for himself, received a request from Philip II to renounce it for the sake of peace, and although there was no hole in the wall, as in the conclave of 1559, the political message nonetheless did get through despite Pius IV's strict decree on papal elections. Farnese withdrew and within twenty-four hours, on 13 May 1572, Cardinal Ugo Boncompagni was elected pope.

Born in Bologna on 1 January 1502, he had studied law there becoming later a professor at his University, then secretary to Cardinal Parisio in Rome, where he entered the ranks of the Catholic reformists, getting experience at Trent. Appointed bishop by Paul IV, he became a cardinal under Pius V, and a sympathiser of Carlo Borromeo: "*Ecce vir in quo dolus non est,*" the pope said to him while giving him the purple hat. His past as a layman, however, had not been entirely saintly.

He had had a son, Giacomo, whom he had legitimatized, but once he had become a priest, he had not strayed again from the serious and blameless conduct Catholic morality demanded. And in the same manner he was to conduct himself as pope, although he did not have the strength to impose his views on people. He would issue strict laws but was incapable of applying them. Indulgent, he would be overcome by remorse and then go back with harshness to his first decisions. He was a hesitant pope, whom Pasquino stigmatized from the very day he was elected: "*Habemus papam negativum.*" Crowned on 25 May 1572, he assumed the name of Gregory XIII.

In some regards, the Romans breathed more easily during his pontificate for he did not approve excessive severity, even if he followed the path of his predecessor. He did not pursue faithfulness with his subjects as much as he did with the ecclesiastics. He established a commission of cardinals to watch over the obedience of conciliar rules, and expected from the pontifical legates a special dedication to the diplomatic work in foreign countries for a control on bishops, priests and deacons. Everything had to go through the Curia with a growing centralizm in which Cardinal Tolomeo Galli, who had been secretary to Pius IV and appointed by Gregory Secretary of State, excelled. In fact he was the first to take up this position in the modern meaning of the title.

So once the reins had been taken off it, Rome became bolder and freer. As Montaigne notes, "life and property were perhaps never so unsafe as during the times of Gregory XIII." It was a "bastard" city which had fallen into the hands of bandits or of nobles who defended themselves arm in hand, while the militia could not even protect itself, and rewards promised for catching the bandits were of no use at all. Duke Piccolomini of Montemarciano was able to enter Rome boldly with his "mob," all of whom had been reported to the police, and have the pope issue a safe-conduct for his retinue. That was an example of the spirit of tolerance then existing with, on the one side, the sovereignty of the pope with his dogmas, and on the other, the most licentious corruption.

Courtesans lost status and could now more vulgarly be called whores, or streetwalkers. Moreover, pederasty was spreading. According to Montaigne, there was a brotherhood (*confraternità*) in the church of S. Giovanni at Porta Latina of homosexuals who would be married to each other during the Mass, "going through the same rites that we use for weddings. They took communion together, read the same nuptial Gospel and then they slept and lived together."

In effect Gregory XIII wanted to govern in a gentle manner, without the need for police, trying to make the Romans aware of a kind of Catholic ecumenism. In that spirit, he had announced the Jubilee Year of 1575, for which he ordered the building of the German, Greek and English colleges. He invited many students from Greece, and he effusively welcomed ambassadors from far-off Japan, the result of the missionary work of the Jesuits. The latter were the faithful right arm of the pope in the work of ecumenical evangelization, as a result of which he made generous contributions to their Roman college, including the annexed library and museum, which became the imposing cultural complex called the Gregorian University.

In this manner, Gregory wanted "to extricate the Papal State from the confines of Apostolic Romanness," as Sarazani observed, making Rome take on the appearance of a cosmopolitan city, which Montaigne had already recognized as such. However, within the city there "continued to be demonstrations of angry starving people against the brigandage and families organized like armed factions."

The pope's intentions proved in vain and even his son betrayed him. He had raised him to the rank of governor of Castel Sant'Angelo and standard-bearer of the Church, and had arranged his marriage to the sister of the count of Santa Fiora, nephew of Cardinal Sforza, obtaining for him from the king of Spain also an appointment as general. When Giacomo then made the mistake of freeing a University classmate from prison, Gregory wanted to throw him out of Rome, but was moved by the tears of his daughter-in-law. However, he realized that even those of his own blood did not understand him, so he had his elder brother who was en route for Rome to collect the manna from heaven, stopped at Orvieto and sent back to Bologna.

The ecumenical spirit of Gregory XIII in effect failed, and its most negative aspect was revealed that terrible night of St. Bartholomew on the 23rd and 24th of August 1572, as a result of which the hopes for religious peace were shattered. The real reasons for that bloodbath were not of a religious nature, but political and personal, instigated by the unscrupulous Queen Catherine. It is clear that the pope knew nothing about this sudden plan and, as a result, had no hand in the preparations or the carrying out of the massacre. Furthermore, the French court declared that it had aborted a conspiracy against the sovereigns.

But it was how Gregory XIII received the news, that gave the massacre an entirely religious twist by blessing the malefactors and by the solemn celebration of a *Te Deum* in St. Mark's as well as a rite of thanksgiving in St. Louis des Français in his presence. He celebrated with lamps and triduums what he deemed to be danger from which the royals of France escaped. He even had a medal struck in commemoration of the event, and commissioned Vasari to fresco the Royal Hall of the Vatican, along with the *Battle of Lepanto*, with *The Night of St. Bartholomew*. All these demonstrations of rejoicing cannot be approved, and certainly "the bloody zeal against the reformists, who were also Christians," observes Giovagnoli, "did not prevent the good Gregory XIII from absolving, spiritually and physically, a priest named Guercino, called 'king of the countryside' from the forty-four, I repeat, forty-four, homicides he had committed, not out of religious fervour but rather to rob, to steal, and to practice openly the 'noble' profession of the assassin.

Two weights and two measures. Typical too was the reply received by the papal nuncio in Spain, Filippo Sega, from the Secretary of State, Cardinal Galli, in the name of the pope to whom the English Catholic Ely had submitted a proposal to kill Queen Elizabeth: "Whoever removes her from this world for the sake of God, not only has committed no sin but acquires merit, especially considering the sentence issued against her by Pius V." This was like a pact between Machiavelli and St. Francis, and "it is beyond doubt," as Seppelt observes, "that by this reply an open and believable approval was given to political assassination, even though it was not the pope who instigated or commissioned the assassin."

Gregory XIII's ecumenical message was contained in the reform of the calendar in such a constructive manner that even now, five centuries later, it is still valid. The order issued to Christendom to strike ten days off the calendar to convert the dating was heeded and, because it was accepted all over the world, had a universal significance which did not stop then. The sovereigns of Italy, Spain and Portugal "obeyed" immediately, so that 5 October 1582, became 14 October. In December, it was the turn of Bavaria and Catholic areas of Germany and Switzerland, between 1586 and 1587, Poland and Hungary, then Prussia in 1610. However, the great victory came in 1700 with adoption of the new calendar by the Protestant countries, including Great Britain, so stubborn and conservative, and probably even more anti-papal than the German States.

This was surely the most positive ecumenical act of Gregory XIII, even though one cannot say to what extent it redeemed him from a certain ignoble mentality, devoid of evangelical spirit, which continued to make him ignore the possibility of pardon. After the night of St. Bartholomew, through Cardinal Orsini, his nuncio to Charles IX of France, he recommended that the sovereign "insist firmly that the cure so well begun with tough medicine not be ruined by inappropriate humanity!" As assassination does not pay, even less can it find justification on a theological level and death must always be considered, if not as a fact of nature, at least as an act of the divine will.

For Gregory XIII death arrived on 10 April 1585. He was buried in the Chapel of St. Peter to which he had caused the removal of the relics of St. Gregory Nazianzen, called therefore the Gregorian Chapel.

227. SIXTUS V (1585–1590)

The story about Cardinal Felice Peretti attending the conclave, bent and in bad health, using crutches, so as to convince his colleagues to choose him as a temporary candidate or, in any event, as a person without energy who could be easily influenced by the Curia was clearly a fabricated one. Nevertheless, it is clear that he schemed to be elected and made an ally of the powerful Cardinal Ferdinando de' Medici who brought along Luigi d'Este so that in the end his candidature was acceptable to all. He was unanimously elected on 24 April 1585, and crowned on 1 May. He chose the name of Sixtus V.

Born at Grottammare in the Marches on 13 December 1521, like Pius V he came from humble origins and had also helped his father as a young lad in the fields, watching over the pigs. In this case too, someone from a higher social level had taken him away from the pigsty; this time an uncle, a Franciscan, had put him into a school and directed him towards a clerical career. At the age of nine he was already with the Friars Minor in nearby Montalto where he showed his considerable talent by rising rapidly to a top position. He studied at Ferrara and Bologna where he was noted for his exposition of complex theological questions, and in 1552 he was in Rome to give Lenten sermons at SS. Apostoli. His tone was clear, without rhetoric, yet in essence firm and severe. Paul IV heard about him and appointed him Inquisitor in Verona. Peretti was unshakeable in his strictness and had quite a few critics within his own Order. Pius V approved him without reserve and made him Vicar General of the Friars Conventual, bishop of St. Agatha of the Goths and subsequently a cardinal.

Under Gregory XIII, Cardinal Montalto, as he was generally called, was kept away from the Curia, being too critical of the tolerance of the pope towards certain aspects of city life, but he knew how to hold his tongue even when his nephew Francesco was assassinated. Everyone knew that the assassin was a powerful nobleman, Paolo Giordano Orsini, the lover of young Peretti's beautiful wife, Vittoria Accoramboni. But summoned by Gregory XIII to ask him how he should react, Cardinal Montalto replied to forget it, time would heal all wounds. Was this magnanimity or postponed revenge?

When the two lovers were married during the conclave in 1585, convinced they had got away with it, the notification that "the martinet had arrived struck them like lightning," as Sarazani puts it, and not simply for those two, since "dark, rigorous and Franciscan days are facing the evil world dedicated to vice, gambling, duels and whoredom. Farewell to joy." Sixtus began by announcing that deeds of banditry would not be tolerated, that there would be the death penalty for those carrying weapons and that nobles and ambassadors who gave bandits asylum would suffer the same fate since they would be interfering with police activity. For cardinals there was the threat of Castel Sant'Angelo. These were not empty words; on the day of the coronation, four young men were hanged at the Sant'Angelo bridge because they were caught bearing weapons.

Paolo Giordano Orsini and his wife understood that the atmosphere was unhealthy for them and they moved to Bracciano, but even there they did not feel safe as Sixtus V was protecting only obedient nobles who marched erect along the road of Christian morality. It was perfectly safe for the first-born sons of the Orsini and the Colonna, named as assistants to the Holy See, for Roberto Altemps who became duke of Gallese, for Alessandro Sforza, duke of Segni, and for Giuliano Cesarini, duke of Civitacastellana. But Paolo Giordano was like an outlaw and had to escape with Vittoria to Venice and then to Padua. He would die of an infection in his leg, while evading papal authority that wanted him hanged, and Vittoria ended up being stabbed to death by assassins sent by Ludovico Orsini.

So Rome became a police state where agents entered the homes of the powerful and a suspicion was enough to send one to the gallows. Those who gave themselves up could not hope to be pardoned and they would be put to death just the same: "If they had not come and presented themselves, I would have caught them" was the icy comment of Sixtus V.

The death penalty was also applied to the "pimps" and to mothers who put their daughters into prostitution. For the prostitutes themselves, the hard times were back and they were again relegated to a place called the Garden of Evil (Ortaccio) and not allowed to walk the streets in the center of the city. A cleansing of the laity, and a cleansing of the clergy! In a bull of 3 December 1586, Sixtus compared the cardinals around him to the Apostles who paid homage to Christ, and made them swear under oath that they would give up their lives in defense of the Catholic religion. Moreover, he would allow no more cardinals with children or grandchildren, and he would prefer Italian cardinals. "A home-made Church" and a "Roman papal nationalism took roots" to use Sarazani's expression, in the organization of which Sixtus V insisted on "a government which precedes the Faith" because, basically, "the Kingdom of Heaven is far away." And here took shape the novel, ingenious conception of Sixtus V, in which the papacy of modern times finds its raison d'être through good order, political restoration and the refusal of an exclusively evangelical Church. All of this thanks to Luther, the real cause of the change, "an enemy, therefore, necessary for the reaction," as Sarazani again notes, "because he had understood the Italians's lack of religion, complaining loudly about the court of Rome, precisely because Rome with its bad examples would have reduced us to sinners without religion."

And so "Luther was for Sixtus V, just as Marx, Lenin and Stalin were for Pius XII." He was "the demon" who justified papal dictatorship, and Sixtus saw it even in the miraculous events which abounded with plebeian fanaticism. For instance, having gone to see a crucifix which was supposed to be bleeding from the wounds, he took up a hatchet and split the image, saying: "As Christ I adore thee; as a piece of wood I split you." However, sponges soaked in blood were discovered in the wood. It was one of his "braggart" acts as a tough pope, the "stubborn pope" (*papa tosto*), as he was described in Belli's sonnet which referred to the incident of the crucifix and gave rise to the proverb, "Pope Sixtus wouldn't forgive Christ Himself."

> Among all who have had the job of being the vicar of Christ,
> we've never seen such a true Roman figure, a stubborn pope,
> a mad pope as Pope Sixtus. He's the fellow who tried to flog
> anyone who tried to get close to him, not forgiving anyone,
> even Christ Himself; and never broke him secretly.
> Let's thank God that he's now gone; it can't happen again
> for a new strong man to come and get the Church
> into such a mess;
> surely there won't appear so soon another pope
> who would choose the name of Sixtus the Sixth!

The reorganization of the offices of the Roman Curia under the aegis of rigid strictness was one of the most important steps taken by Sixtus V, who succeeded in giving the College of Cardinals the structure which it has kept up right to our own century. He established fifteen congregations of cardinals which had the task of doing much of the work that in the past was done by consistories, resulting in a more rational division of labor in the administrative work of the Church, even though all of them had to report to the pope. This restructuring permitted Sixtus V, by virtue of his absolute power, to ignore certain strict rules which he himself had issued about the minimum age for appointment of cardinals, as when he named his nephew, fifteen-year-old Alessandro Peretti, one of them, and favored and enriched his relatives.

Reestablishment of order in the Papal State was the premise for measures that Sixtus V took, also in the interest of the faithful, such as increasing agricultural activity and temporarily draining a part of the Pontine Marshes. Everybody had bread, even if the reorganization of papal finances required new imposts and sales taxes. Giovagnoli notes ironically that "in order to amass wealth for his relatives and the Church, to which when he died he left a patrimony held in Castel Sant'Angelo of five million gold *scudi*, this good pope subjected to a sales tax all food, including wheat, oil, wine, meat, greens, fish, so that the income of the State which, when he ascended the throne amounted only to 1,746,814 *scudi*, by the time of his death had risen to 2,576,814 *scudi*, all at the expense of the people suffering from hunger, misery and desolation."

A dialogue between Pasquino and Marforio echoes him:
MARFORIO:
"How can we live, Pasquino, when all the food costs more
because of the taxes imposed by Sixtus?"
PASQUINO:
"And who told you you have to live under Sixtus?
A few at a time, they must all die on the gallows, no?"

It is true that the enormous amounts raised made possible an increase of the arts and sciences through a huge construction program in Rome. Indeed, Sixtus renewed the water resources of the city, restoring the aqueduct of Alexander Severus up to the "water show" which he called "Felice," in the Monti district, and this led to the building of new houses on the hills of the Esquiline, the Viminal and the Quirinal which until then had been abandoned.

And it was precisely the urban planning which radically altered the city with clearings and opening of new wide streets that, in the pope's mind, would make access by pilgrims to the Seven Churches easier. He actually wanted to organize regular pilgrimages to Rome from all over the world, including America, convinced as he was of the revived conception in the Christian meaning of the *caput mundi*. But the novelty was the erection of the obelisks in Piazza del Popolo and in front of the basilicas of St. John Lateran, St. Mary Major and in the center of the square of St. Peter, beyond which soared the by then completed cupola of Michelangelo. These obelisks really helped to give the revived center of Christianity an original splendor.

Nevertheless, from this christianized *caput mundi* went his message of peace to the whole world, for he would never have wanted a war between Christians. In France, though, there was the war of the three Henry's and Sixtus V's attitude was to wait prudently, while in England, once Mary Stuart had been executed, he realized that Elizabeth was great even in her heresy, and as such invincible. And within himself he must have thought what a shame it was that that queen was a "demon" like Luther. Had she been a Catholic, Pastor records, she would have been his favorite.

However, when Philip II bet everything on the Invincible Armada, though the pope was of the opinion that only war could be used against Elizabeth and even shared the costs of the fleet, in his heart he was convinced that it would be like hitting a stone wall. He did not believe in miracles like Pius V. The logic of a political "system" which did not admit prayer but involved the tough law of the struggle for survival weighed upon him. And England did survive.

This pope of iron could only be vanquished by malaria, and choosing not to follow the advice of his doctors, he was up until the very end, getting out of bed as soon as his strength allowed it to control personally government matters. He died on 27 August 1590, during a violent storm in Rome. People said that he had signed a pact with the devil thanks to which he had risen so high, and that when the agreed time limit had expired, the Evil One had come to take his soul away in the very midst of a hurricane. A myth in the major key of hatred, quite different from that odd one which had him leaning on his crutches during the conclave.

He was buried in St. Mary Major, his beloved church, in the sepulcher he had had built in front of the mausoleum erected by him for his venerated Pius V.

228. URBAN VII (1590)

Sixtus V had not finished the work on a Draconian law for papal elections when he passed away, and, as a result, conclaves which came after him continued to be more or less "open." For a certain period of time the king of Spain controlled them, as guarantor and strenuous defender of Catholicism. His ambassadors had the good taste not to be seen in the neighborhood of the conclave in that month of September 1590, but they did send the Sacred College a list of five cardinals agreeable to the king. There was an agreement on Gian Battista Castagna, very acceptable to the grand duke of Tuscany, and he was elected on 15 September 1590, assuming the name of Urban VII.

Born in Rome on 4 August 1521, he was made a cardinal only in 1583. He had been the archbishop of Rossano Calabro and, on a doctrinal level, he appeared to be close to the ideas of Carlo Borromeo. It seems that he was a very charitable person because as soon as he was elected he had a large part of his patrimony distributed among the poor of the city. He also informed his vast number of relatives that it was not the time to seek benefices and high living, insisting that, aside from managing the Church, his main purpose would be to give assistance to the needy.

Malaria carried him off, however, after only 13 days of pontificate, the briefest in history. In fact, he died on 27 September 1590, leaving his paternal inheritance to the Confraternity of the Annunciation at S. Maria sopra Minerva so that the estate would be distributed as a dowry to wives of indigent husbands. He was buried in the same church in a monument erected for him out of gratitude by the same Confraternity.

229. GREGORY XIV (1590–1591)

During the vacant see period after the death of Urban VII, St. Malachy's prophecy about the popes appeared. I mentioned it in the biography of Celestine II, the first of the popes to whom the famous list of one hundred and eleven sayings made reference.

It might have been a method like another to facilitate betting on a future pope, since in the new conclave there was again a list of seven names acceptable to the king of Spain. But this time the pressure from the ambassadors of Philip II was stronger, trampling on all the rules about "closure," and opposing other candidatures with a real veto.

So Cardinal Niccolò Sfondrati was elected. Born in Somma Lombardo near Cremona on 11 February 1535, he had been sickly as a youth and seemed unlikely to live long, and by his election on 5 December 1590, the College of Cardinals appeared to be biding its time. He was consecrated three days later and took the name of Gregory XIV.

He was not someone prepared for his serious task. An ascetic with angelic habits, he was a friend of Louis Gonzaga who would die of the plague in June 1591. Aware of his inadequacy and his naiveté in affairs of State, he put blind faith in his nephew, Paolo Emilio Sfondrati, whom he appointed Cardinal and Secretary of State, which was the ruin of the policy established by Sixtus V.

The problem was caused by France on whose account the "stubborn pope" had adopted a wait-and-see policy. Gregory XIV promised the Catholic League, supported by Philip II, a subsidy of 15,000 gold *scudi*, excommunicated Henry IV in a bull, and sent to France a mercenary army paid for with the money accumulated by Sixtus V.

Luckily that mad venture came to an end with the death of Gregory XIV on 16 October 1591. He was buried in the Gregorian Chapel in St. Peter's.

230. INNOCENT IX (1591)

During the conclave after the death of Gregory XIV, Philip II instructed his ambassadors not to interfere with the election proceedings, but the cardinals realized that it would be better to hurry in order to avoid pressures. They unravelled the matter in two days and, on 30 January 1591, elected Giovanni Antonio Facchinetti, who was well known to be acceptable to Philip II.

He was another old man, born in Bologna on 20 July 1519, and had been a nuncio in Venice at the time of the league against the Turks. Like his predecessor, he was ailing and was unable to stand on his feet for very long so it was again an interim pontificate. He could hardly get out of bed to be crowned on 9 February with the name of Innocent IX. Then, from under the blankets, he continued to send issue incitements to war against Henry IV and to send financial assistance.

He died on 30 December 1591, and was buried in a simple sarcophagus in the Vatican Grottoes.

231. CLEMENT VIII (1592—1605)

The fifty-two cardinals meeting in conclave after three popes had died in the course of one year were in agreement on one thing, that it was vital to elect a person who could provide assurance about his health to ensure a lengthy pontificate. For the rest, they were divided over whether the new pope should be severe or conciliatory with the Protestants and what stance to take with France. The cardinals were split into two groups, one meeting in the Sistine Chapel, the other in the Pauline. The favorite was the Cardinal of Sanseverino, the most ardent supporter of Spain, and toughest member of the Inquisition, with fingers also in France's pie. His involvement in everything to be was too much to be elected. Meetings between the parties and debates went on for nearly a month and there were those, such as Cardinal della Rovere, who died before the work was completed. But they ended by coming to an agreement on the last cardinal wanted by Spain, Ippolito Aldobrandini, who was elected on 30 January 1592.

Born in Fano in 1536 in a family of Florentine origin, hostile to the Medici, according to Muratori, he was considered a person "of great merit, for the chastity of his habits, his brilliant mind, his writings and his experience in worldly matters." He had been a member of the Sacra Rota, and Sixtus V had raised him to the rank of cardinal, sending him then as a legate to Poland. He was crowned on 9 February and took the name of Clement VIII.

He continued his path of piety also as pope, along the dietetic-spiritual lines of Pius V. He fasted very often and strictly, went to confession every day, meditated and prayed at fixed hours, celebrated Mass every day and was evidently moved during the solemn act of consecration. Every year, during the course of one day, he made fifteen pilgrimages to the principal churches of Rome. The apex was reached during the Jubilee of 1600, with ceremonies of penitence and devotion organized in a definite and systematic manner, and with commissioners for lodging and the supply of food. So Rome took on a serious look.

Away with gambling and Carnival amusements! In came choreographic performances "with crosses, flags and sumptuous images of blessed saints," as announced in the published Notices. An example was the sacred performance given on 9 May by the Company of Mercy from Foligno which, "by torch light wound through the city, carrying the mysteries representing the passion, death and resurrection of Christ."

That Holy Year was also to be, in the pope's intention, a restoration of peace between him and the Romans, who had witnessed the two famous trials of the Cenci and of Giordano Bruno, both of which ended in death sentences and which the people, for the most part in favor of the condemned persons, considered typical expressions of a dictatorial regime.

As is well known, the beheading of the lovely Beatrice Cenci has often seen as a judicial error and, between the legend and the reality, the Roman noble lady became a martyr and a heroine of numerous literary pieces as in Stendhal's chronicle, Guerrazzi's novel, Moravia's play, and Drudi's recent text. It is true that Beatrice, along with her brother Giacomo and with her stepmother Lucrezia, had their father Francesco, a dissolute and brutal man, killed and that she was condemned according to the criminal law of that time. There were various reasons for the unexpected and special severity of the verdict, given the semi-impunity of nobles up until then, including strictly political ones, with the quarrel over the family's property which went to the relatives of the pope and all that gave food for thought. And Pasquino recorded it in a dialogue with Marforio:

> MARFORIO:
> "What crimes did the Cenci family commit,
> according to Holy Father Aldobrandini?"
> PASQUINO:
> "They had too much money."

On the other hand, the sentencing of Giordano Bruno, a Dominican priest from Nola, a former professor at the Sorbonne and the author of essays clearly heretical in the framework of a pantheistic philosophical system, was an extreme example of what signified Catholic restoration of that period, which without a drop of human compassion opposed his words, even if not orthodox, with death. It is important to remember how Bruno had replied during a trial in Venice to his inquisitors: "I reject the accusation; I hate all errors, like any doubt about the doctrine of the Church."

In Rome he had earlier explained that the Holy Office had misinterpreted his ideas and that they were not intended to be heretical. The trial took seven years "and between detailed and exhausting interrogations, all kinds of threats, and atrocious torture, his spirit must have been broken," as Molinari observes. Perhaps he finally admitted heresy, by then being incapable of defending himself, because the Avviso of his sentence to be burnt at the stake states he was "a heretic, in full command of his senses." It is almost certain, Seppelt notes that when "the judges of the Holy Office in 1599 issued their sentence of death for Giordano Bruno, they were not at all convinced of his guilt."

And the Holy Year, "which was supposed to be the Year of the Pardon," according to the anticlerical Domenico Berti, witnessed Bruno at the stake on the 17 February on Campo de' Fiori where, in 1889, the Romans erected a monument to him as a symbol of human freedom and of the right to disagree. In fact, fasting and prayers aside, Clement VIII certainly saw in people like Giordano Bruno elements of danger to him because they were critical of his manner of wielding power, and the Dominican was by no means the only victim of the Inquisition of those days.

Yet this pope, no matter how ascetic, liked elegance and luxury,—apart from the parenthesis of the Jubilee Year—as shown by the fact that he began to live in the "summer" residence of the Quirinal, as yet unfinished but already full of splendid frescoes in the sumptuously decorated halls. Perhaps for this reason he so frequently recited the *Mea culpa*.

Moreover, although as cardinal he had criticized nepotism, as soon as he was raised to the papal throne he promoted to the rank of cardinal two nephews, Cinzio and Pietro Aldobrandini, who together took over the Secretariat of State. These two, with the Jesuit Cardinal Roberto Bellarmino, who managed the principal affairs of the Church, received large incomes, as did also another nephew, a layman, Gian Lorenzo Aldobrandini, whose son was named a cardinal when he was barely fourteen years old.

That Cinzio and Pietro patronized the arts, the former by protecting Tasso, by then a psychopath and the official poet of the Counter-Reformation with his blessed *Gerusalemme conquistata*, and the latter by building a sumptuous villa at Frascati, was of no importance since they were only for their personal advantage. Neither the clerical poetry of a mad poet with his bigotry, nor that costly building by Carlo Maderno with its panoramic terraces, its statues and fountains, which merely brought the finances of the Curia to another collapse, were able to save Clement from dishonor.

The most important event of the pontificate of Clement VIII was certainly his reconciliation with Henry IV. The king's abjuration in 1593 at Saint Denis, with his solemn oath to live and die within the Apostolic Roman Catholic Church, earned him the immediate annulment of the excommunication by the archbishop of Bourges, confirmed by the absolution declared solemnly by the pope in St. Peter's two years later. Henry IV was recognized as the king of all the French. "Paris is well worth a Mass," the king announced, which fully explained the entire political significance of his abjuration. Even Pasquino had understood it:

> Henry was not a Catholic but for the love of the crown
> he's willing to become an Apostolic Catholic;
> if he gets his turn, Clement, the Roman Pontiff,
> might become a Turk or a Lutheran tomorrow.

France became again a great Catholic power, a counterbalance to Spain, and between the two, the papacy, although trapped in Italy in the maw of the Spanish dominions, could now joust more freely. So, Clement VIII felt obliged to do what he could to bring these two powers to peaceful settlement, and that took place in 1598 at Vervins. Henry IV compensated Rome by helping the Papal Estate recover Ferrara that had belonged in fiefdom to the Holy See from the time of Matilda of Tuscany, but was ruled over by the Este family.

Duke Caesar had resolved to defend his own possession by force of arms, but, faced with excommunication, the threat of interdiction and the French troops, he had to give up in January 1598. He lost the duchy but was able to retain the feudal right, the archive, the library and the family's art collection. Clement VIII was so happy to recover the territory that, despite his gout and the expenses of travelling, he wanted to move himself and his whole court to Ferrara to reside there until the Holy Year.

Clement was a restless soul and, as soon as he was able to, he travelled, not for apostolic reasons but simply because he loved to. To keep up that life, given the precarious state of the Curia's treasury, he obviously had to levy new taxes and reorganize the entire fiscal system of the Papal State. So, after he had got rid of the fifteen committees of cardinals created by Sixtus V, he ran the business office by himself, with help from his dear nephews. He insisted also on the application of the decrees of the Council of Trent and, for example, he published a new Index of Prohibited Books, while having printed a large number of religious works to spread the new Catholic teachings.

On this score he did not gain much from Henry IV whose Edict of Nantes was in fact an "edict of tolerance" and which, if it carried with it the reestablishment of the Catholic faith throughout France, recognized at the same time the freedom of worship of the Huguenots. Clement mistakenly thought he could restore in France, as in Spain, yet another Inquisition, which would stamp out any opposition to Catholicism, but he had to give in when he was faced with the obligation that the French sovereign had assumed toward his subjects. While England was ever more inexorably lost, in Spain Clement found satisfaction in the activities of the Inquisition, although the new king, Philip III, was a bigot with no realistic political attitude. All these were the warning signs of the Thirty Years War.

Gout continued to torment the pope, forcing him in later years to spend much time inactive in bed. Then he suffered a stroke during a session of the Inquisition tribunal and never recovered. He died on 3 March 1605, and was buried in St. Peter's. However, Paul V later had a mausoleum built for him in the Borghese Chapel of St. Mary Major, although the work took a long time and his remains could only be moved there in 1646.

What Muratori, reporting the words of Cardinal Bentivoglio, wrote about Clement is significant, because he saw in his death and the extinction of the Aldobrandini family a sort of divine punishment. "Pope Clement died, Cardinal Aldobrandini also following some revolting disputes with Paul V; as well as five nephews, including two cardinals; all the males of that family died and at the end there was no one to carry on the line or all the grandeur of their own blood." There are those who see in this result a certain justice for Giordano Bruno.

232. LEO XI (1605)

At the death of Clement VIII, Spain was still able to dominate the conclave and Philip III gave precise instructions to his ambassador to have a cardinal elected who would not be opposed to his policy of hegemony. It was difficult to lobby sixty-two cardinals and there were those, such as Bellarmino, who cried "scandal!" when they found out that, contrary to the rules, many of the votes were for three cardinals not yet twenty years old.

Men of conscience like him favored Baronio, who was especially hated by the Spaniards because of his harsh criticism of their privileges in southern Italy. However the Spanish cardinals did not make it. The French, led by François de Joyeux, joined forces with Pietro Aldobrandini, and so, on 1 April 1605, Alessandro de'Medici was elected.

Born in Florence on 2 June 1535, into an offshoot of the famous family, he had worked in the Curia under Gregory XIII as the representative of Grand Duke Cosimo. Later he had been bishop of Pistoia and archbishop of Florence, becoming a cardinal in 1583. Under Clement VIII, as emissary to France, he had helped reduce the influence of the Huguenots and to shore up the Catholic Church.

He was crowned on 10 April, taking the name of Leo XI, and he moved into the Lateran on 17 April, but on that very day he fell ill and so was not able to accomplish anything. He is said to have belonged to the group of cardinals opposed to worldliness and devoted to the ascetic lifestyle. He died on 27 April 1605, and was buried in St. Peter's.

233. PAUL V (1605–1621)

Despite the numerous papal decrees, Catholic nations such as Austria, France and Spain went on using more or less unscrupulous methods to get the papacy for a candidate of theirs. On the death of Leo XI, Philip III managed only to avoid the election of Baronio and of Bellarmino, who once again voiced his indignation over certain intrigues. There were stormy sessions for eight days until on 16 May 1605, Cardinal Camillo Borghese, a member of no particular faction, was elected.

Born in Rome on 17 September 1552, into a middle-class family of Siena, he had studied and practiced law in Perugia and Bologna until he had entered the ecclesiastical career, and had become a diplomat in Spain under Clement VIII who had made him a cardinal. As Vicar of Rome and an Inquisitor, he had not involved himself with any particular faction in order to avoid making enemies. He was crowned in St. Peter's on 17 May and assumed the name of Paul V.

A zealous reformer, he was resolved to apply the decisions of Trent to the clergy and did so immediately, from the obligation of residence imposed also on cardinals, without exception, to the respect for the strict cloister for the religious Orders practicing it. For this reason, he approved the charters of new congregations, such as the Oratory of St. Philip Neri and the Chierici. He conceded privileges also to the Theatines, the Barnabites, the Camillini, and the Capuchins, who became important for the internal reform of many European countries.

Impressive too was the development of missions in America, India and Africa with the significant concession that the Jesuits managed to obtain from the pope for China where the use of Chinese was authorized for the liturgy, an exceptional event that considerably facilitated the spreading of the Gospel. This modern concept was extended to the rest of the world only after Vatican Council II.

All these initiatives would lead one to think of a pope dedicated exclusively to works to do with the faith according to a rigorously ordered mind, yet one open to new ideas. In actual fact, Paul V gradually revealed "an increasing personalization of power," according to the historian, Alberto Caracciolo, which ended by his "moving further down the road of absolutism."

That he would not accept any kind of criticism regarding his work was clear just a few days after his coronation when he condemned to death a certain Piccinardi of Cremona, author of a defamatory pamphlet against Clement VIII, in which Piccinardi compared Clement's atrocities with those of the Roman Emperor Tiberius, even though the piece was not published. Then came a disagreement with Venice, which had prohibited the establishment of monasteries in its territory as well as legacies of property to clergymen, without permission from the Senate of the republic.On top of this the city-state refused to extradite to Rome two priests found guilty of common crimes. The pope thought that was an insult to his authority, a rebellion by the diocese of Venice against the primacy of the Roman see, and he issued an interdiction against the Lagoon city-state.

The dispute became absurd since Mass continued to be celebrated regularly in Venice, despite the papal decree. Not only that, but the Orders were divided in defense of one or the other position, with, on the one hand, Paolo Sarpi, consultant of the republic and obedient to the doge and on the other, the Theatines, the Capuchins and the Jesuits led by Bellarmino, loyal to the pope. A lively "war of pens" ensued which, in view of the prestige of both Sarpi and Bellarmino, put into turmoil Catholic Europe and the dispute was only resolved due to the mediation of Cardinal François de Joyeux and Henry IV.

The pope would not give in, however, and making the best of a bad show issued strict directives to the legates at the various States and detailed rules for governments in an *Istruzione* concerning their duties. He insisted on respect and firm cooperation against whoever raised a critical voice or did not conform. He could count blindly upon Spain and the Habsburgs, and then there was the Thirty Years War.

As for internal policy, being a clever economist, Caracciolo notes, and faced with "many serious failures of banks" and the "desire to avoid excessive interference by private capitalists in the work of the Papal Office," Paul took the measure "little noted at first but in the long run very significant, of creating a depository bank at the Hospital of Santo Spirito which was in line with the first public banks being established in other countries."

These actions, however, would not suffice to put right the finances of the Papal State, because Paul V also went ahead with a limitless nepotism, lover as he was of elegance and art. His nephew, Scipione Caffarelli, aged only twenty-six was elevated to the rank of cardinal and received the name and the coat-of-arms of the Borghese family. Paul V loaded him with lucrative titles to the extent that this nephew had an annual income of about 140,000 scudi. Scipione's brothers also received important positions and huge sums of money, and the Borghese family attained a high level in Roman society, showing off their wealth with luxurious living. Pasquino, of course, raged about it:

> After the Caraffa, the Medici and the Farnese,
> now we have to enrich the Borghese.

One way to invest this money was to set up a precious gallery of paintings and sculptures, ancient and modern, with which the palaces and the villas of the entire family were adorned. Among all the buildings, the Villa Borghese near Porta del Popolo on the Pincio benefited mostly from the precious artistic treasures, as desired by Cardinal Scipione, who ended up being considered a great man also for his generosity, and being called the "Delight of Rome."

But the pope himself wanted to leave the mark of his own personal generosity through an architectural embellishment of the city. These included hydraulic works to control the sources of the Tiber and prevent the frequent floods, and the aqueduct ending at the fountain of the Acqua Paolo on the Janiculum, the building of the Pauline Chapel in the Quirinal, and the façade of the basilica of St. Peter by Maderno.

All of this required huge sums of money, and the measures taken were clearly inadequate, without taking into account that "for political purposes the Church directed public money for expenses especially outside the State," as Caracciolo again observes, which meant that "things were going toward a debit situation that circumstantial income or attempted reforms in public administration and finance could not resolve." To think that at the outbreak of the Thirty Years War in 1618, Paul V agreed to grant large amounts of money to the league of the Catholic princes which cost the Curia 625,000 florins in two and a half years!

All that for a war which was seemingly only religious, but in reality political from all points of view. And that for a pope who had declared that he did not want to get involved in politics. Which goes to prove how expensive it can be to make false statements. He drew consolation from the victory at Montagna Bianca in 1620 which guaranteed domination for the Catholic faction within the empire for another ten years. There were solemn hymns of thanksgiving on 3 December of that year in the church of the Germans in Rome, S. Maria dell'Anima.

While the subject of religion, it must be recalled that under Paul V the theologians of the Holy Office condemned on 24 February 1616, the Copernican theory, making one of the most awful errors in history. In particular, the claim that "the sun is the center of the world and thus incapable of moving" was deemed to be "stupid and absurd popular science, heretical in form" for disagreeing with the literal meaning of Holy Scripture. Moreover, the proposition "that the earth is not the center of the world or immovable but rather moves by itself" was banned because it was erroneous from a religious point of view.

Two days later, Galilei, the great man who had hurried to Rome to defend Copernicanism, in a private talk with Cardinal Bellarmino took note of the matter, but had the cardinal give him a certificate that he had received no penance for his defense of the Polish scientist, but merely a *denuntia* in the *Index*. Instead, Father Seguri, a personal enemy of Galilei, wrote a fantasy on the a "private talk" which claimed that the cardinal had warned the scientist to abjure the forbidden opinion under pain of prison, ordering that he should not teach or defend it in any way. Galilei is supposed to have consented and promised to obey that "command."

This report is considered apocryphal and if Seguri wrote it he did so on his own initiative, thereby creating something which could be useful to him in the future. The occasion arose during the trial which Galilei underwent under Urban VIII. Bellarmino was to die in 1621 and could not testify in Galilei's favor even if he had wished to. The ecclesiastical tribunal thus committed an unpardonable mistake, the origins of which point to the pontificate of Paul V who, by his condemnation of Copernicus, had given the go-ahead for this infamous action.

Paul V died on 28 January 1621, and was buried in the Vatican but was later moved to the Borghese Chapel in St. Mary Major.

234. GREGORY XV (1621–1623)

The ambassadors from the Catholic princes did not manage this time either to put their own candidate on the papal throne, despite the fact that the French one stayed as long as he could with the French cardinals before the conclave began on 8 February 1621. The Sacred College was more than ever determined to choose a person who was politically neutral and devoted only to the interests of the Catholic Church, so the choice fell on Alessandro Ludovisi.

Born in a noble family in Bologna on 9 January 1554, he had been a pupil at the Jesuit College in Rome, a guarantee of the continuation of a doctrinal position. Having degrees in civil and canon law from Bologna, he had been named by Paul V archbishop of Bologna and later cardinal. He was not a very healthy man and many thought his pontificate would again be an interim one. In some regards it would be, considering that he would reign only for two years, but he would leave his imprint through important initiatives. He was crowned on 14 February 1621, and took the name of Gregory XV.

He followed the tradition of scandalous nepotism between pope and nephew and this time it was the turn of Ludovico Ludovisi, also a student of the Jesuits, appointed a few days after the coronation as the cardinal chamberlain, and endowed with lucrative ecclesiastical benefices. The enormous wealth amassed by Ludovico was used to acquire the duchy of Zagarolo from the penniless Colonnas, for the building of the magnificent Villa Ludovisi, and for the establishment, now in fashion, of a precious gallery of many antique artistic works, including the famous Ludovisi Throne. In brief, the Ludovisi family achieved the heights of the other great families, following the example of the Borgheses. Perhaps it was through a twinge of conscience over the accumulation of so much money off the backs of the contributors and the stealing of lands of the Church, that they gave so much money away to the poor. Ludovico himself gave annually 32,000 scudi to charitable institutions and, during periods of famine, he maintained at his expense 150 hospital beds at the Lateran and provided meals to the poor. In particular, to repay the Church for what he had extorted, he built the church of St. Ignatius to be run by the Jesuits. So the traffic in money closed its circle; a Jesuit pope had enriched his Jesuit nephew who repaid his Society with a new church after that of the Gesù, already in function.

Although Gregory XV had been elected because of his peaceful nature and because he was outside any of the political factions, he ended up, like his predecessor, by surmounting the earlier neutrality of the nations involved in the Thirty Years War, and urged the Catholic forces of the empire to take the offensive. He was even disposed to contribute financially to the undertaking, promising to pay to the emperor and the Catholic league about two million florins within two and a half years. Not counting that this attitude of his brought serious quarrels with France, which was then led by the famous Cardinal Richelieu, and papal diplomacy had to take great pains to avoid the risks of new schisms within the Catholic States.

Gregory XV knew basically that he could not ignore what should be his chief task, which was the establishment of missionary activity, and he did this by founding the Congregation of the *Propaganda Fide* which became the headquarters of all the missionary lands. It was created on 6 January 1622, "in the conviction that the highest priority of the Pastor is the spreading of the Christian faith," according to his own words. In fact, this institution is a milestone in the history of the Church of Rome and as well as a decisive development in universal evangelization. It was an activity of profoundly Christian inspiration, even if it meant at the same time it had a civil duty to establish the mission program by means of compromises in the countries to be evangelized.

The compromises left signs of martyrdom but also determined the interference of the Holy See in the internal problems of some nations through political involvement with religious aims.

It was also to Gregory XV's merit that he provided two new constitutions for papal elections, which were still at the mercy of the three great Catholic countries of that time. The *Aeterni Patris* of 1621 and the *Decet Romanorum Pontificem* of 1622 reaffirmed the conclave and the two-thirds majority statutes, as well as regulating the procedure and format of the ballot, all in accord with a detailed ceremonial rite. Those rules have remained substantially in force until the present century, but Gregory XV was wrong in thinking he had thereby stopped the Catholic powers from interfering with the election. Their interference justs assumed a different form and consisted of the right to veto to which they would always have recourse in order to oppose any unacceptable candidate. In sum, the Church of Rome was unable to get off its back interference by lay powers in the choice of its head because compromises went on, regardless of Reformation and Counter-Reformation, and continued to affect, in a thousand different ways, the Church's "pastoral" function in the world.

Gregory XV died on 8 July 1623 in the Quirinal Palace and was buried in the Church of St.Ignatius.

235. URBAN VIII (1623–1644)

In a hot summer, with malaria spreading, the cardinals went into conclave in July 1623, to elect the successor to Gregory XV, and did everything except follow scrupulously the rules which that pope had laid down about respecting the closure and the non-interference of persons outside the Sacred College. It was a struggle among three politicized factions of the various tendencies, which the Thirty Years War had made even more evident. They moved ahead by exclusion, under the decisive control of Spain, and nearly came to blows. Then the conclave began to look like a hospital with more than ten of the cardinals down with a fever. Out of fear of malaria, they reached an agreement on Matteo Barberini, who was elected on 6 August. He was crowned on 29 September and assumed the name of Urban VIII.

Born in Florence in 1568 to a wealthy family of merchants, he had been the nuncio to Paris and Paul V had raised him to cardinal in 1606 because of the good work he had accomplished in France. That nation was to remain close to his heart as pope, influencing the final fatal political errors of the Papal State on the international level.

Urban VIII in fact participated in the Thirty Years War under the illusion that there was a religious reason involved, demonstrating his lack of political sense before the great Richelieu. The latter, although he was a cardinal in the Church of Rome, tended exclusively to the interests of the French nation, making alliances with the Lutheran princes, halting the Catholic restoration in Germany and thus causing the final collapse of the pope as arbiter and intermediary among the nations in conflict. "Raison d'état" was the absolute determining factor for Richelieu in order to break up the threatening power of the Habsburg empire in Europe, which made any Counter-Reformation a secondary priority. Urban VIII sent the emperor and the Catholic league financial subsidies, but he allowed himself to be "tricked and strongly influenced by the unscrupulous policies of Richelieu," as Seppelt observes, and certainly "his attitude should have been different had he subordinated all his efforts to the great goal of the Catholic restoration, instead of making decisions mainly as the temporal head of the Papal State."

However, from Urban VIII one could not expect that. He was chiefly a patron of the arts and an outrageous nepotist, and, as such, was mediocre through the very provincialism of his political outlook. Moreover, he was a poet. Even as a young man he had composed poems in Latin and in the vulgate, in the rich baroque style of the period, and continued to produce them, polishing them with extreme care often to the detriment of the content. He had them published, in 1637, as the work of *Maphei Cardinalis Barberini*, but as pope got them praised by those poets he had invited to court in order to enhance the Christianization of poetry in line with the Counter-Reformation.

The best known of these were Francesco Bracciolini who had ridiculed pagan gods in his comic-heroic poem, *Lo scherno degli Dei* (The Scorn of the Gods), for which he won the citizenship of Rome, and Giovanni Ciampoli who, in his poems, exalted the coronation of the pope and his efforts toward peace among peoples. Gabriello Chiabrera from distant Savona praised him on the occasion of the Holy Year of 1625:

> The great Urban reopens the Doors of Grace and Pardon,
> and guides our footsteps where one can enjoy it.

But the poets closest to Urban were two Jesuits, a Pole named Casimir Sarbiewski and an Alsatian, Jacques Balde, who helped him revise hymns in the *Breviario romano* (Roman breviary). But, as Castiglioni notes, "the editing of the hymns, which the pope-poet himself supervised, resulted in a form metrically correct but often at the expense of the thought and inspiration."

It was, to be sure, a divertissement in line with the poetic concessions of the times, and in this pope there was a hint of Leo X who was also a poet and protector of would-be poets. It pleased him to entertain them in his summer residence at Castel Gandolfo and to see them inspired by the splendid villa redecorated by Carlo Maderno! Each one declaimed his lines in that peaceful place which the pope himself praised in a Latin poem dedicated to his friend, Lorenzo Magalotti.

However, Pope Barberini's patronage did not stop here. It was he who gave Rome its baroque imprint having recognized the genius in Lorenzo Bernini. This artist was responsible for the solemn bronze baldachin above the tomb of St. Peter with its bas-reliefs marking the concept of *Mater Ecclesia* with the face of a birth-giving mother in pain and of a baby born smiling at life, the design of the sepulchral monument which was supposed to be erected in St. Peter's for Matilda of Canossa, and the pope's mausoleum which was to be placed on the right side of the apse in the Vatican basilica. So, after 170 years of work, Urban VIII was finally able to consecrate the new church in 1621, even though the work of the embellishment would continue inside and the finishing of the piazza with the famous colonnade would be achieved only in 1667.

But, again, the buildings of this pope were not limited to the completion of the church of the Prince of the Apostles. Many buildings in the city bear the emblem of the bees, the sign of their restoration by the Barberini pope, but also of the generous nepotism which characterized him. In fact, he "celebrated" what a chronicler of the period sarcastically called the "feast" of nepotism, by the way in which he enriched all his relatives with money, property, important positions and incomes, so that the heraldic bees of the Barberini, originally gadflies, infested all Rome:

> Pasquino:
> "Bees that Heaven sent to Roman ground
> to ruin whatever of beauty there is,
> show us now the wax as we eat the sweet honey you have made."
> The Bees:
> "Greedy pigs, what do you want?
> Crude wax and honey are at war
> and the blood which is shed on the earth is for us."

Urban VIII raised his Capuchin brother and two nephews to the rank of cardinal, while the father, Carlo Barberini, received such large donations that he was able to buy huge areas of land, quickly becoming one of the richest landowners in the Papal State. Ranke, Pastor, and Grisar wrote long disquisitions on the actual amount of money received by Cardinal Francesco and by one nephew, Taddeo. It is not very important whether those sums amounted to one hundred million *scudi* or not, but it was unjustifiable and shameful that relatives of the pope should have taken all this money that belonged to the Papal State. And this is not counting the benefices obtained by the other Barberini cardinal, Antonio, with the income from twenty abbeys, priories and *commende*, as well as the money frequently given to all the relatives through the banks in Bologna, Perugia, and Ferrara.

The construction of the Barberini Library with its collection of precious manuscripts and books in the Palazzo Barberini at the foot of the Quirinal, and numerous churches, all commissioned to famous artists such as Carlo Maderno, Pietro da Cortona, and Andrea Sacchi, in addition to Bernini, mentioned above, did make for a splendidly baroque Rome. But the people, as usual, paid the price through various taxes levied to meet the expenses, since the sums paid for indulgences during the Jubilee of 1625 would not have been sufficient.

> And the pope earned the nickname of "the taxing pope"
> because of the new taxes:
> Urban the Eighth with the handsome beard,
> when the Jubilee ended, laid on the taxes.

And there was a series of *Pasquinades* on the subject, as in the case of the tax on wine to pay for the work on the Trevi Fountain:

> Since Urban soured the wine with his taxes,
> the folks in the Quirinal added the water.

Again, a chronicler of the day noted that "Rome was flooded with drawings showing a poor priest who was begging for alms from the Church to keep him alive and the Church responding as follows: 'Alas, I do not have a cent: Barberini has all my money.'"

To complicate matters was the war resulting from Barberini's desire to take over the duchy of Castro and Ronciglione, belonging to Odoardo Farnese, who managed to defend his property and, after being excommunicated, to advance on Rome with his troops, and defeat the papal army. This was a blow for the pope and his family; the vassal had won against his sovereign, who had to lift the excommunication and back-pedal. But it also showed the need to reinforce the "defenses" of Rome and the Papal State with new techniques and war machines. Bastions were added to Castel Sant'Angelo, countless fortifications were built in several cities such as Castelfranco, called "Urban's Fort," and especially in Civitavecchia which was fitted out like a military port.

To furnish the pieces of artillery for these fortifications, the bronze beams from the atrium of the Pantheon were used. And Pasquino did not miss this opportunity to apply his biting sarcasm, coining the famous quip: "*Quod non fecerunt Barbari, fecerunt Barberini.*" In brief, it is obvious that the pope and his relatives were disliked, and in his last years that hatred provoked in Urban VIII a crisis of conscience, to the extent that he set up a committee to decide the limits of the pope's rights to dispose of the income of the Holy See.

Its first decision was very generous, allowing the pope to spend any amount he wished, but even Urban turned that down so a second one limited the pope's spending to one-quarter of the annual income of the Church. These decisions of the committee appear scandalous and show again to what extent Rome did not understand what the honesty and spirituality of papal power meant.

Infamous and of no help to Urban VIII's reputation, even at a religious level, were the bulls he issued about beatification and the veneration of the saints, or the one which took an early position against Jansenism. In this latter case, only treatises on grace or free will were prohibited, referring back to what had been decided by the Council of Trent. In other words, no strong stand was taken.

There were slanderous attacks on Urban VIII at various levels, and he sought to react to popular criticism, which he always feared, by going back to old habits and reviving pagan-like public holidays to win over the population, with a renewal of rowdy parties with hunts, gambling and scenic performances, which caused further deficits in the public finances. In fact, top prelates such as the Cardinals Medici, Borghese and Ludovisi continued with their fast living and gambled away entire fortunes. The cardinals displayed pomp and splendor, in line with the customs of the time, and strutted around like princes although they were lower in rank than them. They pressured the pope to give them titles corresponding to the position they held in society, and Urban VIII obliged them in June 1630. From then on, they were no longer "*Illustrissimi*" but "*Eminentissimi*" and the title of "*Eminenza*" (Eminence) was indeed high-sounding! Poor Don Abbondio in the *Promessi Sposi* reminds us with his bantering: ". . . he must be addressed as Your Eminence, you understand? Because the pope, may God save him, ordered that from the month of June one must give this title to cardinals. And do you know why he came to this decision? Because the "*Illustrissimo,*" which was reserved for them and certain princes, you can see now what it has become, how often it is given, and how eagerly it is lapped up!"

A title does not wipe out the infamy of an anti-evangelical life, just as the recent rehabilitation of Galilei by John Paul II does not wipe out the disgrace of that trial which the famous scientist underwent during the time of Urban VIII in 1633. After the "strict examination," that is, after torture, he was forced to abjure a book issued with the *imprimatur*, which, according to the accusation, he had fraudulently extorted. In effect, he did not tell the clerical authorities that Bellarmino in a "precept" in 1616 had forbidden him to teach or defend the

Copernican theory. However, the truth is, as I have mentioned in the biography of Paul V, that Bellarmino merely held a clarifying talk with Galilei and that the written record of the "precept" was false. The scientist died two years before Urban VIII to whom he had undeservingly dedicated *Il Saggiatore* (The Assayer); in that pope distrust of reason was deeply rooted.

Following the infamy of this distrust and of the most impudent nepotism, with all the consequences that the lack of credibility the papacy managed to foster in Europe by not keeping up with the times, Urban VIII died on 29 July 1644, after he had survived two conspiracies. The Romans ran about Rome holidaying, exclaiming their joy over the end of a bloodsucking nepotism, thinking it would be for the last time. They would have wanted to carve this epitaph on the Bernini mausoleum: "The bee got fat and the flock got shorn." But other bees would come to suck in the thick honey.

236. INNOCENT X (1644—1655)

The conclave, which met in full summer in 1644, seemed to be in the hands of the Barberini, who could count on a large number of cardinals in their debt and were backing the election of Cardinal Sacchetti, though with little success. There were disputes within their own ranks as Francesco Barberini was disappointed over his treatment by the Spaniards, and they even came to blows. The summer sun was beating down on them and, as usual, some of the purple-hatted began to feel ill, so they agreed upon a "creature" of Urban VIII, Giovan Battista Pamphili, who was elected on 15 September 1644, even though he was notoriously anti-French. Mazarin, Richelieu's successor in the leadership of France, was not able to interpose his veto in time.

Giovan Battista Pamphili, born in Rome on 6 May 1574, had been a consistorial lawyer and auditor at the Rota, as well as nuncio in Naples. He had also accompanied Cardinal Barberini on his mission to France and was indebted to him for his purple hat. And for that reason, the family that had grown wealthy under Urban VIII hoped to continue their rich lifestyle alongside him. But they were wrong. As soon as he was consecrated pope on 4 October, with the name of Innocent X, he proceeded immediately to take action against the Barberini, detested by the public for their illegal enrichment. He appointed an investigative committee and charged the noble family with the costs of the war of Castro, considered a kind of private war carried out at the expense of papal finances.

Within a few months the Barberini cardinals fled to France, a flight that was seen as self-admitted guilt. They were deposed from their positions and their assets were confiscated. At this point Mazarin made himself heard with the queen sending protests in writing to the pope, and Innocent understood that it would be best not to go any further. With negotiations in progress to end the

Thirty Years War and the Jansenist heresy flourishing in that kingdom, he could not make an enemy of France forever.

Innocent had to give in, and the work of the investigating committee was forgotten. The Barberinis would return to Rome with full honors, and Mazarin's brother got a purple hat. Papal diplomacy had taken another beating. Then, on the matter of Westphalia, the pope was excluded totally from the lengthy negotiations. His representative, Fabio Chigi, assisted impotently at the decisions taken by the great powers on territorial and religious questions concerning recognition of new States and the affairs of the empire. The congress had officially recognized the heresy and through a whole lot of provisions had resolved problems of ecclesiastical laws, granting to sovereigns and princes who adhered to the confession of Augsburg, the benefices of the Church as perpetual fiefdoms.

Innocent X could do nothing but protest, in his bull of 26 November 1648, against the provisions which conflicted with the rights of the Church of Rome and interfered in the internal regime of the clergy. But his protest was ignored. The bull was not even published in Vienna, and it was the end of a myth. The Papal State was ignored politically on the international scene, and the voice of its monarch was no longer considered in a position to dictate the choice of religion by the citizens of a foreign State. Catholic France had signed the treaties alongside Protestant Sweden, and Europe discovered its exclusively political order, the religious one taking second place. The Catholics of the whole world would go on viewing the pope as the "vicar of Christ" but his voice from then on would be contrasted by the freedom of conscience which was nourished by contingent circumstances, dictated by ever broadening rationalism.

Confirmation of this state of affairs would come with the bull issued against the Jansenists in 1653. It was accepted by everybody, acknowledged to be correct in the reasons for its condemnation by the greatest universities, such as Louvain and Paris, and even by the followers of Jansenism themselves. The latter, in fact, recognized the infallibility of the pope to judge whether a proposition was heretical or not, but they denied in this case that one could declare heretical the meaning of Jansenism. It was indeed the issue of freedom of conscience, and on this question it was clear that everything was subject to opinion. The controversy continued, enlivened by Antoine Arnaud and Blaise Pascal, linking itself to the Port-Royal movement. Jansenism infiltrated the cultural realm in various ways, staying alive in certain intellectual circles in Europe right to the dawn of Romanticism. It was a controversy at the level of religious Orders, in which the Jesuits were involved, but it never became a heresy of the common people, and basically left its stamp only in France which, notwithstanding repeated condemnations from various pontiffs, remained divided into two opposing camps.

Disappointed by a Europe now too large for such a small temporal sovereign, Innocent X adapted to the situation, accepted being snubbed by the great powers, and concentrated his policy to within his Papal State and Rome where he pursued a form of "new" nepotism, enriching his relatives and raising them to positions of lay or clerical power. However, with his nephews who were cardinals, things did not go well. Not one of them was capable of helping him in the administration of power, though a woman, Olimpia Maidalchini, the widow of his brother, Pamphilio, was to impose herself.

It is by now evident that the relationship between the two in-laws, about whom Gualdi spoke maliciously in his *Vita di Donna Olimpia Maidalchini* published in 1666, was pure fantasy, "a novel consisting of apocryphal news items and from chimeric fantasies," Ranke observed. But it is also beyond doubt that this ambitious and greedy woman completely dominated the aged pontiff who gave her substantial donations from the very beginning of his pontificate, ranging from the castle of S. Martino al Cimino to the palazzo in Piazza Navona where he was born.

She was the most powerful person in the Curia to whom, as a genuine "popess," ambassadors, cardinals and prelates went in order to obtain what they wanted from the pope.

> Whoever seeks some favor from the sovereign,
> the road to the Vatican is rough and long;
> but if the person is clever,
> he will run to Donna Olimpia with his hands full,
> and will obtain what he seeks.
> It is the broadest and the shortest road.

That is how Pasquino records her, and it was true since everyone paid her homage and sought to win her over with sumptuous gifts. Her portrait was on the walls of apartments along with that of the pope, and she was considered a sovereign. With her, splendor in the arts, in public life and in clothes was assured in Rome, obviously in the purest baroque style of the era. And with the effulgence, vice and depravity reappeared, especially at upper class levels, and the prostitutes themselves recovered their respectability as courtesans under her protection, as was announced in an Avviso on 30 August 1645. It said that prostitutes "ride in carriages in great solemnity because Donna Olimpia, having been showered with gifts by them, is pleased to take them under her protection and allowed them to install her coat of arms over their door and has granted them permission to ride in carriages as if they were honorable people."

She naturally looked after her own interests, insatiably acquiring limitless wealth, and did not hesitate to take shameful advantage of the famine in 1647 and 1648, as Pasquino noted:

Grain and rations were taken by the greedy laws,
And all could see abundance returning.
Abundance that was destroyed because too much was stolen.

This woman's son, a certain Camillo, had only the embarrassment of choice for an outstanding future. Appointed General of the Church by his uncle, supreme commander of the fleet and Governor of the Borgo, he dropped those positions at a certain point to become, for a while, a cardinal collaborating with the Secretary of State who at the time was Panciroli. Then he changed his mind and returned to lay life to marry the young widow of Prince Borghese, Olimpia Aldobrandini. His mother was not in favor of that marriage because her future daughter-in-law had a similar nature to hers and she feared competition. However, Innocent accepted his resignation as cardinal, on condition that the young couple go to live in Frascati, to please the "popess" who did not want rivals in her domination of Rome's elite.

This woman reached the summit of her prestige during the Jubilee Year of 1650, a holy event which was celebrated with worldliness in accord with a ritual ordered in advance by her. "The sacred liturgy was transformed into an arrogant rhetorical exercise: preachers became stage actors," Castiglioni observed, "people go to a sermon as if it were a stage play; Donna Olimpia invites them to her palazzo" in Piazza Navona given to her by the pope, "to listen to the sermon preached by the famous Jesuit priest, Father Oliva, and invites ladies and gentlemen to hear him for their amusement." Papal audiences achieved an unimaginable solemnity. The ambassador of Philip IV arrived with a retinue of 300 carriages, each one accompanied by liveried Moorish footmen and splendidly harnessed horses.

Then a family crisis arose between the pope and his sister-in-law when he appointed Olimpia's seventeen-year-old nephew, Francesco Maidalchini, as cardinal to take the post of Camillo Pamphili. He was unsuitable, however, and Innocent got rid of him, replacing him with another cardinal nephew, Camillo Astalli, a distant relative of hers. However, she flew into a temper as this did not form part of her plans. The old man had had enough of her, it seems, and he threw her out. Astalli's prestige increased but not enough to take the place of Panciroli when the latter died in 1651. The new Secretary of State was Cardinal Fabio Chigi.

The pope then had Camillo Pamphili return to Rome with his wife, all set to become the new "popess," but she overdid it and, according to Ranke, the aging Olimpia was recalled to court "to keep order in the house." In fact, there were intrigues and insults between the two Olimpias both of whom Innocent tolerated until "the harlot of Piazza Navona," as the Romans referred to the Maidalchini, regained her post as the undisputed lady of the house with the blessing of the eighty-year-old pontiff.

While his sister-in-law held the keys of the house, the pope devoted himself to beautifying Rome, though he had to worry about finances, since he had to find money somehow for that insatiable bloodsucker around his neck as well as for all the building activity. But in this he proved to be "energetic, capable and decisive," Ranke notes, and "he forced the nobles to repay their debts," and his action in this connection with the duke of Parma was exemplary. His creditors were pressing Innocent to make Ranuccio Farnese pay, so the old man made his move. Following the assassination of the bishop of Castro, for which the duke's people were believed responsible, he ordered that the property of Farnese be put up for sale, and in 1649 the papal troops set off for Castro to take possession of it.

Ranuccio thought he could save himself as his father Oduardo had with Urban VIII, but this time the European powers, now at peace, would not allow it. So Castro was destroyed. However, the amount of his debts was so great that the duke would never have been able to pay off his creditors, and for this Spain's mediation was needed.

And then came the tax surcharges. For the erection of the obelisk in Piazza Navona at the Fountain of the Four Rivers by Bernini and the four fountains of the Acqua Vergine only, there was a sales tax of a penny per pound of meat and salt, plus the increase in the price of flour, which led Pasquino to remark:

> We want more than lilies and fountains;
> we want bread, bread, bread!

Piazza Navona, until then the main market for fruit and vegetables, lost its rural character and was gentrified with the rebuilt Palazzo Pamphili and the church of St. Agnes, both of them the work of Borromini, and it became the "Pamphili kingdom." Many of the city's streets were widened and put in order, and the urban planning started by Sixtus V and Paul V was continued. A bit of modernity even reached the prisons when in the "New Prisons" in Via Giulia, a structure of cells with hygiene and security was installed for the first time in Europe. Finally, on the Janiculum, in a quarter called Belrespiro, the Pamphili family had their villa built by Algardi. Innocent's nephew, Camillo, went to live there with his Olimpia.

Innocent X died on 7 January 1655, following a lengthy and agonizing illness which allowed various relatives to loot what they could and deposit their wealth in safe places. Donna Olimpia was last seen taking everything she could from the papal apartments. His corpse lay for three days while none of his relatives bothered to bury him, and when the Curia turned to Donna Olimpia to have her pay the expenses, she answered that she was only a "poor widow" and could not afford it. No other relative felt in any way obligated toward the deceased. His remains were finally transferred to a storehouse and laid out on a temporary bier and only later, Camillo, his nephew, repented and erected a funeral monument in his memory in the church of St. Agnes.

The Romans at last were able to breathe, but they chiefly wanted to do away with Donna Olimpia:

> The fury is finished over that sofa in Piazza Navona.
> Call in the hangman. The fury is finished.
> . . . Dead is the Pastor, the cow survives.
> Let's have a feast: cut out her heart.
> Dead is the Pastor.

Alexander VII, Innocent X's successor, was to become the indirect interpreter of the people's will. Once elected, he ordered her to leave Rome and retire at the frontier in S. Martino al Cimino. A lawsuit was begun against her for "unjust enrichment" with State money and she was condemned to return it. She would never do so, however, and she died of the plague at S. Martino al Cimino in 1657.

237. ALEXANDER VII (1655–1667)

It was an unusual conclave that was held between January and early April of 1655, as the usual group of cardinals, those nephews of the preceding pope able to control the situation, were not there. Astalli did not constitute a faction by himself, since nobody "owed" him anything, so the largest group of cardinals finally felt free to decide openly. They wanted to be guided in the choice by religious reasons only, in an aura of political neutrality and without the influence of foreign States. The Spanish ambassador called them the "flying squadron." However, they really did not know whom to choose since the candidature of Giulio Sacchetti always had the Spanish veto, like that of Fabio Chigi with the opposition of Mazarin. The situation was only unblocked when the French candidate sent a personal letter to the minister of Louis XIV to induce him to lift the veto against Innocent X's former Secretary of State. On 7 April 1655, Fabio Chigi was elected.

Born in Siena on 13 February 1599 in a famous family of bankers, he had represented the Holy See at Münster during the peace negotiations at the end of the Thirty Years War, which was when he had earned the hostility of Mazarin. He had not achieved much through his diplomacy and had had to sit idly by while the interests of the Church suffered. Innocent X had nevertheless made him a cardinal in 1652, calling him to Rome from his nunciature in Cologne and giving him the portfolio of Secretary of State at the death of Panciroli. He was consecrated pope on 18 April, and assumed the name of Alexander VII.

He was a man of profound religious feelings, inspired by an innate sense of humility. According to the chronicles, he did not want to be carried into St. Peter's for the ritual veneration by the cardinals, and during the ceremony held a large crucifix in his hands to indicate that the adoration was for Christ and not for himself. Neither did he want triumphal arches or decorations in the streets when he went to take possession of the Lateran, and he showed edifying piety and disdain for material things, especially for power. For this reason, he had Bernini sculpt a bier for him that he kept in his bedroom, while on his desk he kept a skull. He also declared that he was against nepotism.

Then, as Ranke notes, people began to say "that it was not fitting for relatives of the pope to live like private citizens," and that "one could not avoid rendering princely honors to his family in Siena, his home town," since if he did not it could be taken as an insult to the grand duchy of Tuscany. The great preacher, Oliva, a Jesuit, went so far as to say that the pope would be committing a sin if he did not call to him his nephews, in other words, that he was risking damning his soul, and then that he should go along with the times and give a good example, otherwise, "what kind of pope would he be!"

Alexander VII finally submitted the question of whether it was good or not for him to make use of relatives in the affairs of the Church to a consistory in April 1656. The response could only be in the affirmative, and acceptable even on a theological level, although Pallavicini advised the pope to set limits on the authority of the relatives. So the scruples of Urban VIII were repeated. However appearances having been saved, the way was cleared for the "invasion" from Siena, or, as Pasquino called it, the "procession," and Alexander was overwhelmed and involved perhaps more that he expected. If one wants to think that until then he had simply "played a role," let us say that he had managed to spread an aura of legality over a scandalous institution, and could rest in peace with his conscience.

His brother, Don Mario, received the best paid positions, from Superintendent of the Food Reserves to the administration of justice in the Borgo. His nephew Flavio, following his noviciate with the Jesuits, became a cardinal and assisted Giulio Rospigliosi in the Secretariat of State, essentially laying his hands on ecclesiastical incomes which quickly reached the amount of 100,000 scudi. Another nephew, Agostino, was chosen to begin the princely family of the Chigis. Remaining a layman, as the warden of Castel Sant'Angelo, he gradually received splendid properties, such as Ariccia and the family palazzo in Piazza Colonna, and was married to Maria Virginia Borghese.

So, once Alexander VII had started on the path of nepotism, he could not restrain himself, extending his favors even to distant relatives, such as the Commendatore Antonio Bichi, who was made a cardinal. It was a real and exclusive escalation to riches, while the "political" reason which supposedly justified nepotism, that is, to give the pope a way to find a man he could trust in the management of the Church among his relatives, was put aside. No one had authority to deal with such problems and the pope himself was not interested in the papacy as an instrument of power.

So the Congregations of State, which had been put aside during previous pontificates, appeared again. They had the power to decide on questions of public order, from problems of war or peace to taxes and international issues, while the pope saw to religious matters and pious works, as in fact he did in May 1656, when the plague infested Rome. Showing great charitable spirit, he assisted those who were stricken, supervised their food supply and, to isolate the contagion, erected a hospice on the island of S. Bartolomeo.

Pope Chigi loved the peaceful life at Castel Gandolfo where he stayed two months during summer, but also the Roman afternoons when he listened to poets who read their poems aloud in his court. He probably put aside the funeral bier and the skull and began enjoying a bit of worldliness that was provided by the arrival of Christina of Sweden, who had been converted to Catholicism after she had abdicated her crown. She was happy to accept the invitation of the pope to move to Rome in 1655.

The princess received an impressive welcome, entering the city in an elegant carriage made from a design by Bernini. The pope received her in consistory and confirmed her with a new name, Alexandra. However, this lady was to give Alexander VII both joys and sorrows. Cultivated, haughty, and eccentric, she realized she could dominate the field as far as fashion in Baroque Rome was concerned. There is no question about the sincerity of her religious feelings, although she criticized the outward manifestations of certain cults, and knew how to take advantage of her position and enjoy life. One could well apply to Christina of Sweden the famous remark of Henry IV, as Cesare D'Onofrio justly underlined in his book about her: "Rome is well worth an abjuration." Christina gained a great deal by becoming a Catholic, foreswearing Protestantism and leaving boring, cold Sweden for a warm, happy-go-lucky city like Rome.

From Palazzo Farnese where she first resided by courtesy of the duke of Parma, Christina in fact ran the carefree life of the city, becoming the "queen of the social life of the great Roman world," as Castiglioni recalls. "She was sought after and acclaimed everywhere, and her vanity no longer knew any bounds. Splendid receptions, tourneys, concerts and masked balls were organized in her honor by high clerics and by the Roman nobility. The students at *Propaganda Fide* greeted her with homages in twenty-two languages, while the Jesuit priest, Atanasio Kircher, presented to her a little obelisk with a laudatory inscription in twenty-three languages, and the University of Rome could not do less to honor the illustrious guest."

Among the most splendid events was the pre-Lenten Carnival of 1656, which raged on in such an atmosphere of immorality that Alexander VII regretted that he had ever invited that "lost sheep" to Rome who, returning to the fold at St. Peter's, should have converted the masses by her example. But these were only vain dreams. In fact, the cardinals themselves swarmed about her and played the game, from Chigi to Azzolini who became her close friend and, perhaps, lover.

She was also a kind of Mata Hari of the times, plotting with Mazarin a conquest of Naples, but betrayed by her equerry, Gian Rinaldo Monaldeschi, who sold the lady's secret plans to the Spaniards and whom she did not think twice about having killed. These were neverending diplomatic headaches for Alexander VII who dearly loved his tranquillity, and he was only able to breathe a little when Christina left Rome to see to her financial position after the death of her father, Gustave Adolphus. When she returned, she seemed calmer, less eccentric. She moved into Palazzo Riario and devoted herself to the intellectual life, which appeared to give her at last the satisfaction she did not get from politics. Her salon, frequented by writers and artists, became a sort of Academy, a forerunner of the famous one which, a year after her death in 1689, would take the name of Arcadia.

Meanwhile, after the death of Mazarin in 1661, Alexander VII was to suffer, as the "sovereign" pontiff, still another humiliation in the international field, directly from Louis XIV. The reason for the conflict between them was the pope's dream of a league of Catholic States against the Turks on the pope's part while, the Sun King's part, to get the Sublime Porte to make war against Austria. He needed a pretext to shut the mouth of the pope and get him to stop his appeals for a holy crusade. And to furnish the Sun King the pretext was his new ambassador in Rome, the duke of Créqui.

This gentleman came to the city in June 1662 with 200 armed men, expecting to receive from the pope honors superior to those reserved for other ambassadors. He requested that the diplomatic immunity, which already applied to his residence, the Palazzo Farnese, be extended to the surrounding area. His guards displayed an insolent attitude, and it was evident that sooner or later there would be a diplomatic incident. One took place in the evening of 20 August.

A dispute broke out between some Corsican soldiers in the service of the pope, stationed near the Palazzo Farnese, and three Frenchmen; and from words it went to blows. The Corsicans got reinforcements, shots hit the ambassador's carriage as it was returning to the palazzo, and a page was killed.

The Curia was prepared to give satisfaction to the ambassador, but he seized the opportunity to depart from Rome declaring that his personal security was in danger and refusing all attempts at reconciliation. Paris's reaction was immediate. The papal nuncio was ordered out of the country, while France occupied and annexed Avignon and the Comté Venaissin. Furthermore, an army got ready for a punitive expedition against the Papal State.

Spain's mediation was successful, and a humiliating peace was reached at Pisa in February 1664, by which Cardinal Flavio Chigi, as a nephew of the pope, and Cardinal Imperiali in his capacity as Governor of Rome, had to go to Paris to present the official excuses to the Sun King. In addition, Corsicans were no longer allowed in the service of the pope, despite a summary trial which had already condemned to death two of the guardsmen involved in the attack. Finally, a pyramid was to be erected in front of the barracks of the Corsicans bearing an inscription in perpetual memory of their "crime." Finally, Castro passed again to the Farnese family, the condition for regaining Avignon. It was a degrading peace treaty for the papacy and showed the slight political clout the Papal State wielded in the international context by then.

Alexander VII consoled himself by continuing to beautify Rome. He had the University of the Sapienza restored, decorated many rooms at the Quirinal and at the villa in Castel Gandolfo, put the piazza of the Pantheon in order, and had an obelisk raised on the back of a marble elephant in the piazza of the Minerva. Finally, he saw the completion of the colonnade of St. Peter's. However, he was also interested in military and financial works, such as the building of the arsenal at Civitavecchia and the mint near the Vatican garden.

He died on 22 May 1667, and was buried in St. Peter's in the grandiose mausoleum built for him by Bernini. The customary "kidney stones," which had tortured other popes in the past, were the cause of his death. Pasquino records it as follows:

> Don't weep, Alexander, if your hard luck with the stones
> Has led to your death, a death for thieves
> but not for heroes,
> Your peers had to leave their happy state on earth
> because of these stones.

238. CLEMENT IX (1667—1669)

Eighteen days of conclave were needed to elect the successor to Alexander VII. Between the pro-Spanish and pro-French factions, the "flying squadron" headed by Cardinal Azzolini again got the upper hand, and Giulio Rospigliosi was elected on 20 June 1667. The French ambassador bragged about the selection since Rospigliosi was the second name on the list of possible candidates acceptable to the Sun King, and the Spaniards also recognized him as their favorite, having been a welcome nuncio in Madrid. One might say instead that he won because of his traditional spirit of neutrality which would bear fruit despite the brevity of his pontificate.

Giulio Rospigliosi was born in Pistoia on 28 January 1600, into a family of nobles. A student of the Jesuits in Rome, he had earned a degree in theology in Pisa where he had also been a teacher. Having entered the papal diplomatic corps, he had held various posts, and had found time to write melodramas which enjoyed a certain success in Rome. As vicar of St. Mary Major, he also obtained honorary citizenship of Rome. In 1657 Alexander VII had appointed him cardinal and Secretary of State. He was consecrated pope on 26 June 1667, with the name of Clement IX and took the emblem of a pelican with the motto "*Aliis non sibi Clemens,*" meaning "Clement for others, not for himself." This motto reflected his policy of charity, along with his favorite expression: "We concede!" He was to lower the tax on flour, and every day he gathered at his table thirteen poor people to whom he himself sometimes served the meal. His visits to the sick in the hospital of the Lateran and the daily confessions he heard in a confessional erected for the purpose in St. Peter's got him a reputation of holiness, and the people venerated him as their benefactor.

"He was the best and the kindest man that could be found," Ranke observes, but "more than active, he was full of good intentions; he was compared to a tree full of branches which put out lots of leaves and perhaps even flowers but no fruit." These are words worth meditating on and which take on a particular significance when read together with the "praises" written by Pasquino upon his election:

> The people of Christ will have a peaceful world as a treasure
> And enjoy a golden century.
> This is the papacy of the great Clement IX:
> He speaks with all in soft accents,
> Fills Rome with useless relatives,
> Reduces grain taxes for the poor,
> Foolishly forgives every sin,
> Keeps evil-minded ministers,
> Without ever baring them his fangs,
> And he is content to play the clown.

In effect, Clement IX did not persecute the relatives of Alexander VII by throwing them out of office. The Chigis kept their positions, as did all the Sienese in their group, to the dismay of the people from Pistoia who were expecting to catapult themselves on Rome and seize the benefices. But everything remained as it was. "In place of that continual flow of outsiders seeking their fortune, of that unending exchange of people who had obtained positions, now there was calm blended with caution," Ranke again observes. This was because the power of those families who had already made it was being consolidated and any new ones were excluded.

The papal throne was by this time surrounded by a powerful and wealthy aristocracy which was unwilling either to give up its position or share it with others. And the "merit" for this new management of power went to the "flying squadron" which had put Clement IX on the throne, as the appointment of Decio Azzolini as Secretary of State shows. The distribution of more than 600,000 scudi in the first month of the pontificate to the cardinals and other important members of the Curia was a gift that resembled a percentage cut, and under other circumstances Simony might have been mentioned.

But Clement IX was not a nepotist, at least he was one within the limits set by that great censor, Pallavicino, who on this subject had recommended "that in future no titles such as prince, duke . . . be awarded to relatives of the popes, that all funds received by the State, by the License Office, from the sale of offices and from other entitlements of the apostolic see be used only for the good of souls and for thanksgiving to the people." So his brother Camillo was appointed General of the Church and his nephews Giacomo and Tommaso respectively became cardinal and warden of Castel Sant'Angelo, but all three of them found their income limited to the salaries paid for those jobs.

Of course, the Rospigliosi tried all the same to make their way up within the Roman aristocracy. They built a splendid house, organized banquets and balls and equipped a theater where brilliant performances were held, such as the *Conversion of Saint Baldassare*, composed by Anton Maria Abbatini but based on a text which was said to have been written by the pope himself, and using scenery designed by Bernini. In this way the Rospigliosi spent fortunes, but the pope gave them no public properties or banks to compensate them, yet they managed to stay on the crest of the wave, thanks also to the marriage of a young representative of the family to a wealthy heiress, a Pallavicini from Genoa.

So his relatives were not included among those to be taken care of but Rome itself was, and as a result the city was beautified with the last works of Bernini, the statues for the colonnade of St. Peter's, and the access bridge to Castel Sant'Angelo. Marginal groups such as the Jews were also favored by the abolition of the "race" to which they had to submit for the amusement of the Christians during Carnival time. Also included was that spirit of brotherhood and peace which, in line with the intentions of Clement IX, was to become from then on the "political" obligation of the Papal State in the international context, and which was a way for it to regain a certain religious credibility in the world which the popes of the Renaissance period had, in great measure, lost.

So the pope, favorably viewed as he was by Louis XIV, was able to maintain better relations with France and regain a certain dignity following the humiliating peace accord at Pisa. The French themselves demolished the pyramid erected in Rome in front of the barracks of the Corsicans and thereby removed the symbol of an unpleasant diplomatic incident.

Following this papal diplomatic rehabilitation, it was possible for the pope to do some good in France on a religious level, calming the Jansenist disputes with the "Clementine peace." The Sun King even had a coin minted as "a souvenir of the unity of the Church," even if for the Jansenists the signature of a statement imposed on them by the Estates General was a compromise, a formal acceptance of doctrinal decisions.

And when in 1667 Louis XIV's troops entered Spanish Holland and rapidly wiped out the main fortresses, again it was the Holy See which was the mediator of the peace reached a year later between France and Spain at Aix-la-Chapelle. Finally, the pope induced the Sun King to support Venice against the Turks. It was a matter of defending Crete and the pope had already put his galleys at the disposal of Venice. France sent troops clandestinely, because it did not want to spoil its good relations with the Sublime Porte by fighting under the pope's flag with the papal troops. But the rediscovered spirit of the crusade could not avoid the fall of the Candia fortress on 6 September 1669.

The news was extremely disconcerting for the pope. He had an apoplectic stroke at the end of October and died of heartbreak on 9 December 1669, as Pasquino noted in Latin, which can be translated as:

> You who seek his grave, he lies here,
> Clement the Ninth. For Crete he turned to ashes.
> *(Tr. note: a pun on Crete: creta means "clay" in Italian.)*

Temporarily buried in St. Peter's, Clement was later entombed in a sepulcher erected for him by Rainaldi in St. Mary Major.

239. CLEMENT X (1670–1676)

The conclave to elect a successor to Clement IX lasted almost five months. The dispute between the pro-French and the pro-Spanish cardinals went on and on, and led to a direct intervention by the ambassadors of the two kings. The French ambassador vetoed Cardinal D'Elce, and the Spanish ambassador vetoed Cardinal Brancaccio. The result was the election on 29 April 1670 of another neutral, Cardinal Emilio Altieri.

Born in Rome on 13 July 1590, a former bishop of Camerino, he was for a long time the papal nuncio in Poland, a country which remained dear to him as pope, and had been made a cardinal by Clement IX shortly before his death. He was a humble man, not used to power who tried to refuse the nomination, but had to resign himself to it with the motto, "*Jesu, tibi sit gloria!.*" He was consecrated pope on 11 May 1670, and took the name of Clement X.

He would have liked to have followed the line of his predecessor but could not. When Louis XIV resumed hostilities for the conquest of Holland, his appeals for peace went unheeded, so there was trouble again between the Holy See and France, and the Sun King seized the opportunity of the Jansenist "*mai domo*" movement to increase his interference in ecclesiastical matters. He took over the "royalties," that is, the right to collect the income from the larger benefices in the episcopal "vacant sees," and the pope's protests were ignored. Clement X's only consolation came from Poland where a Catholic king, John Sobieski, was elected after managing, thanks to Louis XIV, to overcome the internal forces opposed to his candidature. The pope sent him substantial sums of money, trusting in his military forces to block the advance of the Turks. Poland was in a sense the farthest bulwark of European Catholicism.

Under the banner of this crusading spirit, the aging pope celebrated the fifteenth Jubilee Year in 1675. The crowds of pilgrims were not very large because of the wars dividing Europe, but Clement in his naiveté hoped that the Holy Year could work the miracle and bring peace. He was ill but did not stop carrying out the sacred rites with great devotion. "If during the Jubilee Year the pope was able to give his blessing only seven times and visit the Seven Churches only five times, that is understandable in view of his poor health," Pastor notes.

"Gout and catarrh tormented the eighty-five-year old man. But he took part in the eighth holy day of the Rosary at the church of S. Maria sopra Minerva and personally recited the entire Rosary aloud to the edification of the multitude present."

And the management of the Church? It was not his line and he chose as collaborator Cardinal Paluzzo Paluzzi, whose nephew, Paluzzo Albertoni, was married to a niece of his. The nepotism of this pope, who had no male nephews, was transferred to the Paluzzis and he finished by granting them every possible favor. Albertoni even took on his wife's family name and became an Altieri.

Clement wanted only to be supported in his works of charity, and Cardinal Paluzzi showed himself generous for those enterprises if careless in collecting taxes, thus nullifying the work of the managers in the Secretariat of State. Pasquino said that then there were two popes, one "to bless and make holy, and the other to regulate and govern." Gregorio Leto wrote a sonnet entitled *Who Was the Pope, Paluzzo Paluzzi or Emilio Altieri*, which begins like this:

> Who of the two was pope, I do not know,
> For the first gave up power and the second his name.

And naturally the Paluzzi-Altieri became as rich as they wanted, and completed the construction of the splendid Palazzo Altieri in record time, perhaps afraid that the source of their prosperity would disappear at any moment.

That happened on 22 July 1676. Clement X was buried in St. Peter's in a large funeral monument that was built for him by a "grateful" Cardinal Paluzzi.

240. Innocent XI (1676–1689)

To resolve the usual arguments, the cardinals were in conclave for two months and because of the continual pressure from Louis XIV, they wound up electing on 21 September 1676 a person who would be especially inimical to him, Cardinal Benedetto Odescalchi.

He was born in Como on 16 May 1611 to a family of wealthy merchants. He arrived in Rome, still a layman, at the age of twenty-five, with his degree in law, and that haughty Spanish-like air, well depicted by Manzoni in so many characters in his novel. He arrived with his sword and pistols, intending to become a "young gentleman" in the kingdom of Naples or to make his way in a military career. Had he stayed on a "branch of Lake Como" he probably would have become a Don Rodrigo or, better, given his talents, an "*Innominato.*" Instead, Benedetto Odescalchi met his cardinal before embarking on the "wrong" road, and so took up a priestly career.

Apostolic Prothonotary and President of the Apostolic Chamber under Urban VIII, he was later the Commissar of the March of Ancona and Governor of the March of Macerata. He declined the court fees that he earned for they were the "price of blood" and he did not want them to contaminate his soul.

He was already a cardinal by the age of thirty-four and Innocent X sent him to Ferrara as papal legate, convinced of the purity of the evangelical spirit which motivated this young cardinal. "We are sending the father of the poor people," he commented when giving him the assignment, and in a spirit of self-denial, Benedetto Odescalchi hastened to combat the famine which was afflicting that city.

Appointed bishop of Novara, he showed even more his generosity towards the needy people, at the same time demonstrating a civil and religious strictness which recalled the times of Pius V and Sixtus V. To a chronicler of his time, he was merely a "big stick," a bigot, and Pasquino was convinced that he would not be elected by the conclave of 1676:

> Odescalchi, that big fellow, is hoping in a conclave,
> but the keys don't go to one who's a bigot.

But he was elected. It is said that he was very reluctant to accept the nomination, even throwing himself on his knees before the cardinals and pleading with them to find someone else. But he had to accept and was consecrated pope on 4 October, taking the name of Innocent XI. They presented to him a symbol which referred to the name he had chosen and on which was written: "*Innocens manibus et mundo corde.*" He found it flattering and substituted it, referring to Peter's boat, with the following: "*Domine, salva nos, perimus!*"

A pope so austere and strict in his habits was a panacea for the financial management of the Papal State, where there was no balance between income and expenses and the deficit was so great that it was threatened with bankruptcy. Innocent XI managed to restore order through drastic measures of economy, resulting in a positive balance at the end of his pontificate.

He reached that result also because he abstained totally from nepotism. He would have liked to abolish that plague forever and wanted the cardinals to swear to respect a bull in that regard. But the Sacred College unanimously opposed such a decree. As for himself, he summoned the only nephew he had, Livio, the son of his brother Carlo, and told him to continue his studies with the Jesuits to achieve a position solely through his own ability, to get out of his head any thought of gifts or honoraria, and to count only on whatever would be left to him by his uncle's estate. To the imperial ambassador who promised to guarantee special protection to the Odescalchis, he replied that the pope had neither home nor family, just the position that God had lent him.

He assigned the Secretariat of State to his friend, Cardinal Alderano Cibo, in whom he trusted blindly, and with him went into action against the abuses and scandals at court, denouncing any kind of corruption. In a consistory he ordered the cardinals to give up carriages and liveried servants in favor of a more priestly lifestyle, while with a series of laws called "*Innocentine*" he lowered the fees of tribunals to cleanse them of any appearance of venality.

In his strict observance of moral principles was included his severe stand against "laxist probability" which was then specifically sustained by certain Jesuits. To stifle any tendency of living against rules he found a strong supporter in Tirso Gonzales, professor at the University of Salamanca, who became the General of the Society. His earnest concern to maintain pure the Catholic doctrine in questions of faith and usage was evident in his tough action against "quietism," a secret mystical current headed by a Spanish secular priest, Miguel de Molinos. Arrested and brought before the Inquisition tribunal, de Molinos admitted the errors of his teachings which tended to ignore all practices of external piety, and abjured them, but was nonetheless condemned to life imprisonment. All his followers were persecuted, including a cardinal, Pietro Petrucci, author of certain writings inspired by Molinos. Innocent avoided having him appear before the Inquisition, for the trial of a cardinal would have been a scandal for the Holy See, and he let him keep all his privileges, though his writings were put on the Index.

Poor Innocent! He did not know he was all "alone" in his effort of moralization. He was full of illusions and should not even have trusted Cardinal Cibo. Instead, he kept close to him, as Pasquino recalls with sarcasm:

And Odescalchi is a starving animal
who demands food
from morn to eve.
(Tr. note: cibo means "food")

But even Cibo betrayed him because, as Giuntella records, "unbeknown to the pope, he received a pension from the king of France," which is to say from the pope's enemy, with whom the pope was fighting a tough battle.

Everything hinged on the question of the "royalties" which had arisen under Clement X. The Sun King had absolutely no intention of giving up that crown privilege. He considered it inalienable, and was supported in this by the French clergy who were bent on opposing the pope's authority in a new and insurgent spirit of national independence. This was evidenced in the famous "Declaration of the Gallican clergy on the power of the church," formulated in 1682 by the bishop of Meaux, approved by the ecclesiastical assembly and recorded by the Estates General on orders from the king.

Made up of four points, it set forth the independence of the laity from the clergy, the superiority of the council over the pope, the invulnerability of French canonical traditions, and the inviolability of the pope in matters of faith, conditioned however on the consent of the Universal Church. The "Declaration" was, and continues to be, a kind of manifesto of Gallican freedoms which Louis XIV raised to the rank of an article of faith to be taught as doctrine in all the schools, and if the pope abstained from definitive condemnation of the four points, it was because he was hoping for an amicable settlement. He merely reproved them, that is, he refused to approve all the nominee bishops proposed by the king who had participated in the Assembly. As a result, a good thirty-five French bishoprics remained vacant and though the new nominees could use the income of the dioceses they could not be ordained and, therefore, could not exercise the ecclesiastical functions of bishops.

So Louis XIV decided to prove his good intentions as a perfect orthodox by provoking a bitter campaign against the Huguenots. It was expected that the pope would give in as a result of this fine service rendered to the Catholic Church and to the Inquisition, which should have gladdened the heart of a Gregory XIII. But, Innocent's reply left him dumbfounded: "Christ did not use this method; it is necessary to lead people to the temple, not drag them inside." It was a denial of the coercive methods of Pius V.

Thereupon, Louis XIV provoked the pope in another way. When in 1687 a bull declared that the "freedom of the quarter," in other words, that the diplomatic immunity of an Embassy in the Roman quarter of its location, was terminated, France refused to respect the decree, even if it was accepted by the other nations. It was in reality dictated by rules of public order to broaden papal judicial and police powers, and thus was a protection for the Embassy itself.

The French ambassador, Henri Lavardin, came to Rome with a couple of cavalry squadrons, and defiantly asserted the right of asylum over a wide area. "They come with horses and carriages," Innocent remarked, "while we wish to proceed instead in the name of the Lord," and, placing an interdiction against the church of St. Louis he excommunicated the ambassador. The Sun King responded by calling for an ecumenical council to deal with all the disputes, but meanwhile had Avignon occupied, and prevented the papal nuncio, Angelo Ranuzzi, from returning to Rome by putting him under arrest. He then threatened to invade the Papal State, but did not go so far as that.

It was a complete break in relations between France and the Church of Rome, with a schism which, if not openly declared, was not to be resolved in the immediate future what with so many questions left unanswered. Innocent XI, however, intended to strike at Louis XIV by discrediting him on an international level and, supported by those States in Europe which opposed the king's hegemony, he found himself, without intending, allied with the Protestants.

In fact, he sent substantial amounts of money to Prince William of Orange who had assumed supreme command on the Rhine in defense of the empire and the Church against Louis XIV, while in the dark about the English plot to dethrone the Catholic King James and offer the throne to the princess of Orange. And an absurd situation ensued by which, while "at the court of Rome they were cementing an alliance, the purpose of which was to free Protestantism in western Europe from the grave danger that threatened it, and also guaranteeing forever that the throne of England would be in Protestant hands," as Ranke admirably demonstrated, "the Protestants on their part, in defending the equilibrium of Europe against "exorbitant power," had contributed to make the latter give in to the ecclesiastical claims of the papacy."

At the same time, Innocent was involved in one more crusade against the Turks which did have two valuable results. The first occurred in 1683 in the battle for the defense of Vienna when the Christians scored a great victory, succeeding also in snatching the Turkish flags. These trophies were sent to Rome and deposited in the new church of S. Maria della Vittoria, and the pope ordered that the feast of the Name of Mary be celebrated by the entire Church in perpetual remembrance.

The other success came in 1686 with the liberation of Buda by Charles of Lorraine who, a year later, won a great victory at Mohacz, and paved the way to the freeing of a great part of the Balkan region from the Ottoman yoke. This grand event, as reported by the chronicles of the period, was celebrated by the ringing of all the bells in Rome for a whole hour.

So all at once the crusade appeared to make sense for European states, even if the motivations were, of course, political. Its Catholic tint served Innocent XI to counterbalance the Protestant compromise in a "tête-à-tête" with Louis XIV.

So was it the universalization of the pope's Christian action transcending doctrinal issues or Catholic propaganda in the vests of political opportunism? The
times were not ripe for the first hypothesis, nor were the Gallic pretentions so
docile as to be muffled by the festive ding-dong of Roman bells. More likely is
the second hypothesis, by which the holy figure of the pontiff helped the Papal
State regain international credibility through bloodshed, even if this were under
the sign of the cross. For Pasquino it was "hypocrisy," as he stigmatized it at the
death of Innocent XI on 12 August 1689:

> I still cannot find in old annals a worse animal than
> one which hypocritically uses others' blood
> to stain beak and wings.

Others, however, praised this pope, such as an anonymous person quoted by
Castiglioni:

> Innocent is dead, died as he lived:
> Wise, holy, devout, unbowed and strong.

Pius XII beatified him in 1956. He is buried in a splendid mausoleum under
the altar of St. Sebastian in St. Peter's basilica.

2 4 1. ALEXANDER VIII (1 6 8 9 — 1 6 9 1)

The conclave to elect a successor to Innocent XI lasted nearly two months.
In addition to France and Spain, this time Austria also sent an envoy. The cardinals wanted to elect a man of the Church rather than a politician and found
themselves agreeing on Cardinal Pietro Ottoboni. To begin with Louis XIV was
not pleased by his candidature because he had supported Innocent XI in the
question of the "royalties," and was ready to interpose his veto.

However, after Ottoboni aired a certain criticism about the strictness of the
deceased pontiff in front of the French representatives, he earned himself the Sun
King's approval. The latter ended by warmly supporting his election when
Ottoboni's nephew promised the French ambassador that his uncle would be
very accommodating to the wishes of the sovereign. He was elected on 6
October 1689, and consecrated on the 16th with the name of Alexander VIII.

Pietro Ottoboni was born in Venice on 22 April 1610. Coming to Rome at
the age of twenty in search of fortune, he had qualified as a jurist, occupying various positions in the Curia, and Innocent X had elevated him cardinal in 1652.
With this new prestige he did not forget his relatives or his hometown and, once
cardinal, sent funds to his native city and business to his brother Anthony and

to his son, who bore his own name. And he remembered them also as pope, so marking a triumphant return of nepotism to the chair of Peter.

Alexander VIII reigned for only sixteen months but that was enough to enrich his relatives in a scandalous fashion, rapidly annulling the efforts of his predecessor. In fact, as soon as he was elected, he summoned them to Rome, and hastened to give them highly remunerative jobs. His brother was appointed General of the Church, and his nephew Peter, barely eighteen, was made a cardinal. Of the latter, Pasquino said:

Pietro stripped Pietro in order to dress Pietro.

Indeed this cardinal adopted a lifestyle for which he never had enough money what with gambling and the banquets he organized as a great patron of the arts, and he was continually asking his uncle for funds that were never denied him. Alexander seemed to be in a hurry to make his relatives wealthy and, given his advanced age, he was afraid he would die before he brought them contentment. So, urging them to take more, he would say: "Let us hurry because the eleventh hour has rung!"

And as usual in such cases, there was also the ridiculous aspect in the distribution of appointments. Marco, the son of another brother of the pope, although hunchback and lame, became superintendent of the papal galleys and also duke of Fiano by marrying Tarquinia Colonna, the grandniece of Cardinal Altieri.

Louis XIV meanwhile was waiting for Alexander VIII to keep his promises, and showed his good will by returning Avignon and renouncing the "freedom of the quarter" for his embassy in Rome. But the pope, aside from making a cardinal of Toussant de Forbin Janson, the bishop of Beauvais, who had pressured the sovereign, did nothing else and the French clergy was clamouring for the ecclesiastical ordinations which had not arrived for those bishops who had taken part in the assembly of 1682.

As Mario Dell'Arco records, "Pierre-Philippe de Coulanges made fun of his fellow nationals, relieving Alexander of the accusation of failing to honor his promises made in the conclave to win his election, and advising them to await patiently the bulls which would lift the interdiction of the French clergy" with this song:

Wishing to hasten too fast, one often must fall back;
stop fidgeting; you shall have more and more bulls.
For the happy choice of Ottoboni, have no concern;
from this good and wise pope will come a harvest
of bulls, bulls, bulls.
Prelates, we think you should save your jokes,

for the cardinals are revolted by free rides
on the bulls, bulls, bulls.

Dell'Arco records also that De Coulanges's song circulated around Rome and
that Pasquino could not fail to recognize that the witty cavalier had mocked
with much aplomb the French nobles and their wait for the papal bulls. Wanting
to give his own twist, he added this ending to the lines:

Don't believe the promises of Ottoboni;
I know Pantalon, and you will receive only the song
of the bulls, bulls, bulls.

Indeed Alexander VIII conceded nothing and, at least in this way, did not
betray the work of Innocent XI. Rather, by bringing the matter of the Jansenist
proposals up again, he condemned more of them in 1690, and recommended the
Sun King to impose with authority the respect for Orthodoxy.

Venice continued its private crusade against the Turks, and Alexander took
care of his hometown with money subsidies, as well as seven galleys with 2000
troops for the military campaign in Albania.

Everything seemed to be done in a hurry, in a race against death during
his pontificate, yet Alexander found time even for a cultural project, that of
purchasing for the Vatican, with his own money, the library of the deceased
Christina of Sweden. He managed also to make himself popular with the
peasants by reducing to the minimum the tax on flour and by granting free
trade in wheat. For this action coins were minted with the inscription: "*Re
frumentaria restituta.*"

He died on 1 February 1691 and was buried in St. Peter's. Pasquino sum-
marized his short but active pontificate in this manner:

Here lies a Venetian, finest of politicians,
Peter's successor in the Vatican,
who cured the madmen, straightened the lame,
raised children to adults,
and awakened the dead.
Modestly born and grown,
he lived mundanely
and died of wine.

242. INNOCENT XII (1691–1700)

The longest conclave of the century began on 12 February 1691. The see of
Rome was vacant for exactly five months, and in Rome there were riots and

demonstrations because of the scandalous continuation of clashes in the conclave between the cardinals's different political factions, while the "flying squadron" of the neutrals tried in every way to get the upper hand. At a certain moment there was even the beginnings of a fire and, for a while, they proceeded with the doors open, or, in other words, with an interruption of work. The occasion was a good one to settle disputes and they finally elected one of the Zelanti on 12 July, who was determined however to end the struggle with the Church of France. Cardinal Antonio Pignatelli was consecrated pope on 15 July and took the name of Innocent XII.

He was born on 13 March 1615, in a noble Neapolitan family, in the castle of Spinazzola in Puglia, and was closely linked to Naples. He had been archbishop of the city since 1687, after having served in several nunciatures and reached the rank of cardinal in 1681. Pasquino was to call him *"Pulcinella,"* partly through usual irreverence, but also because he considered him a Neapolitan and, especially, for his long nose and pointed beard typical of the puppet. However, he was the last pope to sport a beard, as after him clean-shaven faces were the rule. His past credited him with a generous and charitable nature towards the poor, and he would not abandon them even as pope. He would place the Lateran Palazzo at the disposal of women unable to work, since it was no longer the residence of the popes, while he put the men into the hospice of S. Michele at the Ripa Grande. Later, between the plague, the earthquake and the flooding by the Tiber in 1695, he used the papal treasury to help continuously those whom he used to call his real "nephews." He cared for the sick and the indigent, as well as for the education of their children. He was a "good pope" and beloved for this by the people who knew that they had found in him a true father.

His relatives, the Pignatelli, did not set foot in the Vatican. Innocent XII was determined to put a stop to nepotism and on 13 July 1692, published a constitution, *Romanorum decet Pontificem*, the drafting of which had been assigned to Giovanni Francesco Albani, the future Clement XI. To justify the bull, the pope asked Celestino Sfondrati to write a pamphlet explaining its historical basis and the deleterious results of the boundless love of popes for their relatives. This was *Nepotismus theologice expensus, quando nepotismus sub Innocentio XII abolitus fuit*. In essence, the pope would no longer under any pretext confer offices, positions or property of the Church to relatives who, in any case, if priests, would receive emoluments equal to those of prelates unrelated to the pontiff. The bull was sworn to by Innocent himself and by the thirty-five cardinals present in Rome. The Protestants applauded this initiative, although by now they were only distant onlookers. When, towards the end of his pontificate, Innocent had to proceed with the appointment of certain cardinals, some of them proposed the archbishop of Taranto as a very worthy person, but he replied: "That is true, but he is my nephew." And he was struck from the list.

The worldly life in Rome felt the effects of this measure, since many Roman families counted on the newly rich who "on the death of a pope" organized banquets and parties at the expense of the uncle or grandfather in order to put themselves on show. They complained that the city was becoming a sort of monastery, and it was surely not a poor man who wrote the following *Pasquinade* to complain about the ban on nepotism, accusing Innocent especially of not acting in good faith:

What result will the Holy See ever have from
ostracising nephews
if those who reign cannot be trusted?
How much better it would be to have nepotism,
the splendor of Rome and the foundation of government,
than nourish Jansenism with favors!

Moreover the demolition of the Theater of Tor di Nona in 1697 gave rise to much criticism, after it had been "enlarged and, one might say, built" since it was at first made of wood, "at a cost of a hundred and more thousand *scudi* a few years ago," observed the minister of the duke of Savoy, a certain Giobbe De Gubernatis. And Pasquino commented:

But what is this, you built me with your own hands,
and suddenly you are destroying me?

On the other hand, Innocent XII established the maritime customs office at Ripa Grande, while the land customs office finished up behind the basilica of Antonino. The tribunals were in large measure joined together in the Innocentian Curia, that is, the Montecitorio Palace, built by Carlo Fontana, one of the most imposing creations of late Baroque.

In essence, this pope was a profound man of the Church who devoted all his attention to the religious reform of the Roman clergy, after he had cleansed the higher ranks of nepotism. He ordered the priests to wear cassocks in Rome and to do spiritual exercises twice a year. He also established a "Congregation for the discipline of the clergy" which oversaw the dignity of the prelates. Resistance was considerable because "laxity" was always just around the corner. But the principle to be respected was clear: either be a priest or be a layman. But critical periods were about to arise in this field, and the principle would be ignored.

Innocent's religious dedication spread throughout the entire world and there was a notable increase in missions in the Americas, Asia, and Africa. Here, too, the pope invested great sums of money, though new problems arose in these mission lands, especially in China, through the attempt to reconcile millennial local traditions with the Gospel message, resulting in controversies which only time would partially resolve. But, Innocent had no intention of making concessions to the disadvantage of the pontifical dignity of the Apostolic Throne. He tried conciliation without compromise where it was possible, though he was not very successful with Louis XIV.

The negotiations to settle the dispute with the Church of France lasted for two years and the French clergy finally had to declare that whatever had been deliberated during the famous assembly in 1682 was to be considered undecided. "Prostrate at the feet of Your Holiness, we declare that we are ineffably sorry," said the candidates for the episcopal vacancies, and they were thereby granted canonical rule. The Sun King, for his part, withdrew the decree about the observance of the four Gallican propositions, so all was well up to this point. However, the king clarified that he had only cancelled the obligation to teach them but that he could not prevent by force anyone who so wanted to declare their adherence to the propositions. And that was what conciliation meant.

Yet there was a compromise in the fact that the pope had to accept the extension of the right of "royalty." It is true that the Curia thereby recovered a nation which it risked losing, and the danger of a schism had been avoided which was a great achievement. Gallicanism stayed alive and would be heard in all its force in the French Revolution and in Napoleon, but Innocent could not have avoided that.

On the European level, however, the diplomatic action by the Curia was in the circumstances well viewed, and led Charles II of Spain, who had no children and did not know to whom he should leave his throne, to ask the pope for his opinion. The question was examined by a committee of cardinals, including Albani, which rendered an opinion in favor of the sons of the Dauphin of France, the husband of Maria Theresa, elder sister of Charles II. That opinion was accepted and included by the king in his testament. But things would not go smoothly and the succession to the throne of Spain would start a war which Innocent XII was never to see.

He ended his pontificate during the splendor of the Jubilee of 1700. Peace appeared to reign in Europe and the occasion seemed to him propitious to have the Great Powers come together in front of the Holy Door; it was the last dream of this "good pope" who, despite his gout, tried to give audiences to the pilgrims as long as he had the strength.

He did not see the end of the Holy Year but died on 27 September 1700. He was buried in the Vatican in the modest sarcophagus that had been prepared for him. Subsequently Benedict XIV would erect a monument to him between the Chapel of St. Sebastian and the Chapel of the Most Blessed Sacrament.

243. CLEMENT XI (1700–1721)

The first conclave of the eighteenth century, taking place in the midst of the Holy Year, could not prolong matters with lines of pilgrims in front of the Holy Door. Rapidity was essential for a Europe, which appeared ready to tear itself apart in new wars. More than ever a neutral pope was needed who would continue the religious effort for peace started by Innocent XII. The "flying squadron" had that in mind, but did not have the two-thirds control.

On 1 November arrived the news of the death of Charles II. On the 6th, Louis XIV greeted his nephew Philip V as the new king of Spain with the exclamation, "Now the Pyrenees no longer exist!" which Emperor Leopold I resented. It was therefore necessary to take a decision, and a compromise was reached with the pro-French cardinals. On the 23rd Cardinal Giovanni Francesco Albani, a person clearly close to Louis XIV and to Philip V, was elected and though he displayed neutrality, this was more an indication of his insecurity than anything. In fact, he was to be called *cunctator* or "temporizer," and his behavior would cost the Holy See dearly.

Born in Urbino on 23 July 1649 to a family of nobles, Albani became Governor of Rieti and of Orvieto, and was made a cardinal by Alexander VIII. He had been very close to his predecessor in the work of reforming the Papal State. This was a guarantee of his anti-nepotism, even though it was not as wholehearted as with Innocent XII. His vulnerability was revealed from the moment of his election when he declined the appointment, advancing various pretexts such as the fact that he had not received all the priestly ordinations. Basically, he foresaw the grave problems that the new century would bring the pontiff, and he wanted to stay clear of them. He was honest and recognized that he was incapable of handling them.

He was reminded that to refuse the election was like an act of rebellion against the judgment of God since the Holy Spirit had selected him. So he had to acquiesce and on 30 November was consecrated bishop, then on 8 December pope with the name of Clement XI.

The early days of his pontificate were excellent and in line with his predecessor's. To his brother Orazio who came to him with his entire family, he said: "You have lost your natural relative; now in me you have only a father in common with all of the faithful." He forbade any relative of his to meddle in political or religious affairs, to accept offices or adopt titles. The Albanis in fact would never get any money from Clement and when his nephew Annibale later became a cardinal and reached the rank of chamberlain, he achieved those because of his personal merits cited by the Sacred College itself. Furthermore, his uncle took pains to make sure that no money reached his nephew's pocket in excess of the prescribed amount.

However, with the closing of the Holy Door at the end of the Jubilee Year, the war drama began for Clement. The papal couriers of peace sent to the three sovereigns accomplished nothing, partly because Clement had given Philip V grants from Church funds. His neutrality appeared ambiguous and that "dual position as universal father and chief of a temporal State left him perplexed and hindered him in his actions," Castiglioni notes. The eternal dilemma reemerged, despite the past blows suffered at the international level, and while Clement XI tried to show his good and holy intentions, basically he was unable to take a clear stand.

The European States were by now too mature to be fooled by equivocal positions and Austria with Joseph I found outlets in the Papal State at which to oppose France. Mantua, Parma, Piacenza, and Comacchio ended up in the imperial domain and the pope's protests were in vain. France did not come to his aid and Rome itself was threatened. In January of 1709 Clement had to sign a treaty by which he recognized Archduke Charles as king of Spain.

It was a complete about face in respect to Philip V and Louis XIV, but it was chiefly the result of the pope's political ineptness on an international level, and certain 'temporizations" cost him dearly by then. The French ambassador left Rome indignantly and Archduke Charles, who had become Emperor under the name of Charles VI, hoodwinked the pope and did not return Comacchio as Joseph I had promised him in the treaty of 1709.

Then the Utrecht territories which the pope had considered as papal fiefdoms were assigned to new princes without his having any say. Southern Italy and Sardinia went to Austria while the House of Savoy assumed the title of King of Sicily. The duchy of Parma and Piacenza, which had been universally recognized for two centuries as under papal sovereignty with investiture to the Farnese family, now on its way to extinction and with it the regular payment of tribute, remained under Austrian dominion. The pope's protests had no effect.

If until then the Papal State had resisted assaults from the princedoms of the peninsula, from then on even its "Italian" prestige would decline. "The temporal authority of the papacy was so shaken among the bordering States also," Ranke comments, "that this situation had repercussions on the controversies concerning ecclesiastical jurisdiction, so closely connected with political relationships."

The conflicts would grow and the Holy See would no longer have the internal strength to keep its own faithful to it in the Papal State and in Italy generally, while laicism, which had become an anticlerical "system," spread more and more. The bull *Unigenitus Dei Filius* of 1713, for example, with its repeated condemnation of the Jansenists, simply revived the basic disagreements, and with it appeals for a council and doubts about papal infallibility. "In Rome, if one considered matters as a whole, if one looked about oneself, one had to admit that there was a danger of losing everything," Ranke again observes.

The first to realize this had to be Clement XI who ended by isolating himself within his state. He passed out in alms and pious works about a million *scudi* of his own money, trying to gain the favor of the poor as Innocent XII had done. Even the authorized resumption of the lottery game, which had existed in Rome at the time of Alexander VII but had been suppressed, formed part of this policy.

The Lotto "started being extracted in the courtyard of the Pamphili Palazzo," the diarist Francesco Valesio narrates, giving us all the ins and outs of a "drawing" of the times. "Under the double portico of that palazzo which divides the two courtyards, stood a structure of the same length as the arch, above which the judge of the Lotto, one of the solicitors from the Chamber called Pian Castelli, sat on his chair. On his right there was a desk where a notary wrote, and on the stand there were two urns surrounded by glass, in one of which were the white tickets corresponding to the number of the others, among which were those yielding prizes. Two small boys picked out the tickets and a curious man, Mattia Matto, read the numbers out to the public. Six armed soldiers from the Castello were at hand for the drawing."

However, Clement XI's saving grace within the Papal State was his role as a patron of the arts. He enriched the Vatican Library with many Oriental manuscripts and gave a big boost to archaeology with the first scientific excavations among the catacombs. In the Capitol he established an academy of painting and sculpture, and ordered the protection of the city's artistic works. But it was above all the building projects which earned the praise of his subjects, with the famous meridian in S. Maria degli Angeli, the erection of the obelisk in the Pantheon piazza and the creation of the port of Ripetta on the Tiber. The latter would go on functioning until the construction of the Cavour bridge, which unfortunately lead to its demolition.

Clement XI's building activity was also carried on in other cities of the Papal State, with the completion of the aqueduct in Civitavecchia, and the building of a viaduct at Civitacastellana. Urbino, as the pope's birthplace, enjoyed his patronage, with the cancellation of the debts of the Commune, the building of a school for the young, the restoration of the palaces of the archbishop and the duke, as well as that of the city walls, and the foundation of a public library with new privileges granted to the university which has maintained a great reputation up to the present day.

One can say that the benefits denied to his relatives were transferred by Clement to his birthplace and, under certain aspects, this was another form of nepotism. Pasquino could not ignore it in one of his exchanges with his "colleague" Marforio:

MARFORIO:
Tell me, Pasquino, what are you doing?
PASQUINO:
Well, I am guarding Rome lest it move to Urbino.

Clement XI died on 19 March 1721 and was buried beneath the floor of the choir in St. Peter's, as he had wished. A simple marble slab commemorates him.

244. INNOCENT XIII (1721–1724)

The conclave to choose a successor to Clement XI lasted five weeks, and its progress was no different from what had now become customary since the middle of the seventeenth century. The usual political divisions occured this time pitting Spain and France against Austria, with a right of exclusion or veto on the part of the sovereigns for candidates more or less acceptable. In any event, it was a conclave very often "open" to contact with the outside world, as a *Pasquinade* written for the occasion records:

> Guards surround the great portal,
> custodians are at the doors,
> they wall up the windows on the balcony
> and yet, as though these strong men
> were old maids from the Conservatory
> they commit a thousand frauds against the closure,
> and turn the windows into parlours.

Cardinal Fabrizio Paolucci, the Secretary of State under Clement XI and pro-French, was excluded by imperial veto, even though bribery was attempted to get him elected. In the end, the usual neutral candidate, Michelangelo Conti, peaceful, pious, sickly, and inoffensive, who was acceptable to the Great Powers and would continue to do their bidding, was elected on 8 April 1721.

He was born on 13 May 1655, at Poli near Palestrina, a descendant of the noble family of the counts of Segni which had given the Church various pontiffs, the most famous of whom was Innocent III. Governor of various cities in the Papal State, he had been the bishop of Osimo and Viterbo, the nuncio in Switzerland and Portugal, and had been made a cardinal by Clement XI. He was consecrated pope on 18 April and, in memory of his famous ancestor, took the name of Innocent XIII.

He was certainly not his equal. Apart from his chronic sickly condition, he did not have the weight to bring new prestige to the Chair of Peter. Pasquino said: "He's always asleep." But, however calm and quiet and condemning of nepotism, he could not refuse a favor to his brother, Bernardo

Maria, whom he made a cardinal. However, he did nothing else of an authoritarian or personal nature.

He put Paolucci back into the position of Secretary of State and followed the policy of his predecessor, recalling the terms in the bull Unigenitus. The Jesuits gave him a few headaches in China, where they were being criticized by the missionaries from other religious Orders, as well as by the papal legate in the Far East. The pontiff turned the matter over to the Secretary of *Propaganda Fide*, Luigi Caraffa, who sent a decree to the General of the Jesuits in 1725 with the accusation of their having been "inciters and promoters of the incarceration of missionaries, giving scandal by serving as spies and jailers." The Jesuits submitted a memorial in their defense and the polemics went on and on, too much so for such an insecure pope. Pastor, however, considered that decree as a precursor of the "Brief" which suppressed the Society in 1773.

Nothing else shook the pontificate of Innocent XIII. The investiture of Naples and Sicily, which the pope granted in 1722 to Charles VI, was a completely formal matter. Naples was already his since Utrecht, and, at The Hague in 1720, he had exchanged Sicily for Sardinia—the other island ignored by the European powers and over which, in the dark Middle Ages, the pope had claimed a right of sovereignty. Parma and Piacenza remained Austrian territory, and nothing was ever said about the restitution of Comacchio.

Innocent XIII died on 7 May 1724, and was buried in St. Peter's where a rightly modest epitaph remembers him. Also what Pasquino wrote seemed correct:

> Pope Conti has died,
> he who did not do much good
> because he didn't want to,
> And didn't do much bad
> because he wasn't able to.

245. BENEDICT XIII (1724—1730)

In the conclave that began on the death of Innocent XIII, the favorite once again was Paolucci, Secretary of State to two popes. However, the Austrian ambassador, Maximilian von Kaunitz, used the imperial veto against him, causing a rumpus in the "closed" assembly of cardinals, but by this time no one was scandalised by certain events, and the "flying squadron" of Zelanti again managed to put up their own representative. Old enough not to be too energetic for the European sovereigns, he was both austere and full of kindness. This was Cardinal Pier Francesco Orsini, who was elected on 29 May 1724 and consecrated pope on 4 June with the name of Benedict XIII.

He was born on 2 February 1649, at Gravina near Bari, but was a member of the Roman family of nobles, the Orsini, traditionally linked to the papal throne. As a very young man he had entered the Dominican Order, renouncing his inheritance of the duchy of Gravina, but no doubt his belonging to the famous family facilitated his appointment as cardinal at only twenty-three years of age. He had ruled successively over the dioceses of Manfredonia, Cesena, and Benevento, to which he was especially close and which were to remain dear to him also as pope.

Benedict XIII, as Cardinal Lambertini described him "did not have the least idea of what it means to govern." He was ascetic and continued to be so as pope, not changing his simple, nearly poor lifestyle. His favorite occupation was to conduct religious services and to consecrate churches. "He thought only about having the baptisteries in Rome altered so he could baptise by immersion as was done formerly," Montesquieu wrote in his Voyage d'Italie. The French writer in this circumstance cites an event by which he seems to ridicule the "untiring" religious attitude of this pope: "Three years ago he was baptising some Jews and performed the ceremony in accordance with ancient custom. A cold wind was blowing and he stayed for three hours, bareheaded, at the door of St. Peter's which even the laymen present could not manage. The same day he forgot that in the morning he had said his Mass, so he said it twice, because he never stops."

In his deeply mystical zeal he promoted veneration of the saints and to that end he made a series of canonizations, including those of John of the Cross and Luis Gonzaga. With special vigor he decried the display of wealth by the cardinals and prohibited the use of wigs and beards by ecclesiastics, who had to wear long robes but without trains. In addition, there were severe penalties for transgressors of disciplinary rules and a special jail was built at Corneto for them. He forbade, too, the Jesuits from engaging in polemics, and with the bull *Pretiosus* he renewed the concepts of *Unigenitus*, continuing the Jansenist controversy, though that movement had begun to lose strength on a strictly doctrinal level.

His religious zeal was fully satisfied with the Jubilee Year of 1725. For that event, the imposing staircase of the Piazza di Spagna was opened, joining the piazza below with the church of Trinità dei Monti above. The official poet of that Holy Year was a member of the Arcadia, a mediocre improviser of poems, Bernardino Perfetti, whom Benedict XIII wanted to crown in the Capitol.

And in the atmosphere of austerity which the pope decreed for the occasion in Rome, he even abolished the lottery, seeing therein something almost sinful, in the interest payments which came from it to the public treasury for which the drawings were held. For women, more infected by this vice, jail was contemplated, as well as an order for all of them to go before the Inquisition. However, the prohibition served no purpose as it was limited to the Papal State and the

Romans continued to gamble in other States, with the result that big amounts of money went over the border to fatten the treasuries of other sovereigns. Rome should have become a holy city and Benedict XIII its pastor, but that was not what happened. "Public simony rules today in Rome," Montesquieu observed. "One has never seen in the government of the Church crime reigning so openly, while evil men are promoted to jobs from all sides." However, it was not the fault of the pope, unworldly and inexpert in managing the affairs of the government, but rather that of a base individual, Niccolò Coscia.

As his secretary he had already seemed irreplaceable to Benedict XIII when he had been cardinal and archbishop of Benevento, so he brought him to Rome and had him appointed cardinal, entrusting him with all the political and financial affairs of the Papal State. Coscia abused his authority, causing the finances of the Church to fall into total chaos. "There is no doubt that he was one of the most accomplished scoundrels ever to carry on his evil deeds in the Curia," Seppelt observed. "In a very brief time he organized a shameless traffic in favoritism, managing to fill the most influential posts with fellow crooks whilst tirelessly working to enrich himself."

It is likely that "the pontiff, absorbed as he was in religious matters, was not aware of anything," hazarded Castiglioni, but this "ignorance" is not to his credit. Understandably, Montesquieu could but confirm that Benedict XIII was "greatly hated by the Roman population." The Romans were not about to die from hunger, as the French writer asserted, but they were still unhappy because, through the fault of Coscia, the people of Benevento were preferred to them. "All the money in Rome winds up in Benevento," notes Montesquieu again, because the pope hasn't "any idea about worldly business . . . The people from Benevento exploit his weakness and, since they themselves are persons of no worth, they push ahead people of no worth."

The Sacred College repeatedly tried, in vain, to get the pope to open his eyes about Coscia's crimes, but he thought they were all lies and, as a result, Coscia stayed safely in his job until the death of Benedict XIII.

Needless to say, on the international level the Papal State continued to suffer humiliations, though it did regain possession of Comacchio, but only by huge concessions to the Habsburgs on ecclesiastical matters. Also Vittorio Amedeo II of Savoy was recognized as king of Sardinia, in the face of the ancient papal sovereignty over that island, and obtained rights over all the Sardinian dioceses from Coscia, who was, of course, well compensated.

This authentic "criminal," as Seppelt called him, would be put on trial by Clement XII. Excommunicated and sentenced to ten years in prison in Castel Sant'Angelo, he would manage to get away scott-free, despite the sentence that he pay back every cent and a fine of one hundred thousand *scudi*. He would even participate fully in the conclaves of 1730 and 1740, and in the end Benedict XIV actually freed him from prison.

Benedict XIII died on 21 February 1730, and the Romans, of course, took to the streets wanting to kill Coscia, but he had already disappeared with his band of following. The pope was buried in a magnificent mausoleum in S. Maria sopra Minerva. His subjects could only vent their fury with an epitaph:

This tomb encloses the bones of a little monk;
more than an admirer of the saints,
he was a protector of brigands.

246. CLEMENT XII (1730—1740)

The conclave for the election of a successor to Benedict XIII lasted more than four months and was one of the longest and most corrupt of the eighteenth century. In addition to the factions supported by various Catholic States, the Savoy family also had their own representative in Cardinal Albani, although the one who campaigned most was the House of the Medici, on its way to extinction like the Farneses.

Foreseeing the loss of the Grand Duchy of Tuscany, in theory a fiefdom of the pope, the ancient Florentine family tried to assure itself the favors of the next pope. It seems that, through their banks in London, Paris, and The Hague, they managed to buy votes for Cardinal Lorenzo Corsini who came from a wealthy Florentine family. They succeeded because Spain vetoed Lorenzo Imperiali, supported by the Zelanti, while the exclusion against Corsini, declared by Austria and France, vanished. He was elected on 12 July 1730, and consecrated pope on the 16th under the name of Clement XII.

Lorenzo Corsini was born in Florence on 7 April 1652. After studying at the Roman College and law at the University of Pisa, he got a position in the Chancery in Rome through his uncle the cardinal, though on his uncle's death the young man returned to Florence. He was recalled by Innocent XI who ordained him a priest and gave him back his position, later sending him as nuncio to Vienna even if Corsini had shown his best under Alexander VIII as the treasurer of the Apostolic Chamber. Clement XI had raised him to the cardinalate, and from 1725 on he had been the bishop of Frascati.

He perhaps understood financial matters better than other ecclesiasticals and could have been the right man to clean up the disastrous situation of the papal accounts. But, apart from the immediate remedies, such as the trial of Coscia and the eviction from the Curia of the Beneventans, and the ending of long-term abuses like the cancellation of the concessions, the deficit was too big to be eliminated. Moreover, income from various States to the Holy See came to a halt because "royalties" had been taken away from the previous popes in France, southern Italy, and Sardinia.

The Roman people did not believe that the financial mess could not be put right and they considered the high prelates only spendthrifts. They had a prejudice against the new pope when he had been a cardinal and was rumored to have kept a prostitute in Piazza Scossacavalli, a woman named Clarice. Thus according to Pasquino:

> When romantic Corsini goes to see his sweetheart,
> he finds her in such sorrow that he cannot
> pull away from her.

But he could not forget her when he reached the papal throne. Again Pasquino teased him:

> I have been a wealthy abbot, a comfortable prelate,
> an impoverished cardinal and an uprooted pope.

It certainly did not improve the financial situation of the State to print paper money or to reintroduce the lottery but it perhaps helped Clement XII become dearer to the people. In fact, the lottery was permitted from 1732 onwards, and the threat of excommunication by Benedict XIII was revoked by a decree that specified that the proceeds would be invested in charities and in beautifying the city and the Papal State. Thus, no income was available for the treasury.

The reasoning by which the pope justified a gambling game considered sinful by Benedict XIII, was that it was a kind of indirect sales tax and voluntarily paid by the citizen who wanted to try his luck with his own money. Therefore there was no coercion by the Apostolic Chamber which would continue to run the lottery. The first drawing of the new Lotto took place on 14 February 1732 at the Capitol, as Valesio recalls in his diary: "A stand was erected on one side behind the statue at the top of the steps; the stand was decorated with damask and velvet, as was the top of the stand, but it was completely open in front. There sat several clerical officials from the Chamber." The drawing lasted from 5 P.M. to 7 P.M., and the following numbers were drawn: 56, 11, 54, 18, and 6.

Then there were a large number of public works. The Trevi Fountain was finished as was the Palazzo of the Consulta on the Quirinal, and the façade of the basilica of St. John Lateran with, in the interior, the splendid Corsini Chapel dedicated to St. Andrew, the patron saint of the pope's family. There was also the construction on the Capitol of the museum of ancient statues, embellished with imperial busts and inscriptions, and the Teatro Argentina which was inaugurated, as Sergio Delli records it, "with the Berenice of Domenico Sarro, masterfully sung by the boy soprano Farfallino, whose real name was

Giacinto Fontana." Outside Rome there were the restoration and draining of the Val di Chiana, hydraulic projects in the Ravenna area, and the new pier in the port of Ancona.

It should also be noted that, from 1733 on, the pope was completely blind, and with the usual aches and pains of old age increasing, he often had to take to his bed. Overseeing all these temporal and ecclesiastical matters was difficult for him, and he did not have anyone in whom he could fully trust. His nephew Cardinal Neri Corsini did not have the talents to guide his uncle, though he tried to be an art patron like him, and it was he who built the new Palazzo Corsini, embellishing it with paintings and a precious library. So business matters were handled largely by officials of the Curia and favoritism and clientism flourished, despite everything.

Under such conditions it is understandable that the Papal State's prestige declined and this became apparent during the War of the Polish Succession. "Papal lands were overrun and devastated by the belligerents, who paid no attention to the rights of that neutral State. Indeed, the Spaniards went so far as to recruit soldiers in Rome itself," as Castiglioni notes, "provoking serious riots among the population which did not want to hear any more about those wars or put up with the depredations of foreign armies. On 13 March 1736, the people of Trastevere, rioting, forced the Spanish commanders to free the soldiers they had rounded up. They went on to attack Farnese Palace, to tear down the emblems of Don Carlos, and then to the Palazzo of Spain where they were repelled by the militiamen. At Velletri the anger of the people caused some Spanish soldiers to jump from the walls."

The results of the peace treaty of Vienna of 1738 were harmful to the Papal State. Don Carlos of Bourbon took possession of Naples and Sicily while, as a result of bribes during the conclave, the Lorraines took over Tuscany where the Medici dynasty had died out.

The ancient feudal rights of the clergy were definitively lost and concordats with the new sovereigns would be needed to save what could be preserved in the running of the dioceses. However the Habsburgs retained control of Parma and Piacenza, and papal protests had no effect.

Clement XII had not been up to the expectations of those who had elected him in the hope that he would give a new direction to the management of the State, seeing him a politician and an economist more than a man of the Church. Instead, he turned out to be a real spiritual head of the Holy See. But not because he had canonized St. Vincent de Paul, nor because he had sent a naïve and useless letter to the Protestants in Saxony assuring them that,should they return to the Catholic Church, they would retain ownership of church property which had been taken over, nor because he had supported financially yet another victorious crusade of Philip V against the Moors occupying the city of Oran.

Rather, his position as the head of the apostolic see soared with his stand against Freemasonry. The famous secret society showed up in Florence in 1733, and two years later it arrived in Rome with the propaganda of Tomaso Crudeli di Poppi, the writer of anticlerical poems. The bull of condemnation by Clement, *In Eminenti*, was issued on 28 April 1738, and meant the excommunication of anyone who joined that society because, as the pope specified, it brought together people of any religion or sect under the appearance of doing acts of natural ethics, binding them with an oath and the threat of punishment to keep secret all discussion in the various "lodges,"

The power of Freemasonry was certainly not damaged by that bull or those of later popes, but it did establish what appeared to be the definite position of the Church of Rome. And yet, with time, a dialogue would be reached between the parties which, with John Paul II, would lead to the abolition of the excommunication in the new Code of Canon Law.

The pope was also very interested in the missions, especially in the East where there occurred two significant events of this evangelical work. First was the readmission into the Church of Rome of 10,000 Copts together with their patriarch, and second was the establishment of the Orsini College at Ullano in Calabria, funded from the family's patrimony, to facilitate the return of the Greek Orthodox to Catholicism.

Clement XII died on 6 February 1740, and was buried in the splendid Corsini Chapel in St. John Lateran. Perhaps Pasquino exalted him somewhat saying that he "died a beggar." But if Clement was ever a "spendthrift," he was that with his own family's money and for the good of the Church.

247. BENEDICT XIV (1740–1758)

The conclave following the death of Clement XII lasted for six months and showed it could beat all previous records. After a dispute about the candidature of Cardinal Ottoboni, which dragged on and ended with his death on 28 February, the battle moved onto two fronts, the Austro-French on one side and Spain, Naples, and Tuscany on the other. One group of cardinals were for Neri Corsini and another for Annibale Albani, and no compromise was possible. In the end, Pompeo Aldobrandini, positively viewed by the three Powers, seemed to be in the best position, but one more vote was needed.

So the proceedings continued, with long faces and grimaces, until a phrase was tossed in by Cardinal Prospero Lambertini with his sense of humor, which would become proverbial: "You want a holy man? Elect Gotti. You want a politician? Elect Aldobrandini. You want a good man? Elect me." His words seemed like a cool breeze under the summer sun and a panacea. Not "almost through inspiration" but "almost through desperation," on 17 August 1740,

Prospero Lambertini was unanimously elected. When he was asked, as was the custom, whether or not he accepted, he replied in the affirmative, and for three reasons: "The first, not to make light of your kindness; the second, not to oppose the manifest will of God, which I deem it to be as I have never aspired to such lofty vanity; the third, to bring these meetings to an end since I believe that they are a scandal for the whole world because of their length."

Prospero Lambertini was born in Bologna on 31 May 1675. A student in Rome of the Somaschi, he had later studied theology and law. Having become a cleric, he gained a reputation as a consistorial lawyer, doing his apprenticeship in the office of Monsignor Alessandro Caprara, a judge on the Sacra Rota. Clement XI had appointed him a canon in St. Peter's and from then on he had had a brilliant ecclesiastical career as a result of his sound cultural preparation. He became a consultant to the Holy Office, an associate with the Congregation of Ceremonies, and Rector of the Sapienza University, but it was Benedict XIII who promoted him to the high levels of the priesthood. In 1726 he became bishop of Ancona and the following year a cardinal. Clement XIII then appointed him archbishop of Bologna.

What inspired Lambertini in those years was a fruitful apostolate carried on with profound zeal. He was a pastor active in his diocese who kept himself informed about the conditions of the poor, issued orders to lighten punishment, and established a committee to do charitable works, such as visiting and comforting the sick. He was not a bigot but he was against certain theatrics in religious ceremonies and he prohibited them in a series of notices. He sought simplicity and that earned him some criticism. He was not the sort, though, to bear resentment.

He knew how to command, and he accompanied his sudden outbursts with the four letter interjection, a bad habit which remained in his vocabulary even as pope, so that he would say: "I want to sanctify that word by granting a plenary indulgence to whomever will say it ten times a day!" It was the mark of his unequalled spirit, of one who speaks bluntly and calls a spade a spade; the Cardinal Roncalli of the eighteenth century. In addition, he would be the John XXIII of that century, as Falconi brilliantly noted, attributing to him "a conception of the Church and the papacy which showed that he was a modest but convinced precursor of the ideas of John." He was consecrated pope on 22 August 1740, and took the name of Benedict XIV.

The comparison of Lambertini and Roncalli is apt, and one can begin to see it in the relationship which the two men had with the faithful laity of Rome, where both the popes acted with them like any ordinary priest. Benedict XIV went about in every quarter of the city, talking amicably with the poor, a method of contact by which he learned first hand about the precarious conditions of the life of the people, and he was totally involved in saving the State from famine. He limited the expenses of the court, reduced the staff, lowered the salaries of the officers and the wages of the troops. Although it was not the technique of an economist but rather the optimism of the improviser, he succeeded in bettering the finances of the State. "I am the pope before I am a sovereign," he defended himself before his critics for some of the measures he took more from humanitarian than administrative reasons. For example, in an encyclical he granted the poor peasants the right to collect straw from any of the fields in the Papal State regardless of the landowners who wanted to prevent them, and imposed a fine of 30 *scudi* for violators to be distributed among the poor themselves.

He offered further evidence of apostolic charity during the Jubilee Year of 1750. According to a chronicler of that period the Trinità Hospital, which by its charter had to accept poor pilgrims for three consecutive days, in the month of April alone gave out forty-three thousand meals." Benedict often stopped to chat with the pilgrims and, ignoring any protocol and putting aside his mitre and staff, would slip into the line to enter the Holy Door.

In the same spirit of simplicity, he dealt with politics and religion. At a time of great difficulty for the Church, Benedict was aware that in the absolutism of sovereigns the principle of a State religion was growing ever stronger, while with the spread of enlightenment, Christianity itself was in danger of a crisis in an ever more secular world. The only means of saving it was to avoid a policy of hostility and trust in tolerance with a spirit of universal conciliation, the "peace policy," which Falconi records, reproducing some phrases in letters written by Lambertini to Cardinal Pierre Guerin de Tencin: "The sword does not fit well in the hand of him who, however unworthy, is the vicar of Jesus Christ," in other words, the pope "is and must be unarmed."

In the light of this ideal, it did not matter that the lands of the Papal State became battlefields during the War of the Austrian Succession. The pope himself offered free passage to the troops and, to achieve his purpose, he was happy to bear "the martyrdom of neutrality." The loss of Parma, Piacenza, and Guastalla at Aix-en-Provence was sad—they passed to Philip of Bourbon—but it was a sacrifice in the name of an evangelical ideal, an adapting to the changing times. In view of this, it is permitted to suspect, as many men in the Curia already did, that Benedict, at the bottom of his heart, was convinced that with time he would eliminate a great part of the temporal power of the papacy. Thus, all the concordats stipulated with the various European nations is justified, which he treated mildly, convinced as he was that renunciation of temporal rights would favor the spiritual rebirth of the Church of Rome. Hence there was the concordat with the king of Sardinia, who was named the apostolic vicar for the papal fiefdoms in that country, the one with the king of Naples, which limited ecclesiastical immunities, that with Spain which gave the king universal right of patronage by which he could grant to anyone twelve thousand existing benefices, leaving Rome with only fifty-two, and the concordat with Portugal in which Benedict granted to the king the title of Most Faithful King in an appropriate constitution.

Again, this pope permitted Empress Maria Theresa to tolerate Protestants in her domains, while recommending that she seek, with Christian tenderness, to convert them, and officially recognized the king of Prussia, until then considered by the Holy See merely the margrave of Brandenburg. However, in compensation, this sovereign favored the Catholics in his State. "One might say that he discerned," as again Falconi notes, "the origin of the decline of papal prestige in the trend of the popes to behave like sovereigns, claiming universal superiority," by then historically outdated. This was not imprudent behavior but rather the shrewdness of someone who "does not see in the Church a mechanism for power but simply a complex of administrative offices in the service of all the local churches."

Although Benedict XIV was a meteor in the heavens of the Church of Rome which would reappear only two centuries later with John XXIII, that does not take away the fact that he was a shock for the papacy, with "the abandonment of the rigid *non possumus*, with eyes opened finally on the reality, and recognition of the situations created by the reforms of the sixteenth century," as Zizola notes.

This pope, in fact, had a clear view of strictly ecclesiastical problems, clearing up uncertainties and gaps, respecting other opinions and having the ability to distinguish between dogmas and theories. Hence, we see him cancelling holy days of obligation, which amounted, not counting Sundays, to thirty-six according to a constitution of Urban VIII, and we see him putting pressure on the bishops to watch more closely the training of priests in the seminaries. He approved two new religious Orders, the Passionists of St. Paul of the Cross and the Redemptorists of St. Alphonsus de' Liguori. He also threw himself body and soul into a reform of the Breviario, which he would not complete, while leaving behind principles which would remain valid, like the limitation on holy days. He was not against the veneration of saints and in this he was guided more by a principle of credibility, and the usefulness that he hoped would be reaped from their veneration.

For this reason he was cautious in recognizing miracles and canonizations as, for example, when he opposed the canonization of Cardinal Bellarmino, explaining his position by declaring that it could be a "pretext for anyone who wishes to say bad things about us." And so he also abolished the Inquisition in Tuscany. In the arguments over the Jesuits he took a prudent position, though he was to die before he could settle the problems that they had created for him in Portugal by their activities in politico-commercial matters. Ranke notes, "it is probable that he would not have destroyed the Society but he would have submitted it to a complete and radical reform."

However, he did renew the condemnation of Freemasonry and was also an ardent defender of the marriage bond. He busied himself, too, with the missions, and concerning the controversies that arose in China, he told the missionaries to eliminate the customs that he considered pure superstition. With the Near East, he displayed an open mind; Eastern Christians could remain faithful to their rites and the Latin missionaries were not to coerce them into a Western liturgy.

All this apostolic activity is documented in a series of writings and bulls which basically show the great culture of this pope, modern and anticipative in many aspects. The pontificate of Benedict XIV can be considered "a government from a desk," according to a definition dear to Falconi, and one which was naturally stigmatized in a *Pasquinade* written by some official in the Curia as *"Maximus in folio, minimus in solio,"* a variation of the benign *"Vir bonus in folio, vir bonus in solio."*

Because, basically, the populace did not complain about him, Pasquino, ended "philosophically" by praising him:

> Here is a pope who was good for Rome.
> He possessed enough faith,
> advanced the business of his class
> and knows how to take the world as it comes.

Moreover, Benedict XIV did not refrain from urban projects, either of a humanitarian nature, such as the enlargement of the hospitals of S. Spirito and S. Gallicano, or a religious one. He had the church of S. Marcellino built, he restored the façade of St. Mary Major and arranged the construction in its interior of the splendid baldachin at the papal altar. And in the center of the Colosseum, he had a cross raised, declaring that place to be sacred because of the blood shed by Christians, according to an ancient, yet false, tradition. Obviously, however, by sanctifying the amphitheater, the pope simply wanted to preserve it from further pillaging, so that it would no longer be considered a travertine quarry.

Benedict XIV was a patron of the arts in a new sense, as a protector of scientific as well as of artistic activity. He proved that by giving a more liberal interpretation to Boniface VIII's bull *De cadaverum sectione* to encourage a broader study of anatomy, and by propagating the sacrosanct freedom of a writer to express his own ideas. With this in mind he recommended to the consultants of the Index to examine books with the diligence of the Inquisitors, but also with a mind free of all prejudice and putting aside, with the impartiality of the faith, any feeling of nationality or partisanship. Thus many books were removed from the Index, which explains the dedication by Voltaire of the Mohammed in the following distich:

Lambertini here is the honor of Rome and
father to the world,
Teaching the world by his writings and
adorning it by his virtues.

On the intellectual level, recognition of his personality knew no frontiers as can be seen by his correspondence with Protestant schismatics, Russian Orthodox or atheists, his dissertations about poetry and art, and his recognition that all people are children of God, despite their differences in religious faiths or ideologies. Then there was what, in our times with John XXIII, would be termed the "opening" to non-believers and a "dialogue" with Protestants from whose representatives Benedict XIV received official recognition. The son of the English minister, Lord Walpole, in fact, had a monument erected to him, and the inscription attests to the esteem of the Anglicans for "the best of the pontiffs."

It was not simply through modesty that, knowing he was dying and aware that he would not have a follower immediately among his successors, he said at the Quirinal Palace on 3 May 1758, to the motto of *Sic transit gloria mundi*: "Now I shall fall silent and be forgotten, as I deserve." Unfortunately, the papacy would efface his achievements within the next two centuries. The esteem of the Anglicans, the dedication by Voltaire, or the famous comedy of Testoni in the beginning of the twentieth century would not make history except to generate a meagre "sympathy," or, adversely, much criticism and "antipathy" for him, including the later condemnations of his policies by Pius XII. His pastoral lesson of evangelical humanity required more mature scholars.

Perhaps even the solemn funeral monument raised in St. Peter to his memory by the sixty-four cardinals he had created, contributed to his being discredited. The image of him in a theatrical pose with his robes swirling about does not match his appearance which was always simple in its apostolic grandeur.

248. CLEMENT XIII (1758–1769)

At the beginning the conclave that opened on 15 May 1758, appeared to be moving along calmly, in the style of the late pontiff. Austria and France, overcoming their antipathies, seemed in agreement with Spain and the other Catholic States in wanting to have a pope in the "good shepherd" mould, as much like Benedict XIV as possible: a neutral, but one who would work in a constructive way. But then a dispute arose on the problem of the Jesuits, left in abeyance by Pope Lambertini, and basically the French vetoed every candidate. They did not even like Cardinal Cavalchini, bishop of Ostia, who had displayed a character similar to the predecessor, but was clearly in favor of the Jesuits.

After seven weeks, on 6 July, a neutral was elected in the narrowest meaning of the word, pious but prejudiced, educated but not cultured and tradition-minded, judging by the way he fought in vain for the canonization of Bellarmino. Colorless and weak-willed and never having taken a position on the burning question of the Jesuits, such was Cardinal Carlo Rezzonico.

He was born in Venice on 7 March 1693, to a family originally from Como. He had studied with the Jesuits at Bologna and received degrees in theology and law at Padua. He had been governor of Rieti and Fano and a judge on the Rota at Venice. In 1737 Clement XII had promoted him to cardinal-deacon of S. Niccolò in Carcere, and Benedict XIV had entrusted him with the archbishopric of Padua. He had carried out all these tasks with unfailing zeal, and in the city of the Saint, the people of Padua had ended by calling him "the Saint" as well. One could not expect from him breadth of view, as the times required, following the teaching of Benedict XIV, and politically he did not intend to give up any of the temporal rights of the Church of Rome. Moreover, he was a sickly man with heart trouble, an hereditary condition. His mother did not survive her emotion when they told her of his election, and she died two days later. He was consecrated pope on 16 July, taking the name of Clement XIII.

All Venice, however, was elated to have one of its citizens on the Throne of Peter, and though it had always been a little turbulent as a diocese and leaned toward independence, it proved quickly to be favorable to Clement. Indeed, the Senate abrogated an old decree which prohibited Venetians from applying to the Curia for the solution of any dispute, and the pope hastened to thank the Republic of St. Mark. Pasquino exulted in his own way:

> Long live St. Mark, long live the Venetians
> who finally have a Venetian pope.
> Let the Church in joy raise hands to heaven,
> knowing always how to get good out of bad.
> The children of the Adriatic, now more human,
> will admit the Pope's power;
> this time they will be Christians and set the Arsenal
> ablaze for joy.
> Now Saint Peter no longer fears to die, and grows
> in the hands of St. Mark and his sons,
> and has given him the keys to the gates of Heaven.
> He is right to enjoy and be consoled,
> seeing his ship consigned
> to the hands of sailors and boatmen.

Clement XIII was able to display his great charitable spirit in 1763–1764 when a terrible famine struck Latium and southern Italy. Mobs of starving people descended on Rome from their unproductive farms, and a special congregation of cardinals was set up to look after them.

A new bank called the Abundance was established to furnish subsidies, and grain was imported from other nations while temporary shelters were built in the Baths of Diocletian for men, and near S. Anastasia for women. Once the famine was over, a solemn procession of thanksgiving was held on the Feast of Pentecost, 11 June 1764, after which the peasants returned to their lands to begin a new life. It was undoubtedly a meritorious deed.

He was, however, a bigot as attested to by the decree in which he ordered that the nudity of classical works of art in the papal museums should somehow be covered, a measure that was criticized also by Winckelmann who had to carry out this act of censorship in his capacity as Papal Prefect for the Antiquities.

Nothing else is of much interest in this pontificate, and on the problem of the day—that of the Jesuits— Clement XIII showed clearly his lack of personality.

Powerless, he watched the expulsion of the Jesuits from most of the European nations, including Portugal, France, Spain, and Naples. Even the Bourbon of Parma joined his relatives, but with him Clement reacted suddenly by resorting to papal feudal dominion over those lands, and by prohibiting the clergy and the laity from collaborating in any way with the measures prescribed by the Bourbon against the Jesuits. However, when he threatened to excommunicate the duke, warning him to reverse his decisions, considered null and void since issued by a mere vassal of the Church, there was resentment from all the European sovereigns.

It was this severe tone which especially irritated the Bourbons, and there were immediate reprisals with the occupation of Avignon, of the Comté Venaissin, of Benevento, and Pontecorvo. Only Austria remained aloof. Maria Theresa was very fond of the Jesuits, but in any case the principles of "Josephism" were already beginning to be applied there which would create a true State Church, able to face up to Rome on more than one issue.

In effect, this pope lost control of the Church and the relationships of Christian love woven together by Benedict XIV vanished. Although the basic dispute to be resolved immediately was the problem of the Jesuits, behind this there was a new Europe that was losing its Christian and religious character and becoming anticlerical.

At this point, the sovereigns, forced by the intransigent attitude of the pope, demanded once and for all the complete suppression of the Society, or confirmation of the ban placed on the Society in their States. And they tightened their ranks. In January 1769, the ambassadors of Spain, France, and Naples submitted a request to the Curia to that effect, while the pope responded that he would decide the issue with all the cardinals in a consistory called for 3 February. His bitterness was profound and it must have been very sad for him to have to go to that meeting which would have certainly voted for the dissolution of the Society. His heart did not survive the strain and he died on 2 February 1769, the day before. He was buried in St. Peter's and his relatives commissioned Canova to erect that funeral monument which shows him on his knees and absorbed in prayer, in a pose so in line with his spirit of devotion.

249. CLEMENT XIV (1769–1774)

The Church of Rome was in a sad state after the sudden death of Clement XIII, with the Catholic sovereigns in Europe in open conflict with the Holy See to the advantage of the Protestants and the schismatics who were gaining ground in public opinion. The faithful were divided with the spread of Enlightened Theism and the anticlericals would gladly have prevented the election of a new pope because for them it was "bad news to have a pope," as Abbot Ferdinando Galliani wrote.

In this climate of hostility the conclave began in Rome on 15 February 1769. The cardinals were split in the usual two formations of "court" people and of "Zelanti," or fanatics. The basic conflict was over the dissolution of the Society of Jesus and, in a wider sense, over a Church dedicated to spiritual and not temporal matters, as opposed to tradition anchored in the old "disorder" of things. Each group of "courtier" cardinals had received precise instructions for the election, with four lists of "*papabili*," of "indifferent ones," of those "to be avoided" and, in the final analysis, "to be excluded."

The disputes and conflicts were very violent and the voting had to be repeated 179 times, with the conclave lasting for three months. The most exciting event was the unexpected arrival in the middle of March of the eldest son of Maria Theresa, the archduke Joseph, who asked and received permission to enter the conclave in order to present his compliments to all the cardinals, a good and proper intrusion. He had discussions with the cardinals for several days during which he assured them that his mother, the empress, although a good friend of the Jesuits, would take no step to prevent the dissolution of the Society, and he expressed the wish that a pope be elected who would be in favor of this decision, which could no longer be postponed.

The talks between the various ambassadors continued through April and into the beginning of May, completely overriding the secrecy of the conclave's work, which now seemed farcical. The diplomatic manuvers, coordinated by the various European monarchs, finally achieved their purpose. The candidate who appeared the most likely to suppress the Society of Jesus was Cardinal Giovanni Vincenzo Antonio Ganganelli, elected unanimously on 19 May 1769.

According to Castiglioni, "to speak of simony in the selection of Ganganelli or of a formal promise by him to dissolve the Jesuits is an outright lie spread by his enemies long after his death." "He had refused to make any promise in writing about the question," agrees Giancarlo Zizola, stating however, "Given that Cardinal di Bernis, the ambassador from France to Rome, submitted to him a document like a 'capitulation' or 'oath' in use in imperial elections, the candidate had promised him orally that he considered it to be possible and welcome to dissolve the Society. He had furnished similar written guarantees to the Spanish cardinals."

Giovanni Vincenzo Antonio Ganganelli was born on 21 October 1705, in Sant'Arcangelo at Rimini where his father was a physician but had left him early an orphan. The future pope did his studies at Rimini and Urbino where at the age of eighteen he entered the Franciscan Order. He became known as a capable preacher from the pulpits of various cities, and Benedict XIV appointed him a consultant to the Holy Office, while he owed his appointment as cardinal to Clement XIII. He had never had a bishopric so he was consecrated bishop on 28 May, before being crowned pope on 4 June 1769 and adopting the name Clement XIV.

Despite the "compromises," which accompanied his election, the program he set for himself was particularly arduous. Taking Benedict XIV as his role-model, he wanted to make peace for the Holy See with all the Catholic governments and regain credibility for the pope in a brotherhood spirit. He evidently tried to, but without success, mainly because he surrounded himself with unreliable prelates who looked after their personal interests and followed a "libertine" ecclesiastical conduct in keeping with the times.

His intentions were good, as when in 1770 he ordered that there be no further public reading on Holy Week Thursday of the famous bull *In Coena Domini* which, among other things, attacked reactions to jurisdiction by the Church and secular violations of ecclesiastical exemptions and immunities. These were precepts that irritated the sovereigns who therefore greeted with satisfaction the papal order against publication of the bull with the usual solemnity, although in effect the bull remained in force.

Similarly, Clement restored diplomatic relations with Portugal, interrupted when an attempt against the king occurred which aroused the suspicion that it was the work of the Jesuits. The pope intoned in St. Peter's a solemn *Te Deum* for the sovereign's escape from that danger, made a cardinal of Paolo de Carvalho, brother of the prime minister, and created new bishoprics in Portugal. So the papal nuncio was readmitted to Lisbon.

And it was in a spirit of peace that he approached the king of Spain, but Charles III brought him back to reality. His message to Clement was, either he dissolve the Society of Jesus or it was useless to talk of peace, and all the

European sovereigns echoed him in this. Clement XIV tried to circumvent the issue in order to avoid taking the final measure, and began to prepare a reform of the Society. But half-measures did not satisfy the sovereigns. Basically, the pope was alone, surrounded by intrigues and maneuvers even by persons in whom he had most placed his faith. They simply helped him slide down the slippery slope, giving rise to slander and satire which only served to discredit Clement's own image and inflame people against the Jesuits even more.

Pasquino aimed at the whole entourage of the pope, beginning with his favorite, Monsignor Bontempi, apparently a man of humble origin:

> Bontempi was born between the soup and the dishes,
> his home a stable or storeroom,
> he became a monk and what the cats left
> he gobbled down everything and said his Mass.

Another prelate on everybody's lips was Cardinal Alessandro Albani, whom a delightful *Pasquinade* presented under the name of Don Pasquale with his pretty Pimpa, his girlfriend, another Donna Olimpia, in a series of double-meaning "*pimpanti:*"

> When she looks in the mirror, Don Pasquale plays from behind.
> If her coat is worn in style, he arranges the tail;
> if the dress is wrapped,
> he unwraps it; if a fly lights on her face,
> Don Pasquale swats it off;
> if she gets a louse on her breast, he takes the mite by hand.
> When Pimpa is a bit sweaty, he dries her and blows on her.
> If she soils her shoe, Don Pasquale shines it for her.
> When Pimpa has bread in her hand,
> Don Pasqual brings the dog to her.
> If you whisper what I am reporting, you are wrong.
> Get my meaning correctly, don't condemn Pimpa and him,
> because they have done no wrong,
> pretty Pimpa and Don Pasquale.

Surrounded by such persons, Clement XIV could certainly not hope to save the Society of Jesus. Forced into a corner, he finally had to issue the decree which basically was the means by which he reached the papal throne. After so many delays, he could no longer hold back. He personally wrote the "Brief" of dissolution, *Dominus ac Redemptor*, drafted in November 1772, subscribed in final form on 21 July 1773, and communicated to the Jesuits on the 17th of the following month. Clement reserved for himself the right to verify the implementation of the "Brief" in order to avoid any disturbing incidents, and for that purpose appointed a papal commission, though he failed to impede arrests or trials. Among these, the best known was the one against the General of the Society, Lorenzo Ricci, who ended up in Castel Sant'Angelo where he died before the trial was finished.

Needless to say, all the European Catholic sovereigns expressed their full satisfaction. The Bourbons particularly felt obliged to demonstrate their "sincere" gratitude by handing back the domains of Avignon, Benevento and Pontecorvo, which they had occupied earlier. Clement gave no hint of joy as he was evidently in a crisis of conscience. He was only concerned that the sovereigns issue special regulations to the effect that the ex-Jesuits should not be persecuted and should resume all their rights as secular priests. However, in Russia and Prussia, two non-Catholic states, the papal decree was not applied, thus allowing the Society to survive in these countries until it was reconstituted in 1814.

The final year of the pontificate of Clement XIV was a sad one as he neglected his health. When he went on horseback to S. Maria sopra Minerva for the religious ceremonies of the Feast of the Annunciation, he was caught in a rainstorm on the street, but would not turn back and stayed in his wet clothes until the end of the liturgy. That aggravated the herpes illness which had deformed his face. People said that he was terrified by "absurd fears and superstitions," and that he suffered from visions. He died at the Quirinal on 22 September 1774, after a long agony. The rumor, which soon circulated, about a supposed poisoning, was pure fantasy, like the calumny that the culprits were, of course, the Jesuits. They, however, labelled their "enemy" on the occasion with a Pasquinade in Latin which spits venom even in Italian:

> He came as a fox, deceitful;
> He ruled as a wolf, an impostor;
> He died as a dog, wickedly.

Others praised him, rewording the invective above:

> He came as an angel, from God;
> He ruled like Solomon, as a wise man;
> He died like Sixtus, from poison.

His remains, buried at first in St. Peter's, were then moved in 1802 by Pius VII to the church of the Most Holy Apostles and placed in a superb mausoleum sculpted by Canova.

250. PIUS VI (1775—1799)

The conclave to elect a successor to Clement XIV could not have been other than stormy with the usual fighting between the "Zelanti," the "fanatics" of traditionalism, who wanted a return to the intransigent policy of Clement XIII, and the anti-Jesuit "courtier," bound body and soul to the ambassadors of the European sovereigns, who competed as to who could be the most corrupt. It went on for almost five months, with fights and insults which reached beyond the conclave doors, and there were always eavesdroppers ready to report things to Pasquino.

In fact, there were stacks of *Pasquinades* about the various candidates at first proposed and then rejected, which were malicious in the best of cases but mostly slanderous. A masterpiece was the satirical drama in three acts, entitled *The Conclave of 1774*, which exposed forty-four cardinals to public scorn. There was a reaction to that huge farce and on 16 November the cardinalate's commission, on grounds of public order, commanded that the slanderous play be burned in Piazza Colonna. Cardinal Bernis managed to lay his hands on the author, a Florentine priest, Gaetano Sartori, and threw him into Castel Sant'Angelo. The Italian cardinals protested, however, because he had imprisoned a priest on his own initiative without the permission of the vicar of Rome.

After things had calmed down, agreement was reached on one of the "Zelanti" with the consent of the "courtiers," and Cardinal Angelo Braschi was elected unanimously on 15 February 1775. It was Cardinal Bernis who assured Louis XVI that, although he was a member of the group of those "to be avoided," if one looked closely he seemed "reasonable and anxious to have the benediction and the protection of the princes so one need not fear unpleasant surprises from him." On this point he was quite right, but when he added that "nepotism need not be feared either," he was wrong.

Giovanni Angelo Braschi was born in Cesena on 27 December 1717 into a noble family, perhaps related to the Ghislieri of Pius V. At the age of seventeen he already had a law degree and, because of his experience in that field, Cardinal Ruffo took him on as secretary in the bishopric of Velletri. At thirty-eight he became a priest, entering the service of the two most recent Clements as general treasurer. Deeply involved in Vatican finances, he was able to gain experience which would prove to be useful to him as pope. Clement XIV made him a cardinal in 1773 with S. Onofrio as his titular church, but he had never run a diocese, so on 22 February he was simultaneously consecrated a bishop and crowned pope. He assumed the name of Pius VI.

He promptly put into action the program of his pontificate which, under many viewpoints, would recall the splendor of the Renaissance, beginning with the Holy Year which Clement XIV had been unable to open after he had announced it. The Jubilee Year had a festive character, clearly breaking away from the penitential atmosphere, with the artificial lamps lit on the Capitol, traditional banquets and the picturesque Barbary horse race along the Corso. The pilgrim of distinction was Maximilian, archduke of Austria, guest of the Roman nobles at balls and sumptuous receptions.

However, Pius VI was the real figurehead of that Holy Year. To make a good impression on the pilgrims when he went out in public, he had himself combed and pomaded, displaying his small graceful feet like a real Narcissus, as Pasquino satirised him:

> Rome, behold Pius! He is not pious:
> Look how he flaunts his wavy hair and his tiny feet!

His Christian dignity was probably irreproachable, but under many aspects he seemed to be a prince like the one mocked by Parini in the Giorno. However, he was impressive in his looks, and Goethe himself called him "the best looking man" when he saw him one day officiating at a ceremony in the Pauline Chapel. It was perhaps exactly this outward appearance of the man which had suggested to the diabolical de Sade to depict him in the *Histoire de Juliette* as a demon of atheism, lust and cruelty, constrained to celebrate black masses in St. Peter's to obtain the favors of the heroine of the *Prospérités du vice*—the fantasy of the mad genius and a confirmed atheist, though also the product of the extravagant humor of the "divine Marquis."

Pius VI had proudly had a coat of arms designed with the noblest symbols of heraldry: the eagle, the lily, the stars, and the Borea or north wind. And Pasquino advised him:

> Give the eagle back to the empire,
> the lily to the king of the French;
> give the stars back to heaven;
> the rest, Braschi, is for you.

It was a reminder of the vanity of earthly things which the north wind would have blown away, but Pius VI had "dreams about appearing to posterity as a patron and benefactor of the arts," Bruno Cagli records, and certainly could not listen to the voice of the people and think about problems of corruption among the ruling class, of systematic injustice or of the poverty of the lower classes.

He wanted to be generous but to those who paid court to his princely ways, hence the granting of favors to prelates and nobles who agreed with his policy to bring back prestige, now more external than anything, to the Papal State. So he arranged to complete the organization of the Lateran museum, named the Pius-Clementine, since Clement XIV had been the first to show interest in it, and which Ennio Quirino Visconti was to illustrate in a monumental publication in four volumes. He also erected obelisks on the Quirinal, at Trinità dei Monti, and at Montecitorio, and built on the old design of Juvara the new sacristy of the Vatican basilica.

Outside Rome, aside from the construction of the church and the college at Subiaco, he was involved with the draining of the Pontine marshes, a reclamation project which took ten years, cost a million and a half gold *scudi*, and then yielded a harvest for only two years. In fact, floods and the overflowing of river-banks occurred again, and the marshland returned. Monti was ready to praise the project in his *Feroniade*, depicting the pope as the image of Jupiter, but he left it unfinished, as in effect was the work of reclamation. In 1789, the pope managed to restore the Ancient Appian Way and its monuments for a distance of thirty-four miles in the direction of Terracina, which was inaugurated with great splendor. But Pasquino was right when he reflected the resentment of the people for the excessive expenses, both for the church in Subiaco and for the workshop of the sacristy in St. Peter's:

> The marshes, Subiaco and the sacristy,
> three stupidities of Your Lordship.

Pius VI completed his image, in miniature, of a Renaissance pope by renewing nepotism, on a "small scale" for the times, yet always substantial. About this Pasquino commented:

> Verdant and fruitful are the meadows of Holy Church,
> and even the Braschi family can get fat there.

His nephew, Luigi, benefited from his nepotism and built that splendid palazzo in Piazza Navona with the profits received from the absent landowners on the temporarily reclaimed Pontine area. Belli described it in a short sonnet as the final miracle of St. Peter:

> Although St. Peter is now filling flasks.
> His last miracle in our days was Palazzo Braschi.

However, the paternalistic and party-giving world of this pope-prince was fated to undergo mortal blows on an international level. The first conflict was with Austria where Joseph II had carried on all the reforms started in the last years of his mother's reign. From 1780, "Josephism" triumphed, and the emperor subjected the publication of the pope's and bishops's decrees to his own veto, while his government took over the management of the Church, suppressing monasteries, convents and seminaries.

Pius VI protested, but Kaunitz, Joseph II's minister, replied that the imperial dispositions were strictly internal affairs of State, which did not affect articles of faith, and he accused the pope of gratuitous interference. Encouraged by the successful result of that operation, the emperor's brother, Peter Leopold II, grand duke of Tuscany, took the same measures in theological questions and even talked about a national Church. It is obvious that contempt for the rights of the Church of Rome was spreading, together with that of its very primacy in the Catholic world.

Pius VI then reckoned he should do something and, in 1782, decided to pay a visit to Vienna to convince the emperor to stop his anticlerical policies. He was received with great honors, but he returned to Rome without having achieved anything. It was a new humiliation for the pope, and Belli, as satirical as ever, recalls the event in one of his sonnets:

> Perhaps he went to Vienna to punish the arrogance
> of a king who was walking too fast.
> He arrived, he spoke, said everything;
> and when he finished, the German king
> responded very drily:
> "My dear Pius VI, go screw yourself and give me . . . "
> Then the Pope who recognized the cold weather
> returned with his tail between his legs.

It was "Canossa in reverse," as Pasquino himself stressed, leaving the pope to find written on his prie-Dieu, when he returned from the disappointing trip: "What Gregory VII, the greatest of the popes had built, Pius VI, the lowest of priests, destroyed."

But the fatal blow the pope received was from the French Revolution and its rising star, Napoleon. In 1789, with the abolition of the privileges of the clergy and the nationalization of Church property, the freedom of worship, the civil constitution of the clergy with bishops and pastors being elected by the people without any approval by the pope, it was total blackness for Pius VI.

His "Brief," which condemned the laws of the National Constituent Assembly was publicly burned in May 1791 in the Palais Royal of Paris amid the cheers of the revolutionaries. Moreover, on 14 September the legislative Assembly, declared that Avignon and the Comté Venaissin, papal fiefdoms, formed part of the French national territory. The pope had no way to stop the deluge that was engulfing him.

Revolutionary propaganda came to Rome with the ardent republican, Hughes Basville, though things did not to go well for him. On 13 January 1793, the fateful year of the regicide, the Romans smelled a rat and stoned his carriage, while an unknown hand stabbed him. In the eyes of the French, Pius VI became the enemy of the Revolution; he would be punished when the occasion came—Napoleon would take care of that during his Italian campaign.

Bologna, Ferrara, Ancona were all in the hands of the young general, as well as two cardinals. Peace terms were onerous. They ranged from reparations and penalties for the assassination of Basville, to the withdrawal of the "Brief" condemning the constitution governing the French clergy. At the signing of the peace treaty of Tolentino on 19 February 1797, the terms concerning indemnification were even heavier with Avignon, the Comté Venaissin, Bologna, Ferrara, and Romagna definitively ceded. The Directoire demanded the end of the Papal State, but Napoleon wanted to move more slowly.

In December 1798, General Duphot arrived in Rome with instructions to arouse the people against the papal regime. On 28 December, the Revolution was underway and Duphot was in the midst of the rebels shouting: "Long live the Republic! Death to the tyrants!" when papal soldiers fired and he was killed. He was the martyr France was waiting for to invade with an army. General Berthier occupied Rome on 15 February 1798 and, in the name of the Directoire, deposed Pius VI as a temporal sovereign and proclaimed the Roman Republic. Then the sacking of Rome began with many treasures of the Vatican and museums winding up in France.

On 20 February Pius VI was deported from Rome to Siena in the custody of Grand Duke Ferdinand III. It was the beginning of his martyrdom. He would never return to Rome. He was moved to a monastery in Florence where he remained a prisoner for six months, and there the king of Sardinia, Carlo Emanuele IV, another of those persecuted by the Revolution, came to pay him his respects. On 28 March 1799, Pius VI was moved again to Parma, and via Siena and Turin to Briançon as the Directoire feared that someone might try to liberate him. Then he was transferred to Grenoble and, exhausted, on to Valence where he arrived on a cot.

There he died on 29 August 1799, far away from Rome, in a kind of martyrdom which clearly redeemed his mundane and elegant pontificate, or at least compensated for it. Pasquino basically canonized him when he wrote the epitaph for him:

To preserve the faith, a Pius lost the see.

His remains were placed in a basement in Valence, but Napoleon himself saw to it that he was moved to the city cemetery until 1802 when he allowed his transfer to Rome. Only in 1822 was the grandiose monument in St. Peter's finished by Canova.

251. Pius VII (1800—1823)

In the republican and Jacobist climate that reigned in Italy at the end of 1799, almost all the cardinals were living in Venice under the protection of Austria. Emperor Francis II could hardly believe it that he could manipulate in peace the conclave to elect a successor to Pius VI, and made available the monastery on the island of S. Giorgio Maggiore for the cardinals, putting at their disposal large sums of money for expenses to make them feel comfortable. He had only one condition: a "veto" for all cardinals coming from France, Spain, Naples, Genoa, and Sardinia.

However, the conclave was able to begin only on 1 December and thirty-four cardinals participated. There was a hint of polemics between the usual factions of the traditionalists and the moderates, but these did not last long. On 12 December, detailed instructions arrived from the emperor who wished to see Mattei of Rome elected. There was a reaction to that imposition, especially from Spain, which managed to make known its own choice, which had to be taken it into account, even if they were "guests" of Austria. In the end, the eloquence of the Roman prelate, Consalvo, Secretary of the Conclave, and the diplomacy of the Spanish Cardinal Despuig won the day. On 14 March 1800 by unanimous vote Cardinal Barnaba Chiaramonte was elected.

He was born in Cesena on 14 April 1742, from a noble family, his father being a count, his mother a *marchesa*. He had studied with the Jesuits at Ravenna and then had joined the Benedictine Order. He had been the abbot at S. Callisto, and Pius VI had appointed him bishop of Tivoli and later of Imola, raising him to cardinal in 1797. He was not politically compromised and in the end it was this that won the election for him. However, the emperor was not pleased with this choice and therefore ordered that the coronation be held in the church of S. Giorgio Maggiore and not in the basilica of St. Mark. This took place on 21 March, and he took the name of Pius VII.

Then the emperor, perhaps to make up for his snub, and to ingratiate him in the new atmosphere of restoration which was taking place in Italy with the fall of various republics, invited him to stay in Vienna. Pius VII declined, since his see was Rome and he wished to go there. Moreover, to accept the invitation of Francis II would mean breaking any possibility of an agreement with Napoleon who had returned from his operations in Egypt and had imposed himself in France with his first "coup d'état."

Pius VII reached Rome on 3 July, recalled there by King Ferdinand of Naples who had liberated the city from the French. One of the first actions in his pontificate was the appointment in August of Consalvi as a cardinal to whom, in reality, he owed his pontificate.

He assigned to him the Secretariat of State and the Prefecture of various Roman congregations and he would be the pope's right arm in both spiritual and temporal matters.

But neither Pius VII nor his secretary could dam the torrent of Napoleonic power. The concordat defined in Paris by Consalvi between May and August 1801 recognized Roman Catholicism as the State religion in France with a series of clauses which partially improved existing relations between the Holy See and the Bourbon kings. It was subsequently altered by the First Consul, with the mediation of Cardinal Giovanni Battista Caprara sent to Paris as a legate "*a latere*" for the application of the concordat. Napoleon insisted, among other things, of his approval on the publication of papal documents and on the residence in France of papal nuncios. Protests, as usual, were of no avail.

And it was the same for the concordat with the new Italian Republic, as Napoleon insisted on a decree by which the government retained for itself not only the administration of Church property, but also the whole of ecclesiastical discipline—by now "Josephism" had gained adherents! Caprara tried to do what he could, but Napoleon was categorical; Roman Catholicism otherwise would not be proclaimed the religion of the State.

However, in this manner, Pius VII managed for the time being to keep his wobbly papal throne, while Pasquino accused the pope of cowardly surrendering to the wishes of France, contrasting it to the "martyr-like" conduct of his predecessor:

A Pius lost his see to save the Faith;
a Pius lost his Faith to keep his see.

Then, Napoleon wanted to become emperor and insisted that the pope come to Paris to crown him. Pius VII was so angry about this that he made himself sick. It was inconceivable for him to consecrate a son of the Revolution which had guillotined a Catholic king. And under what title, since Francis II of Austria considered his the crown of the Holy Roman empire? On the advice of Consalvi and other cardinals, he ended by consenting to go, in hopes of wresting back from Napoleon some of the clauses added to the concordat of 1801. The coronation took place at Notre Dame on 2 December 1804, but Pius VII simply gave his blessing to the new emperor and his wife. As is well known, Napoleon crowned himself and he also placed the crown on Josephine's head.

The pope gained no concession and was a "guest" of the emperor for the whole winter. It was in fact a forced residence, because permission to leave for Rome, requested continually, never arrived, and a terrible presentiment assailed Pius VII as he recalled the fate of his predecessor. Then, after five months of residence in the Pavillon de Flore in the Tuileries, the pope was finally able to leave for Rome in April 1805. Waiting for him at his see was a homage from the emperor consisting of a precious tiara, eight tapestries, two enormous carpets and two candelabras from Sèvres. The Romans considered it the payment for a deed traditionally viewed as a religious act, that of an "anointment," and felt duty-bound to protest to the pope, who was accused of always praising Napoleon as a liberator:

> But, Holy Father, wherein have we sinned?
> You have anointed him and we have licked his boots.

But a definitive rupture between the pope and the dictator-emperor came about without Consalvi and Caprara being able to save the Holy See. From Vienna which he had entered in triumph, Napoleon decreed in May 1809 the end of the temporal power of the papacy, punishing the pope for failing to close the port of Civitavecchia to English ships, an excuse to resolve a controversy which, for the prestige of his empire, could no longer be postponed. The Papal State became part of the French empire and Rome was declared a free city where the pope could reside only as the head of the Church. He was granted an annual income of two million Lire and the immunity of the apostolic palaces.

Protests were of no avail. General Miollis took possession of the city, and Pius VII had recourse to the bull of excommunication against Napoleon which was affixed to the doors of the basilicas. The emperor's reaction was instantaneous, he ordered Miollis to arrest the pope. This was done by General Radet during the night of the 5th-6th of July for fear of a popular uprising. The pope ordered the Swiss Guard to put up no resistance, certain he was acting correctly by not opposing force with force. He would win by kindness to which he always had recourse when confronted by the emperor's bullying, because all "popes have the words on their side," according to a line from Belli in the famous sonnet *Li papi de punto* which recalls the event, pointing satirically to the delusion of Pius VII:

> At the time of his deportation,
> what said he to the priests at the window?
> "I leave as a lamb and I shall return as a lion."
> But he was wrong. That good lamb
> left a seed and came back an idiot.

The pope and the deputy Secretary of State, Cardinal Bartolomeo Pacca, were forced to climb into a carriage, which, by way of Florence, brought them to Grenoble where the two prisoners were separated. Pacca wound up at Fenestrelle where he would remain until 1815, while Pius VII was taken to Savona.

Napoleon wanted to force the pope to move his residence to Paris, but he got nowhere. The emperor then convened a national council of bishops and cardinals which he wanted to have annul all the bulls issued by the pope, but the members stated honestly that this was not within their jurisdiction. Napoleon was furious and, making no headway, dissolved the council.

But then he had another problem to solve. He had to punish the czar, so he put aside religious polemics. But before leaving for Russia he ordered that the pope be transferred to Fontainebleau, which was to be the final stop of his Calvary.

On his return from the disastrous expedition against Russia, Napoleon had become a ghost of the former conqueror and, shortly afterwards, the Great Powers would defeat him. But Pius VII at Fontainebleau was in the dark about that. On the evening of 19 January 1813, Napoleon called on him, repenting his conduct, embracing and kissing him several times. The pope was moved. In brief, Napoleon succeeded, as Belli might have said, in tricking him into signing on 25 January a new concordat that was supposed to rehabilitate the emperor in the people's eyes. To show his good intentions, Napoleon freed thirteen cardinals who had been under house arrest. But his behavior was not credible and when a *Te Deum* was celebrated in St. Peter's to mark the reestablishment of good relations between the papacy and the emperor, Pasquino made this abundantly clear:

> We praise Thee, O God, and we believe in Thee,
> but we do not believe in Bonaparte.

However, in a hand-written letter on 14 March, Pius VII informed Napoleon that he personally considered the concordat null and void and refused to be bound by it.

But the European sovereigns had the emperor in a grip after his defeat at Leipzig in October 1813 where he had lost all chance of recovery. On 23 January 1814 came the order to free Pius VII. On 4 May, Napoleon reached the island of Elba, and twenty days later the pope returned to Rome.

There were still the "Hundred Days" to come, and the pope would again have to leave his residence and seek refuge at Genoa under the protection of Victor Emanuel I. But as of 7 June 1815, his reentry into Rome would be definite, and Vienna would have fully returned the Italian territories to him.

It was the Restoration. On the religious side, Pius VII reconstituted the Society of Jesus, and on the political one he resumed an absolutist regime.

An uprising at Macerata in 1817 led to numerous arrests, a trial and eleven death sentences, later commuted to life imprisonment. "The 'Carbonari' (literally, "charcoal burners") movement gave Consalvi quite a few headaches, and he attempted to repress the movement harshly, but without too many excesses," as Candeloro notes. However, he "tried to cut the bridges not only with new movements but also with everything that smacked of organized culture," says Bruno Cagli, to a degree that "almost nothing was saved of the Napoleonic laws. And yet for his successors he passed as a somewhat liberal person." And on 21 September 1821, Pius VII published a bull of condemnation against the Carbonari and all the politico-religious sects.

In the final days of his pontificate, after so much suffering, this pope tried to take to heart again the fine arts and he commissioned Canova to negotiate with Louis XVIII for the restitution of precious relics and works of art taken by Napoleon, though with little success, while in 1822 he had the obelisk erected in the large square of the Pincio.

On 7 July 1823, he broke a leg and the wound could not be cured. Then on 16 July a violent fire devastated the basilica of St. Paul about which he was not informed so as to avoid making his agony worse. He died on 20 August 1823, and was buried in St. Peter's in a splendid mausoleum erected by Thorwaldsen.

252. LEO XII (1823–1829)

The conclave to elect a successor to Pius VII opened in the Quirinal Palace on 2 September 1823. Aside from the usual split between the Zelanti and the "moderates," according to the report of the Austrian ambassador Apponyi "the dominant moods were passion, hate and vengeance . . . to humiliate Consalvi and to destroy his creation was, so to speak, the price of papacy." He was in effect excluded by both factions. The candidate of the conservatives was Gabriele Severoli, of whom Austria put its veto as he was opposed to the inter-ventionist policy of Metternich, though the accusation of political connivance with the Carbonari was a figment of the imagination. The candidate of the other faction was Castiglioni, but he was too openly on the side of Austria. The Zelanti won again with their candidate, Cardinal Annibale della Genga, an inde-pendent conservative well known to Pasquino, who had bet on him:

> Whoever wants to put order on the Throne
> should pray for the election of Genga.

Born in the castle of the noble family of Genga near Ancona on 20 August 1760, he had studied in Rome at the Academy of Nobles. His priestly career had been rapid under Pius VI, who appointed him archbishop of Tiro and later nun-cio at Lucerne and Cologne. He owed his promotion to cardinal to Pius VII who at one time had recalled him to Rome as vicar and archpriest at St. Mary Major. The Romans, however, said he had had an affair with the wife of the Captain of the Swiss Guards and, when he became pope, the usual Pasquinade circulated:

Passing Della Genga, a foreigner asked:
"That is the Holy Father, isn't it?"
But the Captain of the Swiss Guards who heard him said:
"Holy, no; Father, yes."

He was elected the Roman pontiff on 28 September 1823, and consecrated in St. Peter's on 5 October, taking the name of Leo XII. It was a solemn coronation with various amnesties and concessions to win over public opinion. He had a *paolo* (silver coin issued under Paul V) distributed to all the poor who came to the Belvedere Courtyard, drew lots for one hundred dowries of thirty *scudi* each for the "unmarried ladies," gave out coupons to the unemployed for bread and meat, and cancelled all debts to pawn shops.

But by then Pasquino's portrait of him had already been drawn and even the concessions would not serve to make him beloved by his subjects:

With a tall frame and a small heart,
limited in talent and thought,
Unmoved by esteem or honor,
ungrateful and impolite;
His face always pale,
he sits enthroned but sees little,
Always surrounded by ne'er-do-wells whom he likes.
O, unlucky ones at the Quirinal,
once masters of the world,
Now reduced by destiny to misery,
you must bear your fate,
Clad in black and weeping while Leo still lives.

Furthermore, odd regulations were issued which confirmed his mediocrity. As Castiglioni records, "since there were fights and injuries and swearing in the taverns, the pope ordered that they be closed with gates. Adventurers could drink wine but they had to stand outside and have the wine poured through the gate!" Then, he enlarged the ghetto considerably and abolished the commission for smallpox vaccinations, and Marforio screamed:

This pope always in bed,
enlarges the ghetto in Rome,
and puts gates on wine
This is Mohammedan law,
O cursed government!

As soon as he was elected, he admitted that his health was not good. He really wanted to renounce the honor and he said to the cardinals: "Do not insist. You are electing a corpse." It was said that he had received the last sacraments seventeen times, one of them after the stresses of the coronation, and since he got better after they had given him up on Christmas Eve, they called it a miracle. Legend has it that the bishop of Macerata, Vincenzo Strambi, a friend of his, had prayed so devoutly to God to the point of offering his own life for that of the pontiff that his prayers were heard. Leo XII survived but Strambi died on New Year's Day.

As for the political orientation of the State, Leo had dismissed Consalvi, and fully embraced a strictly reactionary approach. He appointed Della Somaglia to the Secretariat and cancelled many of the legislative reforms issued by Pius VII. He assigned the job of combating banditry to a special legate, Cardinal Antonio Pallotta, without making a distinction between common criminals and the Carbonari. In June 1825, a meeting place of theirs was discovered in Rome, founded by a man from Brescia, Angelo Targhini, and a doctor from Romagna, Leonido Montanari, whose practice was in Rocca di Papa. They were guillotined in November, in Piazza del Popolo, according to a plaque on the wall of the present barracks, of the Carabinieri, but at the time of the papal police having been found guilty of "crimes of lèse majesté and aggravated assault." A year later in 1826, that same Piazza witnessed the last punishment by simple axing, that is without quartering, of Giuseppe Franconi who had killed a priest during a robbery, and was executed by Mastro Titta.

But the nemesis of the Carbonari was Cardinal Agostino Rivarola, envoy extraordinary with unlimited authority in Romagna. He proceeded with mass arrests and, on 31 August, 1825, personally rendered a verdict against 508 defendants with, according to Candeloro, "Seven sentenced to death (all commuted to life in prison), thirteen to forced labor for life, six to life in prison, two to exile for life, ninety-four to forced labor or prison for various periods, and three hundred eighty-six to surveillance and to 'political precept,' that is, subjected to strict vigilance by the police and to a series of prohibitions and obligations of a particularly vexatious nature, such as not leaving one's city, going to confession once a month, and performing religious exercises for three days in a monastery."

The following year Rivarola escaped an attempt on his life, and the pope recalled him to Rome, replacing him with Monsignor Filippo Invernizzi who began a trial for the attempt in question. The trial ended in 1828 with five persons condemned to death, four of whom were executed, while one sentence was commuted to life imprisonment.

In the bloody wake of these men who, perhaps accidentally like many Carbonari of that time, were the first martyrs of Risorgimento, Leo XII was capable of announcing a new Jubilee Year, which Pius VII had prudently avoided in the Jacobin climate of 1800. Instead, "one of the first ideas of Pope Leo was to announce the universal Jubilee for 1825," as D'Azeglio records it, "which meant the transformation of Rome for twelve months into a huge establishment of spiritual activities. No theaters, no banquets, no balls; just sermons, missions, processions, rituals."

In that Holy Year the pilgrims numbered more than a half million, but the Secretary of State was watchful, fearing "the coming into Rome of political conspirators and members of secret societies who, disguised as pilgrims, could feel safe and plan assassinations." There were the already mentioned executions of Targhini and Montanari without a hint of that Christian mercy which should have been even more the case in an atmosphere of indulgences and pardons of a Holy Year. One can understand Belli's disdain:

> Thanks be to God, we have finally reached a Holy Year!
> Congratulations, Meo: the Pope has announced a Jubilee
> For all baptised Christians.
> All sinners are blessed for a whole year,
> Everybody gets a new conscience!
> Unless you are a Jacobin or a Jew
> Or some other kind of unknown dog.
> You can shed the chains of Purgatory
> And, by Christ, even of Hell this year.
> You can do and say anything you want.
> Go visit the Seven Churches, singing hymns;
> Put some ashes on your head,
> And you will have Paradise at your command.

In 1827, the Secretariat of State passed from Della Somaglia, who had resigned, to Cardinal Tommaso Bernetti who instituted a softer approach, aware that the sentences did not accomplish much as the victims became martyrs, thus gaining new converts to the liberal cause. A so-called "spontaneous" amnesty was granted to all who stated in writing that they had quit the secret society, and some took advantage of it. But the true Carbonari continued to plot, and in 1829, a new meeting place was discovered in Rome. A trial was held under Pius VIII that would lead to a number of life imprisonment sentences.

Leo XII died in Rome on 10 February 1829, and was buried in St. Peter's opposite the altar of St. Gregory the Great. The Romans could breath again, and the epitaph dictated by Pasquino attests to the unpopularity of this pope:

> Here lies della Genca,
> for his—and our—peace.

253. PIUS VIII (1829—1830)

After the death of Leo XII, the vacant see lasted for fifty days. No man of outstanding personality could be found among the usual two factions of Zelanti and "courtiers," and the result was the election of a pope of transition, even if acceptable to Austria, in the person of Cardinal Francesco Saverio Castiglioni. He was ill and did not expect to mount the papal throne: "Fat, fat, with sagging jowls, he thanked the acclaiming people, weeping in consolation, I suppose," D'Azeglio commented, seeing him the day after the election on 31 March 1829 in a procession from the Quirinal to St. Peter's.

Belli records the occasion in his very sarcastic sonnet, where he describes the way that this not very edifying figure appeared meek and downcast :

> My goodness! What a flower of a Pope they have made.
> With due respect, he looks like shit.
> Charming courtesy to daddies and mommies
> to have an ogre for their snotty kids!
> He has herpes all over, even his teeth;
> he is cross-eyed and bow-legged;
> leaning to one side and stupid,
> he comes to bring peace to the parents.
> Look at this fellow who comes
> as the vicar of Christ on earth. A madman,
> stuffed with meat and sausage.
> When the sales clerk at the goldsmith's
> saw him in church, she cried out:
> "My God, they gave us an ugly nag for a Pontiff!"

Castiglioni was born in Cingoli near Macerata on 20 November 1761, into a famous family from Milan to which Pope Celestine IV had belonged. He received his degree in Bologna, but it was in Rome that he made an impression as jurist. Pius VII and Consalvi had consulted him about the Napoleonic concordats, and he had been sent into exile by Napoleon for refusing to swear loyalty to the Italian Republic. When he returned, he continued his rapid ecclesiastical career, and by 1816 he was a cardinal and bishop of Cesena. Then he moved to the diocese of Frascati. He suffered from gout, especially in his legs, and from herpes, as we know from the verses of Belli, but he also had an enormous boil on his neck which forced him to hold his head to one side. In this state of human decadence he was consecrated pope on 5 April in St. Peter's, and took the name of Pius VIII. However, he was aware of his limits and entrusted all political matters to Cardinal Giuseppe Albani whom he named Secretary of State. Austria thought it could maneuver him and the sick pontiff as it wished, but that did not happen. The only occasion the two supported Metternich was with the monarchy in July when the legitimists in Paris hoped that Pius VIII would call for an armed intervention from Austria. Instead, non-intervention won the day.

The pope recognized "our dearest son of Christ, Louis Philippe" as king, and recommended him to protect the religion and the clergy. The policy of the commoner king would bear fruit in a Catholic Belgium separated from Protestant Holland so, basically, the sick pope had not made a mistake. He would certainly not have been up to dealing with the revolutionary aftermath of that monarchy in Italy, but death would soon free him from certain problems that would be inherited by his successor.

He was much too tranquil to get deeply involved in such a complex political situation. And he certainly didn't want his relatives to create other problems for him. He did not want them in Rome and wrote to his brothers not to delude themselves that they would get concessions or favors from him: "No job, no pomp, no promotion! We shall remain humble and console each other about the burden that the Lord has bestowed upon us. Not one of you should move from your work or your homes."

Under his pontificate, a large Catholic community was being formed in the United States, which had recently become independent, and in the first diocese in that new nation, Baltimore, was held the first council in North America. In the East, Pius VIII obtained from the Sublime Porte civil rights and religious freedom for the Armenians, who were assigned a primate for their Church.

The biography of this pope holds nothing more for us. Perhaps in his heart he was awaiting death to free him from his physical suffering. "He was born, he wept, he died;" that epigram summed up the lack of personality of this pontiff, which was confirmed more explicitly in a similar epitaph that added: "And thank God, nobody noticed it."

He died in Rome on 30 November 1830, and was buried in St. Peter's.

254. GREGORY XVI (1831—1846)

In the days following the death of Pius VIII, certain Bonapartists in Rome, headed by Charles Louis Napoleon, the future Napoleon III, planned an insurrection. Taking advantage of the vacant see, the coup was aimed to take over Castel Sant'Angelo and other strategic points, and make the city the center of a hypothetical kingdom of Italy to be handed over to l'Aiglon, the "King of Rome." But someone betrayed them and the conspiracy, obviously not well organized, was discovered on 11 December 1830, and the main conspirators were arrested. Charles Louis Napoleon was expelled from Rome and joined his mother and brother, Louis, in Florence.

Going into the conclave on 14 December in the Quirinal, the cardinals decided to conclude the new election quickly, as it was necessary to have a sovereign pontiff capable of facing up to the revolutionary situation which was placing the Papal State in continual ferment. Despite the best intentions, however, more than 50 days and one hundred ballots were needed to achieve a result.

As usual, the division among the cardinals was between those who backed political independence and those bound to foreign powers, especially with the Holy Alliance to Austria which was prepared to intervene on its own initiative to put down uprisings of the Carbonari where sovereigns were unable to. Cardinal Albani was still the spokesman for Austria and ready to use his veto against candidates not acceptable to Metternich, but the candidature of Cardinal Mauro Cappellari suddenly popped up and caught Albani off his guard. Although he had precise instructions from Vienna for the veto, since Cappellari was known to the imperial court as a liberal, he was not in time to prevent his election that took place on 2 February 1831.

Born in Belluno on 18 September 1765, Mauro Cappellari had become a Camaldolite monk and had held several posts in that Order before being transferred to the monastery of St. Gregory on the Celio in Rome. While General of the Camaldolite Order, he was made a cardinal in 1825 by Leo XII and put in charge of the *Propaganda Fide*. His missionary zeal continued as pope, and he established more than 500 bishoprics in America, Asia, Africa, and Oceania. He was crowned pope on 6 February 1831 with the name of Gregory XVI.

He had not even had time to ascend to the throne than he had to cope with the consequences of a vast revolutionary uprising which broke out on 4 February in Bologna where papal symbols were torn down to the shouts of "long live freedom!" and the tricolored cockade made its appearance. The deputy legate, Monsignor Nicola Paracciani Clarelli, replacing Cardinal Bernetti who was in Rome for the conclave, turned authority over to a commission of liberals with the task "of preserving public peace in the city and in the province, and to protect the lives and property of the citizens."

If temporal power had changed hands in a peaceful way, one had yet to see how the pope would take it. Then, the matter grew in importance.

Between the 5th and 9th of February the insurrection spread to Romagna, Umbria, and the Marches, and civic guards, under tricolored flags, were formed everywhere. The situation took a nasty twist in the front ranks of the agitators who were once again the Bonapartes. Louis Napoleon wrote to the pope inviting him to renounce temporal power, counting on Louis Philippe and his non-intervention. Gregory XVI and his Secretary of State, Tommaso Bernetti were slow to take action and, however ironic Belli was in his *Memorial* in which he exhorted the pontiff to move against the liberals, he was not far from the truth, even if Gregory no longer needed to be urged:

Pope Gregory, don't be an ass! Wake up!
St. Paul gave you the sword,
St. Peter the keys and the chain.
So now you must show some fire,
lift your arm against these jokers;
put a curse on them, cross them out.
Bare your fangs, throw them all out;
excommunicate them!
Let them rot like the stinkers they are.
Excommunicate them, by Christ and the Madonna,
and they will tremble like the palazzo of Prince Colonna.

When on 12 February the liberals tried to take advantage of the confusion of Carnevale and the parade along the Corso to provoke an uprising, the pope took action. The riot in Piazza Colonna was easily put down and the people of Trastevere joined the papal troops showing, as Candeloro records, "lively feelings of affection towards the new pope." One of them reportedly said to him: "Be not afraid, Holy Father, we are here." And he "bared his teeth."

Having little faith in Gregory's repression, the Austrian Army arrived from the north, occupied Ferrara and Bologna and ousted the "peaceful" revolutionary government. Louis Napoleon died at Forlì, while his brother had taken refuge in Spoleto with Archbishop Giovanni Mastai Ferretti, the future Pius IX, an asylum that would be repaid in 1849 when he defeated the Roman Republic and then staunchly defended the pope's temporal power. For the others, there were trials and sentences to death or life imprisonment, all commuted to exile.

Gregory XVI had been pope for less than a month and could not turn cruel so quickly. He had bared his "fangs" and that was enough. He wanted to pursue the tradition of beginning a pontificate with generosity and amnesty to secure the affection of the people. "More or less the usual tune," according to another of Belli's sonnets written especially for the election of this pope, which ends as follows:

He begins by cancelling debts and
letting thieves out of jail,
by moving the usual levers, and a few weeks later,
like all the other Holy Fathers, God forgive me,
he will become a dog.

But more was needed, that is, long-term reforms, and the reality of the situation could no longer be ignored. On 21 May 1831, the sovereigns of Austria, France, England, Prussia and Russia informed the pope of this in a *Memorandum*, explicitly inviting him to make concessions, but Gregory would not listen to them, convinced that it was a question of a few rebels of no importance. That might well have been the case, but there was no doubt that to go on with a reactionary form of government would result in a total collapse of agriculture, industry and trade throughout the Papal State.

Confirmation of that lay in the fact that the deficit in the books "was getting worse and worse from 1831 on," as Candeloro notes, and "to meet the situation the government turned to a tax increase and worse, increased the public debt. Between 1831 and 1846 the government was forced to take out seven loans," five of which were from the Rothschild Bank in Paris. Pasquino made jokes about that:

> Pope Gregory is rather imprudent,
> a clever fellow, I think almost a liberal.
> And if we talk about enriching the State,
> he is smart enough, by God,
> to borrow money from a Jew.

However, it is obvious that as a result of this policy of tax and custom increases the revolutionary uprisings began again and, in 1832, he had to officially request the intervention of the Austrian army, which put down the revolts in the various provinces with bloodshed, and Austria had to think again about Gregory being a "liberal." France, not wanting Vienna to have unchallenged dominion over the Papal State, also intervened on its own initiative and Gregory protested vainly since the French remained in Ancona until 1838, and ended by being an incentive to the liberals.

The pope then established a special corps of policemen called "Commanders" and "Centurions" who were a kind of counterespionage group, a clear sign of his opposition to any political change. An encyclical of 15 August 1832, *Mirari vos*, condemned freedom of conscience, of the press and of thought, viewed as the result "of a cynical perversion, of shameless science, of liberty without limits." Fifteen days later, *Sollicitudo ecclesiarum* reiterated that Christians must follow the maxim according to which "civil obedience must be rendered to whomever holds authority." From such an unconstitutional "constitution" one could expect nothing good.

There were other uprisings in 1836, all put down by Austria. Bernetti, disgusted by Metternich's interference, resigned and was replaced by Cardinal Luigi Lambruschini, but the changing of the guard did not change the disorder. In Rome a section of the "Giovine Italia" (Young Italy) was discovered to which three Augustinian friars belonged. To make matters worse, cholera broke out. Between putting down the uprisings and the epidemic, thousands died. Marforio and Pasquino commented bitterly:

MARFORIO:
What silence, what peace! True, Pasquino?
Everything quiet in Rome.
PASQUINO:
Just like a cemetery.

Amid all these crises, Gregory XVI did not forget his relatives who found ways to get rich, and he also took care of their future in his testament, exempting them from payment of inheritance taxes. Of course, he tried to cover up this nepotism with a series of public works, such as the straightening of the Aniene river, works at the mouth of the Tiber and on the port of Civitavecchia, as well as the completion of the Verano cemetery. And as he wanted to be known for his patronage of the arts, he encouraged excavations at the catacombs and in the Roman Forum.

In terms of religious functions he ended up by letting his conscience bother him, and he did the opposite of what he had pronounced in the encyclical *Mirari vos*; in fact, he abolished the derogatory custom of affixing lists of those who had not fulfilled their Easter duty outside the church of S. Bartolomeo on the island. In his own way, he wanted the obligation for the faithful to go to confession and receive Communion at least once a year to remain a matter of personal conscience, without the conduct of defaulting Christians being made public.

By this he was probably protecting himself too, as he evidently thought of himself as a "pope-cum-man" having, in fact, a mistress. Stendhal mentions it in a letter to the duke of Broglie in 1835. The pope "likes to rest in the company of the wife of Gaetanino. This lady, who may be about thirty-six years old, is neither beautiful nor homely. Four years ago, Gaetanino had no money and now he buys real estate for 200,000 francs." Gaetanino Moroni was the pope's waiter and his wife's name was Clementina Verdesi, called "the most blessed prostitute" by Belli who records in this manner the liaison *d'Er papa omo*, (the man-pope):

There is a garden at the Papal Palace,
with a little wood and a pavilion,
furnished with Turkish sofas,
easy chairs and bottles of wine and liqueurs.
Among other rooms there is a tiny bedchamber
with a back door and a dresser,
whereon sits a ladder to the room of Gaetanino,
a married man;
his wife is well mannered and very devoted

to the vicar of God,
who may or may not absolve from sin.
But I must change the topic:
Indeed, I did wrong to describe each detail
as if it were a crime!

But, aside from the relationship with Clementina which, as a good Christian, he would have had on his conscience like anyone who had not fulfilled his Easter duty, Gregory XVI did as he pleased as the sovereign pontiff. And "in that violent, disoriented climate, in this country where hatred of the government was spread wider than in any other part of Italy," Candeloro observes, "in this State governed by an eighty-year-old pope, whose death was awaited by everyone with the mixed feelings of hope and fear, a moderate movement began to take action in 1845 through Massimo D'Azeglio." His book, *Degli ultimi casi di Romagna* (On the Last Cases in Romagna), attacked the papal government for not making reforms. And there was also the *Manifesto di Rimini* edited by Carlo Farini that contained relatively moderate demands, which would later, in large part, be accepted by Pius IX.

But the Manifest was followed in September 1845 by armed revolts which made "the persecutions more violent and at the same time reconfirmed the incapacity of the priesthood to run a modern State," commented a republican, Aurelio Saffi.

Revolutionary ardour spread throughout the Papal State, and Gregory XVI looked on powerless at the crisis which was crushing a temporal power now in disintegration and cursed with bad administration. The ideas of de Maistre and Lamennais propounding the possibilities of a social function for the papacy were for him unintelligible. The neo-Guelphism of Gioberti could never have found him the ideal pope, even if he had not died.

Slowly consumed by cancer, Gregory XVI died in Rome on 1 June 1846, "abandoned by everyone in a bed full of excrement," as Giordani nastily put it, but "blessedly," Castiglioni assures us. He was buried in St. Peter's in a splendid mausoleum, unpopular as one can tell from the numerous *Pasquinades* that circulated like epitaphs. Among them, the meanest was the following:

He was a baker, then the cream of a monastery,
by the choice of the good ones, he gained the tiara,
crazy and besotted, he visited his kingdom.
He had some unearned triumphs but blew only hot air,
he gave out a little of what he took, and tipped off the spy.
A scoundrel who cheats you,
got his purple hat as a decoration.

Instead of the laws he used a scythe; once our play thing,
he's now our punishment,
opening schools of debt and usury.
A new Sardanapalo, happy on the throne,
adoring Bacchus more than Christ,
he died without forgiving his enemies.

2 5 5. PIUS IX (1 8 4 6 — 1 8 7 8)

The conclave to elect the successor of Gregory XVI met on 14 June 1846, at the Quirinal. Although the majority of the cardinals were reactionary, in view of the extreme gravity of the moment the opinion of those who wanted a new person, not compromised by the reactions of the predecessor, won the day. There were only four ballots and between Gizzi supported by a few liberals, and Lambruschini, Secretary of State under Gregory XVI, sponsor of a strict intransigence, the choice fell on Giovanni Maria Mastai Ferretti, noted for his moderate attitude, who was elected on 16 June.

Born in Senigallia near Ancona on 13 May 1792, into a family of provincial nobles, Mastai Ferretti had studied with the Scholopians in Volterra but then had returned home due to nervous fits of an epileptic type which he overcame by the time he had reached the age of thirty. In 1814, he had already moved to Rome with a *monsignor* uncle, and five years later was ordained a priest and appointed to the management of the orphanage of "Tata Giovanni." From 1823 to 1825, he was in Chile as a judge with the papal legate, and when he returned to Rome he managed the Hospice of S. Michele. But his great apostolic assignment was his appointment as archbishop of Spoleto and later of Imola, after which in 1840, Gregory XVI had made him cardinal. On 21 July he was consecrated pope in St. Peter's and assumed the name of Pius IX.

His past testified chiefly to an intense piety and a profound religious zeal with no particular political slant. The asylum offered at Spoleto to Charles Louis Napoleon was due to a charitable attitude that had no political undertones. However, the terrible crisis of the Papal State prompted Pius IX, in spite of himself, to make reforms. It all began with a normal administrative step, previously taken by other popes at the beginning of their pontificates, i.e. an amnesty for the political prisoners of 16 July.

There was an outburst of enthusiasm and, as Candeloro wrote: "As soon as the notices with the amnesty decree were affixed along the streets of Rome, groups of citizens began to move toward the Quirinal to express to Pius IX the general gratitude. At nine o'clock in the evening, a huge crowd filled the Piazza bearing thousands of candles . . . In the following days, the demonstrations increased in intensity . . . So, between lanterns and candles, parades and demonstrations, hymns and songs of praise, the myth about Pius IX was born, that of the pope of liberation and renovation . . . But as the days went on, the never-ending parties and the acclamations were an expression not only of satisfaction for what the pope had done, but especially of the wish that he would deal quickly with the much hoped-for reforms."

So along came the reforms, modest ones, "more grabbed by the piazza than handed out spontaneously, introduced slowly and with much hesitation, and which did not deal with the basic problems," to quote Martina. In this slow process, without any particular enthusiasm, Belli saw things clearly:

> Good is very good, but too much is too much;
> between the anvil and the hammer,
> he decided to move cautiously,
> as he should have done before
> rather than after.

There was limited freedom of the press, a Council of Ministers, and a Consultative Assembly with no legislative powers, until 14 March 1848 when, with a radical change in the Italian situation, Pius IX finally granted a constitution. It was "the final attempt to save his temporal power by transforming it into a State with a constitution," Martina notes, recalling that this provision was greeted by Mamiani "as beneficial and necessary because it freed the pope from any political responsibility and allowed him to live 'in the peaceful serenity of dogmas . . . (where) he can pray, bless and forgive sins.'" But there was little openly new in this constitution which was in reality a compromise. Pius IX, in fact, had no intention of radically changing the Papal State. He had let himself be carried along by the patriotic excitement of the moment and an equivocal phrase declared on 10 February, "Great God, bless Italy!," with the permission granted to volunteers and some regular troops to leave for the north to join the Piedmont army against Austria, had simply caused ambiguities.

However, on 29 April, these were clarified when Pius IX gave a speech in which he unequivocally refused to participate in the war. The vicar "of He who is the author of peace" embraces "all peoples . . . with an equal share of pater-nal love." The myth of the liberal pope died, and, by reflex action, that of the treacherous pope was born. Pius IX tried to placate the public by calling into the government Terenzio Mamiani, but the basic contrast resurfaced. The pope was unwilling to play a simple walk-on part as he felt it would lessen his image of a constitutional sovereign. However, with the new government headed by Fabbri, there were no problems. Problems did come with Pellegrino Rossi who was assassinated on 15 November and that was the beginning of the revolution and of a new government headed by Monsignor Muzzarelli. But Pius IX was making concessions only to gain time to make preparations for his flight. On the evening of 24 November, dressed as a simple priest, he escaped from Rome and sought refuge in Gaeta where Ferdinando II offered him protection and hospitality.

As of 9 February 1849, Rome experienced its dream of a revived republic, and decreed the end of the temporal power of the popes. Of course, that didn't last more than five months. The triumvirs Mazzini, Saffi, and Armellini, as well as Garibaldi and his wife Anita, and then Mameli and Manara, found days of glory in a secular Rome. But on 3 July, the French, under General Oudinot took possession of the city and on 12 September, the pope granted amnesties from Gaeta before returning and abrogating the constitution. He was helped in his restoration by Cardinal Antonelli who was appointed Deputy Secretary of State, and on 12 April 1850, he returned to Rome. Obviously there was no enthusiasm on the part of the population, but the atmosphere was one of dignified respect.

However, the history of Italy was on the move while Pius IX was destined to remain behind, watching powerless the loss of ecclesiastical rights, first in Sardinia, then in the entire nation. Events occurred rapidly between 1850 and 1861, then more slowly until 1870. With the Siccardi laws of April 1850 of the Piedmont government under D'Azeglio which brought the end of the ecclesiastical court and the right of asylum, and then the laws of May 1855 under Cavour relating to the suppression of religious orders not devoted to preaching and to the confiscation of property, began the initial phase of the concept, "a free Church in a free State," which would never be accepted by Pius IX.

The Holy See excommunicated the Piedmontese. Antonelli, promoted Secretary of State in 1851, a position he would maintain up until his death in 1876, was determined to save the absolute authority of the pope: "As we must come to an end, it is better to continue to be what we are with our great ideals and all the symbols of our past grandeur," he would continue to declare in defense of his action. And Pius IX would follow him, reserving to himself the most absolute freedom of decision on problems of a strictly religious nature.

Next came the annexation by Piedmont of the rebellious legations of Emilia and Romagna, to which the pope responded on 24 March 1860, with a second excommunication of the Piedmontese government. Then the army of Victor Emanuel II crossed the border of the Papal State and routed the few papal volunteers of Lamoricière at Castelfidardo. The plebiscites of the 4th and 5th November 1860, decreed the additional annexations of the Marches and Umbria to what was, by then, the kingdom of Italy, officially proclaimed on 17 March 1861. Finally, on 27 March, Parliament proclaimed Rome the capital of Italy and, two days later, the third excommunication was issued, this time against the Italian Government.

There was no other defense action from the Church. The words of Cavour, seeking to convince Pius IX that the independence of the Church could be protected in a safe and effective way by the loyal separation of the two powers, the civil and the religious, went unheeded "Holy Father . . . renounce, and we shall give you that freedom which you have sought in vain for three centuries from the great Catholic powers . . . What you have never been able to achieve . . . we can offer to you fully. We are ready to proclaim in Italy the grand principle of a free Church in a free State."

But, "how could the supreme head of Catholicism accept, within his tiny kingdom, the equality of religions and so many other aspects of modern civilization?" Molinari rightly asks. Pius IX was essentially a *homo religiosus* who believed that "the strength of his pontificate are rooted in deep faith, in a strong sense of the supernatural, and in the primacy of the spiritual over the political."

That explains the dogma of the Immaculate Conception proclaimed on 8 December 1854, and of the marble column erected exactly two years later in Piazza di Spagna at the top of which is the statue of the Madonna. And it further explains the simultaneous publication in 1864, also on 8 December, a date dear to Pius IX, of the encyclical *Quanta cura* and the famous Syllabus containing the condemnation of all the anti-Catholic teachings of that time, from Pantheism to Naturalism and Rationalism, Socialism, Communism, and Liberalism. It also reaffirmed the divine origin of both the Church and the State, as well as the impossibility of any reconciliation by the Roman pontiff "with progress, liberalism, and modern society."

That is the key to what Zizulo described as "an apocalyptic pontificate, without nuances or distinctions, ready to condemn errors, incapable of discerning in The Manifest of Marx anything other than disintegration and anarchy, without any analysis of the social situation, indeed sceptical of achieving the possibility of economic and social equality, responsible in the name of the Kingdom of Heaven for the poor at the barrier."

Crowning it all, there was the Vatican I Council, the twentieth ecumenical in the history of the Church that opened on 8 December 1869. In addition to repeating the condemnation of modern thinking in all its rationalistic forms, it proclaimed the authenticity of Catholic doctrine as the product of Revelation and of Faith and restated the primacy and infallibility of the pope. On this last matter there were many controversies to overcome and the definition of the primacy of papal jurisdiction over the entire Church, with reference to solemn descriptions ex cathedra of doctrines of faith and morals, was reached only on 18 July 1870. The exclamation attributed to the pope in one of the last audiences, "I am the tradition!," was his way of emphasizing his authority and independence from the episcopate, and it is symptomatic of the state of excitation in which the assembly finally gave its approval.

Pasquino made his comment on the conclusion of Vatican I:

The Council was convened,
and the bishops have decreed
that two persons are infallible:
Moscatelli and Pius IX.

To understand the irony of this *Pasquinade*, as Sergio Delli explains, "one needs to know that in Viterbo there was a match factory of a certain Moscatelli and on the match boxes was printed in big letters Moscatelli-Infallible." Nastier was the telegraphic quip:

I.N.R.I.
I Do Not Recognize Infallibility.

Still more perverse and spiteful seems the *Pasquinade* found in St. Peter's on 17 September 1870:

Blessed Holy Father,
this poor fellow would give you this umbrella.
It's not very good, but I have nothing better.
You ask "What use is it to me?"
Dear old chap, hear the thunder.
What if a rainstorm comes?

In fact, three days later Porta Pia was stormed and on 20 October, the Council was suspended for an indeterminate time.

It is likely that Pius IX did not view that event as dramatic, "he did not plunge into anguish and desperation," according to Franco Molinari who nevertheless places "amongst the legends" what Giulio Andreotti related in his book, that the pope spent that fateful night of 20 September "composing charades and funny sayings. But if the story was not true, it was well invented. In fact, one must marvel at the optimism and faith in providence which sustained the tormented pontiff even during the worst periods of his life."

For years Pius IX probably found relief from the state of siege in which he lived in his little kingdom by solving charades and giving vent to jokes and quips. To deal with the Garibaldi movement in October and November 1867, there were the chassepot (rifle brigade); for Villa Glori and the Cairoli brothers, Antonelli and the few remaining papal troops sufficed; against other possible coups, Napoleon III was a guarantor with his perfectly equipped expeditionary force. The pope had his religious functions and in 1867 he celebrated in a special Jubilee Year the XVIII centenary of the martyrdom of the Apostles Peter and

Paul along with 10,000 pilgrims who had come to Rome despite the guerrilla activities. The indestructible "man of faith" received demonstrations of homage and devotion. As Molinari observed, this was "the characteristic grandeur of a pope as short-sighted in historico-political views as he was profound in his vision of the supernatural in the human adventure."

However, it was in the name of this religious grandeur that on 24 November 1868, the last persons condemned to death by the temporal regime, Monti and Tognetti, were executed. Pius IX refused to show them mercy despite the intervention of Victor Emanuel II on their behalf. On the beheading of those two patriots, Pasquino wrote as follows:

> The plant of the Faith will languish
> unless the priest, with great care,
> waters it with tears and with blood!

Aside from charades and religious martyrs, in all these crises Pius IX found time to devote himself to what would be the final building works in Papal Rome, that is the restoration of the basilica of St. Paul, the Termini main railway station and the Pius-Marcius aqueduct with its fountain. A simple round basin at ground level, inaugurated just ten days before the breach of Porta Pia, where now stands the monument to the fallen of Dogali, it was only in 1885 that the Italian government arranged to move it to the Piazza dell'Esedra where the "immodest Naiads" also appeared.

And then came the end of Papal Rome. On 1 November 1870, Pius IX issued yet another excommunication of those responsible for taking "his" city away, and on 16 May of the following year, in the encyclical *Ubi nos*, he rejected the law of solemn guarantees, declining any indemnity and trusting in the support of the faithful through "Peter's pence." Then there appeared in the terminology of the Sacred Penitentiary the expression "*Non Expedit*" regarding participation by Catholics in political elections. The kingdom of Italy was not recognized and the excommunication was repeated. The Jubilee Year of 1875 was announced, but the opening of the Holy Door in the four basilicas of Rome, no longer Papal Rome, did not take place. It was a Holy Year with Doors closed, a protest action though there were a certain number of pilgrims.

"The protests continued during the following years," as Martina states, "especially in the sermons to the pilgrims in the Vatican, full of bitterness and pessimism on the future of the new Italy, with a pope now incapable of grasping the historical significance of the events of which he was the victim, and had his faith in a miraculous Providence which somehow would assure the Church's triumph."

The realities would obviously negate that, and the last bitter pill came from Bismarck's Germany in the Kulturkampf. In the "battle for civilization" against prejudices and superstitions, the Catholic Church was swamped by a series of laws adopted between 1873 and 1875 which took away its control over education, made civil marriages compulsory, dissolved religious orders, and expelled the Jesuits. In 1876, Cardinal Antonelli died, and the new Secretary of State, Cardinal Simeoni, would not make history carrying out routine administration. The aged pope, still lucid, did understand that the Church would have to adapt itself, but this could not come from him. He was waiting for the change of guard. "Everything is different around me, my organization and my policies have had their time, but I am too old to change direction; it will have to be done by my successor."

Pius IX died in the Vatican on 7 February 1878. Temporarily laid to rest in the Vatican basilica, his remains were buried three years later in St. Lawrence outside the Walls. However, the transfer there underwent a terrible outrage by the anticlericals, for the most part Freemasons, who had organized a demonstration to throw who they called the "rotter" into the Tiber. This took place late at night on 12 July 1881, and there was insufficient police protection for the funeral procession, especially near the Sant'Angelo Bridge. For the entire remainder of the route to the Verano cemetery, insults and stones were thrown at the Catholic priests and laymen surrounding the bier. The remains were finally buried in an ark of bare stone, in accordance with the last will of the pontiff, with no funeral monument, merely the inscription as follows: *Ossa et cineres Pii Papae IX*.

256. LEO XIII (1878–1903)

Given the general situation of Europe at the end of the nineteenth century, a conclave no longer interested the Chanceries of States as it had for years and centuries. Italy was a European nation, the Church of Rome was not a state, so there was less interest on the part of the Great Powers in influencing the election of a pope. The exercise of the right of "veto" lost a lot of its former importance and the various nations worked instead to obtain from the Italian government guarantees for freedom and security of the proceedings in the conclave, which was opened in Rome on 18 February 1878. In fact, the Minister of the Interior, Francesco Crispi, assured its protection by stationing in the square of St. Peter and adjacent areas an adequate number of armed forces. As a result there were no incidents.

Sixty of the sixty-four cardinals of the Sacred College participated in the conclave, which lasted a very short time, barely thirty-six hours. On 20 February 1878, as of the third ballot, Cardinal Gioacchino Pecci was elected. He had defeated Cardinal Bilio, who passed as the author of the Syllabus, whereas

Gioacchino Pecci "had clearly been in opposition during the pontificate of Pius IX," as Giancarlo Zizola notes. "He had lived all those years in exile in Perugia where he had created a little Vatican, frequented by intellectuals and artists, and where he wrote pastoral letters in direct contrast to encyclicals of Pope Mastai, facing up to the problems of the day with a positive attitude." Maybe he was the successor that Pius IX hoped for when he realized that a man like him was no longer of this world.

Vincenzo Gioacchino Pecci was born in Carpineto Romana near Anagni on 2 March 1810, into a family of ancient nobility. He had studied with the Jesuits and later at the academy of noble ecclesiastics. Ordained a priest in 1837, he was legate to Benevento and Perugia, and later nuncio at Brussels. Made archbishop of Damietta and finally of Perugia, he reached the level of cardinal in 1857. He was consecrated pope in St. Peter's on 3 March 1878, and took the name of Leo XIII. Instead of blessing the people from the outside loggia looking over the piazza, he did it from the loggia inside the basilica, A controversial change.

In fact, during the first ten years of his pontificate, Leo XIII did not distance himself from Pius IX's attitude with regard to Italy, and Catholics were expected to be faithful to the *Non expedit* and refuse to participate in public life. "Neither elected nor electors" was the formula behind this crusade aimed at making known to the whole world the situation of a Holy See "prisoner" of an Italian anticlerical State.

Two months after his election, Leo XIII repeated the refusal to accept the loss of temporal power in the encyclical *Imperscrutabili*, and the closure to Italy was total. The attack of 13 July 1881 on the funeral procession which carried the remains of Pius IX to S. Lorenzo was the tangible evidence of this "cold war." Leo XIII wrote to Franz Josef, the emperor of Austria, expressing his wish to leave Italy. He feared that if he remained in Rome under the oppression of a government which could not propose more than the law of solemn guarantees, the condition of stalemate in which the Catholic world was living would not improve. But all his hopes were dashed when the following year the Triple Entente was born and Austria became the ally of Italy. Plans for flight were put aside and Leo remained entrenched in the Vatican.

Thus, Leo continued to refuse to recognize anything that smacked of anti-clericalism, he opposed both naturalism and socialism and insisted upon the return to Christian virtues by all Catholic ecclesiastics and laity. In an oppressive State, even the poor person will find solace in the simplicity of religious practices with nothing more than prayer and resignation. The papacy's refusal to meet this need in its refusal to participate in public life did not fulfill expectations of Catholic intellectuals who had anxiously awaited Leo's election as pope. The very learned pontiff pleased them only when he opened to scholars the secret archives of the Vatican Library.

But where was the cardinal "exiled" in Perugia, the anti-Pius IX, "the future pope" praised by Ruggero Bonghi as the first Roman pontiff without any territorial sovereignty who would shine forth in his grand spiritual majesty? Did he himself not declare, a few hours after his election: "I want to have a great policy"? He could not have taken it all back closing himself behind an iron curtain.

Indeed, in 1887 the thaw suddenly began, and Leo XIII found himself again. During a speech on 27 May he hopes for renewal of peace between Italy and the Holy See, to be achieved in conditions "by which the Roman pontiff will not be subject to the power of anyone and will enjoy complete and genuine freedom." This seemed a step towards further possible negotiations. Crispi, the man who wanted to pass as the renovator of the Italian State, in his reply speech from Naples linked the "three great names" of God, Fatherland, and King, and proposed a kind of God's truce.

This was followed by the delirious, if prophetic, pamphlet of Father Tosti, the Benedictine abbot of Montecassino, entitled *The Conciliation*, which foresaw a forthcoming religious peace. "We will see the gestatorial chair carried on the shoulders of thirty million Italians . . ." However, the dream did not last long. In 1888, the mayor of Rome, Duke Leopoldo Torlonia, made an official call on the cardinal vicar to proffer to the pope his congratulations on the fiftieth year of his priesthood. But the following day the mayor was replaced as the Italian Government did not approve of his action. On the other hand, a book about councils published anonymously by the bishop of Cremona, Bonomelli, entitled *"Rome, Italy and the Realities,"* is placed on the Index. On Easter Sunday, 1889, Bonomelli publicly declares in the cathedral of his city that he is the author and he asks the pope to pardon him.

1889 is in fact the year of the crisis. As Armando Ravaglioli records, "on 9 June at the Campo de' Fiori in Rome, where Giordano Bruno was burned at the stake, his statue by Ettore Ferrari was inaugurated to the applause of all those who profess 'freedom of ideas.' The battle cries of 'death to Leo XIII!' and 'Death to the Holy Spirit!' are heard in the major Italian piazzas where the pope's effigy is hanged."

There was something odd in the conciliatory impatience of the Italian Catholics who had established the "Italian Catholic Union for Social Studies" in Padua with Giuseppe Toniolo, since anticlericalism appeared clear-cut and impenetrable. But this time, Pope Pecci was not discouraged and had the support of his Secretary of State, Cardinal Rampolla. Vatican diplomacy, in crisis in Italy, looked for a solution abroad, and Europe became the field of action for the renewal. First came Germany, where the frontal encounter with Bismarck was shelved and a compromise sought. And, with Wilhelm II's visit to the Vatican on 12 October 1888, the battle of the Kulturkampf was officially ended. The Great Powers of the world appreciated the diplomatic talents of the Church of Rome which, in two cases, became the arbiter of important international disputes, one between Spain and Germany over the Caroline Islands, the other between Spain and the United States over Cuba.

Catholic intellectuals also did not give up the fight. In the provinces of Bergamo, Brescia, Verona, Vicenza, and Padova, signatures were collected for a petition for a "pacification" between the parties. Twenty-six Catholic newspapers were set up to dialogue with the secular press. Leo XIII did not abandon them. Given the ferment now circulating throughout the Catholic world in cultural, historical, and theological fields, he decided to give the Church a rigid organization and formation so as to give it back the capacity to expand again with an authority not limited to Italy but extended throughout the entire world.

On 15 May 1891, the *Rerum Novarum* came out with its social proposals, inviting government leaders to observe the moral law of justice, to avoid class warfare, to provide concrete assistance to the needy and the poor, and to foster a dialogue of cooperation between employers and employees. This was the first position taken by the Catholic Church pertaining to the problems of the world's workers. On the one hand, the encyclical tended to attack the liberal, mainly anticlerical classes who were dominating the policies of the European States, and, on the other, to woo the working masses away from the increasing socialist influence. Although the encyclical had an enormous impact, it arrived too late; socialism had already taken over the masses and, moreover, Pope Pecci spoke like the aristocrat he was.

As a result, as Carlo Falconi observed, the encyclical was fairly limited and "capitalism" was not even mentioned, much less condemned. In reality, the ideal behind the encyclical, according to Guido Gerosa, "was neither social nor even evangelical but the corporativism of medieval Guelph communes. To stop the great spread of socialism, Leo XIII had nothing better than to call for a return to the medieval corporation." Nevertheless "a pope in favor of the right to strike, and a pope who did not oppose the creation of Catholic unions, was a sign of the times, it was already the twentieth century."

And the aim of the great politician that Leo XIII revealed himself to be took form. Papal power, vanquished by the cannon blasts at Porta Pia, would rise again through the organization of the Christian political masses. Although severe and polemical, in that regard the words of Emile Zola seem fitting. For him this pope "is more intellectual than sentimental, with unbounded pride, having from his youth had the highest ambitions, demonstrating everywhere and in everything he did, the determination, once pope, to rule, to rule at all costs, to rule as the absolute, omnipotent monarch!" His new political program to enable him to rule began to take shape with the numerous initiatives of the Catholic intellectuals.

In 1892, the first sign came from Genoa with a national congress of Catholic scholars on social issues. Giuseppe Toniolo founded the "International Review of Social Sciences," the purpose of which was to "refashion with scientific rigour and in a Catholic spirit what Marx, Engels, and Loria have done." The F.U.C.I. (Federation of Italian University Catholic Students) was created and the Office of Catholic Congresses and Committees formed. In 1898, Romolo Murri founded in Rome another review, "Social Culture" in which the Catholic mission to uplift the lower classes became a political program. What this would in fact achieve would be recorded in the history of the new century. It is possible that the social thinking of the Catholics in these years had "only academic value," as Antonio Gramsci noted, "an ideological element like an opiate tending more to preserve certain states of mind in passive expectation of a religious nature, but not as one of political and historical activity." But it is true, too, that the Popular Party, or the Christian Democracy or whatever it was to be called, was already in its beginning form in Murri's programs. In 1899, the young Christian Democrats were preparing in Turin the political lines of the entire movement.

In this climate of renewed Catholic enthusiasm around the figure of the pope, Leo XIII could again announce the Jubilee for the Year 1900, a celebration which, apart from the one with "Doors closed" under Pius IX, had not been observed for seventy-five years. A Socialist poet, Giovanni Pascoli, praised it in his *Odes and Hymns* "The Holy Door." But in this unusual celebration by a secular person a doubt arises about the useful function which the pope and the Church could still have in the new century:

> Oh Man, when with feeble murmurs the world sings to you,
> pale hero, guardian of that other Hall of God:
> Remove your hand from the task, forever weary one!
> Loosen your white apron, oh meek servant of God:
> The Door is still a dream! The flocks still want to enter it.
> Oh our first-born, pure among pure linens,
> the stones you immure with graceful hand.
> seem to enclose all your brothers in the sepulcher
> with three seals all of mankind.
> Only white Death so closes the door that will not reopen!
> Oh! Your hands tremble.
> Where will you be when the new century
> through prayer will remove the three stones.

The "Counter-Jubilee" organized by the Freemasons on 20 September was the actual indication of an ideological battle between the anticlerical world and the Catholic one, and it is therefore reasonable to share the "doubt" raised by Pascoli. This unique demonstration planned a visit to the "four secular basilicas": the Pantheon where Victor Emanuel II was buried, the Janiculum where the monument to Garibaldi was raised, Porta Pia, symbol of the collapse of the pope's temporal power, and the Capitol with the monument to Cola di Rienzo, rediscovered as the putative father of a lay and anticlerical Rome.

It was one incident among many at the time, perhaps a bit more dramatic because intentionally so irreverent and iconoclastic. At the end of the Holy Year, Pasquino left written on his statue a *volemose bene* (let's get on together) in verse. His wish to throw water on the fire was perhaps the last *Pasquinade* in history, at the close of his career as the "talking statue:"

> Let's make peace, Holy Father;
> what has happened, happened;
> Take my hand and let's all of us thank Almighty God!

However, Pope Pecci again appeared undecided. In the encyclical *Graves de communi re* of 1901, he recognized the Christian Democratic movement but limited the sphere of its activity. He warned that the very name of "Christian Democracy" rang badly in the ears of many good people who saw in it something ambiguous and dangerous. "That they were afraid of it for more than one reason because they thought that in this way one could cover up the political goal of bringing the people to power through fostering that form of government rather than others." In other words, it was an invitation to remain in the ranks of "corporativism."

France disappointed him. There was a return of anticlericalism and, in the tension between the Church and the State, reminiscent of Napoleonic times, could be found the failure of the universal spirit of social christianization. Italy also disappointed him. In 1902, the new Prime Minister, Zanardelli, tried to introduce divorce. The pope intervened desperately, without calling for a new crusade, but nonetheless succeeded in eliminating that attack on the sacrament of matrimony.

However, from some aspects, Leo XIII seemed more and more disoriented by the growth of the Catholic movement, and towards the end, in a moment of political meditation, wanted to stop it. In his desire to return the papacy to its supreme temporal function and to involve it in Italy's economic and social problems, he no longer trusted the Catholic intelligentsia. From this moment onward a breach appeared between those who stayed in the ranks of the hierarchy and the independents who would look towards modernism.

Leo XIII's enthusiasm came to an end, and with it his life, on 20 July 1903. Buried temporarily in the Vatican, he would be transferred twenty years later to a splendid mausoleum in St. John Lateran, the work of Giulio Padolini.

257. ST. PIUS X (1903—1914)

The favorite candidate at the conclave that began on 1 August 1903 to elect the successor of Leo XIII, was his Secretary of State, Cardinal Rampolla, because he meant the continuation of the papal policy of the *Rerum Novarum*. And Rampolla was in the lead after the first two ballots but without reaching a quorum, and the presentation of a veto against him by Emperor Franz Joseph through the bishop of Cracow, Cardinal Kniaz Puzyna, gave rise more to surprise than anything. Even on the third ballot Rampolla kept his lead, as if to say that the veto had the opposite effect of what was expected. However, Rampolla would not achieve the majority because more than a third of the conclave was implacably opposed to him.

They pretended to support the emperor's candidature of Cardinal Gotti but in reality wanted the patriarch of Venice, Giuseppe Sarto, who had a reputation of being a deeply religious man. At this point, "there was perhaps an attempt at intimidation through poisoning," states Giancarlo Zizola, and it was true that "many cardinals were ill during the final night, so that there were fifty prescriptions for the pharmacy in the morning."

Cardinal Sarto had come to Rome from Venice never dreaming that he could be elected. To a French cardinal who did not recognize him and had predicted that he would never be elected as pope because he "did not know French," Cardinal Sarto replied to him, "thanks be to God, as I bought a round-trip ticket!" A similar reply would be given by Angelo Roncalli, like him the patriarch of Venice, who would also become pope. In the same manner Giuseppe Sarto, seeing the votes in his favor accumulating, had pleaded with the cardinals: "For the love of God, forget about me; I do not have the qualities to be pope." Instead, on the seventh ballot on 4 August they elected him and, after he had burst into tears, he responded: "I accept, as one accepts a cross."

He was born in Riese near Treviso on 5 June 1835, in a large, poor family. His father was a doorman for the town and his mother a seamstress working at home. As a small child he showed a Christian spirit like St. Francis. For example, when he was eleven years old and was going to school in Castelfranco, he would walk barefoot from Riese carrying his shoes on his shoulders to avoid wearing them until he arrived at the entrance to the school. He succeeded in entering the seminary at Treviso through the remarkable gifts he demonstrated in his studies, and was ordained a priest at the age of twenty-three. His first parish was at Tombolo, a town of cattle breeders used to drinking and swearing, for the most part illiterates who wanted to learn how to read and write. He agreed to instruct them in the evenings and his only payment would be that they stop swearing. At the parish in Treviso where he went in 1875, he kept his old black cassock, refusing one in silk bordered in red to which he was entitled under a Venetian diocesan decree. He did not want any sign of prestige or wealth. He behaved the same way when he was named bishop of Mantua and his old parishioners would say of him:

He came to us with a worn jacket and left without a shirt.

And it was true. He gave everything to the poor, even his own clothes. And as he gradually rose in his priestly career, his spirit of charity and humility increased. When he was appointed cardinal in 1893 and elected as Patriarch of Venice, he sent his gold watch to the pawnshop and declined a new cardinal's cape. Patched up with care by his sisters, his predecessor's cape would suit him fine!

With these credentials, Giuseppe Sarto had presented himself at the conclave and, precisely because of them, he was elected. He was consecrated pope in St. Peter's on 9 August and took the name of Pius X. As pope he was to keep the habits of a "country priest," and when speaking of himself, was to abolish the plural *majestatis*, as John XXIII was also to do, as well as the custom of applause in St. Peter's in honor of the pontiff. He explained that it was not "fair to applaud the servant in the home of the Master." He disliked eating by himself and he would always have a guest to keep him company. And then, he wanted no Swiss Guard at his door while he was asleep; the poor soldier also had the right to sleep at night.

He did not know what nepotism was. His brother Angelo remained a postal clerk in a suburb of Mantova and did not even get a promotion. His three maiden sisters came to live in Rome in a modest apartment. To the heraldic committee that asked Pius X what titles they should have, such as countess or princess, he replied that they should be called simply "sisters of the pope." And he also made jokes. To a gentleman who asked him for a cardinal's hat on behalf of a friend, he replied: "Ah, you've come to the wrong place; I am not a hatter, I am only a tailor" (Sarto=tailor). He himself told the story of an elderly woman at a public audience who looked at him ecstatically and murmured: "Holiness, how are you, your Holiness?" and he had replied, "Bless you, how do you want me to be? Like a pope!."

And as pope, this "country priest" did know how to be one, despite all his humility and simplicity, because "necessarily," as he himself put it, "he had to concern himself with politics, in which he was decidedly conservative. As such he had demonstrated this when he was the patriarch of Venice, opposing the social renewal of the Christian Democrats and in favor, instead, of alliances between moderate liberals and the "parochial" faithful. "Catholic liberals are wolves in sheep's clothing," he had opined and, addressing the priests of Venice, had declared: "You will be called papists, clerics, retrogrades, intransigents. Be proud of it!"

His nemesis was modernism which offered a broad approach in matters of tradition and obedience, a reconciliation of science with faith and freedom of conscience for the Catholic in political choice. Piux X reacted violently and firmly, assisted by the Secretary of State, Merry del Val, ordering the dissolution of the "Office of Congresses." At the same time he softened the significance of the "*Non expedit*" in order to support unofficial alliances between moderate Catholics and liberals, out of which would come in 1913 the Gentiloni Pact.

Everything began in the encyclical *Pascendi* of 1907 with the condemnation of modernism as having trampled on progressive elements in Catholic culture. An author like Fogazzaro made a timely act of submission, but a priest, Ernesto Buonaiuti, the author of writings in direct conflict with the encyclical, was defrocked. Moreover, in a "*motu proprio,*" *Sacrorum Antistitum*, of 1910 the pope ordered priests under a special oath to refuse all modernist thinking. Yet on the other hand, the new organizations approved by Pius X himself were blessed, including the Populist Union, the Economic-Social Union, and the Electoral Union, of which Gentiloni was the president. To those organizations was given, in a sort of "crusade," the task of watching over the Catholic votes, by now officially snatched from the Christian Democrats, from people like Murri, who was suspended *a divinis*, or like Sturzo.

Pope Sarto, "in the face of the evils of Socialism" which, in his opinion, would not admit that it is "in conformity with the order established by God that there exist in society sovereigns and subjects, employers and workers, rich and poor, educated and ignorant," had chosen the lesser evil, a tacit clerical-moderate alliance. The global condemnation of modernists and progressives in general was clearly a reflection of integralist positions as in the Middle Ages, including the abolition of even the "corporative socialism" of Leo XIII. The worst of it was the fact that, because of the inquisitorial and persecutive methods by which the condemnation was applied, a number of authentically Catholic voices were reduced to silence, voices which later would form the future Christian Democracy, that is to say, the Populist Party.

Above all, Pius X's political engagement was of a decidedly provincial nature as seen in this typically Italian struggle in which he was guided by more than one personal vendetta. On the international level, where Leo XIII had regained so much ground, Pius X created a vacuum around himself and diplomatic relations with other States were reduced to a minimum. One example, among many, was France where in his anti-historical and retrograde view he favored the return of the monarchy, and he kept in constant touch with the men of the *Action française*. Meanwhile, the concordat of 1801 had gone by the board in an open break with the French Republic, while in 1905 the French arrived at the separation of State and Church, and which personified the failure of his integralism.

"From the doctrinaire integralism of Giuseppe Sarto came the operative one in the government of the Church, the structure of which," as Cesare Marchi reminds us, "he reformed in an authoritarian, centralized sense, prohibiting priests from going to the theater, under pain of suspension ipso facto, and recommending people not to buy newspapers which were not in line with the Church. He reformed the liturgical singing, the sacred music and expelled from the temple trumpets, drums, pianos and secular instruments . . . permitting only hymns in Latin and no women in the *schola cantorum.*" The 1912 Catechism, containing questions and answers to be memorised in the preparation for First Communion, and which remained in use until the Second Vatican Council, was the symbol of a certain policy of his, the "restoration" in Christ of each one of the faithful, which had been announced in his first encyclical, *Instaurare Omnia in Christo.* The clergy, of course, whom he wanted better educated, were involved in all this, and in the modernizing of the clergy's culture one should not forget the establishment of the Pontifical Biblical Institute and the revision of the Vulgate.

However, Pius X's determination to get rid of any manipulation of the papacy by secular powers was praiseworthy. The constitution *Commissum nobis* of 1904 abolished the veto, however manifested, by a State during a conclave and declared unlawful any interference by civil authority in a papal election. Any cardinal who had become spokesman for an exclusion by any government would be excommunicated by the future pope.

The Church canonized Pius X and therein is reflected all his goodness and gentleness, but there was also his intransigence and intolerance in the religious and ecclesiastical field, or what Loisy called "genuine pandemonium of fanaticism and stupidity." I think it edifying that at the same time this pope declared that the right to private property was inviolable and exhorted the poor to patience and resignation since, where justice was concerned, they could expect nothing of what was owned by the rich. Here are set down the ultimate terms of a heavenly holiness which is sublimated through earthly injustice, fully ignoring the *Rerum novarum.*

It also attests to his reaction to the hints of the First World War. He expressed only his commiseration and no condemnation. According to the words of a biographer, "he did not raise the strong voice of a prophet before a world already in a tempest but rather stretched out himself on the altar as a victim." It was the martyrdom of his holiness. To the Austrian ambassador who asked him to bless the Austro-Hungarian troops about to invade neutral Belgium, he correctly responded: "I shall bless Peace." This was a testament which his successor, Benedict XV, would take up and make the symbol of his own pontificate.

Pius X died in Rome on 20 August 1914 and was buried modestly in the Vatican Grottoes.

258. BENEDICT XV (1914–1922)

The conclave which began on 1 September 1914, to elect the successor to Pius X included fifty-seven cardinals of the sixty-five who made up the Sacred College, and ten ballots over three days were necessary to reach a conclusion. In effect, the choice was between the progressive policies of Leo XIII and the renunciatory ones of Pope Sarto. Despite the sanctions threatened by the latter's constitution, as Zizola notes, "political pressures and the nationalistic diversities of individual groups of the cardinals did not allow the conclave to be a mystical hothouse even this time." There was a detailed memorandum from the Austrian Minister of Foreign Affairs to his Ambassador to the Vatican, but those instructions, assuming the Austro-Hungarian group of cardinals received them, had no effect. In the existing climate of war, they all wanted a quick conclusion, and on 3 September, to the surprise of the minority, Cardinal Giacomo Della Chiesa was elected.

Had Belli been alive at that time, he would have criticized what happened, as he had done in the case of Pius VIII who had seemed so sickly to him. Della Chiesa was a skinny man who was known in the Curia as "the little one." Moreover, he had a visible curvature of the spine and a pallid thin face. Voting for him, someone might have thought he would not last very long, and would have a meaningless, fleeting pontificate, but he would have been wrong. Within a few hours of his election, Della Chiesa showed that he had the situation well in hand, issuing detailed indications of his policies and appointing, a few days later, the pro-French Cardinal Ferrata as Secretary of State. He displayed self-assurance, despite his precarious physical appearance. One cardinal expressed aloud his bewilderment: "My goodness, we have an already professed pope, not a novice!"

Giacomo Della Chiesa was born in Genoa on 21 November 1854, to a very noble family. His father, a marquis, was a descendant of Berengar II and Calixtus II, his mother a Migliorati, and one of his ancestors was Innocent VII. He had studied in his hometown up to his degree in law in 1875, when he had moved to the Capranica College in Rome to pursue his studies in theology. He was ordained a priest in 1878 but continued his studies at the Academy for noble ecclesiastics. Monsignor Mariano Rampolla del Tindaro wanted to have him as his secretary and this gave him experience in high diplomacy. He had special assignments including several in Vienna and, thanks to his diplomatic talents, was appointed Deputy Secretary of State in 1901 while simultaneously a professor of diplomacy at the same Academy where he had studied earlier. However, Pius X blocked his career by naming him archbishop of Bologna in 1907, which was a kind of exile for the "little one." Born as he had been for politics, he could have been a hindrance to the retrograde policies of the saintly pope, but Pius X could not refrain from making him a cardinal on 25 May 1914, just before he died, and within little more than three months Della Chiesa was pope.

He was crowned on 6 September 1914 taking the name of Benedict XV. However, he wanted the ceremony to be held in the Sistine Chapel rather than in St. Peter's, and this was already a novelty. All was done without pomp and ceremony, with a small reception for some cardinals and a few ambassadors, and a frugal meal. Even his clothing was modest and it was a problem for the tailor, who had to adjust even the shortest of the three white vestments, prepared for the new pontiff, by pinning it up with ordinary pins.

His strategy was to restore to the Church of Rome the credibility which Pius X had lost on a political and diplomatic level. For Benedict XV, the terrain on which to rehabilitate it was the First World War. Like a suicide, he played the role of a harmless prophet among the Great Powers who believed only in the usefulness of war, and he was great precisely because he was unheeded and covered with insults.

In his very first message on 8 September 1914, he spoke about "the scourge of the wrath of God." He repeated it on 28 July 1915, when Italy entered the war, which he called a "horrendous bloodbath which dishonors Europe," in his Christmas appeal of that same year to the world "which had become a hospital and a cemetery," again in 1916 when speaking on 4 March of "the suicide of civilized Europe," and once more on 31 July, when talking about the "darkest tragedy of human hatred and human madness."

Benedict reached the apex in the note of 1 August 1917, in which he declared himself neutral in "perfect impartiality towards all of the belligerents, as becomes someone who is the common Father and loves all his children with equal affection," inviting the Great Powers "to stop this tremendous struggle which seems, more so every day, to be a useless massacre." Then came the insults from the "irredentists" who called the pope's peace plan "white," meaning indolent, and accused him of cowardice towards the French who claimed that his appeal was influenced by the Central Powers and who, speaking through Clemenceau, called him the "*pape boche*," "*boche*" being the scornful nickname given to German soldiers.

They were mistaken, they did not understand him, which was logical. Until then the Church had never been impartial in any war, and at times had even been more or less a direct participant in them. Now, fifty years before John XXIII, the Church was declaring "Peace on earth." Thus the dismay of nations and of the Curia itself was understandable, as was to be the case when faced with the actions of Pope Roncalli. And it cannot be denied that, from this point of view, Benedict XV was the real precursor of John XXIII in the context of a Church, which, through both of them, showed it was more interested in mankind than in itself as the center of power. However, his messages were followed by concrete assistance. Thanks to his intervention, in 1915 many civilian prisoners were able to return to their homes and, a year later, tubercular Italian ones could go back to their homeland. He had established an "Office for Prisoners" in the Vatican which dealt with about 700,000 requests for information and 40,000 cases of repatriation while also maintaining, as far as possible, contact between the soldiers at the front and their families.

Through bishoprics and nunciatures he was everywhere where the war, directly or indirectly, was causing ruin. He sent money to the Russian peasants who were victims of famine in the first years of the Bolshevik revolution as well as to the Chinese peasants hit by great calamities in 1921. He personally handed out more than eighty million Lire for these welfare works, according to his secretary, Cardinal Gasparri. He had proclaimed that: "It is the duty of every person to run to help another human being who is in danger of death," and he did it in that true spirit of Christian charity which must not look at the color of a person's skin, overcoming ideologies to demonstrate the highest meaning of the Gospel through a *"miserere super turbam."*

Nor could he overlook the problem of the participation of Catholics in Italian politics. He dealt with it by trying to give greater freedom to various currents for a concrete dialogue that would safeguard a degree of unity within the movement itself. It seemed reasonable at this point to abrogate the *Non expedit* on 12 November 1919. He accepted, without blessing it but also without condemning it, the Populist Party founded by Don Sturzo, although he recommended a clear distinction between "Catholic Action," established as he had wished with a completely evangelical mission, and the actions of Catholics in the economic and political areas. That was an indication of his lucidity which was also evident in numerous other initiatives, such as the founding of the Congregation of Seminaries and Studies, the promulgation of the Code of Canon Law, and the approval in 1920 of the Catholic University of the Sacred Heart at Milan.

Benedict XV died on 22 January 1922, in Rome, after only four days of pneumonia. He was buried in the Vatican Grottoes in front of the tomb of Pius X, and a monument, sculpted by Canonica, was erected to him later in the Chapel of the Presentation in St. Peter's.

259. PIUS XI (1922–1939)

Fourteen ballots and four days in conclave were needed for the fifty-three cardinals gathered in the Sistine Chapel on 2 February 1922, to elect the successor to Benedict XV. There were repeated black smoke signals for the impatient crowd in St. Peter's Square, who were following the voting going on inside for the two candidates, the French Merry del Val, Secretary of State to Pius X, and Cardinal Maffi, archbishop of Pisa, and then of Cardinals La Fontaine and Gasparri. The final choice on 6 February of Achille Ratti, archbishop of Milan, was a compromise between the progressive and the conservative factions.

The man elected decided to take the name of Pius XI and immediately made a gesture which had not been done since the time of the breach at Porta Pia; he appeared on the external balcony of the basilica and imparted his blessing "*urbi et orbi.*" The crowd applauded with a shout: "Viva Pius XI! Viva Italy!," a clear sign of the times. To solve the "Roman question" once and for all, the pope was speaking directly to Italy and with no half-meanings. He was crowned on 12 February in St. Peter's.

Achille Ratti was born in Desio near Milan on 31 May 1857, to a lower middle-class family, his father being a director of a spinning mill. At the age of ten he entered the seminary at Seveso, where he distinguished himself by his precocious seriousness, and the archbishop of Milan, during a pastoral visit, noticed him and thought him "a young old man." At twenty-two he was ordained a priest, but his great interest was in history, especially of secular and clerical events in Lombardy. He published numerous articles on these subjects, and in 1888 got his doctorate at the Ambrosiana Library. He seemed destined to spend his life with books when he became prefect in that same Library in 1907; nothing else appeared to attract his interest. Only mountaineering, his hobby, could pull him away from his "sweaty papers." He had climbed Mount Rosa, spending a night on a rock at 11,880 meters above the abyss, and had also scaled the Mont Blanc and the Matterhorn.

Then in 1911 he received higher orders with Pius X wanting him in Rome at the Vatican Library, so he left Milan. But he was not destined to end up among books. Benedict XV sensed his diplomatic talent and sent him as apostolic nuncio to Poland, Lithuania and Silesia. By 1921 he was ready for the cardinal's hat, and with that rank he returned to Milan as archbishop. It took him only a year to understand the political situation there with the continuous disorders and a government incapable of controlling matters.

In a discourse to his diocese he declared that "the pope is the greatest treasure of Italy" and in a chaotic situation like the one the nation was then experiencing, it was incredible the "prestige and advantages that could come to our country from his presence, when one takes into account his international and supranational sovereignty." He was convinced that the pope had to regain possession of his temporal power and, once he was elected, he would devote himself to achieve that.

The year 1922 was that of the "March on Rome." It appears that the Black Shirts had received precise orders to respect the clergy as they advanced on the capital where there was to be a demonstration in favor of the pope in St. Peter's square. In the *Osservatore Romano* of 29 October of that year one read: "It has been announced that the Honorable Mussolini intends to bring into the government . . . men from all parts, especially those devoted to the interests of the people." It was not praise but it was at least "an attitude of cautious optimism towards the Fascist regime," Giacomo Martina wrote. Pius XI understood very well with whom he had to deal, but he played his cards like a great diplomat and with authority.

Mussolini held his hand out to the Catholics because he recognized the importance of the Christian religion in the history and the life of the Italians, and he was ready to grant concessions to the Church. The new pope was in favor of solutions at a summit meeting rather than through democratic mediation. The "National Union" of Catholics like Mattei-Gentile and Carapelle was acceptable, but not the Populist Party of Don Sturzo, who left and went into exile in London, and priests were forbidden to join any party. "Catholic Action" was also acceptable as it was reorganized on the basis of four branches (boys, men, girls and women) and was active in every parish. According to Tramontin, "this cell formation was to contribute to the spread of the social regime of Christ in the villages."

That was the path on which, to echo Carlo Falconi, through the proclamation of 1925 of the Feast of Christ the King, the new temporal situation of the Church in Italy was to be based, sanctioned by the famous Lateran Pacts of 11 February 1929, which contained as is well known a political agreement, a financial convention, and a concordat. The Holy See was to rediscover itself territorially in the Vatican City, but in effect it was the rebuilding of a theocracy which would spread gradually throughout the world, with Pope Ratti ready to seize any opportunity to establish relations with all and any state, whatever may be the characteristics of their regimes, and to place again the Catholic bastions in schools and political parties with which to consolidate the neo-temporalism of the Holy See around the world.

It was a policy of being active and on the spot through a series of concordats, from the one with Latvia in 1922 to the ones with Rumania and Lithuania in 1927, from those with Germany and Austria in 1933, to those with Yugoslavia in 1937 and Poland in 1939. All motivated, certainly, by religious obligations but through which Pius XI accomplished the masterpiece for an ample "restoration." By the totally spiritual goal of leading humanity back to the Christian principles which spread from the See of Peter, came the inevitable reaffirmation of a territorial sovereignty of the papacy, including concessions and privileges providing for economic security of ecclesiastical institutions.

The outstanding politician in him is revealed in two distinct moments. Initially, when forming certain "repugnant alliances" such as those with dictators like Dollfuss, Horthy, Salazar, Hitler, Franco, and, of course, Mussolini, and then, once he had achieved his purpose, armed with his own recovered prestige, he appeared prepared to condemn them or at least to regret them as a Head of State by then universally recognized.

Then in 1931 came the encyclical, in Italian, *Non abbiamo bisogno* (We do not need), of 5 July against Fascist doctrines and practices and in defense of his "Catholic Action," which was threatened by the organizations inspired by the Fascist ideology that Pope Ratti did not hesitate to condemn as "Pagan Adoration of Statehood."

However, in *Quadragesimo anno* of 15 May, he had acknowledged the "absolute necessity of resisting the ranks of subversive parties, as a united front," thereby justifying his renouncement of the Catholic unions and approval of the corporatist organization in a kind of Clerical-Fascist marriage.

In 1937 came the encyclical in German, *Mit Brennender Sorge*, beginning with a protest against harm done to German ecclesiastics and church property, and then going on to a true condemnation of Hitlerian paganism. It denounced "violations of the concordat, the many forms of oppression of the freedom of organized religion, the idolatry in glorification of race and blood, the horrendous campaigns of scandal against the clergy, the battle against Catholic education, the suppression of the press." Pius XI would have liked to have broken off relations and recalled his nuncio from Berlin, but he was restrained from doing so by his Secretary of State, Eugenio Pacelli, the future Pius XII.

Again in 1937 Pope Ratti condemned Communism in another encyclical, *Divini Redemptoris* by which he categorically opposed any dictatorship which would preclude the religious freedom of Catholics.

Fundamentally, the entire concordat policy of Pius XI towards the totalitarian powers resulted in a "confrontation." remarkably well assisted in this by Secretaries of State like cardinal Gasparri and Pacelli successor in 1930. Pius knew how to defend the fundamental principles of the Church by condemning as soon as the rights of Catholics were suppressed. The danger clearly lay in compromise, which he always avoided, at least in his functions as the Head of the Church of Rome.

Such was, generally speaking, Pope Ratti, head of a religious force which he had succeeded in renewing throughout the world by the establishment of 128 archbishoprics and 113 apostolic prefectures in a closely woven network of missions spread between the five continents, to the degree that he passed into history as the "missionary pope." Especially notable in this field was the founding in Rome in 1927 of the "Missionary League of Students" and the creation of "indigenous clergy," including the first colored priests and bishops.

His image of "Pastor" was reflected in the canonization of thirty-three saints, including Don Bosco, as well as the beatification of 500 persons and the celebration of three Jubilees. That of 1925 was a normal one and was a Holy Year marked by the pilgrimages of different social categories. There were those of the railway workers, of the metallurgists and of the students, all more or less under the banner of corporatism. However, European sovereigns came too, including Queen Olga of Greece with her three children, two Belgian princesses and the Habsburg archduchess. That year also saw the attempt on Mussolini's life, upon whom Pius XI was still "working" to obtain whatever he had in mind in the "Lateran Pacts." He, of course, called the attempt a "criminal" act and stated: "Just the thought of it makes us sad, as his escape from it causes us to give thanks to God." The other two Jubilees were extraordinary, the one in 1929 on the occasion of the fiftieth anniversary of his priesthood, and the other in 1933 on the occasion of the nineteenth centenary of the Redemption of Christ.

As a person, he had an affable manner and a sense of humor, as had many of his predecessors, but he had especially a confidential and familiar tone of voice, particularly in audiences with common people. He was also the first pope to have a woman among his domestic helpers, a certain Teodolinda Banfi, who was his chambermaid for more than forty years. When it was pointed out to him that no pontiff had ever allowed a woman to work in the Vatican, he simply responded: "That means I shall be the first."

February 1939 marked the tenth anniversary of the "Conciliation" of the Holy See with Italy, the seventeenth anniversary of his coronation and the sixtieth of his ordination as a priest, all in a moment of extreme gravity for Europe. Pius XI had convened in Rome the entire Italian episcopate for a meeting on the 11th and 12th of February where he was to give a speech on which he had worked for several months. In that speech he planned to denounce the violation of the Lateran Pacts by the Italian Government, as well as the racial persecutions in Germany and German preparations for war. But he was not able to deliver that speech, some excerpts of which were published only in 1959 by John XXIII, since he passed away during the night of 10 February 1939 of a heart attack.

In a memorial attributed to Cardinal Tisserant and published in 1972 by Paris-Match and Panorama, it was alleged that Pius XI had been assassinated on the orders of Mussolini who feared excommunication. The actual killer was said to be Professor Francesco Petacci, the father of Claretta, effected by means of an injection of poison, but Cardinal Confalonieri, the special assistant to the pope, said that those were "all lies." The episode has passed into history as the "Tisserant murder mystery," but the mystery remains.

However, according to Carlo Falconi, Pius XI's entire life was an "enigma," through his power games with dictatorial regimes which he could shout at, smile with, yet about which he could, on other occasions, remain silent. But that is the image of the great and truly enigmatic politician which Pius XI was. As Franco Molinari has observed, a convincing historical biography of this pope has yet to be written. Perhaps all the mystery will be revealed when the Vatican documents, still labelled "top secret," can be examined. In the meantime, not even the splendor of the sarcophagus containing his remains in the Vatican Grottoes can enlighten us in that regard.

260. PIUS XII (1939–1958)

The conclave that began on the evening of 1 March 1939, was the shortest in recent times due certainly to the imminent outbreak of war. The balloting began on 2 March and the same day the "white smoke" appeared. Towards 6 PM the new pope, Cardinal Eugenio Pacelli, who took the name of Pius XII, appeared on the Vatican balcony.

He was born in Rome on 2 March 1876, into a family belonging to the papal nobility. He had attended the Visconti high school in Rome, and received his degree in theology at the Gregorian University. At twenty-three, he was ordained a priest and, two years later, became an apprentice in the Secretariat of State, making a name for himself with Cardinal Gasparri in the new codification of canon law. He carried out his work while steering clear of religious reforms and zealous orthodoxy, displaying already an extreme diplomatic caution.

In 1917 came the results of that impassive diligence. He was appointed apostolic nuncio at Munich, and three years later at Berlin, where he carried on intense diplomatic activity, achieving concordats with Bavaria and Prussia. These were years which strongly influenced the visceral attachment of the then Monsignor Pacelli to Germany. He was clearly struck by the seriousness, the scientific dedication, the moral conscience and the organizational efficiency of the German people. And it was perhaps in Munich where, together with his fondness for Germany, his antipathy toward Marxism was born. "In the Communist city of Munich Eugenio Pacelli had a dramatic experience," recorded by Franco Molinari, "when a crazed troop of red soldiers pointed a revolver at his temple." He somehow managed to escape, but the incident was one of those which leave their mark.

In 1929 he was appointed cardinal and a year later succeeded Gasparri in the Secretariat of State, making frequent journeys as a papal legate. In Argentina, at Lourdes, Paris, in the United States and Budapest, he acquired an international reputation that facilitated his election to the See of Peter.

Pius XII succeeded a pope who was preparing to denounce vehemently crimes of violence in Italy and in Europe, without worrying about anyone. Pius XII would not do that, always afraid of doing more damage than that already done. He rejected explicit condemnation as he did the "neutrality" of Benedict XV, and would declare his "impartiality," "Neutrality could be understood in the sense of passive equivalence which would not be fitting for the supreme head of the Church faced with so many realities," he is said to have explained in a letter to the archbishop of Munich, Cardinal Faulhaber, on 31 January 1943. "Impartiality means for us the judgment of matters in accordance with truth and justice." But nothing came of this "impartiality."

On 3 March 1939, the day after his election, in a radio transmission to the world he invited nations to make peace. On 12 March he was crowned in St. Peter's and three days later the Germans invaded Prague. On 1 April he sent a telegram with his benediction to General Franco; on 7 April, Good Friday, Italian planes bombarded Tirana and Albania was occupied. Finally, on Easter Sunday, Pius XII spoke; it was "an allocution, prepared before the events," wrote a Catholic, Emanuel Mounier, in the *Voltigeur* of 5 May. "In very general terms, he calls upon the peoples to make peace. In more precise words, he condemns the violations of promises made. The world, sadly surprised, does not hear a single word from him on that bloody Good Friday." On 16 April, ignoring Guernica and the thousands of corpses, he sends a congratulatory message to Spain which, Mounier wrote bitterly, "should increase our concern. It was no longer a matter of silence but of approval. His Holiness congratulated 'the healthy part of the Spanish population' for having embarked on a war "for the purpose of defending the ideals of the Christian faith and civilization." He praised the 'very noble Christian sentiments to which the Chief of State and many faithful collaborators have attested' and he considered that the procedure used to protect Spain against destabilising forces is 'the best evidence' one can provide of the supremacy of religion and the spirit." This was not "impartiality;" he had justified a war, but a war is never just.

And the war spread through the rest of Europe. On 23 August, Hitler and Stalin signed the Treaty of Friendship to divide up Poland. The following day, the French ambassador to the Holy See, François Charles-Roux, called on the pope and begged him "to denounce in advance such an aggression against a Catholic country in the hope of preventing it," notes the historian, Anthony Rhodes, and "the pope preferred not to issue such a condemnation, believing that it might have encouraged the aggressors. Nevertheless, he decided to speak on the radio that same evening from Castel Gandolfo, having his speech translated into the best known foreign languages. It was his final appeal for peace, an appeal containing one of his most famous remarks: "Nothing is lost through peace. Everything can be lost through war," a statement suggested by Monsignor Montini, the future Paul VI, then the deputy for Foreign Affairs in the Secretariat of State.

On 20 October 1939, the encyclical *Summi Pontificatus* was issued condemning the joint Russian-German invasion of Poland which stigmatized the "idolisation of the State by dictators," as Franco Molinari notes, but it is not clear why it was not felt necessary to mention names, since everyone understood that the condemnation was of Hitler and also of Stalin. Now, it was at this point that the "silence" of Pius XII began. This was made clear in the special issue of *L'Osservatore Romano* of 13 December 1981, in an article by Michele Maccarrone, "It is true that Pius XII, accused of being 'a diplomatic pope,' did not practice 'grand diplomacy.' He made no appeal to the belligerents to stop the war, as Benedict XV had done in August 1917, no call for crusades, no excommunications, nor did he utter that solemn, clamorous 'denunciation' of the crimes and the Nazi criminals, demanded of him by Hochhuth in the play, *The Vicar*."

One may defend him as much as one wants, recalling his intervention on behalf of people in occupied countries, the rescue of Jews and internees in concentration camps through his representatives in various countries. Also, as Molinari notes, "Nenni, hidden in the Lateran, was called Don Emiliani and the leaders of atheistic Communism played the role of paunchy monsignors, while Jews went about in long cassocks." And finally there was his visit to St. Lawrence outside the Walls ignoring the danger to see the damage from the bombardments. But it was not enough. All that formed part of the apostolic spirit of the vicar of Christ, gratified moreover to be considered again the *defensor Urbis* by weeping Romans.

It is reasonable to believe that "the very sensitive Pius XII suffered from the tragic uncertainty of the situation . . . between discretion and prudent silence, or speaking openly and taking strong action." One cannot say certainly that he became disinterested in these dramatic events, only the statement released to Alfieri, the Italian ambassador, was not at all exhaustive about the cruelty of the Nazis in Poland, according to a report to him of 11 May 1940 from the Italian Consul who had fled from Warsaw: "We ought to be shouting words of damnation against such things, and we are restrained from doing so only in the knowledge that we would, if we spoke out, be making the situation of those unhappy people still more difficult."

But it was already "more difficult," as the tragic news from Czechoslovakia would confirm, with Jewish girls being deported to Germany destined for the houses of prostitution. Events would have grown worse but the "words of damnation" would never come because the pope continued to view them as counterproductive. And it does not seem to me that "the absence of a spectacular, clamorous declaration by Pius XII finds a convincing explanation in any humanitarian or realistic motivation," as again Molinari maintains.

It is probable that a spectacular protest against Hitler would not have obtained anything but, as Hochhuth declares in his *The Vicar*, "the pope had to make an effort, he should have offered himself as the scapegoat. Where did those proud statements at the beginning of his pontificate end up?" "We have to fight; I am not afraid," he had said to the cardinal-archbishops from

Germany summoned to the Vatican. He had repeated that in 1940, informing Mussolini, who had had enough of his public appeals for peace, that "he had no fear of going to a concentration camp." He should have done so spontaneously, faced up to martyrdom and not, on the contrary, declare after certain information was verified at the beginning of 1944: "To leave here, it will not be enough to invite me to do so, they will have to chain me. Still not enough, even chained, they will have to drag me away by force."

Finally, there was the German reprisal action in Rome leading to the massacre at the Ardeatine Caves. In the beginning, Pius XII was unaware of it, but later Cardinal Nasalli Rocca, at that time his secret chamberlain and the chaplain of the Regina Coeli prison in Rome, who heard about it during the night between the 24th and 25th of March 1944, reported it all to the pope, who said: "It's not possible, I cannot believe it." And he took immediate action: "It is confirmed that Pius XII sent the Salvatorian priest, Pancrazio Pfeiffer, who was the contact between the occupiers and the Vatican," as Giulio Andreotti reports, "to plead for mercy at the command post. The response was that Hitler could not be reached and that it was already a favor to multiply only by ten instead of one hundred the number of victims of the reprisal."

But this was the chance for a martyrdom which would have given the papacy the glow of sanctity it had at its very beginnings. The world would have seen, would have understood the deep meaning of the sacrifice. Whoever did not believe might have discovered, or rediscovered, the faith, according to the words of a layman like Dino Buzzati and recalled in the introduction to this series of biographies: "If it was not to be so, it is the sign that opportunism had come into play, the predominant problem of 'survival.' And some failings of the spirit must be paid for."

In any event, the war was nearing its end, and the Church had its victims. Among the many was the Polish priest, Maximilian Kolbe, in the Nazi lager of Oswiecim, who gave up his life to save the life of the father of a family. John Paul II would canonize him. In Germany, the Jesuit theologian, Alfred Delp, arrested in July 1944, after the famous attempt on Hitler's life, was hanged on 2 February 1945, at Plötzense in a martyrdom against which no accusation was received from Rome. The words of this martyr are a condemnation of Pope Pacelli: "An honest history of the Church must contain bitter chapters on the contributions of the churches to the rise of the common man, of collectivism, and of dictatorial power."

The behavior of Pius XII was not "cowardly" but it was a will to "survive" with eyes closed during a pontificate that was characterized more and more by autocracy. When Cardinal Maglione, the Secretary of State, died in August 1944, the pope did not want to appoint a successor, preferring to follow personally the running of the Church. To the Deputy Secretary Tardini, he stated, "I do not want collaborators; I only want executors."

So he went into isolation. The post-war problem was no longer Nazi Germany but rather the countries of Eastern Europe in the orbit of the Soviet Union and under Communist regime, with the persecution which the Church was certainly undergoing beyond the "curtain," called by Pius XII "the Church of silence." Proof of this was the case against the archbishop of Zagreb, Stepinac, and the Primate of Hungary, Mindszenty, as well as the imprisonment undergone by Beran, archbishop of Prague, and by the Polish Cardinal Wiszynsky.

A dialogue with the Communist regimes to assist the "Church of silence" would probably have been as unrewarding at it would have been with Hitler. However, while there was no excommunication against Nazism or Fascism, there certainly was against Marxism. The anticommunism of Pius XII, already in evidence during the war, became tangible in 1949 with a decree of the Holy Office which excommunicated the Marxists and those who *scienter et libere* joined or collaborated with the Communist Party. The decree was posted in every parish.

So, though the real war was over, a "cold war" had started, imposed by Pope Pacelli through his dogmatic rejections that found their widest echo in the celebration of the Jubilee Year of 1950, the year in which the dogma of the Assumption was also announced. "The defense of the Church against renewed attacks by its enemies, penetration of the true faith by erring people, the infidels, the 'Godless,'" was one of the purposes of that Holy Year, a personal triumph of the pope through an impeccable organization. The most eminent personalities of the new Italian State, of the newly born republic, with which the new clerical union was to be established were present at the opening of the Holy Door.

Indeed, the religious commitment that marked the final eight years of the pontificate of Pius XII, including numerous canonizations, such as that of Pius X in 1954, which was also the Marian Year, became, in effect, an anti-Marxist crusade for the exaltation of the "supremacy of religion and of spirituality." The religious commitment became political, linked to old and outdated programs within which there was no place for the lay groups of renewal with figures like La Pira or Dossetti. The pope did not trust them and avoided them, listening more to Sister Pasqualina Lehnert with whom many tried to curry favor, Giulio Andreotti noted, "as a result of her confidential position with the Holy Father."

One of the few on whom Pius XII relied blindly was Father Riccardo Lombardi, nicknamed "God's microphone" because of his great preaching ability. A "Movement for a better world" arose for reconciliation among peoples on an ecumenical level. But, in effect, it was the "Crusade of Kindness" against the "red barbarism," with Luigi Gedda close to him. Moreover, a big encouragement was given to "Catholic Action" which resumed its activity in a broader sphere, and "Civic Committees" were established through which Catholic assent to the Christian Democracy took place.

Then came a certain modernizing of the liturgy, put into official form in the encyclical *Mediator Dei* following more up-to-date instructions, but they were only temporary. The old regulations about fasting before Communion were modified, evening Mass was permitted and ceremonies for Holy Week were restored to their original format. All of which could have been the prelude to a total renewal. According to Giacomo Martina, "an accurate and detailed analysis would show that from 1940 to 1958 a whole series of factors were in the phase of preparation, some supported, others suppressed by Pius XII, which would result in the renewal which would take place during and after the council." The recent publication of certain documents prove the interest of Pope Pacelli for a council, to the extent that he is spoken of as the precursor of Vatican II. Franco Molinari is convinced of this. "The project of a council does not bear the stamp of John but rather of Pacelli." Yet it is a fact that the "opening toward a future rich in broader developments" did not take place, and a basically static outlook prevailed. Avant-garde figures such as Mazzolari and Maritain paid the price, while Montini, still a monsignor, who was in favor of a broader dialogue with the world of today, was "exiled" to Milan as its archbishop.

Pius XII was probably the victim of his autarchic attitude and of his tendency to political compromise, faults from which John XXIII was immune, and in that sense the image of the *"pastor angelicus,"* prophesied for him by Malachy and defended by the Pacelli faction in a purely mystical context, has no reality. No matter how tough they may seem, the words that the poet, Pier Paolo Pasolini, puts in the mouth of this pope in a poem are nonetheless significant because they delineate in a clear way the image of the fetishistic and Pharaonic pope which, in the final analysis, he showed himself to be:

> I am a Pope-politician and hence unfathomable;
> my charity is buried in my attitude.
> And perhaps my voice has become arrogant and querulous
> (Counterpoint of Our every breath)
> I protect myself. It is my duty as Pope. I am a single block.
> Church and laymen are united in their behavior.
> Dogma has only one other possible face: the Deed.
> And for a layman isn't the Deed the same as Attitude?

His last years were certainly not serene. "Nor did the rumors about miracles and visions which he was said to have during a serious illness do him honor," as Mario Pancera notes, "and people propagated them for purely commercial purposes, abusing his good faith."

Then they made him die twice. He was at Castel Gandolfo in the summer of 1958 and he had extended his stay there because of his illness. On 8 October, he was dying and someone imprudently closed the shutter of a window, which was read as a "signal," and the Roman newspapers issued special editions announcing his death. There had been no official notification and indeed the denial was flashed to the press agencies. "The Pope is still alive, it was a mistake." Meanwhile, his personal physician, Riccardo Galeazzi, was taking photographs of Pius XII in agony that would travel around the world. This scandal ended in a lawsuit.

Pius XII actually died, following a nine-hour agony, during the night of 9 October, stricken by an ictus. During the afternoon of the 10th, his remains were moved in a solemn procession to St. Peter's where they were laid on an enormous bier. The respects of the faithful lasted four days. The papal staff had his corpse wrapped in cellophane to avoid decomposition but the stench was awful.

During the night between the 13th and 14th of October, when the doors of the basilica were closed, the doctors finished the laborious embalming of his remains, and the next day he was temporarily buried in St. John's, and finally laid to rest in the Vatican Grottoes. A bronze monument, sculpted by Francesco Messina, was to be erected to him in St. Peter's.

261. JOHN XXIII (1958–1963)

There was a great deal of uncertainty about the result of the conclave which began in Rome on 25 October 1958. The fifty-one cardinals who participated in it were theoretically lined up on the usual two positions of the traditionalists and of the progressives. But even after his death Pius XII's personality weighed indirectly on the conclave, through the precise characteristics he had given the papacy, and which was influencing the various candidatures for very different reasons. Basically, however, the Sacred College did not have the courage to take a position for one or another. The names of Ruffini and Siri, of the Frenchman Tisserant, of the Russian Agagianian, and of the American Spellman came up most often in the forecasts, and the newspapers evaluated the qualities of this or that cardinal, weighing the pros and cons of the different personalities, but without openly compromising themselves.

In this atmosphere of uncertainty, a lengthy conclave was foreseen, which for the first time seemed to involve both the Sacred College and public opinion. Instead, it was all over in three days after eleven ballots. On the evening of 28 September 1958, the new pope, the patriarch of Venice, Angelo Giuseppe Roncalli, appeared on the balcony of benedictions. He was probably the least *papabile*, "an old man of florid complexion, fat, huge, with a serene and peaceful face," as Carlo Masina recorded. It is true that all of us, including me, aged twenty, there in St. Peter's Square "were immediately taken by that good-natured face framed by those two enormous ears." Personally I was struck by his choice of name, John XXIII, which had been that of an antipope. It had not been a casual one and suggested something that was already "anti," that broke the succession of Piuses, Benedicts, and Gregorys. But who indeed was this new pope? The newspapers were slow in finding news about him, mainly because they had been caught by surprise. He was, in any case, elderly. Many immediately thought that the cardinals had chosen, rather rapidly, in favor of a pontificate of "transition." That may have been the case since he ruled for only five years, but he ruled in such a revolutionary way, fortunately, as to renew the Church in a manner that was irreversible.

Angelo Roncalli was born at Brusicco di Sotto il Monte near Bergamo on 25 November 1881, into a peasant family, the fourth of thirteen children. He began his education privately in a parish of the nearby town until, as with all of the gifted children from such a humble background, he was accepted into the diocesan seminary of Bergamo at the tender age of eleven. There was no doubt about his vocation. At the age of seventeen, he received his minor orders and two years later, thanks to a scholarship, he went to Rome to the Apollinare seminary where he received his degree in theology. He was ordained a priest in 1904 and a year later Monsignor Radini Tedeschi, the bishop of Bergamo, made him return there as he wanted him as his secretary. He stayed with him for ten years and accompanied him in his travels to various European countries. The bishop then left him free to preach and to teach in the seminary and at "the House of the People," where the young prelate got involved in a series of social and religious initiatives for poor people. In 1909, he even participated in fundraising for the workers on strike, and, in Rome, there were insinuations that some of his actions smacked of modernism. But war broke out and Roncalli became a medical sergeant and then as a chaplain with the rank of lieutenant. He got first hand experience of that world "of hospitals and cemeteries" and witnessed that "useless massacre." He cherished the messages for peace from Benedict XV, and founded a "House for the Soldiers," busying himself with the search for dispersed soldiers. Perhaps even then he was thinking along the lines of Pope Della Chiesa about "pacem in terris." When he was discharged from service, he gave his "moral support" to the Populist Party. However, Benedict XV, evidently aware of an identity of views, wanted to have him in Rome and appointed him head of the Propaganda Fide.

Then, under Pius XI, he resumed his travels as an apostolic visitor. From 1925 to 1934 he was in Bulgaria, a land of the Orthodox and distrustful of Rome, but where he succeeded in being admired. He sought a link between the Catholics and the Orthodox faithful because, "in his heart he believed in a final religious unity," as Richard Cushing observed, and so he succeeded in accomplishing the task entrusted to him, and the establishment of diplomatic relations between the Vatican and Bulgaria was his doing. Pius XI transferred him as apostolic delegate to Turkey and to Greece, again two nations distant from Rome, one Islamic and the other Orthodox. But Roncalli was once more successful. He understood particularly the Turkish way of thinking and enjoyed the good will of the Turkish Prime Minister, Ataturk, whom he convinced that the patriotic feelings of Christians were just the same as those of the Moslems. He arranged to have the epistles and gospels read in Turkish, and managed to have the basilica of Santa Sofia declared a historical monument, thereby preserving its appearance as a sanctuary.

When the Second World War started Roncalli remained in Turkey. The country became the center of international intrigue and espionage and, in constant contact with the Vatican, he managed to assist numerous Jewish refugees in escaping from the Nazis and finding asylum in Palestine. One night he signed false certificates of baptism for Jewish children - the peak of his diplomatic intrigues in the name of Christ. From January 1945, to January 1953, he was the apostolic nuncio in Paris. There were the worker-priests there but Roncalli did not understand them. This was one of his "sins," to use a word dear to Franco Molinari, a flaw in the mythicizing of his progressivism, through which one tended to correct a great deal of the anecdotal panegyric circulating about Pope Roncalli. In any case, it was in Paris that he came to know and love Abbé Pierre and Maritain, unjustly treated by Pius XII.

In 1953 he was appointed as cardinal and became patriarch of Venice, where his socially advanced tendencies manifested themselves fully. In 1957, he did not hesitate to welcome the Socialists who held their congress there, although at the same time he invited "the faithful to pray that those who thought the heavens were falling apart would not imagine they could build a social structure without reference to the Gospel," as Cushing notes. At this point, however, his fate had been decided. When he left Venice to attend the funeral of Pius XII and the conclave, he promised to return in fifteen days. They were a sailor's promise or of a *"pastor et nauta"* according to Malachy's prophesy. He would not keep them, just as fifty years earlier Pius X had not kept them. On the nineteenth day of his absence he was elected pope.

That first impression of sympathy which we Romans formed while witnessing his blessing from the balcony with that easy going air of his, was not unfounded, and Masina was right in saying that "Pope John continued in those first days to please everyone especially because of his physical appearance and his extraordinary joviality. Just looking at him made one feel happy and his rotund solidity inspired even more confidence. It was similar to that other peasant who had got to the top, that kind of atheistic pope of the Muscovite creed, Nikita Khrushchev, who had thawed the Stalinist ice," which my youthful enthusiasm linked in their genuine "improvisation." And then came that speech on the day of his coronation on 4 November (yes "with the ancient ceremony reminding one of Renaissance splendor," another of his "sins," as Franco Molinari also notes) when he spoke to us in words never before heard coming from the mouth of a pope. In him we would no longer find "a statesman, a diplomat, a scientist. The new pope, through the course of his life's experiences, was like the son of Jacob who, on meeting his brothers in human misfortune, reveals to them the tenderness of his own heart and cries aloud: 'It is I . . . your brother Joseph.'" He said this on that day, insisting that he wanted to be "that splendid image of the Good Shepherd." And that he achieved fully.

I shall not run through here all the stages in his constant relationship with people. However, a few are sufficient to recall the spirit of this pope about whom Don Mazzolari felt able to declare, from his house arrest in Bozzolo from which Pope Roncalli would extricate him a few days after his election: "We have a pope made of flesh and bones and the whole world is relieved. Fatherhood is not aerial, so much so that the Son of Man is God made flesh."

John XXIII demonstrated that immediately, going on his first Christmas as pope to visit the sick in the Roman hospitals, S. Spirito and Bambino Gesù and the next day the prisoners in Regina Coeli. It was particularly that going into the jail, as in the very ancient times of the papacy, which fully typified the mark of this new pontificate. "So, here we are. I came, you have seen me. I have looked into your eyes, I have put my heart close to yours," is what he said that day to those looked upon as excluded by society. And to eliminate any distance between them, he told them that one day a relative of his, for who knows what naughtiness, had wound up in prison too. In other words, the pope, even indirectly, was "one of them." From that day on, for us Romans John XXIII became "the good Pope," and he continued to be so, leaving the Vatican more than a hundred times on visits, especially to the slums, with his old red cap on his head and exclaiming: "First of all, I seek your benevolence for this man who simply wants to be your brother, friendly, approachable, and understanding." And he was welcomed in just that way.

Smiles aside, Pope John knew that he would not live long and already on 25 January 1959, he informed the cardinals gathered at S. Paolo fuori le Mura of three decisions he had made, namely that the problems of the Diocese of Rome would be analysed by a synod, that as soon as possible there would be an ecumenical council, and finally that there would be a reform of canon law. Needless to say, the cardinals were amazed since what was supposed to be a pontificate of transition turned out to be, in effect, an earthquake. "The Church is a garden to be tended not a museum of antiques!" was said to have been his reply, and he requested the help of all those who were a part of it, giving back the right of speech to the bishops who had been downgraded by the First Vatican Council to the role of "extras," because "the head of the Church is Christ and not the pope" and, moreover, "the Church belongs to everyone but above all to the poor." The ultimate goal was to smooth the way for the unity of Christians, but "the stimulus is for a Christian community which places at its own center the oppressed, the marginalized, the powerless," as Giancarlo Zizola has emphasized, and that "is much more than a change of class. It is a culture leap." This was to be sensed in the reform issued in the *"motu propri"' Summi Pontifici electio* in September 1962, which "sees the election as an ecclesiastical act, not a political one, and declares that all the cardinals must be bishops linked together in one Church."

John XXIII did not have a detailed program for all this. It is true that he let himself "be carried by God, just like a child is who goes to Mass or to the village fair on the shoulders of his earthly father" noted Franco Molinari in a new and realistic depiction of this pope. "But it is his disarming sincerity with which he recognizes before God the burden of his own limitations that the fascination of a true human being shines out. In this world full of lies and hypocrisy, he probably impressed mankind by his courage to be himself." In this sudden change of course, he would be helped by Cardinal Domenico Tardini, the Secretary of State, and by Loris Capovilla, his private secretary, while an aging Jesuit, Cardinal Agostino Bea, would race around the world in the Catholic and non-Catholic countries carrying the peace greetings of John XXIII.

The famous encyclical of 15 July 1961, *Mater et Magistra*, was addressed not only to the Church but to all men of good will, as he wanted to send a message of justice and peace all over the world. In his 'ingenuousness' he was trying to get close to everyone, including those he called "rascals," but not to get them back, rather to show them his good intentions, his evangelical discretion, his human burden. He declined all 'political' caution, sought relations even with the China of Mao and received warmly in a private audience the Soviet journalist, Adzhubey, Khrushchev's son-in-law, and his wife. As Giulio Andreotti recalls, "John XXIII firmly believed that the Soviet Union, with its twenty million deaths during the Second World War, could want only peace. He said so to the American vice-president, Johnson, amongst others, urging him to work for a détente with Russia."

Then there was the problem of Cuba and the pope addressed a letter to Khrushchev, which was effective precisely because of its non-political nature. It ended as follows: "If you have the courage to withdraw your missile ships, you will prove your love of your neighbor not only for your nation but for the entire human family. You will pass into history as one of the pioneers in a revolution of values based on love. You can claim not to be religious, but religion is not simply a collection of commandments, rather it is the dedication to acts out of love for all humanity which, when genuine, is joined to the love of God, on account of which one is religious even if one does not use the word." Khrushchev gave the order to the ships to reverse course, and on 15 December 1962, sent the following note: "To His Holiness Pope John XXIII. On the occasion of the holy feast days of Christmas, I beg you to accept my best wishes and congratulations from a man who wishes health and strength for You in your constant struggle for peace, happiness and welfare."

However, the pope was not well. On 11 October of that year he had opened the Second Vatican Ecumenical Council with the secret hope of bringing it to a quick conclusion. More than 2,500 delegates from all over the world and 35 non-Catholic observers and guests, for the most ecclesiastics representing 17 Protestant and Orthodox groups, were present. At a special audience, he told them that he was burning with "the desire to work and to suffer so that the hour would come when Jesus' prayer at the Last Supper *Ut unum sint* would become a reality for all." But the problems were enormous and he himself had to accept the fact that the preparatory work of the Council, which he had hoped to conclude, would have to be resumed and developed. On 8 December, he decided to end the first session which, in effect, had discussed only "liturgical life, social relations, and the relations of the Church with the modern world." However, the discussions would be the basis for its resumption. "The brilliant beginning of the Council was the introduction to the grand project which has been undertaken," he would say to express his pleasure in his closing speech. But the cancer was already consuming his body, and John XXIII knew that he would not be the one to reopen the assembly. The "good Pope" was also to receive the Balzan Peace Prize in 1963, though this created a bit of controversy for it seemed superfluous to award the pope a Peace Prize. Yet, if one looks at the history of the papacy, that reaction seems gratuitous. Other criticisms of the "good pope" were expressed which he probably did not even hear in his lengthy agony. They saddled him with the status of being the "Bolshevik of the Holy Spirit" and the famous encyclical *Pacem in terris*, promulgated on 9 April would be contorted to *Falcem in terris*, because he was deemed guilty for having caused the electoral advance of the PCI (Italian Communist Party) in the elections of 1963. An Italian cardinal would go so far as to say on his deathbed: "Fifty years will be needed to repair the damage he has done to the Church in the five years of his pontificate."

His stomach cancer was clearly incurable, but Pope John did not want the people to be suffering for him under his window at which he appeared to tell a fib: "My health is returning, indeed I am already well again!" And we in the square below play with the old man and death, applauding him through our tears of commotion. He turns away with words too of consolation for the doctors: "Do not worry about me. My bags are packed and I'm ready to depart."

He died on 3 June 1963 and was interred in the Vatican Grottoes. A panel by Manzù has immortalized him on the door of St. Peter's.

262. PAUL VI (1963–1978)

With Pope Roncalli, there had been an "earthquake" in the Church of Rome, and finding a successor to him was not going to be easy. The "Johnist approach" could not be ignored, with an ecumenical council left at midpoint, while the conservative faction of the cardinals did not want to give in to unlimited progress and even less to improvisation. They wanted a more cautious and methodical pontiff, basically one able "to loose and to bind," and to keep a foot in both camps whose motto ought to be, like Manzoni's Ferrer, "Peter, go ahead, use your judgment." A pope like that was found in the person of Giovanni Battista Montini, archbishop of Milan. He was elected on the fourth ballot on 21 June 1963, and took the name of Paul VI in honor of the "Apostle of the Gentiles." He sought to signify in this way his intention to strike out on a new path, with a broader program for the faith in a dialogue with "persons of good will." The "Johnist approach" would therefore be somehow continued.

Giovanni Battista Montini was born on 26 September 1897, in Concesio near Brescia to a middle-class family. His father had been a member of Parliament for three terms and was a supporter of the Catholic Social Movement. He had studied with the Jesuits, entered the seminary at the age of twenty and at twenty-three had been ordained a priest. He moved to Rome and took courses at the Gregorian University, but in 1923 Monsignor Pizzardo, a deputy in the Secretariat of State, had sent him to Warsaw as assistant in the apostolic nunciature. When he returned to Rome a year later, he obtained a degree in canon law, joining immediately the staff of the Secretariat of State as attaché, and later as a militant. He was particularly active in the FUCI, the Federation of Italian University Catholic Students, and, as spiritual assistant to this Catholic university students' organization, he came to know those who would be the future leaders of the Christian Democratic Party, people such as Scelba, Fanfani, Moro, and Gonella. He avoided any collaboration with the Fascist Federation of University Students and displayed on various occasions a personal aversion to the regime, although in a very diplomatic way.

And he would certainly improve his talents in diplomacy in the Secretariat of State which employed him on a full time basis beginning in 1933, first as a deputy for Ecclesiastical Matters and later as Deputy Secretary with Monsignor Tardini. He had two decades of active collaboration with Pope Pacelli, whose right arm he came to be considered in the immediate post-war period. However, his progressivist orientation was not welcomed in the Vatican, despite the fact that Pius XII continued to praise him. Moreover, he was not raised to cardinalship, since the pope had explained that both Montini and Tardini had asked "to be excused from such a very high dignity." Montini was appointed to the archbishopric of Milan in November 1954. Was it "exile?" There was talk of disagreement between the two Deputy Secretaries, though doubtless Monsignor

Montini wanted to carry forward the liturgical reforms that Pope Pacelli was authorizing, which would explain his new appointment. As the Archbishop, Montini carried out important missions in America and Africa, displaying that modern opening towards the world which would be confirmed in his trips as pontiff.

However, when Pius XII died, he was finally elevated to cardinal in December 1958. Pope Roncalli knew him well and shared his ideas. When he announced in 1959 the ecumenical council, Cardinal Montini dedicated himself to setting up Vatican II. John XXIII found in him a special adviser, although the cardinal began even then to demonstrate what would be the "limits" to his conciliatory approach. Shortly before leaving for Rome to participate in the ecumenical assembly, he had ordered the suppression in his diocese of the fortnightly *Adesso* (Now), founded by Don Mazzolari with the charge of "unrestrained criticism of the hierarchy" in a revolutionary conception of the autonomy of the laity. Ten years later he would act similarly with the ACLI (Catholic Action of Italian Workers) of Gabaglio for their Socialist "leanings." So in the cardinal could already be seen the future pope.

His attitude was clear right from the start with his coronation speech on 30 June 1963, in which he seemed to want to reassure the conservatives: "We shall defend the Holy Church from errors of doctrine and of custom." A controlled reformation became evident throughout the Council, which he reopened and presided on 29 September of the same year, taking care that the progressive movement remained within an effectively moderate program. The conservatives were in a minority but managed to be heard by him and to limit the significance of provisions that the majority was requesting. For example, on the third point of the program, *De ecclesia*, Paul VI weakened the importance of the episcopal college, confirming that it was under the direction of the Roman pontiff. And again on the hot issues such as the celibacy of the priesthood and birth control, he ended by asserting his authority and the right to give his views on the subjects, depriving the bishops of the possibility of discussing them because "a public debate would not at all be appropriate." Or, like when on his own initiative he abolished the "*Index of Prohibited Books,*" and the Holy Office which he replaced with the "Congregation for the Doctrine of the Faith" that would basically maintain a character if not inquisitorial in nature, nonetheless one of control. Finally, to please the majority, he established the Synod of bishops, though he emphasized the exclusively consultative function that such an organization would have. It was a halfway reform that Paul VI would allow to come out of the Council because he opposed whatever initiative might weaken dogmatic tradition or papal primacy.

Despite the above, when Vatican II was officially ended on 8 December 1965 after three sessions, it is beyond any doubt that the basis for a renewal was underway. It was not so much the liturgical reforms which provided this new image, which included celebration of the Mass in national languages and the limitation of veneration of the Madonna to exclude certain exaggerated expansions, with statues and side altars made to disappear from churches, reducing the rites to a single main altar. Rather, it was the concept of the universality of the Church, "the people of God," on the march through history, in a mission which was realized through the promotion of peace in the community of peoples, in an active dialogue with Protestants and Orthodox, with non-Christian religions, with atheists, and Marxists, in what was the *Lumen gentium*.

It was the program that Paul VI was already putting into effect even before the Council finished its labors, and one that he had contemplated in his first encyclical on 9 August 1964, *Ecclesiam Suam*, a dialogue with the separated Christians and with non-believers through the foundation of related congregations to cope with the anguishing problems of contemporary man. His visits began that very year. He went to Palestine and symbolically embraced the patriarch of Constantinople, Atenagora, then went to the Eucharistic Congress in Bombay, India, where he appealed to the Great Powers to stop the arms race and use their wealth to help a Third World assailed by hunger. And in September 1965, in New York, before the delegates to the United Nations, he had the courage to plead for peace when, for the first time in history, the vicar of Christ was recognized as having an approach of "neutrality" in the international context. What should be the only true "policy" of the Holy See, rediscovered by Benedict XV but not heeded, and resubmitted by John XXIII in his simplicity, seemed to have found in Paul VI its strongest and safest spokesman. The Church, shorn of all royal pretensions, became "the pilgrim on this earth" ready to establish new relationships between the peoples of the West and the East.

And under the banner of this credibility, which the papacy had reacquired after so many centuries, came the exhortations for peace in Vietnam, and New Year's greetings for 1966 sent to Hanoi, Saigon, Moscow, and Beijing. Following the private colloquy which Pope Roncalli had had with Khrushchev's son-in-law, the dialogue broadened with the Communist countries because, as Franco Molinari observed, "Paul VI went further, developing through an everyday realization of the prophetic intuition for which Roncalli had been the unwitting and supernatural spokesman." It is a praiseworthy merit one must give Pope Montini during this period, as attested by what developed between 1966 and 1967, on an ecclesiastical level, with the reform of the Curia within the diocese of Rome, and outside by continuing the ecumenical dialogue and receiving the head of the Anglican Church, the archbishop of Canterbury. While on the "political" one, with his trip to Turkey, to which he returned as a sign of peace the flags captured during the Battle of Lepanto, and by finally receiving the visit of Podgorny, the Soviet President, a symbol of the rapprochement between the

Vatican and the countries of Eastern Europe. As from 1970, Gromyko met regularly with the pope on each of his trips, and Monsignor Casaroli, Secretary to the Minister of Foreign Affairs, is said to have accomplished diplomatic miracles, initiating a period of close contacts between the Vatican and the Soviet Union in an atmosphere of détente. However, 1967 was the height of the papacy of Paul VI with *Populorum progressio* which, through its social content committed the Church as never before. It was an invective against the power of the oppressors, but it was also a theology of liberation because it encouraged people to react to oppression in the name of God. The encyclical became a reference point for many Latin American Catholics in revolt against dictatorships and in league with Marxist forces. In Brazil, Helder Camara was to be its interpreter, "the red Archbishop," as Paul VI is said to have called him during a meeting in the Vatican. "Here is our 'Communist' pope," was apparently the reply of the Brazilian prelate. It is an anecdote reported by José Gonzalez in a famous book of his. Whether true or not, it reflects an outlook that the encyclical was developing.

Instead, next came the years of contestation, and Paul VI's authority is stunned if not actually shaken, so much so that he feels that he must review what he has written and clarify the 'limits' within which his encyclical is to be understood, which he does during his trip to Bogotà in August 1968. "We shall continue to denounce social injustices," he declares to the *campesinos* of Colombia, but he tells the Latin American bishops that the weapon of denunciation and opposition is love and not violence. What Franco Molinari states could be true, and that is, that it was necessary "to be able to read both the lines and between the lines, not to approach the papal texts with the wrong viewpoint (for example, the political one and the Marxist one, which can catapult the class struggle right into the conclave)" for the message had obviously been distorted, and there had not been "the familiarity of prolonged reflection." But that was understandable because, behind Paul VI, despite his great personality, there was always Pope Roncalli, "mischievous and malicious," as Molinari called him, and thus people had grown accustomed to look "beyond," and maybe dream of "fleeing forward."

Then there was the ebb tide, the delusion: with the *Humanae vitae* which, squashing the conclusions favorable to birth control of a commission selected by the pope himself, opposed the use of anti-conceptional means, and with the *Sacerdotalis Coelibatus* which reaffirmed the obligation of celibacy of priests. In addition, there was the repudiation of the Dutch catechism and the repeated declaration of the primacy of the pope at the World Council of Churches Congress in Geneva in 1969 in a statement which diminished considerably the significance of the work of a mixed Catholic-Anglican commission for a theological rapprochement between the two Churches. These are the positions taken by a pope who rediscovers his absolutism. He issued ecumenical messages but basically he used them to shore up the "castle" shaken by the "earthquake" of his predecessor. He always used the tiara and the gestatorial throne, and the majestatis plural sounded coldly once again on his lips.

And yet the journeys of Paul VI followed on each other inexorably giving more than ever the picture of a "pope-tourist." But there is no longer the former enthusiasm. In 1970, in Cagliari, youngsters throw stones at him, while in Manila, a South American artist, Benjamin Mendoza, makes an attempt on his life; as he is mentally deranged he will only receive a sentence of only a few years in jail, thanks to the fact that the Vatican does not want to sue him for damages. If it is true that "Montini edified the world when he discretely pardoned his clumsy attacker in Manila," as Franco Molinari pointed out, it is also true that "forgiveness does not die. The civility of love continues" and "in the years of his pontificate he did not fling out a single excommunication, either against the dromedaries of the traditional right (Lefebvre) or against the impatient colts of the militant left (Franzoni). He avoided schisms." All this is true, but I would not say that "the other things are cupboard gossip trifles."

Questions arise about his interference in the work of the Parliamentary commission in charge of examining the constitutionality of the legislation on divorce? "Claiming for himself an inconceivable right, he in fact said that a self-appointed authority had adopted a principle of doubtful legitimacy," Vittorio Gorresio observed in an article written a few days after the pontiff's death. Furthermore, he correctly commented that: "He should not have allowed himself to do that. It is one thing for the Pastor of the Church to preach and to speak against divorce and to deprecate its adoption; it is quite another matter for him to go so far as to deny the legitimacy of the deliberations of a State institution." As is well known, his attitude brought a split within the clergy and the laity. But openly supporting the anti-divorce referendum sponsored by Gabrio Lombardi, Paul VI violated the principle of the separation of State and Church in his attempt to prevent the faithful from acting independently as citizens.

And what to say about the Jubilee of 1975, proclaimed unwillingly by the pope, in a world growing ever more distant from the Church, as he noted in a famous speech on 11 September 1974, with his "postal benediction." All one had to do was to fill out a form and send it to the Alms Officer of the Vatican, Antonio Travia, the titular bishop of *Termini Imerese,* and the apostolic blessing would reach you through the postman for only 2,000 Lire; if you wanted one on rice paper, the price went up to 30,000 Lire. It was a "holy" racket that blurred the ray of light forming the background of the dove with the olive branch in the poster of that Holy Year.

Something was not clear in the personality of this pope "both fragile and very strong," "the Hamlet from beyond the Tiber." But on the other hand it is also true that he is too close to us to be able to speak of him calmly and without controversy.

What I personally maintain illuminates his image in an unequivocally evangelical manner is the way in which he penetrated deeply into the dramas of our times, ready to immolate himself in them as a martyr or to live them in direct contact between God and his own conscience. As when a Lufthansa aircraft was hijacked by German terrorists to Mogadishu and he offered himself as a hostage or again, during the Moro case, when he wrote a letter on 21 April 1978 to the "men of the Red Brigades" before whom he went on his knees, begging in vain. But these are also flashes of light which no longer blinded the masses, by now nihilistic about the value of certain words and gestures.

On 13 May 1978, at St. John Lateran on the occasion of the funeral ceremony for Moro, he said: "Oh Lord, hear us . . . in this day of a sun which inexorably sets . . . Lord, hear us." They seemed to be the words of a prophet in contemplation of death. He died at Castel Gandolfo barely three months later, on 6 August of pulmonary edema, and was buried in the crypt of the Vatican basilica.

2 6 3. John Paul I (1 9 7 8)

The evening of 25 August 1978, 111 cardinals entered the conclave and as only twenty-seven of them were Italians, a minority, the general view was that the new pope would probably not be an Italian. There were three main factions; the traditionalists, the progressivists, and the centrists or Montinians who had an orientation towards candidates who would have had difficulty in reaching the quorum. A fallback on a "candidature in common" was foreseeable, and one did prevail on the third ballot on 26 August. So after barely twenty-six hours a new pope was elected in the person of the patriarch of Venice, Albino Luciani.

In fact the crowd in St. Peter's Square and the T.V. viewers who were following the event on world television were not sure that a positive conclusion of the voting had been reached as the smoke that came out of the chimney of the Sistine Chapel at 6:24 P.M. did not seem to be completely white. The firestoking cardinal must have been up to something odd because the uncertainty lasted for an hour, after which all doubt was eliminated by the opening of the windows on the balcony, and the top cardinal-deacon announced that for the first time in history a pope was to have a double name: Albino Luciani was to be John Paul I.

And it was indeed something new for which it was not necessary to await the explanation given by the newly elected pope the next day at noon on the occasion of his first Sunday benediction. Symbolically the double name meant that it was his intention to "continue the work of Paul VI along the lines already agreed and laid down by the great heart of John XXIII." Then, when he put aside the majestatis plural, he made a brief, simple speech to the faithful in which he chose to state without any false modesty: "I do not have the *sapientia cordis* of Pope John, nor the education and experience of Pope Paul, but I am in their position and I must try to serve the Church. I hope you will help me by your prayers." It was a genuine way of winning over the crowd which applauded the simplicity and the smiling tone of his words. "We needed a smiling pope," it was said. And again, "it seems we're back in the times of Pope Roncalli." Others, already informed about him, hazarded a rapprochement: "His father was a Socialist and like Pertini, his mother was a devout person; they will get on together."

Albino Luciani was born in Canale d'Agordo near Belluno on 17 October 1912. His father was indeed an anticlerical Socialist, a laborer who had immigrated to Latin America to find work until he returned to settle in Murano. His mother instead was very devout and had raised four children in the Christian way. Albino entered the seminary at Feltre when he was eleven years old, and later had gone to the one in Belluno. He was ordained a priest at the age of twenty-three and moved to Rome where he earned a degree in theology at the Gregorian University, submitting a thesis on Rosmini. Then he returned to his birthplace as chaplain at Canale, subsequently at Agordo and finally to teach various subjects at the seminary in Belluno. He had carried on his activity peacefully in his diocese as deputy chancellor and deputy vicar, devoting himself chiefly to teaching catechism and writing his teaching experience in a little book entitled, *Bits and Pieces of the Catechism (Catechesi in briciole)*. It was a sign of a good, rustic background, and Pope Roncalli approved of it, appointing him bishop of Vittorio Veneto in 1958.

Then he had to face up to problems of a different nature, such as the scandal of two diocesan priests involved in swindles and bounced checks. He was a traditionalist and for him even Vatican II was somewhat traumatic. He had to review all his training and update himself on the subject of freedom and religious conscience. Paul VI thought well of his intervention on "responsible motherhood" and raised him to be patriarch of Venice in 1969.

In that position, he proved to be inimical to a dialogue with the Marxists but he did not get worked up when Communists became members of the government in the Lagoon City. Moreover, his speeches were simple, somewhat allegorical, and in that spirit he wrote articles for St. Anthony's Messenger in the form of letters addressed to historical, biblical, literary, and even imaginary characters, which he collected together in a little volume called *Illustrissimi*. Once he was elected pope, the giants of the publishing world, especially the English and the Americans, flung themselves on that modest cultural work to get the publishing rights, though the market for the options naturally deflated at the author's sudden death.

His pontificate was in fact very brief, a total of thirty-three days. The time to be consecrated on 3 September in St. Peter's with a ceremony reduced to the minimum, without the tiara, throne or gestatorial chair, with the celebration of a Mass on a white altar, and then to take possession of St. John Lateran on 23 September as the bishop of Rome. For the rest, he had intended to reconfirm all of the heads of Vatican departments, beginning with the Secretary of State, Jean Villot, in order to continue with the careful reformism begun by Paul VI. Meanwhile, in the audiences that he began to hold from 6 September onwards, those few Wednesdays which he still had to live, there was such a flood of faithful to the Nervi Hall as had not been seen for a long time. In those four audiences he talked about himself with anecdotes and candid, if artless, remarks denoting a "fragmented culture," according to Ignazio Majore. It was not the technique of a strategist to compare the soul with an automobile, to say that God is Mommy, or to quote from Pinocchio; these were "all indications of a pope who was like a factory worker, like a peasant from the Abruzzo," Alfonso di Nola observed. But they were positive signals, these initial clues, destined to be the only ones. Perhaps had he lived longer, John Paul I would not have responded to the wishes of great electors like Benelli and Felici who were convinced they had found a pope "who could be influenced by a Curia whose needs were very worldly, very political." He might have "become what a pope should be, a man like all others, disposed to abandon the Vatican, even in his white robes, and go to live in Merulano or some other quarter of Rome in a three-room apartment." These words of di Nola recalled the image, dreamed about years before by Pier Paolo Pasolini, of a pope who would go and "set himself up in clerical garb with his aides in some basement at Tormarancio or Tuscolano."

The Curia began to murmur as its embarrassment increased. John Paul I freed them from that, just as quietly and simply as he had accepted the high appointment. He was ill. In his last audience on 26 September, dedicated to the sick, he himself told the story of his eight hospitalizations and four surgical operations. He was found dead with the volume *Imitations of Christ* in his hand, on the morning of 29 September, and the physicians certified that he had died from a heart attack at 11 P.M. of the previous day, the 28 September. He was buried in the crypt of the Vatican basilica.

Some newspapers carried reports of death by poisoning but they were groundless, and later would be published two books—*La vraie Mort de Jean Paul II* by J.J. Thierry and *In God's name* by David Yallop—both of which described his death as an assassination, the result of a plot in the Vatican itself.

264. JOHN PAUL II (1978–)

Sixteen days after the unexpected death of Pope Luciani, 114 cardinals came back for a conclave on 14 October 1978. The Italian cardinals were in the minority and, although they quickly lined up behind Siri and Benelli, they achieved nothing. Their attitude simply made it clear that the next pope would not be an Italian. This time, the diplomacy that a month and a half earlier Benelli had undertaken on behalf of Luciani was absent; he had "burnt his bridges" by declaring his candidature. As a result, the candidacy of a non-Italian, that of Wojtyla, sustained by the German cardinals, gained ground. The Polish cardinal was not well known to all the electors. It seems that the Guatemalan Cardinal Casariego was going about asking who was this cardinal whose name sounded something like *"bottiglia."* When they learned about him, a large part of the College adopted his candidacy and it is probable that earlier relations between the Polish cardinal and *Opus Dei* reflourished, since the latter was indirectly present in the conclave through certain cardinals linked to that Spanish organization, still a "pious union" if already powerful as a politico-financial ecclesiastical association. Rapidly the votes for Wojtyla surpassed the necessary quorum. Only three days and eight ballots had been needed to elect a pope who looked young and healthy, a guarantee for a long-term pontificate, perhaps another determining reason for his election. Certainly the choice of a non-Italian pope did not present a problem for the cardinals; if anything, it did for the one chosen.

When he came to the balcony of the Vatican basilica, there was no doubt that the crowd was surprised and confused that evening of 16 October by the announcement not only of an unfamiliar name but also of a non-Italian; in 455 years, since Hadrian VI of Holland, no "foreign" pope had been bishop of Rome. There was a moment of silence, then a murmuring which gradually changed into the first applause of encouragement for John Paul II, the name chosen by this cardinal whose nationality the people at that moment did not even know, and who stood with his hands joined as if in prayer, tense amidst the commotion. Then, as silence returned to the square, he introduced himself as "one from afar," speaking Italian well, but requesting to be corrected when necessary, and this way of presenting himself then gave rise to enthusiastic applause from the people. That he was a "child of Poland" they would soon learn, but by 22 October, the day of his consecration, he was recognized as the "Roman" he himself declared he had now become.

Born in Wadowice near Cracow on 18 May 1920, the son of an Army officer who dreamed of becoming a writer, Karol Wojtyla was orphaned by his mother's death when he was only nine years old. His infancy and childhood reveal a profoundly Christian upbringing, spent between his studies at the diocesan high school, his love of athletics, which he would continue to cultivate, and that of school dramatics. His friends called him Lolus. He graduated from high school in 1938 and registered at Cracow in the Department of Literature but, with the Nazi invasion, he had to find a job to avoid being sent to a labor camp in Germany. He managed to find work in a stone quarry, so was able to continue his studies, even if secretly. Then he got a job in the Solvay chemical factory. But during those war years he lost both his father and a brother, and his only consolations in his grief were his studies and his love of the theater. Ignoring curfews and SS roundups, he and some companions staged various performances in a "Rhapsody Theater" at home. Karol was the actor and his frequent partner was an eighteen-year-old girl, Regina Reinsenfeld, who would go to Rome forty years later to pay her respects to him as pope. His friends now called him by the nickname Lolek and he stayed with them until 1943 when he decided to enter a seminary.

Three years later he was ordained a priest in a Poland, no more subjugated by the Nazis and liberated by the Soviets, and he was able to come to Rome and finish his studies at the Angelicum. Then he was sent on missions to many European nations, studied various languages, and returned to Cracow as pastor of the church of St. Florian. No longer Lolus, nor even Lolek, now he was affectionately called "little uncle" by the children in the parish, for whom he organized day trips, especially into the mountains. He became an expert skier, and also threw himself into the rapids in his canoe. Meanwhile, he matured ecclesiastically and in 1953 became a professor at the seminary in Cracow, then at the Catholic University of Lublin and, at only thirty-eight, was named auxiliary bishop of Cracow and thereafter the titular archbishop. He was the ward of Wyszynski and participated actively throughout the entire Second Vatican Council; in 1967 Paul VI named him cardinal, with St. Cesarius on the Palatine as his titular church.

But in the meantime, while devoting himself to ecclesiastical activities, he did not forget the artistic ones. He wrote poetry and a play in three acts, *La bottega dell'orefice* (The Goldsmith's Shop), came frequently to Italy, among other reasons to preach at the Vatican during Lent, and also found occasion to indulge in sports—he was seen swimming in the Sea of Palidorus and skiing on the snows of Terminillo. This information was made available once Karol Wojtyla was John Paul II. With the two volumes translated into Italian and entitled *Pietra di luce* (Stone of Light) and *Il sapore del pane* (The Flavor of Bread) he became the pope-poet, then the pope-athlete who had a swimming-pool built at Castel Gandolfo equipped with trampolines for diving, and the pope-actor who could even have happily acted in the film on his life produced by Krzystof Zanussi, destined to be shown around the world. All this created the "personage" of "that seducer" of the masses which, according to a definition by Diego Fabbri, in the final analysis he showed himself to be.

This is the characteristic aspect of John Paul II, the keystone of his personality, which allows him to stand out from the events that occurred during the first fourteen years of his pontificate and known to everybody, like the trips he undertook, in his own words, "to spread the Gospel . . . to strengthen brothers in the faith . . . to unify the Church . . . to encounter mankind," the attempt on his life on 13 May 1981 with all that mess of international espionage connected to it, the affaire of the I.O.R., *Istituto per le opere di religione* (Institute for Religious Works), related to the bankruptcy of the Banco Ambrosiano, and the developments in his own Poland and in eastern Europe, which subjected him to criticism for his entirely "Polish" political nature in a strongly reactionary pontificate.

He is a pope at the center of many controversies, often echoing those which swept Paul VI into an isolation like Hamlet's, but by which his own temperament does not appear to have been at all disturbed. Within the Church itself, in front of complaints launched against him by Cardinal Pellegrino for his anti-council tendencies, as well as those of the Jesuits about the reproaches to their Order in the Spring of 1980, John Paul reaffirmed the severity of the discipline precisely in order to straighten out post-council confusion. Thus he succeeded in redimensioning the case of the conservative Archbishop Lefebvre, a sort of antipope who was against the Second Vatican Council and who died in 1991, in taming the Dutch Church, and restoring the Ukrainian one in 1983 by naming the first cardinal in the Soviet Union, well before the fall of the Communist regime, where the East-policy of the former Secretary of State, Cardinal Casaroli, evidently bore its fruit. And again, during the campaign for the referendum on abortion, having been accused of interference in violation of the Concordat between the Italian State and the Holy See, he rejected the accusations, invoking his obligation to intervene whenever fundamental values, human and spiritual, appeared to be threatened. Thus, in the broadest sense, he reaffirmed categorically the defense of a Christian view of sexuality and of the family: "Matrimony is indissoluble and irrevocable; sexual relations outside of matrimony are immoral; homosexual behavior is morally wrong; and it is necessary to reaffirm the right to life, including that of new-born infants."

As Desmond O'Grady has observed: "The conclusion, however surprising it may be, is that although John Paul may intend to go against the trend of society and many tendencies of the post-Council Church, his pontificate has been thus far less controversial than that of Pope Paul VI." Indeed, it is beyond discussion that he appears extremely decisive, that he is not a Hamlet. But one cannot know to what extent this way of standing firmly on his own positions and not backing down except through agreements or at least confrontations, can be productive for the Church itself. Only the future will be able to clarify it for us at the completion of his pontificate.

What should be emphasized is that John Paul II, with his personal and authoritarian participation in the daily life of mankind, has on his side the applauding masses, but as Benny Lai has noted, "the question remains whether this manner of carrying on the function which affects the institution, really serves to change the masses surrounding Wojtyla into a consensus." And here enters into play the "personage," John Paul II, who has indeed changed the figure of the pope, surpassing the careless simplicity of Pope Luciani and the stormy goodness of Pope Roncalli. If you approach him you see, before the pope, the man who has your own habits as when, concluding his talk, he salutes the crowd saying "The night is made for sleeping; so go to bed" or else, "It is time for dinner. May you enjoy your food."

Distances disappear and, in this dimension, his "own" Poland, a permanent point of reference for his pastoral activity, must be viewed in a special light. It is not his personal "homeland," it is the reflection of all homelands, as he himself explains in a poem written in 1979:

> When I think "patria"—I express myself,
> I reach for my roots,
> it is the voice of my heart, the secret frontier that
> from me radiates to others,
> to embrace all, right to the oldest past of each one:
> From this I emerge . . . when I think "patria"
> almost hiding a treasure within myself.
> I ask myself how to enlarge it,
> how to increase the space it occupies.

At least, so it appears. And his journeys would seem to confirm it, inspired as they are by a universal opening up of Catholicism, especially to the countries of the Third World, in Africa and Latin America. One might ask, however, whether political motives inspire him. Certainly a question of prestige is involved, a projection of himself, more than the apostolic significance of his words. Nor is it clear whether the people around the world see in him principally an evangelical spokesman or a Head of State. At any rate, political necessities appear to prevail over the emergence of individual churches in the service of Peter.

At the beginning especially, distances disappeared particularly in those trips and in his relation with the faithful. The image that the Polish pope gave of himself was more international, demonstrating in certain situations the man himself and his typical way of fraternization; as for example, his putting on the hat worn by people whom he is meeting. The Alpine cap when he was speaking with the "Black Feathers," the sombrero among the Mexicans at Puebla, and even the headdress with multicolored feathers of the Masai warriors with the Kenyotes in Nairobi. Again, he let himself relax with boyish escapades as when he sang to the sound of their guitars with the youths who came to visit him at Castel Gandolfo, and joined them in circling around a bonfire. And then he broke with protocol. He picked up babies, raised them towards heaven, kissed them, and put them back in the arms of the parents, and he personally blessed the wedding of the daughter of a street cleaner.

These attitudes partly disappeared, or somehow mellowed as the years passed, up to the surgery to remove a benign tumour in July 1992. Beyond doubt, the operation changed his physique, if not his apostolic spirit, which still remained engaged on all fronts.

In any case, Rome and Italy became mission territory for John Paul II who undertook a full episcopal work, since the capital of Italy is for three-fourths the capital of the Third World. The pope carried out his visits to the parishes as did Paul VI, in an even more decisive spirit, aware that a "devastating secularism," according to the ex-vicar Poletti, "is affecting the city." Rome needed a new evangelization where distances had to disappear, also on a religious level in an ecumenical embrace which reached out to the Jews. And, on 8 February 1981, the pope received a delegation from the Roman Synagogue led by the Chief Rabbi, Elio Toàff in the church of S. Carlo ai Catinari. Wojtyla recalled the massacre of the Jews of Cracow, Toàff recalled "the painful past of humiliation in the ghetto." It was an event of historical significance, noted by Antonello Trombadori, the last "Bellian" poet, in a sonnet entitled *Le risate d'Elia* (The Laughs of Elijah):

> After his sermon in Latin,
> did you see what Wojtyla did for you?
> Upright and brainy pope that he is,
> at San Carlo he didn't run away like a thief.
>
> He said: "Run to the Rabbi in the ghetto
> and tell him it's 2000 years,
> and that the days of Cain are over;
> to meet with us, no one needs to stand in line."
>
> Never before seen at the Catinari!
> Toàff entered with robe and rings,
> smiling amidst his fellow leaders.
>
> "That's the way to make an historical event,"
> said a priest. And, from his grave, Belli speaks:
> "Who laughs at this? Show your teeth!"
> *(translated from Romanesque)*

Then followed the return visit. On 13 April 1986, for the first time a pope entered the Synagogue of Rome and called the Jews "our elder brothers." But then unexpectedly came the cleavage during an audience with the faithful on a Wednesday, as always crammed, in August of 1989, when he referred to the Jews as "infidels," as if they were traitors to the alliance with God. And, strangely, a little later a controversy about the Carmelite convent at Auschwitz broke out, in which the Vatican declined to honor an agreement to remove the nuns from the Nazi concentration camp. It was only in April 1993 that the pope ordered the convent to be abandoned. But it was not an easy decision. For John Paul II, once again "his" Poland was involved, and the Jews were automatically relegated to ancient theological conceptions. These preconceptions did not disappear when, in 1992, the new vicar of Rome, Cardinal Ruini, was not exactly tender with the Jews and the question of their guilt in the crucifixion of Christ emerged again. In short, there was a great deal of ambiguity.

It is a strongly political papacy which identifies itself with the restoration of an ecclesiastical power capable of infiltrating the sinister fibers of international finance, accompanied by a hard line towards an international society burdened with spiritual needs, and by positions which seem in recent years to have brought the Church of Rome to take a leap backwards relative to those of the Second Vatican Council. In this work of restoration can be seen the important role played by Opus Dei, which in 1982 became the "personal prelacy," in effect a juridicial autonomy with free access to all the important offices in the Church of Rome. It is not by chance that its founder, José Maria Escrivà de Balaguer, was proclaimed Blessed following a lightning search for the "heroic nature of his virtues," while Pope John XXIII has been resting twenty years in "the odor of sanctity." For many, the beatification on 17 May 1992, of the monsignor who founded Opus Dei, profoundly desired by the pope, confirms the ideological affinity between John Paul II and the so-called "Octopus of God," on whose account Pasquino parodied the Agnus Dei in these words:

> Opus Dei, who takes away
> the wealth of the world,
> Give us a part.

Moreover, since 1984 the chief of the Press Office of the Vatican, or spokesman of the pope for the mass media, has been Joaquin Navarro Vallis, a Spaniard of Opus Dei. But he is clearly not the only representative of the "personal prelacy" at the service of the pope. This ecclesiastico-political organization has become, above all, the salvation of the Vatican's finances. Thanks to it all traces of anything that obscured the IOR, or the Vatican Bank, which had its troubles from 1982 to 1989 with the failure of the Banco Ambrosiano and the death of Roberto Calvi, were swept away. Monsignors Donato De Bonis and Paul Marcinkus were discharged, evidently incapable of handling money which, unhappily, remains "the instrument in the service of the Church," as Marcinkus himself explained. Clean money and a fresh approach, especially in the management of that .8% of IRPEF, was the authentic novelty in the Vatican's finances.

Finally, in May 1993, on the occasion of his trip to Sicily, John Paul II suddenly displayed a new image by taking a strong position against the Mafia. It was an anathema that appeared all at once to redeem a certain reactionary policy with a view to a decisive apostolic mission, recalling the purest element of the social duty of the Church of Rome. It could signify a change of policy.

This has been confirmed by the last four encyclics with, on 5 October 1993, the *Veritas splendor* in which the position of the Church on moral and ethical questions are reaffirmed in answer to "those who no longer recognize any moral values;" on 31 March 1995 the *Evangelium Vitae* with its condemnation without possible appeal of abortion and euthanasia; on 31 May 1995 the *Ut unum sint*, with its proposal to other Christian Churches to find again the way to unity and to confront, among other subjects of discord; even that of the pope's role: and on 15 October 1998, the *Fides et ratio*, with thoughts "on the path which leads to true wisdom" for bishops, theologians and whoever "is seeking truth."

Meanwhile, John Paul II's state of health becomes a matter of concern with, in 1993, a dislocation of a shoulder, in 1994, a fracture of the thigh, in 1996, an "obscure operation," and the Parkinson's disease which has afflicted him since 1997. What the pope appears to live for is the Jubilee of 2000, which was announced on 10 November 1994 in the apostolic letter *Tertio Millennio adveniente* and officially proclaimed with the bull *Incarnationis misterium* on 29 November 1998. In Rome it is expected to be a memorable event and not only on a religious level. One may say it will be the fulfilment of the extraordinary apostolic engagement which has always guided John Paul II and, in retrospect, signified by the announcement in 1998 on the occasion of the twentieth anniversary of his pontificate. A pontificate which, from a numerical point of view gives: 218 voyages, of which 84 outside Italy, taking him to 116 countries, 274 visits to Roman parishes, 877 audiences and meetings in the presence of 13,833,000 faithful, 36 visits and 548 audiences and meetings with Heads of State, 182 with Prime Ministers, 12 synods of bishops and 7 concistories, 112 ceremonies of beatification for the proclamation of 805 "blessed," 35 for the canonization of 280 saints, and 13 encyclics.

All of this is behind John Paul II who is certainly a personality of tremendous prestige, helped in part by the ephemeral support of the mass media behind which there is often ambiguity, a lack of sincerity if not a downright material give and take. Because he sings, makes recordings and cassettes, is a songwriter, a journalist with reprints of homilies published throughout the world, and is the actor in films and comics, his image influences the market, and that is not in the evangelical spirit of a Christian message. In this sense the criticisms directed toward him for his "superstar" poses appear significant; the Australian writer and Nobel Prize winner, Patrick White, pointed to his "theatricality" and jokingly asked if John Paul II had his "colors on his helicopter." But I would say that it is the masses that want him like that, and the times favor a "cult of personality." It is pointless to conceal it, and Pope Wojtyla has adapted to this image, giving it substance to the level of perfection. That is not to say that in his extemporaneity he does not know how to find in himself the small dimension of everyday life that one's nameless next door neighbor has. And one day it could also happen that he might ring your doorbell in person.

The Holy Year arrived with the opening of the Holy Door at St. Peter's in the Vatican on Christmas Eve 1999 which became a new opportunity for the pope to appeal for a spirit of ecumenism. This moment so awaited by him, saw him put aside his role of protagonist and reveal himself as the spokesman of a worldwide homage to Christ for representatives of many continents, who gave voice to a message of universal peace with flowers and products of their countries exposed on the threshold of the basilica. Up to the opening of the Holy Door at St. Paul's outside the Walls on 18 January 2000, when, at his invitation, the archbishop of Canterbury, George Carey, and the Orthodox Metropolitan, Athanasios, pushed open the double door with him. Behind them, fifty delegates from twenty-two Churches and Committees as well as the ecumenical Council of Geneva crossed the threshold in the greatest concentration of Christian Churches gathered in Rome since the Second Vatican Council.

Thereby John Paul II reaped the fruits of what has probably been the event of major importance in his pontificate, because he has already achieved the purpose of the Holy Year, which is that of re-evoking the two thousandth anniversary of Christ's birth through the union of Christians, and the multiple celebration at the Basilica of St. Paul can be viewed as the beginning of that process of unification. John Paul II, no matter how ill, thus carries out his mission, steadfastly, not intending to fail in what is his life's purpose.

To those, such as the German bishop, Karl Lehmann, who might wish that he abdicate, admitting that he is no longer as lucid as he used to be as a result of the poor health resulting from his eighty years of age, he said with firmness and confidence: "I am not old!" And, indefatigable, he proved this by marking another fundamental moment in his pontificate, regarding the "pardon."

He had begun it in the spirit of the Holy Year when, during a solemn ceremony in St. Peter's on 12 March 2000, he carried an ancient Crucifix and stopped in front of Michelangelo's Pietà asking "pardon" for the errors, contrary to the pure apostolic Christian spirit, committed by the Church of Rome in the past, from the death sentences of the Inquisition and the forced conversions, to the hostility towards the Jews. "Never again, never again!" he had said.

And he repeated it regarding the Jews, for the mortal hatred of certain Christians towards them, and for the camps of extermination. And this he reaffirmed with heartfelt intensity during his recent two voyages to the holy places in the Sinai and then in Jordan, and in Israel from 21 to 26 March, at the Mount of the Beatitudes at the Holy Sepulcher, at the Mausoleum of the Shoah and finally at the Weeping Wall where, as would a Jew, he left his written note, renewing his message of peace and the request for pardon for all humanity — a note which was an act of universal love.

APPENDICES

This list is based on the *Annuario pontificio* (Pontifical Yearbook). Of the two dates given for the beginning of a pontificate, the first refers to the date of election, the second to the date of consecration. The names of the antipopes are italicized in parentheses and are not preceded by a number.

1. St. Peter, Simon of Bethsaida (Galilee). In the year 30 he received pontifical power from Jesus Christ to be transmitted to his successors. He resided at first in Antioch and later, according to the *Chronograph* of 354, for twenty-five years in Rome where he was martyred in 67.
2. St. Linus, from Volterra (Tuscia), 67–76
3. St. Anacletus, Rome, 76–88
4. St. Clement I, Rome, 88–97
5. St. Evaristus, Bethlehem (Judea), 97–105
6. St. Alexander I, Rome, 105–115
7. St. Sixtus I, Rome, 115–125
8. St. Telesphorus, Terranuova (Calabria), 125–136
9. St. Hyginus, Athens, 136–140
10. St. Pius I, Aquileia, 140–155
11. St. Anicetus, Syria, 155–166
12. St. Soter, Fondi, 166–175
13. St. Eleutherus, Nicopolis (Epirus), 175–189
14. St. Victor I, Africa, 189–199
15. St. Zephyrinus, Rome, 199–217
16. St. Callistus I, Rome, 217–222
    (St. Hippolytus, Rome, 217–235)
17. St. Urban I, Rome, 222–230
18. St. Pontianus, Rome, 21 July 230–28 September 235
19. St. Anteros, Greece, 21 November 235–3 January 236
20. St. Fabian, Rome, 10 January 236–20 January 250.
21. St. Cornelius, Rome, March 251–June 253.
    (Novatianus, Rome, 251)
22. St. Lucius I, Rome, 25 June 253–2 March 254
23. St. Stephen I, Rome, 12 May 254–2 August 257
24. St. Sixtus II, Greece, 30 August 257–6 August 258
25. St. Dionisius, birthplace unknown, 22 July 259–20 December 268

26. St. Felix I, Rome, 5 January 269–30 December 274
27. St. Eutychianus, Luni (Etruria), 4 January 275–7 December 283
28. St. Caius, Dalmatia, 17 December 283–22 April 296
29. St. Marcellinus, Rome, 30 June 296–25 October 304
30. St. Marcellus I, Rome, 27 May 308–16 January 309
31. St. Eusebius, Greece, 18 April 309–17 August 309
32. St. Miltiades, Africa, 2 July 311–11 January 314
33. St. Sylvester I, Rome, 31 January 314–31 December 335
34. St. Mark, Rome, 18 January 336–7 October 336
35. St. Julius I, Rome, 6 February 337–12 April 352
36. St. Liberius, Rome, 17 May 352–24 September 366
    (Felix II, Rome, 355 - 22 November 365)
37. St. Damasus I, Spain, 1 October 366–11 December 384
    (Ursinus, 366–367)
38. St. Siricius, Rome, 15 or 22 or 29 December 384–26 November 399
39. St. Anastasius I, Rome, 27 November 399–19 December 401
40. St. Innocentius I, Albano, 22 December 401–12 March 417
41. St. Zosimus, Greece, 18 March 417–26 December 418
42. St. Boniface I, Rome, 28 or 29 December 418–4 September 422
    (Eulalius, 27 or 29 December 418–419)
43. St. Celestinus I, Campania, 10 September 422–27 July 432
44. St. Sixtus III, Rome, 31 August 432–19 August 440
45. St. Leo I, the Great, Volterra (Tuscia), 29 September 440–10 November 461
46. St. Hilary, Sardinia, 19 November 461–29 February 468
47. St. Simplicius, Tivoli, 3 March 468–10 March 483
48. St. Felix III, Rome, 13 March 483–1 March 492
49. St. Gelasius I, Africa, 1 March 492–21 November 496
50. St. Anastasius II, Rome, 24 November 496–19 November 498
51. St. Symmachus, Sardinia, 22 November 498–19 July 514
    (Lawrence, 498 and 501–505)
52. St. Hormisdas, Frosinone, 20 July 514–6 August 523
53. St. John I, Tuscia, 13 August 523–18 May 526
54. St. Felix IV, Sannius, 12 July 526–22 September 530
55. Boniface II, Rome, 22 September 530–17 October 530
    (Dioscuros, Alexandria, 22 September 530–14 October 530)
56. John II, Mercurius or Mercurialis, Rome, 2 January 533–8 May 535
57. St. Agapetus I, Rome, 13 May 535–22 April 536
58. St. Silverius, Campania, 1 June 536–11 November 537
59. Vigilius, Rome, 29 March 537–7 June 555
60. Pelagius I, Rome, 16 April 556–4 March 561

61. John III, Catelinus(?), Rome, 17 July 561–13 July 574
62. Benedict I, Bonosius(?), Rome, 2 June 575–30 August 579
63. Pelagius II, Rome, 26 November 579–7 February 590
64. St. Gregory I, the Great, Rome, 3 September 590–12 March 604
65. Sabinianus, Blera (Viterbo), 13 September 604–22 February 606
66. Boniface III, Rome, 19 February 607–12 November 607
67. St. Boniface IV, Marsica, 25 August 608–8 May 615
68. St. Adeodatus I, Rome, 19 October 615–8 November 618
69. Boniface V, Naples, 23 December 619–25 October 625
70. Honorius I, Campania, 27 October 625–12 October 638
71. Severinus, Rome, 28 May 640–2 August 640
72. John IV, Dalmatia, 24 December 640–12 October 642
73. Theodore I, Greece, 24 November 642–14 May 649
74. St. Martin I, Todi, July 649–16 September 655
75. St. Eugene I, Rome, 10 August 654–2 June 657
76. St. Vitalianus, Segni, 30 July 657–27 January 672
77. Adeodatus II, Rome, 11 April 672–17 June 676
78. Donus, Rome, 2 November 676–11 April 678
79. St. Agatho, Palermo, 27 June 678–10 January 681
80. St. Leo II, Sicily, 17 August 682–3 June 683
81. St. Benedict II, Rome, 26 June 684–8 May 685
82. John V, Antioch, 23 July 685–2 August 686
83. Conon, birthplace unknown, 21 October 686–21 September 687
84. St. Sergius I, Palermo, 15 December 687–8 September 701
     (Theodore, 687)
     (Paschal, 687)
85. John VI, Greece, 30 October 701–11 January 705
86. John VII, Greece, 1 March 705–18 October 707
87. Sisinnius, Syria, 15 January 708–4 February 708
88. Constantine, Syria, 25 March 708–9 April 715
89. St. Gregory II, Rome, 19 May 715–11 February 731
90. St. Gregory III, Syria, 18 March 731–28 November 741
91. St. Zacharias, S. Severina (Calabria), 10 December 741–22 March 752
92. Stephen II, Rome, 26 March 752–26 April 757
93. St. Paul I, Rome, 29 May 757–28 June 767
94. Stephen III, Sicily, 1, 7 August 768–24 January 772
     (Constantine, Nepi, 28 June, 5 July 767–769)
     (Philip, 31 July 768)
95. Hadrian I, Rome, 1, 9 February 772–25 December 795
96. St. Leo III, Rome, 26, 27 December 795–12 June 816
97. Stephen IV, Rome, 22 June 816–24 January 817

98. St. Paschal I, Rome, 25 January 817–11 February 824
99. Eugene II, Rome, 11 May 824–August 827
100. Valentine, Rome, August 827–September 827
101. Gregory IV, Rome, 827–January 844
102. Sergius II, Rome, January 844–27 January 847
    (John, January 844)
103. St. Leo IV, Rome, 10 April 847–17 July 855
104. Benedict III, Rome, July, 29 September 855–17 April 858
    (Anastasius, August 855–September 855)
105. St. Nicholas I, the Great, Rome, 24 April 858–13 November 867
106. Hadrian II, Rome, 14 December 867–14 December 872
107. John VIII, Rome, 14 December 872–16 December 882
108. Marinus I, Gallese, 16 December 882–15 May 884
109. St. Hadrian III, Rome, 17 May 884–September 885
110. Stephen V, Rome, September 885–14 September 891
111. Formosus, Rome, 6 October 891–4 April 896
112. Boniface VI, Rome, April 896
113. Stephen VI, Rome, 896–August 897
114. Romanus, Gallese, August 897–November 897
115. Theodore II, Rome, December 897
116. John IX, Tivoli, January 898–January 900
117. Benedict IV, Rome, January, February 900–July 903
118. Leo V, Ardea, July 903–September 903
    (Christopher, Rome, July or September 903–January 904)
119. Sergius III, Rome, 29 January 904–14 April 911
120. Anastasius III, Rome, April 911–June 913
121. Lando, Sabina, July 913–February 914
122. John X, Tossignano (Imola), March 914–May 928
123. Leo VI, Rome, May 928–December 928
124. Stephen VII, Rome, December 928–February 931
125. John XI, Rome, February, March 931–December 935
126. Leo VII, Rome, 3 January 936–13 July 939
127. Stephen VIII, Rome, 14 July 939–October 942
128. Marinus II, Rome, 30 October 942–May 946
129. Agapetus II, Rome, 10 May 946–December 955.
130. John XII, Octavian of the Counts of Tusculum, Rome, 16 December 955–14 May 964
131. Leo VIII, Rome, 4, 6 December 963–1 March 965
132. Benedict V, Rome, 22 May 964–4 July 966
133. John XIII, Rome, 1 October 965–6 September 972
134. Benedict VI, Rome, 19 January 973–June 974

(Boniface VII, Francone, Rome, June, July 974 and August 984–July 985)

135. Benedict VII, Rome, October 974–10 July 983
136. John XIV, Peter, Pavia, December 983–20 August 984
137. John XV, Rome, August 985–March 996
138. Gregory V, Bruno of the Dukes of Carinthia, Saxony, 3 May 996–18 February 999

    (John XVI, John Filagato, Rossano Calabro, April 997–February 998)

139. Sylvester II, Gerbert, Belliac (Auvergne), 2 April 999–12 May 1003
140. John XVII, Siccone Sicconi, Rome, May 1003–December 1003
141. John XVIII, Fasano, Rome, January 1004–July 1009
142. Sergius IV, Peter, Rome, 31 July 1009–12 May 1012
143. Benedict VIII, Theophylactus of the Counts of Tusculum, Rome, 18 May 1012–9 April 1024

    (Gregory, Rome, 1012)

144. John XIX, Romanus of the Counts of Tusculum, Rome, April, May 1024–1032
145. Benedict IX, Theophylactus of the Counts of Tusculum, Rome, 1032–1044
146. Sylvester III, John, Rome, 20 January 1045–10 February 1045
147. Benedict IX (for the second time), 10 April 1045–1 May 1045
148. Gregory VI, John Gratian, Rome, 5 May 1045–20 December 1046
149. Clement II, Suidger, Morsleben and Honburg, Saxony, 24, 25 December 1046–9 October 1047
150. Benedict IX (for the third time), 8 November 1047–17 July 1048
151. Damasus II, Poppone, Bavaria, 17 July 1048–9 August 1048
152. St. Leo IX, Brunone of the Counts of Egisheim-Dagsburg, Alsace, 12 February 1049–19 April 1054
153. Victor II, Gebhard of the Counts of Dollnstein-Hirschberg, Germany, 16 April 1055–28 July 1057
154. Stephen IX, Frederick of the Dukes of Lorraine, Lorraine, 3 August 1057–29 March 1058
155. Nicholas II, Gerard, Chevron (Savoy), 18 April 1058, 24 January 1059–27 July 1061

    (Benedict X, John, Rome, 5 April 1058–24 October 1059)

156. Alexander II, Anselm, Baggio (Milan), 1 October 1061–21 April 1073

    (Honorius II, Cadalus, Verona, 28 October 1061–1072)

157. St. Gregory VII, Hildebrand of Sovana (Tuscia), 22 April, 30 June 1073–25 May 1085.

    (Clement III, Gilbert, Parma, 25 June 1080, 24 March 1084–8 September 1100)

158. Victor III, Desiderius, Benevento, 24 May 1086–16 September 1087
159. Urban II, Eudes de Lagery, Châtillon-sur-Marne (France), 12 March 1088–29 July 1099
160. Paschal II, Raniero, Blera (Viterbo), 13, 14 August 1099–21 January 1118
    (Theodoric, Bishop of St. Rufina, 1100–1102)
    (Albert, Bishop of Sabina, 1102)
    (Sylvester IV, Maginulf, Rome, 18 November 1105–1111)
161. Gelasius II, John Caetani, Gaeta, 24 January, 10 March 1118–28 January 1119
    (Gregory VIII, Maurice Bourdin, France, 8 March 1118–1121)
162. Calixtus II, Guy, Burgundy, 2, 9 February 1119–13 December 1124
163. Honorius II, Lambert, Fiagnano (Imola), 15, 21 December 1124–13 February 1130.
    (Celestine II, Theobald Boccadipecora, Rome, December 1124)
164. Innocent II, Gregory Papareschi, Rome, 14, 23 February 1130–24 September 1143
    (Anacletus II, Peter Pierleoni, Rome, 14, 23 February 1130–25 January 1138)
    (Victor IV, Gregory, birthplace unknown, March 1138–29 May 1138)
165. Celestine II, Guido, Città di Castello, 26 September, 3 October 1143–8 March 1144
166. Lucius II, Gerard Caccianemici, Bologna, 12 March 1144–15 February 1145
167. Eugene III, Bernard, perhaps the family of the Paganelli of Montemagno,
    Pisa, 15, 18 February 1145–8 July 1153
168. Anastasius IV, Conrad, Rome, 12 July 1153–3 December 1154
169. Hadrian IV, Nicholas Breakspear, Langley (England),
    4, 5 December 1154–1 September 1159
170. Alexander III, Roland Bandinelli, Siena, 7, 20 September 1159–30 August 1181
    (Victor IV or V, Ottaviano Monticelli, Tivoli, 7 September, 4 October 1159–20 April 1164)
    (Paschal III, Guido, Crema, 22, 26 April 1164–20 September 1168)
    (Calixtus III, John, Abbot of Strumi, Arezzo, September 1168–29 August 1178)
    (Innocent III, Lando, Sezze, 29 September 1179–1180)
171. Lucius III, Ubaldo Allucingoli, Lucca, 1, 6 September 1181–25 November 1185
172. Urban III, Uberto Crivelli, Milan, 25 November, 1 December 1185–20 October 1187

173. Gregory VIII, Albert de Morra, Benevento, 21, 25 October 1187–17 December 1187
174. Clement III, Paul Scolari, Rome, 19, 20 December 1187–March 1191
175. Celestine III, Hyacinth Boboni, Rome, 30 March, 14 April 1191–8 January 1198
176. Innocent III, Lothario of the Counts of Segni, Gavignano (Rome), 8 January, 22 February 1198–16 July 1216
177. Honorius III, Cencio Savelli, Rome, 18, 24 July 1216–18 March 1227
178. Gregory IX, Ugolino of the Counts of Segni, Anagni, 19, 21 March 1227–22 August 1241
179. Celestine IV, Geoffrey Castiglioni, Milan, 25, 28 October 1241–10 November 1241
180. Innocent IV, Sinibaldo Fieschi, Genoa, 25, 28 June 1243–7 December 1254
181. Alexander IV, Rinaldo of the Counts of Segni, Jenne (Anagni), 12, 20 December 1254–25 May 1261
182. Urban IV, Jacques Pantaléon, Troyes (France), 29 August, 4 September 1261–2 October 1264
183. Clement IV, Guy Foulkes, St. Gilles (Nîmes), 5, 15 February 1265– 29 November 1268
184. Gregory X, Tebaldo Visconti, Piacenza, 1 September 1271, 27 March 1272–10 January 1276
185. Innocent V, Pierre de Taranteise, Savoy, 21 January, 22 February 1276–22 June 1276
186. Hadrian V, Ottobono Fieschi, Genoa, 11 July 1276–18 August 1276
187. John XXI, Pietro Juliani, called Pietro Ispano, Lisbon, 8, 20 September 1276–20 May 1277
188. Nicholas III, Giovanni Gaetano Orsini, Rome, 25 November, 26 December 1277–22 August 1280
189. Martin IV, Simone de Brion, France, 22 February, 23 March 1281–28 March 1285
190. Honorius IV, Giacomo Savelli, Rome, 2 April, 20 May 1285–3 April 1287
191. Nicholas IV, Girolamo Masci, Lisciano (Ascoli Piceno), 22 February 1288–4 April 1292
192. St. Celestinus V, Pietro Angeleri, Isernia, 5 July, 29 August 1294–13 December 1294
193. Boniface VIII, Benedetto Caetani, Anagni, 24 December 1294, 23 January 1295–11 October 1303
194. Benedict XI, Niccolò Boccassini, Treviso, 22, 27 October 1303–7 July 1304

195. Clement V, Bertrand de Got, Villandraut (Gironde),
     5 June, 14 November 1305–20 April 1314
196. John XXII, Jacques-Arnaud d'Euse, Cahors (France),
     7 August, 5 September 1316–4 December 1334
     (Niccolò V, Pietro Rainallucci, Corvaro, Rieti, 12, 22 May 1328–25
     August 1330)
197. Benedict XII, Jacques Fournier, Savardin (Foix),
     20 December 1334, 8 January 1335–25 April 1342
198. Clement VI, Pierre Roger, Malmont (France), 7, 19 May 1342–6
     December 1352
199. Innocent VI, Etienne Aubert, Mont-Beyssac (France),
     18, 30 December 1352–12 September 1362
200. Urban V, Guillaume de Grimoard, Grisac (Auvergne),
     28 September, 6 November 1362–19 December 1370
201. Gregory XI, Pierre Roger de Beaufort, Rosier-d'Egleton (France),
     30 December 1370, 5 January 1371–27 March 1378
202. Urban VI, Bartolomeo Prignano, Naples, 8, 18 April 1378–15 October
     1389
     (Clement VII, Robert of the Counts of the Cenevois (France),
     20 September, 31 October 1378–16 September 1394)
203. Boniface IX, Pietro Tomacelli, Naples, 2, 9 November 1389–1 October
     1404
204. Innocent VII, Cosimo Migliorati, Sulmona,
     17 October 11 November 1404–6 November 1406
205. Gregory XII, Angelo Correr, Venice, 30 November, 19 December
     1406–4 July 1415
     (Benedict XIII, Pedro de Luna, Aragon, 28 September, 11 October 1394–23
     May 1423)
     (Alexander V, Pietro Filargo, Crete, 26 June, 7 July 1409–3 May 1410)
     (John XXIII, Baldassarre Cossa, Naples, 17, 25 May 1410–29 May
     1415)
206. Martin V, Oddone Colonna, Genazzano (Rome),
     11, 21 November 1417–20 February 1431
207. Eugene IV, Gabriele Condulmer, Venice, 3, 11 March 1431–23
     February 1447
     (Felix V, Amedeo VIII, Duke of Savoy, Savoy,
     5 November 1439, 24 July 1440–7 April 1449)
208. Nicholas V, Tommaso Parentucelli, Sarzana, 6, 19 March 1447–24
     March 1455
209. Calixtus III, Alonso de Borja, Jàtiva (Valencia), 8, 20 April 1455–6
     August 1458

210. Pius II, Aeneas Silvius Piccolomini, Corsignano (Siena),
      19 August, 3 September 1458–15 August 1464
211. Paul II, Pietro Barbo, Venice, 30 August, 16 September, 1464–26 July
      1471
212. Sixtus IV, Francesco della Rovere, Celle Ligure (Savona),
      9, 25 August 1471–12 August 1484
213. Innocent VIII, Giovanni Battista Cibo, Genoa,
      29 August, 12 September, 1484–25 July 1492
214. Alexander VI, Rodrigo de Borja, Jàtiva (Valencia), 11, 26 August
      1492–18 August 1503
215. Pius III, Francesco Todeschini Piccolomini, Siena,
      22 September,1, 8 October 1503–18 October 1503
216. Julius II, Giuliano della Rovere, Albisola (Savona),
      31 October, 20 November 1503–21 February 1513
217. Leo X, Giovanni de' Medici, Florence, 9, 19 March 1513–1 December
      1521
218. Hadrian VI, Adriaan Florensz, Utrecht, 9 January, 31 August 1522–14
      September 1523
219. Clement VII, Giulio de' Medici, Florence, 19, 26 November 1523–25
      September 1534
220. Paul III, Alessandro Farnese, Canino (Viterbo),
      13 October, 3 November 1534–10 November 1549
221. Julius III, Giovanni Maria Ciocchi del Monte, Rome,
      7, 22 February 1550–23 March 1555
222. Marcellus II, Marcello Cervini, Montepulciano (Siena), 9, 10 April
      1555–1 May 1555
223. Paul IV, Gian Pietro Caraffa, S. Angelo della Scala (Avellino),
      23, 26 May 1555–18 August 1559
224. Pius IV, Giovan Angelo de' Medici, Milan,
      25 December 1559, 6 January 1560–9 December 1565
225. St. Pius V, Michele Ghislieri, Bosco Marengo (Alessandria),
      7, 17 January 1566–1 May 1572
226. Gregory XIII, Ugo Boncompagni, Bologna, 13, 25 May 1572–10 April
      1585
227. Sixtus V, Felice Peretti, Grottammare (Ascoli Piceno),
      24 April, 1 May 1585–27 August 1590
228. Urban VII, Giovanni Battista Castagna, Rome, 15 September 1590–27
      September 1590
229. Gregory XIV, Niccolò Sfondrati, Somma Lombardo (Cremona),
      5, 8 December 1590–16 October 1591
230. Innocent IX, Giovanni Antonio Facchinetti, Bologna,
      29 October, 3 November 1591–30 December 1591

231. Clement VIII, Ippolito Aldobrandini, Fano, 30 January, 9 February 1592–3 March 1605
232. Leo XI, Alessandro de' Medici, Florence, 1, 11 April 1605–27 April 1605
233. Paul V, Camillo Borghese, Rome, 16, 29 May 1605–28 January 1621
234. Gregory XV, Alessandro Ludovisi, Bologna, 9, 14 February 1621–8 July 1623
235. Urban VIII, Maffeo Barberini, Florence, 6 August, 29 September 1623–29 July 1644
236. Innocent X, Giovanni Battista Pamphili, Rome, 15 September, 4 October 1644–7 January 1655
237. Alexander VII, Fabio Chigi, Siena, 7, 18 April 1655–22 May 1667
238. Clement IX, Giulio Rospigliosi, Pistoia, 20, 26 June 1667–9 December 1669
239. Clement X, Emilio Altieri, Rome, 29 April, 11 May 1670–22 July 1676
240. Innocent XI, Benedetto Odescalchi, Como, 21 September, 4 October 1676–12 August 1689
241. Alexander VIII, Pietro Ottoboni, Venice, 6, 16 October 1689–1 February 1691
242. Innocent XII, Antonio Pignatelli, Spinazzola (Bari), 12, 15 July 1691–27 September 1700
243. Clement XI, Giovanni Francesco Albani, Urbino, 23, 30 November, 8 December 1700–19 March 1721
244. Innocent XIII, Michelangelo Conti, Poli (Palestrina), 18 May 1721–7 March 1724
245. Benedict XIII, Pier Francesco Orsini, Gravina (Bari), 29 May, 4 June 1724–21 February 1730
246. Clement XII, Lorenzo Corsini, Florence, 12, 16 July 1730–6 February 1740
247. Benedict XIV, Prospero Lambertini, Bologna, 17, 22 August 1740–3 May 1758
248. Clement XIII, Carlo Rezzonico, Venice, 6, 16 July 1758–2 February 1769
249. Clement XIV, Gian Vincenzo Antonio Ganganelli, S. Arcangelo (Rimini), 19, 28 May 4 June 1769–22 September 1774
250. Pius VI, Giovanni Angelo Braschi, Cesena, 15, 22 February 1775–29 August 1799
251. Pius VII, Barnaba Chiaramonti, Cesena, 14, 21 March 1800–20 August 1823

252. Leo XII, Annibale Sermattei della Genga, Genga (Ancona),
     28 September, 5 October 1823–10 February 1829
253. Pius VIII, Francesco Saverio Castiglioni, Cingoli (Macerata),
     31 III, 5 April 1829–30 November 1830
254. Gregory XVI, Bartolomeo Mauro Cappellari, Belluno, 2, 6 February
     1831–1 June 1846
255. Pius IX, Giovanni Maria Mastai Ferretti, Senigallia (Ancona),
     16, 21 June 1846–7 February 1878
256. Leo XIII, Gioacchino Pecci, Carpineto (Anagni),
     20 February, 3 March 1878–20 July 1903
257. St. Pius X, Giuseppe Sarto, Riese (Treviso), 4, 9 August 1903–20
     August 1914
258. Benedict XV, Giacomo della Chiesa, Genoa, 3, 6 September 1914–22
     January 1922
259. Pius XI, Achille Ratti, Desio (Milan), 6, 12 February 1922–10
     February 1939
260. Pius XII, Eugenio Pacelli, Rome, 2, 12 March 1939–9 October 1958
261. John XXIII, Angelo Giuseppe Roncalli, Brusicco di Sotto il Monte
     (Bergamo),
     28 October, 4 November 1958–3 June 1963
262. Paul VI, Giovanni Battista Montini, Concesio (Brescia),
     21, 30 June 1963–6 August 1978
263. John Paul I, Albino Luciani, Forno di Canale d'Agordo (Belluno),
     26 August, 3 September 1978–28 September 1978
264. John Paul II, Karol Wojtyla, Wadowice (Krakow), 16, 22 October
     1978

COMMENTS ON THE LIST AND VARIOUS ANOMALIES

Many doubts persist regarding the chronology and the number of the Roman pontiffs, because of conflicting historical sources and certain controversial questions about popes elected but not crowned due to sudden death, and popes who reigned more than once, as well as the legitimacy or lack thereof on the part of some of them.

According to the *Annuario pontificio* itself, up until a few years ago the number of pontiffs, including the current one, was supposed to be 265; indeed, a Stephen elected in 752 between Zachary and Stephen II was also considered a pope. However, since he died three days following his election, without, of course, having been consecrated, the most recent Annuario pontificio cancelled his name and the number was fixed at 264, which is incongruous because other popes as well died before they had been consecrated yet nonetheless their names appear in the list.

Other uncertainties come from the antipopes, that is, from those popes who disputed the dignity and the Roman See against pontiffs already enthroned and who, in many cases, appeared to have been canonically elected. The Church recognizes only 37, as appears from the above list, but in reality they numbered 39. Clement VIII (1423–1429) and Benedict XIV (1425–1430) are not included in the list (of the Church).

With regard to the antipopes the following questions still persist. Leo VIII (No. 131 in the list) should have been an antipope up to the death of John XII (No. 130 in the list) and the same is true of Benedict V (No. 132) up to the death of Leo VIII. The case of the triple election of Benedict V (No. 132) is especially symptomatic: Sylvester III (No. 146 in the list) and Damasus II (No. 151) should in fact be counted among the antipopes if their depositions in 1044 and 1048 are to be considered illegal.

Regarding the popes who ascended to the throne of Peter, the following "anomalies" may also be indicated.

DURATION OF PONTIFICATES

The six shortest pontificates in order of brevity were:
1. Urban VII: 13 days
2. Boniface VI: 15 days
3. Celestine IV: 17 days
4. Marcellus II: 20 days
5. Theodore II: 20 days
6. Sisinnius: 21 days

The six longest pontificates in order were:
1. St. Peter: 37 years
2. Pius IX: 32 years
3. Leo XIII: 25 years
4. Pius VI: 24 years
5. Hadrian I: 23 years
6. Pius VII: 23 years

THE POPES WHO ABDICATED WERE:

Five popes renounced the papal throne:
1. Clement I in 97
2. Pontianus in 235
3. Benedict IX in 1045
4. Celestine V in 1294
5. Gregory XII in 1415

THE DEPOSED POPES WERE:

These nine popes were deposed for various reasons:
1. Silverius in 537
2. Martin I in 654
3. Romanus in 897
4. Leo V in 903
5. John XII in 963
6. Benedict V in 963
7. Leo VIII in 964
8. Sylvester III in 1046
9. Benedict IX in 1044 and 1048

THE POPE WHO REIGNED MORE THAN ONCE WAS:

Benedict IX. Elected in 1032, he was deposed in 1044; he regained the throne in 1045, abdicating that same year; for the third time he was on the throne in 1047 and was definitely deposed a year later. His name occurs three times in the list of popes which as far as names are concerned means in fact 262 and not 264.

THE POPES WHO TOOK THE NAMES OF THE ANTIPOPES WERE:

Ten popes who, as soon as they were elected, took the name which had previously been taken by antipopes in order to emphasize irreversibly the illegitimacy of their election:

1. Honorius II (1124–1130) took the name of the antipope Honorius II (1061–1072)
2. Celestine II (1143–1144) took the name of the antipope Celestine II (1124)
3. Gregory VIII (1187) took the name of the antipope Gregory VIII (1118–1121)
4. Clement III (1187–1191) took the name of the antipope Clement III (1080–1100)
5. Innocent III (1198–1216) took the name of the antipope Innocent III (1179–1180)
6. Nicholas V (1447–1455) took the name of the antipope Nicholas V (1328–1330)
7. Calixtus III (1455–1458) took the name of the antipope Calixtus III (1168–1178)
8. Clement VII (1523–1534) took the name of the antipope Clement VII (1378–1394)
9. Benedict XIII (1724–1730) took the name of the antipope Benedict XIII (1394–1423)
10. John XXIII (1958–1963) took the name of the antipope John XXIII (1410–1415)

It should also be recalled that Clement VIII (1592–1605) took the name of a Clement VIII (1423–1429) not officially recognized as an antipope by the Church; the same applies to Benedict XIV (1740–1758) who took the name of a Benedict XIV (1425–1430) likewise not recognized by the Church as an antipope.

NAMES OMITTED IN THE SERIES OF POPES:

In the series of pontiffs who bear the same name the following eight were omitted, the first five of whom were antipopes:
1. Gregory XVI, antipope (997–998)
2. Felix II, antipope (355–365)
3. Boniface VII, antipope (974 and 984–985)
4. Benedict X, antipope (1058–1059)
5. Alexander V, antipope (1409–1415)
6. John XX: in reality never existed and was omitted just like John XIX and John XXI.
7-8. Martin II and Martin III in reality never existed, or possibly they were confused with the names of Marinus I and Marinus II so that from Martin I one went directly to Martin IV.

THE FAMILIES THAT HAD MOST POPES:

There were sixteen families that had more than one representative of theirs on the papal throne.

Counts of Tuscolo (5)	John XII
	Benedict VII
	Benedict VIII
	John XIX
	Benedict IX (pope three times)
Counts of Segni (4)	Innocent III
	Gregory IX
	Alexander IV
	Innocent XIII
Savelli of Rome (3)	Gregory II
	Honorius III
	Honorius IV
Orsini of Rome (3)	Celestine III
	Nicholas III
	Benedict XIII
Medici of Florence (3)	Leo X
	Clement VII
	Leo XI
Anici of Rome (2)	Felix III
	Gregory I, the Great
Caetani of Gaeta (2)	Gelasius II
	Boniface VIII
Borgia of Játiva (2)	Calixtus III
	Alexander VI
Colonna of Rome (2)	Hadrian I
	Martin V
Castiglioni of Milan (2)	Celestine IV
	Pius VIII

Della Rovere of Savona (2)	Sixtus IV
	Julius II
Fieschi, counts of Lavagna (2)	Innocent IV
	Hadrian V
Piccolomini of Siena (2)	Pius II
	Pius III
Roger of Beaufort (2)	Clement VI
	Gregory XI

Unknown is the name of the roman family to which belonged the two papal brothers Stephen II and Paul I and that of the family from Frosinone, who also produced two popes, Hormisdas and Silverius, father and son.

THE CHANGE OF NAME

In accordance with a tradition more than a thousand years old, at his election a new pontiff must change his baptismal name. Indeed St. Peter adopted this change of name—imposed on him by Jesus—and, as first pope, no longer called himself Simon. But after him every pope kept his baptismal name until 532 when John II, who was called Mercurial or Mercury, felt it sounded too pagan. Two others who maybe changed names were John III in 561 whose baptismal name was apparently Catelinus, and his successor, Benedict I, whose was probably Bonosius though information about their Christian names is far from certain.

The second one who certainly changed name in 955 was John XII who was called Octavian, another pagan and imperial name. After a further five more popes who kept their original names, another substitution, the most important, was recorded in 983: "*Johannes qui est Petrus*," and this was John XIV. Since then the name of Peter has been "taboo," and the name change became a custom which was never set aside. The abandonment of the name of the first "birth" tends to imply a "second" birth to which one is summoned for the supreme election, in a profoundly mystical signification. Curiously, in certain cases, it was not the newly elected who chose the name, but the first cardinal-deacon, as "godfather" who imposed it on him as happened at the election of Cardinal Cencio Savelli and of the first Avignon pope.

The number of names is limited to about seventy, of which fewer than half have been repeated. The names, which for some centuries have appeared more frequently, are those of Clement, Innocent, Pius and Benedict. However, the motives which led to the choice of one rather than another name are obviously different in each case and at times inscrutable.

In analyzing the motives of some, for example, I recall that Aeneas Silvius Piccolomini is said to have been moved to take the name Pius II from Virgil's districh, "*Sum pius Aeneas.*" Alexander VI, instead, wanted to emulate the great Macedonian conqueror, and Giuliano della Rovere, Julius II, the dictator Caius Julius Caesar. Finally, numerous were those who wanted to pay homage to the pontiffs who had conferred on them the rank of cardinal and hence assumed the same name.

MALACHY'S PROPHECY

Malachy was a Cisternian monk, bishop and primate of Ireland, who lived between 1094 to 1148. He was the author of *De summis pontificibus* in which he prophesied the end of Rome and the world for a specific year, identifiable as 2026, following the ascent to the papal throne of the last pope named Peter II. He would be the 112th pontiff of a list which begins with Celestine II, and in which the name of each pope is indicated symbolically by a motto in Latin.

This prophecy, as much discussed as it was feared, was not always precise in setting forth a clear relationship between the motto and the elected pope.

Concerning the pontiffs closest to our times, the following are the Latin attributions and their likely meanings:

101. Pius IX – *Crux de cruce*, to signify the tribulations of the Church in the context of the formation of the Italian State.
102. Leo XIII – *Lumen coeli*: in the shield of Pope Pecci there appears a comet in the form of a serpent.
103. Pius X - *Ignis ardens*, to signify the heart burning with faith of this "holy" pope.
104. Benedict XV – *Religio depopulata*, bearing in mind that his pontificate occurred during the First World War when millions of Catholics died.
105. Piux XI – *Fides intrepida*, signifying the faith battling with totalitarian regimes.
106. Pius XII – *Pastor angelicus*: for some the "pastor" par excellence, with an "angelic" way of being.
107. John XXIII - *Pastor et nauta*, because he was the Patriarch of Venice and travelled a great deal.
108. Paul VI - *Flos florum*, because there were three flowers in his shield.
109. John Paul I – *De medietate lunae*, to signify the brevity of his pontificate which lasted little more than one lunar month.
110. John Paul II – *De labore solis*: according to many, this could refer to his unflagging activity.

The present pontiff is supposed to be succeeded by someone called *De Gloria olivae* (111) in a hoped for sign of universal peace, following whom would come the catastrophe with the 112th. "*In persecutione extreme Sanctae Romana Ecclesiae sedebit Petrus Romanus qui pascet oves in multis tribulationibus, quibus transactis septicolis diruentur et Judex tremendus judicabit populum suum. Amen.*"

BIBLIOGRAPHY

AA. VV., *I papi*, Novara 1974.

AA. VV., "Paolo VI, la sua vita, la sua difficile missione," *Epoca*, 10 August 1978 (contains texts by V. CORRESIO, D. O'GRADY and M. BELLACCI).

AA. VV., *Fatti e figure del Lazio meridionale*, Rome 1978.

AA. VV., *Storia della Chiesa* (edited by H. JEDIN), Milan 1975–80.

AA. VV., *Il papa, I mille giorni di Wojtyla*, Milan 1981 (contains texts by D. FABBRI, B. LAI, D. O'GRADY, G. PAMPALONI, B. SORGE and G. ZIZOLA).

AA. VV., *L'Osservatore Romano*, 1861–1981, only edition, 13 December 1981.

AA. VV., *100 punti caldi della Storia della Chiesa*, Rome 1982.

AA. VV., *Sisto IV e Giulio II mecenati e promotori di cultura*, Savona 1985.

AA. VV., *I papi del XX secolo*, Turin 1990.

AA. VV., *Pio II e la cultura del suo tempo*, Milan 1991.

AA. VV., *Giovanni Paolo II*, Milan 1992–1993.

AA. VV., *Mondo Vaticano*, Vatican City 1995.

ADEMOLLO G., *Alessandro VI, Giulio II e Leone X nel Carnevale di Roma*, Florence 1866.

AGNELLO ANASTASO L., *Istoria degli antipapi*, Naples 1754.

AGNELLO DI RAVENNA, *in Rerum Italicarum Scriptores* by L.A. MURATORI, Bologna 1924.

ALIGHIERI D., *Epistolae*, Oxford 1920.

ALIGHIERI D., *Rime*, Florence 1956.

ALIGHIERI D., *La Divina Commedia* (edited by N. SAPEGNO), Florence 1959.

AMMIANO MARCELLINO, *Rerum gestarum*, London 1939. "Annales Fuldenses," in *Monumenta Germaniae Historica, I*, Hannover 1826.

ANDREOTTI G., *La sciarada di papa Mastai*, Milan 1967.

ANDREOTTI G., *Pranzo di magro per il cardinale*, Milan 1978.

ANDREOTTI G., *A ogni morte di papa*, Milan 1980. *Annuario Pontificio*, Vatican City,1995.

ARETINO P., *Sonetti lussuriosi e pasquinate*, Rome 1980.

ARIAS J., *L'enigma Wojtyla*, Milan 1986.

AUDISIO G., *Storia religiosa e civile dei Papi*, Rome 1864–65.

BACCHIEGA, M., *Silvestro II papa mago*, Foggia 1981.

BARBAINI P., *Celestino V anacoreta e papa*, Milan 1936.

BARGELLINI P., *Mille santi del giorno*, Milan-Florence 1980.

BARONIO C., *Annales Ecclesiastici*, Lucca 1744.

BATTIFOL P., *Saint Grégoire le Grand*, Paris 1928.

BEDA, *Historia Ecclesiastica gentis Anglorum*, Oxford 1896.

BEGNINI U., *Storia sociale della Chiesa*, Milan 1906.

BELLARMINO R., *Opera*, Venice 1731.

BELLI G.G., *Tutti i sonetti romaneschi* (edited by B. CAGLIA), Rome 1980.
BENOIT F., *Avignon au double visage*, Paris 1940.
BERGERE M., *Quattro papi e un giornalista*, Rome 1974.
BERNAREGGIA A., *I papi*, Milan 1940.
BERNI F., *Rime, poesie latine e lettere*, Florence 1885.
BERTI D., *Giordano Bruno da Nola*, Turin 1889.
BERTHELET G., *L'elezione del papa. Storia e documenti*, Rome 1891.
BERTOLDI S., *A futura memoria*, Milan 1981.
BERTOLINI G., "La fine del pontificato di papa Silverio" in *Arch. R. Soc. Rom. Storia Patria*, 47, 1924.
BIANCHI GIOVINI A., *Storia dei papi*, Milan 1864.
BOCCACCIO G., "De claris mulieribus," in *Tutte le opere*, Milan 1967.
BONANNO C., *L'età medievale nella critica storica*, Padua 1973.
BRAIVE M.F., *Avignon*, Paris 1949.
BREZZI P., *Roma e l'impero medievale*, Bologna, 1947.
BREZZI P., *Fonti e studi di storia della Chiesa*, Milan 1962.
CALLOVINI C., *I papi e la Chiesa Romana odierna*, Rome 1980.
CANDELORO G., *Storia dell'Italia moderna*, vol. I-IX, Milan 1956–81.
CAPELLO G., *Gregorio I e il suo pontificato*, Saluzzo 1905.
CARAVALE M.- CARACCIOLO A., *Lo Stato pontificio da Martino V a Pio IX*, Turin 1978.
CASARIEGO A., *Los papas pecadores*, Madrid 1992.
CATERINA DA SIENA, *Lettere*, Siena 1913–30.
CENCIARINI A.C.-GIACCAGLIA M., *Rocche e castelli del Lazio*, Rome 1982.
CESAREO G.A., *Pasquino e pasquinate nella Roma di Leone X*, Rome 1938.
CHACON A., *Vitae et res gestae Pontificium Romanorum et cardinalium*, Rome 1677.
CHELINI J., *La vie quotidienne au Vatican sous Jean-Paul II*, Paris 1985.
CHIABRERA G., *Rime*, Milan 1808.
CORNWELL J., *Un ladro nella notte. La morte di Papa Giovanni Paolo I*, Naples 1990. *Corpus Christianorum*, Paris, 1844–64.
CRUCITTI E., *Roma pagana e cristiana. Le persecuzioni*, Rome 1978.
CUSHING R., *Mi avete amato*, Rome 1976.
D'AZEGLIO M., *I miei ricordi*, Turin 1949.
DELAHAYE K., *Ecclesia mater chez les pères des trois premiers siècles*, Paris 1964.
DELL'ARCO M., *Pasquino statua parlante*, Rome 1967.
DELLI S., *Le strade di Roma*, Rome 1975.
DELLI S., *I ponti di Roma*, Rome 1977.
DELLI S., *Le strade del Vaticano*, Rome 1982.
DEL RE N., *La Curia capitolina*, Rome 1993.
D'ERME V., *La palude dei Papi*, Rome 1982.
DE ROSSI G.B., *Roma sotterranea*, Rome 1861–77.
DE STEFANO A., *Civiltà medievale*, Palermo 1937.
DI FRESCO A., *Misteri e segreti dell'anno santo*, Milan 1974.
D'ONOFRIO C., *Roma val bene un'abiura*, Rome 1976.

D'ONOFRIO C., *La papessa Giovanna*, Rome 1979.

DOTTI U., *Galilei*, Milan 1971.

DRUDI G., *Beatrice e C.*, Turin 1979.

DUBOIS P., *Supplication du peuple de France au roi contre Boniface*, Paris 1655.

DUCHESNE H., *Histoire ancienne de l'Èglise*, Paris 1906–10.

DUCHESNE H.-QUENTIN H., *Le Liber Pontificalis*, Paris 1886–1925.

DUPRE THESEIDER E., *Roma dal Comune di popolo alla Signoria pontificia*, Bologna 1952.

DUPRE THESEIDER E., *I papi di Avignon e la questione romana*, Florence, 1939.

DURRELL L., *La papessa Giovanna*, Milan 1979.

EGINARDO, "Vita Caroli" in *Monumenta Germaniae Historica, II*, Hannover 1829.

Enciclopedia cattolica, Vatican City1947.

Enciclopedia del papato, Catania 1961.

Epistolae pontificum romanorum ineditae, Liepzig 1885.

EUSEBIO DI CESAREA., *Storia ecclesiastica*, Leipzig 1932.

FABRETTI N., *I vescovi di Roma*, Cinisello Balsamo 1986.

FALCO G., *La Santa Romana Repubblica*, Milan 1959.

FALCONI C., *I papi del XX secolo*, Milan 1967.

FALCONI C., *Storia dei papi e del papato*, vol. 4. Milan 1966–72.

FALCONI C., *I papi sul divano*, Milan 1975.

FEDELE C.-GALLENGA M., *Strade, corrieri e poste dei papi dal Medioevo al 1870*, Modena 1988.

FERRARA O., *Il papa Borgia*, Novara 1969.

FERRER BENIMELI J.A.-CAPRILE G., *Massoneria e Chiesa cattolica*, Rome 1982.

FLODOARDO DI REIMS., *Oeuvres*, Reims 1857.

FUHRMANN H., *Storia dei papi*, Bari 1992.

GATTO TROCCHI C., *Leggende e racconti popolari di Roma*, Rome 1982.

GERVASO R., *I Borgia*, Milan 1976.

GIANNONE P., *Il Triregno*, Bari 1940.

GIORDANI I., *Le encicliche sociali dei papa*, Rome 1956.

GIORDANI, P., *Opere*, Milan 1854–63.

GIOVAGNOLI R., *Passeggiate romane*, Milan s.d.

GIOVANNI DI SALISBURY., *Policratraticus*, Oxford 1909.

GIOVANNI XXIII, *Il giornale dell'anima* (edited by L.F. CAPOVILLA), Rome 1964.

GIOVANNI XXIII, *Lettere ai familiari* (edited by L.F. CAPOVILLA), Rome 1968.

GIOVANNI PAOLO I, *Lo spazio di un sorriso. I venti discorsi del suo pontificato*, Rome 1978.

GIOVIO B., *Vita Leonis X*, Basle 1578.

GIOVIO B., *Vita Hadriani VI*, Basle 1578.

GIUNTELLA V.E., *Roma nel Settecento*, Bologna 1971.

GLIGORA F.-CATANZARO B., *Storia dei papi*, Padua 1989.

GNOLI D., *La Roma di Leone X*, Milan 1938.

GONZALES J., *Helder Camara*, Rome 1970.
GORRESIO V., *Il papa e il diavolo*, Milan 1973.
GRAF A., *Attraverso il '500*, Turin 1888.
GRAMSCI A., *Quaderni del carcere*, Turin 1966.
GRANT M., *Storia di Roma antica*, Rome 1981.
GREGORIO MAGNO, *Epistolae*, Hannover 1887–89.
GREGORIO MAGNO, *Dialoghi*, Rome 1924.
GREGORIO DI TOURS, *Historia Francorum*, Hannover 1883.
GREGOROVIUS F., *Storia di Roma nel medioevo*, Rome 1972.
GRISAR H., *Analecta Romana*, Rome 1899.
GRISAR H., *San Gregorio Magno*, Rome 1902.
GRISAR H., *Roma alla fine del Mondo antico*, Rome 1930.
GUALDI, *Vita di Donna Olimpia Maidalchini*, Cosmopoli 1666.
GUARDUCCI M., *La tomba di Pietro*, Rome 1984.
GUERRAZZI F.D., *Beatrice Cenci*, Milan 1869.
GUGLIELMO DI MALMESBURY., *Gesta Regum*, Pordenone 1992.
GUILLEMAN B., *La Cour pontificale d'Avignon*, Paris, 1962.
GUITTON J., *Paolo VI segreto*, Rome 1981.
HASLER A.B., *Come il papa divenne infallibile*, Turin 1982.
HAYWARD F., *Histoire des papes*, Paris 1929.
HEFELE CH.-LECLERCQ H., *Histoire des Conciles*, Paris 1911.
HERGENROTHER G., *Storia universale della Chiesa*, Florence 1908.
HOCHHUTH R., *Il Vicario*, Milan 1964.
HOCK C.F., *Gerberto o sia Silvestro II papa ed il suo secolo*, Milan 1846.
JACOPONE DI TODI, *Laudi* (edited by S. CARAMELLA), Bari 1930.
JANNATTONI L., *Roma fine Ottocento*, Rome 1979.
JEDIN H., *Girolamo Seripando*, Würzburg 1937.
JEDIN H., *Breve storia dei Concili*, Rome 1960.
JOURNET C., *Il primato di Pietro nel pensiero cristiano contemporaneo*, Bologna 1965.
KELLY J., *Grande dizionario dei papi*, Casal Monferrato 1989.
KNOWLES M.D., *Nouvelle histoire de l'Eglise*, Paris 1968.
KRATHEIMER R., Roma. *Profilo di una città* (312–1308), Rome 1981.
LAI B., *I segreti del Vaticano da Pio XII a papa Wojtyla*, Bari 1984.
LECLERCQ H., *Liber Diurnus romanorum pontificum*, Paris 1930.
LEONE M., "*Dietro quel sorriso,*" Panorama, 3 october 1978.
LEPELLEY C., *L'impero romano e il cristianesimo*, Milan 1970.
LIUTPRANDO, "*Antapodosis,*" in *Monumenta Germaniae Historica, III*, Hannover 1826.
LIUTPRANDO, *De rebus gestis Ottonis imperatoris*, ibidem, Hannover 1826.
LUCIANI A., *Illustrissimi*, Padua 1976.
MANODORI A., *Anfiteatri, circhi e stadi di Roma*, Rome 1982.
MANZONI A., *I promessi sposi* (edited by L. RUSSO), Florence 1956.
MARCHETTO A., *Episcopato e primato pontificio nelle Decretali pseudoisidoriane*, Rome 1971.

MARCORA C., *Storia dei papi*, Milan 1966–72.

MARTINA G., *Pio IX* (2 vol.), Rome 1974 and 1986.

MARTINA G., *La Chiesa in Italia negli ultimi trent'anni*, Rome 1977.

Martirologio romano, Vatican City 1955.

MARUCCHI O., *Il primato di papa Damaso nella storia della sua famiglia*, Rome 1905.

MASSON G., *Cortigiane italiane del Rinascimento*, Rome 1981.

MASTRIGLI F., *Il portone di bronzo*, Rome 1928.

MELLONI A., *Innocenzo IV*, Genova 1990.

MELZI C., *L'insegnamento sociale di Leone XII, Pio XI, Pio XII*, Milan 1961.

MISTRALI F., *I misteri del Vaticano*, Milan 1862.

MOLINARI F., *I peccati di papa Giovanni*, Turin 1975.

MOLINARI F., *I nuovi tabù della storia della chiesa*, Turin 1979.

MOLLAT G., *Les papes d'Avignon*, Paris 1930.

MONTAIGNE M. DE., *Journal de voyage en Italie*, Paris 1946.

MONTANARI F., *Il cardinale Lambertini*, Milan 1943.

MONTESQUIEU, *Viaggio in Italia*, Bari 1971.

MORAVIA A., *Beatrice Cenci*, Milan 1958.

MORGHEN R., *Medioevo cristiano*, Bari 1962.

MOSCATI S., *Nuove passeggiate romane*, Rome 1980.

NICHOLS P., *Le divisioni del papa*, Milan 1981.

PALERMO F.S., *Monsignore Illustrissimo*, Rome 1980.

PANI ROSSI E., *Le centosettantuna ribellioni dei sudditi pontifici dall 896 al 1859*, Florence 1860.

PAOLO DIACONO, *Vita di Gregorio Magno*, Paris 1675.

PAOLO DIACONO, *Storia dei Longobardi*, Milan 1970.

PAOLO OROSIO, *Historiae adversus paganos*, Vienna 1882.

PAPARELLI G., *E. S. Piccolomini (Pio II)*, Bari 1950.

PARAVICINI BAGLIANI A., *Il corpo del papa*, Turin 1994.

PASCHINI P.-MONACHINI V., *I papi nella storia*, Rome 1961.

PASCOLI G., *Poesie*, Milan 1939.

PASOLINI P.P., *Trasumanar e organizzar*, Milan 1971.

PASTOR L. VON, *Storia dei papi dalla fine del Medio Evo*, Rome 1910–34.

PECCHIAI P., *Roma nel Cinquecento*, Bologna 1948.

PETRAI G., *I dieci Pii*, Rome 1903.

PETRARCA F., *Senilium rerum libri*, Basle 1581.

PETRARCA F., *Rerum familiarium libri*, Florence 1933–42.

PETRARCA F., *Rerum memorandarum liber*, Florence 1943.

PETRARCA F., *Rime*, Milan-Naples 1951.

PETRARCA F., *Prose*, Milan-Naples 1955.

PEZZELLA S., *Cosa ha veramente detto Giovanni XXIII*, Rome 1972.

PICCOLOMINI E.S., *Opera inedita*, Rome 1883.

PICCOLOMINI E.S., *I Commentari*, Siena 1972–76.

PINTONELLO A., *I Papi*, Rome 1980.

PLATINA, *Le vite dei pontefici*, Venice 1715 (First part: *dal Salvatore Nostro a*

Paolo II; second part: *da Sisto IV a Clemente XI,*) described by Honofrio Panvinio and other more modern authors).

PLINIO IL GIOVANE, *Lettere ai familiari*, Rizzoli 1961.

PLINIO IL GIOVANE, *Carteggio con Traiano e Panegirico di Traiano*, Rizzoli 1963.

PLUMPE J., *Mater Ecclesia*, Washington 1943.

PROCOPIO, *Storia segreta*, Rome 1972.

PROCOPIO, *La guerra gotica*, Rome 1974.

PRODI P., *Il sovrano pontefice*, Bologna 1982.

PSEUDO ISIDORO, *Decretales Pseudo-Isidorianae* (edited by H. HINSCHIUS), Liepzig 1863.

QUERCIOLI M., *Le mura e le porte di Roma*, Rome 1982.

RAHNER H., *Chiesa e struttura politica nel cristianesimo primitivo*, Milan 1970.

RANKE L. VON, *Storia dei papi*, Florence 1968.

RAVAGLIOLI A., *Roma ieri e oggi*, Rome 1982.

REGINONE DI PRÜM, "Chronicon," in *Scriptores Rerum Germanicarum*, Hannover 1890.

RENDINA C., *Il Vaticano, Storia e segreti*, Rome 1986.

RENDINA C., *Pasquino statua parlante*, Rome 1991.

RENDINA C., *La papessa Giovanna*, Rome 1994.

RENDINA C., *Il papa. Sacro e profano*, Rome 1995.

RENDINA C., *Il Vaticano. Storia e tesori*, Udine 1995.

RICHARDS J., *Il console di Dio*, Florence 1984.

RHODES A., *Il Vaticano e le dittature 1922–1945*, Milan 1975.

RICHERO DI REIMS., *Historia*, Rome 1826.

RIZZATI M.I., "Avignone, rifugio dei Papi," *Storia illustrata*, August 1968.

ROMANO G., *L'origine del potere civile e della signoria territoriale dei Papi*, Pavia 1905.

ROSSETTI B., *La Roma di Bartolomeo Pinelli*, Rome 1981.

ROUX A., *Le pape Gélase I*, Paris 1880.

SABA A.-CASTIGLIONI C., *Storia dei papi*, Turin 1939.

Sacra Bibbia, Rome 1973.

SADE D.-A.-F. DE, *Histoire de Juliette ou les prosperités du vice*, Paris 1966.

SAFFI A., *Storia di Roma dal 9 gennaio 1846 al 9 febbraio 1849*, Florence 1893.

SALLUSTIO SALVEMINI C.G., *Il potere temporale del papa*, Rome 1992.

SARAZANI F., *La Roma di Sisto V*, Rome 1979.

SARPI P., *Istoria del Concilio Tridentino*, Bari 1935.

SAVIO F., *La questione di papa Liberio*, Rome 1907.

SAVIO F., *Il papa Zosimo*, Rome 1908.

SCHNEIDER B., *Pius XII*, Rome 1966.

SEPPELT F.X.-SCHWAIGER G., *Storia dei papi*, Rome 1962–64.

SGARBOSSA M.-GIOVANNINI L., *Il santo del giorno*, Rome 1978.

SILENZI F., *Pasquino, cinquecento pasquinate*, Milan 1932.

SILONE I., *L'avventura di un povero cristiano*, Milan 1968.

SILVANI L., *Storia degli antipapi*, Milan 1971.

SIMONETTI M., *La letteratura cristiana antica greca e latina*, Florence 1969.

SPADOLINI G., *Il papato socialista*, Milan 1982.

STACCIOLI R.A., *Roma entro le mura*, Rome 1979.

STEFANESCHI J., "Opus metricum," in *Monumenta Coelestiniana*, Paderborn 1921.

STENDHAL, *Correspondance*, Paris 1937.

STENDHAL, *Cronache italiane*, Turin 1959.

STENDHAL, *Passeggiate romane*, Bari 1973.

STEVENSON J., *La civiltà delle catacombe*, Rome 1979.

TAGLIOLINI A., *I giardini di Roma*, Rome 1980.

TEODORETO DI CIRO, *Storia ecclesiastica*, Berlin 1954.

TEOFANE, *Cronografia*, Liepzig 1885.

TESTINI P., *Le catacombe e gli antichi cimiteri cristiani in Roma*, Bologna 1966.

TESTONI A., *Il cardinale Lambertini*, Bologna 1933.

THIERRY J.-J., *La vraie mort de Jean-Paul I*, Paris 1984.

TRAMONTIN S., *Profilo di storia della Chiesa italiana dall'Unità ad oggi*, Turin 1980.

TREZZINI C., *La legislazione canonica di papa S. Gelasio I*, Locarno 1911.

TROMBADORI A., *Sonetti romaneschi*, Rome 1988.

ULLMANN W., *Il papato nel Medioevo*, Bari 1975.

VALENTINI N.-BACCHIANI M., *Il papa buono che sorrideva*, Milan 1978.

VILLANI G., M. e F., *Cronache*, Florence 1823–26.

VILLARI R., *Storia medievale*, Bari 1978.

WEST M.I., *Nei panni di Pietro*, Milan 1964.

WOJTYLA K., *Pietra di luce*, Vatican City1979.

WOJTYLA K., *Il sapore del pane*, Vatican City1979.

YALLOP D., *In nome di Dio*, Naples 1985.

ZACCAGNINI C., *Le ville di Roma*, Rome 1976.

ZEPPEGNO L., *I rioni di Roma*, Rome 1978.

ZEPPEGNO L.-BELLEGRANDI F., *Guida ai misteri e piaceri del Vaticano*, Milan 1974.

ZEPPEGNO L.-MATTONELLI R., *Le chiese di Roma*, Rome 1975.

ZIZOLA G., *L'utopia di papa Giovanni*, Rome 1976.

Index of Popes and Antipopes*

*The antipopes are italicized.